Lecture Notes in Computer Sc

Edited by G. Goos, J. Hartmanis and J. va

Springer
Berlin
Heidelberg
New York
Barcelona
Hong Kong
London
Milan
Paris
Singapore
Tokyo

Mokrane Bouzeghoub   Zoubida Kedad
Elisabeth Métais (Eds.)

Natural Language Processing and Information Systems

5th International Conference on Applications
of Natural Language to Information Systems, NLDB 2000
Versailles, France, June 28-30, 2000
Revised Papers

Series Editors

Gerhard Goos, Karlsruhe University, Germany
Juris Hartmanis, Cornell University, NY, USA
Jan van Leeuwen, Utrecht University, The Netherlands

Volume Editors

Mokrane Bouzeghoub
Zoubida Kedad
University of Versailles, PRiSM Laboratory
45 av. des Etats-Unis, 78035 Paris, France
E-mail: {Mokrane.Bouzeghoub,Zoubida.Kedad}@prism.uvsq.fr

Elisabeth Métais
CEDRIC Laboratory, CNAM
292 rue Saint-Martin, 75003 Paris
E-mail: elsa@cnam.fr

Cataloging-in-Publication Data applied for

Die Deutsche Bibliothek - CIP-Einheitsaufnahme

Natural language processing and information systems : revised papers / 5th International Conference on Applications of Natural Language to Information Systems, NLDB 2000, Versailles, France, June 28 - 30, 2000. Mokrane Bouzeghoub ... (ed.). - Berlin ; Heidelberg ; New York ; Barcelona ; Hong Kong ; London ; Milan ; Paris ; Singapore ; Tokyo : Springer, 2001
(Lecture notes in computer science ; Vol. 1959)
ISBN 3-540-41943-8

CR Subject Classification (1998): H.2, H.3, I.2, F.3-4, H.4, C.2

ISSN 0302-9743
ISBN 3-540-41943-8 Springer-Verlag Berlin Heidelberg New York

Springer-Verlag Berlin Heidelberg New York
a member of BertelsmannSpringer Science+Business Media GmbH

http://www.springer.de

Typesetting: Camera-ready by author, data conversion by Boller Mediendesign
Printed on acid-free paper SPIN: 10781022 06/3142 5 4 3 2 1 0

Preface

This book includes the papers presented at the fifth International Conference on Application of Natural Language to Information Systems (NLDB 2000) which was held in Versailles (France) on June 28-30. Following NLDBí95 in Versailles, NLDBí96 in Amsterdam, NLDBí97 in Vancouver, and NLDBí99 in Klagenfurt, NLDB 2000 was a forum for exchanging new research results and trends on the benefits of integrating Natural Language resources in Information System Engineering.

Since the first NLDB workshop in 1995 it has become apparent that each aspect of an information system life cycle may be improved by natural language techniques: database design (specification, validation, conflict resolution), database query languages, and application programming that use new software engineering research (natural language program specifications). As information systems are now evolving into the communication area, the term databases should be considered in the broader sense of information and communication systems. The main new trend in NLDB 2000 is related to the WEB wave: WEB querying, WEB answering, and information retrieval.

Among 47 papers submitted from 18 countries, the program committee selected 29 papers to be presented during the conference. Besides these regular papers, two invited talks (given by Pr. Reind P. van de Riet and Pr. Maurice Gross), and a set of posters and demonstrations are also included in these proceedings.

This conference was possible thanks to the support of three main sponsors : the University of Versailles Saint-Quentin-en-Yvelines (Versailles, France), the PRiSM Laboratory (Versailles, France), and the Vrije University of Amsterdam (The Netherlands). We would like to thank them for their support.

We would also like to thank the secretaries and the PhD students of the PRiSM laboratory who put all their competence, enthusiasm, and kindness into making this meeting a real success.

January 2001

Mokrane Bouzeghoub
Zoubida Kedad
Elisabeth MÈtais

Conference Organization

Conference Chair

Mokrane Bouzeghoub

Program Chair

Elisabeth MÈtais

Organization Chair

Zoubida Kedad

Program Committee

Alfs T. Berztiss, University of Pittsburgh, U.S.A.
Mokrane Bouzeghoub, PRiSM, UniversitÈ de Versailles, France
Hans Burg, Ordina Alignment Consulting, The Netherlands
Isabelle Comyn-Wattiau, UniversitÈ de Cergy, France
G¸nther Fliedl, Universit‰ Klagenfurt, Austria
Nicola Guarino, CNR, Padova, Italy
Jon Atle Gulla, Norsk Hydro, Norway
Udo Hahn, Freiburg University, Germany
Paul Johannesson, Stockholm University, Sweden
Zoubida Kedad, PRiSM, UniversitÈ de Versailles, France
Christian Kop, Universit‰ Klagenfurt, Austria
Paul McFetridge, Simon Fraser University, Canada
Henrich Mayr, Universit‰ Klagenfurt, Austria
Ana Maria Moreno, Universidad Politecnica de Madrid, Spain
Odile Piton, UniversitÈ de Paris 1, France
Reind van de Riet, Vrije Universiteit Amsterdam, The Netherlands
Ans Steuten, Vrije Universiteit Amsterdam, The Netherlands
Veda Storey, Georgia State University, USA
Bernhard Thalheim, University of Cottbus, Germany
Roland Wagner, University of Linz, Austria
Werner Winiwarter, University of Vienna, Austria
Christian Winkler, Universit‰ Klagenfurt, Austria
Stanislaw Wrycza, University of Gdansk, Poland

Table of Contents

Linguistics in Information Systems Design

Temporal Databases

Word-Sense Disambiguation

Semantic Relationships in Databases

Semantic and Contextual Document Retrieval, Traceability

Natural Language Generation for Answering E-Mail and OLAP

NLP Techniques for Information Retrieval

WEB Information Retrieval

Technical Databases

Users and Interactions in WEB Querying

Conceptual Patterns

Posters and Demonstrations

WordNet++: A Lexicon Supporting the Color-X Method

Ans A.G. Steuten, Frank Dehne, and Reind P. van de Riet

Vrije Universiteit, Amsterdam
Faculty of Sciences
Division of Mathematics and Computer Sciences
De Boelelaan 1081a, 1081 HV Amsterdam
The Netherlands
{steuten,frank,vdriet}@cs.vu.nl

Abstract. In this paper we discuss what kind of information can be obtained from WordNet and what kind of information should be added to WordNet in order to make it better suitable for the support of the Color-X method. We will present an extension of WordNet (called WordNet++) which contains a number of special types of relationships that are not available in WordNet. Additionally, WordNet++ is instantiated with knowledge about some particular domain.
Keywords: Linguistic relations, Conceptual Modeling, WordNet, CASE tools, Object Orientation, Ontology, Consistency Checking.

1 Introduction

An important phase in the software development process is *requirements engineering* which can be defined as the process of analysing the problems in a certain Universe of Discourse (UoD), representing the observations in various formats and checking whether the obtained understanding is accurate. An essential part of the requirements engineering phase is the process of *requirements specification*, also called *conceptual modelling* [1]. During this process the requirements document, which is a natural language (NL) description of the UoD and the problems that occur in it, is represented in models. According to [22], a conceptual model is an abstract representation of the behaviour of the UoD, understandable and understood in the same way by the users and developers of the system. The developer can find in the requirements document relevant candidate concepts such as classes, relationships and events.

In this paper, we will focus on the information or knowledge that is necessary for conceptual modelling by the Color-X method [1] [1]. Color-X is based on linguistic and object-oriented modelling concepts. Color-X uses two kinds of models: the static object model and the event model and both are founded on Cpl [6], a formal linguistically based specification language that is based

[1] **Co**nceptual **L**inguistically based **O**bject-oriented **R**epresentation Language for Information and Communication Systems (Ics is abbreviated to X).

M. Bouzeghoub et al. (Eds.): NLDB 2000, LNCS 1959, pp. 1–16, 2001.

on a theory called Functional Grammar (FG) [8]. The COLOR-X Static Object Model (CSOM) [3] presents the objects and their classes in a UoD as well as the relationships between them and the static constraints upon them. The COLOR-X Event Model (CEM) [2] presents the dynamic aspects of the UoD which are the events that could and should take place.

For the construction and verification of COLOR-X models, a lexicon can be used that supports the relevant concepts. [7] pointed out that information systems that use some form of NL need a lexicon because in here the building blocks with which natural languages express information are found. [13] stated it differently by asserting that an ontology can be fruitful in the development of information systems. According to him, especially ontological knowledge in the sense of some fundamental ontological distinctions can help the designer in his task of conceptual analysis.

In [4] is described how COLOR-X modelling can be supported by WORDNET [17, 10] and used in a COLOR-X tool environment. WORDNET is a lexical database that links word forms to sets of synonyms, that are related by different semantic relations such as *hyponymy*, *meronymy* and *antonymy*. [16] used WORDNET for the NL-OOPS system, a CASE tool that supports natural language analysis by extracting the objects and their associations for use in creating object models. Core of this tool is the NLP system LOLITA that is built around SEMNET, a large graph that holds knowledge that can be accessed and expanded using NL input and has been merged with WORDNET. [15] proposed some additions to WORDNET by assigning thematic roles to nouns that occur in particular sample sentences. This addition is also relevant for COLOR-X as will be explained later.

In Sect. 2 we will give an introduction to the object-oriented and linguistic concepts on which COLOR-X models are founded. In Sect. 3 we will focus on the representation forms of the COLOR-X models, i.e. as diagrams or as a database of PROLOG facts. In Sect. 4 we will present our WORDNET++ lexicon. In Sect. 5 we show an experiment for how WORDNET++ can be used for the semantic verification of a COLOR-X model. Finally, Sect. 6 contains our conclusions. Appendix A contains the requirements document and diagrams of our test case.

2 Concepts of Color-X Models

The static object model (CSOM) has four basic concepts, namely *classes* (and *objects* as instances of classes), *attributes*, user-defined and standard *relationships* and *constraints*. The event model (CEM) has as basic concepts *events*, *modalities* and *constraints*.

2.1 Classes

The concept of *class* refers to a group of objects in a UoD that all have a structure and behaviour in common. For example, in the domain of hotels there are classes *'client'* and *'hotel_room'*. A class is always denoted by a (composite) noun. These nouns can be characterised by semantic features like *+/- living*,

+/- human, *+/- animate* and *+/- individual* (see also [21]) ('+feature' means 'feature is true', '-feature' means 'feature is false'). A +animate class is a class, which is not necessarily living or human but can act as a human. For example, you can consider a hotel, that is taking part in the process of booking a hotel room, an agent because it is able to initiate or perform some action.

2.2 Standard Relationships

In a CSOM, several types of static relationships between two or more classes or objects exist and two subsets are distinguished: *standard relationships* and *user-defined relationships*. The following standard relationships are discerned:

- *Generalisation* (*is_a* relationship), which is a relationship between two classes. Class A generalises class B if each instance of B is also an instance of A.
- *Aggregation* (*part_of* relationship), which is a relationship between classes that indicates that instances of one class are parts or members of another class. An example is: *'hotel has_as_part a hotel_room'* or the reverse: *'hotel_room is_part_of a hotel'*.
- *Attribute* (*has_a* relationship), which is a relationship that relates data types to classes. An example is *'client has_a name: string'*. In COLOR-X, names of attributes should be (composite) nouns. In COLOR-X, attribute and aggregation relationships are distinguished by the fact that an aggregation is a relationship between classes and an attribute is a relationship (function) between a class and some simple data type (string, integer etc.).
- *Instantiation* refers to one or more instances of the class involved; for example, an instantiation of the class *'hotel'* is the object *'Hotel Astoria'*. In general, instances are not found in a lexicon.

2.3 User-Defined Relationships

Another type of relationship in the CSOM is the user-defined or intra-State of Affairs (SoA) relationship, which denotes associations between two or more objects. For example, in a hotel-domain the following intra-SoA relationships could be specified: *'book'*, *'check in'*, *'check out'* and *'pay'*. The establishment of these relationships contains important information for the system. For instance, the establishment of the *'check in'* relationship between a client, a number of rooms, some period of time and the hotel itself contains information about the occupation of a room for that period of time and the client who occupied it.

In COLOR-X, user-defined relationships are denoted by a verb and, like classes, they can be characterised by semantic features. Common semantic features of verbs [21] are *+/- telic*, *+/- durative*, *+/- dynamic*, *+/- controlled* and *+/- transitive*. These features are the major parameters for the typology of State of Affairs as proposed by [8], except the feature of *transitivity* that was introduced by [14]. Related to this typology is the assignment of semantic functions and satellites [8] which is in line with [11]. Semantic functions correspond to semantic or thematic roles and describe the roles objects play in conjunction with some verb (see for instance [18]). Example roles are *agent*, *goal* and *recipient*. For example, the semantic function of the first argument in a *+dynamic* SoA, which is *+controlled*, must always be 'agent'. Consequently, this argument must be a living, a human or an animate class (see also [12]). *Satellites* are also a notion from FG and can be informally defined as lexical means to specify additional information in a sentence. Common examples of satellites are *source*, *direction*, *time* and *location*. For a more detailed definition and information about the modification of different layers of a clause by satellites, we also refer to [18].

2.4 Events

Dynamic aspects of the UoD are represented in the CEM. An example of an event is *'the client pays the bill to the hotel'*, or in a CPL notation: *pay (agent=client) (goal=bill) (beneficiary=hotel)*. According to [1] occurrences of certain events, indicated by verb V in the CEM have as a consequence that the user-defined relationship named V in the CSOM starts to hold. The remarks we made for the user-defined relationship also apply to events because the event specifications are built up in the same way as the user-defined relationships. Verbs that denote events should have the feature *+dynamic* (i.e. they indicate some change). This means that verbs that indicate some static situation can not denote events (although it is possible that they denote a user-defined relationship).

Other important information related to events is the so-called *antonym relationship* between verbs. We can distinguish two types of antonymy namely *perspective antonymy* and *complementary antonymy* (see [4]). In perspective antonymy, the verbs refer to the same event or relationship but subject and (direct or indirect) object are interchanged and the semantic functions associated with them are different. Consider for example the perspective antonyms *'to buy'* and *'to sell'* in the following sentences: 'the client *buys* a computer from the trader' and 'the trader *sells* a computer to the client'. Complementary antonymy applies to reverse events and an example is *'to check in'* which has a reverse *'to check out'*.

Finally, another type of relationship between verbs is the *entailment relationship*, which provides information about effects of a certain event or relations between events and user-defined relationships. We distinguish the following types of entailment (basically the same as mentioned in [9]):

- *Backward presupposition*: the event denoted by the entailed verb precedes always the event denoted by the entailing verb. For example, the event of *to book* a room goes always before the event of *to cancel* the reservation.
- *Cause*: the entailing verb describes the causation of the state or action to which the entailed verb refers. For example, the event of checking in in a hotel causes that the client occupies a hotel room.
- *Troponymy*: the entailing verb is a *particular way of* the entailed verb, e.g. *to pay* is a particular way of *to transfer*.
- *Proper inclusion*: an example of this is *to buy* that includes *to pay* because there is some period of time in which buy and pay occur at the same time

whereas there is no period of time in which buying occurs and paying does not.

2.5 Requirements for a Lexicon

Summarising, a lexicon that supports COLOR-X modelling has the following requirements:

1. Nouns that represent the classes and attributes of classes.
2. The semantic features of nouns.
3. The generalisation relationship.
4. The 'part-of' relationship, both for aggregation as for attribute relationships.
5. Verbs that represent user-defined relationships and events.
6. The semantic features and semantic roles of verbs.
7. The perspective and complementary antonymy relationship between verbs.
8. The four different types of entailment, i.e. backward presupposition, cause, troponymy and proper inclusion.

3 Representations of Color-X Models

3.1 Graphical Specification of COLOR-X Models

COLOR-X models can be represented by a diagram technique resembling that of UML [19]. The main concepts of COLOR-X were already introduced in the former section. Here we will mention briefly the notation that is used for the two kinds of diagrams. An example of a static object diagram can be seen in Fig. 3 in the appendix. A static object diagram contains:

- *Classes*, notated as rectangular boxes listing the class name and the attributes and *objects*, notated as rounded boxes listing the class name and the attribute values.
- *User-defined relationships*, notated as diamonds. Lines connect a diamond with the two or more classes that participate in this relationship. The relationship name is written inside the diamond together with an optional *modality* (see Table 1). Each line from a diamond to a class is adorned with a role name (see Table 2). Roles are either semantic functions or satellites. Also, each line has an optional cardinality (such as 1-10 or 1+) that constrains how many objects of a certain class can participate in the occurrences of this relationship. The cause and troponym entailment relationship between two user-defined relationships can be notated by a dotted arrow between the two diamonds, labeled respectively *cause* and *subset*.
- *Generalisations*, notated as lines from the subclass to the superclass, with a little white triangle pointing to the superclass.
- *Aggregations*, notated as lines from the part-class to the whole-class, with a little white diamond pointing to the whole-class.
- *Instantiations*, notated as dashed arrows from objects to classes.

Table 1. Modalities in COLOR-X models. Only in CSOMs the 'factual' modality is allowed.

Modality	Meaning	Corresponding Logical Operator
must	should be	deontic obligation
nec (essary)	has to be	modal necessity
permit	allowed to be	deontic permission
factual	happens to be	– (first order logic)

Table 2. Role types in COLOR-X models. Only roles used in this paper are listed.

Role		Meaning
agent	**ag**	entity controlling an action
beneficiary	**ben**	animate for whose benefit the SoA is affected
goal	**go**	entity affected by the operation of agent
location	**loc**	place where event takes place
recipient	**rec**	entity into whose possession something is transferred
source	**src**	entity from which something moves/is moved
time	**tmp**	point in time when event takes place
zero	**zero**	entity primarily involved in a state

An example of a COLOR-X event diagram can be seen in Fig. 4. An event diagram contains:

- One *start node*, denoted by a black dot and one or more *final nodes*, denoted by an encircled black dot.
- *Event-boxes*, which are numbered boxes that denote the states of the system. The boxes have three compartments that contain:
  - A modality (see Table 1).
  - One or more events [2]. An event is specified in CPL notation and consists of a verb and one or more terms. A term consists of a role name, class name and optionally a variable name.
  - Constraints formulated in CPL to which the events should obey.
- *Positive event occurrences*, notated as arrows between event boxes, labeled with the number of the event occurring. For each event in a box a positive event occurrence should depart from this box.
- *Negative event occurrences*, notated as lightning arrows between event boxes. They have the same type of labels as positive occurrences. A negative event occurrence is an event that did not take place within an (expiration) time.

[2] Actually, *processes* of multiple events related by the operators *and*, *or* and *followed_by*, can be specified but for simplicity we will only treat single events here.

Table 3. PROLOG facts for representing COLOR-X-models.

Color–X element	Prolog fact name and arity	Example Prolog fact
Class	cso_class(1)	cso_class(client).
Attribute	cso_attribute(3)	cso_attribute(hotel, name, string).
Generalization	cso_generalization(2)	cso_generalization(client, person).
Aggregation	cso_aggregation(2)	cso_aggregation(bathroom, hotel_room).
User defined relationship	cso_relationship(3)	cso_relationship(pay, factual, [[ag, client], [go, residence], [rec, hotel]]).
Event	ce_event(3)	ce_event(send, nec, [[ag, hotel], [go, invoice], [rec, client]]).

This time should be specified as a constraint in the box from which this arrow originates.
An event box labeled *NEC* (necessary) describes what the system itself has to do and negative event occurrences do not depart from this type of box (otherwise the system itself would be inconsistent). An event box labeled *MUST* describes what some external agent has to do and for each event in a *MUST* box a negative event occurrence should depart from it, in case this agent does not do what it must do. A *PERMIT*-box describes what an external agent is permitted to do and therefore it is not necessary that it contains expiration time constraints.

3.2 Textual Specification of COLOR-X Models

COLOR-X models are founded on CPL, which means that each syntactically correct CSOM or CEM is equivalent to a specification in CPL. CPL has a semantics based on dynamic, deontic and temporal logic. The direct use of CPL as a representation of COLOR-X models is rather impractical. Instead we will use a simple representation in the form of PROLOG facts, that is equivalent to the diagrams (minus the graphical layout features). See Table 3 for some of these facts.

4 Structure of WordNet++

WORDNET is an on-line lexical reference system whose design is inspired by current psycholinguistic theories of human lexical memory. More than 90,000 English nouns, verbs, adjectives and adverbs are organised into synonym sets, each representing one underlying lexical concept. Different types of relationships link these synonym sets. The main similarities and differences between the concepts and relationships of WORDNET and COLOR-X are listed in Table 4. In the third column of that table we show the WORDNET++ relations that correspond with the COLOR-X concepts.

Table 4. Linguistic concepts of WordNet versus Color-X model elements versus the relationships in WordNet++.

WordNet concept	Color–X concept	WordNet++ relation
noun	class name	noun(Word, SynsetID)
noun	attribute name	noun(Word, SynsetID)
verb	user–defined relationship name	verb(Word, SynsetID)
verb	event name	verb(Word, SynsetID)
adjective	attribute value	adjective(Word, SynsetID)
adverb	––	––
homonym	–– (preferably no multiple meanings in the same model)	––
synonym	–– (preferably no synonym words in the same model)	––
glossary	comment or annotation in the model	glossary(Word, Gloss).
hypernym	generalization of classes.	hypernym(Noun1, Noun2)
part meronym	aggregation (class to class) or attribute (class to data type)	consists_of(Noun1,Noun2) or attribute(Noun1,Noun2)
member meronym	aggregation (class to class) or attribute (class to data type)	consists_of(Noun1,Noun2) or attribute(Noun1,Noun2)
substance meronym	––	––
––	object and instantiation relationship	––
––	data type (string, integer, date etc)	––
––	cardinality constraint.	––
attribute	possible attribute value	value(Noun, Adjective)
antonym	perspective antonym: alternative specification (verb frame) of the same relationship or event.	p_antonym(Verb1, Verb2)
antonym	complementary antonym: "inverse" event in the event model.	c_antonym(Verb1, Verb2)
entailment	backward presupposition: in every possible execution of CEM event1 (Verb1) always precedes event2 (Verb2).	precede(Verb1, Verb2)
entailment	proper inclusion: used in specification of activities (an extension of Color–x that is not treated in this paper).	include(Verb1, Verb2)
cause	event1 in a CEM leads to a NEC–box with event2 or cause constraint occurs between relationships in a CSOM.	cause(Verb1, Verb2)
troponym	subset constraint between two relationships denoted by Verb1 and Verb2. The verb frame of Verb1 is an 'extension' of that of Verb2.	subset(Verb1, Verb2)
sentence frame	specification of roles in relationships and events.	verbframe(Verb, ObligedRoleList, PermittedRoleList)
––	modalities of events and relationships (must, necessary, permit).	––

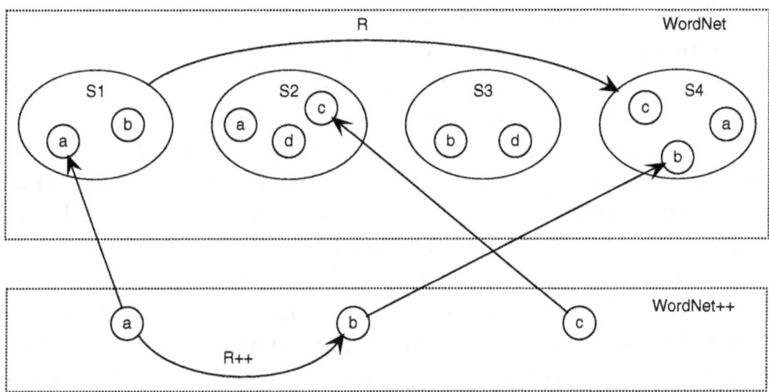

Fig. 1. Mapping of the WORDNET++ words a, b and c to WORDNET synsets $S_1 \ldots S_4$. Synset S_1 is related to S_4 by relationship R. Consequently, words a and b are related by relationship R^{++}, the counterpart of relationship R in WORDNET++.

4.1 The Relations of WordNet++

Words in WORDNET++ are divided into three categories: nouns, verbs and adjectives (adverbs are not used). The predicates `noun`, `verb` and `adjective` link these words to a synonym set (synset) in WORDNET. A `SynsetID` uniquely identifies a synset. With WORDNET++ it can be checked that names that are used in COLOR-X have the right category. WORDNET++ does not contain synonyms and homonyms as is illustrated with an example in Fig. 1. This is because we do not want ambiguities in our models. From each synset in WORDNET we include at most one word in WORDNET++ and each word in WORDNET++ comes from exactly one synset in WORDNET. If in WORDNET some relationship occurrence $R(S_x, S_y)$ (R is one of homonym, meronym, ...) exists between synsets S_x and S_y and WORDNET++ contains the words $w_x \in S_x$ and $w_y \in S_y$ then in WORDNET++ also the corresponding (see Table 4) relationship occurrence $R^{++}(w_x, w_y)$ should exist (see for example the arrows R and R^{++} in Fig. 1).

In principle, each noun in WORDNET++ is a possible class or attribute name in a COLOR-X-model. Verbs in WORDNET++ are possible relationship or event names in COLOR-X-models. All the nouns in WORDNET++ form a taxonomic structure via the `hypernym` relation. The names of the semantic features of nouns (entity, human, living_thing ...) are nouns as well and form the top layers of this taxonomic structure. This means that a certain noun has some semantic feature if it has the name of this feature as a hypernym (generalisation) in the taxonomic structure. This top of the taxonomic structure is domain-independent.

Both part and member meronymy can be found in WORDNET. COLOR-X, like most other OO modeling methods, does not distinguish between parts and members. WORDNET has also a third form of meronymy called *substance meronymy*. Substances (masses) are not identifiable objects and hence not included in COLOR-X and WORDNET++. Both COLOR-X aggregations and COLOR-X attributes can be seen as a form of part/member meronymy. In the WordNet lexicon no distinction is made between aggregations and attributes, because WordNet does not distinguish nouns for classes from nouns for attributes. WordNet++ supports Color-X and makes therefore a distinction between aggregations and attributes. In WordNet++ the aggregation relation is renamed to `consists_of` so it can be read in the same direction as `attribute`. Nouns that occur as second argument in an `attribute` relationship are possible attributes. Nouns that occur as second argument in `consists_of` are possible part/member classes of classes.

Confusingly, WordNet contains also a relationship named "attribute" which is a relationship that links a possible value (adjective) to a noun. For instance, the noun *'quality'* has in version 1.6 of WordNet the attributes *'good'* and *'bad'*. This makes that WordNet attributes are possible values of Color-X attributes. So, WordNet++ could contain the relation `value(quality, bad)`, where `quality` can be used as an attribute. Objects, cardinality constraints and data types are not included in WordNet++ because in most of the cases they denote knowledge about some specific application not of a domain in general.

In contrast with WordNet, WordNet++ distinguishes between the two types of antonyms that are discerned by Color-X. Also, WordNet++ has all four different kinds of entailment, whereas WordNet has only three (proper inclusion and backwards presupposition are jointly called "entailment" in WordNet). WordNet contains so-called *sentence frames* which illustrate the types of simple sentences in which the verbs can be used, for example Somebody —-s something. This concept is extended further in WordNet++ where for each verb it is specified which roles it has (some are obliged, others are optional) and what semantic features the nouns should have that play this role. Indirectly the semantic features of verbs (controlled, dynamic, ...) are part of these verb frames as each type of verb has some typical combination of roles. For example, a verb frame of an *action* (a +controlled and +dynamic verb, e.g. *'to send'*) should always include an *agent* and a *goal* as roles. A frame of a *state* (a -controlled and -dynamic verb, e.g. *'to occupy'*) should always have a *zero* role, but never an agent or a goal.

4.2 Domain-Specific Knowledge in WordNet++

In contrast with WordNet, WordNet++ contains domain-specific knowledge. The words in WordNet++ are however a subset of all the words in WordNet. For each domain (hotel-domain, library-domain, insurance-domain) a distinct instance of WordNet++ is created that contains all knowledge from WordNet that is relevant for this particular domain. Knowledge that is particular for single applications should not be included in WordNet++, e.g. in our example hotel-domain in WordNet++ we did not include specific knowledge about Hotel Astoria but only about hotels in general. On the other hand, not everything in WordNet++ is domain-dependent. The structure of the lexicon itself and the inference rules that WordNet++ uses are all domain-independent. The domain-dependent part of WordNet++ is mostly instantiated by hand. This task is supported however by WordNet++ which contains (domain-independent) rules

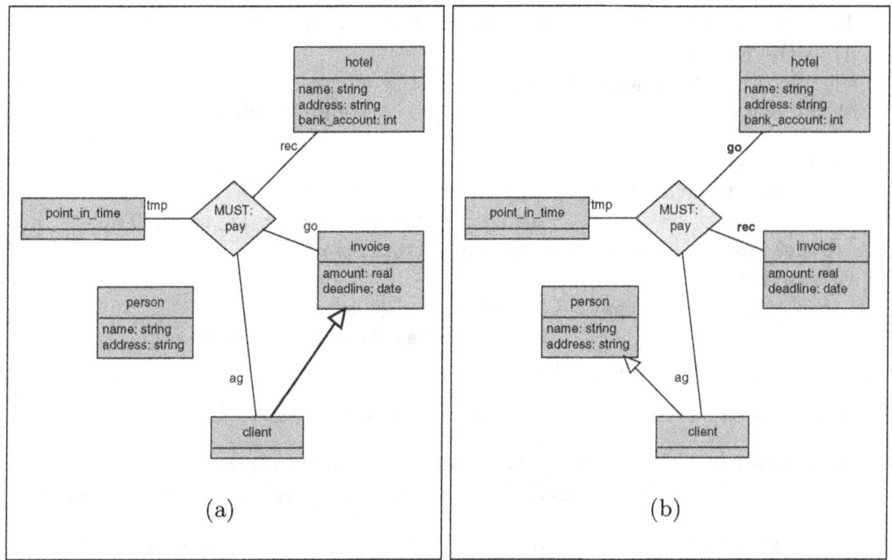

Fig. 2. Diagrams fragments for experiments 1 and 2.

to extract candidate words and relationships from WordNet based on the current contents of WordNet++, to check the consistency between WordNet and WordNet++ and to check the internal consistency of WordNet++ itself.

5 Prototype and Some Experiments

The Color-X-method is supported by a Case tool [1, 20]. The Figs. 3 and 4 were made by this tool that is based on Tcm [5]. The tools are able to check syntactical correctness (e.g. the nodes have only correct connections, labels have correct Cpl-syntax). This functionality is mostly provided by Tcm. What is interesting for this paper, is checking the semantic correctness of models by using WordNet++. We will show some small tests for a small case about doing business in a hotel. The requirements document of this case and a possible solution in the form of two diagrams that are found to be correct by WordNet++ are in appendix A. The methods and techniques that are used to create a model from a requirements text are not treated here (they can be found in [1]). We restrict ourselves to the semantic checking of a possibly incorrect Color-X model by using WordNet++.

1. Look at Fig. 2(a), which is a fragment of Fig. 3 where the generalisation arrow from `client` is drawn to `invoice` instead of to `person`. This is a syntactically correct diagram, but semantically checking this diagram will reveal:

```
These generalisations do not exist as hypernym in WordNet++:
    cso_generalization(client, invoice)
```

This is because the relation `hypernym(client, invoice)` cannot be inferred from the lexicon.

2. Fig. 2(b) is a fragment of the same CSOM where only the `rec` and `go` labels of the `pay` relationship are interchanged. A semantic check would give:

```
role error:
  cso_relationship(pay, [[ag,client],[go,hotel],
                        [rec,invoice],[tmp,point_in_time]]):
  hotel is not one of [possession,abstraction,act]
role error:
  cso_relationship(pay, [[ag,client],[go,hotel],
                        [rec,invoice],[tmp,point_in_time]]):
  invoice is not one of [agent]
```

This is because the verb frame for `pay` in WORDNET++ is:

```
verbframe(pay, [[ag,agent],[go,possession,abstraction,act],
               [rec,agent]],[[tmp,point_in_time],[loc,location]]).
```

The first list of roles are required in every occurrence of the indicated event or relationship. The roles in the second list are optional. For each role the possible hyponyms as argument, are specified. Note that for the goal of `pay` three nouns are specified in the verb frame. The actual noun that has the goal-role should then be a hyponym (specialisation) of (at least) one of them.

3. Suppose we had forgotten to add box number 4 in the CEM of Fig. 4. This box contains the `check_out` event. Analyzing that diagram would result in:

```
Of the following complementary antonym verb pairs only the first
verb is found in the event model: [check_in|check_out]
```

This is because WORDNET++ has inferred the relation `c_antonym(check_in, check_out)` and only the first event can be found in our CEM. This indicates that the model should be repaired with the complementary antonym, `check_out` and in such as way that a `check_in` always precedes `check_out`. This order is relevant because `precede(check_in, check_out)` can also be derived from WORDNET++.

6 Conclusions

COLOR-X tries to bridge the gap between NL and traditional modelling techniques such as ER or UML. This is achieved by using CPL, a specification language based on NL that has a graphical notation and by making use of a lexicon in NL that defines the words and how these words can be used in the models. In this paper we presented WORDNET++, a lexicon based on WORDNET. WORDNET++ has been developed to accommodate COLOR-X as much as possible with semantic knowledge about specific domains. WORDNET++ contains a number of relationships that are not found in WORDNET itself. We have shown in Sect. 4 that WORDNET++ fulfills all eight requirements for a COLOR-X lexicon that were listed in Sect. 2.5. In order to be used in the hotel-domain, WORDNET++ has been filled with knowledge. This knowledge is based on an internally consistent subset of WordNet, and this knowledge is valid only for this domain. In other words, WordNet++ provides a *domain ontology* based on WordNet. We have presented a prototype implementation of the WordNet++ lexicon in an example domain and showed some examples of how it performs the automatic checking of the semantic correctness of Color-X models. The next logical steps in our research would be the application of WordNet++ in a larger, real-world domain and improving our prototype implementation of the lexicon and integrate it better within our Case tool.

A The Hotel Case

Hotel Astoria books rooms of type single, double or suite for clients for a specific period and clients are allowed to book one or more rooms. Each type of room has a specific price per night and this includes breakfast. Each room has a bathroom with bath and toilet. Also, suites have a mini-bar and air-conditioning. A reservation has a date of arrival and a date of departure and reservations should be made in advance. When clients made a reservation they have to check in on the date of arrival before 6:00pm, in case they did not cancel their reservation. Cancelation must be done before 1:00pm, on the date of arrival. Clients who do not check in and did not cancel on time must pay a fine to the hotel. Clients should pay this fine within six weeks. Clients have to check out on the day of departure before 12:00am and they should pay at departure. If a client does not pay s/he will receive an invoice that should be paid within six weeks.

References

[1] J.F.M. Burg. *Linguistic Instruments in Requirements Engineering.* PhD thesis, Vrije Universiteit, Amsterdam, 1996. ISBN 90 5199 316 1 (IOS Press), ISBN 4 274 90144 0 C3000 (Ohmsha).

[2] J.F.M. Burg and R.P. van de Riet. Color-x: Linguistically-based event modeling: A general approach to dynamic modeling. In J. Iivari, K. Lyytinen, and M. Rossi, editors, *The Proceedings of the Seventh International Conference on Advanced Information System Engineering (CAiSE'95)*, number 932 in Lecture Notes in Computer Science, pages 26–39, Jyvaskyla, Finland, 1995. Springer-Verlag.

[3] J.F.M. Burg and R.P. van de Riet. Color-x: Object modeling profits from linguistics. In N.J.I. Mars, editor, *Towards Very Large Knowledge Bases: Knowledge Building & Knowledge Sharing (KB&KS'95)*, pages 204–214, Enschede, The Netherlands, 1995. IOS Press, Amsterdam.

[4] J.F.M. Burg and R.P. van de Riet. Color-x: Using knowledge from wordnet for conceptual modeling. In C. Fellbaum, editor, *WordNet: An Electronic Reference System and Some of its Applications.* MIT Press, Cambridge, MA, 1996.

[5] F. Dehne, H. van de Zandschulp, and R.J. Wieringa. Toolkit for conceptual modeling, user's guide for tcm 2.0. Technical report, Faculty of Computer Science, University of Twente, September 1999. URL http://www.cs.utwente.nl/~tcm.

[6] F.P.M. Dignum. *A Language for Modelling Knowledge Bases. Based on Linguistics, Founded in Logic.* PhD thesis, Vrije Universiteit, Amsterdam, 1989.

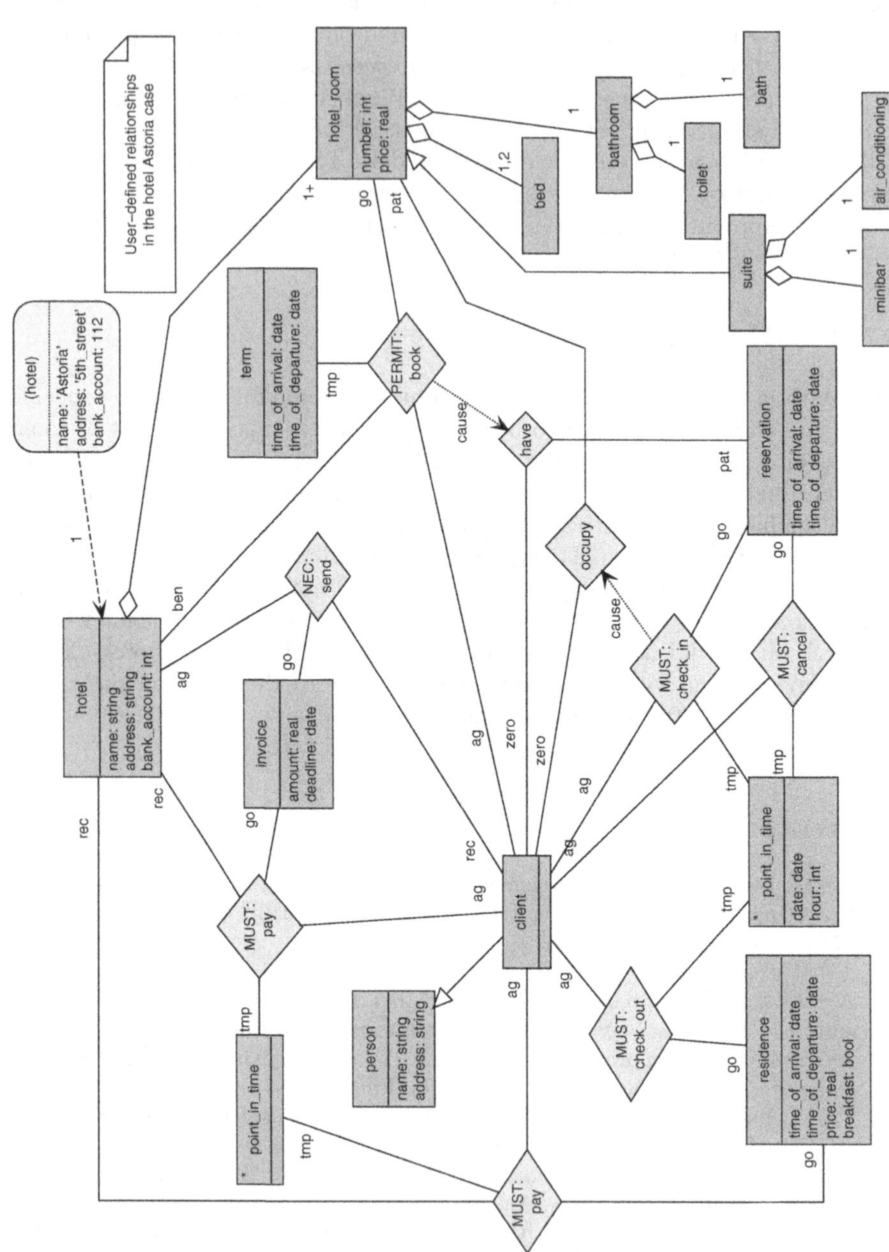

Fig. 3. Static object model of the hotel.

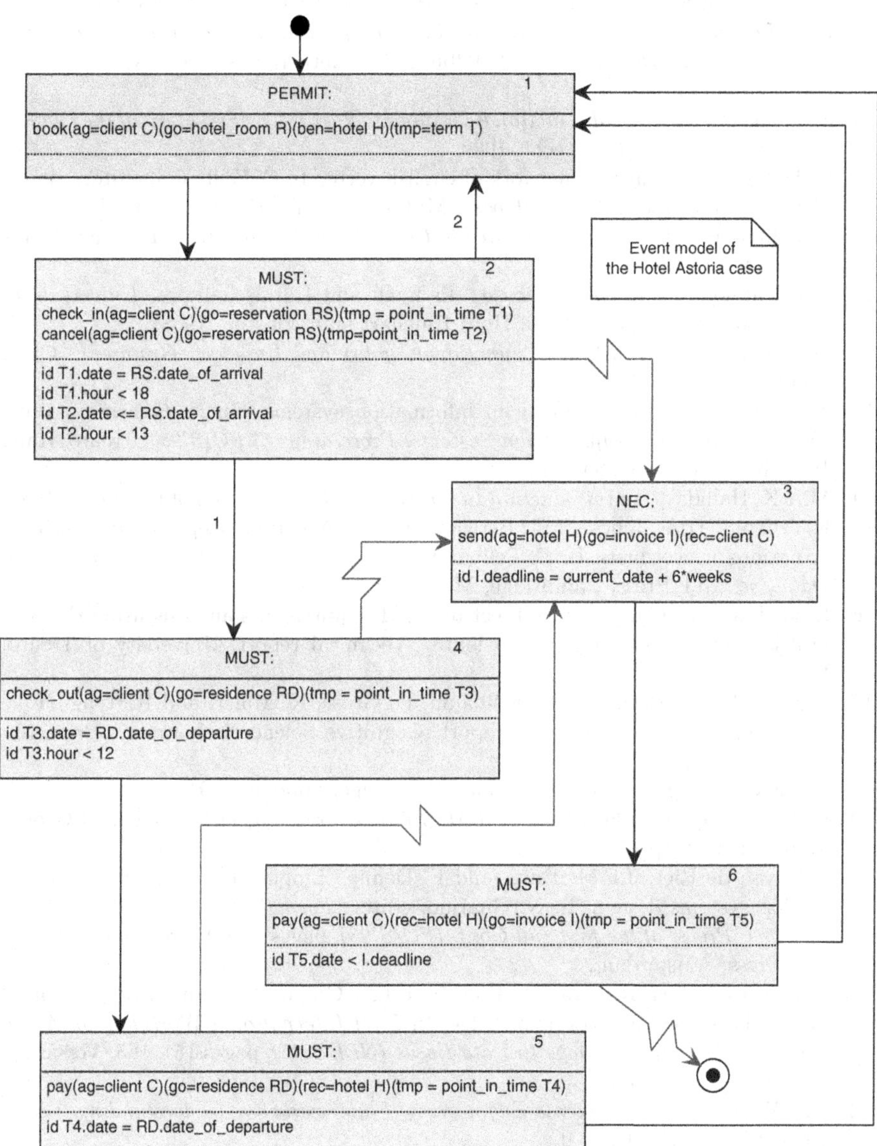

Fig. 4. Event model of the hotel.

[7] S. Dik, W. Meijs, and P. Vossen. Lexigram: A functional lexico-grammatical tool for knowledge engineering. In R.P. van de Riet and R.A. Meersman, editors, *Linguistic Instruments in Knowledge Engineering: Proceedings of the 1991 Workshop on LIKE*, pages 19–52, Tilburg, The Netherlands, January, 17-18 1991. North-Holland.

[8] S.C. Dik. *The Theory of Functional Grammar. Part I: The Structure of the Clause.* Floris Publications, Dordrecht, 1989.

[9] C. Fellbaum. A semantic network of english verbs. In C. Fellbaum, editor, *WordNet: An Electronic Lexical Database.* MIT Press, Cambridge, MA, 1998.

[10] C. Fellbaum, editor. *WordNet: An Electronic Lexical Database.* MIT Press, Cambridge, MA, 1998.

[11] C.J. Fillmore. The case for case. In Bach and Harms, editors, *Universals in Linguistic Theory*, pages 1–90. Holt, Rinehart and Winston, 1968.

[12] W. Foley and R. van Valin. *Functional syntax and Universal Grammar.* CUP, Cambridge, 1984.

[13] N. Guarino. Formal ontology in information systems. In N. Guarino, editor, *Formal Ontology in Information Systems. Proceedings of FOIS'98)*, Trento, Italy, 1998. IOS Press, Amsterdam.

[14] M.A.K. Halliday. *An introduction to Functional Grammar.* Arnold, London, 1985.

[15] K.T. Kohl, D.A. Jones, R.C. Berwick, and N. Nomura. Representing verb alternations in wordnet. In C. Fellbaum, editor, *WordNet: An Electronic Lexical Database.* MIT Press, Cambridge, MA, 1998.

[16] L. Mich and R. Garigliano. Object oriented requirements analysis using the natural language processing system lolita. Technical report, University of Trento, Italy, 1996.

[17] G.A. Miller, R. Beckwith, C. Fellbaum, D. Gross, K. Miller, and R. Tengi. Five papers on wordnet. Technical report, Cognitive Science Laboratory, Princeton University, 1993.

[18] A. Siewierska. *Functional Grammar.* Routledge, London, 1991.

[19] UML Revision Task Force. *OMG UML Specification.* Object Management Group, March 1999. http://uml.shl.com.

[20] R.P. van de Riet, J.F.M. Burg, and F. Dehne. Linguistic instruments in information systems design. In N. Guarino, editor, *Formal Ontology in Information Systems. Procs. of the first Intl Conf. (FOIS'98)*, pages 39–60, Trento, Italy, 1998. IOS Press, Amsterdam.

[21] A.J. van der Vos, R.P. van de Riet, and J.A. Gulla. Verification of conceptual models based on linguistic knowledge. In *First International Workshop on Applications of Natural Language to Data Bases (NLDB'95)*, pages 151–165, Versailles, France, 1995. AFCET.

[22] R.J. Wieringa. *Requirements Engineering: Frameworks for Understanding.* Wiley, 1996. ISBN 0 471 95884 0.

Generating Narratives from Plots Using Schema Information

Antonio L. Furtado and Angelo E. M. Ciarlini[1]

Departamento de Inform· tica - PontifÌcia Universidade CatÛlica do R.J.
R. MarquÍs de S. Vicente, 225 - 22.453-900 Rio de Janeiro, Brazil
{furtado,angelo}@inf.puc-rio.br

Abstract. The temporal dimension adds to databases the capability of functioning as repositories of narratives about the objects involved. Database narratives correspond both to sequences of past events and to simulated future events. This work addresses the problem of displaying such narratives in natural language. We focus here on the first kind of narrative, that is, we analyze a segment extracted from a log of the execution of pre-defined application-oriented operations, which is treated as a plot of the narrative in question. The main point in the presentation is that a three-level conceptual schema of the database provides a sound basis for interpreting such plots, although it should be complemented with further linguistic processing for the sake of fluency and conciseness. The schema-driven method for generating narratives from plots is described. A prototype Prolog implementation of the method is operational. A simple example is used to illustrate the discussion.

1. Introduction

Temporal databases can be said to contain, implicitly, *narratives* of the events concerning the objects about which they keep information [4]. So, if employee "Mary" is one of these objects in some specific database, it should be possible to pose a query, such as *"What happened to Mary between time instants t1 and t2?"*, and have the option to receive an answer in natural language.

Here, we shall concentrate on the generation [7,12] of the textual response, rather than on how the query is expressed, thus leaving aside any aspects related to natural language understanding. As will be argued in the present paper, a useful *Text-Generator* (henceforward, **TG**) can be constructed if two requirements are met: (a) a comprehensive database schema is specified and made accessible, including, among other features, the definition of application-oriented *operations*; and (b) the temporal database installation supplies a *log* to register all executions of these operations, together with the respective time stamps.

We specify schemas at three successive levels. The first is the *static level*, where the types of facts to be stored in the database are declared, according to the Entity-Relationship model, extended with is-a hierarchies for entity types. Operations are defined, in a STRIPS-like formalism, at the *dynamic level*. A third level, the

[1] The work of the second author was supported by FAPERJ - FundaÁ‚o de Amparo ‡ Pesquisa do Estado do Rio de Janeiro - Brazil

M. Bouzeghoub et al. (Eds.): NLDB 2000, LNCS 1959, pp. 17-29, 2001.

behavioural level, is added to model the predicted patterns of database usage, by the various classes of agents involved.

For answering the kind of query indicated above, the first step is to extract from the log the sequence of time-stamped executions of operations, performed during the time interval t1-t2, associated with the object of interest and other related objects. This sequence, regarded as the *plot* of a narrative, is then analyzed, on the basis of the three-level schema, to produce the textual narrative proper.

Processing for text generation is generally divided into two stages [17,12]. The first (producing the strategic component) determines "what to say", i.e. the contents and structure of the discourse, whereas the second (tactical component) finds out "how to say", realizing in natural language the message produced by the strategic component. Until now, we have mainly directed our efforts to the strategic component, which means that we have taken very little from the powerful instrumentality offered by Computational Linguistics [8,12,13]. As a result, although readable, the texts generated by our experimental **TG** Prolog prototype are lacking in conciseness and fluency. With the continuation of the project, besides exploiting more fully the potential of our behavioural level features in order to provide more information about collaboration and competition situations among agents, we intend to revise the **TG** architecture to introduce stylistic improvements in a well-balanced way, so as to achieve better quality texts.

For practical usage, the environment we have in mind integrates a temporal database with a number of logic plus constraint programming facilities, including **TG**, an interactive plot generator, and knowledge discovering tools.

The paper is organized as follows. Section 2 presents the three-level modelling concepts, emphasizing the visualization of plots of narratives as the result of *plans* of the various agents. Section 3 describes the method for generating narratives from plots using schema information. A small example is used throughout the paper to illustrate how the process works. Section 4 contains concluding remarks.

2. Three-Level Specifications

The concepts used at each level will be introduced with the help of the very simple example of a Company Alpha's database. Schemas are specified, at each level, in a notation compatible with logic programming. Convenient onomastic criteria are recommended, in anticipation of the needs of the text generation process.

2.1. The Static Level

At the static level, *facts* are classified according to the Entity-Relationship model. Thus, a fact may refer either to the existence of an entity instance, or to the values of its attributes, or to its relationships with other entity instances. Entity classes may form an *is-a* hierarchy. Entities must have one privileged attribute, which identifies each instance at all levels of the is-a hierarchy. For the time being, we are concentrating on single-valued attributes and binary relationships without attributes. All kinds of facts are denoted by *predicates*.

The example static schema — given in Figure 1 — includes, among the entity classes, person, company, and course; in addition, class employee is a specialization of person, and client a specialization of company. The identifying attributes are name (for person, and also for employee), denomination (company and client) and title (course). For the attribute level (of employee) there are only two possible values: 1 and 2, corresponding to different salary levels. Account is an attribute of client, referring to the status of the clientís account, whose only value that will concern us here, because of its criticality, is "inactive". Relationship serving is defined between employees and clients; employees and courses are related by taking. With respect to onomastic criteria, notice that nouns are used to name entity classes (e.g. person) and attributes (e.g. level). For relationships, we favour past or present participles (e.g serving).

The set of all predicate instances of all types holding at a given instant constitutes a *state*. In temporal database environments, one can ask whether or not some fact F holds at a state S associated with a time instant t.

```
% COMPANY ALPHA EXAMPLE
dbowner('Company Alpha').

% Facts

entity(person, name).

entity(employee).
is_a(employee, person).
attribute(employee, level).

entity(company, denomination).

entity(client).
is_a(client,company).
attribute(client, account).

entity(course, title).

relationship(serving, [employee, client]).

relationship(taking, [employee, course]).
```

Fig. 1. static sub-schema

Examples of predicates representing facts are: (a) entity instance: person(Mary); (b) attribute of entity: level(Mary,1); (c) relationship: serving(Mary,Beta).

2.2. The Dynamic Level

The dynamic level covers the *events* happening in the mini-world of interest. A real world event is perceived in a temporal database environment as a *transition* between database states. Our dynamic level schemas — figure 2, for the current example — specify a fixed repertoire of *operations*, as the only way to cause state transitions [6]. Accordingly, from now on we shall equate the notion of event with the execution of one of these operations.

As in STRIPS, each operation is defined through its signature, pre-conditions, and post-conditions or effects. Both pre-conditions and effects are expressed in terms of facts, thus establishing a connection with the static level. Pre-conditions are conjunctions of positive (or negated) facts, which should hold (or not hold) before execution, whereas effects consist of facts added and/or deleted by the operation.

When defining the signature of an operation, we declare the type of each parameter (which implicitly imposes a preliminary pre-condition to the execution of the operation) and its semantic role, borrowing from Fillmore's case grammars [5]. From the cases proposed by Fillmore, we retained *agent* (denoted by the letter "a") and *object* ("o"); we found convenient to denote the other cases (e.g. *beneficiary*, *instrument*, etc.) by some preposition able to suggest the role when used as prefix. The agent is, of course, whoever is in charge of executing the operation. In our example, operation complain is the only one whose definition indicates the agent explicitly. If none of the parameters is indicated as playing the role of agent, the database owner is assumed by default to have the initiative. Thus the clause oper(replace(E1,E2,C), [employee/o, employee/by, client/for]) allows us to interpret the event "replace(Mary,Leonard,Beta)" unambiguously as: "Company Alpha replaces employee Mary by employee Leonard for client Beta".

```
% Operations

oper(sign_contract(C), [company/ with]).
added(sign_contract(C), client(C)).

oper(hire(E), [person/ o]).
added(hire(E), (employee(E), level(E, 1))).

oper(assign(E,C), [employee/ o, client/ to]).
added(assign(E,C), serving(E,C)).
precond(assign(E,C),
  ((not serving(E,C1)), (not serving(E1, C)))).

oper(enroll(E,T), [employee/ o, course/ in]).
added(enroll(E,T), taking(E,T)).
deleted(enroll(E,T), account(C,inactive)).
precond(enroll(E,T), (serving(E,C),
                      not taking(E,T1))).

oper(promote(E), [employee/ o]).
added(promote(E), level(E,2)).
deleted(promote(E), level(E,1)).
```

```
precond(promote(E),
  (serving(E,C), not account(C,inactive),
   level(E,1))).

oper(replace(E1,E2,C),
      [employee/ o, employee/ by, client/ for]).
added(replace(E1,E2,C), serving(E2,C)).
deleted(replace(E1,E2,C), (serving(E1,C),
        account(C,inactive))).
precond(replace(E1,E2,C),
        (serving(E1,C), not serving(E2,C1))).

oper(fire(E), [employee/ o]).
deleted(fire(E), (employee(E), level(E,N))).
precond(fire(E), (not serving(E,C))).

oper(complain(C,E),
      [client/ a, employee/ about]).
added(complain(C,E), account(C,inactive)).
precond(complain(C,E), serving(E,C)).
```

Fig. 2. dynamic sub-schema

The other clauses defining the operation (cf. figure 2) give its preconditions and effects. As a consequence of these clauses, as the reader can verify, this particular replace event will indeed produce a state transition, whose net effect is that, in the next state, Leonard, instead of Mary, is serving Beta.

The other operations make it possible for company Alpha to sign a contract with a company (so as to make it one of its clients), to hire a person as employee with initial level 1, to assign an employee to the service of a client, to enroll an employee in a training course, to promote an employee by raising the level to 2, and to fire an employee. To clients it is allowed to formally complain about the service rendered by the assigned employee, with the contractual effect of suspending all ongoing business transactions (account = "inactive").

Pre-conditions and effects are usually tuned in a combined fashion, aiming at the enforcement of integrity constraints. It can be shown that the integrity constraints below, among others, will be preserved if, in consonance with the abstract data type discipline, the initial database is consistent and these pre-defined operations are the only way to cause database transitions: an employee can serve at most one client and a client can be served by at most one employee(i.e. serving is a 1-1 relationship); an employee can only be fired if currently not serving any client; and to have a level raise, an employee must be serving a client whose account is not inactive.

Verbs are employed to name the operations, possibly with trailing prepositions or other words or particles, separated by underscore.

2.3. The Behavioural Level

Carefully designed application-oriented operations enable the various agents to handle the database in a consistent way. The question remains of whether they will coexist well with a system supporting such operations, and, if so, what actual usage patterns will emerge. Ideally, the designers of an information system should try to predict how agents will behave within the scope of the system, so as to ensure that the specification at the two preceding levels is adequate from a *pragmatic* viewpoint.

To model the reactions of prospective users, our behavioural sub-schema for the Company Alpha example — given in figure 3 — contains a few illustrative *goal-inference rules*, and *typical plans* (represented as *complex operations*).

A goal-inference rule has, as antecedent, some *situation* which may arouse in a given agent the impulse to act in order to reach some *goal*. Two rules refer to Company Alpha, the database owner. The first one indicates that, if employee E is not currently serving any client, Alpha will want E to cease being an employee. The goal in the second rule is that Alpha will make an effort to placate any client C who, being dissatisfied with the employee assigned to its service, has assumed an inactive status. A goal is indicated for employees: if E1 has merely level 1, whilst some other employee E2 has been raised to level 2, then, presumably moved by emulation, E1 will want to reach this higher level.

In [2], we have used the three-level schemata for *simulation* purposes, with the help of a plan-recognition / plan-generation method, combining Kautz's algorithm and the AbTweak planner. In that context, a simulated process is enacted, whereby, at each state reached, the goal-inference rules are applied to propose goals by detecting situations affecting each agent. For attempting to fulfill such possibly collaborating or conflicting goals, *plans* are taken from a library or built by the plan-generator component. In turn, the execution of such plans leads to other states, where the goal-inference rules are again applied, and again plans are obtained and executed, so that the multistage process will continue until it reaches a state where no more goals arise, or until it is arbitrarily terminated.

We mention this use of goals and plans to call attention to the important assumption that plots generally reflect the interaction of diverse plans — not always totally executed and successful with respect to the intended goals — undertaken by the various agents. Here, however, we are not looking at simulation runs, but rather at observed actions, which may not be entirely *rational*. Hence, our use of goal-inference rules falls into an *abductive* mode of reasoning, as explained in the sequel. Assume that a rule R indicates that agent A, confronted with situation S, will have the desire to achieve a goal G. Now suppose that in the plot being examined an operation (or sequence of operations) O is present, with the effect of achieving goal G for A, and suppose further that, in the state before the execution of O, the motivating situation S prevailed. We then formulate the *hypothesis* that the event can be explained by this rule R, i.e. that agent A executed (or was able to induce an authorized agent A' to execute) operation O because A previously observed the occurrence of S, being thereby motivated to achieve G. This kind of reasoning is no more than hypothetical, because there may exist other reasons (possibly expressed in other goal-inference rules) that may better explain why O was executed.

So, goal-inference rules help us to suggest an *interpretation* for the events in a narrative. To fulfill this purpose, they are complemented by *typical plans*, expressed here as complex operations. We call the operations introduced in the previous section *basic operations*. Then, a *complex operation* can be defined from the repertoire of basic operations (or from other complex operations, recursively) by either *composition* (part-of hierarchy) or *generalization* (is-a hierarchy). In case of composition, the definition must specify the component operations and the ordering requirements, if any (noting that we allow plans to be *partially-ordered*). In case of generalization, the specialized operations must be specified.

In our example, complex operation renovate assistance is composed of basic operations hire, replace, and fire. In turn, complex operation improve service generalizes basic operation enroll and complex operation renovate assistance. (A minor technical detail: the fact "serving(E,C)", introduced by ":" in the first is_a clause is needed to identify C, which is not in the parameter list of enroll). Notice that the two (specialized) forms of improve service have, among others, the effect of removing the undesired de-activation of a client's account. Both can be regarded as reflecting customary strategies (typical plans) of Company Alpha to placate a complaining client: it either trains the faulty employee or "renovates" the manpower offered to the client. Both are adequate to achieve the goal expressed in the second rule of figure 3. So, as an additional feature in the interpretation of a plot, where only the basic operations are recorded, we can detect and call the user's attention to conjectural occurrences of typical plans (simple like enroll or composite like renovate assistance, both in turn classifiable as ways to perform improve service).

```
% Goal-inference rules and typical plans

goal('company Alpha', (not serving(E,C)),
                      not employee(E)).

goal('company Alpha', account(C,inactive),
                      not account(C,inactive)).

goal(employee(E1), (level(E1,1),level(E2,2)),
                   level(E1,2)).

op_complex(renovate_assistance(C,E2,E1),
           [client/ to, employee/ with,
            employee/ 'in the position of']).
```

```
components(renovate_assistance(C,E2,E1),
        [f1: hire(E2), f2: replace(E1,E2,C),
         f3: fire(E1)], [f1-f2, f2-f3]).

op_complex(advance_the_career(E), [employee/
of]).
components(advance_the_career(E),
        [f1: enroll(E,C), f2: promote(E)],
        [f1-f2]).

op_complex(improve_service(C), [client/ for]).
is_a(enroll(E,T),
     improve_service(C): serving(E,C)).
is_a(renovate_assistance(C,E2,E1),
improve_service(C)).
```

Fig. 3. behavioural sub-schema

Complex operation advance the career has an apparent peculiarity, in that it deviates from the usual norm of plan-generation algorithms, whereby operations are chained together exclusively as needed for the satisfaction of pre-conditions. Here, however, the component operation enroll is not required for satisfying a pre-condition for promote (except in the special case where training is the chosen way to remove the effects of a pending complaint). Our notion of typical plans, similarly to scripts [15], allows however a looser interpretation. A plan is typical if it reflects the usages and policies, imposed or not by rational reasons, that are observed (or anticipated) in the real-world environment. Thus, we may imagine that the employer, company Alpha, is sensed to be more favourable to promoting employees who, even in the absence of complaints against their service, seek the training program.

3. From Plots to Textual Narratives

As described in the sequel, our method (and, consequently, the implemented **TG** prototype) is fully parameterized on the schema specified. Hence, different applications can be handled by simply replacing the three-level specification.

3.1. Displaying the Operations

An elementary pattern-matching device is readily provided by logic programming languages. The two clauses:

```
read_as(replace(E1,E2,C),  ['Company Alpha replaces employee ',E1,' by employee ',E2,' for client ',C]).
disp(T) :- read_as(T,P1), concat(P1,P), write(P), nl.
```

are enough to display, by entering the calling statement:

```
:- disp(replace('Mary','Leonard','Beta')).
```

the expected natural language equivalent:

```
Company Alpha replaces employee Mary by employee Leonard for client Beta
```

A more general but still small program, loaded together with the example schema, will, given the plot [complain('Beta','Mary'),replace('Mary','Leonard','Beta')], yield "Beta complains about employee Mary, Company Alpha replaces employee Mary by employee Leonard for client Beta".

The reader will notice that this narrative conveys more precise information than the originating plot, in that the semantic roles of the parameters are expressed unambiguously. Thus, the use of the schema to drive text-generation already pays-off, even with this trivial version of **TG**.

3.2. Unravelling Pre-conditions and Effects

Exactly as in the previous section, distinct events in a plot (denoted by executions of operations) are the syntactical units of the narrative for the fuller **TG** that we have thus far developed. What establishes their conjectured coherence is the chaining of pre-conditions and effects, entailed by the assumption (mentioned before) that plots incorporate plans.

Separate sentences, ending with a period, correspond to each event. The scheme for expressing an event is: As <pre-conditions>, <operation>, so <effects>

The words 'as' and 'so' were chosen as being relatively neutral to express various kinds of enablement and consequence, so as to accommodate as many cases as possible with minimum strain. In the next section, we shall introduce additional *textual markers* [16] more suggestive of motivation.

All operations have, at least, the trivial pre-condition that the actual arguments be of the types indicated for their parameters. Thus, given hire('Mary'), the system will check if Mary is a person. Yet such obvious pre-conditions are not spelled out in the generated text. As a consequence, no pre-condition will be listed for certain events. When more than one pre-condition (or effect) is present, they are separated by 'and'.

The chaining of pre-conditions and effects is verified by a conventional holds meta-predicate, which, incidentally, is the basis for simple plan-generators based on STRIPS formalisms. A fact F holds after an operation O is executed at the state reached by executing a previous sequence of operations P if either: (a) O is s0, which denotes the initial state (P being empty), and F already belongs to the database, or (b) F is among the facts declared to be added by O, and the pre-conditions of O hold at the state after the execution of P, or (c) F already held at the state after the execution of P and is not among the facts declared to be deleted by O.

Notice that (2) and (3) make the process recursive (fixing the pre-conditions as sub-goals, or looking for F in P), and that (3) is a standard solution for the frame problem (facts not affected by O continue to hold). By using holds we not only check coherence but also provide for the instantiation of those variables in the pre-conditions and effects that do not correspond to the parameters. If a variable remains uninstantiated even after that, it is replaced by an adequate word, such as 'undefined', 'any' or 'no' (the two last ones being needed for negative expressions).

TG classifies the effects into (1) creation of entity instance; (2) deletion of entity instance; (3) assignment of value to attribute; (4) removal of value of attribute; (5) creation of relationship instance; and (6) deletion of relationship instance.

Cases (1) and (2) include acquiring or loosing membership in a specialized class, e.g. a person gaining or losing the condition of employee. Coupled occurrences of the pairs (4)-(3) or (6)-(5) are duly recognized and treated as *modifications*, rather than independent deletions-creations.

In Example 1 below, operation s0, with no parameters or pre-conditions, has as effect to introduce an initial database. In this example, it merely consists of facts asserting the existence of persons Mary, John and Leonard, companies Beta and Omega, and course c135. The presence of s0 in the plot is translated by the word 'beginning'. Notice that assign is the only operation in the plot with (non-trivial) pre-conditions. The past tense is employed. Effects involving creation of specialized entity instances in a class, and assignment of value to attributes are uniformly introduced by "became", whereas the creation of a relationship instance is prefixed by "started to be". Deletion of entity instances from a class, removal of values of attributes, and deletion of relationship instances are all introduced by "ceased to be". Underscores are everywhere removed.

Example 1: *Plot* - [s0,hire(Mary),sign_contract(Beta),assign(Mary,Beta)]
Narrative: Beginning. Company Alpha hired person Mary, so person with name Mary became employee and the level of employee with name Mary became 1. Company Alpha signed contract with company Beta, so company with denomination Beta became client. As employee Mary was not serving any client and no employee was serving client Beta, company Alpha assigned employee Mary to client Beta, so employee with name Mary started to be serving client with denomination Beta.

3.3. Reasoning about Goals and Typical Plans

If, on examining an event E and the part of the plot coming before its occurrence, **TG** decides that a declared goal-inference rule applies, it uses for E the expanded scheme
Since <situation> and as <pre-conditions>, then <event>, so that <goal> and, in addition, <effects>

The consideration of goals thus results in a refinement of the input / output characterization of events. A fact F that is both a pre-condition and part of a motivating situation can be said to both *enable* and *motivate* the operation. Since the latter relation carries greater significance, F will be displayed only once under the stronger "since" textual marker. (Notice, incidentally, that a fact can be part of <situation> without being a pre-condition: e.g. an employee can be led to strive for level 2 if some other employee was able to reach it, but this is exclusively a motivation, not a required condition for his actions). For analogous reasons, effects that are also part of a goal are emphasized, being separately introduced by "so that".

Also, if TG conjectures that a typical plan was used to achieve the goal, it introduces a parenthetical comment, following the scheme:

(thus, <complex operation by composition>, and, in this way, <complex operation by generalization>)

where one or the other kind of complex operation may be missing.

For Example 2, s0 establishes as initial the state resulting from the execution of the plot in Example 1. While Mary was attached to company Beta's service, the client complained of her service, which, according to the definition of complain, signals that Beta's account was automatically made inactive. The plot suggests that Alpha responded with the training strategy (consisting of a single basic operation) to improve the service rendered to Beta.

Example 2: *Plot* - [s0,complain(Beta,Mary),enroll(Mary,c135)]
Narrative: Beginning. As employee Mary was serving client Beta, client Beta complained about employee Mary, so the account of client with denomination Beta became inactive. Since the account of client Beta was inactive, and as employee Mary was serving client Beta and employee Mary was not taking any course, then company Alpha enrolled employee Mary in course c135, so that the account of client with denomination Beta ceased to be inactive, and, in addition, employee with name Mary started to be taking course with title c135 (in this way, company Alpha improved service for client Beta).

Example 3 illustrates the other way to improve service. The initial database is the same as for Example 2. As explained before, this strategy does involve composition and, as the last component operation (fire) is analyzed, and after checking the sequence of occurrence (not necessarily contiguous) of the components against the partial order requirements, **TG** signals the occurrence of renovate assistance. Modification of relationship instances, illustrated here by Leonard replacing Mary in Beta's service, is indicated by "<new entity instance > instead of <old entitity instance>".

Example 3: *Plot* - [s0,complain(Beta,Mary),hire(Leonard),replace(Mary,Leonard,Beta),fire(Mary)]
Narrative: Beginning. As employee Mary was serving client Beta, client Beta complained about employee Mary, so the account of client with denomination Beta became inactive. Company Alpha hired person Leonard, so person with name Leonard became employee and the level of employee with name Leonard became 1. Since the account of client Beta was inactive, and as employee Mary was serving client Beta and employee Leonard was not serving any client, then company Alpha replaced employee Mary by employee Leonard for client Beta, so that the account of client with denomination Beta ceased to be inactive, and, in addition, employee with name Leonard, instead of Mary, started to be serving client with denomination Beta. Since employee Mary was not serving any client, then company Alpha fired employee Mary, so that person with name Mary ceased to be employee, and, in addition, the level of person with name Mary

ceased to be 1 (thus, company Alpha renovated assistance to client Beta with employee Leonard in the position of employee Mary, and, in this way, company Alpha improved service for client Beta).

The current prototype does not consider the possibility that there may exist more than one goal-inference rule applicable to the interpretation of an event.

3.4. Extracting a Plot from the Log

Plots that we want to tell are generally focussed on some topic or object. The query indicated at the beginning, as suggesting the theme of this paper: "What happened to Mary between time instants t1 and t2?", presupposes our ability to extract from among the many records in the Log all events directly or indirectly involving Mary.

First of all, how can the Log be structured? In an earlier work [3], we showed that one possibility (compatible with a relational DBMS implementation) is to use a separate table in correspondence with each basic operation. The name of each table can be that of the operation, and its columns correspond to its parameters, adding one more column for the time stamps. Then each row, of course, stores an event (execution) of this particular operation. The entire Log is viewed, therefore, as a virtual sequence of tuples coming from the separate tables, merged together in the sequence induced by the time stamps.

Regardless of what file structure is used to keep the Log, we should be able to take from it a subsequence **L** of all events in the time interval t1-t2, and then consider suitable criteria to extract from it a plot P, where, intuitively, we require that an event E in **L** should be copied in P if and only if it concerns an indicated object Obj. In our example query, Obj is the entity instance "employee Mary".

Our first approximation to an extraction method (a Prolog implementation is operational), which we expect to revise after further study and experimentation, is described informally in the sequel. The method proceeds by examining **L** in reverse order, and considering one event E in **L** at each step. E should be copied in P if (1) it has Obj as one of its arguments, or (2) if it contributes to fulfilling the pre-conditions of an event E' already copied in P, or (3) if it contributes to creating a situation inducing a goal (as defined in a goal-inference rule) to be achieved by some event E' already in P. If E is added to P by (1) or (2), then the literals (positive or negative) constituting pre-conditions of E are added to a set Sp and the literals (again, positive or negative) that are part of the triggering situation of a goal to which E contributes (again, as defined in a goal-inference rule) are added to a different set Ss. It is by checking against these sets that tests (2) and (3) will be performed at subsequent steps on other (earlier) events in **L**. Note that, if E is accepted for reason (3), none of the two sets will be updated, a criterion that we chose to adopt to avoid stretching the length of P by propagating events not so clearly pertinent to Obj.

In Example 4, the already described goal of interest to employees is considered. If Mary, still at level 1, sees that a colleague, John, has been promoted, she will be motivated to seek an advancement in her career. As seen, a typical plan towards this objective is to take a course, in the expectation that this will attract the employer's favourable attention. Let **L**, the segment of the Log in the given time interval t1-t2 (preceded by s0 to denote the state current at t1, which we shall assume to be the same as the state at the end of Example 1), be as follows:

L = [s0,sign_contract(Omega),hire(John),assign(John,Omega),promote(John),hire(Leonard), enroll(Mary,c135),promote(Mary), fire(Leonard)]

From **L** we proceed to extract P, as the plot focussed on events pertaining to employee Mary. Notice that Leonard's admission and termination are discarded as irrelevant. John's promotion is retained, as the event that provokes Mary's ambition, but none of the other events involving him or his assignment to client Omega is kept.

P =[s0,promote(John),enroll(Mary,c135),promote(Mary)]

The narrative generated for P follows. Two remarks are in order. Firstly, because the preliminary events about John were omitted, **TG** is unable to verify that the pre-conditions for John's promotion are fulfilled. To cope with this unavoidable consequence of the limiting criterion adopted, we supplied a noncommittal "as reported" clause. The second remark is that the agent of promote is not, of course, the employee involved, but the employer. Accordingly, the clause "as <agent with the goal> wished", precedes the information about the execution of the event by the actual authorized agent. Mary's level raise illustrates the modification of an attribute value, phrased as "the <attribute> of <entity> was changed from <old value> to <new value>".

Example 4: *Narrative*: Beginning. As reported, company Alpha promoted employee John, so the level of employee with name John became 2. As employee Mary was serving client Beta and employee Mary was not taking any course, company Alpha enrolled employee Mary in course c135, so employee with name Mary started to be taking course with title c135. Since the level of employee Mary was 1 and the level of employee John was 2, and as employee Mary was serving client Beta and the account of client Beta was not inactive, then, as employee Mary wished, company Alpha promoted employee Mary, so that the level of employee with name Mary was changed from 1 to 2 (thus, company Alpha advanced the career of employee Mary).

4. Concluding Remarks

We have not yet fully used our conceptual modelling theory for the task of text generation. Features related to the characterization of multi-agent environments with collaborating and, especially, conflicting goals, such as *conditional* and *limited* goals [2] are still to be examined in the context of the generation of narratives. In particular, we intend to adapt our **TG** to deal with plots generated by simulation, as those we treated in [2]. For simulation, one must cope with partially ordered sequences of events, taking into account the interactions between different goals of one or more agents, and using goal-inference rules that are more general than those used here.

Moreover, the second stage of text generation, corresponding to the *tactical component* of the process, needs much more attention, which will be given with the continuation of the research. The characterization of the nature of the connections between events, with their pre-conditions, effects, and goal-oriented aspects, may be refined through a revision in terms of *rhetorical structure theory* [13], followed by a more principled choice of *textual markers* [16] (at the present state of our work limited to "as", "since", etc.) for the rhetorical relations [9] identified.

Some rules for stylistic enhancement should be added, based, for instance, on *coordination*, *ellipsis*, *anaphora*, and *relativization* [1]. Also, due stress on the *nucleus* components, as opposed to their attending *satellites* [13], can often be achieved by *embedding* [16]. Consider the awkwardness of the following passage in

Example 1: "Company Alpha hired person Mary, so person with name Mary became employee and the level of employee with name Mary became 1". The dominating effect of hire is clearly the creation of a specialized instance of employee, but the circumstance of the initial value of an attribute received here the same attention. By eliding the redundant elements, and through a judicious use of anaphora and embedding (of the reference to level), a shorter and more natural rendering is obtainable: "Company Alpha hired person Mary, so she became employee with level 1".

Finally, an interdisciplinary approach may offer clues along the continuation of the research. Literary research and semiotics have contributed extensively to the understanding of how narratives are structured (structuralism, narratology), mutually interfere with each other (intertextuality), and act upon the people who observe them (reader reception); our treatment of application-oriented operations was greatly influenced by the use of functions in [14]. The different needs of different classes of users posing queries to be answered by narratives must also receive a differentiated treatment, tuned to a level of detail that is neither insufficient nor over-helpful [8], which in turn increases the demand that *user-modelling* be taken into account. How to detect usage patterns [11,10], so as to discover goal-inference rules and typical plans is the problem to which we are currently dedicating more effort.

References

1. G. Brown and G. Yule. *Discourse Analysis*. Cambridge University Press, 1983.
2. A. E. M. Ciarlini and A. L. Furtado. ìSimulating the interaction of database agentsî. In Proc. *DEXA'99 Database and Expert Systems Applications Conference*, Florence, Italy, 1999.
3. A. L. Furtado and M. A. Casanova. "Plan and schedule generation over temporal databases". in Proc. of the *9th International Conference on the Entity-Relationship Approach*, 1990.
4. A.L. Furtado and A. E. M. Ciarlini. "Plots of narratives over temporal databases". in Proc. of *the 8th International Workshop on Database and Expert Systems Applications*. R. R. Wagner (ed.). IEEE Computer Society, 1997.
5. C. Fillmore. "The case for case". In *Universals in Linguistic Theory*. E. Bach and R. Harms (eds.). Holt, Rinehart and Winston, 1968.
6. A. L. Furtado and E. J. Neuhold. *Fornal Techniques for Data Base Design*. Berlin: Springer-Verlag, 1986.
7. B. J. Grosz, K. S. Jones and B. L. Webber (eds.). *Readings in Natural Language Processing*. San Mateo: Morgan Kaufmann, 1986.
8. H. P. Grice. "Logic and conversation". In *Syntax and Semantics*, vol. 3, P. Cole and J. Morgan (eds.). Academic Press, 1975.
9. E. H. Hovy and E. Maier. "Parsimonious or profligate: how many and which discourse structure relations?". Announced for *Discourse Process*. Currently available from http://www.isi.edu/natural-language/discourse/text-planning.html.
10. J. L. Kolodner. *Case-Based Reasoning*. San Mateo: Morgan Kaufmann, 1993.
11. C.J. Matheus, P.K. Chan. and G. Piatesky-Shapiro. "Systems for knowledge discovery in databases". *IEEE Transactions on Knowledge and Data Engineering*, 5, 6, 1993.
12. K.R. McKeown. *Text Generation: Using Dscourse Strategies and Focus Constraints to Generate Natural Language Text*. Cambridge: Cambridge University Press, 1992.
13. W. C. Mann and S. A. Thompson. "Rhetorical structure theory; toward a functional theory of text organization". *Text*, 8, 3, 1988.

14. V. Propp. *Morphology of the Folktale*. Laurence Scott (trans.). Austin: University of Texas Press, 1968.
15. 16. R.C. Schank and R.P. Abelson. *Scripts, Plans, Goals and Understanding*. Lawrence Erlbaum Associates, Hillsdale, NJ, 1977.
16. D.R. Scott and C.S. de Souza. "Getting the message across in RST-based text generation". In *Current Research in Natural Language Generation*. R. Dale, C. Mellish and M. Zonk (eds.). Academic Press, 1990.
17. H. Thompson. "Strategy and tactics: a model for language production". In *Papers 13th Regional Meeting Chicago Linguistic Society*, 1977.

Temporal Granularity Enlightened by Knowledge

Sylviane R. Schwer*

L.I.P.N. UPRESA CNRS 7030
Institut Galilée, Université Paris 13
99, Bd J-B Clément
Fr. 93430 Villetaneuse
schwer@lipn.univ-paris13.fr

Abstract. The formalization of periods of time inside a linear model of Time are based on the notion of intervals, that can or not contain their endpoints. It is quite insufficient when these periods are expressing in terms of coarse granularities with respect to the event taken into account. For instance, how to express the inter-war period in terms of a *years* interval?
This paper presents a new type of interval and the extension of operations on intervals to this new type, in order to reduce the gap between the discourse related to temporal relationship and its translation into a discretized model of Time in databases.

Keywords: time, granularity, intervals.

1 Introduction

Human activities are heavily related to calendar units and clock units (e.g. *years*, *weeks*, *months*, *hours* and *seconds*). System support and reasoning involving these units, also called granularities [5] or chronologies [13] or time units [14], have been recognized to be an important issue. Many different definitions of granularities exist in the literature and data conversions among different granularities are proposed. These conversions are proposed when two granularities are comparable, as *months* and *years* are, but as *months* and *weeks* are not. The method is always the same. If a granularity f, say *months*, is finer than a granularity g, say *years*, an occurrence of f, a *month*, is translated into the occurrence of g, the *year* that contains it: $June2000$ is so converted into 2000. In the other way, an occurrence of g is converted into the interval of all occurrences of f that is contained in it: 2000 is converted into $[January2000,\ December2000]$. This is obviously a good way to manage as far as granularities are taken into account regardless to any timestamped information. This becomes far from what is expected when relationship between periods of validity of facts or events is concerned. It has been remarked [8,4] that a constraint about a temporal relationship in one granularity may not be preserved in another granularity. As an example, if a constraint says

* This work is partially supported by REANIMATIC project.

M. Bouzeghoub et al. (Eds.): NLDB 2000, LNCS 1959, pp. 30–41, 2001.

that an event must happen in the *day* that follows the *day* when another event happens, then this constraint cannot be translated into one in terms of *hours* because it is incorrect to say that the second event must happen within 24 hours after the first event happens. The reader can see that the solution is x hours for some x such that $1 \leq x \leq 47$. This constraint cannot be also translated automatically into one in terms of *months* because the first event may occur the last day of a month, the next day taking then place in an other month.

In Databases framework, the same problem was risen [7]. In fact, it is clear that, when the Time line, supposed to be continuous, is partitioned into intervals with non-null length, called granules of time, any instant is approximated with such a granule. Exactly in the same manner as any measurement is an approximation of what is measured. Two instants that are located within the same granule, inside a granularity may be strictly ordered inside a finer granularity. It has been proposed, for dealing with that problem of precision or indeterminacy, different approaches based on fuzzy sets or probabilistic functions. Much attention has been paid about the conversion of temporal expression from one granularity to another, about an information which is supposed to be timestamped with the good granularity according to its management.

But no attention has been paid to discrepancy between the time granularity expressed in the discourse and the time granularity induced by the knowledge level, that induces temporal relationships on finer granularity that are contained in the knowledge level, but not expressed in the discourse.

For instance, the worldwide II war is called 1939-1945 war, which express the fact that this war began in the course of the year 1939 and ended in the course of year 1945. The same thing can be said about 1914-1918 war. And the period between these two wars is obviously, for a human being, the period 1918-1939.

This problem is concerned with how to express indeterminacy related to the expression *in the course of* which can be expressed or simply inferred by the knowledge of he context.

That is the problem we address in this paper, *i.e.* how to express the difference between endpoints of intervals that are wholly included in the validity period of the fact taken into account and the endpoints of intervals that are partially included in it and how to manage with it inside a granularity and going from one granularity to another one.

The paper is organized as follows. We begin with two examples that motivate this work. The first one is taken from a book about french history, the second one is inspired by the REANIMATIC project, which is devoted to a medical datawarehouse. Then we propose a new kind of interval over the set of natural integers, that takes into account the notion of imprecision when converting a period from a granularity to a finer one, as well as operators to deal with intervals. We end the paper with the resolution of the Reanimatic's example and a short conclusion.

2 Examples Analysis

In this section, we outline our work on the example about worldwide wars, and then we show how, with that formalism, it is possible for an hospital, to have an hospital day (that is: a bed) paid two or even three times.

2.1 The Inter-war Period

In the dictionary [9], one can read "entre-deux-guerres : The inter-war period (1918-1939)". Following this notation, the first worldwide war period is (1914-1918) and the second worldwide war period is (1939-1945). Everybody understands that these three periods are adjacent, or following Allen's vocabulary [2], (1914-1918) *meets* (1918-1939) and (1918-1939) *meets* (1939-1945). It would be a pity not to be able to maintain this knowledge when storing it in a database, without the precise date (with the granularity *days*).

A granularity, temporal elements provided by usual Data Models for Time are either points, intervals or subsets of a linear and discrete set, such as the set of positive integers $\mathbb{N}$, or as the set of integers $\mathbb{Z}$. As a point is an interval with only one element and as any subset of $\mathbb{N}$or $\mathbb{Z}$ can be rewritten as union of intervals, temporal elements of Data Model for Time are reduced to intervals. It is not possible to express the periods of validity of 1914-1918 war and of 1939-1945, respecting the semantics of it, inside the granularity *year*. With the endpoints 1914 and 1918, with the 4 types of intervals that can be used in $\mathbb{N}$and $\mathbb{Z}$: a closed interval such as [1914, 1918], an open interval such as]1914,1918[, right-open interval such as [1914, 1918[and left-open interval such as]1914, 1918]. The endpoints are included or not included, depending on whether the interval is closed or open or closed-open or open-closed, depending whether the endpoints are contained or not in the period. None of them modellize the sense of *in the course of*, that is the endpoint is in part included, so that this other part will be included to any period that meets the interval by that endpoint. None of the fourth kinds of intervals allows to do that. For that purpose, we need a new kind of interval that mentions the fact that its endpoints can be shared with a meeting interval of that kind. In order to have a compromise between the dictionary way of writing and the databases timestamping with intervals notation, we propose to denote such new kind of interval: (1914,1918), that is to convert "–" into "," which has the following meaning: the period of time containing the period of years 1915, 1916, 1917, a starting period of 1918 and a finishing period of 1914.

The fact is that granules are thought as abstract points, hence as atomic objects, they are not sharable. In fact, they are atomic objects, with respect to a granularity coarser than their own granularity, they are sharable but not decomposable with respect to their own granularity and decomposable with respect to a finer granularity.

This notion of sharing is close to the notion of S-letters defined in [6]. A S-letter describes the Russel definition of an instant, which is the set of all events occurring at this time. A granularity induces a sequence of points on the physical time line, which are the meeting points of granules. Each point can be viewed as the representative of the granule that just follows it (in the sense of the arrow of Time). In that sense, a granule is the set of all events occurring during that period of time.

2.2 Allen's Work Read Again

The 13 possible relations between two symbolic intervals were set by Allen [1] and we show in Figure 1.

Fig. 1. Allen's relations between two symbolic intervals

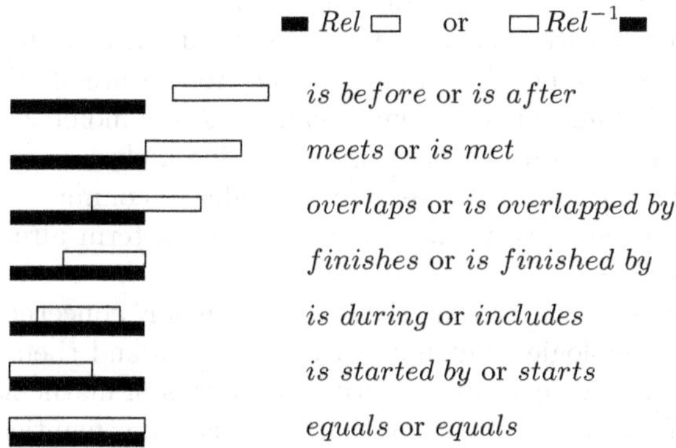

In [2], the relation *meet* is proved to be the generator of the 13 Allen relations, and induces the notion of Russel's point as an equivalence class. Also in [2], in order to avoid confusion between the span of time taken by an event and its mathematical representation, the term *period* is preferred to the term *interval*, but they are not themselves periods, not even very short ones. Two periods *meet* where there is no time between the two periods, and no time that the periods share. Points in time are places where periods meet. A point is then an abstract object, the nature of which is different from the interval nature. Note that all physical use of Allen's work has been made in terms of numerical intervals.

A time period is the sort of thing that an event might occupy. Even a flash of lighting, although pointlike in many ways, must be a period because it contains a real physical event. Other things can happen at the same time as the flash. They then set the following definition:

Definition 1 (Moment and Periods).
A period *is a convex time duration of an event or a fact.*
A moment *is an indivisible period.*

Moments have many of the properties of points: if a period has moments at its ends, then these moments are unique, and they uniquely define the period between them. But moments also differ from points in many ways, for instance they have distinct endpoints.

2.3 Chronology Revisited

In [13], a chronology was defined as a couple $\langle \alpha, U \rangle$ where α is an ordinal such that $0 < \alpha \leq \omega$, named its temporal domain, and U is its unit.

An ordinal can be viewed has an element of any ordinal greater than itself or the well-ordered set of all ordinals smaller than it. Ordinals have the two natures of indivisibility or divisibility, depending of what Hobbs [10] calls a change of granularity.

Inside a chronology, a unit is the thickness of the now. α is the number of units taken into account, often called *time-windowing function*, for example in [14]. As such, it is the well-ordered set. The α elements of the ordinal α are its elements. But neither α nor its elements, that we yet call units, are those which are thought when devising of the two natures of an ordinal. These two natures are connected with the change of granularity. But nothing is said about ordinals inside a chronology. We argue that the true nature of an ordinal inside a chronology is something between elements and sets, as a moment is between point and period. That is to said that an ordinal inside a chronology as a thickness but is indivisible. As adopted in temporal databases community [5] we use the term of *granule*, even if we would prefer *chronon*, a term already used for an other purpose in [11].

In this paper, we argue that all these works are only concerned with relationships between chronologies, but not between periods and their representations inside a chronology. All periods are written in terms of mathematical intervals. It is the aim of this paper to show that periods are semantically richer than intervals as far as temporal (or spatial) relationships are concerned.

A granule is not a point, but an atomic interval. It is not possible to cut it, (which is unacceptable for an atomic object,) but there are four possible relations for a period of validity inside a granule as shown in Figure 2.

Fig. 2. The four relations between a period and the granule g that contains it

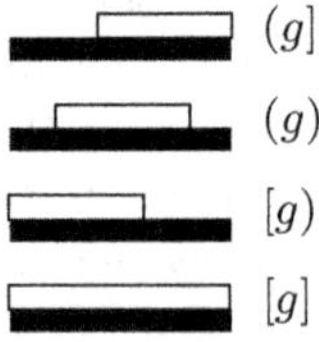

For instance, the relation between the intersection of period of the first worldwide war with year 1914 is (1914], with 1915 is [1915], with 1916 is [1916], with 1917 is [1917] and with 1918 is [1918). The symbols [and] have the same meaning as for usual intervals. The two others symbols "(" [resp. ")"] mean that the point, thought as an ordered set is not wholly taken but only a finishing [resp. a beginning] section of it is taken.

Thus an endpoint of an interval can be either excluded, or included or partially included. We then have nine type of intervals depending of the status of the two endpoints. These types are only qualitative because nothing is said about the part which is included. But this suffices to answer correctly to the following question: "Knowing the two worldwide war periods (14, 18) and (39, 45), what is the inter-war period?" The answer is (18,39).

In a french hospital, a day begins at 8 a.m. and lasts 24 hours. If Jack goes to the hospital at 2 p.m. on monday march 13*th* and leaves at 10 a.m. on friday march 17*th*, he will be registered and will be requested to pay for 5 days. If George goes to the same hospital at 6 p.m. on monday march 6*th* and leaves at 10 a.m. on monday march 13*th*, he will be registered and will be requested to pay for 8 days. If Karl goes to the same hospital from 11 a.m. to 4 p.m. on monday march 13*th*, he will be recorded and will be requested to pay for 1 day.

Suppose that they occupy the same bed, let us say bed 13. The registration database is described by Table 1.

Table 1. The relational table of staying days in the hospital

Bed	Name	admission-day	exit-day
13	Jack	03/13	03/17
13	George	03/06	03/13
13	Karl	03/13	03/13

Now, the occupation basis of the hospital (and the payment involved) derived from this is given by Table 2.

The stay includes the two endpoints days, even if they are partial. That so, the day 03/13 is paid three times instead of one time, since according to the hospital database, for the same bed, 5+8+1=14 days have been accounted from 03/06 until 03/17 (that is for 12 days) thought at any moment there is at most one person in the bed. The solution that consists in changing the time unit to hours would induce perhaps less liberty for a patient to leave the hospital and a change inside the database of the hospital.

Table 2. The closed interval's solution: the usual case

Bed	Name	stay [x,y]	days due=y-x+1
13	Jack	[03/13, 03/17]	5
13	George	[03/06, 03/13]	8
13	Karl	[03/13, 03/13]	1

Let us show that none of closed, open, open-closed or closed-open intervals, with the same endpoints, are able to modellize this reality, that is to make the social security to pay only one day per bed, when a bed is occupied (partly or not) this day without to change the granularity. *Days due* computes the number of days inside the interval.

The open interval choice gives Table 3:

Table 3. The open interval's solution

Bed	Name	stay]x,y[	days due=max{0,y-x-1}
13	Jack	] 03/13, 03/17[	3
13	George	]03/06, 03/13[	6
13	Karl	] 03/13, 03/13[	0

Only 3+6+0=9 days will be accounted, which is obviously not enough. The closed-open (or the open-closed) interval choice gives Table 4:

Table 4. The closed-open interval's solution

Bed	Name	stay [x,y[	days due=y-x
13	Jack	[03/13, 03/17[	4
13	George	[03/06, 03/13[	7
13	Karl	[03/13, 03/13[	0

The total due for bed 13, during the period beginning at 03/06 and ending at 03/17 is 4+7+0=11. If bed 13 is not used on 03/18, the day 03/17 is not perceived and all the day 03/13 is due by Jack, Karl paying nothing.

With respect to that framework, the choice of the hospital is the good one but one of these solutions gives the good result: 12 days.

Our proposition consists in the offer of a best approximation of what is due to the hospital, *i.e.* the possibility of signifying if an endpoint day is totally or partially occupied by a patient. Our solution gives the good solution and the number of user of a same bed per day. Our proposition offers a good compromise between the hospital interest and patients' one. It will be possible to write that 03/13 has been shared by three patients, but of course, without knowing proportionality because staying inside the same time unit.

3 Our Proposal

In mathematics, the general definition of intervals inside a lattice $\langle L, \leq \rangle$ is

[a,b]= $\{x \in L | a \leq x \leq b\}$

[a,b[= $\{x \in L | a \leq x < b\}$

]a,b]= $\{x \in L | a < x \leq b\}$

]a,b[= $\{x \in L | a < x < b\}$

These four types are derived from the two ways that exist for typing each of the two endpoints: included or excluded. So we have

- $[x, -$ left included endpoint
- $]x, -$ left excluded endpoint
- $-, x]$ right included endpoint
- $-, x[$ right excluded endpoint

Let us set $\sim$ the algebraic operator that converts an endpoint of an interval to the corresponding endpoint of the adjacent interval (that meets it in that endpoint), as shown in Table 5:

Table 5. Complementation

	$[x,-$	$]x,-$	$-,x]$	$-,x[$
$\sim$	$-,x[$	$-,x]$	$]x,-$	$[x,-$

The binary operators union and intersection of two intervals that share a same endpoint are given in Table 6:

Table 6. Union and Intersection

$\cup$	$[x,-$	$]x,-$	$-,x]$	$-,x[$
$[x,-$	$[x,-$	$[x,-$	$-,-$	$-,-$
$]x,-$	$[x,-$	$]x,-$	$-,-$	$-,x[\cup]x,-$
$-,x]$	$-,-$	$-,-$	$-,x]$	$-,x]$
$-,x[$	$-,-$	$-,x[\cup]x,-$	$-,x]$	$-,x[$

$\cap$	$[x,-$	$]x,-$	$-,x]$	$-,x[$
$[x,-$	$[x,-$	$]x,-$	$[x]$	$\emptyset$
$]x,-$	$]x,-$	$]x,-$	$\emptyset$	$\emptyset$
$-,x]$	$[x]$	$\emptyset$	$-,x]$	$-,x[$
$-,x[$	$\emptyset$	$\emptyset$	$-,x[$	$-,x[$

Mathematics works on ideal objects with null dimension: the points. A point is essentially atomic. In the set of real number $\mathbb{R}$, any point is the limit of any infinite set of fitting together intervals which contain it [12, Weierstrass theorem]. This is due to the completeness of $\mathbb{R}$. The physical time line is usually modellized by a convex part of $\mathbb{R}$.

Calendars, in the databases community, are defined upon the discrete ordered set of chronons, which is a partition with finite intervals of the physical time line. A chronon, which is a finite non vacuous interval of $\mathbb{R}$, is treated exactly as if a mathematical point. But it is not a mathematical point because it is very large with respect to the Planck time, so that lots of sequential things may appear during this leap of time inside the system, but the system will work on them as if they where simultaneous.

It has been shown in [13], that calendars are essentially discrete well-orders and that their limits, if not discrete are certainly not calendars. A chronon, as any time unit inside a calendar is then neither a point nor a true interval (*i.e.* with more than one element) inside its chronology [13]. We suggest, following Allen, to adopt the denomination of a *moment* for any point inside a chronology. We now recall the vocabulary of [13] and add a new definition concerning the moment and derived from Allen's work. A chronology is potentially made for cover all the physical Time line, but the need for changing units brings to the definition of calendars, to go from a unit to a coarser or a finer one. Hence we set:

Definition 2 (chronology).
A chronology *is a couple* $\{\alpha, U\}$ *where* α *is an ordinal such that* $0 < \alpha \leq \omega$, *named its temporal domain, and* U *is its unit.*

Definition 3 (atomic calendar).
Let $\langle \alpha, U\rangle$ and $\langle \beta, V\rangle$ be two chronologies such that $\alpha \leq \beta \leq \omega$ and let f_{UV} a morphism from α into β. The data $\langle U, V, f_{UV}\rangle$ defines a structure named an atomic calendar.
If $\alpha = \beta = \omega$ then $\langle U, V, f_{UV}\rangle$ is an atomic ω-calendar.

An atomic calendar has two commensurable units. A calendar is a directed acyclic graph where the set of nodes is the set of units, the set of vertices is the set of morphisms such that, if U and V are neighbors, f_{UV} is the vertex between them.

Hence, we set:

Definition 4 (moment, point, interval).

1. *Let $\langle \alpha, U\rangle$ be a chronology.*
   $x \in \alpha$ is a moment *of the chronology $\langle \alpha, U\rangle$.*
2. *Let $\langle \alpha, U\rangle$ and $\langle \beta, V\rangle$ be two chronologies and $\langle U, V, f_{UV}\rangle$ be an atomic calendar.*
   $x \in \alpha$ is an interval *with respect to the chronology $\langle \beta, V\rangle$.*
3. *Let $\langle \gamma, X\rangle$ and $\langle \alpha, U\rangle$ be two chronologies and $\langle X, U, f_{XU}\rangle$ be an atomic calendar.*
   $x \in \alpha$ is a point *with respect to the chronology $\langle \gamma, X\rangle$.*

An interval inside a chronology has a mathematical meaning, but a period of the linear time line, mapped inside a chronology is not exactly an interval as far as its limits are concerned. It can be useful to say if the entire moment is taken or not. This is why we add a new type of endpoint for partially included end-moment that we note:

- $(x, -$ for a left moment
- $-, x)$ for a right moment

In $\mathbb{R}$, the closure of an interval is the closed interval with the same endpoints, the opening of an interval is the open interval with the same endpoint. That allow us to extend the $\sim$ operator and these two topological operators (in $\mathbb{R}$) as described in Table 7.

Table 7. Extended $\sim$, opening and closure operations

	$[x, -$	$(x, -$	$]x, -$	$-, x]$	$-, x)$	$-, x[$
$\sim$	$-, x[$	$-, x)$	$-, x]$	$]x, -$	$(x, -$	$[x, -$
opening	$]x, -$	$]x, -$	$]x, -$	$-, x[$	$-, x[$	$-, x[$
closure	$[x, -$	$[x, -$	$[x, -$	$-, x]$	$-, x]$	$-, x]$

It is important to know how two periods share the same partial endpoint. They are three different kinds of union: one with a non vacuous intersection, which is denoted by "-,-", one with the meet relations, which is denoted by

"-,g)(g,-" and the other with an interval gap in between which we name disjoint-union and denote by "-,g)$\bigoplus$(g,-".

The two operators are extended as shown in Table 8. We set "x,-" for "x,y", y being any moment following x; and we set "-,x" for "y,x", y being any moment preceding x. where "$\cup\cap$" stands for "(x)" or "$\emptyset$" and "$\cup\cup\cup$" stands for "$-,x)\bigoplus(x,-$" or "$-,x)(x,-$" or "$-,-$".

Table 8. Extended union and Extended intersection

$\cup$	$[x,-$	$(x,-$	$]x,-$	$-,x]$	$-,x)$	$-,x[$
$[x,-$	$[x,-$	$[x,-$	$[x,-$	$-,-$	$-,-$	$-,-$
$(x,-$	$[x,-$	$(x,-$	$(x,-$	$-,-$	$\cup\cup\cup$	$-,x[\cup(x,-$
$]x,-$	$[x,-$	$(x,-$	$]x,-$	$-,-$	$-,x)\cup]x,-$	$-,x[\cup]x,-$
$-,x]$	$-,-$	$-,-$	$-,-$	$-,x]$	$-,x]$	$-,x]$
$-,x)$	$-,-$	$\cup\cup\cup$	$-,x)\cup]x,-$	$-,x]$	$-,x)$	$-,x)$
$-,x[$	$-,-$	$-,x[\cup(x,-$	$-,x[\cup]x,-$	$-,x]$	$-,x)$	$-,x[$

$\cap$	$[x,-$	$(x,-$	$]x,-$	$-,x]$	$-,x)$	$-,x[$
$[x,-$	$[x,-$	$(x,-$	$]x,-$	$[x]$	[x)	$\emptyset$
$(x,-$	$(x,-$	$(x,-$	$]x,-$	$(x]$	$\cup\cap$	$\emptyset$
$]x,-$	$]x,-$	$]x,-$	$]x,-$	$\emptyset$	$\emptyset$	$\emptyset$
$-,x]$	$[x]$	$(x]$	$\emptyset$	$-,x]$	$-,x)$	$-,x[$
$-,x)$	$[x)$	$\cup\cap$	$\emptyset$	$-,x)$	$-,x)$	$-,x[$
$-,x[$	$\emptyset$	$\emptyset$	$\emptyset$	$-,x[$	$-,x[$	$-,x[$

Let us set, by the end, how these types are converted inside atomic calendars hence, (and hence by transitivity, inside calendars).

Let $\langle\alpha, U\rangle$ and $\langle\beta, V\rangle$ be two chronologies such that $\alpha \leq \beta \leq \omega$, let f_{UV} be a morphism from α into β and $\langle U, V, f_{UV}\rangle$ the atomic calendar. The reader will convince her/himself that Table 9 is true.

Table 9. From one chronology to another one

	[	(	]	)
$\alpha \rightarrow \beta$	[	(or [	]	) or]
$\alpha \leftarrow \beta$	(or [	(	) or]	)

4 Examples Resolution

4.1 The Inter-war

The period of the inter-war is the period between the two periods (1914,1918) and (1939,1945). These two intervals cover only a part of their endpoints. Hence, the period between has to cover the parts of the two endpoints 1918 and 1939 which are not covered by the two war periods and all the years between 1918 and 1945. This period is then the intersection between the complementary of the two intervals "-,1918)" and "(1939,-". It is obtained first by using the ∼ operator on both endpoints "-,1918)" and "(1939,-" which provides the two intervals "(1918,-" and "-,1939)", secondly by the intersection of them which gives (1918,1939).

4.2 The Hospital

Jack's period in the hospital is "(03/06, 03/13)", that is two partial days (one beginning and one ending) and 5 full days.

George's period is "(03/13, 03/17)", that is two partial days (one beginning and one ending) and 3 full days.

Karl's period is "(03/13, 03/13)", that is one partial day (middle).

The global period is obtained by union of three periods with "-, 03/13)"," (03/13,03/13)" and "(03/13,-".

The table gives "-, 03/13) ∪∪∪ (03/13,03/13) ∪∪∪ (03/13,-".

There is *a priori* 3 × 3=9 *scenarii.* But it is obvious to any one that bed 13 cannot be shared by two patients at the same time and that there is a gap between two patients used this bed, so that, according to the knowledge of the domain, there is thus only one *scenario* which is "(03/06, 03/13)⊕ (03/13)⊕ (03/13, 03/17)". The length of this period is the length of its closure. The closure of a union is the union of the closure, hence this period is: "[03/06, 03/13]∪ [03/13]∪ [03/13, 03/17]" = "[03/06,03/17]". Its length is 12 days.

All these informations may help the social security and the patients to have a fairer fee to pay!

5 Conclusion

In this paper, we introduced a new type of interval and the extension of operations on intervals to this new type of interval based on the three different meanings of what it is usually called a granule inside a chronology, depending on whether it view*above*, *under* or inside its chronology. We showed on two examples how to use these new tools. We are going, in the REANIMATIC project, to implement them and to provide translation functions between all kinds of chronologies inside a calendar.

This new type of interval is adequate not only for expressing time life period inside a chronology, but also for translating Allen's relations between symbolic intervals inside a chronology. This concept of *partially included end-moment* is very close to the theory of granularity, inside which it would be used a lot.

References

1. Allen, J.: An Interval-Based Representation of Temporal Knowledge. In: proceedings of the International Join Conference in Artificial Iintelligence (1981) pp221-226.

2. Allen, J., Hayes P.: A common-Sense Theory of Time. In: proceedings of the International Join Conference in Artificial Iintelligence (1985) pp528-531.
3. Allen, J., Hayes P.: Short Time Periods. In: proceedings of the International Join Conference in Artificial Iintelligence (1987) pp981-983.
4. Bettini C., Wang S., Jajodia S.: A general framework for time granularity and its application to temporal reasoning. Annals of Mathemetics and Artificial Intelligence 22 (1998) pp29-58.
5. Bettini C., Dyreson C., Evans W., Snodgrass R, and Wang S.: A Glossary of Time Granularity Concepts. In Temporal Databases - Research and Practice. In Lecture Notes in Computer Science, Vol 1399. Springer-Verlag, Berlin Heidelberg New-York (1998) pp 406-413.
6. Dubois M., Schwer R. S.: Classification topologique des ensembles convexes de Allen. In: Proceedings of Reconnaissance des Formes et Intelligence Artificielle, vol III (2000) pp59-68.
7. Dyreson C. E., Snodgrass R. T. Valid-time Indeterminacy. In: Proceedings of the International Conference on Data Engineering. Vienna, Austria, (1993) pp335-343.
8. Euzénat J. An algebraic approach for granularity in qualitative space and time representation. In: Proceedings of the International Join Conference in Artificial Iintelligence (1995) pp894-900.
9. Harrap's shorter dictionnaire. Français-Anglais, Anglais-Français. Bordas. 1978.
10. Hobbs J. Granularity. In: Proceedings of International Join Conference in Artificial Iintelligence (1985) pp432-435.
11. Jensen C. *et al.* The Consensus Glossary of Temporal Database Concepts. In: Temporal Databases - Research and Practice. In Lecture Notes in Computer Science, Vol 1399. Springer-Verlag, Berlin Heidelberg New-York (1998) pp 406-413.
12. Rudin W. Principles of Mathematical Analysis. McGraw-Hill. ISBN 07-085613-3,3rd ed.,1975.
13. SchwerS. R., Vauzeilles J.. Calendars inside the framework of finite ordinals category. *In* Proceedings of the Workshop Spatial and temporal reasoning. In: Proceedings of the European Conference in Artificial Intelligence (1998) pp65-73.
14. Wang S., JajodiaS., Subrahmanian V. S. Temporal Modules: An Approach Toward Federated Temporal Databases. In SIGMOD/5/93 (1993) pp227-236.

Coping with Different Types of Ambiguity Using a Uniform Context Handling Mechanism

Martin Romacker and Udo Hahn

Text Knowledge Engineering Lab, [logo] Group, Freiburg University
http://www.coling.uni-freiburg.de/

Abstract. We introduce a uniform context mechanism which is able to adequately represent and manage different forms of ambiguities as they occur in the course of text understanding. Different lexical, syntactic and semantic interpretations are clearly separated by assigning each alternative a single context space for local reasoning. The mechanism we propose directly supports the task of disambiguation at all levels of text analysis, since it also incorporates constraints from the discourse context, as text understanding proceeds.

1 Introduction

The notion of context turns up in at least two varieties (for a discussion cf. [10]). Contexts are either considered as *formal objects* at the level of knowledge representation proper [11], with corresponding extensions to logic formalisms [3, 1], or they are taken as a basic construct for dealing with the *interpretation of natural languages.* The latter usage includes the pragmatics of situations, beliefs of the hearer or speaker, common-sense world knowledge, and metaknowledge about the situation in which utterances occur [5].

The work presented in this paper integrates both of these different views by treating contexts from a knowledge representation as well as from a natural language understanding perspective. In the application framework of a text understanding system [8], we propose an extension of its knowledge representation backbone by applying such a context mechanism. The way we use contexts for understanding natural language leads to the creation of hypothesis spaces for its content representations which, at the same time, account for different levels of ambiguity. In order to keep the number of context spaces small, we make direct use of constraints for disambiguation purposes that are inherent to the particular discourse context provided by the input text. Generally, we consider an interpretation to be invalid, if adding an axiom (originating from the analysis of the input text) to a formal context leads to a set of axioms that is no longer satisfiable [6]. The 'context' in which the analysis of an input text evolves with respect to the satisfiability of a set of logical axioms consists of the *static* context, as given by the a priori modelled domain knowledge, and the *dynamic* context as resulting from the incremental processing of a text [16], whose new information (interpretation constraints) is made continuously available.

M. Bouzeghoub et al. (Eds.): NLDB 2000, LNCS 1959, pp. 42–53, 2001.

In this paper, we start with an outline of the architecture of our text understanding system and give an example of how its different knowledge sources interact during sentence analysis (Section 2). Then, we briefly describe a formal extension of description logics on which the context mechanism is grounded (Section 3). Finally, examples are given in order to demonstrate how contexts are used to allow for reasoning within clearly separated content representations of ambiguous natural language input (Section 4).

2 An Overview of the System Architecture

Grammatical knowledge for syntactic analysis is based on a fully lexicalized dependency grammar [9]. A dependency grammar captures binary valency constraints between a syntactic head (e.g., a noun) and possible modifiers (e.g., a determiner or an adjective). These include restrictions on word order, compatibility of morphosyntactic features and semantic integrity conditions. For a dependency relation $\delta \in \mathcal{D} :=$ {*specifier, subject, dir-object, ...*} to be established between a head and a modifier, all valency constraints must be fulfilled. Figure 1 depicts a sample dependency graph in which word nodes are given in bold face and dependency relations are indicated by labelled edges.

At the parsing level, these constraint checking tasks are performed by lexicalized processes, so-called *word actors*. Word actors are encapsulated by *phrase actors* which enclose partial parsing results (e.g., for phrases) in terms of a dependency subgraph. Syntactic ambiguities, i.e., several phrase actors for alternative dependency structures for the same text segment, are encapsulated by a single *container actor* (cf. [7] for the actor-based model of dependency parsing).

Domain Knowledge used for text understanding is expressed in terms of a standard concept description language ($\mathcal{CDL}$), which has several constructors combining *atomic* concepts, roles and individuals to define the terminological theory of a domain (for a subset, see Table 1; cf. [15] for a comprehensive survey of terminological languages based on a decription logics framework). *Concepts* are

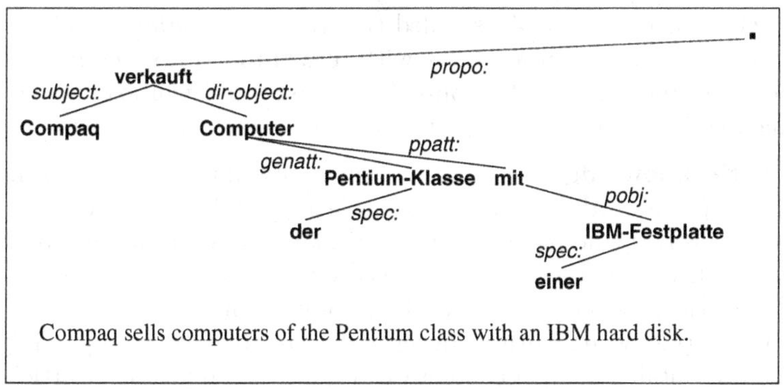

Fig. 1. A Sample Dependency Graph

Syntax	Semantics
C	$\{d \in \Delta^{\mathcal{I}} \mid \mathcal{I}(C) = d\}$
$C \sqcap D$	$C^{\mathcal{I}} \cap D^{\mathcal{I}}$
$C \sqcup D$	$C^{\mathcal{I}} \cup D^{\mathcal{I}}$
$\neg C$	$\Delta^{\mathcal{I}} \setminus C^{\mathcal{I}}$
$\forall R.C$	$\{d \in \Delta^{\mathcal{I}} \mid R^{\mathcal{I}}(d) \subseteq C^{\mathcal{I}}\}$
R	$\{(d,e) \in \Delta^{\mathcal{I}} \times \Delta^{\mathcal{I}} \mid \mathcal{I}(R) = (d,e)\}$
$R \sqcap S$	$R^{\mathcal{I}} \cap S^{\mathcal{I}}$

Table 1. Syntax and Semantics for a Subset of $\mathcal{CDL}$

Terminological Axioms	
Axiom	Semantics
$A \doteq C$	$A^{\mathcal{I}} = C^{\mathcal{I}}$
$A \sqsubseteq C$	$A^{\mathcal{I}} \subseteq C^{\mathcal{I}}$
$Q \doteq R$	$Q^{\mathcal{I}} = R^{\mathcal{I}}$
$Q \sqsubseteq R$	$Q^{\mathcal{I}} \subseteq R^{\mathcal{I}}$
Assertional Axioms	
Axiom	Semantics
$a : C$	$a^{\mathcal{I}} \in C^{\mathcal{I}}$
$a\ R\ b$	$(a^{\mathcal{I}}, b^{\mathcal{I}}) \in R^{\mathcal{I}}$

Table 2. Axioms

unary predicates, *roles* are binary predicates over a domain Δ, with *individuals* being the elements of Δ. We assume a common set-theoretical semantics for this language — an interpretation $\mathcal{I}$ is a function that assigns to each concept symbol (from the set $\mathcal{F}$) a subset of the domain Δ, $\mathcal{I}: \mathcal{F} \rightarrow 2^{\Delta}$, to each role symbol (from the set $\mathcal{R}$) a binary relation of Δ, $\mathcal{I}: \mathcal{R} \rightarrow 2^{\Delta \times \Delta}$, and to each individual symbol (from the set $\mathbf{I}$) an element of Δ, $\mathcal{I}: \mathbf{I} \rightarrow \Delta$.

Concept terms and *role terms* are defined inductively. Table 1 states corresponding constructors for concepts and roles, together with their semantics. C and D denote concept terms, while R and S denote role terms. $R^{\mathcal{I}}(d)$ represents the set of *role fillers* of the individual d, i.e., the set of individuals e with $(d,e) \in R^{\mathcal{I}}$. By means of *terminological axioms* (cf. Table 2, upper part) a symbolic name can be defined for each concept and role term. We may supply necessary and sufficient constraints (using "$\doteq$") or only necessary constraints (using "$\sqsubseteq$") for concepts and roles. A finite set of such axioms, $\mathcal{T}$, is called the *terminology* or *TBox*. Concepts and roles are associated with concrete individuals by *assertional axioms* (see Table 2, lower part – a, b denote individuals). A finite set of such axioms, $\mathcal{A}$, is called the *world description* or *ABox*. An *interpretation* $\mathcal{I}$ is a model of an ABox with regard to a TBox, iff $\mathcal{I}$ satisfies the assertional and terminological axioms. In Section 3, we will extend the syntax and semantics of assertional axioms to cover the context mechanism as well.

Semantic knowledge accounts for conceptual linkages between instances of concept types according to those dependency relations that are established between their corresponding lexical items. Semantic interpretation processes operate on so-called *semantically interpretable* subgraphs of the dependency graph (cf. [13]). By this, we refer to subgraphs whose starting and end nodes contain content words (i.e., words with a conceptual correlate), while all possibly intervening nodes contain only non-content words (such as prepositions, articles etc.). The linkage between content words may be direct (in Figure 1 between *"Compaq"* and *"verkauft"* via the dependency relation *subject*), or it may be indirect

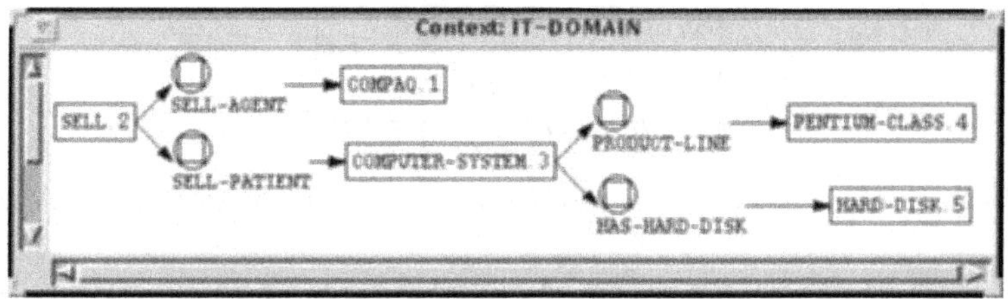

Fig. 2. A Sample Semantic Interpretation

(e.g., between *"Computer"* and *"IBM-Festplatte"* via the preposition *"mit"* and the dependency relations *ppatt* and *pobj*).

The semantic interpretation process consists of identifying relational links in the concept graph formed by the domain knowledge base between the conceptual correlates of the two content words under consideration. As an example, when the first word in our sample sentence, *"Compaq"*, is read, its conceptual correlate, COMPAQ.1, is instantiated. The next word, *"verkauft" (sells)*, also leads to the creation of an associated instance (SELL.2). Syntactically, the valencies of the transitive verb *"verkauft" (sells)* lead to checking the *subject* dependency relation for *"Compaq"*. At the conceptual level this syntactic relation always translates into checking AGENT or PATIENT (sub)roles only, since we statically linked each dependency relation to a (possibly empty) set of conceptual relations by a function $i: \mathcal{D} \mapsto 2^{\mathcal{R}}$ (for example, $i(subject) = \{$AGENT, PATIENT$\}$). In order to infer a valid semantic relation we incorporate knowledge about the concept types of COMPAQ.1 and SELL.2, *viz.* COMPANY and SELL, respectively.

Whenever a semantic interpretation process is triggered, we instantiate a general semantic interpretation schema [13]. As actual parameters the concept types of the two instances involved and the constraints supplied by the dependency relation are incorporated. In our example, the knowledge base is searched whether a COMPANY can be interpreted in terms of an AGENT or a PATIENT of a SELL event. Extracting the roles from SELL, only SELL-AGENT and SELL-PATIENT are allowed for interpretation as they are subroles of AGENT and PATIENT. Checking sortal restrictions (e.g., SELL-AGENT requires a PERSON while SELL-PATIENT requires a PRODUCT) succeeds only for SELL-AGENT (cf. Figure 2).

3 Extending Description Logics by Contexts

In order to enhance description logics by a context mechanism, we first assume the set of context symbols $\mathcal{H}$. Syntactically, assertional axioms internal to a context $h \in \mathcal{H}$ are enclosed by brackets and are subscripted by the corresponding context identifier. For example, $(a : C)_h$ means that in a context h the individual a is asserted to be an instance of the concept C. We then define the set-theoretical semantics of the *interpretation* $\mathcal{I}_h$ relative to a context h for assertional axioms as summarized in Table 3. Accordingly, the TBox $\mathcal{T}$ and the ABox $\mathcal{A}$ for a context $h \in \mathcal{H}$ is given by $\mathcal{T}_h$ and $\mathcal{A}_h$, respectively.

Syntax	Semantics
$(a : C)_h$	$a^{\mathcal{I}_h} \in C^{\mathcal{I}_h}$
$(a\ R\ b)_h$	$(a^{\mathcal{I}_h}, b^{\mathcal{I}_h}) \in R^{\mathcal{I}_h}$

Table 3. Syntax and Semantics of Context-embedded Assertional Axioms

We then define the transitive and reflexive relation $subcontextOf \subseteq \mathcal{H} \times \mathcal{H}$ (cf. Table 4) to account for property inheritance in a context hierarchy. The criterion requires the TBox and the ABox of a parent context to be inherited by all of its child contexts. Since multiple inheritance may occur, we refer to the resulting structure as a "context graph". In our framework, we allow for incremental extensions of the TBox or the ABox specific to a context. However, some restrictions apply:

1. Extensions of contexts by additional terminological or assertional axioms have to be monotonic, i.e., neither are redefinitions of concepts or relations, nor are retractions of assertions allowed.
2. Context-specific assertions which assign an individual to a concept type or to conceptual relations are permitted, while context-specific concept definitions are prohibited. If a concept occurs in two different contexts it must have the same definition.
3. The discourse universe Δ is identical for all contexts. We use the special concept $\top$, the interpretation of which covers all individuals of the domain Δ, $\top^{\mathcal{I}} = \Delta^{\mathcal{I}}$, and assert every individual to be an instance of $\top$ in the uppermost context.

Provided these extensions to standard description logics, the basic idea for the application of the context mechanism is to use a separate context for each assertion added to the text knowledge base during text analysis. Such an assertion represents a statement about the meaning of a word, a phrase or the entire text. Previous assertions (which constitute the discourse context) are made accessible by inheritance between contexts. Since, under ambiguity, alternative statements have the status of hypotheses, they may or may not be true. Whenever an assertion within a particular context turns out to be nonsatisfiable for an a priori fixed TBox[1] and a dynamically extended ABox, we have an indicator that the corresponding semantic interpretation is erroneous and, therefore, has to be excluded from further consideration. An ABox is nonsatisfiable if there exists an individiual a for which the TBox and ABox imply that its interpretation is empty (formally: $\mathcal{T} \cup \mathcal{A} \models a^{\mathcal{I}} = \emptyset$). In this view, contexts provide the representational foundation for managing ambiguities and for computations aimed at their disambiguation.

[1] We assume this TBox to be consistent. That means that there exists no concept C for which the TBox implies an empty extension (formally: $\mathcal{T} \models C^{\mathcal{I}} = \emptyset$).

$subcontextOf(h_i,\ h_j)\colon \Leftrightarrow$ $\quad \forall\ h_i,\ h_j\ \in\ \mathcal{H}$: $\quad \mathcal{T}_{h_i}\ \supseteq\ \mathcal{T}_{h_j}\ \wedge\ \mathcal{A}_{h_i}\ \supseteq\ \mathcal{A}_{h_j}$

Table 4. Inclusion of Terminological and Assertional Axioms for Contexts Related by *subcontextOf*

The linkage between the syntactic level and the evolving text knowledge base consisting of a context graph (contexts related by *subcontextOf*) is made by assigning these contexts to phrase actors. Let $\mathcal{P}$ be the set of phrase actors. Every instance of a phrase actor $p \in \mathcal{P}$ is linked to a (possibly empty) set of contexts $cont_p \subseteq 2^{\mathcal{H}}$ that hold all of p's alternative semantic interpretations.

4 Managing Ambiguities by Contexts

Contexts account for ambiguities at all conceivable levels of language interpretation. We here focus on lexical ambiguity (e.g., polysemous words) and semantic interpretations in terms of different readings for phrases and sentences. Each interpretation alternative is then represented by a different context. In our approach there are three different levels where contexts come into play in the text analysis process:

- *Instantiation*: Different conceptual instances for lexical items contained in an input text are created, each one of them in a separate context.
- *Semantic Interpretation*: Whenever a semantic interpretation relating several conceptual instances is performed, different readings (if they exist) are encapsulated in corresponding alternative contexts.
- *Selection*: The results of analysis processes contained in alternative contexts have to be assessed in order to select the "best", i.e., most plausible reading(s).

Instantiation. At the beginning of the text analysis, we start with an empty text knowledge base, one that contains no assertions at all. Nevertheless, we define the text knowledge base as a subcontext of the a priori given domain knowledge base, thus preserving the information it encodes for subsequent interpretations. By convention, the initial text knowledge base is called NewText. All interpretation contexts created in the course of the text analysis are subcontexts of NewText. As the NLP system incrementally reads the words from an input text, instances are created in the text knowledge base for each content word associated with a concept identifier.

In the instantiation phase, we have to cope with the two different sources of lexical ambiguity. First, one lexical item in a text may refer to different word classes (a kind of part-of-speech ambiguity) and, therefore, requires the creation of different contexts for semantic interpretation. Secondly, a lexical item in a text may relate to more than one conceptual correlate (polysemy). For each concept

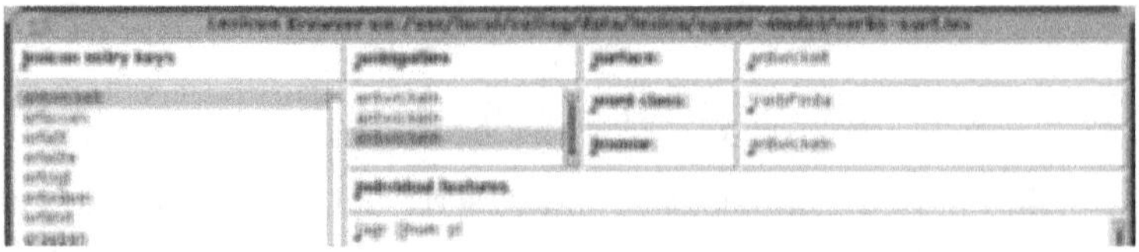

Fig. 3. Fragment of the Lexicon: Lexical Entry for *entwickelt*

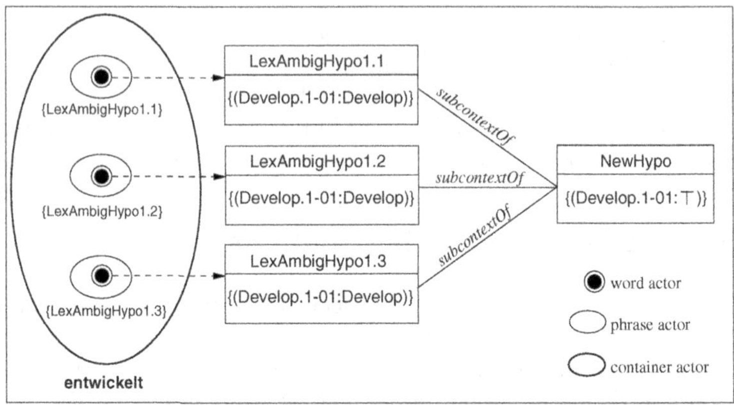

Fig. 4. Instantiation of Text Knowledge Base Objects for Word Class Ambiguity

associated with this lexical item an instance has to be created in a *separate* context.[2]

Consider Figure 4 where the instantiation of contexts for the German lexical item *"entwickelt"* (*develop*) is depicted. In the lexicon, the surface form *"entwickelt"* is linked to three different word classes, viz. VERBFINITE, VERBPARTPASSIVE, VERBPARTPERFECT (cf. the corresponding three entries in the **ambiguities** field in Figure 3, the corresponding word class is only visible for the highlighted entry of the finte verb, viz. VERBFINITE). These word classes refer to the same canonical base form (*"entwickeln"*) which can be found in the **lexeme** field. For each of the three categorial readings a corresponding word actor is created. As the base form is associated with only one concept identifier in the domain knowledge (viz. DEVELOP), each word actor triggers the creation of the same single assertion in a separate context. For example, in Figure 4 the uppermost word actor initializes the creation of the assertion $(Develop.1\text{-}01 : Develop)_{LexAmbigHypo1.1}$. Note that the instance symbol is also introduced in NEWHYPO, the uppermost context, by the assertion $(Develop.1\text{-}01 : \top)_{NewHypo}$. The contexts are then linked to the phrase actors enveloping the single word actors.

[2] By convention, these contexts are named as LEXHYPO, if no ambiguities occur, and LEXAMBIGHYPO, otherwise.

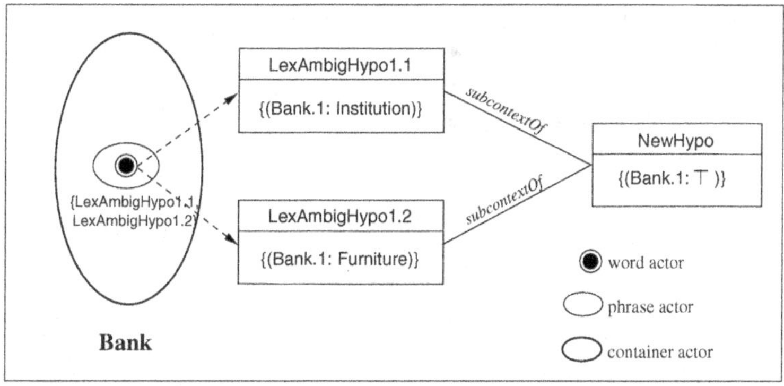

Fig. 5. Instantiation of Text Knowledge Base Objects for Polysemy

In case of polysemy, the lexical entry is linked to more than one conceptual correlate. Again, the instantiation of the corresponding objects in the text knowledge base is controlled by the word actor representing a lexical entry. Since polysemy does not directly affect the parsing process, the text knowledge base constitutes the appropriate representational platform for dealing with it. Consider the German noun *"Bank"* which may refer to a *financial institution* or a *piece of furniture*. Both meanings are linked to a single lexical item belonging to the same word class. In Figure 5 the context instantiation pattern for *"Bank"* is depicted. The corresponding word actor causes the creation of two lexical contexts, with the assertions $(Bank.1 : Institution)_{LexAmbigHypo1.1}$ and $(Bank.1 : Furniture)_{LexAmbigHypo1.2}$. Note that the same instance symbol (viz. BANK.1) receives different interpretations depending on its context.

The interpretation alternatives are administrated by the *phrase actor* which embeds the word actor in terms of a set of contexts. However, according to the principle of information hiding (opaqueness), the phrase actor is ignorant about how many meanings are actually encapsulated in different lexical contexts (i.e., how many contexts are contained in the associated set).

Semantic Interpretation. The semantic interpretation process is invoked whenever two content words are linked by a minimal semantically interpretable subgraph during the sentence analysis process. Conceptual relations are searched for in order to relate the conceptual correlates of the two content words spanning this subgraph. For the computed relation a corresponding assertional axiom is added in a dedicated context. If more than one conceptual relation has been computed a semantic ambiguity is given. Each one of these representational alternatives is encapsulated in a separate context. The resulting contexts are defined as a subcontext of the contexts containing the two content words. They inherit the assertions of their parent contexts and, therefore, contain the interpretation of the dependency graph that emerges after syntactically linking the two content words.

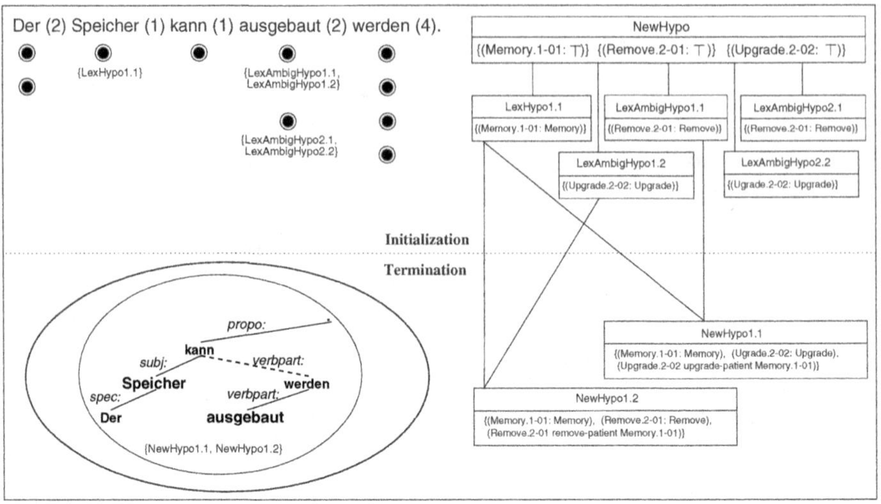

Fig. 6. Interaction of Word Actors and Contexts under Lexical Ambiguity

Let p_1 and p_2 be the phrase actors that contain the word actors for the two content words which negotiate a dependency relation and let all constraints except the semantic one be fulfilled. Let $cont_{p_1}$ and $cont_{p_2}$ be the sets of contexts attached to p_1 and p_2, respectively. A semantic interpretation schema is instantiated for all context tuples contained in $cont_{p_1} \times cont_{p_2}$. Note that an instance identifier - the conceptual correlate of a lexical item involved - may belong to different concept types in different contexts, and that the interpretation space spanned by the assertional axioms necessarily differs for all tuples. All new contexts resulting from the semantic interpretation process are finally included in the set of contexts acquainted with the phrase actor p_3 which is created after the dependency relation under negotiation is finally established and thus encompasses p_1 as well as p_2. All of these semantic computations remain invisible for the syntactic parsing process. The parser is merely informed that the semantic constraints could be satisfied in the evolving text knowledge base. No information of how many interpretation contexts exist and what the particular readings actually are is passed to the parsing component.

In order to illustrate the basic mechanism underlying the interaction of knowledge levels during the text analysis, Figure 6 contains an example of an ambiguous sentence, viz. *"Der Speicher kann ausgebaut werden."* Due to the lexical ambiguity of the German word *"ausbauen"*, one reading of this sentence is given by *"The storage can be upgraded"* while the second reading is given by *"The storage can be removed"*. The left side of Figure 6 depicts the syntactic level, its right side contains the (semantic) context graph. Horizontally, Figure 6 is divided in two layers, the initialization step and the termination step. Since the input sentence consists just of one single semantically interpretable subgraph, no intermediate interpretation steps occur.

The number of word actors that get instantiated at the syntactic level is given in brackets behind each word in the sentence. Accordingly, a corresponding number of word actor symbols is depicted beneath each lexical item. Since *"Speicher"* (*storage*) and *"ausgebaut"* (*upgrade, remove*), being the sole content words, are linked to a conceptual correlate, each associated word actor initiates the creation of instances in separate contexts. For example, *"ausgebaut"* belongs to the word classes VERBPARTPERFECT and VERBPARTPASSIVE. Therefore, two word actors are created that both have two meanings contained in two independent lexical contexts, viz. *LexAmbigHypo1.1 (remove)* and *LexAmbigHypo1.2 (upgrade)* for the word class VERBPARTPASSIVE, as well as *LexAmbigHypo2.1 (remove)* and *LexAmbigHypo2.2 (upgrade)* for the word class VERBPARTPERFECT.

Semantic interpretation is executed, as soon as the word actor for *"kann"* (*can*) tries to govern its modifier *"werden"* (*be*) – which itself already governs the VERBPARTPASSIVE *"ausgebaut"* (*ugrade/ remove*) – by the dependency relation *verbpart*. Identifying the phrase actor of *"kann"* with p_1 leads to $cont_{p_1} = \{LexHypo1.1\}$. Accordingly, p_2 as the phrase actor containing *"ausgebaut"* as VERBPARTPASSIVE results in $cont_{p_2}= \{LexAmbigHypo1.1, LexAmbigHypo1.2\}$. This leads to two different interpretation contexts (two tuples), one with the *upgrade* and the other one with the *removal* reading.[3] As semantic interpretation is here considered as a problem to link the conceptual correlates of the content words spanning the semantically interpretable subgraph – composed of *"Speicher" (memory)* and *"ausgebaut" (removed/upgraded)* – a search for appropriate conceptual relations is conducted in the domain knowledge base. This search retrieves the relations REMOVE-PATIENT and UPGRADE-PATIENT for the concept MEMORY1-01 with regard to REMOVE.2-01 and UPDATE.2-02, respectively. The resulting assertions are added to new interpretation contexts, viz. (UPGRADE.2-02 UPGRADE-PATIENT MEMORY.1-01)$_{NewHypo1.1}$ and (REMOVE.2-01 REMOVE-PATIENT MEMORY.1-01)$_{NewHypo1.2}$. These contexts form the context set $cont_{p_3}$ and are then linked to the phrase actor p_3 that contains the entire dependency graph for the input sentence (cf. Figure 6, left, lower part). Note that there exists a single syntactic structure for two different semantic interpretations.

While incrementally computing the interpretation of the input text, each of the interpretation results resides in so-called *terminal contexts*, i.e., contexts that do not have children. Let $w_1, w_2, \ldots, w_n$ be a sequence of words in a text. For every word increment of the analysis the interpretation results for the text analyzed so far are given by the corresponding set of terminal contexts in the concept graph. Furthermore, each sentence is assigned a set of terminal contexts as sentential reading(s).

Selection. A use of contexts that is not directly associated with the ambiguity problem is made for selection. If several parses or semantic interpretations exist after the analysis of a sentence has been completed, it seems infeasible,

[3] The initial contexts *LexAmbigHypo2.1* and *LexAmbigHypo2.2* are not considered for further interpretation because of syntactic reasons. The VERBPARTPERFECT reading of *"ausgebaut"* cannot be bound by any of the preceeding word actors in the sentence.

at least in a realistic operational framework for NLP systems, to carry on each of these different analyses simultaneously. However, the resolution of anaphoric phenomena [14] necessitate a recourse to referents enclosed in terminal contexts. The question then arises: With which interpretation (which context) should the text analysis continue? At the current stage of implementation, we use several selection heuristics to accumulate different sources of evidence: syntactic coverage, ranking of semantic interpretations (e.g., PP interpretations receive a higher weight than genitives), and the potential of particular assertions to foster additional, reasonable inferences. The weight of a context is determined inductively by the weight of its immediate ancestor contexts in the context graph plus the weight of the context under consideration itself. Selecting the best reading(s) for a sentence then boils down to the selection of terminal context(s) with the maximal weight.

5 Conclusion

Dealing with the full range of ambiguities in the framework of a natural language processing system is a crucial issue, since their number tends to grow at an exponential rate (cf. e.g., [4]). In this paper, we introduced a context mechanism for representing and managing ambiguities. Ambiguities occur at different levels during the text analysis. At the word level a lexical item might be ambiguous with regard to its grammatical category (syntax) or with regard to its meaning (semantics). At the phrase level alternative structural analyses may either lead to different dependency graphs (syntax) or the interpretation of dependency relations yields more than one conceptual relation (semantics).

We claim that the context mechanism we proposed is an appropriate means to capture the representational structure for ambiguities occurring at all levels of text analysis. The most outstanding feature of this methodology is its clean embedding in the reasoning mechanisms underlying the text understanding process. Ambiguities are represented as disjunctions of logical axioms [2], tentatively assumed to hold in their encapsulating contexts. This implies also that all interpretation alternatives be enumerated explicitly (cf. [12] for a different approach using semantic underspecification as a technique to cope with scoping ambiguities of quantifiers, an issue we have not touched upon here).

An important feature of our approach is the clear separation between knowledge levels: lexeme class (categorial) and structural ambiguities are handled at the syntax level (by phrase actors), while polysemic and semantic interpretation ambiguities are dealt with at the context level (by multiple interpretation contexts). The dynamic context extension mechanism which reflects the incremental processing strategy of the input text further constrains the satisfiability of additional assertional axioms and supports the disambiguation of the alternative readings.

Acknowledgements. We would like to thank our colleagues in the CLIF group for fruitful discussions. M. Romacker is supported by a grant from DFG (Ha 2097/5-1).

References

[1] Varol Akman and Mehmet Surav. The use of situation theory in context modeling. *Computational Intelligence*, 13(3):427–438, 1997.

[2] Sasa Buvač. Resolving lexical ambiguity using a formal theory of context. In *AAAI-95 Fall Symposium on Formalizing Contexts, MIT, Cambridge, Massachusetts, November 10-12*, 1995.

[3] Sasa Buvač, Vanja Buvač, and Ian A. Mason. Metamathematics of contexts. *Fundamenta Informaticae*, 23(3):263–301, 1995.

[4] Kenneth Church and Ramesh Patil. Coping with syntactic ambiguity or how to put the block in the box on the table. *American Journal of Computational Linguistics*, 8(3/4):139-149, 1982.

[5] Giacomo Ferrari. Types of contexts and their role in multimodal communication. *Computational Intelligence*, 13(3):414–426, 1997.

[6] Jeroen Groenendijk, Martin Stokhof, and Frank Veltman. Coreference and modality. In Shalom Lappin, editor, *The Handbook of Contemporary Semantic Theory*, pages 179–213. Oxford: Blackwell, 1996.

[7] Udo Hahn, Norbert Bröker, and Peter Neuhaus. Let's PARSETALK: message-passing protocols for object-oriented parsing. In Harry Bunt and Anton Nijholt, editors, *Recent Advances in Parsing Technology*, Text, Speech and Language Technology, page (to appear). Dordrecht, Boston: Kluwer, 2000.

[8] Udo Hahn and Martin Romacker. SYNDIKATE – generating text knowledge bases from natural language texts. In *IEEE SMC'99 – Proceedings of the 1999 IEEE International Conference on Systems, Man, and Cybernetics*, volume 5, pages V–918–V–923. Tokyo, Japan, October 12-15, 1999. Piscataway, NJ: IEEE Press, 1999.

[9] Udo Hahn, Susanne Schacht, and Norbert Bröker. Concurrent, object-oriented natural language parsing: the PARSETALK model. *International Journal of Human-Computer Studies*, 41(1/2):179–222, 1994.

[10] Graeme Hirst. Context as a spurious concept. In *Proc. of the AAAI Fall Symposium on Context in Knowledge Representation and Natural Language. Cambridge, Massachusetts, 8 November 1997*, pages 1–19, 1997.

[11] John McCarthy. Notes on formalizing context. In *IJCAI-93 – Proceedings of the 13th International Joint Conference on Artificial Intelligence*, pages 555–560, Chambery, France, 1993.

[12] Uwe Reyle. Dealing with ambiguities by underspecification. *Journal of Semantics*, 10:123–179, 1993.

[13] Martin Romacker, Katja Markert, and Udo Hahn. Lean semantic interpretation. In *IJCAI'99 – Proceedings of the 16th International Joint Conference on Artificial Intelligence*, volume 2, pages 868–875. Stockholm, Sweden, July 31 - August 6, 1999. San Francisco, CA: Morgan Kaufmann, 1999.

[14] Michael Strube and Udo Hahn. Functional centering: grounding referential coherence in information structure. *Computational Linguistics*, 25(3):309–344, 1999.

[15] William A. Woods and James G. Schmolze. The KL-ONE family. *Computers & Mathematics with Applications*, 23(2/5):133–177, 1992.

[16] Gian Piero Zarri. Internal and external knowledge context, and their use for interpretation of natural language. In *IJCAI'95 Workshop on "Context in Natural Language Processing"*, pages 180–188, August 1995.

WSD Algorithm Applied to a NLP System

AndrÈs Montoyo and Manuel Palomar

Research Group of Language Processing and Information Systems
Department of Software and Computing Systems
University of Alicante, Alicante, Spain
{montoyo,mpalomar}@dlsi.ua.es

Abstract. Nowadays, the need of advanced free text filtering is increasing. Therefore, when searching for specific keywords, it is desirable to eliminate occurrences where the word or words are used in an inappropriate sense. This task could be exploited in internet browsers, and resource discovery systems, relational databases containing free text fields, electronic document management systems, data warehouse and data mining systems, etc. In order to resolve this problem in this paper a method for the automatic disambiguating of nouns, using the notion of Specification Marks and the noun taxonomy of the WordNet lexical knowledge base [8] is presented. This method is applied to a Natural Language Processing System (NLP). The method resolves the lexical ambiguity of nouns in any sort of text, and although it relies on the semantics relations (Hypernymy/Hyponymy) and the hierarchic organization of WordNet. However, it does not require any sort of training process, no hand-coding of lexical entries, nor the hand-tagging of texts. An evaluation of the method was done on both the Semantic Concordance Corpus (Semcor)[9], and on Microsoft¥s electronic encyclopaedia (ÒMicrosoft 98 Encarta Encyclopaedia DeluxeÓ). The percentage of correct resolutions achieved with these two corpora were: Semcor 65.8% and Microsoft 65.6%. This percentages show that successful results with different domain corpus have been obtained, so our proposed method can be applied successfully on any corpus.

1 Introduction

The development and convergence of computing, telecommunications and information systems has already led to a revolution in the way that we work, communicate with each other, buy goods and use services, and even in the way we entertain and educate ourselves. The revolution continues and one of its results is that large volumes of information will increasingly be held in a form which is more natural for users than the data presentation formats typical of computer systems of the past. Natural Language Processing (NLP) is crucial in solving these problems and language technologies will make an indispensable contribution to the success of the information systems.

Designing a system for NLP requires abundant knowledge on language structure, morphology, syntax, semantics and pragmatic nuances. Morphological knowledge provides the tools for building words, while syntactic knowledge combines words to form sentences. Semantic knowledge provides the meaning of a given word, and

M. Bouzeghoub et al. (Eds.): NLDB 2000, LNCS 1959, pp. 54-65, 2001.

pragmatic knowledge helps us to interpret the complete sentence in its true context. All of these different linguistic knowledge forms, however, have a common associated problem, their many ambiguities, which is difficult to resolve. One of the main objectives in designing any NLP system, therefore, is the resolution of ambiguity. Furthermore, each type of ambiguity, whether it be structural, lexical, quantifying, contextual or referential, requires its specific resolution procedure.

In this paper we concentrate on the resolution of the lexical ambiguity that arises when a given word has several different meanings. This specific task is commonly referred to as Word Sense Disambiguation (WSD). This disambiguating of a word's sense is an Ñntermediate taskì [19] and is necessary for resolving such problems in certain NLP applications, such as Machine Translation (MT), Information Retrieval (IR), Text Processing, Grammatical Analysis, Information Extraction (IE), hypertext navigation, etc. In general terms, WSD involves assigning a definition to a given word, in either a text or a discourse, that endows it with a meaning that distinguishes it from all of the other possible meanings that the word might have in other contexts. This association of a word to one specific sense is achieved by acceding to two different information sources, known as Ñcontextì and Ñexternal knowledge sourcesì. The Ñcontextì of a word to be disambiguated is considered as a valuable group of words that contain, not merely general information about the text or discourse in which the target word appears, but which also provide linguistic information about the text, such as syntactic relationships, semantic categories, distance, etc. ÑExternal knowledge sourcesì include encyclopaedias and other lexical resources, in other words, manually operated knowledge sources that provide useful data for associating words and senses.

We should like to make a clear distinction, however, between our method and other approaches to word-sense disambiguation systems, such as that described in [4]. The method we propose in this paper, however, is based on strategic knowledge, i.e., the disambiguating of nouns by matching the context in which they appear with information from an external knowledge source (knowledge-driven WSD).

To accomplish this task, we chose WordNet as it combines the features of both dictionaries and thesauruses, and also includes other links among words by means of several semantic relations, (Hyponymy, hypernymy, meronymy, etc). In other words, WordNet provides definitions for the different senses that a given word might have (as a dictionary does) and defines groups of synonymous words by means of ÑSynsetsì, which represent distinct lexical concepts, and organises them into a conceptual hierarchy (as a thesaurus does).

Most of the recent research done in the field of WSD has been carried out with the knowledge-driven method. Lesk in [5], proposes a method for deciphering the sense of a word in a given context by counting the number of over-laps that appear between each dictionary definition and the context. Cowie in [2] describes a method for lexical disambiguation of texts that uses the definitions given in the machine-readable version of the Longman¥s Dictionary of Contemporary English (LDOCE), as in the Lesk method, but also uses simulated annealing for greater efficiency.
Yarowsky in [20] derives different classes of words, starting from the common categories of words in Roget¥s Thesaurus. Wilks in [18] uses co-occurrence data, extracted from the LDOCE, for constructing word-context vectors and, thus, word-sense vectors. Voorhees in [17] defines a form of construction, called a *hood* that represents different sense categories in the WordNet noun hierarchy. Sussna in [16] defines a

meter-based measurement that takes the semantic distance between the different nouns in a given text into account. It assigns weights, based on its type of relation (synonymy, hypernymy, etc) to WordNet links, and counts the number of arcs of the same type leaving a node, as well as the total depth of the arcs. Resnik in [10] computes the commonly shared *information content* of words, which serves a measurement of the Specification of the concept that subsumes the words included in the WordNet IS-A hierarchy. Agirre in [1] presents a method for the resolution of lexical ambiguity of nouns, using the WordNet noun taxonomy and the notion of conceptual distances among different concepts. Rigau in [13] combines a set of un-supervised algorithms that can accurately disambiguate word senses in a large, completely untagged corpus. Hale in [3] presents the results obtained from using a combination of Roget¥s International Thesaurus and WordNet as taxonomies, in a measurement of semantic similarity (four similarity metrics). Stetina in [15] introduces a general supervised word-sense disambiguating method, based on a relatively small syntactically parsed and semantically tagged training corpus. This method exploits a complete sentence-context and all the explicit semantic relations that occur in a sentence. Resnik in [12] presents a measure of semantic similarity in an IS-A taxonomy, based on the notion of commonly-shared information content, as well as introducing algorithms that exploit taxonomic similarity in resolving syntactic and semantic ambiguity. Mihalcea in [7] suggest a method that attempts to disambiguate all of the nouns, verbs, adverbs and adjectives in a given text by referring to the senses provided by WordNet.

In this paper, we present a method of solving the lexical ambiguity of nouns. Our method relies on knowledge provided by the WordNet noun taxonomy.

2 The PLN System with the WSD Module

In this section we describe, in detail, the architecture employed in developing a NLP system with the WSD module. The text that is to be disambiguated come from different files and are passed through a *prepocessing*. The first step in prepocessing consist of using a part-of-speech (POS) tagger to automatically assign syntactic tags to the text. Next, a partial parsing is used to extract all the words from the sentences whose lexical category is based on the noun, for the subsequent resolution of their morphological ambiguity. These nouns are the input for the WSD module, the output being another slot structure with the corresponding senses.

A grammar (SUG) that recognises every constituent (np, pp, p, verbal chunks) is first defined. Our process, however, only uses the np to disambiguate the nouns of a sentence. This grammar is automatically translated into Prolog clauses. The translator will provide a Prolog program that can parse sentences. The program will return structure (SS) for each parsed sentence. This SS stores the syntactic, morphological and semantic information of the np constituent, thus solving their morphology ambiguity. After a sentence has been parsed, its SS will be the input for the WSD module. This module will consult the WordNet knowledge base for all the words that appear in the context, returning all of their possible senses. The disambiguation algorithm will then be applied and a new SS¥will be returned, in which the words have the correct sense assigned. This process is illustrated in Figure 1. We should like to emphasise that this resolution skill allows us to produce modular NLP systems in which the grammatical rules, the knowledge base (WordNet), the parsing scheme and the WSD module are all quite independent of one other.

In the following section, we describe, from an intuitive point of view, how this module functions, and we define the concept of Specification Marks for word-sense disambiguation.

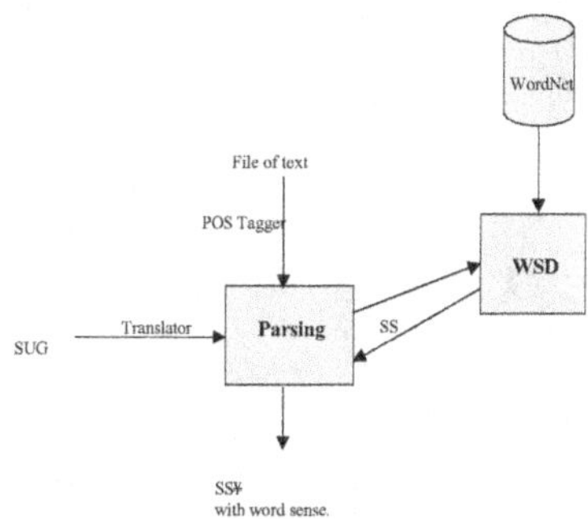

Figure 1. NLP system with WSD module

3 Method with Specification Mark

The method we present here consists basically of the automatic sense-disambiguating of nouns that appear within the context of a sentence, whose different possible senses are quite related. The context is given by the words that co-occur with the given word, within a sentence and by their relations to the word to be disambiguated. The disambiguation is resolved with the use of the WordNet lexical knowledge base (1.6).

The underlying intuition to this approach is that the more similar two words are, the more informative the most specific concept that subsumes them both will be. In other words, their lowest upper bound in the taxonomy. (A Ñconceptì here, corresponds to a Specification Mark (SM). That is to say, the more information two concepts share in common, the more similar they obviously are, and the information commonly shared by two concepts is indicated by the concept that subsumes them in the taxonomy.

The input for the WSD module will be the group of words $W=\{W_1, W_2, ..., W_n\}$. Each word w_i is sought in WordNet, each having an associated set $S_i=\{S_{i1}, S_{i2}, .., S_{in}\}$ of possible senses, and each sense having a set of concepts in the IS-A taxonomy (hypernymy/hyponymy relations). First, it the common concept to all the senses of the words that form the context is sought. This concept is denominated the Initial Specification Mark (ISM). If this Initial Specification Mark does not resolve the ambiguity of the word, we descend from one level to another, through the WordNet hierarchy, assigning new Specification Marks. The number of concepts containing the sub-hierarchy will then be counted for each Specification Mark. The sense that corresponds to the Specification Mark with highest number of words will be chosen as the sense disambiguation within the given context.

To illustrate graphically how the word (W_1) is disambiguated, in Figure 2 the word (W_1) has four different senses and several word contexts. It can be seen that the Initial Specification Mark does not resolve the lexical ambiguity, since the word W_1 appears in three sub-hierarchies with different senses. The Specification Mark with the symbol (*) however, contains the highest number of words from the context (three) and, will therefore be the one chosen to resolve the sense s_2 of the word W_1. The words W_2 and W_3 are also disambiguated by choosing the senses s_1 respectively. W_4 has not been successfully disambiguated, as it is out of the scope of the application of the heuristics.

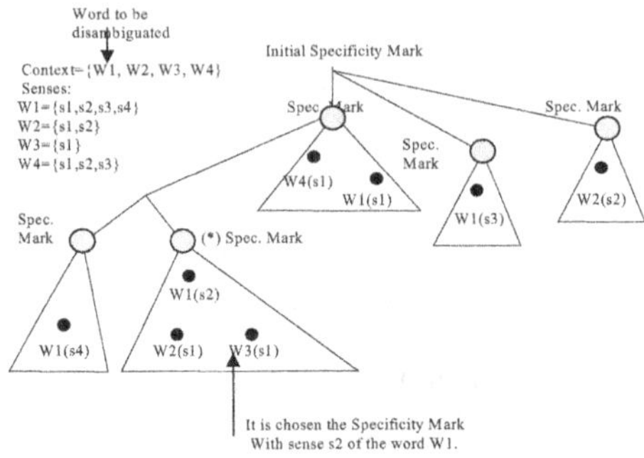

Figure 2: Intuitive example of Specification Marks algorithm.

3.1 Improvement

At this point, we should like to point out that after having evaluated the method, we subsequently discovered that it could be improved, providing even better results in disambiguation. We therefore define three heuristics:

H1 (hypernym): This heuristic solves the ambiguity of those words that are not directly related in WordNet (plant and leaf) but the word that is forming the context, is in some composed synset of a hypernymy relationship for some sense of the word to be disambiguated (leaf#1 ✏ plant organ). To disambiguate a given word, all of the other words included in the context in the hypernyms synsets of each of its senses are checked, and a weight is assigned to it in accordance with its depth within the sub-hierarchy, and the sense that carries the greater weight is chosen. In the case of there being several senses with the same weight, we apply the following heuristic.

H2 (definition): With this heuristic, the word sense is obtained using the definition (gloss used in WordNet system) of the words to be disambiguated (sister, person, musician). To disambiguate the word, all of the other words that belong to the context in the gloss of WordNet for each of the synsets, are checked, and the weight of each word that coincides is increased by one unit. The sense that finally has the greatest weight is chosen. In case of there being several senses with the same weight, the following heuristic is then applied.

H3 (Common Specification Mark): With this heuristic, the problem of fine-grainedness is solved (year, month). To disambiguate the word, the first Specification

Mark that is common to the resulting senses of the above heuristic is checked. As this is the most informative of the senses, it is chosen. By means of this heuristic one it is tried to solve the problem of the fine grainedness of WordNet¥s sense distinguishes, since in most of the cases, the senses of the words to be disambiguated differ very little in nuances, and as the context is a rather general one it is not possible arrive at the most accurate sense.

4 Disambiguation Algorithm

In this section, we formally describe the algorithm with Specification Marks, employing the following five steps and using the three heuristics:

Step 1 Extract all of the nouns to disambiguate from their respective sentences. These nouns constitute the input context. Context={W_1, W_2, ..., W_n}, for example Context={plant, tree, perennial, leaf}.

Step 2 For each word W_i in the context, all of its possible senses, S_i={S_{i1}, S_{i2}, ..., S_{in}} are obtained from WordNet. For each sense S_{ij}, all the hypernyms synsets are obtained and stored in stacks.

Plant#1: Building complex#1, Structure#1, artifact#1, object#1,entity#1
Plant#2: life form#1, entity#1

Step 3

For each word
  For each sense
    For each hypernym.
      The given hypernym synset is looked for in all the other senses of all the words.
      All of the senses in which this hypernym synsets appears are then stored.

For PLANT:
  For PLANT#1:
    Plant#1 ->
    Building complex ->
    Structure ->
    Artifact ->
    Object -> leaf#1,leaf#2,leaf#3
    Entity -> plant#2,plant#4,tree#1,leaf#1, leaf#2,leaf#3,perennial#1

Step 4

For each word
  For each sense
    It must be located within the bottom hypernym synset of the stack and the number of words in the list created in the step 3 are counted.
This number of words is then assigned to that sense.

For PLANT:
  PLANT#1:4 (plant, tree, perennial, leaf)
  PLANT#2:4 (plant, tree, perennial, leaf)
  PLANT#3:1 (plant)
  PLANT#4:4 (plant, tree, perennial, leaf)

Step 5

For each word, select the sense(s) whose number(s) is/are the greatest (MAX).

If there is only one sense (MAX=1), it is obviously chosen.

If there is more than one sense (MAX>1) return to Step 4, lowering by one level within the taxonomy until a single sense is obtained (MAX=1).

In other cases, the heuristics are activated, which means that the word has not been disambiguated with the sole use of the hypernymy relationships that appear in WordNet.

In this case: Max(plant)= {plant#1, plant#2, plant#4} it would be necessary rise within the taxonomy and return to Step 4. When it arrives at the level of <life from>, the only maximum that will be obtained is plant#2, and that sense will therefore be assigned to the word „plant".

We shall now detail the proposed heuristics:

H1 (Hypernym):

Weight=0. // Each sense has an initial weight of 0.

For all of the non-disambiguated words

For all of the non-disambiguated senses. Select hypernyms.

For the rest of the words belonging to the context

Search to verify if it appears in some of the hypernyms.

If it appears, the weight of this sense is increased proportionate to its depth in the taxonomy. The relationship is as follows:

Weight=weight+(deep/total deep).

The sense with the greatest weight is chosen and given as the solution. If there are more than one ambiguous sense, the definition heuristic is applied.

Context: *plant, tree, leaf, perennial.* **Words non disambiguated**: *leaf.* **Senses**: *leaf#1, leaf#2.*

For leaf#1:
=> *entity, something*
=> *object, physical object*
=> *natural object*
=> ***plant** part*
=> ***plant** organ*
=> *leaf#1, leafage*

For leaf#2:
=> *entity, something*
=> *object, physical object*
=> *substance, matter*
=> *material, stuff*
=>*paper*
=>*sheet, piece of paper*
=> *leaf#2, folio*

In this example, therefore, the sense **leaf#1** is therefore selected as the result of the disambiguation, since its weight ((4/6)+(5/6)) is the greatest 1,5.

H2 (Definition):

For all non-disambiguated senses

For all words that belong to the context

These words are sought in the definition of the sense

If they appear, Weight=Weight+1

The sense with the greatest weight is selected and given as a solution.

If there are more than one ambiguous senses, the heuristic Common Specification Mark is applied to them.

Context: *person, sister, musician.* **Words non disambiguated**: *sister, musician.* **Senses**: *sister#1,sister#2,sister#3.*

For sister#1: ✏ Weight = **2**
sister, sis -- (a female **person** who has the same parents as another **person**; "my sister married a **musician**")
For sister#2: ✏ Weight = **0**
Sister -- ((Roman Catholic) a title given to a nun (and used as a form of address); "the Sisters taught her to love God")
For sister#3: ✏ Weight = **1**
sister -- (a female **person** who is a fellow member (of a sorority or labor union or other group); "none of her sisters would betray her")

In this example, the best sense is **sister#1**, because it has is the greatest weight.

H3 (Common Specification Mark):
This heuristic searches the first common synset to the previous resulting senses of the above heuristic because it has the most informative content.

Context: *year, month.* **Words non disambiguated**: *year.* **Senses**: *year#1, year#2, year#3.*

For year#1:
=> abstraction
=> measure, quantity
=> time period, period
=> year#1, twelvemonth

For year#2:
=> abstraction
=>measure, quantity
=> time period, period
=> year#2

In this example, and due to the fine-grainedness of WordNet, *month* does not specify anything about the meanings of Ñyearì it is therefore fine-tuned the sense of *year* is given as **time period**.

5 Evaluation & Discussion

We tested this method on sentences taken from the Semantic Concordance corpus (Semcor) and from Microsoft¥s electronic encyclopaedia (Microsoft Encarta 98 Encyclopaedia Deluxe). With texts that were chosen at random, 90 sentences and 619 nouns for the Semcor and 90 sentences and 697 nouns for the encyclopaedia. The test that was done to evaluate the method was carried out first without and then with heuristics, to demonstrate the percentage of improvement that these heuristics provide.

5.1 Results

The following table show the percentages obtained when the method is applied with the base algorithm and with the heuristics employed here. These results demonstrate that when the method is applied with the heuristics, the percentages of correct resolutions increases, thereby improving word-sense disambiguation. This table provide some statistics for comparing the improvements obtained for the individual application of each heuristics.

	SEMCOR			ENCARTA		
%	Correct	Incorrect	Ambiguous	Correct	Incorrect	Ambiguous
Base algorithm	52í5%	28%	19í5%	55í2%	26í7%	18í1%
1™Heuristic	53%	29í7%	17í3%	56í4%	27í2%	16í4%
2™Heuristic	53í5%	30í2%	16í3%	58í3%	27í5%	14í2%
3™Heuristic	65í8%	32í5%	1í7%	65í6%	33í3%	1í1%

Regarding the above data, we should like to point out that the appearance of 1.7% and 1.1% of ambiguous words is due to the fact that no common synsets are obtained for ambiguous nouns.

5.2 Comparison with Other Work

As indicated by Resnik *et al.* in [11] WSD methods are very difficult to compare, due to the many differences found among the words chosen for disambiguation and because of the different approaches considered (i.e., knowledge-based, corpus-based and statistic-based methods).

Resnik in [10] applied his method to a different task, for the automatic sense-disambiguation of nouns that appear within sets of related nouns. Input for this sort of evaluation comes from the numbered categories of Roget¥s Thesaurus, which makes its comparison with our method rather difficult.

Yarowsky in [21] reported an improvement that afforded a performance of 91.4% correct resolutions. His method, however, focused on just two senses, and for a rather limited number of nouns. It also requires a large training corpus, so we could hardly attempt to make a meaningful comparison.

Mihalcea *et al.* in [7] proposed a WSD method that uses two sources of information. (1) Searching on Internet with queries formed. And the senses are ranked by the order provided by the number of hits. (2) WordNet for measuring the semantic density of a pair of words. Although this method had a reported average accuracy of 85.7 % for nouns, it is tremendously inefficient as it requires a previous filtering due to the combinatorial problem. Our method resolves this problem, because it is fully automatic and requires no filtering process nor any manual query forms on Internet.

We think that the results published by Stetina *et al.* in [15] cannot be compared with ours for several reasons. It presents us with a supervised word-sense disambiguating method and a semantically-tagged training corpus, and therefore requires a training process for one to lean how to use the restricted domain.

We can, however, compare our method with those of Agirre *et al.* in [1] and Yarowsky in [20], since their approaches are the most similar we have seen to ours.

The article [20] had to adapt for working with WordNet, in [1]. The results[1] are those shown in the following table.

%	Coverage	Precision	Recall
Specification Marks	98.5 %	66.6 %	65.7 %
Agirre and Rigau	86.2 %	71.2 %	61.4 %
Yarowsky	100 %	64.0 %	64.0 %

A more ample and detailed comparison to the above methods would be valuable, but this is not yet possible as they have been compared with different version of WordNet and of input sentences. We have used the 1.6 version of WordNet, which implies greater fine-grainedness as well as a greater number of senses for each word than version 1.4 offers.

5.3 Discussion

The obtained results demonstrate that our method improves the recall of the others compared methods. Furthermore, it improves the precision of the Yarowsky method and coverage of the Agirre-Rigau method.

6 Conclusion and Further Work

In this paper, we have presented an automatic disambiguation method for nouns which is based on Specification Marks between words, using word-sense tags from WordNet. This method does not require any training process nor any hand-tagging. Working from a text of any domain, therefore, we can automatically obtain, the senses of words.

The problem found in the experiments carried out with the Semcor corpus and the Microsoft Encarta 98 electronic encyclopaedia is that the method depends on the hierarchical structure of WordNet. There are words that should be related semantically, but WordNet does not reflect such relationship. The words *plant* and *leaf*, for example, both belong to the *flora* context, yet WordNet includes only *plant* in this concept, while *leaf* is assigned to *object* concept. To solve this problem we have defined the Hypernym and Definition heuristics.

WordNet is not a perfect resource for word-sense disambiguation, because has the problem of the fined-grainedness of WordNet¥s sense distinctions [4]. This problem causes difficulties in the performance of automatic word-sense disambiguation with free-running texts. Several authors, like Slator and Wilks in [14], have stated that the divisions of a given sense in the dictionary are too fine for the work of Natural Language Processing. To solve this problem, the Common Specification Mark heuristic was defined since it provides an information concept that is common among such

[1] Coverage is given by the ratio between total number of answered senses and total number of senses. Precision is defined as the ratio between correctly disambiguated senses and total number of answered senses. Recall is defined as the ratio between correctly disambiguated senses and total number of senses.

senses. We feel that the results obtained are promising, considering the difficulty of the task carried out. We used free-running texts, a great number of senses for each word (in WordNet) and there was a considerable lack of *context* in the texts.

In further work we intend to modify the method by using more and better semantic relationships from WordNet and adding more lexical categories for disambiguation, such as verbs, adjectives and adverbs. This should not only give the method more *context* information but should also relate such information much better, in line with the proposal of McRoy in [6], that fledged lexical ambiguity resolution should combine several information sources. More information from other lexical sources, (both dictionaries and thesauruses), are also required.

The most important novelty, however, is probably the use syntactic relationships, combined with different techniques and resources, to produce an all together better word-sense disambiguation.

7 Acknowledgements

We will like to thank German Rigau and Eneko Agirre for revising and discussing this paper.

References

1. Agirre E. and Rigau G. (1996) *Word Sense Disambiguation using Conceptual Density*. Proc. 16th International Conference on COLING. Copenhagen.
2. Cowie J., Guthrie J. and Guthrie L. (1992) *Lexical disambiguation using simulated annealing*. Proc. DARPA Workshop on Speech and Natural Language. 238-242. New York.
3. Hale, Michael L. Mc. A comparison of WordNet and Roget¥s taxonomy for measuring semantic similarity.
4. Ide N. and VÈronis J. (1998) *Introduction to the Special Issue on Word Sense Disambiguation: The State of the Art*. Computational Linguistics. 24 (1), 1-40.
5. Lesk, M. (1986) *Automatic sense disambiguation using machine readable dictionaries: How to tell a pine cone from an ice cream cone*. Proc. 1986 SIGDOC Conference, ACM 24-26, New York.
6. McRoy S. (1992) *Using Multiple Knowledge Sources for Word Sense Discrimination*. Computational Linguistics 18 (1).
7. Mihalcea R. and Moldovan D. (1999) *A Method for word sense disambiguation of unrestricted text*. Proc. 37th Annual Meeting of the ACL 152-158, Maryland, USA.
8. Miller G. A., Beckwith R., Fellbaum C., Gross D., and Miller K. J. (1990) *WordNet: An online lexical database*. International Journal of Lexicography, 3(4): 235-244.
9. Miller G., Leacock C., Randee T. and Bunker R. (1993) *A Semantic Concordance*. Proc. 3rd DARPA Workshop on Human Language Tecnology, 303-308, Plainsboro, New Jersey.
10. Resnik P. (1995) *Disambiguating noun groupings with respect to WordNet senses*. Proc. Third Workshop on Very Large Corpora. 54-68.Cambridge, MA.

11. Resnik P. and Yarowsky D. (1997) *A perspective on word sense disambiguation methods and their evaluation.* Proc. ACL Siglex Wordshop on Tagging Text with Lexical Semantics, why, what and how?, Washington DC.

12. Resnik P. (1999) *Semantic similarity in a taxonomy: an information-based measure and its application to problems of ambiguity in natural lenguage.* In Journal of Artificial Intelligence Research 11. 95-130.

13. Rigau G., Atserias J. and Agirre E. (1997) *Combining Unsupervised Lexical Knowledge Methods for Word Sense Disambiguation.* Proc. 35th Annual Meeting of the ACL, 48-55, Madrid, Spain.

14. Slator B. and Wilks Y. (1987) *Towards semantic structures from dictionary entries.* Proc. 2nd Annual Rocky Mountain Conference on Artificial Inteligence, 85-96. Boulder, CO.

15. Stetina J., Kurohashi S. and Nagao M. (1998) *General word sense disambiguation method based on full sentencial context.* In Usage of WordNet in Natural Language Processing. COLING-ACL Workshop, Montreal, Canada.

16. Sussna M. (1993) *Word sense disambiguation for free-text indexing using a massive semantic network.* Proc. Second International CIKM, 67-74, Airlington, VA.

17. Voorhees E. (1993) *Using WordNet to disambiguation word senses for text retrieval.* Proc. 16th Annual International ACM SIGIR Conference on Research and Development in Information Retrieval. 171-180, Pittsburgh, PA.

18. Wilks Y., Fass D., Guo C., McDonal J., Plate T. and Slator B. (1993) *Providing Machine Tractablle Dictionary Tools.* In Semantics and the lexicon (Pustejowsky J. Ed.) 341-401.

19. Wilks Y. And Stevenson M. (1996) *The grammar of sense: Is word sense tagging much more than part-of-speech tagging?* Technical Report CS-96-05, University of Sheffield, UK.

20. Yarowsky D. (1992) *Word Sense disambiguation using statistical models of Roget's categories trainined on large corpora.* Proc. 14th COLING, 454-460, Nantes, France.

21. Yarowsky, D. (1995) *Unsupervised word Sense disambiguation rivaling supervised methods.* Proc. 32nd Annual Meeting of the ACL.

"Beijing Frowns and Washington Pays Close Attention" Computer Processing of Relations between Geographical Proper Names in Foreign Affairs

Odile Piton[1] and Denis Maurel[2]

[1] CERMSEM, Université Paris 1, 12, place du Panthéon, 75005 Paris, France, piton@univ-paris1.fr

[2] LI/E3i-University of Tours, 64 avenue Jean-Portalis, F37200 Tours, France, maurel@univ-tours.fr

Abstract. We present results of the project Prolex. The aim of the project is the automated analysis of proper names, especially a description of relations between different proper names in a text. The system currently works with geographical proper names (place names, derived adjectives and names of inhabitants) in French.
It consists of a database containing specific types of proper names and relations between the different names. Using these names and relations, the program can group the proper names appearing in a text that may belong together (such as Beijing-Chinese-Pekinese-China; American-United States-Washington). This is done by constructing an association matrix between them and by computing the transitive closure of this Boolean matrix. The method is explained with an example.
Key words: Proper Names, Place Name, Inhabitant Name, Natural Language Processing (NLP), Electronic Dictionary, Relational Data Base, Geographical Proper Names, Computing Method, Transitive closure.

1 Introduction

"Beijing frowns and Washington pays close attention"

"Pékin fronce les sourcils et Washington ouvre l'oeil" (Belgium Newspaper *Le Soir*, 02/25/00)

The Prolex project is a university research project whose purpose is the automatic processing of proper names. In particular, it studies the relations between the various forms of the proper names of a text. This relational aspect is original. Current research about proper names is based on heuristics. Some simply declare as "proper names" all the unknown words starting with a capital letter [14]. More sophisticated ones use local grammars [5,7,3] and propose to classify the identified proper names [10]. Today, the whole of this research often merges with more general research on named entities. This research was the occasion

M. Bouzeghoub et al. (Eds.): NLDB 2000, LNCS 1959, pp. 66–78, 2001.

for various evaluations, especially within the framework of Muc conferences [13]. In NLDB'99, we presented our database of toponyms (place names), inhabitant names and derived adjectives that we constructed for the Project Prolex [12]. We have introduced that we register the links between these words, in the purpose of the automated analysis of geographical proper names. We shall present linguistic and computational aspects of a use of our Geographical Proper Names Database for the Natural Language Processing of a text dealing with international politics.
We have acquired some experiment with the first database made by Claude Belleil [1], for France. We had noticed that the use of a database is much too slow, as concerns NLP. So we have used transducers automatically build from it. We call it "electronic dictionary". It is in fact a minimal transducer, within the meaning of [9]. It is built directly by the algorithm of [8]. **This transducer includes only a part of the direct links of the DB.**
We will explain the method, not the tool that we will make. We study the properties of texts dealing with international affairs (Section 2), then we explain the different steps of our method (Section 3). First we collect information from our database (Section 3.3.1), then we sum it up (Section 3.3.2). Next we build a Boolean matrix of the links between the collected words (Section 3.3.3). Fourth we compute the transitive closure of the matrix (Section 3.3.4). Lastly, we obtain tags to add to the geographical proper names of the text (Section 3.3.5).

2 Properties of the Texts Dealing with International Politics

Our purpose is to automatically compute texts of newspapers. They have some pecularities. Let us look at a text of an example, from the French newspaper *Le Monde* (02/23/00):

> "**Pékin** menace **Taipeh** d'intervention militaire en cas d'enlisement du processus de réunification... C'est un glissement d'importance dans la position de **Pékin** à l'égard de **Taiwan** ...on en trouve trace dans de multiples déclarations de **dirigeants pékinois**... Le raidissement de sa position sur une intervention militaire traduit l'irritation croissante de **Pékin** devant les obstacles placés par les **Taiwanais** sur le chemin de la réunification alors que la récupération de **Hong-Kong** et de **Macao** a été bouclée sans heurts.... Les **Chinois** font certes un geste en acceptant d'ouvrir les discussions sur un pied d'égalité ... Les **Américains** intensifient leurs manouvres diplomatiques afin d'éviter la réédition de la crise des missiles de la présidentielle du printemps 1996. L'objectif de **Washington** est d'ouvrir des canaux de communication au plus haut niveau[1]"...

[1] Beijing has threatened to use force against Taipei in the event of the sinking of the reunification process. It is a modification of importance in the position of Beijing

This text includes the names of six places, three inhabitant names and a derived adjective. Among these toponyms, we find one name of country (*Taiwan-Taiwan-*) and three names of capital cities (*Pékin-Peking-*, *Washington* and *Taipeh-Taipei-*). The The last two are the names of regions that have been united with the mainland (*Macao*, *Hong-Kong*).
One of the inhabitant names (*Taiwanais-Taiwanese-*) is related to a mentioned country (*Taiwan*) but the two others (*Américain-American-* and *Chinois-Chinese-*) are not. The adjective (*pékinois-Pekinese-*) derives from the name of the inhabitants of Beijing (*Pékinois-Pekinese-*).
We wish to give prominence to five groups as on Table 1.

Group of Words
Taiwan, Taiwanais, Taipeh
Pékin, pékinois, Chinois
Washington, Américains
Macao
Hong-Kong

Table 1. Three countries and two concerned areas

It is very important to notice that the different words of each group can be exchanged, without changing the meaning of the text. For example "**Beijing** has threatened to use force against **Taipei**" may be changed into "The **Chinese** have threatened to use force against **Taiwan**" or "**Pekinese** Leaders has threatened to use force against the **Taiwanese**", or any other exchange. In this case we say that there are metonymies between the name of a country, the name of its capital town, the name of its inhabitants and the government of the country (Figure 1). This explains the reason why the text speaks of the US and of China, although these words do not appear in the text. The name of the USA is replaced by *Washington* and *les Américains*, and the name of China is replaced by *Pékin*, *pékinois* or *Chinois*.
To refer to the government, an equivalent nominal group can be made with a word like *les dirigeants* (*the Leaders*), *le gouvernement* (*the Government*) or *les autorités* (*the Authorities*) and a provenance adjective (from the name of the capital or the name of the country). Here we can write *Pekinese Leaders*,

with regard to Taiwan... one can find trace of it in many declarations made by Pekinese Leaders... The stiffening of its position on a military intervention proofs the increasing irritation of Beijing because of the obstacles placed by the Taiwanese on the path of reunification whereas the recovery of Hong-Kong and Macao did not rise any trouble... The Chinese surely are making an effort by accepting to start the negotiations on state-to-state basis... the Americans intensify their diplomatic operations in order to avoid the repetition of the missiles crisis as it had once before during the presidential elections in 1996.. The purpose of Washington is to open channels of communication on the highest level...

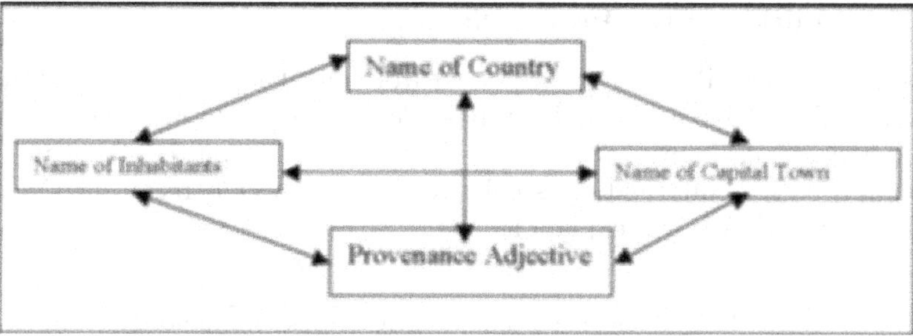

Fig. 1. Metonymies

Chinese Government or *Pekinese Authorities*, or obtain some other equivalent expressions by exchanging the two adjectives together (Figure 2).

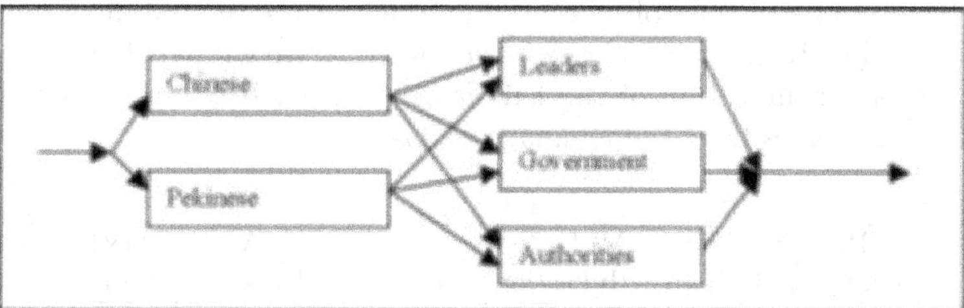

Fig. 2. A local grammar for the Chinese Government

We assume too that in every text that we study, there is either the name of the country or the name of the capital town.
Our method is based on all these remarks.

3 Method

The text is analyzed automatically by the computer. When a Geographical Proper Name is recognized, we automatically collect information about it and about the words that are associated with it from our database. We use a filter to eliminate associated words that are not relevant for our purpose. Our method is explained step by step on the example of the newspaper *Le Monde*. We show the collected information in tables 6 and 7.

3.1 Recognition of the Proper Names

Let us have a look (Table 2) at an extract from our database as regards the six toponyms. They have a key and a type-code ("1" if the toponym is the name of an Independent Country, "2" if it is the name of a Capital, "3" means "is a Region of"...). This information is collected with a special treatment when the Type-Code is "3". We will explain it later.

French word	key	Type-code	French word	key	Type-code
Hong-Kong	T6	3	Taipeh	T10	2
Macao	T7	3	Taiwan	T12	1
Pékin	T8	2	Washington	T13	2

Table 2. Toponyms of the text

In our database, Inhabitant Names and Adjectives are registered as lemmas[2] (see Table 3). They have a key, a code (with the same signification) and an inflection[3] code (This is most often the same thing for the Inhabitant Name as for the derived adjective). Owing to the inflection code, we will be able to recognize *Américains* as an inflection of the lemma *Américain*. It is the same thing for *pékinoise* that comes from the lemma *pékinois*.

INHABITANTS NAMES				DERIVED ADJECTIVES			
French word	Code	Key	Inflection	French word	Code	Key	Inflection
Américain	1	G1	3	américain	1	A1	3
Chinois	1	G2	1	chinois	1	A2	1
Hongkongais	3	G3	1	hongkongais	3	A3	1
Pékinois	2	G4	1	pékinois	2	A4	1
Taiwanais	1	G5	1	taiwanais	1	A5	1
Washingtonien	2	G6	2	washingtonien	2	A6	2

Table 3. Inhabitant name and derived adjective lemmas

For each toponym of the text, we collect the information about associated inhabitant name and derived adjective lemmas.

---

[2] For the names and for the adjectives the lemma is the masculine singular form; for the verbs it is the infinitive form.

[3] The inflections are the four forms, masculine singular, feminine singular, masculine plural, feminine plural.
If code = 1, the four endings are (-, e, -, es) e.g. Chinois, Chinoise, Chinois, Chinoises
If code = 2, the four endings are (-, ne, s, nes) e.g. Washingtonien, Washingtonienne, Washingtoniens, Washingtoniennes
If code = 3, the four endings are (-, e, s, es) e.g. Américain, Américaine, Américains, Américaines

For all the geographical words of the text, we present, Table 4, the associations between toponyms and inhabitants names or between toponyms and derived adjectives. We notice that new toponyms have been collected. For instance, the names *Etats-Unis* and *Chine*, but also the name *Amérique*. Actually, some words are ambiguous. Like *Américain* in French. It means as well inhabitant of the U-S as inhabitant of the Americas. When we compute the text, we have to collect the two associations.

IsNameOfInhabitantsOf				*IsAdjectiveOf*			
Toponym	Key	Key	Inhabitant	Toponym	Key	Key	Adjective
Etats-Unis	T3	G1	Américain	Etats-Unis	T3	A1	américain
Amérique	T1	G1	Américain	Amérique	T1	A1	américain
Chine	T2	G2	Chinois	Chine	T2	A2	chinois
Hong-Kong	T6	G3	Hongkongais	Hong-Kong	T6	A3	hongkongais
Pékin	T8	G4	Pékinois	Pékin	T8	A4	pékinois
Taiwan	T12	G5	Taiwanais	Taiwan	T12	A5	taiwanais
Washington	T13	G6	Washingtonien	Washington	T13	A6	washingtonien

Table 4. Associations between toponyms, inhabitants names and derived adjectives

In Table 5 we collect the associations between the former toponyms, as mentioned above: to be a Capital, a Region, a Country... An other association is relevant for us, it is the association between synonyms (*Taipei* is a synonym of *Taipeh*). We code "4" for the synonyms.

Toponym	key	Included Toponym	key	Type -code
Amérique	T1	Etats-Unis	T3	1
Chine	T2	Hong-Kong	T6	3
Chine	T2	Macao	T7	3
Chine	T2	Pékin	T8	2
Etats-Unis	T3	Washington	T13	2
Pékin	T8	Beijing	T4	4
Taipeh	T10	Taipei	T11	4
Taiwan	T12	Formose	T5	4
Taiwan	T12	Taipeh	T10	2

Table 5. Links between toponyms

As regards names of Countries and of Capital Towns, we must mention an other aspect of the terminology. Some denominations have been pointed out as "official denominations". They are used in all the official documents. The texts of newspapers that we intend to automatically treat, do not only use the official names, but other ones also. In newspapers, the difference is mainly stylistic. In our database these denominations are registered as "canonical forms". All the equivalent expressions are linked to the canonical form. As a result, when two names of a Capital or of a Country are synonymous, either one of them is an official denomination and they have an association, that is to say a direct link, or they are both associated with the official denomination, so they have an indirect link.

Let us sum up what we have collected for the word *Taiwan*: we have collected the links between the names *Formose*, *Taiwanais*, *Taipeh*, and the adjective *taiwanais*. Besides there is a link between *Taipei* and *Taipeh*.

The name of most countries has two official forms (here we have only collected one) and lot of toponyms have many synonyms. Our purpose is to introduce our method, not to be exhaustive. In this presentation, we have reduced the number of collected words, otherwise the Boolean matrix (next step) would be too big. For this reason, we eliminate the adjectives for the next steps of our presentation. The treatment of the adjectives can be inferred from the treatment of the names of inhabitants. Nevertheless we notice that the number of collected words is growing. That is not a problem for automatic analysis.

3.2 Organization of the Collected Data

The program only collects the keys and the Type-Code. For each word we have the list of the associated keys. Remember that when the type-code is 3 (like for *Macao* and *Hong-Kong*) we have a separate treatment: **we do not collect the link with the country including the region**. Let us sum up the words of our example, in the Table 6 and the Table 7, and, for each word, sum up the list of associated word keys. We add the full words to be clear.

Name	Key	Type-code	Associated links	Associated Names list
Amérique	T1	5	G1	Américain
Chine	T2	1	G2, T8	Chinois, Pékin
Etats-Unis	T3	1	G1, T13	Américain, Washington
Beijing	T4	4	T8	Pékin, Chine
Formose	T5	4	T12	Taiwan
Hong-Kong	T6	3	G3	Hongkongais
Macao	T7	3		
Pékin	T8	2	G4, T2,T4	Pékinois, Chine, Beijing
Taipeh	T10	2	T12, T11	Taiwan, Taipei
Taipei	T11	4	T10	Taipeh
Taiwan	T12	1	G5, T10, T5	Taiwanais, Taipeh, Formose
Washington	T13	2	G6,T3	Washingtonien, Etats-Unis

Table 6. Toponyms

Inhabitant Name	Key Key	Associated Links	Associated Names List
Américain	G1	T3, T1	Etats-Unis, Amérique
Chinois	G2	T2	Chine
Hongkongais	G3	T6	Hong-Kong
Pékinois	G4	T8	Pékin
Taiwanais	G5	T12	Taiwan
Washingtonien	G6	T13	Washington

Table 7. Inhabitant Name

3.3 Building of an Association Matrix between the Associated Words

We build a square Boolean matrix with a row and a column for each collected word. We put a "1" at the intersection between rows and columns of associated words. Each "1" at the intersection between line i and column j means that there is a direct link between the word i and the word j, either in the Table 6 or in the Table 7.
The geographical words of the example are *Pékin*, *Taipeh*, *Pékin*, *Taiwan*, *Pékinois*, *Pékin*, *Pékin*, *Taiwanais*, *Hong-Kong*, *Macao*, *Chinois*, *Américains*, *Washington*.We deal with the first occurrence of each word.
For each word, step by step, we build the matrix with the collected links (Figure 3).

1. We write the first word in a table, on the first row.

2. We look for the associated keys: G4, T2, T4 (*Pékinois*, *Chine*, *Beijing*).

3. The next word is *Taipeh* (T10). We add it into the matrix on the fourth line. There is no association between *Taipeh* and the former words. We introduce the link with T12, T11 (*Taiwan*, *Taipei*).

4. The next word is *Taiwan* (T12). We have the line 7 for it. We have already registered the association with *Taipeh*. It also has a link with G5 and T5 (*Taiwanais*, *Formose*).

5. The next word is *Pékinois* (G4). It is already line 2. Its link with *Pékin* is already registered. Next is *Taiwanais* (G5). It is line 8. The next word is *Hong-Kong* (T6), it has a link with *Hongkongais* (G3).

And so on... Lastly we obtain a 18x 18 matrix.

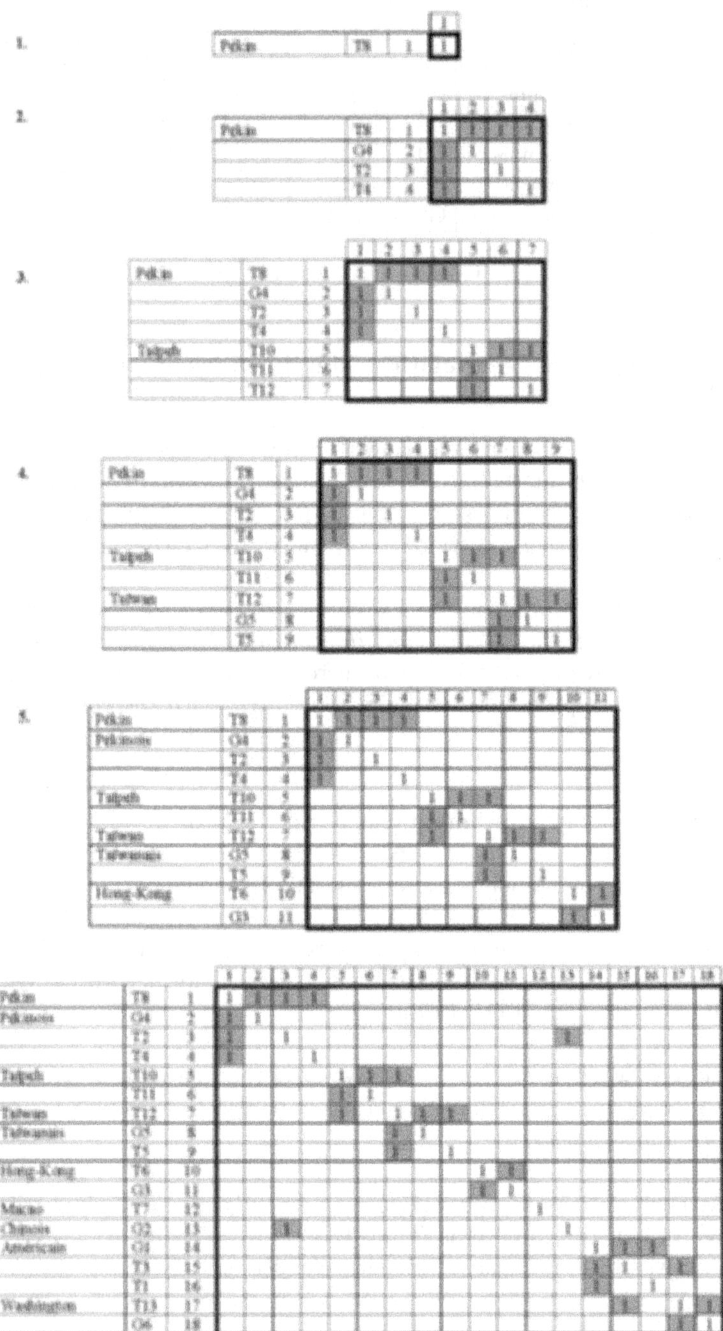

Fig. 3. Association matrix between the geographical words of the text

3.4 Compute of the Indirect Links between the Selected Words

The Boolean matrix registers the links between two words of the text. It is symmetrical. Other links can be performed by transitivity: so we compute the transitive closure of the Boolean matrix [4].
The algorithm of transitive closure is performed in that way: we note O_x -x being the number of the lines in the matrix- the operation whose effect is to copy each "1" that belong to the line x in every line having a "1" in column x.
First we perform O_1. All the "1" of the first line are written in the lines having a "1" in the column 1. Here it affects the second, the third and the fourth lines. Then we perform O_2. The "1" of the second line are written on the first, the third and the fourth lines. We go on until O_{18}. Then we obtain the association matrix after the transitive closure (Figure 4).

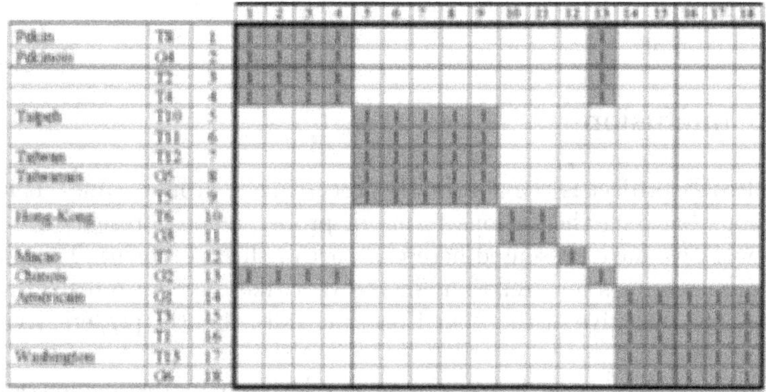

Fig. 4. Associated matrix after the transitive closure

Every "1" in the matrix at the intersection of the column i and the line j shows a transitive link between the word number i and the word number j.

3.5 Results

On the matrix obtained by the transitive closure, we only keep the lines corresponding to the words of the text, and we group the similar lines together. So we obtain the words of the text that have to be put in the same group. We obtain the matrix of the Figure 5.
We recall that our transducer (Section 1) contains only a part of the direct relations of the data base. The Figure 5 pools the words of the text that have either a direct relation or an indirect relation. We have labeled each group. We will use it as a tag (Figure 6) for the key of the pool.

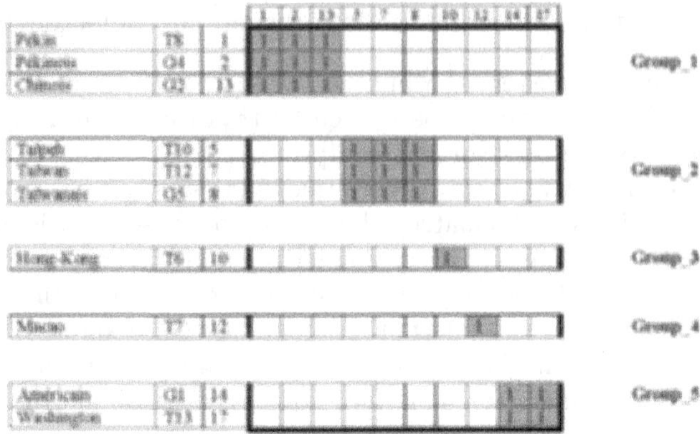

Fig. 5. Groups of the associated words of the text

4 Conclusion

The Prolex project is the automatic processing of proper names. It includes the relations between the various forms of proper names present in a same text. The work we have presented here is a part of this treatment. The purpose is to tag proper names and relations in the text like on Figure 6. In this example, we use the directive of the Text Encoding Initiative (http://etext.virginia.edu/TEI.html) [2].

We are now dealing with proper names relatives to foreign countries. This second step needs the merging of the first database with different thesaurus of geographical proper names relatives to the foreign countries. It is in progress. A study of the long names of countries [11] has lead to local grammar rules. With these rules we are able to recognize expressions that are not in our dictionary. This rules are connected to the short names. So we will be able to connect these expressions with the countries.

Among the other development of the Prolex project, we can cite three of them (at the University of Tours, either at the Computer Laboratory (LI) or at the theme Language and Information technologies (LTI): To translate proper names: to day, Thierry Grass works on German-French comparison. To build local grammars about the determination and modification of proper names (Nathalie Garric). To apply the Prolex knowledge on proper names for text classification and clustering (Nathalie Friburger).

```
<name type="Toponym/Country capital" key="group_1">
      Pékin </name>
menace
<name type="Toponym/Country capital" key="group_2">
      Taïpeh </name>
d'intervention militaire en cas d'enlisement du processus de réunification...C'est un glissement
d'importance dans la position de
<name type="Toponym/Country capital" key="group_1">
      Pékin </name>
à l'égard de
<name type="Toponym/Country" key="group_2">
      Taïwan </name>
...on en trouve trace dans de multiples déclarations de dirigeants
<adjective type="Toponym/Country capital" key="group_1" reg=«pékinois»>
      pékinois </adjective>
... Le raidissement de sa position sur une intervention militaire traduit l'irritation croissante de
<name type="Toponym/Country capital" key="group_1">
      Pékin </name>
devant les obstacles placés par les
<name type="Inhabitants/Country" key="group_2" reg=«Taïwanais»>
      Taïwanais </name>
sur le chemin de la réunification alors que la récupération de
<name type="Toponym/Region" key=" group_3">
      Hong-Kong </name>
et de
<name type="Toponym/Region" key=" group_4">
      Macao </name>
a été bouclée sans heurts....Les
<name type="Inhabitants/Country" key="group_1" reg=«Chinois»>
      Chinois </name>
font certes un geste en acceptant d'ouvrir les discussions sur un « pied d'égalité »...Les
<name type="Inhabitants/Country" key="group_5" reg=«Américain»>
      Américains </name>
intensifient leurs manœuvres diplomatiques afin d'éviter la réédition de la " crise des missiles " de
la présidentielle du printemps 1996. L'objectif de
<name type="Toponym/Country" key="group_5">
      Washington </name>
est d'ouvrir des canaux de communication au plus haut niveau...
```

Fig. 6. The encoded text

References

1. BELLEIL C. (1997), *Reconnaissance, typage et traitement des coréférences des toponymes français et de leurs gentilés par dictionnaire électronique relationnel*, Doctoral thesis, University of Nantes.

2. BRUNESEAUX F. (1998), Noms propres, syntagmes nominaux, expressions referentielles: reperage et codage, *Langues*, 1-1, 46-59.

3. COATES-STEPHENS S. (1993), The Analysis and Acquisition of Proper Names for the Understanding of Free Text, *Computers and the Humanities*, 26:441-456.

4. FAURE R. (1970), *Précis de Recherche Opérationnelle*, Dunod Décision.

5. MACDONALD D. (1996), Internal and external evidence in the identification and semantic categorisation of Proper Names, *Corpus Processing for Lexical Acquisition*, 21-39, Massachussetts Institute of Technology.

6. MAE (1995), *Etats et capitales Liste des formes françaises recommandées*, Division Géographique (Archives et Documentation) du Ministère des Affaires Etrangères.

7. MANI I., RICHARD MACMILLAN T. (1996), Indentifying Unknown Proper Names in Newswire Text, *Corpus Processing for Lexical Acquisition*, 41-59, Massachussetts Institute of Technology.

8. MIHOV S., MAUREL D. (2000), Direct Construction of Minimal Acyclic Subsequential Transducers, *CIAA 2000*, to appear in *LNCS*.

9. MOHRI M. (1994), Minimization of Sequential Transducers, *Theoretical Computer Science*.

10. PAIK W., LIDDY E. D., YU E., MCKENNA M. (1996), Categorizing and Standardizing Proper Nouns for Efficient Information Retrieval, *Corpus Processing for Lexical Acquisition*, 61-73, Massachussetts Institute of Technology.

11. PITON O., MAUREL D. (1997), Le traitement informatique de la géographie politique internationale, *Colloque Franche-Comté Traitement automatique des langues (FRACTAL 97)*, Besançon, 10-12 décembre, in *Bulag*, numéro spécial, 321-328.

12. PITON O., MAUREL D., BELLEIL C. (1999), The Prolex Data Base : Toponyms and gentiles for NLP, Third *International Workshop on Applications of Natural Language to Data Bases (NLDB'99)* (Proceedings p. 233-237), Klagenfurt, Autriche,.17-19 juin.

13. POIBEAU T. (1999), Evaluation des systèmes d'extraction d'information: une expérience sur le français, *Langues*.

14. REN X., PERRAULT F. (1992), The typology of Unknown Words : An Experimental Study of Two Corpora, *COLING 92*.

15. ROCHE E., SCHABES Y. ed. (1997), *Finite state language Processing*, Cambridge, Mass./London, England: MIT Press.

16. SILBERZTEIN M. (1993), *Dictionnaires électroniques et analyse automatique de textes - Le système INTEX*, Paris, Masson.

Understanding and Representing Relationship Semantics in Database Design

Veda C. Storey

Dept. of Computer Information Systems
J. Mack Robinson College of Business Administration
Georgia State University
P.O. Box 4015 Atlanta, Georgia, USA 30302
VStorey@gsu.edu

Abstract. Much of the research that deals with understanding the real world and representing it in a conceptual model uses the entity-relationship model as a means of representation. Although the relationship construct is a very important part of this model, the semantics of relationship verbs are usually not considered in much detail, due, in part, to their generic nature. In this research, an ontology for classifying relationships based upon their verb phrases is proposed. The ontology is intended to serve as a useful part of database design methodologies to understand, capture, and refine the semantics of an application. Testing of the ontology on a number of cases illustrates its usefulness.

Keywords. conceptual modeling, relationships, semantics, ontology, entity-relationship model

1. Introduction

The purpose of conceptual modeling is to understand the real world and represent it in an implementation-independent model, such as the entity-relationship model. Entities represent things in the real world; a relationship is usually defined simply as an association among entities. Some of the challenges of conceptual modeling focus on identifying which construct to use; that is, whether something should be represented as an entity, a relationship, or an attribute. The verb phrase of a relationship is usually selected by a designer without a great deal of thought given to finding the one that best reflects the semantics of the application.

One reason for the lack of analysis of verb phrases may be the structure of the relational model where, a one-to-many relationship is represented by a foreign key. Therefore, there is no trace of the verb phrase of the relationship from which the foreign key came. For a many-to-many relationship, however, a separate relationship relation is created [Teorey et al., 1986] with the name of this relation usually some variation of the verb phrase. Understanding the semantics of a verb phrase would be useful for several reasons. First, the verb phrase that most accurately models the real world makes the conceptual design easiest for the end-user to understand. This is

M. Bouzeghoub et al. (Eds.): NLDB 2000, LNCS 1959, pp. 79-90, 2001.

useful when eliciting feedback from the user about the correctness and completeness of the design. Second, it would assist when resolving conflicts among schemas in heterogeneous databases. This is especially so with the increase in the number of web databases and the potential need to integrate them. Third, automated database design tools would benefit from some surrogate for understanding the meaning of relationship verb phrases when checking the completeness of a given design and automatically generating a new design from a generic schema. The objective of this research, therefore, is to: *develop an ontology that would assist in the meaningful classification of verb phrases of relationships.* The contribution is to provide a means of understanding verb phrases so that semi-automated comparisons among relationships can be made for the evaluation or generation of database designs. Our current research is also analyzing how to develop an ontology for relationships using a linguistic approach [Ullrich et al., 2000]. The research reported here, however, is based upon research on data abstractions and other semantic relationships.

2. Related Research

A relationship is of the form *A verb-phrase B*, where *A* and *B* are entities. Although relationships are usually classified according to their cardinalities (unary, binary, ternary, n-ary), much of the semantics of a relationship is captured in its verb phrase. However, it is difficult to understand and represent the semantics of relationship verb phrases because of the generic nature of some verb phrases and the specific or context-dependent nature of others.

- *Generic and context-independent verb phrases:* Many verb phrases are generic; for example, ìhasî (ìhaveî) or ìdoes.î They are found in many different applications and capture different meanings. ìHas,î for example, is used to represent many different kinds of concepts such as part-of, associated-with and is-a. The meaning of other verb phrases may be the same across application domains. For example, ìreservesî has the same semantics whether it is used for a restaurant or airline application. Other examples include ìdeliversî and ìtransportsî.
- *Ambiguous and context-dependent verb phrases:* The meaning of a verb phrase may be domain-specific. For example, ìswitchingî in the railway domain refers to the movement of cars in a railway yard. In a hotel application, it might refer to the changing of shifts. The direction of the verb phrase may be ambiguous because the relationship construct does not have an inherent way of indicating direction.

2.1 Data Abstractions

The most notable research on analyzing the meaning of relationships has been in the area of data abstractions. Even these, though, can sometimes have more than one interpretation. The *is-a* relationship is the most common data abstractions [Bachman, 1983]. An *is-a* relationship may partition an entity (for example, an employee is a part-time or a full-time employee and nothing else) or there may be overlap (an employee is a part-time or a full-time employee and at the same time is a secretary or an engineer). These has been extensively studied and referred to as a generalization hierarchy and a subtype relationship, respectively [Teorey et al., 1986; Goldstein and Storey, 1992]. *Part-of*, or meronymic, relationships have many different meanings. For example, *Desk* part-of *Office* refers to a physical component, whereas in *Slice part-of Pie*, both the *Slice* and *Pie* entities have many attributes that are the same (e.g., kind, texture) and share the same values [Whinston et al., 1987; Storey, 1993]. *Instance-of* may refer to an instantiation (specialization) [Teorey et al., 1986, Motschnig-Petrik and Mylopoulos, 1992]. It may also refer to a materialization, which is a relationship between a conceptual thing and its concrete manifestations, such as that found between a movie and a video or a car model and rented car [Goldstein and Storey, 1994]. *Member-of* relationships have different interpretations that are based upon sets [Brodie, 1981; Goldstein and Storey, 1999; Motschnig-Pitrik and Storey, 1995]. Finally, research on views and perspectives tries to capture different aspects of the real world [Motschnig-Pitrik, 2000].

2.2 Database Design Automation

A number of systems have been developed for automated database design [Bouzeghoub, 1992; Lloyd-Williams, 1997; Storey and Goldstein, 1993]. These tools, however, do not contain domain-specific knowledge to help them reason about the semantics of the application domain. It has been suggested that domain models, which would serve as templates for designers, would be useful [Lloyd-Williams, 1997]. The models could be used to compare an existing design to make suggestions for completeness (reasoning) and to generate new designs. This would require a classification scheme for comparing relationships. In our prior research, we attempted to develop a methodology for automatically generating and classifying application domain models, when reasoning about the quality of a userís (initial) design. This is partially implemented in a system called the Common Sense Business Reasoner [Storey et al., 1997]. From each new design given to the system, an effort was made to ìlearnî about the new application domain. The research involved the development of an entity ontology [Storey et al., 1998] to recognize similarities in entities. For example, *Worker* and *Employee* are both classified as person by the ontology, so they are candidates to be the same during automated comparison of two models. That research, however, considers only the structure of the relationship when comparing two models. To better compare two models, understanding something about the semantics of the relationship verb phrases would be extremely useful.

3. Relationship Ontology

An ontology refers to a set of concepts that can be used to describe some area of knowledge or build a representation of it [Swartout, 1999]. It defines the basic terms and rules for combining them [Neches et al., 1991]. This section presents an ontology for classifying relationships based upon their verb phrases. The ontology classifies a verb phrase into one or more categories such as *temporal*, *part-of*, *transaction/event*, or *generic*. The ontology, which is not yet implemented, requires interaction with a user. An important objective is to minimize the number of questions to ask the user, while still providing a useful classification scheme. This requires that the ontology make a number of inferences automatically (no user involvement). The classification categories were generated from: analysis of data abstractions and problems understanding the semantics of verb phrases; prior experiences in developing an entity ontology; known problems with modeling temporal relationships; and textbook and simulated database design examples.

The purpose of the ontology is to: 1) store and provide information on the meaning of verb phrases; 2) acquire information regarding the meaning of new verb phrases, and 3) facilitate the comparison of two verb phrases to ascertain if and how two relationships might be related. The ontology consists of: a *semantic network* describing the different categories into which verb phrases can be classified; a *knowledge base* containing information on the meaning of verb phrases that have been classified; and an *acquisition component* for interactive extraction of the meaning of verb phrases from a user. It is intended that both the ontological classifications and the knowledge base containing the classified verb phrases will build up over time. Initially, there will be some real-world knowledge encoded in the knowledge base; for example, ìhasî and ìhaveî are the same. In the classification of relationships, use is made of the entity ontology mentioned above.

3.1 Semantic Network

The top of the semantic network is shown in Figure 1. The verb phrases are classified into two types: those with well-defined semantics and those without. This is useful because it immediately separates those verb phases that are relatively straight-forward to classify from those that require more user input.

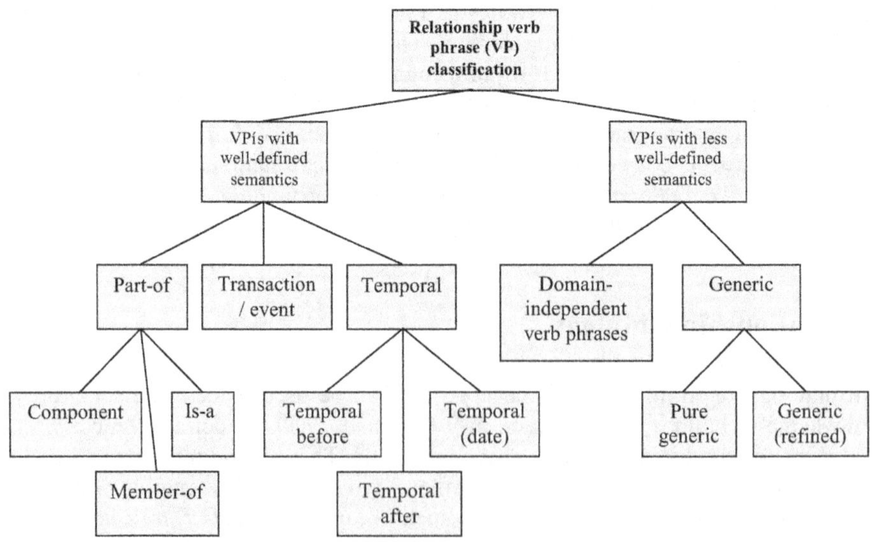

Figure 1: Top Levels of Relationship Ontology

3.1.1 Relationships with Well-Defined Semantics

Relationships with well-defined semantics are: part-of, transaction/event, and temporal. This classification is adapted from Whinston et al. [1987] who first classify semantic relationships into: inclusion, possession, attachment, and attribution. Inclusion generally refers to *is-a* relationships, although Whinston et al. [1987] include a number of *part-of* relationships as types of inclusion. Possession is one interpretation of the generic verb phrase ìhasî [Storey and Goldstein, 1988]. Attachment may have an interpretation under *part-of.* Attribution is captured by entity and relationship attributes.

1. *Part-of:* Although Whinston et al. [1987] identify seven interpretations of part-of verbs, is-a, component, and member-of are most relevant to database design. The best interpretation is found by querying the user. Examples are shown in Table 1.

Relationship	**Interpretation**
Wheel part-of Car	Wheel component-of Car
Secretary part-of Employees	Secretary is-an Employee
Secretary part-of Committee	Secretary member-of Committee

Table 1: Part-of Relationships

In *Secretary part-of Employees*, there is a mistake in the userís input, which can be attributed to mixing singular and plural forms of the verb phrases. The design implications for component relationships are restrictions on the values for the cardinalities, when the component is further classified as relevant, characteristic, or identifying [Goldstein and Storey, 1999].

2. *Transaction/event:* Verb phrases that represent transactions or events include *files, supplies,* and *generates.*

3. *Temporal (before/after)*: Many relationships have timeframes; for example, a *Customer rents Video.* An important design implication is whether both the ìbeforeî and ìafterî relationships need to be included.

For example, *Employee starts Job* and *Employee ends Job* capture different semantics so different attributes are associated with each. For an employee starting a job, previous employment history may be relevant. For an employee terminating a job, information on the date the termination occurred, the circumstances under which it occurred, and so forth, might be relevant.

4. *Temporal (sequence not important):* A relationship may have a time element, but the sequencing may not be important. An order is placed in a given timeframe, but what happens before or after the order is placed is not relevant. The design implication is that ìdateî should be included as an attribute.

3.1.2 Verbs with Less Well-Defined Semantics

Generic verb phrases are: 1) pure generic; or 2) can be further refined.

1. *Pure generic:* Many verb phrases cannot be refined further and so are classified as pure generic. These include ìis-a,î ìuses,î and ìgives,î and are part of the ontologyís initial knowledge base. In Figure 2, *Supporter* and *Manager* are both

classified as person by the entity ontology. *Pledge* and *Raise* are classified as nontradable abstract good. Even though the verb phrases are the same, the relationships differ. Unfortunately, the generic verb phrase does not help one to infer that they are different, illustrating the problems with generic verb phrases. A query to the user is needed for clarification.

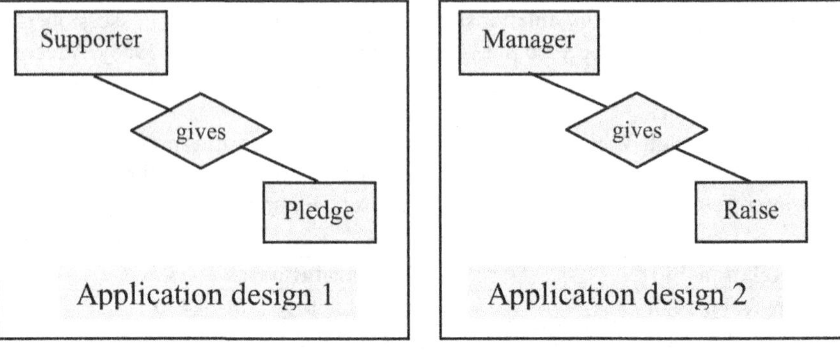

Figure 2: Generic verb ìgivesî; relationships are different

Consider now the relationships in Figure 3. The ontological classifications of the entities signal that the relationships are different. *Manager* and *Professor* are classified as person. *Bonus* is classified as an abstract good and *Lecture* is classified as a tradable document.

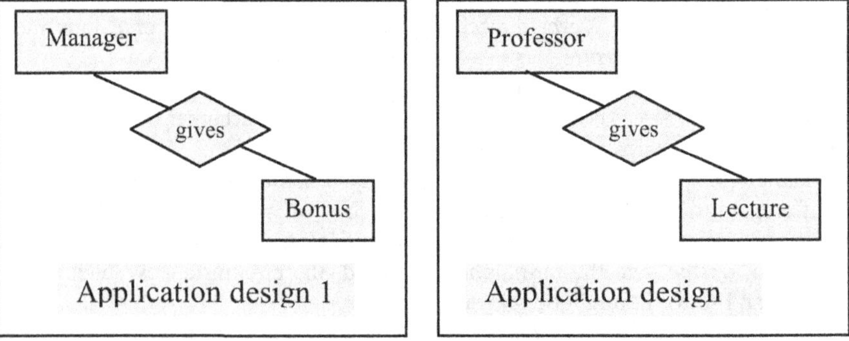

Figure 3: Generic verb ìgivesî; relationships are different

Because of the problem of identifying all generic, and other types of, verb phrases a priori, the ontology is intended to build up over time.

2. *Refined Generic:* Some generic verb phrases may be refined, depending upon the application domain. ìGivenî in the relationship *Employee given Project* can be interpreted as ìassignedî or some notion of ìcontracts-withî. Similar interpretations hold for *Professor given Class*. In another domain, ìgivenî could have a completely different interpretation. For example, the semantics of *Musician given Lesson* is best

captured as written. Many verb phrases can potentially belong in this category. Three of the most common are illustrated below.

Has/Have: The most important verb in this category is ìhasî (ìhaveî). The most frequent interpretations are shown in Table 2.

Interpretation	Classification	Justification
Part-of (physical)	Component-of	Aggregation abstraction
Part-of (membership)	Member-of	Association abstraction
Is-a (non-overlapping subsets)	Is-a	Generalization / specialization abstraction
Is-a (overlapping subtypes)	Is-a	Subtype hierarchy
Possess/owns	Possession	Common sense knowledge
Non-specific interpretation	Associated with	Common sense knowledge

Table 2: Possible interpretations of ìhasî

The design implications such as semantic integrity constraints, primary key selection, and inheritance that are associated with these abstraction categories hold [Goldstein and Storey, 1999], which indicates the importance of identifying the correct interpretation. The questioning scheme is illustrated in Figure 4.

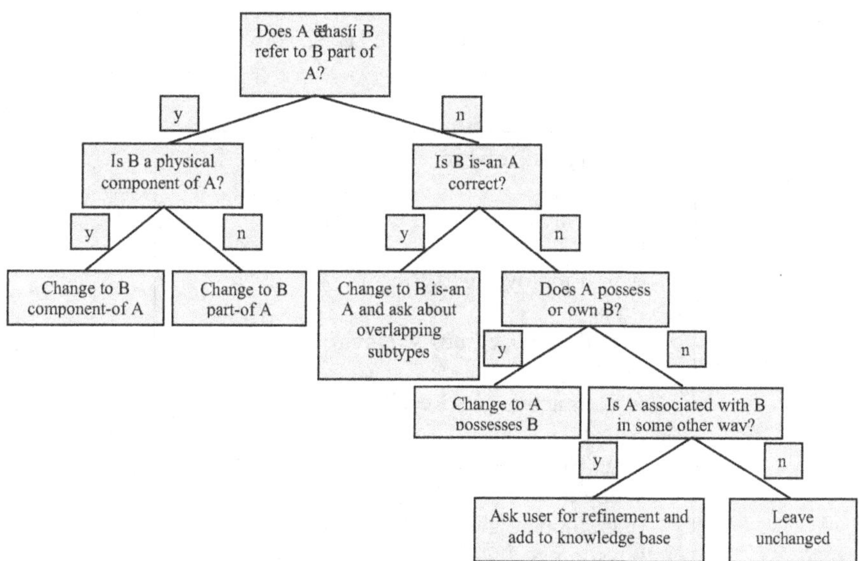

Figure 4: Interpretation of the ìhasî verb phrase

Takes: The interpretation of ìtakesî is domain-dependent. *Student takes Exam,* for example, is much different than *Train takes Passenger.* Common interpretations are shown in Table 3.

Relationship example	Interpretation
Student takes Exam	writes
Passenger takes Train	rides (generalized to transportation industry)
Employee takes Position	accepts
Person takes Responsibility	possesses

Table 3: Possible interpretations of the ìtakesî verb phrase

***Gets**:* The verb phrase ìgetsî can have a number of interpretations. Consider the relationships shown in Figure 5. Both *Customer* and *Passenger* as classified as person. *Loan* is classified as abstract good, as is *Flight*. Refinement of the verb phrase for each relationship will proceed as shown in Figure 6. The actual querying could be similar to that for ìhasî. However, since there are a number of interpretations, it is probably best to use a menu so that all of the options can be seen simultaneously. The user can provide an additional interpretation. Then, the interpretation, along with the application domain from which the userís problem came, will be stored in the ontologyís knowledge base.

Customer gets Loan
(person) (abstract good)

Passenger gets Flight
(person) (abstract good)

Figure 5: Resolution of the ìgetsî verb phrase

Does ìgetsî refer to:
Assigned
(e.g., Player assigned Position)
given
(e.g., Employee gets Raise)
finds
(e.g, Employee finds Archive)
results-in
(e.g., Practice gets Results)
adjust
(e.g., Bicycle gets Repairs)
acquires
(e.g., Student gets Skill)
buys/rents
(e.g., Customer gets Good)
Other (please specify) ______

Figure 6: Resolution of the ìgetsî verb phrase

Finally, many verb phrases are domain independent. This is the most difficult category. Because of their number, they are hard to specify a priori. However, a number of clear categories emerge, examples of which are shown in Table 4.

3.2 Knowledge Base

The knowledge base contains: 1) verb phrases that are included as an initial part of the ontology; 2) verb phrases that are classified by the users; and 3) verb phrases that are identified to be added by the users.

3.3 Acquisition Component

Interaction with a user can take place in two ways. The user can select from a menu of options, to which he or she can add an additional category. Alternatively, the user will be lead through a set of questions that appear to follow a search-tree-like pattern. Additional rules are needed to make inferences that will limit the questioning of the user, making the ontology appear more intelligent.

Verb phrase classification	**User questioning scheme**	**Relationship example**	**Other verb phrases in category**
Augments / diminishes	Does VP indicate up or down?	Campaign improves Ratings	Reduces, augments
Transaction/e vent	Does VP indicate activity?	Manager initiates Meeting	complete, shut-down
Pre-requisites	Is A required for B?	Course requires Pre-requisite	needs, is-a
Discovers	Does A find B?	Digger finds Artifact	learns
Earns/sells	Does VP signal commerce?	Company profits-from Sale	Benefit, sell, earn
Facilitates	Does VP enable something?	Professor allows Waiver	can
Adjusts	Does VP change something?	Repairman fixes Bicycle	Fix, change
Prefers	Does VP indicate preference?	Patron likes Movie	Choose, prefer select
Transports	Does VP refer to movement?	Passenger rides Train	Walks, transports, ships, delivers

Table 4: Classification of domain-dependent verb phrases

Verb Phrase	Classification	Source	Application domain
Is-a	Generic	Initial knowledge	Domain-independent
Part-of	Member-of	User J. Mills	University
Part-of	Component	User H. Stewart	Bicycle retail
Commence	Temporal	User: L. Wallace	Video sales
Starts	Temporal	Initial knowledge	Domain-independent
teaches	Teaches	User G. Rogers added	University

Table 5: Knowledge Base

4. Validation

Testing was carried out by simulating the use of the ontology on two types of problems. The first was a set of textbook-like design problems that had been created for other purposes and, therefore, were not biased to this ontology. The application domains were: student advisory, airline, railway, car rental, video rental, and library. Second, a set of articles was randomly selected from two magazines: *McLean's* and *Fortune*. From these, sample relationships were created. Six subjects played the role of the user. A total of 139 verb phrases were classified. 14.4% of the cases were classified automatically (mostly *is-a* verb phrases). An additional 52.5% of the cases were classified as expected by the subjects for a total of 66.9% ìcorrectî classifications. In 3.5% of the cases, the subjectsí classifications were more general than expected. Although not incorrect, a finer classification would have been preferred. The most common of these was the subject selecting ìassociated withî as an interpretation of ìhasî when, for example, ìcomponent-of,î would have been better. In 14.4% of the classifications, the subject and expected classification differed. This may have been due to the way the questions were asked, the subjectís lack of understanding of the application domain, or a lack of suitable categories. In several cases the subject wanted to use more than one classification. Several implications for the ontology emerged. First, a large number of the verb phrases were classified as transaction/event. This suggests that a finer classification of these verb phrases might be useful (e.g., spontaneous versus planned, instant versus finite time, discrete versus continuous). Second, some domain-independent verb phrases did not appear in the testing, indicating that they do not occur as frequently as previously thought or that refinement is needed. Finally, new verb phrases were added by the subjects. This is consistent with the objective of building the knowledge base over time.

5. Conclusion

An ontology for the classification of relationship verb phrases has been presented. This classification is useful for comparing conceptual designs to identify missing constructs and for building templates of new designs. Testing of the ontology on various application domains illustrates its effectiveness. The ontology will be implemented and incorporated into a database design system. Further testing on real world databases is needed. Learning techniques will be developed to update the knowledge base by category.

Acknowledgement. This research was supported by Georgia State University.

6. Bibliography

1. Bouzeghoub, M., ìUsing Expert Systems in Schema Design,î in Loucopoulos, P. and Zicari, R. (Eds.), *Conceptual Modelling, Databases, and CASE*, Wiley, 1992
2. Brachman, R.J. What IS-A is and isnít : An analysis of taxonomic links insemantic networks, *IEEE Computer,* October, 1983.
3. Brodie, M., "Association: A Database Abstraction," *Proceedings of the Entity-Relationship Conference*, 1981.
4. Goldstein, R.C., and Storey, V.C., ìMaterializationî, *IEEE Transactions on Knowledge and Data Engineerig*, Vol.6, No.5, October 1994, pp.835-842.
5. Goldstein, R.C. and Storey, V.C., ìData Abstractions: ìWhy and How,î *Data and Knowledge Engineering*, Vol.29, No.3, 1999, pp. 1-18.
6. Goldstein, R.C., and Storey, V.C., ìUnravelling IS-A Structures,î *Information Systems Research (ISR)*, Vol.3, No.2, June 1992, pp.99-126.
7. Lloyd-Williams, M., ``Exploiting Domain Knowledge During the Automated Design of Object-Oriented Databases,î Proceedings of the 16th *International Conference on Conceptual Modeling (ER'97),* Los Angeles, 3-6 November, 1997.
8. Motschnig-Pitrik, R., "A Generic Framework for the Modeling of Contexts and its Applications," *Data and Knowledge Engineering*, Vol.32, 2000, pp.145-180.
9. Motschnig-Pitrik, R. and Myloppoulos, J., "Class and Instances," *International Journal of Intelligent and Cooperative Systems*, Vol1, No.1, 1992, pp.61-92.
10. Motschnig-Pitrik, R. and Storey, V.C., ìModelling of Set Membership: the Notion and the Issues,î *Data and Knowledge Engineering*, Vol.16, August 1995.
11. Neches, R., Fikes, R.E., Finin, T., Gruber, T.R., Senator, T., and Swartout, W.R., ìEnabling Technology for Knowledge Sharing, î *AI Magazine*, Vol.12, No.3, 1991, pp.36-56.
12. Storey, V.C., ìUnderstanding Semantic Relationships,î *Very Large Data Bases (VLDB) Journal*, Vol.2, No.4, October 1993, pp.455-488.
13. Storey, V.C., Chiang, R., Dey, D., Goldstein, R.C., and Sundaresan, S., ìCommon Sense Reasoning and Learning for Database Design Systems,î *ACM Transactions on Data Base Systems,* Vol.22, No.4, December 1997.
14. Storey, V.C., Dey, D., Ullrich, H., and Sundaresan, S., ìAn Ontology-Based Expert System for Database Design,î *Data and Knowledge Engineering, Special Issue: ER'97*, 1998.
15. Storey, V.C. and Goldstein, R.C., ìKnowledge-Based Approaches to Database Design,î *Management Information Systems Quarterly,* Vol.17, No.1, March, 1993, pp.25-46.
16. Storey, V.C. and Goldstein, R.C., ìA Methodology for Creating User Views in Database Design,î *ACM Transactions on Database Systems*, Vol.13, No.3, September 1988, pp.305-338.

17. Swartout, W., ìOntologies,î *IEEE Intelligent Systems*, January-February, 1999, pp.18-19.
18. Teorey, T.L., Yang, D., and Fry, J.P, ìA Logical Design Methodology for Relational Databases using the Extended Entity-Relationship Approach,î *ACM Computing Surveys*, Vol.18, No.2, 1986, pp.197-222..
19. Ullrich, H., Purao, S., and Storey, V.C., ìAn Ontology for Classifying the Semantics of Relationships in Database Design,î *Proceedings of NLDB'2000*, Versailles, 28-30 June 2000.
20. Whinston, M.E., Chaffin, R., and Hermann, D., ìA Taxonomy of Part-Whole Relations,î *Cognitive Science*, Vol.11, 1987, pp.417-444.

An Ontology for Classifying the Semantics of Relationships in Database Design

Harald Ullrich[1], Sandeep Purao[2, 3], and Veda C. Storey[2]

[1]Southern Company Energy Marketing
900 Ashford Parkway, Atlanta, Georgia 30338
harald.ullrich@southernenergy.com

[2]Department of Computers and Information Systems
Georgia State University, Box 4015 Atlanta, Georgia 30302

[3]Institutt for Informasjonvitenskap, Agder University College,
Tordenskjoldsgate 65, 404 Kristiansand, Norway
Phone: 404.651.3894, FAX: 404.651.3894
{spurao,vstorey}@gsu.edu

Abstract. Relationships are an integral part of conceptual database design because they represent associations between entities from the real world. With the proliferation of both traditional, corporate, and now, web-based, databases representing similar entities, comparison of relationships across these databases is increasingly important. The ability to compare and resolve similarities in relationships in an automated manner is critical for merging diverse database designs, thus facilitating their effective use and reuse. The key to automating such comparisons is the capture and classification of the semantics of the relationship verb phrases. This research presents a multi-layered ontology for classifying verb phrases to capture their semantics. The fundamental layer captures the most elementary relationships between entities. The next, generic layer combines or arranges fundamental relationships to represent generic, real-world relationships. Finally, the contextual layer instantiates the generic relationships with specific verb phrases in different situations. Empirical testing of the ontology illustrates its effectiveness.

Keywords: Database design, relationships, ontology, semiotics, entity-relationship model, natural language

1. Introduction

Relationships are an important part of conceptual modeling since things in the real world do not exist by themselves, but are somehow connected. In the entity-relationship model, a binary relationship is defined as *A verb phrase B* where *A* and *B* are entity types and the verb phrase describes the association between them. The semantics of verb phrases, however, have not been analyzed in detail. Understanding these semantics can be useful for representing and reconciling relationships for various database design activities. For example, since designers have begun to develop corporate databases, they have been faced with the problem of view integration. With increasing inter-organizational coordination, heterogeneous

M. Bouzeghoub et al. (Eds.): NLDB 2000, LNCS 1959, pp. 91-102, 2001.

database integration has become a necessity. Finally, the maturing of web databases is requiring the integration of databases for ad hoc queries. In general, if the comparison and integration of databases could be carried out in a (semi-)automated way, this would result in less manual effort on the part of the designers. It would also produce better results because the input designs would be completely and consistently compared.

The objective of this research, therefore, is to: *develop a relationship ontology for understanding the semantics of the verb phrases that represent relationships among entities.* The ontology provides a concise, yet exhaustive, organization and classification of the different levels of semantics implicit in relationship verb phrases.

2. Related Research

The semantics of relationships for database design and use have not received much attention. Most database design practices are restricted to the use of *simple* relationships to represent associations between entities. Proposed extensions to design models, such as the type hierarchies (in the extended E-R models [Chen, 1993]) or the categories (in the E-C-R models [Elmasri and Navathe, 1989]), are not widely used. With the introduction of object-oriented concepts and research on data modeling, aggregation and inheritance have added to the understanding of the semantics of relationships [Motschnig-Pitrik, 2000]. The semantics of *simple* relationships, however, have largely been ignored because they are so complex. As a result, important tasks such as comparisons of relationships across databases have been restricted to syntactical properties.

Consider the need to recognize whether two relationships are the same during a comparison of heterogeneous databases. *Customer buys Product* and *Customer purchases Product* capture the same real world situation, even though they use different verb phrases, and should, therefore, be treated as the same. In contrast, *Customer rents Car* and *Customer returns Car* represent different concepts, and must be differentiated. An important consideration for the latter is whether both relationships need to be included in the integrated database. Understanding the semantics of the verb phrases is, therefore, a prerequisite for any automated comparison of relationships.

Research in semiotics and ontologies that deal with capturing and representing the meaning of terms is most relevant. The need to understand and represent the semantics of words has long been recognized. Semiotics, the theory of signs, is concerned with properties of things in their capacity as signs for objects [Morris, 1946]. Semantics is the study of meaning and deals with the association between signs and the objects in the real world to which they are applicable. For example, the sign MSFT represents the stock of Microsoft, Inc., and a red octagon at an intersection represents the instruction to stop a vehicle before proceeding. Semantics is one of the ten semiotic features of information systems identified by Barron et al. [1999]. Stamper [1996] identifies three principles for establishing and utilizing semantics: 1) objectivist meaning, 2) constructivist meaning, and 3) mentalistic meaning. With the objectivist meaning, all users know the mappings from the sign to the real world. For example, ëmaleí and ëfemaleí indicate two genders. The constructivist meaning involves negotiation and reconciliation among users to assign meanings to signs. For example, a product code, say, 0407, although widely accepted, may be changed by negotiation. With a mentalistic meaning, a person establishes a mapping from a sign to a real world object. For example, a rectangle represents an entity in an entity-relationship model, and once used by a designer, the readers are expected to accept this interpretation.

Database design, where a conceptual data model represents an aspect of the real-world, there is little room for negotiating the meanings captured in the database. The constructivist meaning, therefore, is largely absent. The other two, objectivist and mentalistic meanings, play a large role. The aspects of the real world that indicate a shared understanding of the mapping between signs and the real world objects (e.g. ëmaleí and ëfemaleí) are observed in databases; that is, the objectivist meaning. Other aspects of the real world that are captured on the basis of organizational policies (e.g. part number 0407) indicate a negotiated understanding of the meaning of that sign as is captured in the database. Our relationship ontology, therefore, needs to focus on the objectivist and the mentalistic meanings.

Ontologies have been defined in various ways. In artificial intelligence, an ontology is defined within the context of a knowledge-based system, which is based on some abstract, simplified view of the world called a conceptualization. An ontology represents an explicit specification of such a conceptualization [Gruber 1993]. Smith [1999] defines an ontology simply as something that seeks the classification of entities. The term ëentitiesí is used generically to refer to things and not restricted to entities in an entity-relationship model.

An ontology consists of terms, their definitions, and axioms relating them. Terms are usually organized into a taxonomy using one of three approaches [Noy and Hafner, 1997]. The first involves arranging everything in a tree-like concept hierarchy (with possible multiple inheritance). The second is called the distinctions approach, where several parallel dimensions are devised along which one or more top-level categories or subcategorized. The third approach involves developing a large number of small local taxonomies that might be linked together by relations or axioms. Our research uses a distinctions approach because it is more flexible than the concept hierarchy and facilitates the creation of one ontology.

The above perspective on ontology development focuses on classifications and taxonomies to understand distinctions between things. This is different from that of Bunge [1977] who focuses on articulating the properties of things. That view has been applied to information systems by Wand and Weber [1990].. Our approach, instead, is on finding distinctions among relationships. Interesting work on ontology development has been carried out in database design [Embley et al. 1999] and natural language understanding [Dalhgren, 1995]. Kedad and Metais [1999] propose to manage semantic heterogeneity by the use of a linguistic dictionary. Dullea and Song [1999] propose a taxonomy of recursive relationships.

In database design, divergent bodies of data from different sources must be unified. Ontologies can be useful because different databases may use identical names, but have different meanings or the same meaning may be expressed by different names [Smith, 1999]. Database design, in general, is complex because it involves understanding contexts, context overlapping, and relative naming [Theodorakis et al. 1999]. These lead to problems in design automation and reuse, view integration and heterogeneous databases, and web-based databases.

Research on understanding, formalizing, and automating database design, lead to the development of various types of knowledge-based tools for design automation [Bouzeghoub, 1992; Lloyd-Williams, 1997; Storey and Goldstein, 1993]. These tools, however, lack the ability to acquire, organize, and use real-world knowledge. For example, within the hospital domain, *Patient* and *Room* are common, important entities, as is the relationship *Patient assigned-to Room*. If a library of such domain models were available, they could serve as a starting point for new designs, thus facilitating a high-level of reuse.

For domain models to be created automatically, however, application designs need to be automatically compared. A database design system that does so must be able to recognize similarities among constructs when their names differ. This requires comparisons based upon both content and context (meaning and structure). Structural comparisons deal with recognizing the similarities in the positioning of entities, relationships and attributes. Comparisons based upon meanings is much more difficult. In prior research we developed an ontology for the meaning of entities [Storey et al., 1998]. The ontology was then used to assist in the creation of domain models within and across different application domains [Storey et al., 1997; 2000; Storey and Dey, 2000].

View integration is used to obtain all parts of the input conceptual schemas that refer to the same portion of reality and unify their representation. View integration is also used for database integration where different databases are merged to form a single database or data warehouse. In either situation, one is forced to deal with semantic heterogeneity among data elements.

3. Relationship Ontology

This section resents a relationship ontology that serves as a framework for classifying verb phrases. The classification is intended to be robust enough to formalize and analyze the semantics of the vast majority of relationships encountered in database design. The development of the ontology was heavily influenced by several well-known problems. The first is that generic verb phrases (e.g. ëhasí) are used in different ways. In linguistic terms, these are forms of *auxiliary* verbs [UIUC, 1998] that database designers use as primary verbs. A verb phrase can have different meanings in different contexts. The second problem is the inverse of the first, namely, that different verb phrases can be used to capture the same meaning in different contexts (e.g. ëbuysí and ëpurchasesí). This can create a many-to-one mapping between verbs and meanings. These mappings are a direct outcome of the richness of natural language and the desire of database designers to exploit this richness. They can, however, result in use of idiosyncratic, or unclear verb phrases, making understanding and further use of them for database tasks, such as integration, difficult. One solution to these problems is the creation of an ontology that can capture the generic or prototypical verbs or verb phrases that can then be mapped to observed instantiations in different contexts and applications. For example, the verbs ëbuysí and ëpurchasesí may both map to the underlying prototypical verb ëacquires.í Figure 1 shows this separation between observed instantiations and the generic mappings captured in the prototypical verbs.

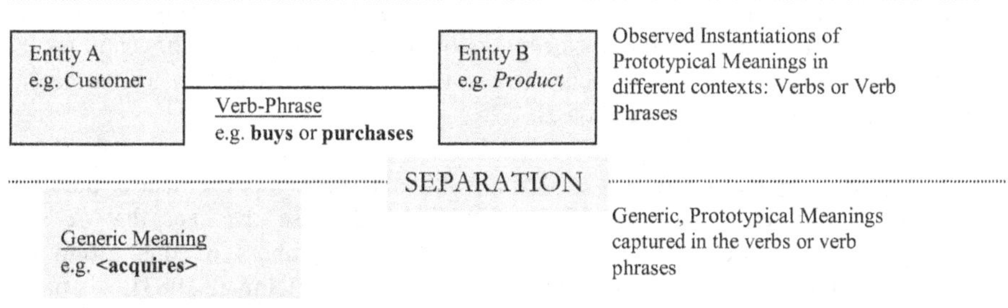

Figure 1: Separating Observed Instantiations from Generic Meanings

Deriving an exhaustive set of prototypical verbs is difficult. Whether such a set is distilled from observed instantiations (e.g. SPEDE 2000) or generated manually, demonstrating completeness is difficult because of the different shades of meaning in natural language. We, therefore, propose a decomposition of the prototypical verbs into fundamental primitives. For example, the verb ëacquiresí usually involves two actions represented by the two primitives, ëintends-toí and ëbecomes-owner-ofí, as shown in Figure 2.

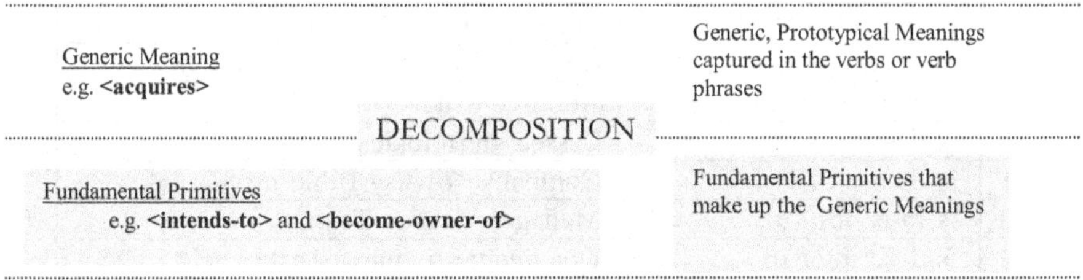

Figure 2: Decomposing Generic Meanings into Fundamental Primitives

Three levels of analysis for verb phrases can now be identified. The first refers to fundamental primitives, which correspond to the objectivist semantics captured in the relationships. The primitives can be combined to create generic or prototypical meanings at the second level (figure 2), which correspond to the mentalistic meaning captured in the relationship verb phrases [Stamper, 1996]. Finally, the prototypical verbs can be instantiated in different contexts at the third level (figure 1). The observed verb phrases are, thus, at the third level, whereas the other two levels capture the deep semantics implicit in these verbs or verb phrases. The ontology mirrors these three levels.

3.1 Layer 1: Fundamental Primitives

Layer 1 captures the fundamental primitives representing connections between entities at a very abstract level. Three groups fully capture these primitives: (a) status,

(b) change in status, and (c) interaction. Status represents the orientation of one entity towards the other entity, e.g. A <is-owner-of> B. A change of status signifies a change in this orientation, e.g. A <becomes-owner-of> B. Interaction captures a communication or operation between entities that does not result in a change in orientation, e.g. A <sends-message-to> B.

Group 1: Status: Primitives describing status describe a permanent or durable orientation of one entity towards the other. They express the fact that A <is something> with respect to B. The most prominent members of this group of primitives include <is-a> (generalization/specialization) [Brachman 1983], <is-part-of> (aggregations) [Smith and Smith 1977], <is-member-of> (membership) [Brodie 1981; Motschning-Pitrik and Storey 1995], <is-instance-of > [Motsching-Pitrik and Mylopoulous 1992], and <is-assigned-to>. This group contains 15 elements that represent a set of primitives to describe status. Table 1 lists these primitives.

	Status Primitives <S>	**Corresponding Real-world Examples**
1	is-a	Pilot <is an> Employee
2	is-member-of	Professor <is member of> Department
3	is-part-of	Car <contains> Engine
4	is-instance-of	VideoTape <is a copy of> Movie
5	is-version-of	Word97 <is a version of> MS Word
6	is-assigned-to	Project <has> Objective
7	is-subjected-to	Industry <is regulated by> Law
8	requires	Construction <requires> Approval
9	is-creator-of	Author <writes> Book
10	is-destroyer-of	Lessee <terminates> Lease
11	is-owner-of	Company <owns> Building
12	is-in-control-of	Manager <leads> Team
13	is-descriptor-of	Document <defines> Task
14	has-attitude-towards	Customer <likes> Product
15	follows-or-precedes	Rental <follows> Reservation

Table 1: Primitives describing Status

A sixteenth element <is-able-to> represents a bridge primitive, that is, it acquires meaning along with other primitives. The bridge primitive is so termed because it can facilitate primitives from the groups that follow; that is, change-of-status and interaction.

	Bridge Primitive	**Corresponding Real-world Example**
16	is-able-to <R>	Programmer <can code in> Language

Table 2: Bridge Primitive describing Status

Group 2: Change of status: Primitives describing change of status describe the transition from one status to another. They express the fact that the orientation A <is something> with respect to B is *transitioning* to A <is something else> with respect to

B. The primitives in this group cannot be used independently of those specified for the first group: status. The change-of-status primitives describe the transitioning life-cycle for each status. They are exhaustive in that they cover the complete life cycle of a status primitive. Consider, for example, status <is-owner-of>. The change-of-status primitives along with this status, then, generate the real-world examples in Table 3. The first row shows an example of the change-of-status primitive <wants-to-be> with the status primitive <owner-of>, that is, <wants-to-be-owner-of>. The sub-column under the change-of-status primitives shows the meanings captured in each: intent, attempt and the actual transition.

	Change of Status Primitives <CS>		**Corresponding Real-World Example for Status: <owner-of>**
1	wants-to-be	*intent*	Customer <wants to own> Product
2	attempts-to-become	*attempt*	Customer <orders> Product
3	becomes	*transition*	Customer <receives> Product
4	dislikes-being	*intent*	Company <wants to sell> Product
5	attempts-to-give-up	*attempt*	Company <offers> Product
6	gives-up	*transition*	Company <sells> Product

Table 3: Primitives Describing Change of Status

Figure 3 shows the status lifecycle captured by these change-of-status primitives. The bridge primitive represents the starting point for this life-cycle. It represents the status from which a change of status can begin.

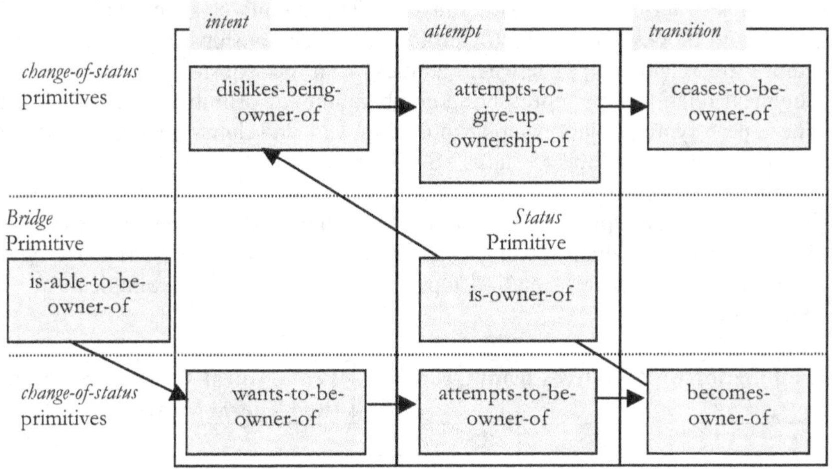

Figure 3: The Relationship Life Cycle

<u>Group 3: Interactions:</u> Interaction primitives describe a short duration communication between or operation on one entity by another. An interaction does

not result in a change of status of either entity. If the result of an interaction is a certain orientation of one entity towards the other entity, it is captured as a status in group 1. This happens when the effect of an interaction is worth remembering and capturing as a verb phrase. Consider the interaction ëcreate.í In some cases, it is useful to remember this status <is-creator-of>, for example, Author ëwritesí Book (see table 1). In other cases, the interaction itself is worth remembering and may not result in a status or a change of status. Consider Waitperson ëservesí Customer. In this case, status may not be relevant but the interaction is important. Primitives describing interaction, therefore, express the fact that A <is doing something> with respect to B. Table 4 lists the interaction primitives.

	Interaction Primitives <I>	**Corresponding Real-World Example**
1	Observes	Analyst <analyses> Requirements
2	Manipulates	Instructor <grades> Exam
3	Transmits	Bank <remits> Funds
4	Communicates	Modem <negotiates with> Phone Line
5	Serves	Employee <serves> Customer
6	Performs	Developer <tests> Software
7	Operates	Pilot <flies> Plane

Table 4: Relationships describing Interactions among Entities

3.2 Layer 2: Prototypical Relationships Representing Generic Meanings

This layer contains definitions of commonly used, context-independent, ìreal-worldî relationships in terms of the abstract layer 1. The primitives specified in layer 1 are the building blocks from which "prototypical relationships representing generic meanings of relationships between entities" can be constructed. There are 117 prototypical relationships representing combinations of primitives identified in layer 1. These prototypical relationships capture context- and domain-independent generic meanings. First, each of the 15 status <S> primitives can be considered by themselves or combined with each of the 6 change of status <CS> primitives, yielding 15*(6+1)=105 prototypical relationships. Next, the 6 interaction primitives can be either considered by themselves or combined with the bridge primitive yielding 6*(1+1)=12 prototypical relationships. Table 5 shows examples of these combinations.

Combination of Primitives from Groups			**Prototypical Verbs to capture the Generic Meaning**
<S>	**<CS>**	**<I>**	
assigned-to			<reserves>
owner-of	attempts-to		<orders>
In-control-of	gives-up		<relinquishes>
		manipulate	<manipulates>
able-to		operate	<can operate>

Table 5: Examples of Generic Relationships and their Mapping to Primitives

3.3 Layer 3: Context and Domain-Dependent Real-World Relationships

Layer 3 captures the numerous context and domain-dependent relationships that must be captured over time as the ontology is populated with examples. Since there can be a large number of such verbs, the knowledge base will be built up using a knowledge acquisition component. Building this layer is important because it ensures that the verbs important to different domains are captured appropriately. Consider the use of the verb ëopensí in a database of Plays and Characters versus in a database of Banks and Customers. One may encounter the relationship Character <opens> Door in the first domain, which may map to the interaction primitive <manipulates>. On the other hand, the relationship, Teller <opens> Account may map to the status primitive <is-creator-of> or Customer <opens> Account may map to <is-owner-of>.

In summary, the ontology is comprised of three layers. Layer 1 consists of fundamental primitives and captures basic, real world, relationships that exist between two entities. It corresponds to objectivist semantics. Layer 2 is a generic knowledge base containing semantic information on domain-independent and context-independent real-world relationship. These relationships represent combinations and arrangements of different fundamental primitives identified in layer 1. It corresponds to the mentalistic meaning captured in the verb phrases [Stamper, 1996]. Layer 3 consists of a contextual knowledge base containing domain- and context-dependent relationships. Given the many-to-many mapping between layers 2 and 3 and the richness of database designs, pre-defining even a small percentage of verbs in layer 3 would require a significant effort. Thus, the layer needs to be built up over time. Figure 4 summarizes our ontology.

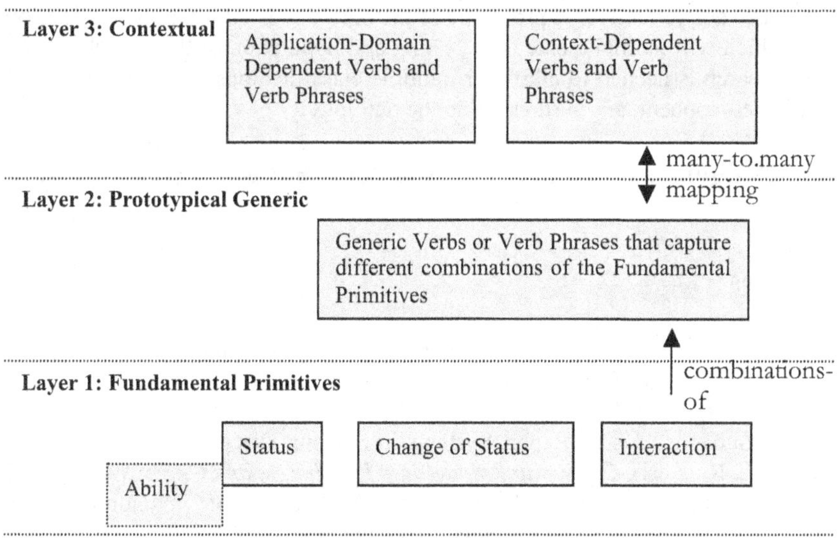

Figure 4: Organization of the Relationship Ontology

4. Knowledge Acquisition Component

To populate layer 3 as well as to ensure that the layered ontology is complete, we classified 99 verb forms found in a collection of generic business processes adapted from the Process Classification Framework produced by the American Productivity & Quality Center [SPEDE,2000].

5. Testing

To test the ontology, an empirical study was carried out. From this the ontology was refined into the form presented above. Relationships for testing the ontology were generated from three sources: 1) textbook cases; 2) class projects; and 3) magazine articles (to test robustness). During the second phrase of testing, seven subjects classified the relationships using a set of dialogs. The ontology created a correct classification (agreement with researchersí classification) 70% of the time or better.

6. Conclusion

A three-layer ontology has been presented that classifies relationship verbs so that automated comparison of database designs can take place. The ontology was developed based upon our understanding of relationship classification problems, natural language, and business ontology development. Testing on the ontology shows it to be reasonably effective. A prototype of the ontology is currently being developed in Java, which will facilitate extensive testing and population of the knowledge base. Further research is needed to allow for multiple classifications, refine the knowledge acquisition component, and further refine the ontology.

Acknowledgement. This research was supported by Georgia State University.

References

1. Barron, T.M., Chiang, R.H.L., and Storey, V.C., ìA Semiotics Framework for Information Systems Classification and Development,î Decision Support Systems, Vol.25, 1999, pp.1-17.
2. Bouzeghoub, M., ìUsing Expert Systems in Schema Design,î in Loucopoulos, P. and Zicari, R. (Eds.), *Conceptual Modelling, Databases, and CASE*, Wiley, 1992.
3. Brachman, R.J., "What IS-A is and isnít : An analysis of Taxonomic Links in Semantic Networks", IEEE *Computer,* October, 1993.
4. Brodie, M., "Association: A Database Abstraction," *Proceedings of the Entity-Relationship Conference*, 1981.
5. Bunge, M., *Treatise on Basic Philosophy: Vol.3: Ontology 1: The Furniture of the World,* D. Reidel publisheing Co., Inc., New York, NY, 1977.

6. Chen, P. , "The Entity-Relationship Approach", In Information Technology in Action: Trends and Perspectives. Englewood Cliffs: Prentice Hall, 1993, pp.13-36.
7. Dahlgren, K., "A Linguistic Ontology, International Journal of Human-Computer Studies, Vol.43, 1995, pp.809-818.
8. Dullea, J. and Song, I.-Y., "A Taxonomy of Recursive Relationships and Their Structural Validity in ER Modeling," in Akoka, J., Bouzeghoub, M., Comyn-Wattiau, I., and Metais, E. (eds.), *Conceptual Modeling – ER'99, 18th International Conference on Conceptual Modeling, Lecture Notes in Computer Science 1728*, Paris, France, 15-18 November 1999, pp.384-389.
9. Elmasri, R. and Navathe, S. B. *Fundamentals of Database Systems*. Menlo Park, C.A. Benjamin Cummings Publishing Co., 1989.
10. Embley, D., D.M. Campbell, Y.S. Jiang, Y.-K. Ng, R.D. Smith, S.W. Liddle, D.W. Quass , ìA Conceptual-Modeling approach to Web Data Extraction, î *Data & Knowledge Engineering*, 1999.
11. Gruber, T.R., ìA Translation Approach to Portable Ontology Specifications,î *Knowledge Acquisition*, Vol. 5, 1993, pp.199-220.
12. Kedad, Z., and Metais, E., ìDealing with Semantic Heterogeneity During Data Integration,î in Akoka, J., Bouzeghoub, M., Comyn-Wattiau, I., and Metais, E. (eds.), *Conceptual Modeling – ER'99, 18th International Conference on Conceptual Modeling, Lecture Notes in Computer Science 1728*, Paris, France, 15-18 November 1999, pp.325-339.
13. Lloyd-Williams, M., ìExploiting Domain Knowledge During the Automated Design of Object-Oriented Databases," *Proceedings of the 16th International Conference on Conceptual Modeling (ER'97)*, Los Angeles, 3-6 November 1997.
14. Morris, C.W., *Signs, Language and Behavior*, Prentice-Hall, New York, 1946.
15. Motschnig-Pitrik, R. and Myloppoulos, J., "Class and Instances," *International Journal of Intelligent and Cooperative Systems*, Vol1, No.1, 1992, pp.61-92.
16. Motschnig-Pitrik, R. and Storey, V.C., ìModelling of Set Membership: the Notion and the Issuesî, *Data and Knowledge Engineering*, Vol.16, August 1995.
17. Motschnig-Pitrik, R., "A Generic Framework for the Modeling of Contexts and its Applications," *Data and Knowledge Engineering*, Vol.32, 2000, pp.145-180.
18. Noy, N.F., and Hafner, C.D., "The State of the Art in Ontology Design: A Survey and Comparative Review,î AI Magazine, Fall 1997, pp.53-74.
19. Smith, B., ìOntology: Philosophical and Computational.î http://wings.buffalo.edu/philosophy/faculty/smith/artices/ontologies.hml, 1999.
20. Smith, J.M., and Smith, C.P. "Database Abstractions: Aggregation and Generalization," ACM Transactions on Database Management Systems, Vol.2, No.2, June 1977, pp.105-133.
21. SPEDE, Cottam, H., Milton, N., and Shadbolt, N., "The Use of Ontologies in a Decision Support System for Business Process Re-engineering," http://www.psychology.nottingham.ac.uk/research/ai/themes/ka/UseofOnto.html Part of the SPEDE project: http://www.psychology.nottingham.ac.uk/research/ai/themes/ka/SPEDE.html.
22. Stamper, R.K., Signs, ìInformation, Norms and Systemsî in B. Holmqvist, P.B. Andersen, H.Klein, R. Rosner (Eds.), *Signs at Work*, De Gruyter, Berlin, 1996, pp.349-397.

23. Storey, V.C., Chiang, R.H.L., Dey, D., Goldstein, R.C., and Sundaresan, S. Database Design with Common Sense Business Reasoning and Learning, *ACM Transactions on Database Systems*, Vol. 22, No.4, 1997.
24. Storey, V.C., and Dey, D., ì A Methodology for Learning Across Application Domains for Database Design Systems,î *IEEE Transactions on Knowledge and Data Engineering*, forthcoming, 2000.
25. Storey, V.C., and Goldstein, R.C. (1993). ìKnowledge-Based Approaches to Database Design,î *Management Information Systems Quarterly*, Vol.17, No.2, March, pp.25-46.
26. Storey, V.C., Dey, D., Ullrich, H., and Sundaresan, S., "An Ontology-Based Expert System for Database Design,î *Data and Knowledge Engineering,* 1998.
27. Storey, V.C., Goldstein, R.C., and Ullrich, H , "NaÔve Semantics to Supported Automated Database Design," *IEEE Transactions on Knowledge and Data Engineering,* forthcoming, 2000.
28. Theodorakis, M., Atalyti, A., Constantopoulos, P., Spyratos, N., "Contextualization as an Abstraction Mechanism for Conceptual Modeling," in Akoka, J., Bouzeghoub, M., Comyn-Wattiau, I., and Metais, E. (eds.), *Conceptual Modeling – ER'99, 18th International Conference on Conceptual Modeling, Lecture Notes in Computer Science 1728*, Paris, France, 15-18 November 1999, pp475-489.
29. UIUC, 2000. http://www.english.uiuc.edu/cws/wworkshop/grammarmenu.htm
30. Wand, Y., and Weber, R., ìAn Ontological Model of an Information System,î *IEEE Transactions on Software Engineering*, Vol. 16, 1990, pp. 1282-1292.

A Very Large Database of Collocations and Semantic Links

Igor Bolshakov and Alexander Gelbukh

Center for Computing Research, National Polytechnic Institute,
Av. Juan Dios B· tiz s/n esq. Mendizabal, col. Zacatenco, 07738, MÈxico DF., Mexico.
{igor,gelbukh}@cic.ipn.mx

Abstract. A computational system manages a very large database of collocations (word combinations) and semantic links. The collocations are related (in the meaning of a dependency grammar) word pairs, joint immediately or through prepositions. Synonyms, antonyms, subclasses, superclasses, etc. represent semantic relations and form a thesaurus. The structure of the system is universal, so that its language-dependent parts are easily adjustable to any specific language (English, Spanish, Russian, etc.). Inference rules for prediction of highly probable new collocations automatically enrich the database at runtime. The inference is assisted by the available thesaurus links. The aim of the system is word processing, foreign language learning, parse filtering, and lexical disambiguation.

Keywords: *dictionary, collocations, thesaurus, syntactic relations, semantic relations, lexical disambiguation.*

Introduction

Word processing and computerized learning of foreign languages include mastering not only the vocabulary of separate words, but also common relations between them. The most important relations are

- dependency links between words, with give word combinations (collocations) occurring in texts with or without interruption (e.g., *fold* → [*in one's*] *arms*, *way* → [*of*] *speaking*, *deep* ← *admiration*, *kiss* → *passionately*, etc.), and
- semantic links of all kinds (*small* ñ *little*, *small* ñ *big*, *apple-tree* ñ *tree*, *house* ñ *room*, *treatment* ñ *doctor*, etc.).

To enable writing a correct text in an unknown language (or sublanguage) with the aid of computer, author needs a linguistic database with registered links of the mentioned types and with the most possible completeness.

In [1, 2], a preliminary description of the *CrossLexica* system was given. It was planned as a very large (unrealizable in the printed form) database reflecting multiplicity of relations between Russian words.

The further research has shown that the basic ideas of *CrossLexica* are equally applicable to other languages, between them English, Spanish or French. The structure of the system contains only few features dependent on the specific language. Properties of morphology, the use of obligatory articles or other determinants of nouns, the

M. Bouzeghoub et al. (Eds.): NLDB 2000, LNCS 1959, pp. 103-114, 2001.

word order, and some other morphosyntactic features can be rather easily adjusted to some universal structure. However, each version of the system is dedicated to a specific language, and another language can be optionally embedded only for queries.

In the past, the valuable printed dictionary of English collocations was created by Benson, Benson, and Ilson [3], while the WordNet project [4] has produced a very large database of only semantic links between English words. The analogous works for Italian [5] and other European languages are also known, whereas in [6] large-scale database of uninterrupted Japanese collocations was reported. However, we are unaware so far of systems covering both semantic and syntactic relations and deriving benefits from this coexistence. It is worth to claim that the combined system is in no way WordNet-like, since its collocation-oriented part can be much more bulky and contain information unprecedented in the modern word processors.

The continuing research has proved a broader applicability of the important property of CrossLexica to use semantic relations already available in its database for predicting collocations that were not yet available in it in the explicit form. Let us call this feature self-enrichment of the database.

Step by step, the set of relations between words, i.e., textual, semantic, and other, has slightly broadened and stabilized in CrossLexica. It became clear how to incorporate to it and to rationally use any complementary language (we have selected English for the Russian version). This dictionary permits to enter the query words in the native userís language and to receive the output data in the language to be referenced.

The opinion has also settled that such systems, in their developed form, permit to create more correct and flexible texts while word processing, to learn foreign languages, to filter results of parsing, to disambiguate lexical homonyms, and to converse the phonetic writing to ideographic one for Japanese [6].

In this paper, the description of the universal structure of the system is given, with broader explanations of its relations, labeling of words and relations, and the inference capability. The fully developed version of the system ñ Russian ñ is described in some detail, as well as some peculiarities of underdeveloped English and Spanish versions. Examples are mainly given in English.

Structure of the System

The structure of the system under investigation is a set of many-to-many relations upon a general lexicon. The types of relations are chosen in such a way that they cover the majority of relations between words and do not depend on the specific language, at least for major European languages.

Textual relations link words of different parts of speech, as it is shown in Fig. 1. Four main parts of speech are considered, i.e., nouns ***N***, verbs ***V***, adjectives ***Adj***, and adverbs ***Adv***, in their syntactic roles. The syntactic role of an adjective or an adverb can be played by a prepositional group as well, e.g., *man* → *(from the South)* or *speak* → (*at random*). Each arrow in Fig. 1 represents an oriented syntactic link corresponding to dependency approach in syntax. It is possible to retrieve such relations from the side of both ruling and dependent word, i.e. moving along the oriented dependency chain or against it.

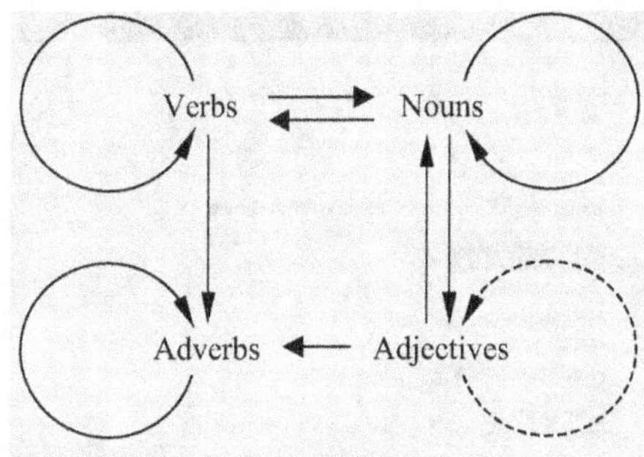

Fig. 1. Various types of syntactic links[1].

A syntactic relation between two words can be realized in a text through a preposition in between, a special grammatical case of noun (e.g., in Slavonic languages), a specific finite form of verb, a word order of linked words, or a combination of any these ways. All these features are reflected in the system entries. Since nouns in different grammatical numbers can correspond to different sets of collocations, the sets are to be included into the system dictionary separately.

All types of commonly used collocations are registered in the system: quite free combinations like *white dress* or *to see a book*, lexically restricted combinations like *strong tea* or *to give attention* (cf. the notion of lexical function in [9]) and idiomatic (phraseologically fixed) combinations like *kick the bucket* or *hot dog*. The criterion of involving of a restricted and praseological combination is the very fact that the combination can be ascribed to one of these classes. The involving of the free combinations is not so evident, and we have taken them rather arbitrary. Nevertheless, as features of Russian version show (see later), the semantics itself essentially restricts the number of possible ìfreeî combinations.

Some idiomatic or commonly used uninterrupted combinations are additionally included to the lexicon as its direct entries. As to 3-ary collocations, the system is not destined to contain them, but a very simple mean, namely dots, is used to represent 2-ary collocation with obligatory third participant or fourth participant.

Semantic relations link words of different parts of speech in any-to-any manner. Usually they form a full graph, cf. Fig. 1. We proceed from the idea that many separate meaning can be expressed in any language by words or word combinations of four main parts of speech. For verbs this is rather evident (see later an example). For living creatures, things, and artifacts this is dubious (what id the verb equivalent in meaning to *fly* or *stone*?). For such terms, the verb group in the set of four POS groups is empty.

User Interface

The easiest way to describe an interactive system is to characterize its userís interface. For English version, it is shown in Fig. 3, with necessary explanations given later.

In standard mode, the screen of the system seems like a page of a book, in which the formatted results of retrieval operations are output. The operations are prompted by the query consisting of a separate keyword of a short uninterrupted collocation and

[1] A syntactic link between two adjectives is possible in some languages with the governor of a special class, for example, Russian *samyj vazhnyj* ëmost importantí.

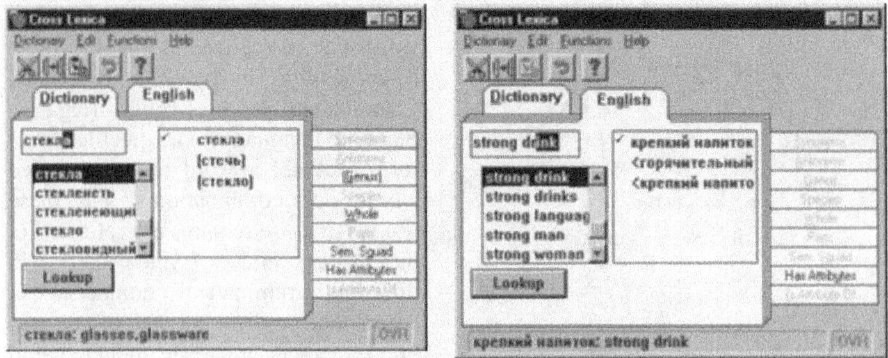

Fig. 2. Two dictionaries of the Russian version.

are performed within the system database. (The keyword is shown in the small window at left higher corner.)

There are two bookmarks with inscriptions at the upper edge and not less that 14 additional labeled bookmarks at the right edge.

The first upper-side bookmark, *Dictionary*, permits a user to enter queries, directly extracting them from the system dictionary. This is dictionary of the basic language of the version, i.e., of the language to get references about or to learn. The entries of the dictionary are presented in alphabetic order in the left sub-window with a slider. To select necessary dictionary item, it is necessary to enter its initial disambiguated part.

In the parallel sub-window at the right side, all possible normalized forms of the string already entered are given. For example, if English wordform *were* is entered, the standard form *be* is given there. In some cases, the results of normalization can be multiple. For example, for the English form *lacking* the normalized forms are *lack* ***V*** and *lacking* ***Adj***, labeled with part-of-speech tags.

The second upper-side bookmark permits a user to select the query in the complementary (usually native language of the user), e.g. in English, within the Russian version of the system. The system does not contain data about the second language, it only permits to introduce queries.

The window of the supplementary language presents a lexicographically ordered list of words of this language. In contrast to the basic language dictionary, the forms can be not normalized and the amount of short collocations in it is much higher, since all these entries are translations from the basic language.

One important function of the system is to assist in the translation of each word of the basic language. It translates them separately, without translating the whole collocation. However, in the opposite direction, i.e., from supplementary language to the basic one, through a special filtering, the system automatically forms correct translation of a whole collocation even in cases, when word-by-word translation might give wrong result. For example, the translation of the English combination *strong tea* to Russian also gives the idiomatic combination *krepkiy chay*, though *krepkiy* has numerous autonomous translations: *firm, robust, strong*, etc.

Main Types of Relations

The numerous bookmarks at the right side of the ìbook pageî correspond to the referential functions of the system. These functions are divided to three groups corresponding to various relations between words, i.e., semantic, syntactic, and the rest.

We describe these functions through English examples.

Semantic Relations

Synonyms gives synonymy group for the query keyword. The group is headed with its dominant, with the most generalized and neutral meaning. Note that only synonyms are used now in the commercial word processors.

Antonyms gives the list of antonyms of the keyword, like *small* for *big* and vice versa.

Genus is the generic notion (superclass) for the keyword. For example, all the words *radio, newspapers,* and *television* have the common superclass *mass media.*

Species are specific concepts (subclasses) for the keyword. This relation is inverse to ***Genus***.

Whole represents a holistic notion with respect to the keyword. For example, all the words *clutch, brakes,* and *motor* give *car* as a possible value of the whole. Of course, each of these words can have different other value(s) of the holistic concept and all the concepts contained in the database are output as a list.

Parts represent parts with respect to the keyword, so that this reflects the relation inverse to ***Whole***.

Sem. Squad represents semantic derivatives of the keyword. For example, each word of the structure

N	*possession*	***Adj***	*possessive*
	property		*possessing*
	possessor		*possessed*
V	*possess*	***Adv***	*in possession*
	be possessed		
	appropriate		

while forming a query, gives the other words of the same structure as its semantic derivatives. All these words correspond to the same meaning, but express it by various parts of speech and from various viewpoints (can play different semantic roles).

Syntactic Relations

Has Attributes represents a list of collocations, in which the keyword, being a noun, an adjective or a verb, is attributed with some other word: an adjective or an adverb.

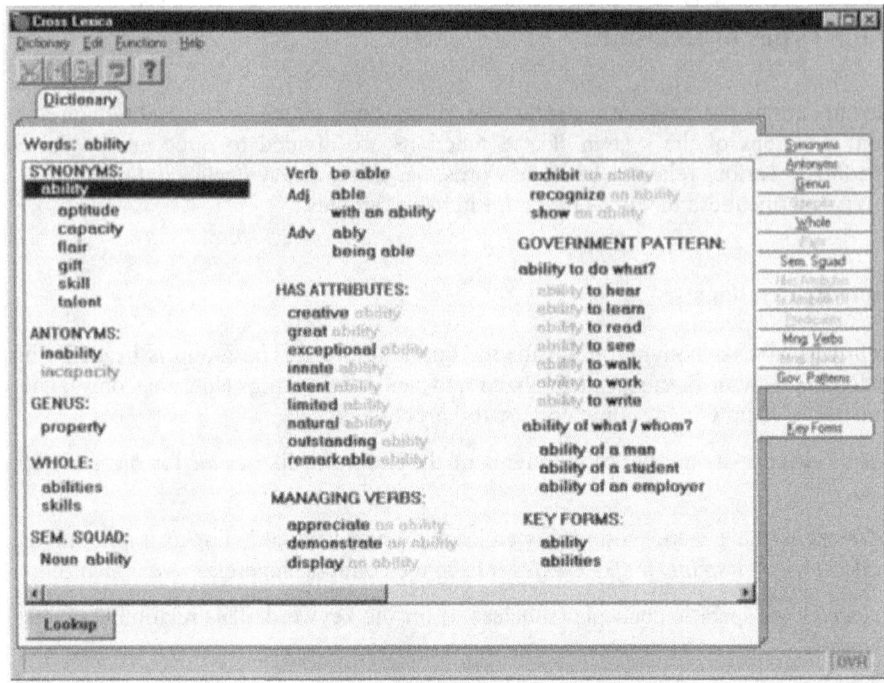

Fig. 3. English version.

For example, the noun *act* can be attributed with *barbaric, courageous, criminal*; the noun *period,* with *incubation, prehistoric, transitional,* etc.

Is Attribute Of is reverse to the previous relation and represents a list of collocations, in which keyword, being adjective or adverb, attributes the other word of any part of speech. For example, the adjective *national* can be an attribute for the nouns *autonomy, economy, institute, currency*; the adjective *economic,* for the nouns *activities, aid, zone*, etc.

In Romance and Slavonic languages, an adjective usually agrees its morphologic form with its ruling noun, e.g., in Spanish, *trabaj**os** científic**os***. In all necessary cases, the agreement is made by the system automatically.

Predicates represents a list of collocations, in which the queried noun is the grammatical subject and various verbs are common predicates for it. For example, the noun *heart* commonly uses predicates *sinks, aches, bleeds*; the noun *money* uses *burns, is close, is flush*, etc.

Mng. Verbs represents the list of collocations, in which the queried noun is a complement and a common verb is its governor. For example, the noun *head* can have governing verbs *bare, beat (into), bend, shake*; the noun *enemy* can have *arrange (with), attack, chase*, etc.

Mng. Nouns represent the list of collocations, in which the queried noun is ruled by various other nouns. For example, the noun *clock* can be ruled by *hand (of), regulation (of)*, etc.

Mng. Adjectives represent the list of collocations, in which substantial keyword is ruled by different adjectives. For example, the noun *rage* can be ruled by *mad (with)*.

Gov. Patterns represent schemes, according which the keyword (usually verb or noun) rules other words, usually nouns, and give also the lists of specific collocations for each subpattern. In the case of verbs, these are just their subcategorization frames, but with unfixed word order in the pair. For example, the verb *have* has the pattern *what / whom?* with examples of dependents *capacity, money, family;* the pattern *in what?* with examples *hand, reach*; and pattern *between what / whom?* with examples *friends, eyes*. Conceptually, this function is inverse to **Mng. Nouns**, **Mng. Verbs** and ***Predicates*** relations. The system forms the patterns automatically, through the inversion of functions mentioned above.

Coordinated Pairs represent a word complementary to the keyword, if the both constitute a stable coordinated pair: *back and forth, black and white, body and soul, good and evil, now and then,* etc.

Relacions of Other Types

Paronyms represent the list of words of the same part of speech and the same root, but with potentially quite different meaning and collocations. For example, *sensation* is a representative of the paronymous group: *sensationalism, sense, sensitivity, sensibility, sensuality, sentiment.*

Key Forms represent the list of all morphologic forms (morphologic paradigm) possible for this keyword. Irregular English verbs have here all their forms explicitly. In Slavonic languages like Russian, the paradigms of nouns and adjectives are rather numerous, not speaking about verbs.

Homonyms

Each homonymous word in the database forms a separate entry of a system dictionary. Each entry is supplied with numeric label and a short explanation of meaning. User can choose the necessary entry or observe them in parallel. It is important, that each homonym have its specific syntactic and semantic links.

Usage Marks

The simple set of usage marks selected for the items of the database seems sufficient for a common user. In contrast to many other dictionaries, it contains only two ì coordinatesî :

- ***Idiomacity*** reflects metaphoric (figurative) use of words and collocations. For an idiomatic collocation, the meaning is not simply a combination of the meanings of its components. Three different grades are considered: (1) literal use (no label);

(2) idiomatic and non-idiomatic interpretations are possible (*kick the bucket*), and (3) only idiomatic interpretation possible (*hot dog*).

- ***Scope of usage*** has five grades: (1) neutral: no label and no limitations on the use; (2) special, bookish or obsolete: use in writing is recommended when meaning is well known to the user; (3) colloquial: use in writing is not recommended; (4) vulgar: both writing and oral use is prohibitive; and (5) incorrect (contradicts to the language norm).

As a rule, the labels of the scope given at a word are transferred to all its collocations.

Inference Ability

The unique property of the system is the online inference ability to enrich its base of collocations. The idea is that if the system has no information on some type of relations (e.g., on attributes) of a word, but does have it for another word somehow similar to the former, the available information is transferred to the unspecified or underspecified word. The types of the word similarity are as follows.

Genus. Suppose the complete combinatorial description of the notion *refreshing drink*. For example, verbs are known that combine with it: *to bottle, to have, to pour*, etc. In contrast, the same information on *Coca-Cola* is not given in the system database, except that this notion is a subclass of *refreshing drink*. In this case, the system transfers the information connected with the superclass to any its subclass that does not have its own information of the same type. Thus, it is determined that the indicated verbs are also applicable to *Coca Cola*, see Fig. 4.

Synonym. Suppose that he noun *coating* has no collocations in the database, but it belongs to the synonymy group with *layer* as the group dominant. If *layer* is completely characterized in the database, the system transfers the information connected with it to all group members lacking the complete description. Thus, a user can recognize that there exist collocations of the type *cover with a coating*.

Supplementary number of noun. If a noun is given in the system dictionary in both singular and plural forms, but only one of these forms is completely characterized in the system, then the collocations of one number are transferred to the supplementary one.

These types of self-enrichment are applied to all syntactic relations except ***Gov. Patterns***, since this transfer reflects semantic properties not always not always corresponding to syntactic ones.

Enrichment of antonyms. Besides of antonyms recorded in common dictionaries, synonyms of these antonyms and antonyms of the synonymous dominant of the word are output as quasi-antonyms. This is the only semantic relation, which is subject to the enrichment.

Precautions in Inferences

In each case, the inherited information is visually indicated on the screen as not guaranteed. Indeed, some inferences are nevertheless wrong. For example, *berries* as superclass can have nearly any color, smell and taste, but its subclass *blueberries* are scarcely *yellow*. Hence, our inference rules have to avoid at least the most frequent errors.

Classifying adjectives. The adjectival attributes sometimes imply incorrect combinations while inferring like **European Argentina* (through the inference chain *Argentina* ⇒ *country* & *European country*). To avoid them, the system does not use the adjectives called classifying for the enrichment. They reflect properties that convert a specific notion to its subclasses, e.g., *country* ⇒ *European / American / African country*. In contradistinction to them, non-classifying adjectives like *agrarian, beautiful, great, industrial, small* do not translate the superclass *country* to any subclass, so that collocation *beautiful Argentina* is considered valid by the system while the enrichment.

Idiomatic and scope labeled collocations are not transferred to any subclasses either. It is obvious that the collocation *hot poodle* based on the chain (*poodle* ⇐ *dog*) & (*hot* ← *dog*) is wrong.

With all these precautions, the hundred-per-cent correctness of the inferences is impossible, without further semantic research.

Parse Filtering and Lexical Disambiguation

The system in its standard form has a userís interface and interacts with a user in word processing or foreign language learning. However, the database with such contents can be directly used for advanced parsing and lexical disambiguation.

If a collocation is directly occurs in a sentence, it proves the part of dependency tree, in which its components plays the same syntactic roles. The collocation database functions like a filter of possible parse trees. It can be realized through augmented weighting of optional trees with subtrees already found in the database. This idea is the directly connected with that of [7].

Different homonyms usually have their own collocations (more rarely, they overlap). For example, $bank_1$ (financial) has attributes *commercial, credit, reserve, saving*, etc., while $bank_2$ (at shore) has attributes *rugged, sloping, steep,* etc. Thus, if the word *bank* is attributed, it can be disambiguated with high probability on the stage of parsing.

Three Versions of the System

Russian. The Russian version of the system is near to its completion, though there are no reasonable limits for the database and lexicon size. Now it has the lexicon (including common uninterrupted collocations and prepositional phrases) of ca. 110,000 entries.

The statistics of unilateral semantic links in this version is as follows:

Semantic derivatives	804,400
Synonyms	193,900
Part/whole	17,300
Paronyms	13,500
Antonyms	10,000
Subclass/superclass	8,500
Total	**1,047,600**

Note, that for semantic derivatives, synonyms, and paronyms, the numbers of unilateral links were counted as $\Sigma_i\ n_i\ (n_i$ ñ $1)$, where n_i is number of members in *i*th group. That is why the links connecting semantic derivatives and synonyms are much more numerous than the derivatives and synonyms themselves.

For syntactic unilateral links, the statistics is:

Verbs ñ their noun complements	342,400
Verbs ñ their subjects	182,800
Nouns ñ short-form adjectives	52,600
Attributive collocations	595,000
Nouns ñ their noun complements	216,600
Verbs ñ their infinitive complements	21,400
Nouns ñ their infinitive complements	10,800
Copulative collocations	12,400
Coordinated pairs	3,600
Total	**1437,600**

Summarizing all relations gives ca. 2.5 million explicitly recorded links. Foe evaluation of the text coverage, 12 text fragments of ca. 1 KB length were taken from various sources (books on computer science, computational linguistics, and radars; abstract journals on technologies; newspaper articles on politics, economics, popular science, belles-lettres, and sport; advertising leaflets). The count of covered collocations was performed by hand, with permanent access to the database. The results varied from 43% (abstracts) to 65% (ads). The inference capability gives not more than 5% rise in coverage so far, since the names of underspecified subclasses turned to be rather rare in texts, and the thesauric part of the system is not yet brought to perfection.

Some statistics on the fertility of different words in respect of collocations is pertinent. If to divide the number of the collocations ìverbs ñ their noun complementsî to the number of the involved nouns, the mean value is 15.7, whereas the division to the number of the involved verbs gives 17.9. If to divide the number of the collocations ìnouns ñ their noun complementsî to the number of the dependent nouns, the mean value is 13.6, whereas the division to the number of the ruling nouns gives 12.8. The mean number of attributes is 15.5.

This series of fertility indicators can be broadened, all of them being in a rather narrow interval 11 to 18. This proves that even the inclusion into the database of collocations considered linguistically quite free gives on average only ca. 20 different

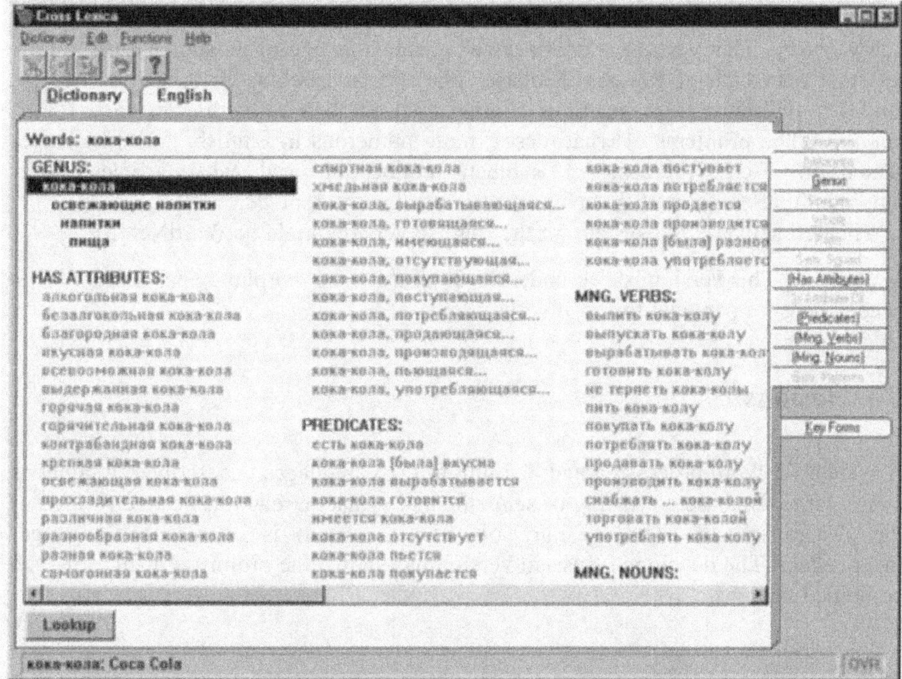

Fig. 4. An example of enrichment: the key *Coca Cola* (Russian version).

words syntactically connected with each given word, in each category of collocations (both dependent and ruling syntactic positions are considered). The evident reason of this constraint is semantics of words, so that the total variety of collocations in each specific case does not exceed the some limits.

The source database of any language has the shape of formatted text files. Besides labels of lexical homonymity, idiomacity, and scope, the Russian version contains numerical labels at homonymous prepositions (they imply different grammatical cases of dependent nouns) and sparse accentuation information. The Russian source files with collocations ìverbs ñ their noun complementsî and ìnouns ñ their noun complementsî contain also dots replacing obligatory complements, which are not participants of the given relation. The dots are not used in the automatic formation of government patterns, since every complement in Russian is expressed through its own combination of a preposition and the corresponding grammatical case.

The methods of automatic acquisition of collocations are well known in the literature on computing linguistics [7, 8]. We used them in a rather limited and ìrussifiedî manner. E.g., one acquisition program searched for only attributes of each textual noun positioned about it as (-3, +1) and agreed with it in number, gender, and case. The major part of the database was gathered manually, by scanning a great variety of texts: newspapers, magazines, books, manuals, leaflets, ads, etc.

At the stage of automatic compiling of the runtime database, morphological lemmatizer reduces indirect cases of nouns and finite verb forms to their dictionary norm. A similar lemmatizer normalizes forms in the query.

English. An example of how English version functions is given in Fig. 3, for the query *ability*. This version is under development, the size of its source base is now less that one tenth of Russian database. The special labeling of its source files includes: a delimiter of prepositions coming after English verbs, like in *put on* | (*a*) *bandage*. The problems of what tenses, more numerous in English, are to be represented in each ìpredicate ñ subjectî collocation and what articles (definite/indefinite/zero) are to given at each noun are not yet solved.

The best semantic subsystem for the English version might be WordNet [5].

Spanish. This version is also under development. The morphological lemmatizer is needed here for personal forms of verbs.

Conclusions

A system for word processing and learning foreign languages is described. It contains a very large database consisting of semantic and syntactic relations between words of the system lexicon. The structure of such a system is in essence language-independent. The developed Russian version has shown the promising nature of such combined systems.

References

1. Bolshakov, I. A. Multifunctional thesaurus for computerized preparation of Russian texts. *Automatic Documentation and Mathematical Linguistics*. Allerton Press Inc. Vol. 28, No. 1, 1994, p. 13-28.
2. Bolshakov, I. A. Multifunction thesaurus for Russian word processing. *Proceedings of 4th Conference on Applied Natural language Processing,* Stuttgart, 13-15 October, 1994, p. 200-202.
3. Benson, M., et al. The BBI Combinatory Dictionary of English. John Benjamin Publ., Amsterdam, Philadelphia, 1989.
4. Fellbaum, Ch. (ed.) WordNet as Electronic Lexical Database. MIT Press, 1998.
5. Calzolari, N., R. Bindi. Acquisition of Lexical Information from a Large Textual Italian Corpus. *Proc. of COLING-90,* Helsinki, 1990.
6. Yasuo Koyama, et al. Large Scale Collocation Data and Their Application to Japanese Word Processor Technology. Proc. Intern. Conf. COLING-ACLí98, v. I, p. 694-698.
7. Satoshi Sekine., et al. Automatic Learning for Semantic Collocation. *Proc. 3rd Conf. ANLP*, Trento, Italy, 1992, p. 104-110.
8. Smadja, F. Retreiving Collocations from text: Xtract. Computational Linguistics. Vol. 19, No. 1, p. 143-177.
9. Leo Wanner (ed.) Lexical Functions in Lexicography and Natural Language Processing. Studies in Language Companion Series ser.31. John Benjamin Publ., Amsterdam, Philadelphia 1996.

Using Terminology Extraction to Improve Traceability from Formal Models to Textual Requirements

Farid Cerbah[1] and Jérôme Euzenat[2]

[1] Dassault Aviation - DPR/DESA - 78, quai Marcel Dassault
92552 cedex 300 Saint-Cloud - France
farid.cerbah@dassault-aviation.fr
[2] Inria Rhône-Alpes - 655, avenue de l'Europe
38330 Monbonnot St Martin - France
Jerome.Euzenat@inrialpes.fr – http://www.inrialpes.fr/exmo/

Abstract. This article deals with traceability in sotfware engineering. More precisely, we concentrate on the role of terminological knowledge in the mapping between (informal) textual requirements and (formal) object models. We show that terminological knowledge facilitates the production of traceability links, provided that language processing technologies allow to elaborate semi-automatically the required terminological resources. The presented system is one step towards incremental formalization from textual knowledge.

1 Introduction

Modern information systems tend to integrate textual knowledge and formal knowledge in common repositories. The informal is richer and familiar to any user while the formal is more precise and necessary to the computer. It is recognized that linking formal knowledge to informal knowledge has several benefits including, (1) establishing the context for formalized knowledge and documenting it, and (2) providing a natural way to browse through formalized knowledge. Two significant examples can be pointed out:

- **Product Data Management.** Design and production data are formalized in product trees. This formalization improves data consistency and evolutivity. The components of the product tree are related to documents, such as maintenance manuals or manufacturing notices. Connecting formal models to informal sources guarantees a better synchronization between technical data and documents.
- **Software Engineering.** Formal models, and more particularly object oriented models are widely used in software development. In this context, textual knowledge represents specification and design documents. These informal sources are used as a basis for building formal models.

M. Bouzeghoub et al. (Eds.): NLDB 2000, LNCS 1959, pp. 115–126, 2001.

Several works focused on the advantages of using a corpus-based terminology for supporting formal knowledge acquisition [4], [1], [2]. These contributions emphasize the central role of terminological resources in the mapping between informal text sources and formal knowledge bases. In the same spirit, the present work uses terminology software support for generation and management of traceability links between initial software requirements and formal object representations resulting from the modeling processes. We describe a fully implemented system that provides high-level hypertext generation, browsing and model generation facilities. From a more technical viewpoint, we introduce an original XML based model for integrating software components.
The rest of the paper is organized as follows. Section 2 introduces the main concepts of our approach and the basic tasks that should be performed by a user support tool which takes advantage of terminological knowledge for improving traceability. Section 3 gives a detailed and illustrated description of the implemented system. Finally, section 4 briefly compares our contribution to related works and the conclusion provides some directions for further research.

2 Principles

2.1 Traceability in Software Engineering

In a software development process, design and implementation decisions should be "traceable", in the sense that it should be possible to find out the requirements impacted, directly or indirectly, by the decisions. This mapping is useful in many respects:

- It helps to ensure exhaustiveness: By following traceability links, the user or a program can easily identify the requirements which are not satisfied by the software.
- It facilitates the propagation of changes: At any time in the development process, traceability information allows to find out the elements impacted by changes (upstream and downstream). For instance, the user can evaluate the incidence on the software design and implementation of a late change in the initial customer requirements.
- When traceability is established with hyperlinks, the browsing capabilities provided by design support tools are increased.

In an object-oriented framework, many traceability links aim at relating textual fragments of the documents in natural language and model fragments. Putting on these links manually is a tedious and time consuming task and current tools for requirement analysis provide no significant help for doing that job.

2.2 The Role of Terminological Resources

In many information systems where both textual knowledge and formal knowledge are involved to describe related concepts, terminology can play an intermediate role. As mentioned earlier, previous works in the fields of knowledge

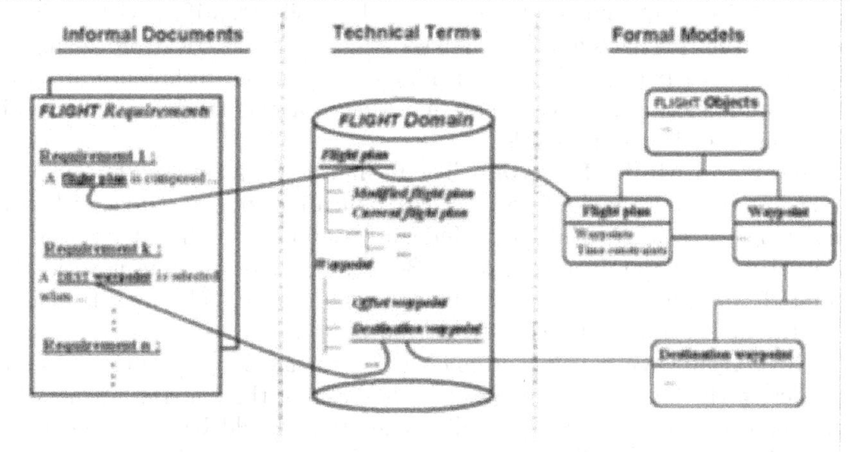

Fig. 1. Using terminological items to link textual requirements and object models

acquisition and natural language processing have shown that terminological resources extracted from corpora can help the incremental formalization processes from texts to formal models.
There exist other demonstrative examples in related domains, such as product data management and software engineering.
For example, in the DOCSTEP project [8], which deals with product data management, terminological resources are used to connect multilingual technical documentation and items of product trees. Hyperlinks are established between term occurrences in documents and corresponding objects in product trees.
In software engineering, the role of terminological knowledge in the modeling process has often been pointed out [15, 10, 3]. One of the first step in the modeling process consists of a systematic identification of the technical terms (simple and compound nouns) in the documents, namely the terminology used to describe the problem. Some of these technical terms represent concepts which will be subsequently introduced in the formal models. These terms can be seen as an intermediary level between the textual requirements and the formal models. (see figure 1).

2.3 Functional View of a System That Exploits Terminology

A system that takes advantage of terminological resources may involve techniques pertaining to several technological areas, and particularly natural language processing, information retrieval and knowledge management:

Terminology Extraction. In technical domains, many precise and highly relevant concepts are linguistically represented by compound nouns. The multiword nature of the technical terms facilitates their automatic identification in texts. Relevant multi-word terms can be easily identified with high accuracy using partial syntactic analysis [4], [11] or statistical processing [6] (or even both paradigms [7]). Terminology extraction techniques are used to automatically build term hierarchies that will play the intermediate role between documents and models.

Document and Model Indexing. The technical terms are used for indexing text fragments in the documents. Fine grained indexing, i.e paragraph level indexing, is required while most indexing systems used in information retrieval work at the document level. Besides, most descriptors used in this kind of indexing are multi-word phrases. The terms are also used for indexing the model fragments (classes, attributes ...).

Hyperlink Generation. The terminology driven indexing of both texts and models with the same terminology is the basis of the hyperlink generation mechanisms. Futhermore, hyperlink generation should be controlled interactively, in the sense that the user should be able to exclude automatically generated links or add links that have not been proposed by the system.

Model Generation. It is quite common that the concept hierarchies mirror the term hierarchies found in the documents. This property can be used to generate model skeletons which will be completed manually.

These features are implemented in the system presented in the next section.

3 A User Support Tool for Improving Traceability

The implemented system consists of two components, XTerm and Troeps. XTerm deals with the document management and linguistic processing functions, more particularly terminological extraction and document indexing. Troeps deals with model management and model indexing. The model generation function is spread over both components.

3.1 XTerm

XTerm [5] is a natural language processing tool that provides two services to end users:

- Terminology acquisition from documents. It analyzes a French or English technical documentation in order to build a hierarchy of potential technical terms. The user can explore and filter the extracted data via a graphical interface.
- Terminology-centred hypertext navigation. XTerm can be seen as a hypertext browser. The extracted terms are systematically linked to their textual contexts in the documents. The user can easily access the textual fragments containing term occurrences.

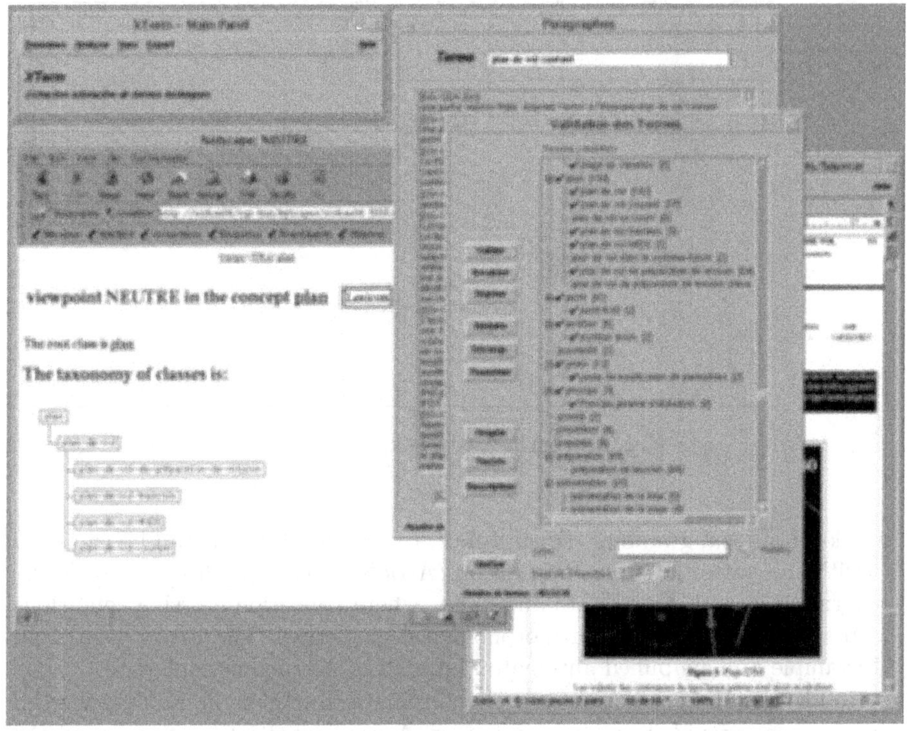

Fig. 2. The integrated system based on XTerm and Troeps.

XTerm is made of four components:

Document Manager. This component provides textual data to the linguistic components. It scans all document building blocks (paragraphs, titles, figures, notes) in order to extract the text fragments. The extracted units are then prepared for linguistic processing.
Additionally, the document manager provides the mechanisms for indexing and hyperlink generation from technical terms to document fragments. Hyperlink generation is a selective process: To avoid overgeneration, the initial set of links systematically established by the system can be reduced by the user.

Part of Speech Tagger. The word sequences provided by the document manager are processed by a tagger based on the Multex morphological parser [14]. POS tagging starts with a morphological analysis step which assigns to each word its possible morphological realizations. Then, contextual desambiguation rules are applied to choose a unique realization for each word. At the end of this process, each word is unambigeously tagged.

Term Extractor. As mentioned in section 2.3, the morpho-syntactical structure of technical terms follows quite regular formation rules which represent

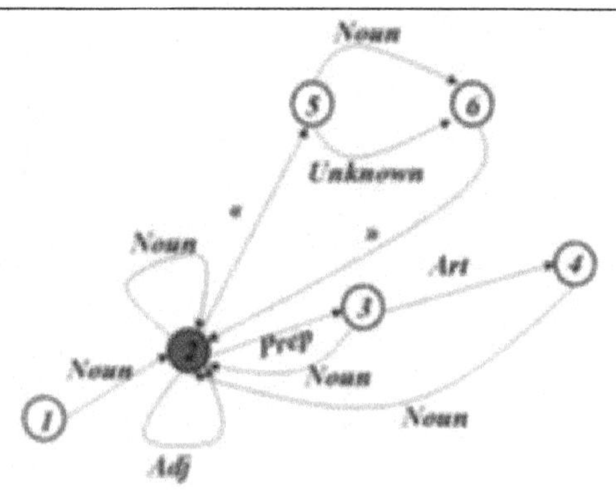

Fig. 3. a term extraction automaton

a kind of local grammar. For instance, many French terms can be captured with the pattern "*Noun Preposition (Article) Noun*". Such patterns can be formalized with finite state automata, where transition crossing conditions are expressed in terms of morphological properties. The figure 3 gives an example of a simplified automaton (state 2 is the unique final state).
To identify the potential terms, the automata is applied on the tagged word sequences provided by the POS tagger. A new potential term is recognized each time a final state is reached. During this step, the extracted terms are organized hierarchically. For example, the term "*flight plan*" ("*plan de vol*" in figure 2) will have the term "*plan*" as parent and "*modified flight plan*" as a child in the hierarchy.
Actually, term extraction with automata is just the first filtering step of the overall process. The candidate set obtained after this step is still too large. Additional filtering mechanisms are involved to reduce that set. In particular, grouping rules are used to identify term variants. For instance, in French technical texts, prepositions and articles are often omitted for the sake of concision (the term "*page des buts*" can occur in the elided form: "*page buts*)"[1]. Term variants are systematically conflated into a single node in the term hierarchy.

Management/Browsing Component. This component ensures the basic term management functionalities (editing, search, validation). XTerm is highly interactive. Many browsing facilities are provided to facilitate the manipulation of large data sets (extracted terms + text fragments). XTerm can be used as an access tool to documentation repositories.

[1] Whose English literal translations are respectively: "*page of the waypoints*" and "*page waypoints*". A plausible equivalent term in English could be "*Waypoint page*".

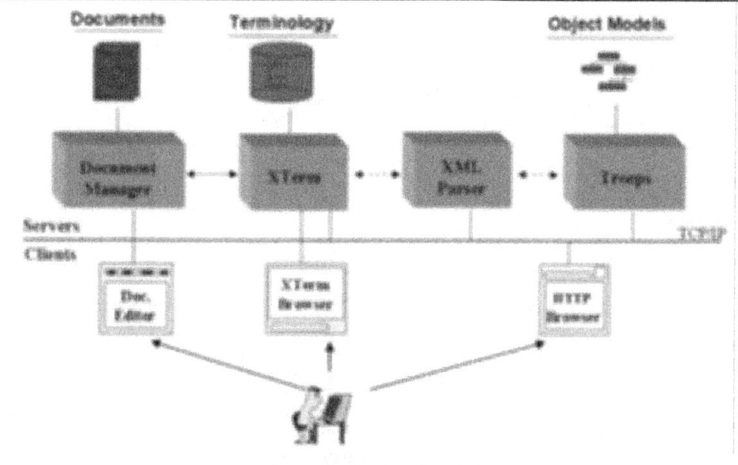

Fig. 4. System architecture

3.2 Troeps

Troeps [12, 16] is an object-based knowledge representation system, i.e. a knowledge representation system inspired from both frame-based languages and object-oriented programming languages. It is used here for expressing the models.

An object is a set of field-value pairs associated to an identifier. The value of a field can be known or unknown, it can be an object or a value from a primitive type (e.g. character string, integer, duration) or a set or list of such. The objects are partitioned into disjoint concepts (an object is an instance of one and only one concept) which determines the key and structure of its instances. For example, the "*plan*" concept identifies a plan by its number which is an integer. The fields of a particular "*plan*" are its time constraints which must be a duration and its waypoints which must contain a set of instances of the "*waypoint*" concept.

Objects can be seen under several viewpoints, each corresponding to a different taxonomy. An object can be attached to a different class in each viewpoint. For instance, a particular plan is classified as a "*flight plan*" under the nature viewpoint and as a "*logistic plan*" under the functional viewpoint. This is unlike other object systems, which usually allow only one class hierarchy.

Troeps knowledge bases can be used as HTTP servers whose skeleton is the structure of formal knowledge (mainly in the object-based formalism) and whose flesh consists of pieces of texts, images, sounds and videos tied to the objects. Turning a knowledge base into a HTTP server is easily achieved by connecting it to a port and transforming each object reference into an URL and each object into a HTML page. If HTML pages already document the knowledge base, they remain linked to or integrated into the pages corresponding to the objects. The Troeps user (through an Application Programming Interface) can explicitly manipulate each of the Troeps entities. The entities can also be displayed on a HTTP client through

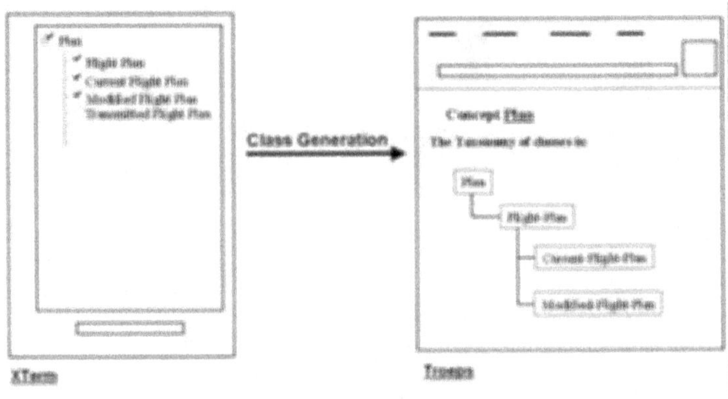

Fig. 5. Class generation

their own HTML page. The Troeps program generates all the pages on request (i.e. when a URL comes through HTTP). The pages make numerous references to each others. They also display various documentation (among which other HTML pages and lexicon) and give access to Troeps features. From a Troeps knowledge server it is possible to build complex queries grounded on formal knowledge such as filtering or classification queries. The answer will be given through a semantically sound method instead of using a simple full-text search. Moreover, it is possible to edit the knowledge base. The system presented here takes advantage of this last feature.

3.3 Communication between the Components

The communication between the linguistic processing environment and the model manager is bidirectional: Upon user request, XTerm can call Troeps to generate class hierarchies from term hierarchies. Conversely, Troeps can call XTerm to provide the textual fragments related to a concept (via a technical term).
For example, figure 5 illustrates the class generation process from a hierarchy of terms carefully validated by the user (a hierarchy rooted in the term "*Plan*"). The class hierarchy constructed by Troeps mirrors the hierarchy of the validated terms (under the root "*Plan*").
At the end of the generation process, the created classes are still linked to their corresponding terms, which means that the terminology-centred navigation capabilities offered by XTerm are directly available from the Troeps interface. As illustrated by figure 6, the Troeps user has access to the multi-document view of the paragraphs which concern the "*Flight-Plan*" concepts[2]. From this view, the user can consult the source documents if required.

[2] More precisely, this view displays the paragraphs where the term "*flight plan*" and its variants occur.

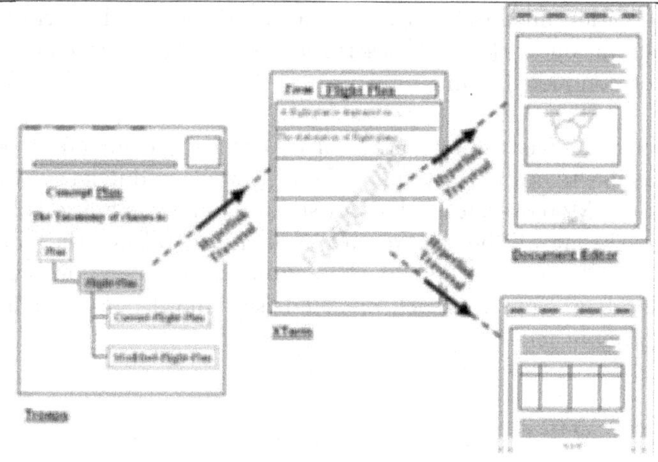

Fig. 6. Traceability through hypertext links.

Data exchanges between XTerm and Troeps are based on the XML language (see figure 4). Troeps offers an XML interface which allows to describe a whole knowledge base or to take punctual actions on an existing knowledge base. This last feature is used in the interface where XTerm sends to Troeps short XML statements corresponding to the action performed by the user. These actions correspond to the creation of a new class or a subclass of an existing class and the annotation of a newly created class with textual elements such as the outlined definition of the term naming the class. For example, to generate classes from the term hierarchy rooted at the term "*plan*", XTerm sends to Troeps an XML stream containing a sequence of class creation and annotation statements. XML representation of object models . We give below an extract of this sequence, corresponding to the creation of classes "*Flight-Plan*" and "*Current-Flight-Plan*":

```
<trp:ADD>
    <trp:CLASS>
       <trp:CLASSDSC name="Flight-Plan">
            <trp:CLASSREF name="Plan"/>
        </trp:CLASSDSC>
    </trp:CLASS>
</trp:ADD>

<trp:ADD>
    <trp:CLASS>
        <trp:CLASSDSC name="Current-Flight-Plan">
            <trp:CLASSREF name="Flight-Plan"/>
        </trp:CLASSDSC>
    </trp:CLASS>
</trp:ADD>

<trp:ANNOTATE label="comment">
    <trp:CLASSREF name="Flight-Plan"/>
    <trp:CONTENT>
             A flight plan is a sequence of waypoints ...
    </trp:CONTENT>
</trp:ANNOTATE>
```

The term definition filled out in the XTerm description of the term is added as a textual annotation in the class description. After these automated steps, the classes can be completed manually.

This XML interface has the advantage of covering the complete Troeps model (thus it is possible to destroy or rename classes as well as adding new attributes to existing classes). Moreover, it is relatively standard in the definition of formalized knowledge so that it will be easy to have XTerm generating other formats (e.g. XMI [13] or Ontolingua) which share the notion of classes and objects.
More details about this approach of XML-based knowledge modeling and exchange are given in [9].

4 Related Work

Terminology acquisition is one of the most robust language processing technology [4, 11, 7] and previous works have demonstrated that term extraction tools can help to link informal and formal knowledge. The theoretical apparatus depicted in [4], [1] and [2] provides useful guidelines for integrating terminology extraction tools in knowledge management systems. However, the models and implemented systems suffer from a poor support for traceability, restricted to the use of hyperlinks from concepts and terms to simple text files. On this aspect, our proposal is richer. The system handles real documents, in their original format, and offers various navigation and search services for manipulating "knowledge structures" (i.e., documents, text fragments, terms, concepts ...). Moreover, the management services allow users to build their own hypertext network.
With regard to model generation, our system and Terminae [2] provide complementary services. Terminae resort to the terminologist to provide a very precise description of the terms from which a precise formal representation, in description logic, can be generated. In our approach, the system does not require users to provide additional descriptions before performing model generation from term hierarchies. Model generation strictly and thoroughly concentrates on hierarchical structures that can be detected at the linguistic level using term extraction techniques. For example, the hierarchical relation between the terms "*Flight Plan*" and "*Modified Flight Plan*" is identified by XTerm because of the explicit relations that hold between the linguistic structures of the two terms. Hence, such term hierarchies can be exploited for class generation. However, XTerm would be unable to identify the hierarchical relation that hold between the terms "*vehicle*" and "*car*" (which is the kind of relations that Terminae would try to identify in the formal descriptions). As a consequence, the formal description provided by our system is mainly a hierarchy of concepts while that of Terminae is more structural and the subsumption relations is computed by the description logic system.
In the field of software engineering, object-oriented methods concentrate on the definition of formal or semi-formal formalisms, with little consideration for the informal-to-formal processes [15, 10, 3]. However, to identify the relevant re-

quirements and model fragments, designers should perform a deep analysis of the textual specifications. The recommendations discussed in section 2.2 on the use of terminological resources can be seen as a first step.
The transition from informal to formal models is also addressed in [17]. The approach allows users to express the knowledge informally (like in texts and hypertexts) and more formally (through semantic networks coupled with an argumentation system). In this modeling framework, knowledge becomes progressively more formal through small increments. The system, called "Hyper-Objet substrate", provides an active support to users by suggesting formal descriptions of terms. The integrated nature of this system allows to make suggestions while the users are manipulating the text, and to exploit already formalized knowledge to deduce new formalization steps (this would be adapted to our system with profit). However, our natural language component is far more developed.

5 Conclusion

We have presented a fully implemented system which:

- analyzes text corpora and generates terminological resources organized in a hierarchical way;
- allows users to validate particular elements of the terminology;
- generates class hierarchies in a formal model and communicates them to the Troeps knowledge server through an XML stream;
- provides a way back from the model to the documents through the federating action of the terminology.

It thus provides both assisted generation of formal models from texts and traceability of these models back to the documents. To our opinion, this is a valuable tool for elaborating structural or formal knowledge repositories (as well as databases or software models) from legacy texts.
To improve the current system, more developments are underway for:

- improving knowledge generation by automatically detecting potential attributes and their types (the same could be possible for events, actions ...);
- implementing definition detection in texts;
- using the knowledge model as an index for providing query-by-formalized-content of the documents.

Acknowledgements

This work has been partially realized in the GENIE II program supported by the French ministry of education, research and technology (MENRT) and the DGA/SPAé.

References

[1] N. Aussenac-Gilles, D. Bourigault, A. Condamines, and C. Gros. How can knowledge acquisition benefit from terminology ? In *Proceedings of the 9th Knowledge Acquisition for Knowledge Based System Workshop (KAW '95)*, Banff, Canada, 1995.

[2] B. Biébow and S. Szulman. Une approche terminologique pour la construction d'ontologie de domaine à partir de textes : TERMINAE. In *Proceedings of 12th RFIA Conference*, pages 81–90, Paris, 2000.

[3] G. Booch. *Object-Oriented Analysis and Design with Applications.* Addison-Wesley, 2d edition, 1994.

[4] D. Bourigault. Lexter, a terminology extraction software for knowledge acquisition from texts. In *Proceedings of the 9th Knowledge Acquisition for Knowledge Based System Workshop (KAW '95)*, Banff, Canada, 1995.

[5] F. Cerbah. Acquisition de ressources terminologiques – description technique des composants d'ingénierie linguistique. Technical report, Dassault Aviation, 1999.

[6] K. W. Church and P. Hanks. Word association norms, mutual information and lexicography. *Computational Linguistics*, 16(1):22–29, 1990.

[7] B. Daille. Study and implementation of combined techniques for automatic extraction of terminology. In J.L. Klavans and P. Resnik, editors, *The Balancing Act: Combining Symbolic and Statistical Approaches to Language.* MIT Press, Cambridge, 1996.

[8] K. Elavaino and J. Kunz. Docstep — technical documentation creation and management using step. In *Proceedings of SGML '97*, 1997.

[9] Jérôme Euzenat. XML est-il le langage de représentation de connaissance de l'an 2000 ? In *Actes des 6eme journées langages et modèles à objets*, pages 59–74, Mont Saint-Hilaire, CA, 2000.

[10] I. Jacobson. *Object-Oriented Software Engineering: A Use Case Driven Approach.* Addison-Wesley, 1992.

[11] J. S. Justeson and S. M. Katz. Technical terminology: Some linguistic properties and an algorithm for identification in text. *Natural Language Engineering*, 1(1):9–27, 1995.

[12] O. Mariño, F. Rechenmann, and P. Uvietta. Multiple perspectives and classification mechanim in object-oriented representation. In *Proceeding of 9th ECAI*, pages 425–430, Stockholm, 1990.

[13] OMG. XML Metadata Interchange (XMI). Technical report, OMG, 1998.

[14] D. Petitpierre and G. Russell. MMORPH – the Multext morphology program. Technical report, Multext Deliverable 2.3.1, 1995.

[15] J. Rumbaugh. *Object-Oriented Modeling and Design.* Prentice-Hall, 1991.

[16] Projet Sherpa. Troeps 1.2 reference manual. Technical report, Inria, 1998.

[17] F. Shipman and R. McCall. Supporting incremental formalization with the hyper-object substrate. *ACM Transactions on information systems*, 17(2):199–227, 1999.

Natural Language Analysis for Semantic Document Modeling

Terje Brasethvik & Jon Atle Gulla

Department of Computer and Information Science, IDI
Norwegian University of Technology and Science, NTNU

{brase, jag}@idi.ntnu.no

Abstract. To ease the retrieval of documents published on the Web, the documents should be classified in a way that users find helpful and meaningful. This paper presents an approach to semantic document classification and retrieval based on Natural Language Analysis and Conceptual Modeling. A conceptual domain model is used in combination with linguistic tools to define a controlled vocabulary for a document collection. Users may browse this domain model and interactively classify documents by selecting model fragments that describe the contents of the documents. Natural language tools are used to analyze the text of the documents and propose relevant domain model concepts and relations. The proposed fragments are refined by the users and stored as XML document descriptions. For document retrieval, lexical analysis is used to pre-process search expressions and map these to the domain model for manual query-refinement. A prototype of the system is described, and the approach is illustrated with examples from a document collection published by the Norwegian Center for Medical Informatics (KITH).

1. Introduction

Project groups, communities and organizations today use the Web to distribute and exchange information. While the Web makes it easy to publish documents, it is more difficult to find an efficient way to organize, describe, classify and present the documents for the benefit of later retrieval and use. One of the most challenging tasks is semantic classification - the representation of document contents. Semantic classification is usually done using a mixture of text-analysis methods, carefully defined vocabularies or ontologies, and various schemes for applying the vocabularies in indexing tasks.

With controlled vocabularies, more work can be put into creating meaningful attributes for document classification and building up document indices. However, even though the words in a controlled vocabulary are selected on the basis of their semantic content, this semantic part is normally not apparent in the classification and retrieval tasks. As far as the information retrieval system is concerned, the vocabulary tends to be a list of terms that are syntactically matched with terms in the documents. The inherent meanings or structures of the terms in the vocabulary are not used to classify and retrieve documents, and we are still left with a syntactic search approach to information retrieval.
There have been a few attempts to add a semantic component to document retrieval. With the inclusion of semantically oriented lexicons like WordNet, it has been

M. Bouzeghoub et al. (Eds.): NLDB 2000, LNCS 1959, pp. 127-140, 2001.

possible to link search terms to related terms and use these links to expand or restrict the search query in a semantic way. Stemming is a technique for reducing a conjugated word to its base form, which may also be used when classifying documents and can be regarded as a way of deducing the underlying concept from the surface text string. There is a tendency, though, that linguistically oriented retrieval systems including such techniques do not easily combine with controlled vocabularies.

An interesting approach to this problem would be to define a controlled vocabulary of terms that can be semantically interpreted by the information retrieval system. For this to be useful, though, the semantic descriptions have to be derived from the way these terms are actually used in the document collection. A general multi-purpose lexicon would give us definitions that in most cases are too generic and will work against the whole principle of using controlled vocabularies. Also, the semantic aspects have to be given a representation that the retrieval system can understand and make use of.

In this paper, we present a document retrieval system that brings together semantic retrieval and controlled vocabularies. Particular to this system is the way conceptual modeling and linguistics are combined to create conceptual models that serve as controlled vocabularies. Section 2 introduces the whole architecture of the system. The construction of the vocabulary is discussed in Section 3, and Section 4 and 5 present the processes of classifying and retrieving documents respectively. A comparison with related work in done in Section 6 and the main conclusions of our work are summed up in Section 7.

2. Semantic Document Retrieval

Semantic document retrieval implies that the documents are classified using interpretable concepts. The classification of a particular document is a structure of concepts that has an unambiguous interpretation and can be subjected to well-defined reasoning. Whereas syntactic retrieval is based on a simple matching of search strings with document attributes, semantic retrieval requires that the underlying meaning of the search expression be compared to the semantic descriptions of the documents. During this comparison, various logical, linguistic or conceptual theories may be applied. Our semantic retrieval approach rests on the following major principles:

- Fundamental to our document retrieval system is the assumption that the documents are all restricted to a domain that can be characterized by well-defined, inter-related concepts. These concepts form the scientific terminology of the domain and are represented as a hierarchical conceptual model of entities and unlabelled relationships that we will refer to as the *domain model*.
- The contents of documents are described using domain model fragments that have clear semantic interpretations. These classifications may be more precise than the domain model by labelling the relationships between the domain concepts.
- Document queries must refer to the concepts included in the domain model. The query is regarded as a fragment of the domain model including the labelled

relationships from the document classifications. Query refinement is done graphically by selecting and deselecting elements of this extended domain model.

The four-tier architecture of the information retrieval system is shown in Figure 1. Using the retrieval system, the user accesses a model viewer implemented in Java that integrates the components of the system. In addition to classifying and retrieving documents, this graphical model viewer is also applied to construct the domain model for the documents. The models shown in the model viewer are based on the Referent modeling language [1], which is an ER-like language with strong abstraction mechanisms and sound formal basis.

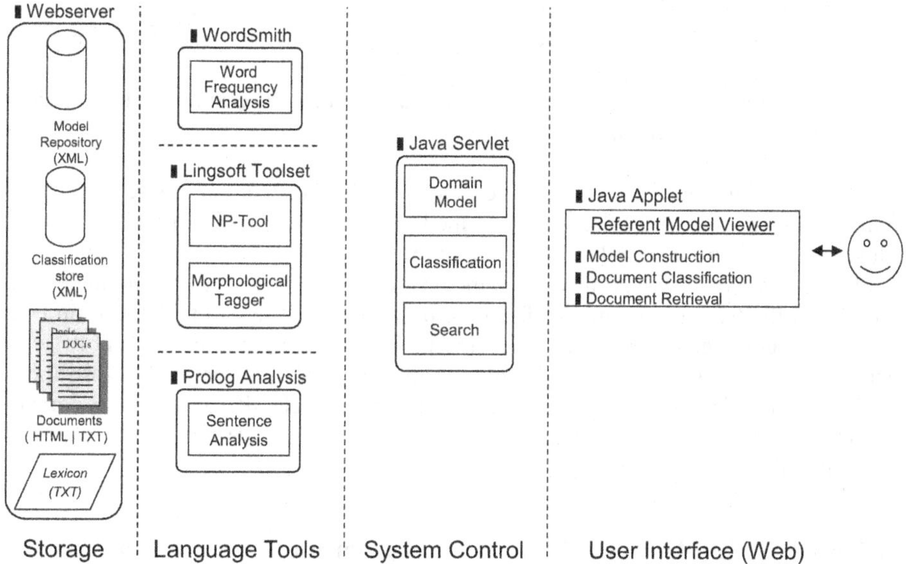

Figure 1 Overview of system architecture

The Java servlets at the next level define the overall functionality of the system. They are invoked from the model viewer and coordinate the linguistic tools incorporated into the system.

At the third level, a number of linguistic tools analyze natural language phrases and give the necessary input to construct domain vocabularies and classify and retrieve documents. The Word frequency analyzer from WordSmith is a commercially available application for counting word frequencies in documents and producing various statistical analyses. A Finnish company, Lingsoft, has two tools for analyzing nominal phrases and tagging sentences that are needed for the classification and retrieval of documents. A smaller Prolog application for analyzing relations between concepts in a sentence is being developed internally at the university. This application assumes a disambiguated tagged sentence and propose relations between the concepts on the basis of classification-specific rules. As an alternative to the tagger and the relation analyzer, we are considering a parser linked to an extensive semantic lexicon.

Finally, the documents and their classifications are stored in HTML and XML format respectively. The domain model is also stored in XML and can be continuously maintained to reflect the vocabulary used in the documents being added to the document collection. The linguistic tools rest on lexical information that is partly stored in XML and partly integrated with the tools themselves.

The functionality of the document system includes three fundamental processes:

- the construction of the domain model on the basis of selected documents,
- the classification of new documents using linguistic analysis and conceptual comparison, and
- the retrieval of documents with linguistic pre-processing and graphical refinement of search queries.

In the following sections, we will go into some more detail of these processes. Examples from the Norwegian centre of medical informatics (KITH) will be used to illustrate our approach. KITH has the editorial responsibility for creating and publishing ontologies covering various medical domains. Today, these ontologies are created on the basis of documents from the particular domain and take the form of a list of selected terms from the domain, their textual definitions (possibly with examples) and cross-references (Figure 3). KITHís goal is to be able to use these medical ontologies directly in a web-based interface to classify and browse domain documents. Our work is related to the ontology from Somatic Hospitals [2], which is currently under construction.

3. Constructing Domain Models from Document Collections

Conceptual modeling is mainly a manual process. However, when the conceptual models are constructed on the basis of a set of documents, textual analysis may be used to aid the process. Our approach is outlined in Figure 2.

The first step of the process is to run the document collection through a word analysis with the purpose of proposing a list of concept candidates for the manual modeling process. In the KITH case, the WordSmith toolkit [3] is used for this purpose. This analysis filters away stop words and it also compares the text of the documents with ìa reference set of documentsî, assumed to contain average Norwegian language.

The result from this analysis is a list of the highest frequented terms in (documents from) this domain. The WordSmith tool offers a word concordance analysis that ñ for a given term - may display example uses of this term in phrases from the text and also compute words that are co-located with this term in the text. The WordSmith tool is based on statistical analysis. An alternative is to use a linguistically motivated tool, like Lingsoftís NPTool [4] which extracts complete noun phrases from running text.

Such an analysis may propose more complete noun phrases as candidates for concepts in the model and may also handle more linguistic variation.

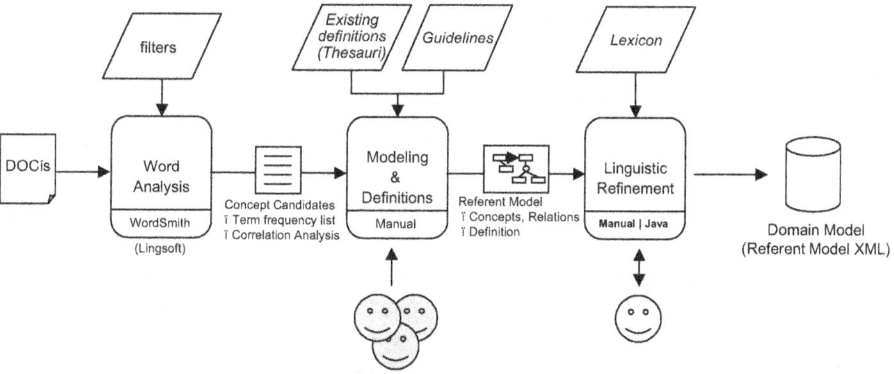

Figure 2 Constructing the domain specific conceptual model

After the word analysis, the conceptual model is created by carefully selecting terms from the proposed list through a manual and cooperative process. In the KITH example, this work is performed by a committee consisting of computer scientists, medical doctors and other stakeholders from the particular domain. Terms are selected and defined ñ possibly with examples from their occurrences in the document text, and related to each other. The concept definition process performed by KITH conforms to what is recommended elsewhere, e.g. in the SpriTerm project [5] and in ISO standards [6]. Typical sources of input for this work are guidelines for terminological work, domain specific thesauri etc.

In the KITH approach a visual conceptual modeling language is used to keep an overview of the central concepts and their relations. In the example model from the domain of somatic hospitals, the initial word analysis proposed more than 700 terms and the final result is a MS Word document listing 131 well defined concepts together with some overview conceptual models ñ shown in Figure 3. As shown, the final domain ìmodelî contains the terms, their definitions and their relations to other terms. Relations between concepts in this model are not well-defined, relations are here merely an indication of ìrelatednessî and are denoted ìcross-referencesî.

To be able to experiment with KITHís term-definition document further in our approach to semantic document classification, we have chosen to use our own conceptual modeling language and tool ñ the Referent Model Language. We translate the input from KITH into a complete Referent model and embed the textual definitions within this model. We also perform what we have denoted a ìlinguistic refinementî of the model in order to prepare the model-based classification of documents. For each of the concepts in the model, we add a list of terms that we accept as a textual designator of this concept. This list of terms may be extracted from a synonym dictionary, e.g. [7]. Today this is performed manually. We then run the

model through an electronic dictionary and extract all conjugations for each of the concepts in the model and its corresponding list of terms.
The resulting Referent Model is stored as an XML file and is now available for browsing and interaction across the Web in a Java based Referent Model viewer.

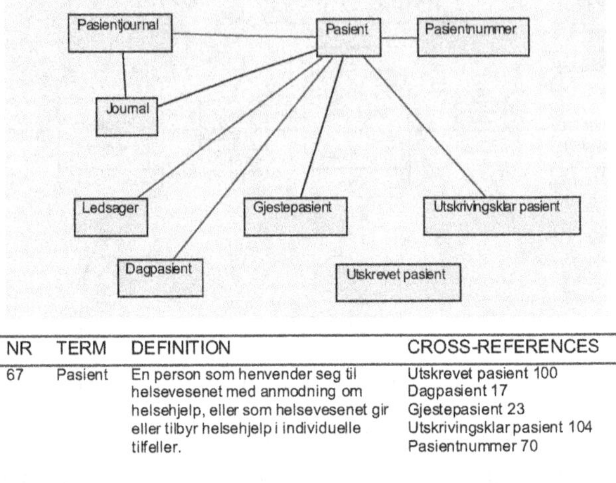

NR	TERM	DEFINITION	CROSS-REFERENCES
67	Pasient	En person som henvender seg til helsevesenet med anmodning om helsehjelp, eller som helsevesenet gir eller tilbyr helsehjelp i individuelle tilfeller.	Utskrevet pasient 100 Dagpasient 17 Gjestepasient 23 Utskrivingsklar pasient 104 Pasientnummer 70

Figure 3 Example concept definitions and model from the domain Somatic Hospitals [2]

Figure 4 shows the exploration of a fragment of the somatic hospital domain model. Using the model viewer, we are able to visualise for the users the conceptual model that will be used to classify documents. As shown, the user may interact with the model - by clicking on a concept, he may explore the concept definitions as well as the list of terms and conjugations for this concept.

4. Classifying Documents with Conceptual Model Fragments

In our approach, a document is semantically classified by selecting a fragment of the conceptual model that reflects the documentís content. Figure 5 shows how linguistic analysis is used to match the document against the conceptual model and hence help the user classify the document.

The user provides the URL of the document to be classified. The document is downloaded by our document analysis servlet, which matches the document text with the concepts occurring in the model. This matching is done by comparing a sequence of words (a concept name in the model may consist of more than one word) from the document with the concepts in the model ñ i.e. it uses the given conjugations found in the conceptís term list. The result of this matching is a list of all concepts found in the document ñ sorted according to number of occurrences ñ as well as a list of the document sentences in which the concepts were found. The concepts found are shown to the user as a selection in our Referent Model viewer. The shown selection in the model viewer of Figure 4 (the greyed out Referents ñ *Patient*, *Health service* and

Treatment) is the result of the matching of the document whose URL is indicated at the top right corner of the model viewer.

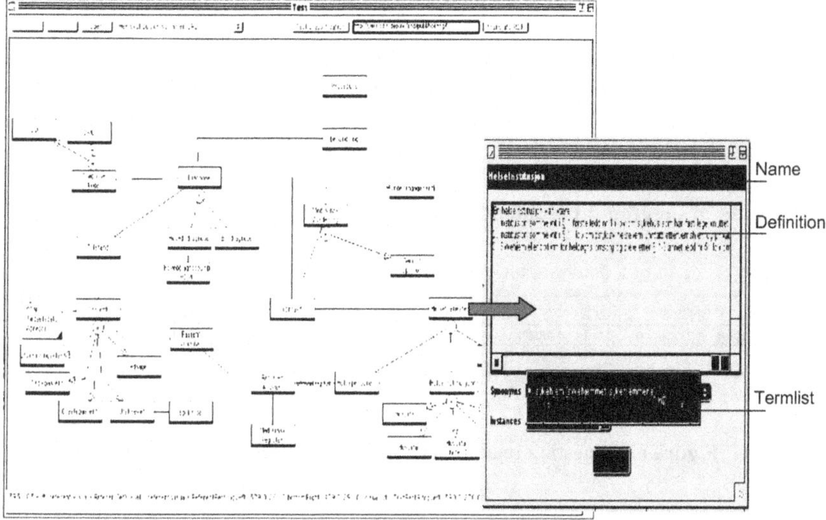

Figure 4 Exploration of concepts and definitions in Referent Model Viewer

The user may then manually change the selection of concepts according to her interpretation of the document. The user may also select relations between concepts in order to classify a document with a complete model fragment, rather than individually selected concepts. Once the user is satisfied with the selected model fragment, this fragment is sent back to the document servlet. In order to add some semantics to the selected relation, it is important also to provide relevant relation names. For each of the selected relations in the model fragment, the servlet chooses all the sentences extracted from the document that contain both concepts participating in the relation. These sentences are first sent to a syntactic tagger [8] and from there to a semantic analyzer in Prolog. The semantic analyzer uses a set of semantic sentence rules to extract suggested names for each relation from the set of sentences.

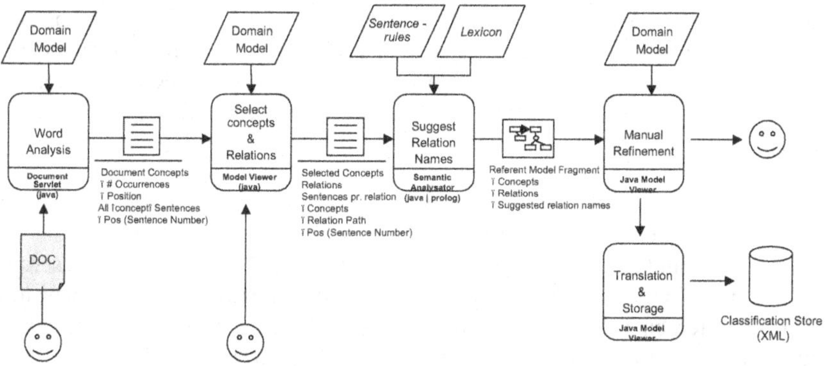

Figure 5 Semantic classification through lexical analysis and conceptual model interaction

As an example, take one of the documents classified in our document retrieval system. There are 11 sentences in that document that contain the domain concepts ì helsetjenesteî (health service) and ì pasientî (patient). One of the sentences is

"Medarbeidere i helsetjenesten må stadig utvikle nye muligheter for å fremme helse, hjelpe pasientene og bedre rutinene" (The employees of the health service must steadily develop new methods to promote health, help the patients and improve the routines)

and the results of tagging this sentence is shown in Figure 6.

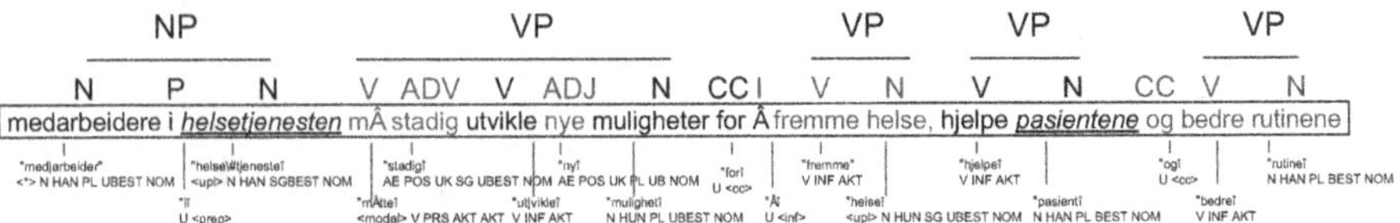

Figure 6 Suggesting relation names - example sentence analysis

When the disambiguation part of the tagger is completed, some syntactic roles will also be added to the tagged sentence. Using the results from the tagger as a basis, the system tries to propose a relation between the two concepts, health service and patient. Currently, the relation is formed by the part of the sentence linking the two concepts that remain after removing irrelevant sentence constituents. Constituents to remove are for example attributive adjectives (ì newî), modal verbs (ì mustî), non-sentential adverbs, and most types of sentential adverbs (ì steadilyî). Also, we remove prepositional phrases and paratactic constructions that do not contain any of the two concepts in question (ì promote healthî and ì improve the routinesî). For the sentence above, the system proposes to use the following words to form a relation between the concepts (proposed words in bold face): *"**The employees of the** health service must steadily **develop** new **methods to** promote health, **help** the patients and improve the routines."*

The user is provided with a list of all proposed relation names extracted from the found sentences, and may select the desired ones. Users may also refine the proposed names or provide their own names for a selected relation. All the relation names used when classifying a document are stored in with the conceptual model and can later be added to the list of proposed relation names, when the next user is selecting the same relation.

The completed model fragment with relation names now serves as the classification of the document. Our goal is to store classifications in conformance with the W3C proposed RDF standard for Web-document descriptions ñ the Resource Description Framework [9]. Thus, we may translate the selected Referent Model fragment into a set of RDF statements. We also let the users specify a set of contextual meta-data attributes selected from the Dublin Core [10] proposal (*Document Title , Creator, Classification Date, URL etc.*) and use Dublin Coreís guidelines generating RDF-

XML syntax. By using the RDF syntax, we hope to be able to use available internet search machinery at a later stage. For now, however, we store the classifications in our own Referent Model XML format and use our own document servlet for searching.

5. Retrieving Documents with NL Queries and Model Browsing

Our document retrieval component includes graphical mechanisms for analyzing the queries with respect to the domain vocabulary. The retrieval interface combines the analysis of natural language query inputs with the subsequent refinement of conceptual model query representations.

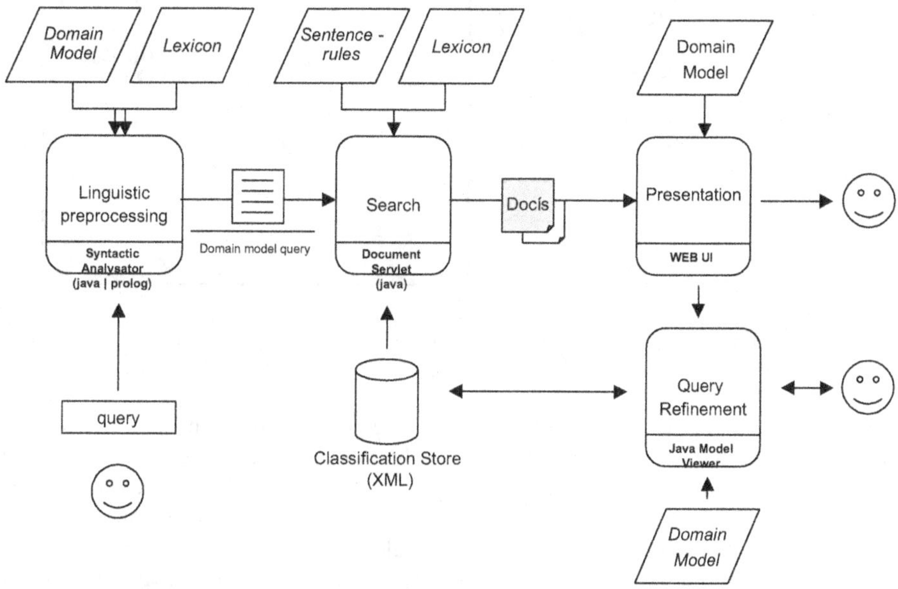

Figure 7 NL & Model based document retrieval

Figure 7 gives an overview of the retrieval process. The users enter a natural language query phrase which is matched against the conceptual model like in the classification process. The domain model concepts found in this search phrase (if any) are extracted and used to search the stored document descriptions. Verbs found in between the concepts in the search phrase are extracted and matched against the stored relation names. Note that the relations are given a simpler analysis than what is done in classification. Using the same sentence analysis here would require that the search phrase is written almost the exact same way as the original document sentence in order to produce a match. Such relaxations have proven necessary also in other works [11].

Our goal is not to develop new indexing or retrieval methods at this level. Storing our document descriptions in a standard format, we intend to use available or standard indexing and retrieval machinery as these are made available. For the prototype interface shown in this paper, we are using our own document servlet, which uses a simple weighting algorithm to match, sort and present documents.

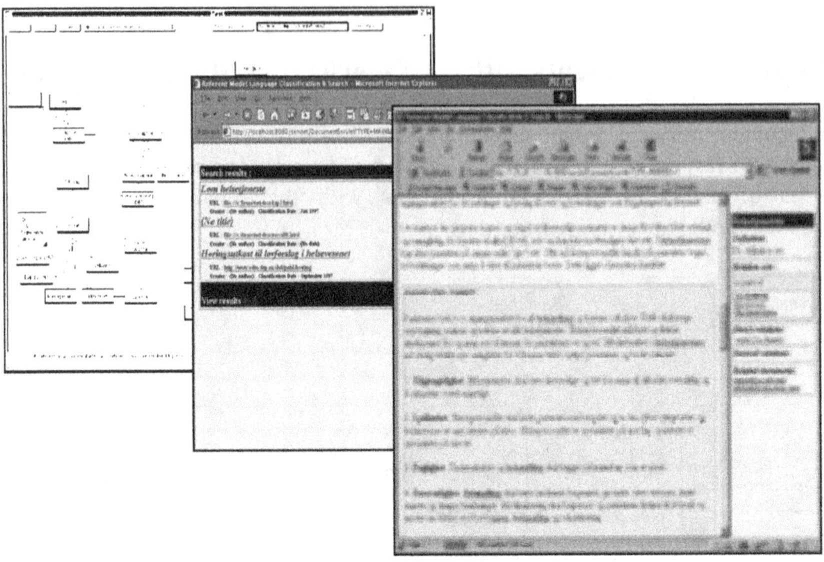

Figure 8 Selecting referents in model -> Ranked list of documents -> Enhanced document reading

Users may now refine their search by interacting with the domain model. Concepts found in the search phrase are marked out in the model. Relation names found in the stored classifications are presented to user in a list format. The search may be narrowed by a) selecting several concepts from the model, b) following the generalization hierarchies of the model and selecting more specific concepts or c) selecting specific relation names from the list. Likewise, the search may be widened by selecting more general concepts or selecting a smaller model fragment, i.e. fewer relations and concepts.

Figure 8 shows our prototype search interface. The figure shows how users may interact with the model and retrieve a ranked list of documents. Documents are presented in a Web-browser interface by using a selection of the stored Dublin Core attributes. The figure also shows what we have denoted ìenhanced document readerî, that is, when reading a document, each term in the document that matched a model concept is marked as a hyper-link. The target of this link is a ìsidebarî with the information regarding this concept that is stored in the domain model, i.e. the definition of the concept, the list of accepted terms for this concept and its relations to other concepts. If relevant, this sidebar also contains a list of documents classified according to this concept. This way, a user may navigate among the stored documents by following the links presented in this sidebar. Such a user interface visualizes the connection between the documents and the domain model, and may aid the user in getting acquainted with the domain model. Note that the ìenhanced document readerî not only works on classified documents, but is implemented as a servlet that accepts any document URL as input.

6. Related Work

Shared or common information space systems in the area of CSCW, like BSCW [12], ICE [13] or FirstClass [14] mostly use (small) static contextual meta-data schemes, connecting documents to for example people, tasks or projects, and relying on freely selected key-words, or free-text descriptions for the semantic classification. TeamWave workplace [15] uses a "concept map"-tool, where users may collaboratively define and outline concepts and ideas as a way of structuring the discussion. There is however no explicit way of utilizing this concept graph in the classification of information. In the ConceptIndex system [16], concepts are defined by attaching them to phrases ñ or text fragments ñ selected from their occurrences in the text. This way the concept-definitions also serve as an index of the text fragments.

Ontologies [17, 18, 19] are nowadays beeing collaboratively created [20, 21] across the Web, and applied to search and classification of documents. Ontobroker [22, 23] and Ontosaurus [24] allows users to search and also annotate HTML documents with "ontological information". Domain specific ontologies or thesauri are used to improve search-expressions. The medical domain calls for precise access to information, which is reflected in several terminological projects, such as [25, 26, 27, 28]

Naturally, in order to facilitate information exchange and discovery, also several "web-standards" are approaching. The Dublin Core [10] initiative gives a recommendation of 15 attributes for describing networked resources. W3C's Resource Description Framework, [9] applies a semantic network inspired language that can be used to issue meta-data statements of published documents. RDF-statements may be serialized in XML and stored with the document itself. Pure RDF does however not include a facility for specifying the vocabulary used in the meta-data statements. The TopicMap ISO standard [29] ñ offers a way of linking various kinds of ìinstancesî (files, pictures, text-fragments, etc.) to a topic, and then navigate in this material by following associations between the topics. Topic maps may be stored using SGML.

Natural Language Analysis enables the use of phrases or semantic units, rather than ìsimpleî words in retrieval. Phrase extraction from text has led to advances in IR and has been the basis for Linguistically Motivated Indexing - LMI - [30, 31, 32, 33] . [34] provides a survey of NLP techniques and methods such as stemming, query expansion and word sense disambiguation to deal with morphological, lexical, syntactic and semantic variation when indexing text. A multiple stream indexing architecture [33] shows how several such ìsimpleî LMI techniques may be applied simultaneously and effectively in the TREC-7 full-text ad-hoc task. In some systems search expressions are matched with a conceptual structure reflecting a linguistic or logical theory, e.g. [35, 36, 37]

Understanding natural language specifications and turning them into formal statements of some kind in a CASE tool has been an old challenge [38]. For ER-like conceptual models, the naive approach is to use nouns and verbs as candidates for entities and relations respectively. Some CASE tools adopt a particular grammar, or accepts only a selective subset of natural language in order to produce model statements. Constructing models from a larger set of documents, however, the system needs more sophisticated techniques for handling linguistic variation when proposing model elements. [39, 40] give examples of CASE tools that have integrated advanced parsing and understanding [38].

7. Concluding Remarks

We have presented an approach to semantic classification of documents that takes advantage of conceptual modeling and natural language analysis. A conceptual modeling language is used to create a domain specific vocabulary to be used when describing documents. Natural language analysis tools are used as an interface to the domain model, both to aid users when constructing the model, to suggest classifications of documents based on the model and to preprocess free-text search expressions. The conceptual modeling language visualizes the domain vocabulary and allows the users to use this vocabulary interactively when classifying documents. Users may browse the domain model and select a model fragment to represent the classification of a document. Natural language tools are used to analyze the text of a document and to propose a relevant model fragment in terms of concepts and named relations.

This paper reports on work in progress, and further work is needed in several directions. Improving the interface between the modeling tool and the linguistic tools, we want to speed up the construction of domain models. To enhance the matching of document texts against the model, further work is needed on the term lists used to match each of the model concepts. Today, synonyms are only added manually and word forms are extracted from a dictionary. There is however work in linguistic IR that uses advanced algorithms for expanding on noun phrases and generating term lists from a corpus. Furthermore, our approach must be interfaced with proper indexing and retrieval machinery, so that the approach can be tested on a larger full-text KITH case.

Acknowledgments:

This work is supervised by professor Arne S¯lvberg at the Information Systems Group at IDI NTNU. Special thanks to professor Torbj¯rn NorgÂrd, department of Linguistics NTNU for providing the Norwegian dictionaries and for helping with the linguistic analysis. Thanks also to Hallvard TrÊtteberg and Thomas F. Gundersen for most of the Java programming, and to ÿ rjan Mjelde and Torstein Gjengedal for the Java-Prolog interface. Parts of this work are funded by the NFR-sponsored CAGIS project.

References:

1. S¯lvberg, A. *"Data and what they refer to"*. in *Conceptual modeling: Historical perspectives and future trends*. 1998. In conjunction with 16th Int. Conf. on Conceptual modeling, Los Angeles, CA, USA.
2. Nordhuus, I., *"Definisjonskatalog for Somatiske sykehus (In Norwegian)"*, http://www.kith.no/kodeverk/definisjonskatalog/defkat_somatiske/default.htm, (Accessed: March 2000)
3. Scott, M., *"WordSmith Tools"*, http://www.liv.ac.uk/~ms2928/wordsmit.htm, (Accessed: Jan 1998)
4. Voutilainen, A., *"A short introduction to the NP Tool"*, http://www.lingsoft.fi/doc/nptool/intro, (Accessed: March 2000)
5. SPRI, *"Methods and Principles in terminological work (In Swedish)"*, . 1991, Helso och sjukvÂrdens utvecklingsinstitutt.
6. ISO/DIS, *"Terminology work - principles and methods"*, . 1999.
7. Lingsoft, *"NORTHES Norwegian Thesauri"*, http://www.lingsoft.fi/cgi-pub/northes, (Accessed: March 2000)
8. Lingsoft, *"Lingsoft Indexing and Retreieval - Morphological Analysis"*, http://www.lingsoft.fi/en/indexing/, (Accessed: March 2000)
9. W3CRDF, *"Resource Description Framework - Working Draft"*, http://www.w3.org/Metadata/RDF/, (Accessed: March 2000)
10. Weibel, S. and E. Millner, *"The Dublin Core Metadata Element Set home page"*, http://purl.oclc.org/dc/, (Accessed: May 199)
11. Sparck-Jones, K., *"What is The Role of NLP in Information Retrieval?"*, in *Natural Language Information Retrieval*, T. Strzalkowski, Editor. 1999, Kluwer Academic Publisher.
12. BSCW, *"Basic Support for Cooperative Work on the WWW"*, http://bscw.gmd.de, (Accessed: May 1999)
13. Farshchian, B.A. *"ICE: An object-oriented toolkit for tailoring collaborative Web--applications"*. in *IFIP WG8.1 Conference on Information Systems in the WWW Environment*. 1998. Beijing, China.
14. FirstClass, *"FirstClass Collaborative Classroom"*, www.schools.softarc.com/, (Accessed: May, 1999)
15. TeamWave, *"TeamWave WorkPlace Overview"*, http://www.teamwave.com, (Accessed: May, 1999)
16. Voss, A., K. Nakata, M. Juhnke and T. Schardt. *"Collaborative information management using concepts"*. in *2nd International Workshop IIIS-99*. 1999. Copenhague, DK: Postproceedings published by IGP.
17. Gruber, T., *"Towards Priciples for the Design of Ontologies used for Knowledge Sharing"*. Human and Computer Studies, 1995. Vol. 43 (No. 5/6): p. 907-928.
18. Guarino, N., *"Ontologies and Knowledge Bases"*, . 1995, IOS Press, Amsterdam.
19. Uschold, M. *"Building Ontologies: Towards a unified methodology"*. in *The 16th annual conference of the British Computer Society Specialist Group on Expert Systems*. 1996. Cambridge (UK).
20. Gruber, T.R., *"Ontolingua - A mechanism to support portable ontologies"*, . 1992, Knowledge Systems Lab, Stanford University.
21. Domingue, J. *"Tadzebao and WebOnto: Discussing, Browsing, and Editing Ontologies on the Web."*. in *11th Banff Knowledge Aquisition for Knowledge-based systems Workshop*. 1998. Banff, Canada.
22. Fensel, D., S. Decker, M. Erdmann and R. Studer. *"Ontobroker: How to make the web intelligent"*. in *11th Banff Knowledge Aquisition for Knowledge-based systems Workshop*. 1998. Banff, Canada.

23. Fensel, D., J. Angele, S. Decker, M. Erdmann and H.-P. Schnurr, *"On2Broker: Improving access to information sources at the WWW"*, http://www.aifb.uni-karlsruhe.de/WBS/www-broker/o2/o2.pdf, (Accessed: May, 1999)
24. Swartout, B., R. Patil, K. Knight and T. Russ. *"Ontosaurus: A tool for browsing and editing ontologies"*. in *9th Banff Knowledge Aquisition for KNowledge-based systems Workshop*. 1996. Banff, Canada.
25. Spriterm, *"Spriterm - hälso och sjukvårdens gemensamma fakta och termdatabas"*, http://www.spri.se/i/Spriterm/i-prg2.htm, (Accessed: March 2000)
26. Soamares de Lima, L., A.H.F. Laender and B.A. Ribeiro-Neto. *"A Hierarchical Approach to the Automatic Categorization of Medical Documents"*. in *CIKM*98*. 1998. Bethesda, USA: ACM.
27. OMNI, *"OMNI: Organisaing Medical Networked Information"*, http://www.omni.ac.uk/, (Accessed: May, 1999)
28. Galen, *"Why Galen - The need for Integrated medical systems"*, http://www.galen-organisation.com/approach.html, (Accessed: March 2000)
29. ISO/IEC, *"Information Technology - Document Description and Processing Languages"*, http://www.ornl.gov/sgml/sc34/document/0058.htm, (Accessed: March 2000)
30. Schneiderman, B., D. Byrd and W. Bruce Croft, *"Clarifying Search: A User-Interface Framework for Text Searches"*. D-Lib Magazine, 1997. Vol. (No. January 1997).
31. Strzalkowski, T., F. Lin and J. Perez-Carballo. *"Natural Language Information Retrieval TREC-6 Report"*. in *6th Text Retrieval Conference, TREC-6*. 1997. Gaithersburg, November, 1997.
32. Strzalkowski, T., G. Stein, G. Bowden-Wise, J. Perez-Caballo, P. Tapanainen, T. Jarvinen, A. Voutilainen and J. Karlgren. *"Natural Language Information Retrieval - TREC-7 report"*. in *TREC-7*. 1998.
33. Strzalkowski, T., *"Natural Language Information Retrieval"*. 1999: Kluwer Academic Publishers.
34. Arampatzis, A.T., T.P. van der Weide, P. van Bommel and C.H.A. Koster, *"Linguistically Motivated Information Retrieval"*, . 1999, University of Nijmegen.
35. Puder, A. *"Service trading using conceptual structures"*. in *International Conference on Conceptual Structures (ICCS'95)*. 1995: Springer-Verlag.
36. Rau, L.F., *"Knowledge organization and access in a conceptual information system"*. Information Processing and Management, 1987. Vol. 21 (No. 4): p. 269-283.
37. Katz, B. *"From Sentence Processing to Information Access on the World Wide Web"*. in *AAAI Spring Symposium on Natural Language Processing for the World Wide Web*. 1997. Stanford University, Stanford CA.
38. MÈtais, E., *"The role of knowledge and reasoning i CASE Tools"*, . 1999, University of Versailles.
39. Fliedl, G., C. Kop, W. Mayerthaler, H.C. May and C. Winkler. *"NTS-based derivation of KCPM Perspective Determiners"*. in *3rd Int. workshop on Applications of Natural Language to Information Systems (NLDB'97)*. 1997. Vancouver, Ca.
40. Tjoa, A.M. and L. Berger. *"Transformation of Requirement Specifications Expressed in Natural Language into EER Model"*. in *12th Int. conceference on Entity-Relation approach*. 1993.

Domain Analysis and Queries in Context

Alfs T. Berztiss[1,2]

[1] University of Pittsburgh, Pittsburgh PA 15260, USA
alpha@cs.pitt.edu
[2] SYSLAB, University of Stockholm, Sweden

Abstract. We are formulating design guidelines for a knowledge system that is to provide answers to natural language queries in context. A query that starts out being very vague is to be sharpened with the assistance of the system. Also, the response to a query is more meaningful when presented in context. We recognize three types of context: essential, reference, and source. Essential context associates the response to a query with a time and place. Reference context provides reference values that help the user determine whether the response to a fuzzy query is true or false. Source context relates to the dependability of the response.

1 Introduction

The DARPA project of high performance knowledge bases (HPKB) [1] is to result in a knowledge base of a million assertions (axioms, rules, frames). At the 1999 AAAI Fall Symposium on Question Answering Systems Marc Light gave the following example of a typical question: "Which architect designed the Hancock Building in Boston?" The answer needs to be correct (I.M. Pei), justified (by a reference to the source of the information), and concise ("The Hancock Building is an example of I.M. Pei's early work"). But do we need the HPKB for this? The Hotbot search engine with search term "Hancock Building Boston" returned a reference to the building as its very first search result, with the index entry naming I.M. Pei and giving the dates 1972-75.

On the other hand, when, for a cross-cultural comparison of technological development in USA and Germany, I had data on the growth in the number of computers in USA, but needed comparable data for Germany, I spent an entire day on an unsuccessful search. I doubt that the HPKB would have done better. Moreover, had the numbers been available, there would still be uncertainty as to what is being counted — the exact definition of what is a computer could have been different for the two sources of information.

We shall differentiate between questions and queries. We call "Which architect designed the Hancock Building in Boston?" a question, but "Which salesman is assigned to Boston?" we call a query. The two expressions have the same form, but differ in the kind of information source used to deal with them. Questions are put to so-called knowledge bases, while queries go to highly structured data bases. This is consistent with standard English usage: to query means to ask questions with some degree of formality. Of course, once a data base of buildings

M. Bouzeghoub et al. (Eds.): NLDB 2000, LNCS 1959, pp. 141–151, 2001.

and their architects has been constructed, the question shown above becomes a query. Here we shall deal with queries alone, to avoid discussion of retrieval of information from unstructured sources. However, we shall see that a knowledge base is needed to establish an appropriate context for the answer to a query.

The answering of queries can be considered from several viewpoints. One is based on queries as functions. Define a query as a function f with a tuple of arguments X. The response to the query is then the value $f(X)$, but some flexibility can be achieved by making f a fuzzy function. Another approach is to consider queries in context. Thus, if on May 15 a user asks "Is it a cold day?" the response could be "The average temperature in Stockholm for May 15 is 6 degrees Centigrade." This provides the user with hints on how to modify the query, and the initial query could be reformulated to, say, "What was the minimum temperature in Pittsburgh on May 15 in Fahrenheit?" A third approach is to partition the informations space into regions, and allow the user to sharpen a query by calling up a sequence of menus.

Here we shall try to integrate the main characteristics of the three approaches. This results in a composite strategy based on a concept space partitioned into regions. Each region corresponds to a concept, such as warmth or locality. A fuzzy term in a query, e.g., "cold" or "here" identifies the region of interest. A menu then allows a user to select the terms appropriate for a query. We realize that the implementation of a knowledge system along these lines is very difficult. Nevertheless, we believe that the expected benefits justify further research. Our aim is to survey problem areas, and thus to suggest directions for this research.

Regions of the concept space will be called domains. Sections 2 and 3 introduce domain analysis in general, identify several interesting domains, and show by examples what complexity is to be expected. In Section 4 we give an example of the processing of a query under our approach. Section 5 is a discussion of the problems that have to be resolved in the course of implementation of a domain-assisted querying facility. The final two sections survey related work, and list our conclusions. We emphasize that we do not offer a ready solution. Rather, our contribution is a framework for the detailed research that needs to be undertaken.

2 Domain Analysis

We define *domain knowledge* as the entire corpus of knowledge regarding a related set of objects, and consisting of (1) the attributes of the objects, (2) their relations to each other, and (3) the processes in which they participate. A *domain model* is an abstraction that consists of only those parts of general domain knowledge that are relevant to a particular application, and *domain analysis* is used to develop appropriate domain models.

Developers of information systems have been constructing domain models for a long time, under various designations, such as conceptual models, enterprise models, and business rules. Software engineers have also become interested in domain analysis and domain models — different purposes of domain analysis are discussed by Wartik and Prieto-Diaz [2]; for a bibliography see [3]; Glass and Vessey [4] survey taxonomies of domains.

Although the importance of domain analysis is now realized, there is considerable confusion as to what domain analysis should mean with regard to query systems. For example, confusion arises when the difference between immutable and mutable objects in a concept space is not being taken into account. Immutable objects, such as the date of birth of a person, never change. Mutable objects, such as the age of a person, undergo changes in time. There are then in general two ways of looking at a concept space. One is a static view, and under this view the user is interested in snapshots of the concept space. The other is a dynamic view, and the concern is with how changes are brought about in the concept space. Primarily our interest relates to the static view. However, trend analysis is an instance in which a dynamic view has to be taken: stock prices, the number of shares traded, passengers carried by an airline, and populations of cities are examples of parameters that change with time. A query system should also allow a user to ask for correlations between specified parameters, such as between the number of shares traded on the New York Stock Exchange and the average temperature for the day.

It should be clear that in an answer to a query regarding a mutable object it is essential to indicate the time to which the answer relates. Thus, if f is the age function, its argument is the pair <person-identifier, date>. Normally the date is implicitly assumed to be that on which the query is being put. But even with immutable objects a context needs to be established. This has three purposes. First, the user must be made aware in what ways the answer to a given query is dependent on the context. For example, although the boiling point of water is immutable with respect to a specific altitude, it does vary with altitude, and the altitude depends on precise location. Hence, in asking for the boiling point of water, one has to specify an altitude directly or by specifying a location. Second, an answer is to be made meaningful by providing it with comparison values. For example, the information that the minimum temperature in locality Q on May 15 was 4 degrees becomes more meaningful when it is known that the average minimum temperature at Q for May is 8 degrees, say. Third, the source of the information may have to be indicated in cases there is uncertainty relating to its dependability. We shall distinguish between the three types of context by calling them *essential, reference*, and *source* context, respectively.

3 Some Interesting Domains

In data base work it has become understood that different domains require different approaches. Two specific developments are temporal data bases and geographical or spatial data bases. If we look at the form of queries, we can see a natural separation of concerns, defined by Wh-queries, which start with What, When, Where, Why, and Who.

The What relates to the main interest of the user, with the other four Wh-forms serving to establish a context. In terms of the coldness query of the introduction, it can be reformulated to "What is the temperature?" We saw that the When and Where are very important here because they establish essential context. Why queries can arise in two ways. One has to do with causes and effects. For example, if the minimum temperature on a particular date was exceptionally low, the system might be able to indicate a reason for it. The other relates to the system querying the user. If the system knows to what purpose the user will put the answer it generates, the answer can be tailored to correspond more closely to the needs of the user.

Let us now turn to the Who queries. Who has relevance in three different ways. The first is the identity of the user: "Who put the query?" By means of profiles of individual interests the system can select a reference context that is adapted to the individual needs of a user. Also, availability of sensitive information depends on the identity of the user. Next we may ask: "Who provided the information?" The answer to this query may help establish the reliability of the information, i.e., it contributes to the source context. Finally, if one requests information regarding a person called Smith, it has to be established who precisely is this person. Thus, from our viewpoint, the query "When was Smith born?" is not a When query, but represents the two queries "Who is denoted by Smith?" and "What is the date of birth of the person denoted by Smith?"

Now consider the query "Was President Roosevelt tall?" As with the date of birth of Smith, we again have two queries: "Who was President Roosevelt?" and "What was the height of this President Roosevelt?" Here the Who helps to reduce the search space to Presidents of the United States, and then a distinction has to be made between Theodore Roosevelt and Franklin Delano Roosevelt. But the height value alone may not be sufficient to allow the user to decide whether Theodore Roosevelt, say, was or was not tall. A reference context, giving the average height of males in the United States who belonged to the same age group as Theodore Roosevelt at the time of his presidency, could help reach a decision. We shall explore this query in some detail.

4 Was Roosevelt Tall?

The title of this section states the query that will be the subject of our analysis. We face three tasks: selection of the right Roosevelt, determination of his height in appropriate units of length, and provision of an appropriate reference context. The objective of this exercise is to show the difficulty of building a knowledge system capable of such analysis.

In identifying the Roosevelt that the user has in mind, the obvious approach is to ask the user to be more specific. However, the user may not recall the first name of the particular Roosevelt he or she has in mind. It may be feasible for the system to generate a list of all Roosevelts with some claim to fame, but with a more common name such as Brown or Smith, the list would be too long. We suggest that a first cut be made on grounds of linguistic usage. In English, women are not referred to by surname alone, which reduces the search space to that of men. However, the query may have been put by a person with limited knowledge of English, so that this is the first chance for moving off in a wrong direction. Also, the past tense is helpful in that it suggests that we can disregard people who are still alive, e.g., Elliot Roosevelt, a prominent writer of detective stories. Again, however, a misinterpretation can arise in case the user assumes a living person not to be alive or a foreigner gets the tenses confused. To guard against such misinterpretations, the system can be made to explain its reasoning, as is common practice with expert systems.

The next step is to refer to a "celebrity index" which would have its own context determined by location and domain of interest. A default location is defined by the place from which the query is put, and the domain of interest by selection from a menu. Thus, suppose the user selects "Politics", the set of deceased male politicians named Roosevelt will be headed by Franklin Delano and Theodore in the United States, but in some town in The Netherlands the first entry in the list could be the popular local mayor Joop Roosevelt. Note that in our case the list would be short enough not to cause any problems, but again we have to be aware of the Smiths and Browns.

After identification of the most feasible Roosevelts, and the determination which of them the user has in mind, the height of this man has to be obtained, and presented in suitable units. Supposing we have Theodore Roosevelt in mind, finding his height should be no problem. On the other hand, the height of Joop Roosevelt might not be available, and then we would come to a stop right there. The units for expressing Theodore Roosevelt's height would be feet and inches in the United States, but centimeters nearly everywhere else.

The definition of the reference context has to be based on a menu. In the preceding section we introduced one option: the average height of males residing in the United States who were in the same age group as Theodore Roosevelt at the time of his presidency. Other options include average height of heads of state at the time of his presidency, and average height of all presidents of the United States. However, such information may not be available today. Note also that the response to the query "How tall was Roosevelt?" should be just a single value. The form of this query shows that no reference context is called for.

A final problem relates again to English usage. Tallness is not an attribute of people alone. We speak also of tall trees and tall buildings. A thesaurus can establish that Roosevelt is not a tree. Also, a tree would not be capitalized. However, if the query were "How tall was the Roosevelt?" then the "the" hints that this Roosevelt is not meant to be a person. Instead it is likely to denote a demolished hotel. Unfortunately, foreigners could quite easily omit the important linguistic marker.

5 A Catalogue of Problems

The problems presented by a query-answering system based on our model can be separated into several categories. One is the interpretation of the query. It has to be converted into one or more Wh-queries. Next these queries have to be related to appropriate domains. The essential context is to be established next.

This should allow the generation of an adequate answer to the query. In some cases, though, the answer can be null, and the system should then give some explanation of why this is so, and, where possible, provide a surrogate answer. The generation of a reference context should come next, and in some cases it may be appropriate to provide a source context as well. Orthogonal to this development there are presentation concerns, such as the choice of appropriate entity, e.g., minimum, maximum, or average temperature, of appropriate granularity, and of the appropriate unit of measurement. An explanation generator has to be provided as well. We have already noted its significance in case the answer to a query is null.

Interpretation of a query. This is largely a concern of linguistics. The query could be analyzed, and its components annotated with markers provided by a (very large) attribute grammar. For example, the "Roosevelt" of "Was Roosevelt tall?" would receive attributes "male" and "deceased". Care has to be taken that the difference between "Was Roosevelt tall?" and "How tall was Roosevelt?" is preserved in the analysis of these queries. A marker should indicate that a reference context is to be provided for the first case. To continue with the concept of tallness, processing of the query "Are pines tall?" would start with the transformation of this query into "What is the height of pines?" and this requires the knowledge that height is the measure of tallness. Similarly, "cold" and "hot" point to temperature, and "far" and "near" to distance. To summarize, fuzzy terms relate to ranges for which there exist metrics. The task of creating a system for the interpretation of queries is well within current technical capabilities, but would still be a complex undertaking.

Domain selection. As we saw earlier, the query "Was Roosevelt tall?" is to lead to the selection of a particular person. Linguistic indicators show that Roosevelt is likely to be a deceased male, and a menu can be used to reduce this domain to politicians. Since height is a fairly standard attribute of persons, the determination of the height of an individual is usually straightforward. In general, once the main subject of a query has been identified, such as "pines" in "Are pines tall?" (actually in "What is the height of pines?") a thesaurus can be used to determine that our domain is that of trees.

Essential context. This relates to time and place, and the time and place of the submission of a query suggest themselves as default values. Time presents no real problems, except that sometimes the time zone on which a time is based becomes important, and sometimes it even matters whether switching to daylight saving time is being practiced. Place is different. A user may be interested in the temperature of a star several light-years away, of his or her office, or of the water in the local swimming pool. Hence the selection of a default value becomes problematic. For example, should the query "How far is X?" become "What is the distance between my exact location and the official center of X?" or "What is the distance between the official centers of my city and X?"

Surrogate answers. Instead of responding to a query with a null response, the system should endeavor to supply the user with a surrogate. Thus, if a query were to be put relating to the temperature of a place for which there are no climatic records, an answer should be generated that relates to the nearest place for which such records exist, where "nearest" refers not only to distance, but to other factors as well, such as a similar altitude. Suppose that the height of President Theodore Roosevelt had never been recorded. Then "How tall was Roosevelt?" cannot be answered, but it may be possible to determine from contemporary records whether Theodore Roosevelt was regarded as tall in his own time. At this point the query becomes a question under our interpretation.

Reference context. Definition of a reference context is perhaps the most difficult of the tasks we are discussing. Obviously the system cannot select the reference context on its own, even when provided with profiles of user interests. So it provides a set of options from which the user is to choose. But this set of options will depend on a highly specific domain, which will vary from query to query even when the queries are formally similar, such as "Was Roosevelt tall?" or "Are pines tall?" or "Was the Roosevelt tall?" or "Was Eleanor Roosevelt tall?" or "Are Swedes tall?" or "Were Vikings tall?" As another example, take the query "Is it far from Pittsburgh to Cleveland?" The obvious response is to give the distance in some appropriate units, but here the reference context could tell how long it would take to cover this distance by car or by plane, including expected delays due to, for example, road repairs or heavy snow. The essential context of time and place provides search keys for accessing such data.

Source context. Indication of the source of an item of information is straightforward by itself, but the assignment of a measure of trustworthiness to the information is not so simple. To begin with, a distinction has to be made between imprecision and uncertainty. If a system responds with an answer "Smith owes Brown USD 500," then under uncertainty we are not sure that Smith owes Brown anything, and under imprecision we know that something is being owed, but are not sure that the amount owed is USD 500.

Presentation of results. As noted above, this relates to appropriateness of the entity selected in response to the query, to granularity, and to the unit of measurement. Thus, in selecting a temperature for a given date, it has to be decided whether it should be the lowest, the highest, or the average temperature for that date. It seems appropriate to respond to a query that refers to coldness with a minimum temperature, to one that refers to warmth with an average, and to one that refers to hotness with a maximum. The query "What was the lowest temperature on May 15?" seems to ask for the lowest temperature on the nearest May 15 in the past, but the query "What is the lowest temperature for May 15?" for the lowest temperature on record for that date. Further, if we are dealing with temperatures close to absolute zero, the granularity would be very fine, and the temperature expressed in Kelvin. On the other hand, the granularity for solar temperatures would be quite coarse, with Centigrade the appropriate scale. On the short-tall scale the appropriate response to "Are pines tall?" is the height of the tallest known pine, but this is probably also the most appropriate answer to "Are pines short?" Finally, when the information used to answer a query can come from anywhere in the world, care has to be exercised with unit conversions. For example, if the flood damage in some German town is estimated at DEM 5,000,000, it would be wrong to show it as USD 2,450,980.

Explanation component. Whenever the system makes a decision, the reasons for making the decision are to be preserved. The trace of how the final response was arrived at is to be presented on demand. It serves as a check that the query has been interpreted to the satisfaction of the user. If this is not so, it should be possible to backtrack along this trace and force a decision to go some other way. A special case arises when data relevant to the response to the query are found to be inconsistent. An attempt can then be made to construct several responses. The responses may turn out to be identical, which happens when the inconsistencies turn out to be irrelevant as far as this query is concerned. If not, we should deal with this as a Who situation. If the sources of the data are known, and their dependability can be estimated, then the system can supply several ranked responses. It is then very important to provide an explanation of how the different responses and their ranking were arrived at.

6 Related Work

The determination of a response to a query under our model has two phases. The query is to be interpreted, and then a response is to be created. The interpretation of a query belongs to natural language processing, which has not been our concern here. In the creation of the response three main concerns arise: inconsistencies in the data base are to be allowed for, a null answer to a query should be avoided, and a context is to be established. Inconsistencies have been considered from two points of view. They can arise in the requirements for a software system, or they can be found in data. We regard the two cases as essentially the same because, in a system that is to support software development, requirements are part of the process data of this system, and such a system can be queried no differently from other specialized information systems. Surveys of how to deal with imperfect information are provided by Klir [5] and by Parsons [6]. Specifically, inconsistencies in software requirements are treated by Balzer [7], Finkelstein et al. [8], Liu and Yen [9], and Burg and van de Riet [10].

An extensive discussion of the null problem (with 68 references) is to be found in [11]. The null-value problem can be treated in two ways. One is to introduce appropriate markers into empty slots in a relational data base. Thus, Liu and Sunderraman [12, 13] extend the relational data model by means of what they call an I-table, which allows indefinite or maybe responses to be provided. Possible values in place of null values are introduced by Kong and Chen [14]. The other approach is to use similarity for arriving at a non-null response [15]. Motro's FLEX system [16] suggests related queries when no answer can be given to the original query.

Related queries bring us very close to the approach we have been taking here. Work on intensionality [17, 18] is even closer. An extensional answer is a set of values, an intensional answer is a condition that defines these values. Intensional answers can be used to reformulate queries to make them correspond better to users' needs. Approximate reasoning [19] and qualitative reasoning [20] are closely related to this work. So is fuzzy reasoning. Klir and Yuan [21] present an excellent introduction to fuzziness — Chapter 14 of their book addresses specifically fuzzy data bases and information retrieval systems. Fuzzy queries to a relational data base are considered in [22].

Query answering by knowledge discovery techniques [23] takes us close to queries in context. For our preliminary investigation of queries in context see [24]. We have also designed an iconic system for constructing a response to a query [25]. Such a system can in principle generate an SQL query in parallel with the construction of the response, and the SQL query can then be modified by the user.

7 Conclusions

We have outlined a research program for the development of a query system that assists the user in developing a meaningful query. For this we suggest that the original query be reformulated by the system into one or more Wh-queries. Moreover, the system should supply the user with reference points that put the answer to a query in a proper context.

Domain models are to assist in the interpretation of vague queries, in guiding a user in the formulation of precise queries, and in defining the context for an answer. For this purpose a suitable domain model is an appropriately partitioned concept space. Two sections of this space are particularly important. They relate to time and location. Others relate to concepts such as heights, temperatures, stock market data, distances, and flight times. The concept space and the procedures for accessing it constitute a highly complex knowledge system for the processing of queries. Such a system does not yet exist, and its development will be an immense undertaking. Our purpose has been to indicate the problems that have to be solved as part of this undertaking.

We have discussed the problems under the headings of query interpretation, domain selection, essential context, surrogate answers, reference context, source context, presentation of results, and explanation. On the surface the problems do not appear difficult, but most of them ultimately reduce to the interpretation of natural language expressions, and this is where the difficulties start. For work with natural language there are no general solutions, but each case has to be analyzed on its own. By means of a few examples we have demonstrated what such analysis entails. The examples show that the development of the query system we are envisaging will require close cooperation of software engineers, domain experts, and computational linguists.

Of immediate interest is the setting up of a priority scheme. This would indicate the order in which the research tasks should be undertaken so as to allow the system to be developed incrementally. As the system becomes more complete, it will become increasingly helpful to a user, but some degree of usefulness is to be there from the very start.

Acknowledgement. This work was performed while the author was on sabbatical leave in Kaiserslautern. Support was provided by the Fraunhofer-Gesellschaft (Einrichtung Experimentelles Software-Engineering) and the University of Kaiserslautern (Sonderforschungsbereich 501). The support is gratefully acknowledged.

References

1. Cohen, P., Schrag, R., Jones, E., Pease, A., Lin, A., Starr, B., Gunning, D., and Burke, M., The DARPA High Performance Knowledge Bases project. *AI Magazine* 18:4 (Fall 1998), 25-49.
2. Wartik, S. and Prieto-Diaz, R., Criteria for comparing reuse-oriented domain analysis approaches. *International Journal of Software Engineering and Knowledge Engineering* 2 (1992), 403-431.
3. Rolling, W.A., A preliminary annotated bibliography on domain engineering. *ACM SIGSOFT Software Engineering Notes* 19:3 (1994), 82-84.
4. Glass, R.L. and Vessey, I., Contemporary application-domain taxonomies. *IEEE Software* 12:4 (1995), 63-76.
5. Klir, G.J., Developments in uncertainty-based information. *Advances in Computers* 36 (1993), 255-332.
6. Parsons, S., Current approaches to handling imperfect information in data and knowledge bases. *IEEE Transactions on Knowledge and Data Engineering* 8 (1996), 353-372.
7. Balzer, R., Tolerating inconsistency. In *Proceedings of the 13th International Conference on Software Engineering*, 158-165. IEEE CS Press, 1991.
8. Finkelstein, A.C.W., Gabbay, D., Hunter, A., Kramer, J. and Nuseibeh, B., Inconsistency handling in multiperspective requirements. *IEEE Transactions on Software Engineering* 20 (1994), 569-578.
9. Liu, X.F. and Yen, J., An analytic framework for specifying and analyzing imprecise requirements. In *Proceedings of the 18th International Conference on Software Engineering*, 60-69. IEEE CS Press, 1996.
10. Burg, J.F.M. and van de Riet, R.P., Analyzing informal requirements specifications: a first step towards conceptual modeling. In *Applications of Natural Language to Information Systems*, 15-27. IOS Press, 1996.
11. Kao, M., Cercone, N., and Luk, W.-S., Providing quality responses with natural language interfaces: the null value problem. *IEEE Transactions on Software Engineering* 14 (1988), 959-984.
12. Liu, K.-C. and Sunderraman, R., On representing indefinite and maybe information in relational databases. In *Proceedings of the Fourth International Conference on Data Engineering*. IEEE CS Press, 1988.
13. Liu, K.-C. and Sunderraman, R., Indefinite and maybe information in relational databases. *ACM Transactions on Database Systems* 15 (1990), 1-39.
14. Kong, Q. and Chen, G., On deductive databases with incomplete information. *ACM Transactions on Information Systems* 13 (1995), 354-369.
15. Ichikawa, T. and Hirakawa, M., ARES: a relational database with the capability of performing flexible interpretation of queries. *IEEE Transactions on Software Engineering* SE-12 (1986), 624-634.
16. Motro, A., FLEX: a tolerant and cooperative user interface to databases. *IEEE Transactions on Knowledge and Data Engineering* 2 (1990), 231-246.

17. Pirotte, A., Roelants, D., and Zimanyi, E., Controlled generation of intensional queries. *IEEE Transactions on Knowledge and Data Engineering* 3 (1991), 221-236.
18. Motro, A., Intensional answers to database queries. *IEEE Transactions on Knowledge and Data Engineering* 6 (1994), 444-454.
19. Yager, R.R., Using approximate reasoning to represent default knowledge. *Artificial Intelligence* 31 (1987), 99-112.
20. Kalagnanam, J., Simon, H.A., and Iwasaki, Y., The mathematical bases for qualitative reasoning. *IEEE Expert* 6:2 (1991), 11-19.
21. Klir, G.J. and Yuan, B., *Fuzzy Sets and Fuzzy Logic: Theory and Applications.* Prentice Hall, 1995.
22. Bosc, P. and Pivert, O., SQLf: a relational database language for fuzzy querying. *IEEE Transactions on Fuzzy Systems* 3 (1995), 1-17.
23. Han, J., Huang, Y., Cercone, N., and Fu, Y., Intelligent query answering by knowledge discovery techniques. *IEEE Transactions on Knowledge and Data Engineering* 8 (1996), 373-390.
24. Berztiss, A.T., Imprecise queries and the quality of conceptual models. In *Information Modelling and Knowledge Bases V*, 174-185. IOS Press, 1994.
25. Berztiss, A.T., The query language Vizla. *IEEE Transactions on Knowledge and Data Engineering* 5 (1993) 813-825.

Using Information Extraction and Natural Language Generation to Answer E-Mail

Leila Kosseim, Stéphane Beauregard, and Guy Lapalme

RALI, DIRO, Université de Montréal
CP 6128, Succ. Centre Ville, Montréal (Québec) Canada, H3C 3J7
{kosseim, beaurs, lapalme}@iro.umontreal.ca

Abstract. This paper discusses the use of information extraction and natural language generation in the design of an automated e-mail answering system. We analyse short free-form texts and generating a customised and linguistically-motivated answer to frequently asked questions. We describe the approach and the design of a system currently being developed to answer e-mail in French regarding printer-related questions addressed to the technical support staff of our computer science department.

1 Introduction

The number of free-form electronic documents available and needing to be processed has reached a level that makes the automatic manipulation of natural language a necessity. Manual manipulation is both time-consuming and expensive, making NLP techniques very attractive. E-mail messages make up a large portion of the free-form documents that are currently treated manually. As e-mail becomes more and more popular, an automated e-mail answering service will become as necessary as an automated telephone service is today.

This paper discusses the use of information extraction and natural language generation to answer e-mail automatically. We describe the design of a system currently being developed to answer e-mail in French regarding printer-related questions addressed to the technical support staff of our computer science department. The original project was prompted by a local corporation for its customer service needs, but because of difficulties in gathering a corpus of e-mail messages from their archives, local e-mails from our department were used to develop the technology.

Unlike typical question answering systems (e.g. [20]) our focus is on *analysing* short, free-form texts and *generating* a customised and linguistically-motivated answer to frequently asked questions. In our view, two main approaches are available to answer e-mail: information retrieval or information extraction. With the information retrieval approach, the incoming message is considered as a query to be matched against some textual knowledge base (e.g. a FAQ). E-mail answering thus becomes a question of finding passages from the textual knowledge base that best relate to the incoming message and sending the passages as is to the user. Although this approach has the major advantage of being domain

M. Bouzeghoub et al. (Eds.): NLDB 2000, LNCS 1959, pp. 152–163, 2001.

independent[1], it does not provide a natural and customised answer. It provides an ergonomically awkward interaction with e-mail users, and it supposes that the e-mail message is short enough so that the process can be computationally efficient. In order to provide a specific response to the user query, we believe that key information from the content of the e-mail must be identified and used to customise the answer. For this reason, whenever the specific discourse domain of the question is known (e.g. through classification), information extraction seems in our view more adequate for analysing the incoming e-mail and template-based natural language generation appropriate to produce a natural answer from pre-written response templates.

2 The Corpus

The system we are developing is aimed at answering printer-related user e-mail received by the technical support staff of our department, where communications are done in French. We have concentrated our efforts on a specific discourse domain in order to obtain good results in information extraction and to be able to manage knowledge representation. The entire corpus covered a 3 year period and is composed of 188 e-mails. The corpus was split into two sets: the first 2 years for analysis and the last year for testing. From the original corpus, we kept only the messages that discussed only one topic and were self-contained, i.e. that do not need information external to the message to be understood. We therefore removed replies (i.e. messages that answer a previous question from technical support), signatures and e-mail headings (except the `from` and `subject` fields). The final analysis corpus contains 126 messages with an average of 47 words per message. This average is smaller than the Reuter-21578 text categorisation test collection [2] (129 words), but larger than the typical questions of the QA track of TREC-8 (9 words[3]) [20]. The messages from the analysis corpus fall into 3 major query types:

- problem reports (67%): For example, reports that a printer is out of paper, a user can't print a particular file, the printer is unreachable, ...
- how-to questions (19%): For example, questions about how to print on both sides of the paper, how to kill a job, ...
- general information (13%): For example, questions regarding properties of the printers (name, location, resolution, ...)

Figure 1 shows a example of a simple e-mail and its English translation (for illustration purposes). Note that for confidentiality reasons, names of persons have been changed.

---

[1] Provided a textual knowledge base exists

[2] www.research.att.com/~lewis

[3] average of the NIST 38 development questions (www.research.att.com/~singhal/qa-dev-set)

From: David Smith <smith@iro.umontreal.ca>
Subject:
Bonjour,
J'aimerais savoir comment je peux imprimer seulement sur un côté de la page sur l'imprimante hp2248. *[I would like to know how I can print only on one side of the page on the hp2248 printer.]*
Merci.
David

Fig. 1. Example of a how-to question from our corpus and its English translation

3 General Architecture

The typical task of answering e-mail can be decomposed into 3 steps [4]: recognising the problem(s) (reading and understanding the e-mail); searching for a solution (identifying predefined text blocks) and providing a solution (customising the text blocks and sending the text). Our interest lies in the first and last steps: understanding the text and formulating the response.

The general architecture of the system is shown in Figure 2. As a printer-related message arrives, information extraction tries to fill pre-defined extraction templates that are then passed to a knowledge-intensive, domain-dependent process that checks the validity of the extracted information. Valid templates are further filled by inferring new information from the extraction templates and a domain knowledge base. Depending on the template content, a set of answer templates is selected, filled and organised by a natural language generation module. The emphasis of the work is on the information extraction and the natural language generation modules (modules in bold in Figure 2).

When responding to an e-mail, four situations can occur:

Answer found: The extraction templates contain correct information and the decision process can find a suitable answer template. In this case, the extraction and the answer templates are passed to the generation module.

Human referral: The extraction templates contain correct information but the decision process cannot find a suitable answer. In this case, a *Human referral* message is produced.[4]

Incorrect information: The extraction templates contain incorrect or incoherent information. This situation can arise from a legitimate error made by the sender in the message, or from an error in the extraction module. Because the source cannot be determined, in both cases a generic *Incorrect information* message is generated.

Incomplete information: The extraction templates do not contain enough material to select an answer template. This can occur if the message did not

[4] Our interest lies in answering the e-mail and not in actually routing it to a clerk or department. A technique based on text classification or case-based reasoning may be used to select the most appropriate clerk to route the e-mail to.

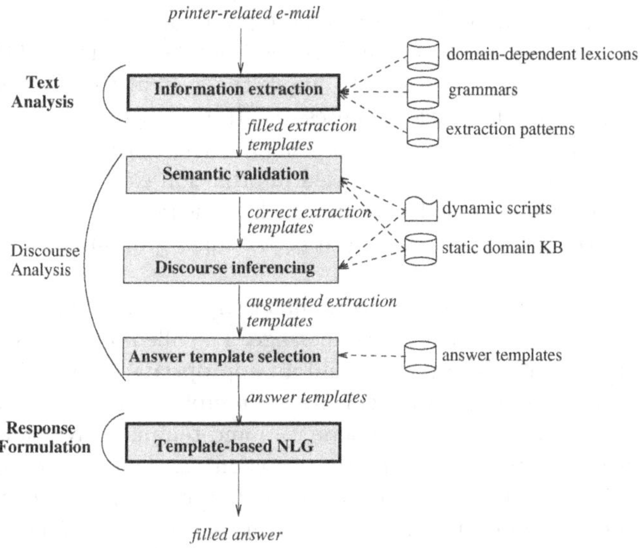

Fig. 2. Architecture of the system

contain the necessary information, or if the extraction module did not find it. In this case, a message of the type *Missing information* is generated. Note that no conversation management is performed to wait for and recover the missing information in subsequent messages.

3.1 Text Analysis

The task of an Information Extraction (IE) system is to identify specific information from a natural language text in a specific discourse domain and to represent it in a structured template format. For example, from a car accident report, an IE system will be able to identify the date and location of the accident, and the names and status of the victims. The filled templates can then be stored in a database for later retrieval or serve as a basis for the automatic generation of summaries.

IE from formal texts usually follows one of two approaches: a linguistic surface approach or a statistical approach. The linguistic approach is based on a lexico-syntactic description of the phrases to be located [1, 2, 12]. With this approach, the text is tokenised, each token is tagged with its most likely grammatical category, and syntactic chunking is performed to group together noun and verb phrases. Next, lexico-syntactic extraction patterns and large dictionaries of trigger phrases (*M.*, *inc.*, ...), of known proper names and of general language are used to identify and semantically tag key phrases. Discourse rules are then applied to relate this key information and to infer new ones. To account for noise in certain kinds of texts, IE is often performed by statistical methods which uses a language model trained on large pre-tagged corpora [11, 17]. Studies have shown that the probabilistic methods yield good results if large corpora are available for training. However, to apply the system to different discourse domains, retraining of the model is necessary. In contrast, linguistic rule-based systems can be tuned more easily from a small corpus. Because our corpus was so small and we already had a rule-based information extraction prototype for French [13], we followed a rule-based approach. As is typically done, we tokenise and lemmatise the texts and make use of lexicons, grammars and extraction patterns.

In our project, the IE module tries to fill a template relation and a set of template elements for each printer-related message. The filled templates will be used to diagnose the printer question and find an appropriate answer. Following the MUC terminology [18], template elements are templates describing named entities (e.g. templates for persons, artifacts, ...) and templates relations represent relations between template elements (e.g. `person1` *is the owner of* `artifact1`). While the design and extraction of some fields are domain independent (e.g. person templates, location templates) and can use publicly available resources, others are domain-dependent (e.g. printer or file templates) for which specific grammars and lexicons must be built. In our discourse domain, the system tries to fill templates for computer users, printers, files, machines and actions performed. These templates are shown in Figure 3. Each field value can either be a free-form string extracted from the document (e.g. `David Smith`), a value from a closed set of possible answers (e.g. a printer name) or a pointer to another template. Template entities are filled through three techniques:

Lexicons: This includes lists of known users, laboratories, software and printer names built from the technical support databases.

Grammars of named entities: This includes such things as regular expressions for recognising file names from unknown words.

Lexico-syntactic extraction patterns: This includes patterns for recognising named entities from their neighboring words. For example, the pattern `printer::name`[5] `in room X` allows us to infer that X is the room number of `printer::name` although it may not follow the grammar of room numbers. Such patterns allows us to be somewhat flexible and recognise named entities that are not well formed.

Because our e-mails are factual and short and because the discourse domain is very specific, template relation extraction can be kept simple. As Figure 3 shows, in most cases, the template elements can only have one relation with other templates. For example, any printer template is assumed to be the job destination (where the user wants to print) and machine templates are always assumed to be the job source (the machine from where the printing job is sent). In the cases of file and user templates, two relations are possible; in these cases, lexico-syntactic patterns are used to disambiguate between relations. For example, if a template entity for files is filled then it can be a `file_to_print` or a `file_printing`. To

[5] The notation `X::Y` refers to field `Y` of template `X`.

identify the correct relation, patterns such as `I wish to print file::name` or `file::name is blocking the queue` are used. Template relations are identifiable this way because the discourse domain is very specific, and the texts are factual and short.

print event template		
Field	*Value*	*Validation*
sender	user template	no
destination	printer template	no
source	machine template	no
file_to_print	file template	no
action_tried	action template	no

user template		
Field	*Value*	*Validation*
name	string	no
e-mail address	set	yes
laboratory	set	yes

file template		
Field	*Value*	*Validation*
name	string	yes
current_format	set	yes
desired_format	set	yes
current_page_size	set	yes
desired_page_size	set	yes
generated_how	set	yes
owner	user template	no
job number	string	no

printer template		
Field	*Value*	*Validation*
name	set	yes
room	set	yes
status	set	yes
file_printing	file template	yes

machine template		
Field	*Value*	*Validation*
name	set	yes
OS	set	yes
laboratory	set	yes

action template		
Field	*Value*	*Validation*
comand_tried	string	yes
error_message	string	yes

Fig. 3. Extraction Template Relation and Template Entities to be filled

Template and field coreference allows us to merge several templates if they refer to the same real-world entity. Several manually coded and automatically learned techniques exist to perform coreference resolution (e.g. [5]). In our system, coreference resolution has not specifically been addressed. We use the strategies of our existing IE system, EXIBUM [13], which merges entities only on the basis of head noun equality. This strategy allows us to determine that the names `David Smith` and `David` refer to the same person and that `smith@iro.umontreal.ca` is the e-mail address of this same person. However, this technique cannot determine that `JD` in the signature of the second message of Figure 1 refers to `John Doe`. Figure 4 shows the templates filled by the IE module for the how-to question of Figure 1.

3.2 Discourse Analysis

Semantic Validation and Discourse Inferencing Once the templates are filled, the field values are validated. This process serves two purposes: making

print event 1	
sender	user1 template
destination	printer1 template
source	
file_to_print	file1 template
action_tried	

printer1 template	
name	hp2248
room	
status	
file_printing	

file1 template	
name	
current_format	
desired_format	single_sided
current_page_size	
desired_page_size	
generated_how	
owner	
job number	

user1 template	
name	David Smith
e-mail address	smith@iro.umontreal.ca
laboratory	

Fig. 4. Extraction Templates after Information Extraction

sure the user communicated correct information, so that a correct answer can be formulated, and more importantly, making sure the information extraction performed a correct analysis of the text. Extraction templates contain two types of field values: those used to select an answer template, and those that do not influence the choice of answer templates but rather are used to customise the answer. The latter fields are not verified, while the former are checked for correctness. Semantic validation is performed through two strategies:

1. Matching filled fields against one another and against a static knowledge base to verify their coherence. For example, if the IE module extracted within the same printer template the fields `printer1::name = hp2248` and `printer1::room = X-234`, but the database does not contain the pair `(name= hp2248, room= X-234)`, then an incoherence is detected.
2. Running dynamic scripts associated to specific template fields. For example, if the IE module extracted within the same printer template the fields `printer1::name = hp2248` and `printer1::file_printing::name= test.txt`, but the script associated with printer names to find the name of the currently printing file (namely, `lpq -P printer::name`) has determined that printer hp2248 is currently printing another file, then an incoherence is detected.

Incorrect templates are flagged and are sent directly to the answer template selection, that will select an *Incorrect information* type of answer. On the other hand, correct templates are further filled by discourse analysis.

The role of discourse analysis is to infer information or relations that is not explicitly stated in the text, but that are known from the discourse itself or the domain. Discourse analysis tries to further fill extraction templates and create new ones. This analysis is performed also by the use of a static and a dynamic knowledge bases, and by the use of default values for empty fields. For example, the fact that `David Smith` is a member of the `artificial intelligence` laboratory can be determined by matching the e-mail address `smith@iro.umontreal.ca` to the static knowledge base; while a dynamic script can determined that printer `hp2248` is currently printing the file `test.txt`, thus creating a new `file` template.

Answer Template Selection Selecting the generic content of the response is done using a decision tree developed specifically for this discourse domain. Conditions of the decision tree relate to field values of the extraction templates, while the leaves of the decision tree are answer templates (see Figure 5). Answer templates can contain canned answers to be used as is, but can also contain command names, options and syntax, special considerations and a location where to find more information, for which the formulation can vary.

For example, a value for the field `file_to_print::desired_format` indicates that the topic of the e-mail is to print a file in a particular format and the corresponding decision tree is traversed. If the extraction templates do not contain enough information to reach an answer template (a leaf), then an *Incomplete information* answer template is selected. If no answer template can be reached because of unpredicted information in the extraction templates, a *Human referral* (no answer found) is selected. Finally, if an answer template is reached, it will be customised by the template-based Natural Language Generation (NLG) module.

canned answer:	∅
command:	lpr
option:	-i-1
syntax:	lpr -P destination::name -i-1 file_to_print::name
special considerations:	*Note that this printing mode should only be used for the final copy of a document.*
more info:	www.theURL/lpr#recto

Fig. 5. Example of an answer template

3.3 Response Formulation

Once an answer template is selected, it must be filled and organised into a cohesive answer. To produce a response, pre-defined rhetorical schemas are followed. Regardless of which situation we are dealing with, the response will contain welcome greetings, a message body (Incorrect info or Missing info or Human referral or a Customised response), closing greetings and a signature. A repertoire of canned answers is available to produce each part of the response. Some canned answers are fully lexicalised, while others contain slots to be filled by information contained in the extraction templates or the answer templates. For example, welcome greetings can simply be `Hello` or `Dear sender::name`. If the extraction templates contain the name of the sender, `Dear sender::name` will be preferred over `Hello`. If several equivalent variants of the same part of the answer have been specified, such as `Dear sender::name` and `Hi sender::name`, one of the variants is randomly selected by the system.

The process of deriving the surface form from the answer template is carried out in two steps. A Prolog definite clause grammar (DCG), specifying the rhetorical schema, the canned text and parameterized slots, and various helper predicates and rules, is used to generate the text level of abstraction [10], that is the full sequence of words and phrases in the response. The final orthographic form is then generated from this sequence of words. Issues such as elision, contraction, punctuation, capitalisation and formatting are handled in this step by the motor realisation module of the SPIN generation system [14].

The customised response is built from the filled answer template selected by the decision tree. "Special considerations" and "Location for more information" are optional parts of the response schemas and will be filled depending on the level of detail desired in the responses. The output for the how-to question of Figure 1 is shown in Figure 6 along with an English translation.

Bonjour David,
Pour imprimer en recto seulement sur la hp2248, il faut utiliser la commande lpr avec l'option -i-1. Faire: lpr -P hp2248 -i-1 <nom du fichier>
Notez que ce mode d'impression ne doit être utilisé que pour la copie finale d'un document.
Pour plus d'info, consutez l'URL: www.theURL/lpr#recto
[To print on only one side of the paper on the hp2248, you must use the command lpr with the option -i-1. Type: lpr -P hp2248 -i-1 <file name>
Note that this printing mode should only be used for the final copy of a document.
For more info, consult the URL: www.theURL/lpr#recto]
Bonne chance,
Support technique

Fig. 6. Generated answer for the how-to question of Figure 1

4 Related Work

Related work on e-mail answering include commercial e-mail answering systems, question answering and e-mail classification.

The simplest level of e-mail answering systems is the so-called *autoresponder*[6]. These systems return a canned document in response to an e-mail according to the presence of keywords in the subject or body of the message. A variant of autoresponders can customise the returned document, if the user filled in a

[6] also known as *AR*, *infobots*, *mailbots* or *e-mail-on-demand*

predefined Web form. An obvious drawback of these systems is that they do not analyse the content of a free-form message. A more sophisticated type of e-mail responder are included in e-mail management systems, and can provide pre-written response templates for frequently asked questions. Slots are usually filled in with information extracted manually from the incoming mail, but some systems seem to perform the extraction automatically [3, 16].

Question answering (QA) tries to find an answer to a natural language question [20] form a large set of documents. The question type is determined by the presence of trigger phrases (e.g. *where, how many, how much, ...*), which indicates the type of the answer required (*location, number, money, ...*). Information retrieval is typically performed to identify a subset of the documents and a set of passages that may contain the answer, named entities are then extracted from these passages and semantically tagged and the string containing the best scoring entity is retained as the answer. QA differs from e-mail answering in several aspects. Generally speaking, e-mail answering is interested in *analysing* a longer text and *formulating* a linguistically-motivated answer, while QA takes a short and explicit question as input and focuses on *locating* the answer. Issues in discourse analysis must therefore be addressed in e-mail answering, but not in QA. In addition, questions in QA are, for the moment, restricted to specific types: *who, why, where, ...* but pertain to an unrestricted discourse domain. On the other hand, in e-mail answering, the questions are of unrestricted type, but the discourse domain is typically restricted.

E-mail classification is another domain related to our work that has been addressed by many research projects. This has been approached both from an automatic learning perspective (e.g. [4, 9]) and from an IE perspective (e.g. [6]). Our work complements those in text classification as it supposes that the incoming e-mail messages have already been classified as printer-related questions. E-mail classification can therefore be seen as a pre-processing module to our system.

On the NLG side, Coch developped a system to generate automatic answers to complaint letters from clients of LaRedoute (a large French mail-order corporation) [7, 8]. As letters are not in electronic format, the reading and extraction is done by humans, but the decision and the production of the response is done automatically. Through a formal blind evaluation, Coch has demonstrated that the best responses (according to specific criteria) are still the human-generated ones, but that the use of a hybrid template-based NLG system produced acceptable responses at a much faster rate.

5 Discussion and Further Research

In this paper, we have described the design of an e-mail answering system we are currently developing. The system relies on information extraction to *analyse* the user message, a decision tree to determine the content of the answer, and template-based natural language generation to produce the surface form of the answer in a customised and cohesive way. Because the discourse domain is specific and high precision scores are desired, a knowledge-intensive approach is used. In order to scale up the approach to larger domains, we believe that new domain-dependent knowledge-bases, extraction rules and answer templates should be developped and that text-classification should be performed prior to IE in order to select the appropriate knowledge bases to use. Although the design of a knowledge-intensive domain-dependent system offers poor adaptability to other discourse domains, it was viewed as a means to reach high precision scores in text analysis; something that is crucial in e-mail answering, as a wrong answer sent to a client can have far-reaching customer satisfaction consequences. We believe the incremental approach to be appropriate; i.e. testing the precision of the system on a small discourse domain, and incrementally enlarging the discourse domain.

As the system is under development, no formal evaluation has yet been performed. As far as further research is concerned, our priority is therefore finishing the implementation of the prototype so that a formal evaluation can be performed. We plan to evaluate the system using 3 measures: a measure of the IE module, a measure of the NLG module and a global measure combining the two. Measuring the IE will be done using the MUC evaluation protocol [19] on the test corpus. Measuring the NLG module will be done through to a blind evaluation protocol similar to [7].

So far, we have not taken into account how textual noise from the e-mail affects the textual analysis. E-mail messages are informal electronic texts that do not follow strict writing guidelines. Textual noise can come from typography (e.g. lack of diacritics and capitalisation), terminology (e.g. informal abbreviations), orthography and grammatical irregularities. Our approach is based on the MUC experiences that have mainly been concerned with homogeneous corpora that follow writing guidelines. The rule-based key-word approach may need to be adapted to account for textual noise.

For the moment, the NLG system fills answer slots directly, without much linguistic knowledge. We plan to increase the cohesiveness and naturality of the responses by using referring expressions whenever possible. The work of Kosseim et al. [15], for example, provides linguistically-motivated guidelines for the generation of such expressions in French.

Acknowledgements

We are grateful to our colleagues from RALI and to the anonymous referees for their relevant comments. This work was supported by a grant from the Laboratoire Universitaire Bell (LUB).

References

[1] J. Aberdeen, J. Burger, D. Day, L. Hirschman, P. Robinson, and M. Vilain. MITRE: Description of the Alembic System as Used for MUC-6. In MUC-6 [19].

[2] D. Appelt, J. Hobbs, J. Bear, D. Israel, M. Kameyama, and M. Tyson. SRI: Description of the JV-FASTUS System Used for MUC-5. In MUC-5 [18].

[3] www.brightware.com. Site visited in December, 2000.

[4] S. Busemann, S. Schmeier, and R. Arens. Message Classification in the Call Center. In *Proceedings of ANLP-2000*, pages 159–165, Seattle, 2000.

[5] C. Cardie and K. Wagstaff. Noun Phrase Coreference as Clustering. In *Proceedings of the Joint Conference on Empirical Methods in Natural Language Processing and Very Large Corpora*, pages 82–89, 1999.

[6] F. Ciravegna, A. Lavelli, N. Mana, J. Matiasek, L. Gilardoni, S. Mazza, M. Ferraro, W. Black, F. Rinaldi, and D. Mowatt. Facile: classifying texts integrating pattern matching and information extraction. In *Proceeding of IJCAI-99*, pages 890–895, Stockholm, Sweden, 1999.

[7] J. Coch. Evaluating and comparing three text-production techniques. In *Proceedings of COLING-96*, Copenhagen, Dannemark, 1996.

[8] J. Coch and J. Magnoler. Quality tests for a mail generation system. In *Proceedings of Linguistic Engineering*, Montpellier, France, 1995.

[9] W. Cohen. Learning rules that classify e-mail. In *Proceeding of the 1996 AAAI Spring Symposium on Machine Learning in Information Access*, 1996.

[10] R. Dale and E. Reiter. *Building Natural Language Generation Systems.* Studies in Natural Language Processing. Cambridge University Press, 2000.

[11] L. Dekan. Using Collocation Statistics in Information Extraction.

[12] R. Grishman. Where's the Syntax? The NYU MUC-6 System. In MUC-6 [19].

[13] L. Kosseim and G. Lapalme. Exibum: Un système expérimental d'extraction d'information bilingue. In *Rencontre Internationale sur l'extraction, le filtrage et le résumé automatique (RIFRA-98)*, pages 129–140, Sfax, Tunisia, November 1998.

[14] L. Kosseim and G. Lapalme. Choosing Rhetorical Structures to Plan Instructional Texts. *Computational Intelligence: An International Journal*, 16(3):408–445, August 2000.

[15] L. Kosseim, A. Tutin, R. Kittredge, and G. Lapalme. Generating Grammatical and Lexical Anaphora in Assembly Instruction Texts. In G. Adorni and M. Zock, editors, *Trends in Natural Language Generation*, LNAI 1036, pages 260–275. Springer, Berlin, 1996.

[16] Y. Lallement and M. Fox. Interact: A Staged Approach to Customer Service Automation. In H. Hamilton and Q. Yang, editors, *Canadian AI 2000*, LNAI 1822, pages 164–175, Berlin, 2000. Springler-Verlag.

[17] D. Miller, R. Schwartz, R. Weischedel, and R. Stone. Named Entity Extraction from Broadcast News. In *Proceedings of the DARPA Broadcast News Workshop*, Herndon, Virginia, 1999.

[18] *Proceedings of the Fifth Message Understanding Conference (MUC-5)*, Baltimore, Maryland, August 1993. Morgan Kaufmann.

[19] *Proceedings of the Sixth Message Understanding Conference (MUC-6)*, Columbia, Maryland, November 1995. Morgan Kaufmann.

[20] *Proceedings of the Text Eighth REtrieval Conference (TREC-8)*, Gaithersburg, Maryland, November 1999.

Using OLAP and Data Mining for Content Planning in Natural Language Generation

Eloi L. Favero[1] and Jacques Robin[2]

[1] Departamento de Inform· tica Universidade Federal do Par· (DI-UFPA)
Par· , Brazil
ellf@cin.ufpe.br
[2] Centro de Inform· tica Universidade Federal de Pernambuco (CIn-UFPE)
Recife, Brazil
jr@cin.ufpe.br

Abstract. We present a new approach to content determination and discourse organization in Natural Language Generation (NLG). This approach relies on two decision-support oriented database technologies, OLAP and data mining, and it can be used for any NLG application involving the textual summarization of quantitative data. It improves on previous approaches to content planning for NLG in quantitative domains by providing: (1) application domain independence, (2) efficient, variable granularity insight search in high dimensionality data spaces, (3) automatic discovery of surprising, counter-intuitive data, and (4) tailoring of output text organization towards different, declaratively specified, analytical perspectives on the input data.

1 Research Context: Natural Language Generation of Executive Summaries for Decision Support

In this paper, we present a new approach to content determination and discourse organization in natural language summarization of quantitative data. This approach has been developed for the HYSSOP[1] system, that generates hypertext briefs of OLAP[2] summaries and data mining discoveries. HYSSOP is the result reporting component of the *Intelligent Decision-Support System* (IDSS) MATRIKS[3]. MATRIKS aims to provide a comprehensive knowledge discovery environment through seamless integration of data warehousing, OLAP, data mining, expert system and *Natural Language Generation* (NLG) technologies.

The architecture of MATRIKS is given in Fig. 1. It advances the state of the art in integrated environments for *Knowledge Discovery in Databases* (KDD) in three ways. First, it introduces a *data warehouse hypercube exploration expert system* allowing automation and expertise legacy of dimensional data warehouse exploration strategies developed by human data analysts using OLAP queries and data mining tools. Second,

[1] HYpertext Summary System of On-line analytical Processing.
[2] On-Line Analytical Processing
[3] Multidimensional Analysis and Textual Reporting for Insight Knowledge Search.

M. Bouzeghoub et al. (Eds.): NLDB 2000, LNCS 1959, pp. 164-175, 2001.

it introduces an *hypertext executive summary generator* (HYSSOP) reporting data hypercube exploration insights in the most concise and familiar way: a few web pages of natural language. Finally, the use of a modern, open software architecture based on encapsulation of services inside reusable components communicating via API. In contrast, currently available KDD environments, even cutting-edge ones such as DBMiner [5] report discoveries only in the form of tables, charts and graphics. They also do not provide any support neither for automating data cube exploration nor for managing exploration heuristics and sessions. Finally, their architectures are monolithic and closed, with no API for external communication, which prevents both their customization and their integration inside larger decision-support and information systems.

The long-term goal of the MATRIKS project is to deliver the first IDSS usable *directly by decision makers* without constant mediation of human experts in data analysis and decision support information technology. Its development started with the implementation of HYSSOP in LIFE [1], a multi-paradigm language that extends Prolog with functional programming, arityless feature structure unification and hierarchical type constraint inheritance. It currently focuses on the implementation of a series of API to connect OLE DB for OLAP [19] compliant OLAP servers to LIFE and other logic programming languages in which the data cube exploration expert system will be implemented.

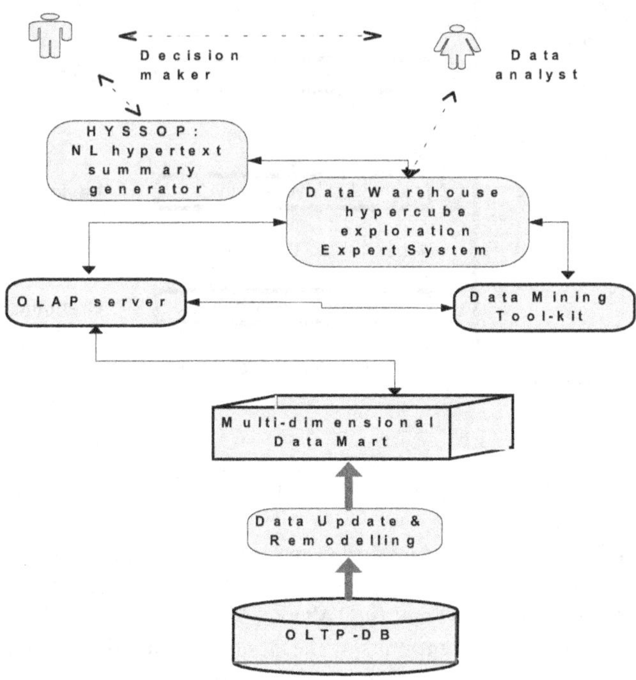

Fig. 1. The architecture of MATRIKS

2 Research Focus: Content Determination and Discourse-Level Organization in Quantitative Domains

The overall task of generating a natural language text can be conceptually decomposed in five subtasks: *content determination*, *discourse-level content organization*, *sentence-level content organization*, *lexical content realization*[4] and *syntactic content realization*. As shown in Fig.2, HYSSOP adopts the standard pipeline generation architecture [21] with one component encapsulating each of these subtasks.

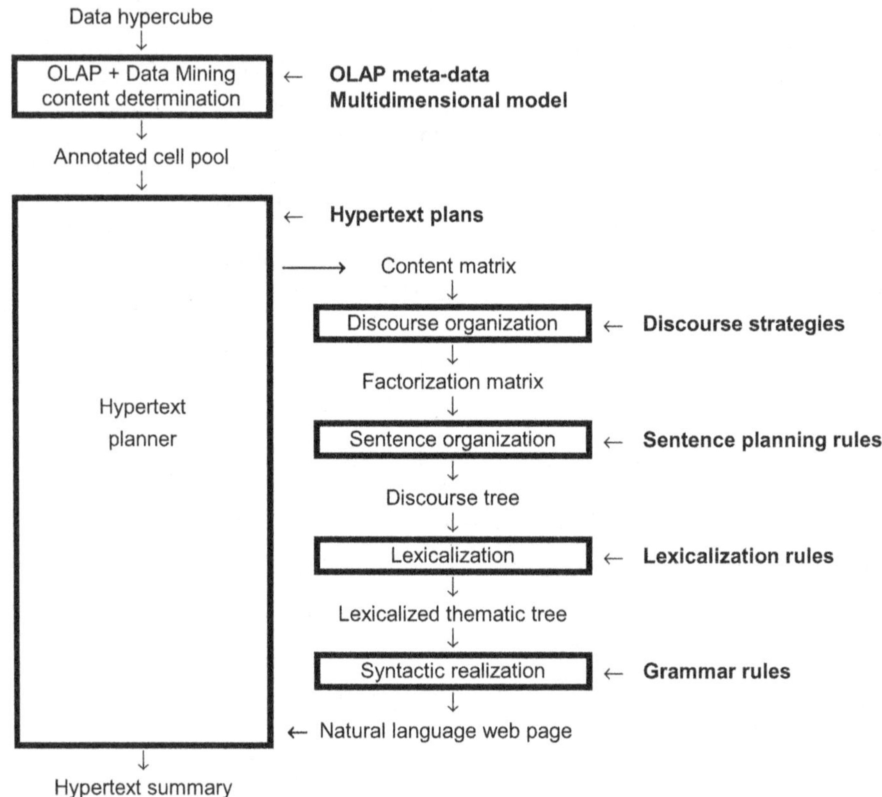

Fig. 2. HYSSOPís architecture

However, HYSSOPís architecture differs in several ways from those of previous NLG Quantitative Data Summarization Systems (QDSS), such as ANA [14], FOG [2], GOSSIP [3], PLANDoc [17] and FLOWDoc [20]. First, *content determination* relies on OLAP to aggregate content units at the desired granularity and on statistical data mining to identify intriguing aggregate values in the multidimensional analytical context provided by the OLAP hypercube. Second, a special, *hypertext planning* component partitions the selected content units among the various web pages of the output

[4] Also called lexicalization or lexical choice.

hypertext, recursively calls the four remaining components of the standard pipeline to generate each of these web pages, and picks the content units to serve as anchor links between these pages. Finally, *discourse organization* relies on OLAP dimension hierarchies, OLAP data visualization operators (rank, pivot, slice, dice) and OLAP aggregation operators (total, percent, count, max, min) to group and order content units in the generated output text, in a regular, domain-independent, principled way that reflects multidimensional data analysis practice.

This architecture in effect *pushes content determination and discourse organization into the database* and outside the NLG system *per se*. This simple move has far reaching effects on the portability of the generator: by implementing content planning using the generic, advanced functionalities of a multidimensional, inductive database, our approach achieves domain-independence for these two tasks that until now were always carried out in a highly domain-specific way. Previous NLG QDSS generally perform content determination by relying on a fixed set of *domain-dependent heuristic rules*. Aside from preventing code reuse across application domains, this approach suffers from two other severe limitations that prevent the generator to report the most interesting content from an underlying database:

- it does not scale up for analytical contexts with high dimensionality, multiple granularity and which take into account the historical evolution of data through time; such complex context would require a combinatorially explosive number of summary content determination heuristic rules;
- it can only select facts whose class have been thought ahead by the rule base author, while in most cases, it is its very unexpectedness that makes a fact interesting to report.

OLAP and data mining are the two technologies that emerged to tackle precisely these two issues: for OLAP efficient, variable granularity search in a high dimensionality, historical data space, and for data mining, automatic discovery, in such spaces, of hitherto unsuspected regularities or singularities. To our knowledge, the development of HYSSOP inside the MATRIKS architecture is pioneer work in coupling OLAP and data mining with NLG. We view such coupling as a synergetic fit with tremendous potential for a wide range of practical applications. Not only are OLAP and data mining the only technologies able to completely fulfill the content planning needs of NLG QDSS, but reciprocally, NLG is also the only technology able to completely fulfill the reporting needs of IDSS based on OLAP, data mining and KDD.

Natural language has several advantages over tables, charts and graphics to summarize insights discovered through OLAP and data mining in an IDSS. First, textual briefs remain the more familiar report format on which business executives base their decisions and they are more intuitive to mathematically naive end-users. Second, natural language can concisely and clearly convey analysis along arbitrary many dimensions. For example the fact expressed by the natural language clause: *"Cola promotional sales' 20% increase from July to August constituted a strong exception"* involves 8 dimensions: product, marketing, sales measure, aggregation operator, variation direction, time, space and exceptionality. In contrast, table and 3D color graphics loose intuitiveness and clarity beyond the fourth dimension. Third, natural language can convey a single striking fact in isolation from the context making it striking. Consider for example, *"Cola sales peaked at 40% in July"*. Using a chart, the values of cola sales *for all the other months* also need to be plotted in the report just to create the visual contrast that graphically conveys the notion of maximum value, even if these other month values are not interesting in their own right. Finally, natural language can freely mix quantitative content with qualitative, causal and subjective content that cannot be intuitively conveyed by graphics or tables.

For these reasons, as the first system to report OLAP and data mining discoveries in *natural language*, HYSSOP makes a significant contribution to IDSS research. It also makes several contributions to NLG research:

1. the first approach to *multiple page, hypertext planning* in the context of NLG starting from *raw data* and generating *summaries* as output (previous hypertext generator such as PEBA [18] and ILEX [13] start from a pre-linguistic knowledge representation and they generate as output didactic descriptions for which conciseness is not a primary concern).
2. a *new approach to sentence planning and content aggregation,* that allows factorizing content units inside complex, yet fluent and concise paratactic linguistic constituents and doing so in a domain-independent way;
3. a *new approach to syntactic realization*, that combines the advantages of both functional unification grammars [12][6] and definite clause grammars;
4. the already mentioned *new approach to content determination*, based on OLAP and data mining, that allows revealing more interesting content and doing so in a domain-independent way;
5. the already mentioned *new approach to linear discourse organization*, also based on OLAP and data mining concepts, that allows grouping and ordering content units following various domain-independent strategies for presenting aggregated quantitative data.

Hypertext output presents various advantages for QDSS. The first is that it allows avoiding the summarization dilemma: having to cut the same input content in a unique output summary, even though such output is geared towards readers whose particular interests are unknown, yet potentially diverse. An hypertext summary needs not cutting anything. It can simply convey the most generically crucial content in its front page, while leaving the more special interest details in the follow-up pages. If the anchor links are numerous and well planned, readers with different interests will follow different navigation patterns inside the unique hypertext summary, each one ending up accessing the same material than if reading a distinct, customized summary. The second advantage is to avoid the text vs. figure dilemma: tables, charts and graphics can be anchored as leaves of the hierarchical hypertext structure. This hierarchical structure makes hypertext output especially adequate for OLAP-based QDSS: it allows organizing the natural language summary report by following the drill-down hierarchies built in the analytical dimensions of an OLAP hypercube. Further details on this first contribution of HYSSOP to NLG are given in [7].

The next two contributions are presented in other publications: the one to content aggregation in [22] and the one to syntactic realization in [8]. The remaining two contributions constitute the focus of the present paper: the one to content determination is presented in section 3 and the one to discourse organization in section 4. In section 5, we review related work in these two sub-areas. In section 6, we conclude and discuss future work.

3 Content Determination by OLAP and Data Mining

HYSSOPís content determination is entirely based on the idea of *On-Line Analytical Mining* (OLAM) [9], *i.e.*, the integration of data mining and OLAP to search for intriguing patterns expressed in terms of a multidimensional, analytical data model. Within this framework, data mining algorithms work on top of an OLAP layer that provides data hypercube queries and exploration operators as primitives. The current version of HYSSOP was built to work with the whole range of OLAP facilities but only a single data mining facility: detection of data cell values (atomic or aggregated) that are *exceptional* in the multidimensional context of the mined data cube. Following Sarawagi [23] and Chen [4], we define exceptionality as the compound statistical deviation of the cell value, along every data cube dimension and at every data aggregation level. This functionality can answer a mining queries such as ì *looks for exceptional monthly sales variations measured as a percentage difference from previous month".* It results in a pool of exceptional data cells extracted from the mined data cube. Because exceptional values are sparsely distributed at different aggregation levels, a cell pool is *not* an OLAP sub-cube. It is a simple relational database table, which fields correspond to the data cube dimensions and measures together with the data mining derived data (in our case, degree of exceptionality). An example cell pool, input to HYSSOP is given in Fig.3. Each cell is described by three dimensions (product, place, time) and two measures (sales-diff, exception).

	Dimensions			Measures	Data mining
cell	product	place	time	sales-diff	exception
1c	Birch Beer	nation	Nov	-10	low
2c	Jolt Cola	nation	Aug	+6	low
3c	Birch Beer	nation	Jun	-12	low
4c	Birch Beer	nation	Sep	+42	high
5c	Cola	central	Aug	-30	low
6c	Diet Soda	east	Aug	+10	low
7c	Diet Soda	east	Sep	-33	medium
8c	Diet Soda	east	Jul	-40	high
9c	Diet Soda	south	Jul	+19	low
10c	Diet Soda	west	Aug	-17	low
11c	Cola	Colorado	Sep	-32	medium
12c	Cola	Colorado	Jul	-40	medium
13c	Cola	Wisconsin	Jul	-11	low

Fig. 3. Cell pool resulting from mining a multidimensional retailing data mart for exceptions (created from the data set discussed in [23])

4 Discourse Organization with the Content Matrix

Content organization deals with the question ìWhen to say what?î. To group and order quantitative content units inside summaries, we introduce a new discourse organization approach that relies on a data structure called the *content matrix*. Essentially, a content matrix is a cell pool where rows and column have been ordered in a way that reflects the desired grouping and ordering of cell descriptions in the output textual summary. This desired grouping and ordering is specified in input using a simple declarative language that refers to the dimensions and measures of the data cube under analysis. The grammar of this *Discourse Organization Strategy Specification Language* (DOSL) is given in Fig.4. An example DOSL specification, called A, is given in Fig. 5. When using this *strategy A* to summarize the cell pool of Fig. 3, HYSSOP generates the natural language page given in Fig. 6, called *version A* summary. In contrast, when using *strategy B* given in Fig. 7, HYSSOP generates the *version B* natural language summary, given in Fig. 8.

OrgSpecif ✐ WithClause GroupSortSeq
OrgSpecif ✐ GroupSortSeq
WithClause ✐ **with count on <identifier>**
GroupSortSeq ✐ GroupClause, SortClause, **then** GroupSortSeq
GroupSortSeq ✐ SortClause, **then** GroupSortSeq
GroupSortSeq ✐
GroupClause ✐ **group_by (measure | dim) <identifier>**
SortClause ✐ **sorted_by (measure | dim) <identifier> (increase | decrease**)

Fig. 4. DOSL grammar

group-by measure exception, **sort-by measure** exception **decrease**
then group-by dim product, **sort-by dim** product **increase**
then sort-by measure sales-diff **decrease**

Fig. 5. Discourse strategy A specified in DOSL

Last year, the most atypical sales variations from one month to the next occurred for:

- Birch Beer, with a 42% national increase from September to October;
- Diet Soda, with a 40% decrease in the Eastern region from July to August.

At the next level of idiosyncrasy came:

- Cola¥s Colorado sales, falling 40% from July to August and then a further 32% from September to October;
- again Diet Soda Eastern sales, falling 33% from September to October.

Less aberrant but still notably atypical were:

- again nationwide Birch Beer sales' -12% from June to July and -10% from November to December;
- Cola's 11% fall from July to August in the Central region and 30% dive in Wisconsin from August to September;
- Diet Soda sales¥19% increase in the Southern region from July to August, followed by its two opposite regional variations from August to September, +10% in the East but -17% in the West;
- national Jolt Cola sales' +6% from August to September.

To know what makes one of these variations unusual in the context of this year's sales, click on it.

Fig. 6. HYSSOP generated textual summary (Version A), resulting from applying discourse strategy A, specified in Fig. 5, to the input cell pool of Fig. 3.

```
with count on all groups
group-by dim product, sort-by product increase
    then group-by measure exception, sort-by measure exception decrease
      then group-by dim dir, sort-by measure dir decrease
       then sort-by measure sales-diff decrease
```

Fig. 7. Discourse strategy B, with count aggregate statistics

Last year, there were 13 exceptions in the beverage product line.
The most striking was Birch Beer's 42% national increase from Sep to Oct.
The remaining exceptions, clustered around four products, were:

- Again, Birch Beer sales accounting for other two mild exceptions, both national slumps: 12% from Jun to Jul and 10% from Nov to Dec;
- Cola sales accounting for four exceptions, all slumps: two medium ones in Colorado, -40% from Jul to Aug and a -32% from Aug to Sep; and two mild ones, -11% in Wisconsin from Jul to Aug and -30% in Central region from Aug to Sep;
- Diet Soda accounting for five exceptions:
    - one strong, -40% in the East from July to Aug,
    - one medium, -33% in the East from Sep to Oct;
    - and three mild: two rises, +19% in the South from Jul to Aug and +10 % in the East from Aug to Sep; and one fall, -17% in Western region from Aug to Sep;
- Finally, Jolt Cola's sales accounting for one mild exception, a national 6% fall from Aug to Sep.

Fig. 8. HYSSOP generated textual summary (Version B), resulting from applying discourse strategy B specified in Fig. 7 to the input cell pool of Fig. 3.

The whole content organization is carried out as a simple process of shuffling rows and columns inside the content matrix, satisfying the grouping and ordering goals of the DOSL specification. In version A, content organization starts with moving the exception columns to second leftmost position, followed by sorting the rows in decreasing order of the values in this column. Since at this point the product column is already in its desired third leftmost position, content organization proceeds by sorting, in product name alphabetical order, the rows of each row group sharing the same exception column value. The final organization step consists in ordering by decreasing values of the sales-diff column, the rows in row sub-groups sharing the same values for both the exception and the product columns. The resulting final content matrix is given in Fig.9. The corresponding final matrix for strategy B is given in Fig.10.

DOSL provides a simple, high-level interface to control the generation of different textual reports organizing the same underlying data in a variety of ways. It allows tailoring the textual summary from a given data analysis perspective, much as OLAP operators such as pivot, slice and dice allow viewing tabular data under various such perspectives.

Cell	exception	product	place	time	sales-diff
4c	high	Birch Beer	nation	Sep	+42
8c	high	Diet Soda	east	Jul	-40
12c	medium	Cola	Colorado	Jul	-40
11c	medium	Cola	Colorado	Sep	-32
7c	medium	Diet Soda	east	Sep	-33
3c	low	Birch Beer	nation	Jun	-12
1c	low	Birch Beer	nation	Nov	-10
13c	low	Cola	Wisconsin	Jul	-11
5c	low	Cola	central	Aug	-30
9c	low	Diet Soda	south	Jul	+19
6c	low	Diet Soda	east	Aug	+10
10c	low	Diet Soda	west	Aug	-17
2c	low	Jolt Cola	nation	Aug	+6

Fig. 9. Final content matrix after applying the discourse strategy A specified in Fig.5 to the input cell pool of Fig. 3

Cell	product	exception	dir	sales-diff	place	time
4c	Birch Beer	high	+	42	nation	Sep
3c	Birch Beer	low	-	12	nation	Jun
1c	*2	*2	*2	10	*2	Nov
12c	Cola	medium	-	40	Colorado	Jul
11c	*4	*2	*2	32	*2	Sep
13c		low	-	11	Wisconsin	Jul
5c		*2	*2	30	central	Aug
8c	Diet Soda	high	-	40	east	Jul
7c	*5	medium	-	33	east	Sep
9c		low	+	19	south	Jul
6c		*3	*2	10	east	Aug
10c			-	17	west	Aug
2c	Jolt Cola	low	+	6	nation	Aug

Fig. 10. Final content matrix after applying the discourse strategy B specified in Fig.7 to the input cell pool of Fig. 3

5 Related Work

Related work in two sub-areas are relevant to the research presented in this paper: content determination in NLG QDSS and discourse organization in NLG in general.

5.1 Related Work in Content Determination in NLG QDSS

Previous NLG QDSS used a wide variety of content determination approaches: production rules (ANA), topic tree object database query methods (GOSSIP), heuristic rules based on aggregated statistics (FLOWDoc). In spite of this apparent variety, these approaches share common characteristics that set them apart from our OLAM-based approach. First, they all involve computing aggregated values (*e.g.,* sum, count, avg, percent, min, max) of content units inside *fixed semantic classes, specific to the underlying application domain.* This makes these content determination approaches both *goal driven* and domain-dependent. Second, they compute aggregate values using either ad-hoc procedures or general tools that were not designed to perform quantitative aggregation on large data set with complex internal structures. By relying OLAP and data mining, content determination in HYSSOP is in contrast, scalable, domain-independent, and *fully data driven.* It does not involve any pre-defined threshold or content unit semantic *class*, but only comparison of content unit attribute *values* in the multidimensional analytical context of the data cube.

5.2 Related Work in Discourse Level Organization in NLG

The discourse organization approaches of most NLG QDSS share the same characteristics than their content determination approaches[5]: processing is driven by iterating through a fixed, domain-dependent set of semantic classes for which instances are searched among the content units produced by content determination. In contrast, the content matrix approach is fully data-driven and domain-independent. It is also considerably simpler than most NLG QDSS discourse organization. Finally, using DOSL, our approach allows tailoring discourse organization towards a wide variety of desired analytical perspectives. Such functionality is not offered by previous NLG QDSS, in which organizational preferences heuristics are generally hard-wired in the content planning algorithm.

Before concluding, let us point out that neither of the three mainstream discourse organization approaches, so widely used in NLG at large, textual schemas [16], topic trees [3], and RST[6]-planning approach [10],[15] are appropriate for QDSS. This is mostly due to the fact that theses approaches are also based on relations between *semantic classes* of content units. They provide no direct way to base content unit grouping and ordering on the *value* of the unitsí attributes. This is problematic for quantitative domain where content units tend to pertain to a very few if not a single semantic class (in our case, cell of a multidimensional data model). Theses units thus form an homogeneous set, sharing the same descriptive attributes, and the main basis to group and order them in a text is the various attribute *value sharing* relations between them. In other words, quantitative domain discourse organization must be data driven and schema, topic tree and RST approaches are goal driven. To make things worst, the goals used by these approaches to drive discourse organization are mostly *interpersonal* (*e.g.* speech-acts, intentions and beliefs). In quantitative domains, the communicative goal tends to be unique and *ideational*: summarize the data.

---

[5] Indeed, many systems perform both tasks together.

[6] RST: Rhetorical Structure Theory.

6 Conclusion and Future Work

In this paper, we presented a new approach to content determination and discourse organization in NLG. This approach relies on two decision-support oriented database technologies, OLAP and data mining, and it can be used for any NLG application involving the textual summarization of quantitative data. It improves on previous approaches to content planning for NLG in quantitative domains by providing: (1) application domain independence, (2) efficient, variable granularity insight search in high dimensionality data spaces, (3) automatic discovery of surprising, counter-intuitive data, (4) tailoring of output text organization towards different, declaratively specified, analytical perspectives on the input data.

In future work, we intend empirically evaluate the various discourse strategies implemented in HYSSOP, with human readers comparing the resulting generated summaries in terms of decision support utility. We also intend to extend HYSSOPís coverage to make it able to summarize other classes of data mining discoveries such as association rules, conceptual clusters, trends and time-series.

References

1. AÔ-Kaci, H. and Lincoln, P.: LIFE ñ A natural language for natural language. *T.A . Informations*, 30(1-2):37-67, Association pour le Traitement Automatique des Langues, Paris France (1989).
2. Bourbeau, L., Carcagno, D., Goldberg, E., Kittredge, R., PolguËre, A.: Bilingual generation of weather forecast in an operational environment. *COLING'90*, Helsinki, (1990).
3. Carcagno, D., Iordanskaja, L.: Content determination and text structuring; two interrelated processes. In H. Horacek [ed.] *New concepts in NLG: Planning, realization and systems.* London: Pinter Publishers, pp 10-26, (1993).
4. Chen, Q.: *Mining exceptions and quantitative association rules in OLAP data cube.* M.Sc. Thesis. Department of CS, Simon Fraser University, B.C., Canada, July (1999).
5. DBMiner: http://db.cs.sfu.edu/DBMiner/index.html, (2000).
6. Elhadad, M. and Robin, J.: An overview of SURGE: a re-usable comprehensive syntactic realization component. *In Proceedings of the 8th International Workshop on Natural Language Generation (*demonstration session). Brighton, UK (INLG'96). (1996)
7. Favero, E.L.: *Generating hypertext summaries of data mining discoveries in multidimensional databases.* Ph.D. thesis, CIn, UFPE, Recife, Brazil.(2000)
8. Favero, E.L. and Robin, J.: Um ambiente para desenvolvimento de gram· ticas computacionais para o PortuguÍs, *Revista de Informática Teórica e Aplicada*, Volume VI, N˙ mero 1, Julho, 1999 pp 49-76, Porto Alegre, (1999).
9. Han, J.: OLAP Mining: An integration of OLAP with Data Mining. In *Proc. 1997 IFIP Conf. Data Semantics (DS-7)*, pp 1-11, Leysin, Switzerland, Oct. (1997).
10. Hovy, E.: Automated discourse generation using discourse structure relations. *Artificial Intelligence,* 63: 341-385, (1993).
11. Iordanskaja, L., Kim, M., Kittredge, R., Lavoie, B., Polguere, A.: Generation extended bilingual statistical reports. *In Proc. of COLING 94*, pp.1019-1023 (1994).
12. Kay, M. Functional grammar. *In proceedings of the 5th Annual Meeting of the Berkeley Linguist Society,* (1979).

13. Knott, A . Mellish, C. Oberlander, J. and OíDonnell, M.: Sources of flexibility in dynamic hypertext generation. *In Proc. of the 8th International Workshop in NLG*, Sussex, UK, (1996).
14. Kukich, K.: *Knowledge-based Report Generation: A knowledge-engineering approach to NL Report Generation*; Department of Information Science, University of Pittsburgh, Ph. D. thesis, (1983).
15. Mann, W C Thompson, S A.: Rhetorical structure theory: Toward a functional theory of text organization. *Text*, 8(3):243-281, (1988).
16. McKeown, K.: Text generation. Cambridge University Press, Cambridge, (1985).
17. McKeown, K., Kukich, K., Shaw, J.: Practical issues in automatic document generation. In Proc. of ANLPí94, pages 7-14, Stuttgart, October (1994).
18. Milosavljevic, M. Tulloch, A . and Dale, R. Text generation in a dynamic hypertext environment. *In Proceeding of the 199th Australian Computer Science Conference*, 417-426, Melbourne, Austria, (1996).
19. MS OLAP Server (www.microsoft.com/sql/productinfo/olap.html)
20. Passonneau, B., Kukich, K., Robin, J., Hatzivassiloglou, V., Lefkowitz, L. Jin, H.: Generating Summaries of Work Flow Diagrams. *In Proc. of the Intern. Conference on NLP and Industrial Applications.* Moncton, New Brunswick, Canada (NLP+IA'96). 7p. (1996).
21. Reiter, E., Dale, R.: Building applied natural language generation system. *ANLPC* Washington DC. (1997).
22. Robin, J. Favero, E.L.: Content aggregation in natural language hypertext summarization of OLAP and Data Mining discoveries. *In Proc. of INLG'2000 Conference (Intern. Natural Language Generation),* Mitzpe Ramon, Israel, June (2000).
23. Sarawagi, S., Agrawal, R., Megiddo, N.: Discovery-driven exploration of MDDB data cubes. In Proc. *Int. Conf. of Extending Database Technology* EDBTí98, March, (1998).

Toward an Enhancement of Textual Database Retrieval Using NLP Techniques*

Asanee Kawtrakul[1], Frederic Andres[2], Kinji Ono[2], Chaiwat Ketsuwan[1], Nattakan Pengphon[1]

[1] NaiST, Computer Engineering Dept, Kasetsart University, Bangkok, Thailand
ak@beethoven.cpe.ku.ac.th
[2] NII, National Institute of Informatics, Tokyo, Japan
{andres,ono}@rd.nacsis.ac.jp

Abstract. Improvements in hardware, communication technology and database have led to the explosion of multimedia information repositories. In order to improve the quality of information retrieval compared to already existing advanced document management systems, research works have shown that it is necessary to consider vertical integration of retrieval techniques inside database service architecture. This paper focuses on the integration of NLP techniques for efficient textual database retrieval as part of the VLSHDS Project -Very Large Scale Hypermedia Delivery System. One target of this project is to increase the quality of textual information search (precision/ recall) compared to already existing multi-lingual IR systems by applying morphological analysis and shallow parsing in phrase level to document and query processing. The scope of this paper is limited to Thai documents. The underlying system is The Active HYpermedia Delivery System-(AHYDS) framework providing the delivery service over internet. Based on 1100 Thai documents, as first results, our approach improved the precision and recall from 72.666% and 56.67% in the initial implementation (without applying NLP techniques) to 85.211% and 76.876% respectively.

1 Introduction

Improvements in hardware, communication technology and database engines had led to the expansion of challenging interactive multimedia applications and services. Typical examples of applications include on-line news, digital libraries and web-based information involving multi-dimension multimedia document repositories. These systems combine various media content with hyperlink structures for user query or navigation. Most of them store contents inside the database systems supporting extenders in order to add application data types with their access methods. However, there is no vertical integration between application IR plug-ins and the database kernel

* This Project has been granted by Kasetsart University Research and Development Institute (KURDI), Kasetsart University, Thailand and National Institute of Informatics (NII), Center of Excellence of the Ministry of Education, JAPAN and National Electronics and Computer Technology Center (NECTEC).

M. Bouzeghoub et al. (Eds.): NLDB 2000, LNCS 1959, pp. 176-189, 2001.

itself. This limitation is an underlying reason for further improvements [6,8,17,18,19]. AHYDS - The Active HYpermedia Delivery System is one prototype as part of a new wave of data or information engine kernels [4,7,16] that facilitates the access to multimedia documents according to the userís requirements and applicationís features over a wide spectrum of networks and media [1].

The VLSHDS-Very Large Scale Hypermedia Delivery System is a cooperation project between NII and NAiST [2,10] that aims to integrate both data delivery service and textual information retrieval service. The AHYDS component is a framework providing open data delivery service, communication service, query execution service and supervision service. The quality of full text retrieval service has been enhanced compared to existing state of the art IR systems both in precision and recall by integrating morphological analysis and shallow parsing in phrase level for document and query processing.

Section 2 gives an overview of the VLSHDS. The role of natural language processing and knowledge base in document processing, query processing and retrieving processing are described in section 3, 4 and 5 respectively. Section 6 gives the conclusion and briefs the next step of the project.

2 An Overview of the Very Large Scale Hypermedia Delivery Systems

The key components of the VLSHDS platform used as textual retrieval platform are shown in Fig 1.

The system consists of a three-tiers architecture. At the client side, queries are sent to the server by using the AHYDS communication support [11]. At the server side, there are three main components: Document Processing, Query Processing and Retrieval Processing. The Document Processing based on the Extended Binary Graph (EBG) structure provides multilevel indices and a document category as document representation. The Query Processing provides query expansion with a new set of queries consisting of phrase terms, heads of phrases and their categories. The Retrieval Processing computes the similarity between queries and documents and returns a set of retrieved documents with the similarity scores.

3 The Role of NLP in Textual Data Based Retrieval

To enhance the performance of full text retrieval service, optimal representation of documents should follow [14], i.e., multi-level indices and document category. Multi-level indices will increase the retrieval recall without the degradation of the system precision. Document category will be used for pruning irrelevant document in order to increase precision while decrease the searching time.

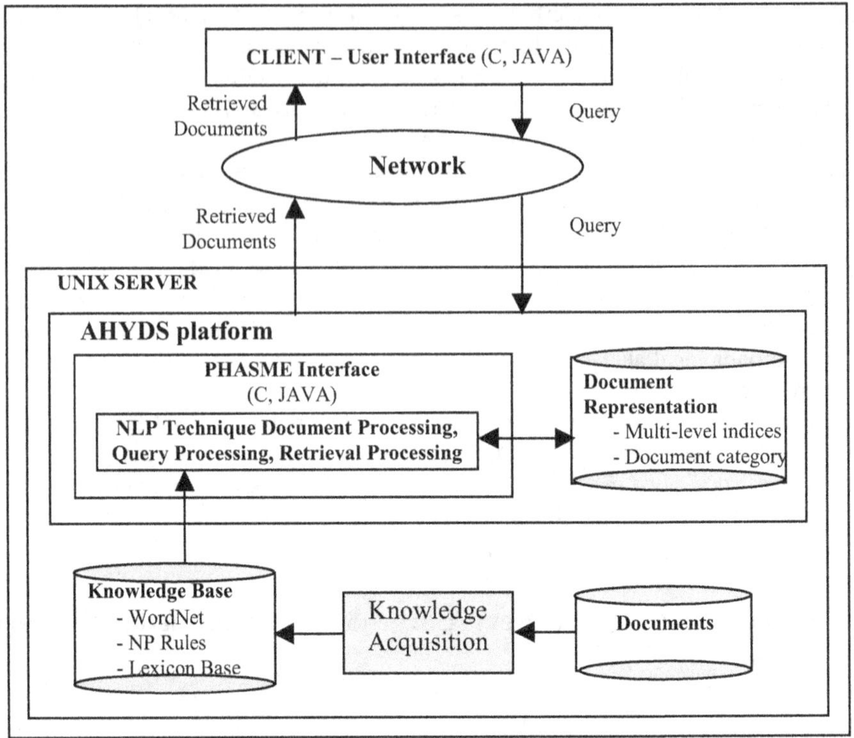

Fig. 1. The Architecture of the VLSHDS Platform for Textual Document Retrieval

However, the primary problem in computing multi-level indices and category as document representation is a linguistic problem. The problems frequently found, especially in Thai documents, are lexical unit extraction including unknown word, phrase variation, loan words, acronym, synonym and definite anaphora [11, 12, 13].

Accordingly, to be more successful, NLP components, i.e., morphological analysis and shallow parsing in noun phrase level should be integrated with statistical based indexing and categorizing.

3.1 The Architecture of NLP Based Document Processing

Fig. 2 shows the overview of Thai document processing. There are two main steps: multilevel indexing and document categorizing. Each document will represented as

$$D_i = \langle I_p, I_t, I_c, C_i \rangle$$

Where I_p, I_t, I_c are the set of indices inphrase, single term and conceptual level, respectively

Ci is the category of a document i-th

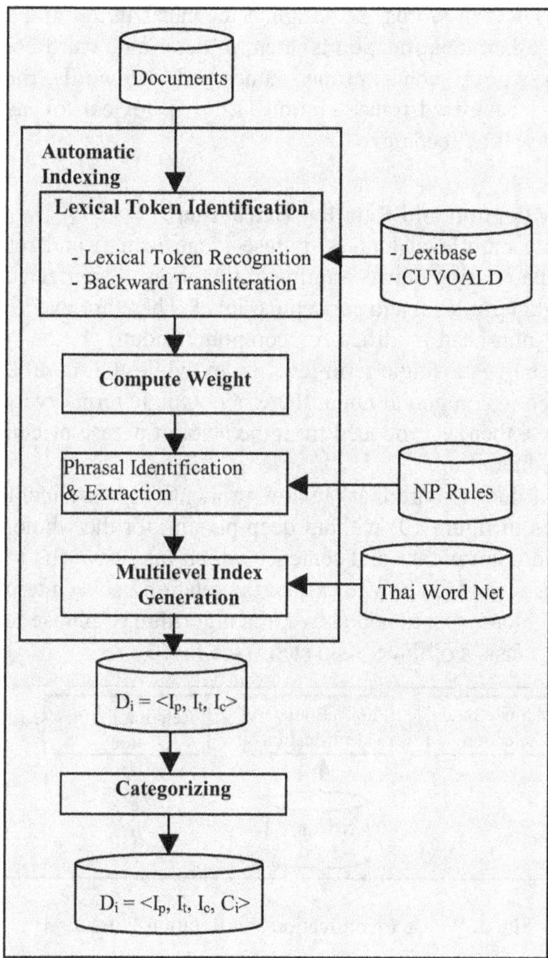

Fig. 2. Overview of Thai Document Processing

3.2 Automatic Multilevel Indexing with Language Analysis

As shown in Fig. 2, automatic multilevel indexing consists of three modules: lexical token identification, phrase identification with relation extraction, and multilevel index generation. Each module accesses different linguistic knowledge bases stored inside the EBG data structure.

3.2.1 Lexical Token Identification

Like many other languages, the problems which effect the performance of Thai text retrieval systems are unknown proper names including proper names like ìMiddle Westî, acronym, synonym and anaphora [10, 11]. However, Thai also has no word delimitation and uses loan words, i.e. English technical terms in Thai orthography. The role of lexical token identification is, then, to determine word boundaries, and to recognize unknown words, such as proper names and loan words. Based on morphological analysis and backward transliteration [12, 13], lexical tokens are segmented and unknown word will be recognized.

3.2.2 Phrase Identification and Relation Extraction

In order to compute multilevel indices, phrase identification and relation extraction are also needed. The relation between terms in the phrase is extracted in order to define indices in single term level and conceptual level. There are two kinds of relations: head-modifier and non-head-modifier (or compound noun). If the relation is head-modifier, the head part is a single term-level index while the modifier is not used as index. If the relation is compound noun, there is no single term-level index. The conceptual level indices, then, is produced from the head of phrase or compound noun by accessing Thai wordnet.

The problems of this step are that (1) how to identify phrase including paraphrase (see some examples in figure 10) without deep parsing for the whole text, (2) how to distinguish between noun phrase and sentence which may have the same pattern (see the third rule in fig. 4) and (3) how to extract the relation between terms in phrase.

To solve the problems mentioned above, the algorithm of phrase identification and relation extraction consists of three main steps (see Fig. 3).

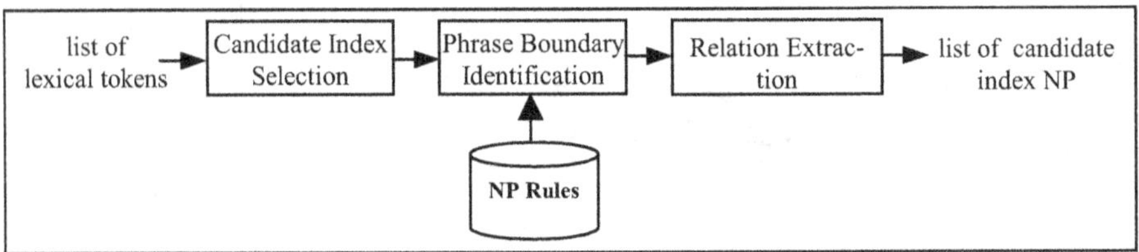

Fig. 3. Phrase Identification and Relation Extraction

The first step is the candidate index selection that is based on Saltonís weighting formula [9], then, the second step is the phrase boundary identification using a statistical-based NLP technique. This step will find phrase boundary for a set of candidate indices (provided from the first step) by using NP rules (see Fig. 4).

At this step, we can describe as 4-tuple:

$$\{T, N, R, NP\}$$

where

T	is the set of candidate terms which have weight $w_i > \theta$ (θ is a threshold)
N	is the set of non-terminal
R	is the set of rules in the grammar
NP	is the starting symbol

NP <- cn + cn + (cn)	กล้วยไม้ป่า
NP <- cn + {cn, pn}	ประเทศไทย
NP <- cn + v + (cn)	วิทยุกระจายเสียง
NP <- cn + (cn) + mod	น้ำปลาหวาน
NP <- cn + prep + cn	คุณค่าทางอาหาร
NP <- cn + v + v	ค่าใช้จ่าย
NP <- cn + num + cl	สัตว์สองเท้า
NP <- cn + NOM	อุตสาหกรรมการกลั่นสุรา
NOM <- prefix + vp	การกลั่นสุรา

Fig. 4. Some examples of Noun phrase rules

The third step is the relation extraction. After the boundary of phrase(s) is identified, we need to compute the relation between a set of words in the phrase in order to find whether that NP is a head-modifier NP or a compound. If the frequency of each word in the candidate NP is the same (see Fig. 5) then the relation of that NP is a compound noun, otherwise the relation of that NP is a head-modifier pair. Head is the term(s) with highest frequency. Modifier is the term(s) with lower frequency.

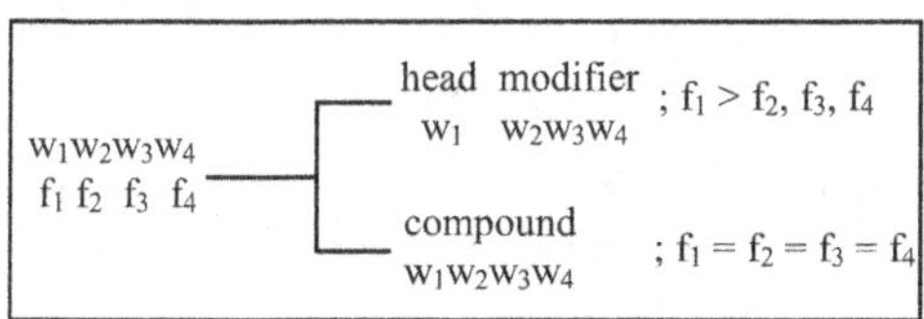

Fig. 5. Relation Extraction

The detail of the algorithm is given in Appendix 1.

3.2.3 Multilevel Index Generation

At this step, each document D_i is summarized and represented in the EBG data structure as a vector of numeric weights, i.e.:

$$D_i =< I_{p_i}, I_{t_i}, I_{c_i} >$$

where

$$I_{p_i} =< W_{p1_i}, W_{p2_i}, \ldots, W_{p3_i} >$$
$$I_{t_i} =< W_{t1_i}, W_{t2_i}, \ldots, W_{t3_i} >$$
$$I_{c_i} =< W_{c1_i}, W_{c2_i}, \ldots, W_{c3_i} >$$

Phrasal level indices (I_p) consist of set of the phrases extracted by using noun phrase rules. Single term level indices (I_t) are the head of each index token in the phrasal level. Conceptual level indices (I_c) are the semantic concepts of each single term level index, given in Lexibase [15]. For example, the document about มะนาว (lemon), may keep ìมะนาวไข่î (A kind of lemon) as phrasal level and keep ìมะนาวî (Lemon) as single term level and ìพืชî (Plant) as conceptual level. Here, ìไข่î (egg) is considered as the proper name instead of common noun.

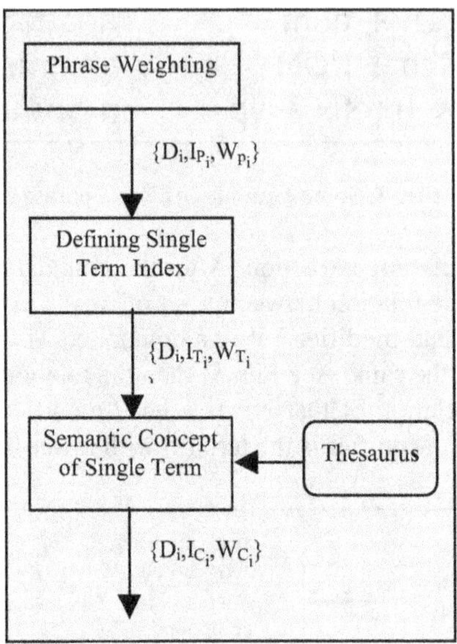

Fig. 6. Multilevel Index Generation

Fig. 6 shows the process of Multilevel Index Generation consisting of phrase level, single term level and conceptual level for each document.

$$V_k^{\,m} = \frac{tf_k^{\,m} \log \dfrac{N_d}{n_k}}{\sum_{j=1}^{l} tf_j^{\,m} \log \dfrac{N_d}{n_j}}$$

tf_k^m = Number of index terms k in document m

n_k = Number of documents that contain term

k

N_d = Number of documents in the collection

l = Number of index terms

We use Saltonís Weight normalization [16] as shown later to compute weights in each level of the index.

Parallel index generation for each document is provided by the AHYDS engine based on the EBG data structure. Details of the algorithm of the multilevel index generation are given in Appendix 2.

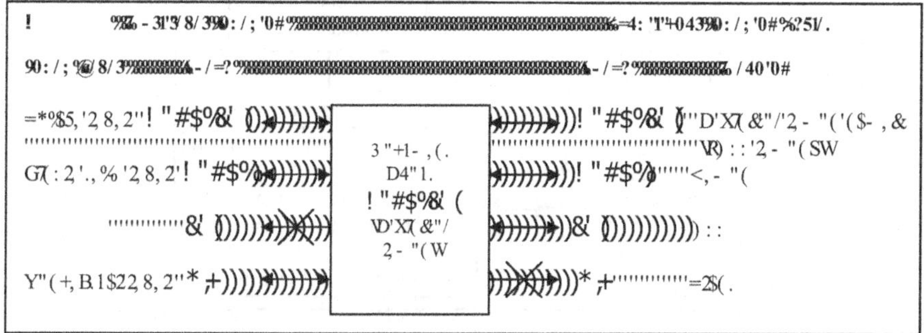

Fig. 7. Example of how Multi-Level Indexing can enhance performance

Fig. 7 shows the comparison between multilevel indexing and traditional indexing system

Using multilevel indexing, ì eggî would not be retrieved, while, in traditional IR, it will be retrieved which degrades the performance of the system.

3.2.4 Document Classification

Even though multi-level indices can cover a very wide range of document retrieval without any degradation of system performance, document clustering for pruning irrelevant documents is still necessary in order to increase precision and decrease searching time.

The text categorization or document clustering consists of two parts: a prototype learning process to provide prototypes for each cluster of documents and a clustering process, which computes the similarity between input document and prototype (see Fig. 8).

Finally, document will be represented as

$$D_i = < I_{p_i}, I_{t_i}, I_{c_i}, C_i >$$

where

$$I_{p_i} = < W_{p1_i}, W_{p2_i}, \ldots, W_{pt_i} >$$
$$I_{t_i} = < W_{t1_i}, W_{t2_i}, \ldots, W_{tt_i} >$$
$$I_{c_i} = < W_{c1_i}, W_{c2_i}, \ldots, W_{ct_i} >$$
$$C_i = < W_{cat\,1_i}, W_{cat\,2_i}, \ldots, W_{cat\,n_i} >$$

The algorithm of document clustering is summarized in Appendix 3.

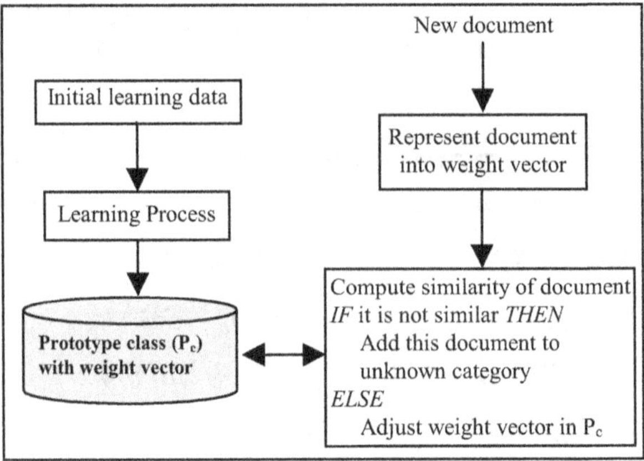

Fig. 8. Text Categorization process

4 Query Processing

In order to obtain those documents which are the best match for a given query, we also need a ìquery guideî. Query Guide is applied by using the cluster hypothesis and query expansions. Our method applies Word-Net for query expression. For example Query = ìน้ำดอกไม้.î (proper name: the name of mango) and its general term (from Word-Net) is ìมะม่วงî (mango). After expansion, the new query is ìมะม่วง-น้ำดอกไม้î (The phrase contains of mango and its specified name).

5 Retrieval Processing

The following retrieval process is implemented in order to enhance the performance retrieval of the system (see fig. 9).

Step 1. Computation of a candidate set (labeled B) of documents by matching the input queries with the inverted index file.
Step 2. Selection of a candidate set (labeled C) of documents that belong to the same category as the query.
Step 3. Calculation of the similarity between the queries of the documents evaluated as the intersection between B and C sets of documents.
Step 4. Retrieval of a set of retrieved documents with related ranks according to the similarity scores.

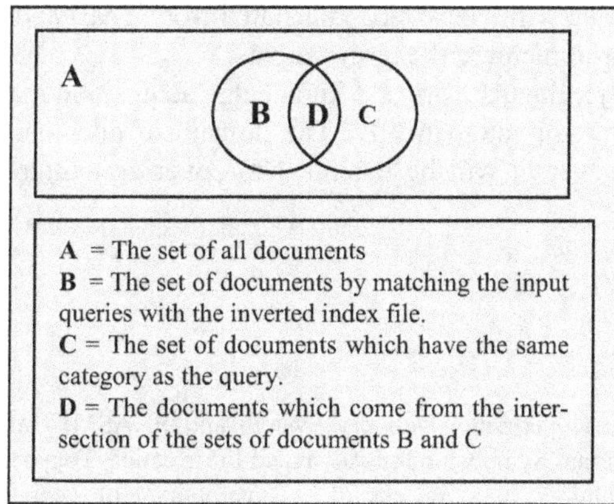

Fig. 9. The Retrieved Documents

6 Conclusions and Future Work

The paper has shown how NLP Techniques enhance textual database retrieval as part of the VLSHDS platform. We focus on describing the innovative implementation of the VLSHDS Platform.

Early benchmarking based on 1100 documents shown that the VLSHDS improved the precision and the recall 72.666% and 56.67% respectively, compared to traditional IR Systems 85.211% and 76.876%, respectively.

Problem	Indexing without NLP Technique		Indexing with NLP Technique	
Phrase variation	การเชื่อมต่อเครือข่าย	0.0082	การเชื่อมเครือข่าย	0.0836
	การเชื่อมเครือข่าย	0.0082		
	การเชื่อมโยงระหว่างเครือข่าย	0.0373		
	การเชื่อมโยงเครือข่าย	0.0299		
Loan word	อินเตอร์เน็ต	0.0073	Internet	0.0165
	อินเทอร์เน็ต	0.0092		
	อีเทอร์เน็ต	0.0117	Ethernet	0.0611
	อีเธอร์เน็ต	0.0494		

Fig. 10. Examples of Applying NLP Technique to solving phrase variation and loan word

Fig. 10 shows the example of an improvement in indexing. Phrase variation or paraphrase such as ìNetwork Connectionî, ìConnection Networkî, ìConnecting to Networkî and ìConnecting with Networkî (translated from Thai) and loan words will be standardized in order to increase the term weights.

At the current state, linguists process knowledge acquisition manually. Next step it will be provided by semi-automatically. The domain of documents is limited to the computer area. However, it will be extended to cover agriculture and general news area.

References

1. Andres F., ìActive Hypermedia Delivery System and PHASME Information Engineî in Proc. First International Symposium on Advanced Informatics, Tokyo, Japan, 2000.
2. Andres F., Kawtrakul A., Ono K. and al., ìDevelopment of Thai Document Processing System based on AHYDS by Network Collaborationî, in Proc. 5th international Workshop of Academic Information Networks on Systems(WAINS), Bangkok, Thailand, December 1998.
3. Andres F., and Ono K. ìThe Active Hypermedia Delivery Systemî, in Proceedings of ICDE98, Orlando, USA, February 1998.
4. Boncz, P.A. and Kerstern, M.L. ìMonet: An Impressionist Sketch of an Advanced Database Systemî In Proc. IEEE BITWIT Workshop, San Sebastian (Spain), July 1995.
5. E. Chaniak, ìStatistical Language Learningî, MIT Press, 1993.
6. Geppert, A. Dittrich, K.R. ìConstructing the Next 100 Database Management Systems: Like the Handyman or Like the Engineer ?î in SIGMOD RECORD Vol.23, No 1, March 1994.
7. Geppers A., Scherrer S., and Dittrich K.R. ìKids: Construction of Database Management Systems based on Reuseî, Technical report 97.01, Institutfur Informatik, University of Zurich, Swinzerland, 1997.
8. Grosky W.I. ìManaging Multimedia Information in Database Systemî in Communication of the ACM December 1997, Vol 40., No 12, page 73-80.
9. G. Salton, ìAutomatic Text Processing. The Transformation, Analysis, and Retrieval of Information by Computerî, Singapore: Addison-Wesley Publishing Company, 1989.
10. Kawtrakul A., Andres F., et.al.,. ìA Prototype of Globalize Digital libraries: The VLSDHS Architecture for Thai Document processing.î 1999. (on the process of submission)
11. Kawtrakul A., Andres F., Ono K. and al., ìThe Implementation of VLSHDS Project for Thai Document Retrievalî in Proc. First International Symposium on Advanced Informatics, Tokyo, Japan, 2000.
12. Kawtrakul A., et.al., ìAutomatic Thai Unknown Word Recognitionî, In Proceedings of the Natural Language Processing Pacific Rim Symposium, Phuket, pp.341-346, 1997.
13. Kawtrakul A., et.al., ìBackward Transliteration for Thai Document Retrievalî, In Proceedings of The 1998 IEEE Asia-Pacific Conference on Circuits and Systems, Chiangmai, pp. 563-566, 1998.
14. Kawtrakul A., et,al, ìTowards Automatic Multilevel Indexing for Thai Text Information Retreivalî, Proc. of IEEE, pp 551-554, 1998.
15. Kawtrakul A., et.al., ìA Lexibase Model for Writing Production Assistant Systemî In Proceedings of the 2nd Symposium on Natural Language Processing, Bangkok, pp. 226-236, 1995.
16. Seshadri P., Livny M., and Ramakrishnan R. ìThe Case for Enhanced Abstract Data Typesî In Proceedings of 23rd VLDB Conference, Athens, Greece, 1997, pages 56-65.
17. Subrahmanian V.S. ìPrinciples of Multimedia Database Systemsî, Morgan Kaufmann, 1997.

18. Teeuw W.B., Rich C., Scholl M.H. and Blaken H.M. ìAn Evaluation of Physical Disk I/Os for Complex Object Processingî in Proc. IDCE, Vienna, Austria, 1993, pp 363-372.
19. Valduriez P., Khoshafian S., and Copeland G. ìImplementations techniques of Complex Objectsî in Proc. Of the International Conference of VLDB, Kyoto, Japan, 1986, pp 101-110.

Appendix 1

<u>**Algorithm Phrase Identification and Relation Extraction**</u>

Input: a list of lexical token $w_1, w_2, \ldots, w_n$
with set of POS tag information $T_i = \{t_1, t_2, t_3, \ldots, t_m\}$,
frequency f_i and weight W_i for each word

Output: set of candidate index NPs with head-modifier relation or compound relation

Candidate Index Selection:
Selecting candidate index by selecting term which have weight $w_i > \theta$ (θ is an index threshold)

Phrase boundary identification:

```
FOR each candidate term DO
        Apply NP rule to find boundary
        IF can not apply rule directly
            Consider weight of adjacent term w_adj THEN
            IF adjacent term has weight w_adj > φ
                (φ is a boundary threshold)        THEN
        Extend boundary to this term
          ELSE
              IF this adjacent term in the preference list
                  Extend boundary to this term          THEN
```

Relation Extraction:

```
FOR each candidate index phrase DO
        To find internal relation we consider term frequency
        in each phrase
        IF the frequency of each word of candidate NP
            has the same frequency                     THEN
            Relation of this NP is compound noun
        ELSE
            Relation of this NP is head-modifier pair :
            Head is the term(s) with highest frequency.
            Modifier is the term(s) with lower frequency.
```

Appendix 2

Algorithm Multilevel Index Generation

Input: 1. A list of lexicon token provided by Lexicon Token Identification and Extraction process w1, w_2,Ö ., w_j with its frequency f_{wi} and weight w_{wi}.
2. A list of candidate Phrasal indices with head-modifier relation or compound relation.

Output: Index weight vector as document representation

$$D_i = \{I_{p_i}, I_{t_i}, I_{c_i}\}$$

Where

$$I_{p_j} = \{w_{p_1}, w_{p_2}, \ldots, w_{p_j}\}$$
$$I_{t_j} = \{w_{t_1}, w_{t_2}, \ldots, w_{t_j}\}$$
$$I_{c_j} = \{w_{c_1}, w_{c_2}, \ldots, w_{c_j}\}$$

Phrasal Level Indexing:

FOR each candidate Index NP *DO*
Recompute Phrase weights in whole documents
IF phrase weight > θ (θ *is* index threshold)
Keep sorted Phrase index token *THEN*

Single Term Level Indexing:

FOR each candidate phrase index NP *OR* each single term *DO*
IF tokens of candidate phrasal index
Extract the head of the token *THEN*
Recompute weight
ELSE
FOR each lexicon token that not appear in phrasal level *DO*
Recompute weight
Keep sorted Single term indices

Conceptual Level Index:

FOR each single term index *DO*
Find Semantic Concept of each single terms
Recompute weight
Keep Sorted Conceptual Level Index

Appendix 3

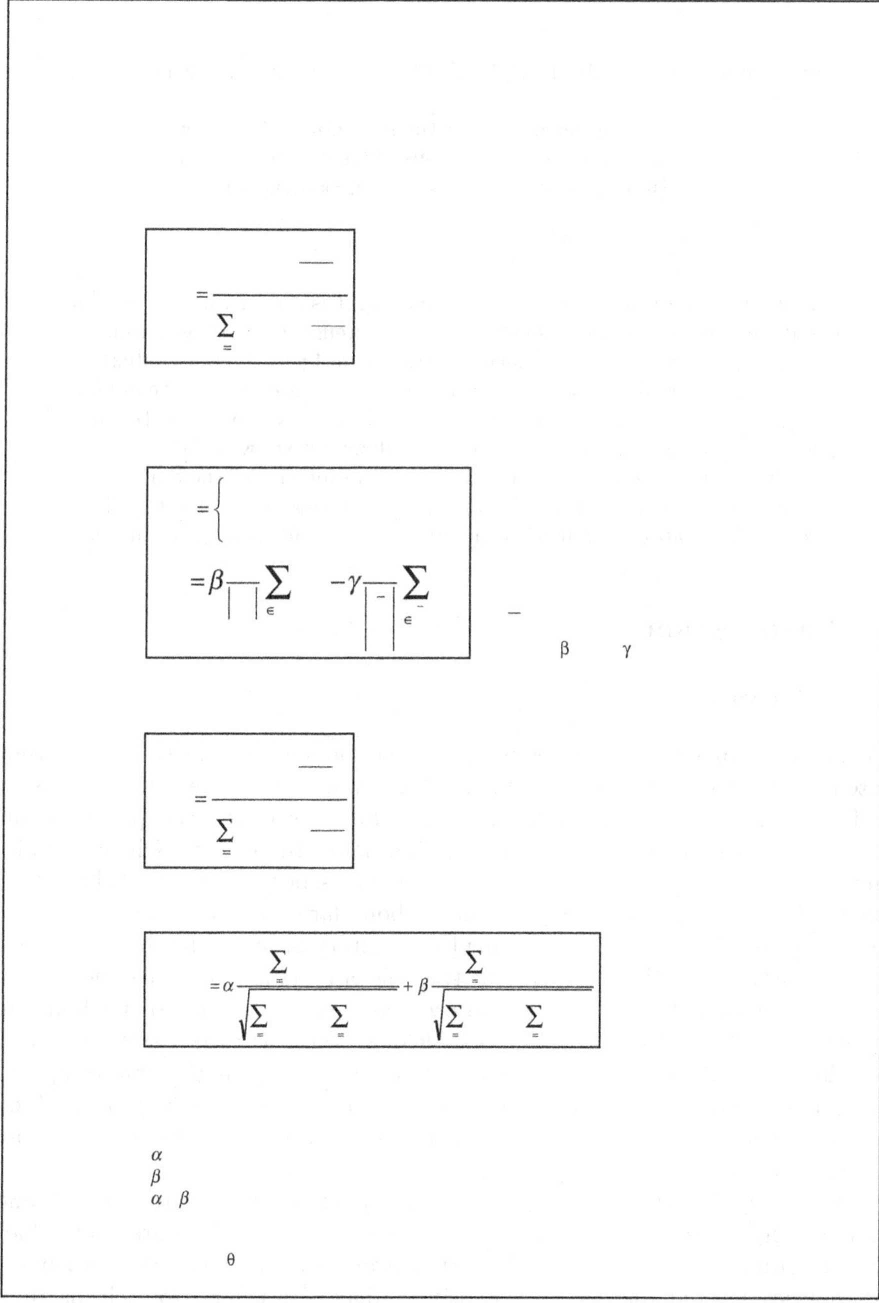

Document Identification by Shallow Semantic Analysis

Abdelhamid Bouchachia, Roland T. Mittermeir, and Heinz Pozewaunig

Universität Klagenfurt, Institut für Informatik-Systeme
Universitätsstrasse 65-67, A-9020 Klagenfurt, Austria
{hamid,roland,hepo}@ifi.uni-klu.ac.at

Abstract. Identifying a matching component is a recurring problem in software engineering, specifically in software reuse. Properly generalized, it can be seen as an information retrieval problem. In the context of defining the architecture of a comprehensive software archive, we are designing a two-level retrieval structure. In this paper we report on the first level, a quick search facility based on analyzing texts written in natural language. Based on textual and structural properties of the documents contained in the repository, the universe is reduced to a moderately sized set of candidates to be further analyzed by more focussed mechanisms.

1 Introduction

1.1 Motivation

People use things they used before, and when looking for something new, they often confine themselves to a familiar search space. We can experience this by self observation when looking for a book or for a set of relevant papers in the library. We get our own experience substantiated by advice on how to build libraries of reusable components (i.e.: be domain-specific) [7], [8]. While there are many arguments for staying within the boundaries of a well known territory, there are also situations where leaving this territory provides the chance to make a substantial innovative step without the cost of making a new invention.

The growth and adoption of the internet as a global information medium can be seen as a chance for such a step outside ones own backyard of software reuse. The increase in functionality of software systems is also a motivation to tap this semi-understood functionality if need arises. Thus, in our ongoing research on software reuse our aim is to provide mechanisms for dealing with larger corpora of (re)usable assets.

Taking stock of the broad spectrum of mechanisms for software retrieval (and description) [9] one has to accept that those mechanisms which are "palatable" for practitioners and, therefore, in rather heavy practical use (keyword based approaches, faceted approach) are relatively weak with respect to their discriminating power. Besides other points of critique, such as maintainability [10], their recall will degenerate with size (and age) of a repository. Thus, small domain

M. Bouzeghoub et al. (Eds.): NLDB 2000, LNCS 1959, pp. 190–202, 2001.

specific repositories are recommended [16] in line with actual demand and current availability of resources. However, when looking at highly discriminative approaches, such as those being based on formal specifications, we find only moderate inclinations of practitioners to formally specify first and reuse later. Additionally, search based on proving whether a complex specification used as query is satisfied by the individual specifications contained in a repository [11] is quite resource and time intensive. This tends to become prohibitive with larger repositories. Therefore, we look for alternative solutions.

Searching for alternatives, a paper on retrieval of images by Guglielmo and Rowe [3] played an important role. Their empirical results showed that allowing for vagueness in general leads to better search results than strict matching of keywords or other sharp concepts. Thus, we were aiming for similar mechanisms to allow for a vagueness in conceptually matching a query against the description of software assets [13]. After an appropriate pre-selection, precise mechanisms are used in order to satisfy the reusers need for accuracy. To do so, we are splitting the retrieval problem into two phases:

(1) A first phase, serving to conceptually "synchronize" a need's description with the descriptions of available reusable assets. Since these descriptions are made by different persons at different times, a certain degree of fuzziness to gain *high recall* is appropriate. The vagueness inherent in natural language descriptions appears to be instrumental to build an intermediate candidate set.

(2) A second phase where criteria aiming for *high precision* filter out previous selected components from the candidate set. In the case of software retrieval, formal specifications could serve this purpose. The intermediate candidate set should be small enough to facilitate the final matching process.

1.2 Contents and Structure of This Paper

In this paper we are focusing on the first phase of the presented approach to match a query expressed in natural language against several natural language descriptions of assets. Actually, this paper is decoupled from the general discussion about software reuse. It would also be beyond its scope to address details of the final matching algorithms. Here, we rather want to present our approach to solve the following requirements by means of processing natural language descriptions. We assume as given:

a) A large set of natural language descriptions, one for each asset.
b) The descriptions are written in a technical natural language. The size of a description might be about one or two pages of text. A good example for such texts are UNIX man-pages.
c) The descriptions adhere to certain "professional standards". Thus, they are written by software engineers and revised by professional software librarians or documentation experts. They do have some internal structure that might even be made explicit.
d) The query text is singular, usually shorter and less professionally written than the asset descriptions.

The system is expected to process the query to identify its semantics. This knowledge is then matched fuzzily against the descriptions of stored assets to gain high recall. Further refinement of the gathered candidate set to identify fitting assets is postponed to the second phase. Due to the number of component descriptions the need to perform match operations efficiently is very important. This should impact the requirement for high recall in the least possible way.

On these preconditions, full linguistic analysis of documents is irrational. Additionally, this is off the point, since the second phase will take care of the assets' (not the descriptions'!) semantics anyway. On the other hand, just relying on keywords is insufficient for the reasons given above. Hence, we must provide an intermediate solution between classical information retrieval and classical natural language comprehension. Taking the example of searching a book in a library, the approach has to imitate a regular customer going to some stack (here: application domain, problem domain, solution category etc.), taking one book after the other and quickly browsing through them to check, whether a book should be scrutinized or whether it should be put back onto the stack. We do this by focusing on *textuality* and *structure* of a document. This combination will lead to a "footprint" of a component that can be held against the "footprint" of the query in order to determine the potential suitability. We refer to this approach as *shallow semantic analysis.*

The sequel of the paper is structured as follows: First, we discuss how to use textual cohesion for identifying a documents semantics. In section 3 we focus on the document's structure. How to combine both views to perform shallow semantic analysis is explained in section 4 and demonstrated in section 5. The paper concludes with a brief discussion.

2 Textual Cohesion as Resource

The notion of textual cohesion is fully defined by Halliday and Hasan in [6] as: "the potential for relating one element in the text to another, wherever they are and without any implication that everything in the text has part in it".

It follows that a text consists of two constituents: elements and relations. The former can be individual words, groups of words or parts of the text. The latter reflects the way these elements form a coherent unit. The authors identified different types of relations. **Reiteration** is the most important relation and exists in the forms of repetition (*write/writing*), synonymy (*delete/suppress*), antonomy (*increase/decrease*), hyponymy (*real/integer*), and meronymy (*class/method*). **Substitution** is also a form of repetition and casually appears in the form of nominal (*the first one, another*), pronominal (*it, these*), verbal (*do*), and clausal (*so*). A special form of substitution is **ellipsis** ("substitution by zero"), where a part of a sentence is omitted (*The first parameter is multiplied but the second [one] is added*). It is related to the mood and is mainly used in question/answer sequences. Another relation is **conjunction** which serves as a rethorical adjunct to relate sentences (*consequently, thus*).

Substitution and ellipsis are grammatical relations, whereas repetition and conjunction are considered as lexical devices. Lexical repetition relations cannot be extracted from the analyzed text directly and are compiled from an external source of knowledge, e.g. a thesaurus. The use of external knowledge is justified by the definition of Halliday and Hasan to grasp the textual items' semantics. Furthermore, we perform no deep analysis of the text.

Based on the defined relations between textual items, Halliday and Hasan analyzed the phenomena of *lexical chains.* Using Roget's thesaurus Morris and Hirst [14] refined this notion by analyzing various lexical relations. Our observation here is that chains represent concepts of the same family, as demonstrated in this example: {*hours, whole day, all day, minute*}. A more consistent chain is {*sorting, sort, increase, order*}. Hence, a chain is merely a cluster of near-synonyms. Morris and Hirst report that the length of chains indicates importance. But the reader should be aware that chains do not provide a means to understand the topic of the text since correlation between words in a large sense is not considered: "The linguistic analysis of literature is not an interpretation of what the text means; it is an explanation of why and how it means what it does" ([6, p.328]).

Analyzing textual cohesion aims at understanding a text. However, the task performed by a lexical binding process is superficial especially if we only consider lexical cohesion. But it helps to relate different parts of a text and consequently, to find important parts, sentences, and chains reflecting the main topics. Hence, it is not ingenious to integrate these lexical and (if possible) grammatical relationships in an analysis system, rather it is a requirement. The problem the vector space model (largely used in information retrieval) is faced with is notably the lack of these considerations. Many researchers have limited the use of lexical devices on the level of query expansion [12]. Query expansion is the set of techniques for modifying a query in order to satisfy an information need. Basically, terms are added to an existing query (focus on short queries), causing a modification of terms' weights. In our approach, we go one step further in integrating lexical knowledge as a resource and taking advantage of the distribution of lexical items by considering the networks they build.

3 Structure as Resource

We consider it important to use different aspects of text analysis. Shallow analysis of texts aims at improving the comprehension of texts by including various resources. In information retrieval the structure of texts is one of these important aspects that has been so far neglected.

To overcome the problem of irrelevant features, characterizing documents and thus impeding effective information retrieval, we take advantage of the cognitive aspect inherent in the organization of texts. Our goal is to find the location of important information. This task needs to be done at the sentence level via intermediate segment level up to the document level. If the position of such important information is known, our chance to avoid irrelevant information increases. Our starting point is the topic-comment theory seen from the functional grammar perspective.

From a structural point of view, a proposition is divided into a *topic (theme)* and a *comment (rheme)*. These notions have been researched by the Prague school of linguists (represented by Daneš) as well as by others led by Halliday and Kintsch. Halliday [5, p.36] defined **theme** as: "...a function in the clause as a message. It is what the message is concerned with, the point of departure for what the speaker is going to say." A theme identifies something known by both speaker and listener. It is the part of the sentence from which the speaker proceeds by presenting the information s/he wants to comment in the remainder of the sentence. However, according to Firbas [15], a theme does not always express known (given) information. So the thematic part of a sentence is not totally equivalent to known information.

The **rheme** then is defined as the remainder of the message, where the theme is developed [5, p.38]. It introduces new information, as a comment, after presenting the topic at the beginning of the sentence. Though rhematic elements generally express new information, they cannot always be considered as equivalent to unknown information [15]. In analyzing a document how can one find the theme? Since it occurs necessarily at the beginning of a sentence, it can take forms such as nominal, adverbial, or prepositional groups. Furthermore, one can distinguish *marked* from *unmarked themes*. If it is unmarked it occurs in the form of the subject (nominal group) of the sentence, whereas the marked theme is in the form of an adjunct (adverbial group and prepositional phrase).(For more details see [5]).

Furthermore, the theme appears in different forms but generally at the beginning of a sentence. New information, on the contrary, normally appears in the rheme part. Writers tend to use the end of a clause to indicate newsworthy information [2]. On the other hand, they use the beginning of clauses to lead their readers to the message in the rest of the clause [5]. Therefore, a clue is to take the last constituent of the clause as the newsworthy information. This is justified by a tendency of writers to remind the reader of valuable information at the last position before moving to the next sentence. In general, finding given and new information based on the position within sentences is no easy task. Daneš observed three schemes of thematic progression in exploring the given-new progression through texts [17]:

- **Simple linear progression**, where the theme is identical to the rheme of the preceding sentence.
- **Continuous theme progression**, where the theme is identical in a sequence of sentences.
- **Derived theme progression**, where sentences are related to an extra theme called hypertheme which is not mentioned in the text explicitly and must be found by external knowledge.

He noted that the important information lies in the theme part. Writers or speakers place their concerns within the message as thematic content. Thus, the content of the rheme tends to represent the details of the theme.

4 Combining Structure and Textual Cohesion

To perform text analysis effectively we exploit both structure and texture. Hence, our attention is put on *what* and *how* something is said. Therefore, we focus on passages where meaningful content is likely to appear. In the following section we discuss two ideas for representing the semantics of documents and how to index documents on that basis: meaningful sentences and stratified abstractions.

4.1 Meaningful Sentences

In a cognitive sense, words or phrases are considered as semantic units. Units describing the concerns of texts are *main features*. Those representing details are *secondary features*. The main idea of a text segment is expressed as themes appearing in the segment. This can be generalized by associating a theme with different levels of text granularity (sentence, segment, document). If no topical units are predefined, we exploit the second resource, the texture expressed in terms of cohesion devices. As a result, coherent units will be constructed by relating themes of the sentences. This fits well into the progression schemes of Daneš [17] since we also try to group sentences related to the same theme into coherent units. Our approach permits managing the intersentences relationships by linking sentences which are about the same topic. Additionally, we take care of the vocabulary distribution over the document, since topical cohesion does not end with the boundaries of sentences. An approach similar to ours was described in [4].

The document's macrostructure can be derived by formalizing the theme as a whole. Van Dijk [18] states that macrostructures are often expressed by titles, headlines, or summarizing sentences. Good candidates for deriving the main idea are summarizing sentences. This is in contrast to Daneš's third option of thematic progression meaning that if a main idea is not stated explicitly, then extra knowledge has to be exploited to infer it. But since we analyze textual surface structures only in technical documents, we assume that the main topic is clearly stated by a few sentences. Given that we are dealing with technical documents, certain stylistic conventions can be taken for granted. For us, the main idea is determined by computing the number of themes appearing in the sentences. Starting from sentence's themes we infer the segment's theme (the main sentence). Then, the set of segments' themes form the document's theme. Thus, a kind of summary is derived and can be understood as a "footprint" for the whole document (see Fig. 1).

Sentences appearing in the footprint are not metaphorical. No inference is used to understand their contents. They are extracted on the basis of their surface based upon a clear appearance of the main items. If used as index, they certainly increase precision and recall. Since the index is extracted from the content of document and includes basic elements of the meaning, it carries the appropriate contents. This is not the case with techniques usually used in digital libraries, where titles serve as indexing basis. Similar to a scientific document structured into an abstract, a list of keywords and the content, themes of the footprint are considered as key-concepts. They are used as a first cue to find the documents the user is interested in (see Fig. 2).

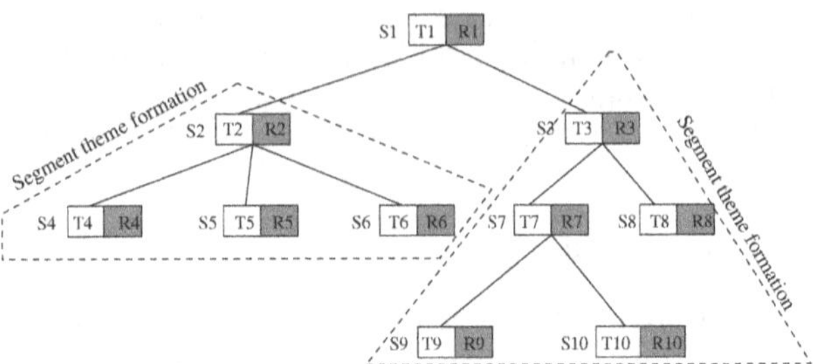

Fig. 1. Footprint formation (Meaningful sentences). The themes of sentences 4, 5 and 6 occur in sentence 2 also, such that 4, 5, and 6 explain sentence 2. Therefore, sentence 2 represents them in the resulting footprint

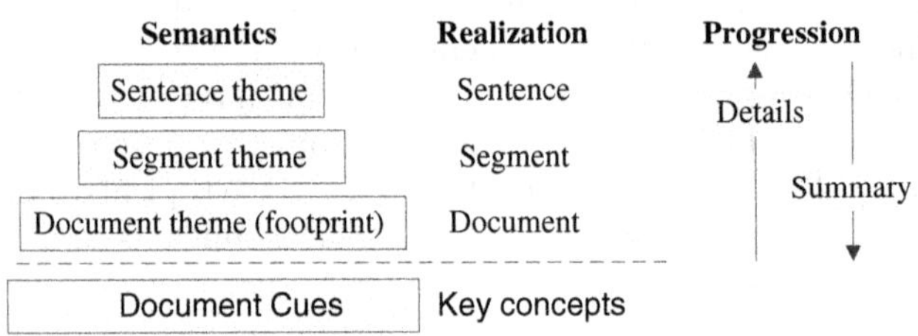

Fig. 2. Levels of abstraction

A questioner formulates a short paragraph that will be abstracted in the same way as the fully fledged stored documents. If the key-concepts are described in a nutshell, the resulting footprint is smaller, but includes already the most important concepts related to the document(s) to be selected. Expert users may express their need by just specifying key-concepts directly. The system compares the key-concepts related to the user query with the key-concepts associated with the available assets in the library first and then presents the abstracts of documents that correspond to matched key-concepts. The questioner can have access to the content of documents if s/he is interested in details. The final selection rests on the users' capability of adequately matching related things. Thus, this approach is interactive. However, one should note that this interaction marks both the power and the limit of the approach.

4.2 Stratified Abstractions

The second idea for semantics extraction is based on the same foundation presented in the previous section. Here, a sentence is not a self-contained semantical unit anymore. Sentences are reduced to two multi-sets that are freed from unnecessary sentential particularities. One consists of concepts serving as themes and the other contains rhematic concepts. Here, "concept" refers to a semantical unit that is represented by a few words. The bridge between textual representation by words and semantical representation by concepts is established by a domain specific dictionary. As discussed above, the main features represent the set of items that are explained by secondary ones. In the first step thematic concepts are identified and weighed. The weights depend on the number of their occurrences as main features (themes). Thus, a similarity to the vector space model [1] can be established. But here we do not remove stop words and take the rest to select the information items representing some concept. Further, we identify the most characterizing concept of a textual unit not just by a straight count of words. The dictionaries help to identify genericity among concepts. Thus, the concept of a higher genericity will obtain its weight from the number of occurrences as direct theme or subconcept theme.

In the second step, the secondary features are exploited. The multi-set of rhematic concepts is linked to its corresponding theme resulting in a set of tree structures. In fig. 3 one can see an example of rhemes forming a forest of concepts.

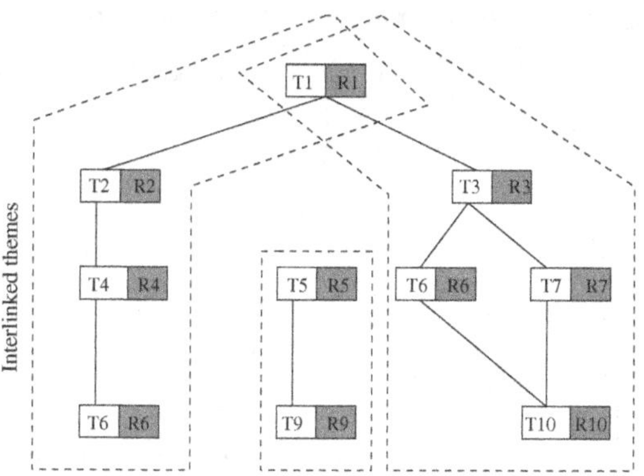

Fig. 3. Footprint formation (Abstract concepts)

In general, several concepts occur in more than one of the thematic lists. In addition to the links between thematic concepts representing the semantic neighborhood of concepts, further links between identical rhematic concepts can be defined. If looking at rhematic concepts linked to their themes, the concept of *"explained by"* pops up which clearly goes far beyond simple term weighing and concept counting.

Due to the *"explained by"* relationships, one can identify the *"best explained"* theme by building an *explanation graph*. In an explanation graph theme concepts are the root of explanation trees and concepts manifested as rhemes form only (unexplained) leaves. Such unexplained leaves are obviously of low interest in comparing documents. To compare footprints, tree pruning is applied, since the *"most explained"* concepts will occur close to the root.

Stored documents are represented by their fully developed footprints built at low cost. The complexity still to be overcome lies in matching document footprints against query footprints. Neural nets, specifically self-organizing ones, can be used for this purpose, if adequately adjusted. A full discussion of matching processes is beyond the scope of this paper and left for future work.

5 A Practical Example

In this section we want to clarify the presented approach by analyzing the description of the Unix command **mkdir** (see Fig. 4). Additionally, cohesion relations forming a network are set.

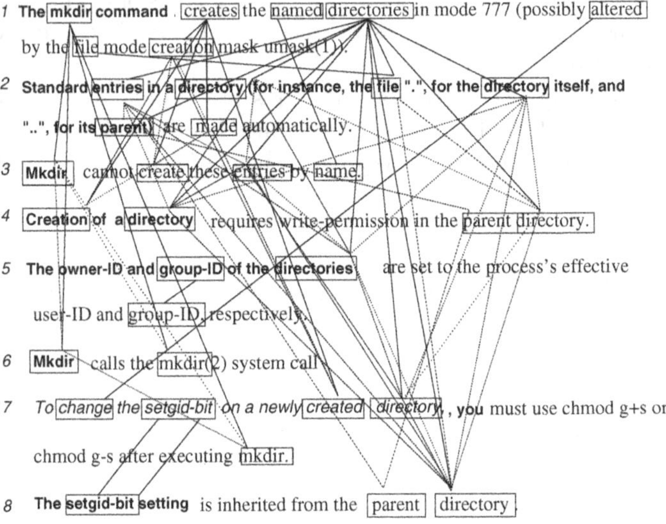

Fig. 4. Example of theme-rheme analysis: a *box* represents a concept, *marked theme* is shown in italic, *unmarked theme* in bold, *solid line* connects a concept with its first occurrence, *dotted line* links two instances of the same concept but not its first occurrence. Occurrence means an appearance in different forms of lexical devices (presented in section 2) such as repetition (*create, creation*), synonym (*create, make*), hyponym (*entry, file*)

The main sentence is found by computing the number of links per sentence. In this example the first sentence is determined as dominating in that way. Furthermore, in most cases the result will be the same, if a domain expert analyzes this page to find the main sentence. An interesting observation is the fact that the first (main) sentence appears in the theme parts (presented in bold and italic fonts) of the remaining sentences. This again reflects the tendency of writers to present the main statement first and explain it in detail by putting each concept as theme later on. In the analysis of this example, we neglect the distinction between marked and unmarked theme.

Because of the short document, no segment themes can be computed resulting to the footprint which is the first sentence. Hence, the abstraction described above cannot be literally respected.

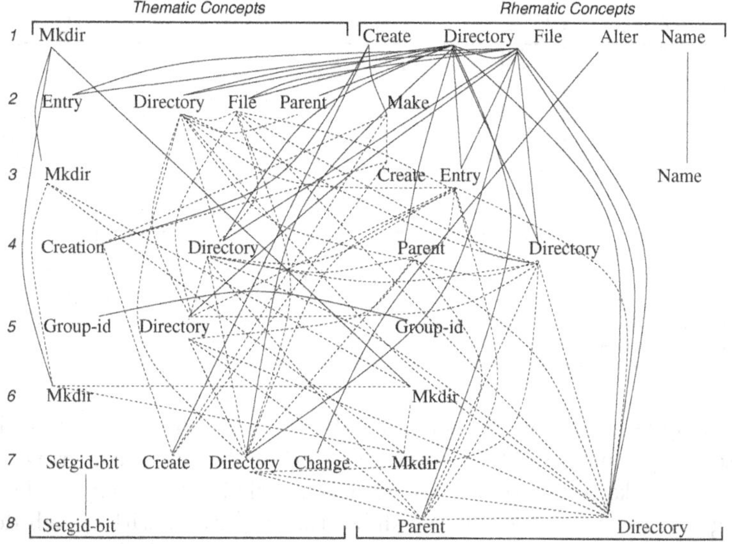

Fig. 5. From text to concepts

According to the second analysis option (section 4.2), we organize the concepts into two multi-sets, themes and their corresponding rhemes. In that way, the content of the first multi-set is explained by the second one (see Fig. 5). For the sake of computation, we transform Fig 5 into an adjacence matrix (Table 1).

One may notice that a concept can occur as theme as as well rheme. From this it follows that an important concept is usually commented. These comments introduce details related to the topic of the concept and represent, in general, various facets of that concept.

In order to quantify the notion of "important concept", we introduce two measures:

- *Explanatory power* measures how well a rhematic concept serves to explain the thematic concepts. It is the number of occurrences of the rhematic concept appearing in the rheme part of a sentence. This value can be used as an associated weight. In the example the most powerful explanatory concept is "Mkdir" with a degree of 6, followed by "Creation" (5) and "Dictionary" (4).
- *Topicality power* measures the centrality of a concept and provides the ability to determine the main objects of the document. It is computed by summing up the number of occurrences of the rhemes explaining that concept. In the example, "Mkdir" is the topical concept of the document with a degree of 9, followed by "Directory" gaining a 5.

Table 1. Thematic and rhematic concepts analysis. *themes* are represented as rows and are indexed by the sentence number they appear in. *rhemes* are represented as columns. A cell $c(i, j)$ indicates the occurrence the concept in column j "explains" the concept of row i along the text

THEME \ RHEME	Creation	Directory	File	Mkdir	Entry	Parent	Group-id	Change	Name	**Topicality Power**
Mkdir <1,3,6>	2	1	1	1	1			1	2	9
Entry <2>	1									1
Directory <2,4,5,7>	1	1		1		1	1			5
File <2>				1						1
Parent <2>	1									1
Creation <4,7>		1		1		1				3
Group-id <5>							1			1
Setgid-bit <7,8>		1		1		1				3
Change <7>				1						1
Explanatory power	5	4	1	6	1	3	2	1	2	

The results of this example are very plausible vis-à-vis human judgment because of the topic of the text. These results can be revised by considering also lexical cohesive links among concepts from a knowledge base (e.g. a thesaurus). Applying this revision, the example shows that the items with a high degree of topicality remain the same. Thus, for example "Directory" will have a topicality degree of 8 instead of 5 after adding the topicality degrees of the concepts which are related to it by use of lexical devices analysis.

Although the example does not show all theoretical aspects discussed earlier, it provides a clear idea about the method we suggest here. Further, we showed that the semantic contents expressed in terms of topical sentences or in terms of the main concepts are successfully determined leading to a highly promising approach.

6 Conclusion

The problem of reducing irrelevant information to a representative one is treated widely in the literature [19]. Although a variety of techniques (e.g. vector space model, probabilistic model, symbolic model, neural nets, genetic algorithms, etc.) are used in the information retrieval area, no significant progress in intelligently understanding documents is achieved. Here, we showed how different aspects for extracting semantics from documents can be used simultaneously. The way we interpret the structure of the document is more consistent and cognitively more acceptable than approaches strictly confined to the level of word analysis. In addition, the use of structure is almost neglected so far in the domain of information retrieval. By exploiting the theme-rheme relationship, it is possible to locate passages of important information.

We see that integrating different resources for the analysis of documents enhances the capabilities of detecting the semantics of documents. Thus, we expect a better effectiveness of the software retrieval system under construction. Our approach offers an engineering solution between information retrieval based on words and full semantic comprehension of texts after complete syntactic and semantic analysis.

Using some relatively simple heuristics and results from linguistics, the role of words can be inferred from their position in a sentence. Linking the role of words within a sentence with semantic information stemming from dictionaries and information about cohesion (currently reduced to genericity as first order approximation), paragraphs and consequently sections and documents can be reduced to abstract "footprints" suitable for quick comparison.

We refer to this approach as shallow semantic analysis. Two variants of such computerized shallow semantic analysis are described. One gives the user interactive control of the matching process. The other is fully automatic, but the user has quite a number of options to control the accuracy of matches.

References

[1] W.B. Frakes. *Information Retrieval: Data Structures and Algorithms*, pages 1–12. Prentice Hall, 1992.

[2] P.H. Fries. *Advances in Written Text Analysis*, pages 229–249. Routledge, 1994.

[3] E.J. Guglielmo and N.C. Rowe. Natural Language Retrieval of Images based on Descriptive Captions. *ACM Trans. on Information Systems*, 14(3), July 1996.

[4] U. Hahn. Topic Parsing: Accounting for Text Macro Structures in Full-Text Analysis. *Information Processing and Management*, 26(1):135–170, 1990.

[5] M.A.K. Halliday. *An Introduction to Functional Grammar.* Edward Arnold, 1985.

[6] M.A.K. Halliday and R. Hasan. *Cohesion in English.* Addison Wesley Ltd, 1976.

[7] I. Jacobson, M. Griss, and P. Jonsson. *Software Reuse.* Addison-Wesley, 1997.

[8] R.J. Leach. *Software Reuse.* McGraw Hill, 1997.

[9] A. Mili, R. Mili, and R.T. Mittermeir. A Survey of Software Reuse Libraries. *Annals of Software Engineering - Systematic Software Reuse*, 5:349–414, 1998.

[10] H. Mili, E. Akhi, R. Godin, and H. Mcheik. Another Nail to the Coffin of Faceted Controlled-Vocabulary Component Classification and Retrieval. In M.Harandi, *Symposium on Software Reusability*, vol. 22, pp 89–98. ACM Press, 1997.

[11] R. Mili, A. Mili, and R.T. Mittermeir. Storing and Retrieving Software Components: A Refinement Based System. *IEEE Tran. on Software Engineering*, 23(7):445 – 460, July 1997.

[12] M. Mitra, A. Singhal, and C. Buckley. Improving Automatic Query Expansion. In *Proc. of the 21st Annual Int. ACM SIGIR Conf. on Research and Development in Information Retrieval*, pp 206–214, Melbourne, August 24 - 28 1998.

[13] R.T. Mittermeir, H. Pozewaunig, A. Mili, and R. Mili. Uncertainty Aspects in Component Retrieval. In *Proc. of the 7th Int. Conf. on Information Processing and Management of Uncertainty in Knowledge-Based Systems*, Paris, July 1998.

[14] J. Morris and G. Hirst. Lexical Cohesion Computed by Thesaural Relations as an Indicator of the Structure of Text. *Ass. for Comp. Linguistics*, 17(1), March 1991.

[15] M. Nystrand. *The Structure of Written Communication.* Academic Press, 1986.

[16] Rubèn Prieto-Diàz. Implementing Faceted Classification for Software Reuse. *Communications of the ACM*, 43(5):88 – 97, May 1991.

[17] F. Daneš. Functional Sentence Perspective and the Organization of the Text. In *Papers on Functional Sentence Perspective*, pages 106–128. Publishing House of The Czechoslovak Academy of Sciences, Prague, 1970.

[18] T.A. van Dijk. *Handbook of Discourse Analysis: Dimensions of Discourse*, vol. 2, pp 103–134. Academic Press, 1985.

[19] Y. Yang and J.P. Pedersen. A Comparative Study on Feature Selection in Text Categorization. In *Proc. of the 14*th *Int. Conf. on Machine learning*, 1997.

Automated Information Extraction out of Classified Advertisements

Ramón Aragüés Peleato, Jean-Cédric Chappelier, and Martin Rajman

Computer Science Dep. – Swiss Federal Institute of Technology (EPFL) – Lausanne

Abstract. This paper presents an information extraction system that processes the textual content of classified newspaper advertisements in French. The system uses both lexical (words, regular expressions) and contextual information to structure the content of the ads on the basis of predefined thematic forms. The paper first describes the enhanced tagging mechanism used for extraction. A quantitative evaluation of the system is then provided: scores of 99.0% precision/99.8% recall for domain identification and 73% accuracy for information extraction were achieved, on the basis of a comparison with human annotators.

1 Introduction

The work reported in this paper has been carried out in the context of the development of a system able to automatically extract and structure information from the textual content of newspaper advertisements. The system consists of three modules, as summarized in figure 1:

1. The task of the first module is to classify advertisements into *a priori* known classes (*real estate*, *vehicles*, *employment* or *other*). This step is needed to identify which thematic form has to be associated with the advertisement, and then used to guide the information extraction process. Classification is performed using a mixture of a naive Bayes classifier and a form-based classifier developed in our laboratory [15]. An evaluation on a test collection of 2,856 manually classified ads produced the very satisfying scores of 99.8% recall and 99.0% precision.
2. The task of the second module, which represents the main focus of this paper, consists in tagging (i.e. labelling) the textual content of the advertisement, in order to identify the information units that have to be extracted to fill in the slots of the associated form. Tagging is achieved by using specialized lexica, regular expressions, word spotting techniques and relative position analysis as described in the following sections.
3. Finally, the structuring module is in charge of transforming the tagged text into structured data (i.e. a filled form). This involves extracting the tagged textual units, standardizing formulations[1], removing inappropriate punctuation, transforming abbreviations, etc. In the current system, this module

[1] for example, using the same format for all price indications.

M. Bouzeghoub et al. (Eds.): NLDB 2000, LNCS 1959, pp. 203–214, 2001.

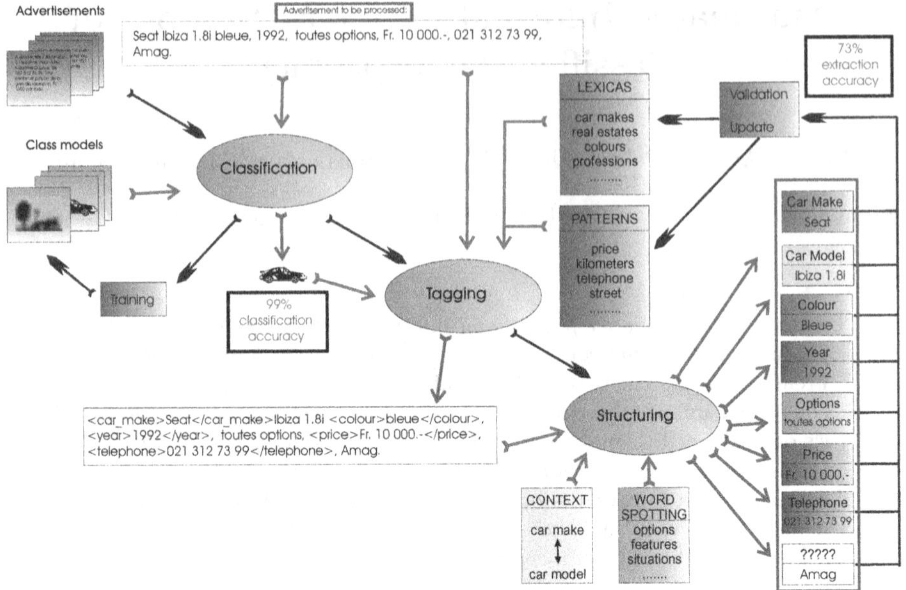

Fig. 1. *Global architecture of the system for automatic processing of newspaper advertisements.*

remains quite simple as the tags used in step 2 closely correspond to the slots present in the associated forms.

The tagging phase can be further decomposed in the following steps:

- Labelling known entities (words, compounds, expressions) using specialized lexica and regular expressions (section 2).
- Identifying the nature of the information that is expressed by the textual units that have not been tagged in the first step (section 3). This is achieved through:
  1. segmentation based on punctuation and prepositions;
  2. word spotting in each segment (subsection 3.1);
  3. contextual tagging using the relative position of the units with relation to already tagged segments (subsection 3.2).

Notice that the design methodology used for our system is different from typical Information Extraction approaches [9] in the sense that, instead of trying to find some specific information in a whole document, it rather tries to identify the nature of the information expressed by each single piece of the text. In addition, the general strategy used by traditional systems [1, 8] consists in searching trigger words and then analyzing their context, while our system first segments using known entities and then analyzes the unknown segments with positional techniques and trigger words. Another specificity of our system is the average length of the processed documents: advertisements are generally short and very concise.

2 Tagging with Lexica and Regular Expressions

As already mentioned, the first step necessary to extract information from advertisements and fill in the automatically associated forms consists in tagging the advertisements for known entities using both specialized lexica and regular expressions [7].

2.1 Lexicon

Lexicon-based tagging simply consists in searching the text for entries contained in an *a priori* build lexicon. This lexicon may contain general words (e.g. *camion* [truck]), specific words (e.g. *airbag*), compounds (e.g. *pneus d'hiver* [winter tires]) and expressions (e.g. *libre de suite* [vacant immediately]) associated with identification labels (e.g. label such as *ville* [city] for the word *Paris*). Elements in the advertisement are tagged with the corresponding label only if they are non-ambiguous in the lexicon (i.e. associated with only one single label).

The tagging lexicon used in our system was created on the basis of a preliminary lexical study of a corpus of 10,700 advertisements, spread over 8 years[2]. A frequency analysis of the vocabulary was performed to serve as a guideline for the creation of the lexicon. For this analysis, a general purpose French lexicon containing more than 550,000 word forms (84,000 lemmas) was used and the following two questions were addressed:

1. what is the overall orthographic quality of the advertisements? The answer to this question determines whether an efficient spelling checker needs to be integrated in the system.
2. what is the proportion of specific vocabulary (i.e. vocabulary that is frequently used in advertisements but unknown to the general purpose lexicon)?

To answer these questions, the following table was built for the identified out-of-vocabulary forms (7270, 38.8% of the vocabulary):

		rare forms	frequent forms
Corrected	short	501 (2.7% of voc.)	514 (2.7% of voc.)
	long	1038 (5.5% of voc.)	
Not corrected		4170 (22.3% of voc.)	1047 (5.6% of voc.)

Rare forms are the forms[3] that appeared less than 3 times in the corpus. *Corrected forms* refer to forms that accept a one spelling error correction[4] in the general purpose lexicon (short/long refers to the number of characters in the form, short standing for less than or equal to 4 characters).

[2] The total vocabulary contained in that corpus was of 18,720 words. Words had an average frequency of 22 and advertisements had an average length of 37 words.

[3] i.e. tokens resulting from a French tokenizer, most often words.

[4] a "one spelling error correction" is any form in the lexicon that is at an edit distance equal to 1 from the considered out-of-vocabulary form.

To interpret the above table, the following hypotheses were used

- frequent out-of-vocabulary forms that are not corrected correspond to instances of the specific vocabulary for the advertisements;
- frequent forms that can be corrected should be carefully analyzed as they might either correspond to systematic errors (frequent) or specific vocabulary that incidentally also corresponds to a correction that belongs to the general purpose vocabulary;
- rare and corrected forms may possibly be spelling errors. This has to be moderated by the length of the form as short forms more easily produce one spelling error corrections in a general purpose lexicon. We therefore decided to only trust corrections for forms with length greater than 4. Short rare forms are ignored, even if they have a correction in the general purpose lexicon.[5]
- rare and uncorrected forms are ignored as they concern infrequent phenomena for which not enough information is available.

With such interpretation rule the table can then be summarized as:

		rare forms	frequent forms
Corrected	short	ignored	manual processing
	long	spelling errors	
Not corrected		ignored	specific voc.

The above results therefore indicate that the corpus is of good orthographic quality (38.8% of out-of-vocabulary forms among which only 5.5% can reasonably considered as errors)[6] and contains a quite high ratio of specific forms (5.6% of identified specific vocabulary and 25%[7] of ignored forms mainly due to rare (personal) abbreviations).

The lexical study was also a good starting point for the creation of the tagging lexicon: first of all, many of the frequent unknown words were directly introduced into the lexicon, thus improving its coverage; but, most of all, all the new words identified were good indicators of what was the kind of vocabulary that can be found in newspapers advertisements. Therefore, when a word corresponding to a label was added to the lexicon (e.g. *Paris* being a city), several other words corresponding to the same label (e.g. all cities in the considered country) were also added. These other words have been extracted from several different sources, mainly Internet public lists. However, a large amount of time needed to be devoted to the validation/correction of these other sources of information. Approximately 45 person·days were spent on the lexical analysis and lexicon construction.

[5] This choice is sensible if the orthographic quality of the corpus is good, as it was the case for us.

[6] This was not surprising as we were dealing with proof-read newspapers advertisements. The results would certainly have been different if dealing with Internet advertisements.

[7] 22.3% + 2.7%

The following table shows examples of labels contained in the tagging lexicon used by our system:

Label	Number of words	Examples
Cantons	97	*GE, Genf, Genève*
Colours	36	*blanche, foncé, métallisée*
Car makes	134	*Renault, Seat, VW*
Car garages	114	*Amag, Croset, ROC*
Real Estates	137	*Chapuis, Gérim, Rêve-Immob*
Professions	539	*pompier, ingénieur, serveuse*
Languages	47	*Espagnol, Anglais, Roumain*
Months	24	*Janvier, Janv., Juin*
Motor bikes	48	*Honda, Yamaha, CBR*
Streets Index	83	*Rue, Av., Ruelle*
Cities	4230	*Lausanne, Zürich, Chur*
Kinds of vehicles	12	*Scooter, Bus, camion*
Kinds of buildings	57	*Halle, Appartement, villa*
Salary expressions	10	*salaire à discuter*

2.2 Regular Expressions

The second method used for directly tagging textual units was to apply descriptive patterns written with regular expressions, as for example dates, phone numbers, prices, surfaces. In order to create the regular expressions a first basic set was build for several *a priori* chosen slots of the forms to be filled. The resulting tagger was then run over a training corpus consisting of textual units corresponding to the chosen slots. New patterns were then gradually created and old ones improved by iterative testing on the reference corpus as long as there were slots with error frequency greater than 1.

The following table describes several different patterns created with this procedure:

Pattern	Examples
Name	*M. Duboux*
Surface	*200 m2 environ*
Kilometers	*100 000 km*
Number rooms	*3 1/2 pièces*
Age	*Agée de 35 ans*
Work Time	*50% ou 75%*
Action	*Cherche à louer*
Date	*Janvier 2000* *1.12.1999*

Pattern	Examples
Free	*libre de suite* *livrable: fevrier 2000*
Email	*pepito.grillo@cdi.com*
Price	*Fr. 3'000.- à discuter* *loyer à négocier*
Charges	*Charges comprises* *+ 50.- charges*
To visit	*Pour visiter: 021 693 66 97*
To treat	*Rens: Régie Houx, 021 693 66 97*
Telephone	*Tél. (021) 312 73 99, le soir.*

2.3 Tagging Known Entities

Using the above described tagging lexicon and regular expressions, the system then scans the whole advertisement and tags all the identified unambiguous textual units with the corresponding label. The output of this process therefore consists in a partially tagged text with remaining untagged parts corresponding to either unknown ambiguous items. Figure 2 gives an example of the result of this first step on a vehicle advertisement.

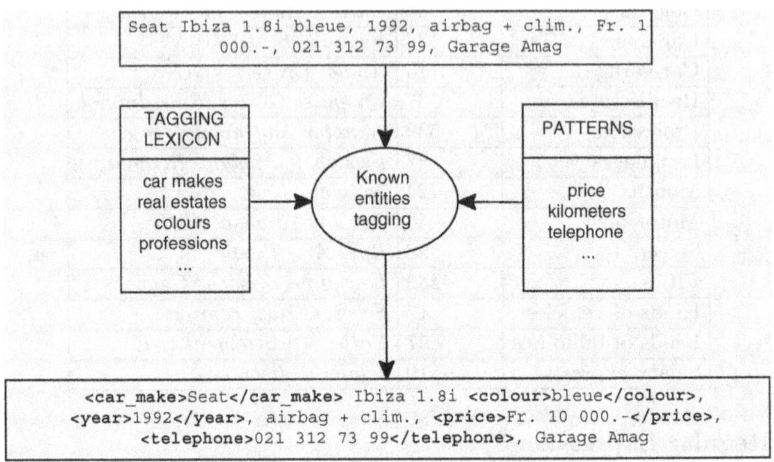

Fig. 2. *Tagging known entities with lexica and patterns. Information is identified by the SGML surrounding tags.*

3 Identifying Information in Unrecognized Parts

Once the advertisement has been tagged for known entities, it still contains several portions that have not been identified (e.g. *Ibiza*, *Garage Amag* in the example of figure 2). To further tag these pieces of text the following three steps were applied:

1. the untagged text is segmented using punctuation and (for employment advertisements only) prepositions, so as to separate different information pieces that may be contained in the same text area[8]. A special treatment using a list of known abbreviations avoids segmenting punctuation used for abbreviations.
2. a word spotting score is computed for each segment on the basis of several trigger lexica (section 3.1).
3. If the word spotting score is not high enough to allow a reliable decision, the segment is tagged according to contextual rules taking into account the nature (i.e. the tags) of its neighbour segments (section 3.2).

[8] These segments may be recombined afterwards (at the end of the process) if they happen to have the same final tag.

3.1 Word Spotting

To compute the word spotting score for a segment, the system uses several *trigger lexica*. A trigger lexicon consists in a list of keywords that are typical for a certain type of information (e.g *climatisation* for vehicle options) and that help to identify the proper label for all the text in that segment. The word spotting score is therefore a measure of the likelihood for a segment to be relevant for a certain type of information [11].

The words selected for the trigger lexica used by our system were extracted from the lexical study described in section 2. They have been extended by running the system over a training corpus containing additional advertisements. Notice however, that trigger lexica differ from the tagging lexicon in the sense that they do not contain words that represent alone an identified information entity. These words rather give an idea on the kind of information that is contained in the text area they appear in.

The following table describes several different trigger lexica used in our current system:

Trigger lexicon	Number of words	Examples
Options (vehicles)	83	*autolook, clim, alarme*
Models (vehicles)	500	*Mégane, Punto, Ibiza*
Dealers (vehicles)	3	*garage, SA, AG*
Price (vehicles, real estate)	13	*prix, CHF, gratuit*
Construction (real estate)	11	*récent, rénover, refait*
Features (real estate)	42	*cheminée, balcon, parking*
Quality (real estate)	11	*spacieux, splendide, charmant*
Situation (real estate)	44	*calme, gare, centre*
To treat (real estate)	12	*renseignements, SARL, vente*
To visit (real estate)	3	*visite, contact, adresser*
Activity (employment)	70	*garder, ménage, nettoyage*
Age (employment)	3	*ans, âge, adulte*
Contact (employment)	6	*offre, contact, soumettre*
Qualifications (employment)	40	*diplômé, connaissances, programation*
Requirements (employment)	15	*curriculum, permis, véhicule*
Salary (employment)	3	*argent, gagner, salaire*
Company (employment)	15	*institution, SA, S.A.R.L.*
Work place (employment)	50	*pizzeria, hôtel, commerce*

As each trigger lexicon is associated with a unique specific tag, the word spotting score for each tag is computed as the number of words of the corresponding lexicon that appear in the segment. Finally, if there is a word spotting score that exceeds the others of a given threshold, the segment is tagged with the label associated with the corresponding trigger lexicon.

3.2 Contextual Tagging

In case where word spotting techniques do not permit to identify the information contained in a segment[9], a tag is allocated to the segment on the basis of the tag immediately preceding (i.e. its left boundary). We call this technique *contextual tagging* as the allocated tag to a segment depends on its (left) context. For example, the contextual tag following the make of a vehicle is "*model*" as, in vehicle advertisements, the car model very often follows the car make. This relation between tag and context is based on an *a prior* analysis carried out on a large amount of advertisements. When no contextual rule can be applied, the segment is tagged as "*undefined*".

The final result of the tagging module is therefore a fully tagged text that can then be directly used to fill the associated form. In the current system the structure obtained by filling the slots is further filtered: unwanted punctuation is removed and slots without relevant information (i.e. less than one normal[10] character) are removed.

3.3 Examples

The following table contain several examples of tags obtained by word spotting and contextual tagging:

Class	vehicles		real estate		employment
Tag	**options**	**models**	**features**	**situation**	**qualifications**
Vocabulary size	291	266	2586	1169	522
Examples	*pneus neufs*	*A 160 Avantgarde*	*meublé*	*centre*	*sérieux*
	3 portes	*Astra Break 16V*	*jardin*	*1er étage*	*dynamique*
	toit ouvrant	*4x4*	*2 salles d'eau*	*situation calme*	*jeune fille*
	5 portes	*LX (241 HSE)*	*place de parc*	*2e étage*	*jeune homme*
	ABS	*Grand Cherokee*	*garage*	*3e étage*	*d'expérience*
	jantes alu		*cave*	*vue imprenable*	*avec expérience*
	radio CD		*balcon*	*vue sur le lac*	*jeune*
	toutes options		*cuisine agencée*	*vue*	
	climatisation			*calme*	

Underlined words are words that appear in trigger lexica (and were used for word spotting).

An example of the the final output of the tagging module for the same vehicles advertisement as in figure 2 is given in figure 3, as well as its corresponding final filled frame.

4 Evaluation of the System

An evaluation of the system described in this paper was done on the basis of a comparison with forms filled by human annotators.

The test corpus consisted of 77 advertisements (41 real estate, 30 employment and 6 to vehicles; a proportion representative of both the whole corpus and week

[9] i.e. all word spotting scores are under the threshold or there is more than one best score (ties).

[10] neither blank nor punctuation.

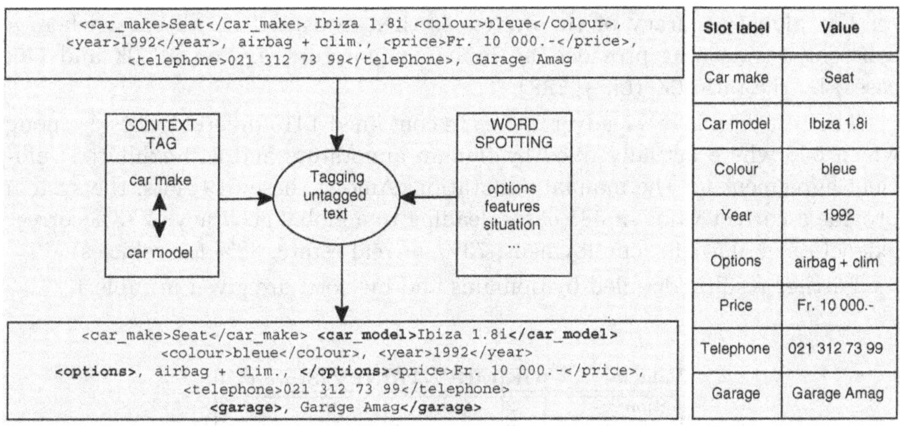

Slot label	Value
Car make	Seat
Car model	Ibiza 1.8i
Colour	bleue
Year	1992
Options	airbag + clim
Price	Fr. 10 000.-
Telephone	021 312 73 99
Garage	Garage Amag

Fig. 3. *Tagging entities with word spotting and context. The frame filled after structuring is also shown on the right.*

ads production). Each of these advertisements was submitted [11] to several human annotators who had to properly fill the corresponding form.

Before the evaluation of the system itself, the manually annotated forms were checked for coherence using a kappa measure [18, 3, 2]. On the basis of the confusion matrices produced for the computation of the kappa scores, several unreliable slots were thus identified and were then either removed or clustered in order to improve the agreement among the human annotators. The final average kappa value obtained was 0.9, thus indicating a satisfying agreement for the reference[12].

The test set was then submitted to the system, and the results were compared to the human references. The rules used to assign a comparison score to a slot were the following:

- If there is no agreement among the manual annotation, the slot is ignored (neutralization (`NTR`) case);
- If no value, neither manually nor automatically, was assigned to the slot, it is ignored (non evaluation (`NEV`) case);
- If both the system and the human annotators agree, the answer is considered as correct (`OK` case);
- In any other case the answer is considered as an error (`ERR` case).

Notice that the evaluation of the slots was carried out manually and the `OK`/`ERR` assessments for the values assigned to the slot by the system and the annotators were therefore judged by humans. On a larger scale, the manual assessment would need to be replaced by automated rules relying for instance on the number of common words in the values assigned.

[11] together with its corresponding form

[12] kappa measure varies between -1 (complete disagreement) and 1 (complete agreement). Values higher than 0.8 are usually considered as indicating good agreement.

The global accuracy of the system is then measured on all cases where a coherent answer was provided by human annotators (i.e. on all OK and ERR cases) by the ratio OK/(OK + ERR).

The test corpus of 77 advertisements contained 1415 different slots[13] among which 556 where actually filled by human annotators and 519 exhibited sufficient agreement for the manual annotation. Among these 519 slots, the system provide a correct value in 381 cases, leading to a global accuracy of 73% correct extractions (70.5% for employment, 73% for real estate, 88% for vehicles).

Further results, detailed by domains and by slots, are given in table 1.

Vehicle	OK	ERR	NTR	NEV	Score (%)
Action	2	0	0	4	100
Kind of vehicle	0	1	2	3	0
Vehicle make	4	0	1	1	100
Vehicle model	4	1	0	1	80
Motor bike	0	0	0	6	–
Colour	3	0	0	3	100
Year	5	0	0	1	100
Expertized	2	0	0	4	100
Kilometers	5	1	0	0	83
Options	4	0	1	1	100
Price	3	1	0	2	75
Dealer	0	1	0	5	0
Contact	0	0	0	6	–
Telephone	6	0	0	0	100
Fax	0	0	0	6	–
E-mail	0	0	0	6	–
Total	38	5	4	49	**88.4**

Real Estate	OK	ERR	NTR	NEV	Score
Action	31	1	2	7	97
Kind of building	28	6	4	3	82
Number of rooms	16	3	1	21	84
Surface	10	2	2	27	83
Story	8	21	6	6	28
Construction	1	3	2	35	25
Features	17	7	2	15	71
Region	24	14	2	1	63
Quarter	0	4	1	36	0
Street	2	5	1	33	29
Price	22	0	0	19	100
Charges	5	4	0	32	56
Entry date	15	4	0	22	79
Real estate	0	1	0	40	0
To visit	0	1	0	40	0
To treat	2	1	1	37	67
Telephone	33	2	1	5	94
Fax	0	0	0	41	–
E-mail	0	0	0	41	–
Total	214	79	25	461	**73.0**

Employment	OK	ERR	NTR	NEV	Score
Action	30	0	0	0	100
Job	17	9	2	2	65
Qualifications	9	13	0	8	41
Age	0	4	1	25	0
Languages	1	1	0	28	50
Entry date	16	2	0	12	89
Work time	3	1	2	24	75
Kind of Company	0	8	0	22	0
Work place	9	8	1	12	53
City	12	1	1	16	92
Quarter	0	0	0	30	–
Street	0	1	0	29	0
Region	3	2	0	25	60
Salary	0	1	1	28	0
Contact	10	3	0	17	77
Telephone	18	0	0	12	100
Fax	1	0	0	29	100
E-mail	0	0	0	30	–
Total	129	54	8	349	**70.5**

Table 1. Precise results of the evaluation of the system for each slot of the 3 forms corresponding respectively to real estate, employment and vehicle advertisements.

[13] 30 x 18 for Employment, 41 x 19 for real estate and 6 x 16 for vehicles.

5 Conclusions and Future Work

The goal of the work presented in this paper was to create a system able to automatically classify and structure newspaper advertisements. As the classified advertisements domain is quite different from other studied information extraction problems [12, 13, 14] specific techniques were implemented, which as shown in section 4 achieve very promising results (73% correct extraction) when compared with human annotators.

However, there is still room for improvements. In particular the presented tagging methodology has one important limitation: when the text that remains untagged after the first segmentation[14] contains information associated with different labels[15], the word spotting technique does not correctly tag the text. Indeed when the untagged text contains keywords for two different trigger lexica[16], a decision about the contents of that information unit is not possible (same score for two trigger lexica means no decision about the kind of content) and the text is then tagged as undefined.

One way of solving this problem is to apply a progressive tagging, in which segmentation is not done on the sole basis of the tagging lexicon and patterns, but delayed until the nature of the information inside the segment is unambiguously identified. The idea is to progressively calculate the word spotting scores for a growing initial sequence of words in the untagged segment and to build a new segment (with an associated tag) only when the difference between the scores assigned by the different trigger lexica decreases. Experiments over the whole corpus of advertisements are being carried out, and future work will evaluate the potential improvements brought by this technique.

Another future research will focus on lowering the dependency on hand-written lexica and patterns. As shown in [10, 16, 17] different techniques allow a system to automatically extract patterns and dictionaries form labelled and unlabelled texts, allowing a faster adaptation of a system when moved to a new domain. Extending the approach to ontologies could also be considered [5, 4, 6].

References

[1] D. Appelt et al. SRI international FASTUS system: MUC-6 results and analysis. In *Proceedings of the Sixth Message Understanding Conference (MUC-6*. Morgan Kaufmann Publishers, 1995.

[2] J. Carletta. Assessing agreement on classification traks: the kappa statistics. *Computational linguistics*, 2(22):249–254, 1996.

[3] J. Cohen. A coefficient of agreement for nominal scales. *Educational and Phychological measurement*, 20:37–46, 1960.

[14] where the system uses tagging lexicon and regular expressions

[15] e.g. "*situation calme et place de parc*" (calm and garage) contains information about the situation and the features of the building"

[16] e.g. keywords for "situation" and "parking place";

[4] D. W. Embley, D. M. Campbell, Y. S. Jiang, S. W. Liddle, Y.-K. Ng, D. Quass, and R. D. Smith. Conceptual-model-based data extraction from multiple-record web pages. *Data and Knowledge Engineering*, 31(3):227–251, 1999.

[5] D. W. Embley, D. M. Campbell, R. D. Smith, and S. W. Liddle. Ontology-based extraction and structuring of information from data-rich unstructured documents. In G. Gardarin, J. C. French, N. Pissinou, K. Makki, and L. Bouganim, editors, *Proc. of of the 1998 ACM CIKM Int. Conf. on Information and Knowledge Managemen (CIKM'98)*, pages 52–59, Bethesda (Maryland), November 1998. ACM Press.

[6] D. W. Embley, N. Fuhr, C.-P. Klas, and T. Rölleke. Ontology suitability for uncertain extraction of information from multi-records web documents. *Datenbank Rundbrief*, 24:48–53, 1999.

[7] D. Fisher et al. Description of the UMASS system as used for MUC-6. In *Proceedings of the Sixth Message Understanding Conference (MUC-6)*, San Mateo, CA, 1995. Morgan Kaufmann Publishers.

[8] R. Grishman. The NYU system for MUC-6 or where is the syntax? In *Proceedings of the Sixth Message Understanding Conference (MUC-6)*, San Mateo, CA, 1995. Morgan Kaufmann Publishers.

[9] R. Grishman. Information extraction: Techniques and challenges. In ed. M. T. Pazienza, editor, *International Summer School SCIE-97*, Springer-Verlag, July 1997.

[10] J.-T. Kim and D. I. Moldovan. Acquisition of linguistic patterns for knowledge-based information extraction. *IEEE Transactions on Knowledge and Data Engineering*, 1995.

[11] A. McCallum and K. Nigam. Text classification by bootstrapping with keywords, EM and shrinkage. In *ACL '99 Workshop for Unsupervised Learning in Natural Language Processing*, 1999.

[12] *Proceedings of the Fifth Message Understanding Conference (MUC-5)*. Morgan Kaufmann, August 1993.

[13] *Proceedings of the Sixth Message Understanding Conference (MUC-6)*. Morgan Kaufmann, San Mateo CA, November 1995.

[14] *Proceedings of the Seventh Message Understanding Conference (MUC-7)*. http://www.muc.saic.com/, 1997.

[15] R. Aragüés Peleato, J.-C. Chappelier, and M. Rajman. Lexical study of advertisements and automatic identification of lexical items through contextual patterns. In *Proc. of 5th International Conference on the Statistical Analysis of Textual Data (JADT'2000)*, volume 1, pages 309–316, Lausanne (Switzerland), March 2000.

[16] E. Riloff. Automatically generating extraction patterns form untagged text. In *Proceedings of the Tenth National Conference on Artificial Intelligence*, pages 50–55, San Jose, CA, 1992. AAAI/MIT Press.

[17] E. Riloff. An empirical study of automated dictionary construction for information extraction in three domains. *Artificial Intelligence*, 85:101–134, 1996.

[18] S. Siegel and N.J. Jr. Castellan. *Nonparametric statistics for the Behavioral Sciences*. McGraw-Hill, second edition edition, 1988.

A Smart Web Query Engine for Semantic Retrieval of Web Data and Its Application to E-Trading

Roger H.L. Chiang[1], Cecil Chua[2], and Veda C. Storey[3]

[1] College of Business Administration
University of Cincinnati, Cincinnati, OH 45221, USA
Roger.Chiang@uc.edu
[2] School of Accountancy and Business
Nanyang Technological University, Singapore 639798
aehchua@ntu.edu.sg
[3] J. Mack Robinson College of Business
Georgia State University, Atlanta, GA 30303-4015, USA
VStorey@gsu.edu

Abstract. Vast amounts of data are available on the World Wide Web. However, the extraction and use of this data is difficult, since web data does not conform to any data organization standard. Search engines provide only primitive data query capabilities, and require a detailed syntactic specification to retrieve relevant data. This research proposes a Smart Web Query (SWQ) approach for the semantic retrieval of web data. The approach uses context and domain information to specify and formulate appropriate web queries and formats to search. The SWQ approach relies on context ontologies to discover relevant web pages. Unlike traditional ontologies, SWQ ontologies are structured on a set-theoretic model, which makes them more flexible, adaptive, extensible, and rapidly deployable. An SWQ engine is being developed to test the approach.

Keywords. Semantic information retrieval, web data, web search engine, ontology development, Smart Web Query Engine

1 Introduction

One of the largest and most easily accessible sources of data is the World Wide Web. However, web searches are often difficult to perform for several reasons. First, search engines are still very primitive. Search statements must be specified as sets of key words separated by boolean operators. Reasonable levels of precision and recall are only achieved when many key words are used. Second, search engines can only retrieve data on a purely syntactic basis. It is not possible to embed common sense, context, or domain specific knowledge into the search engines' queries. Third, web data occurs in a wide variety of heterogeneous formats such as PDF documents and images. Most searches are unable to query such data sources. Finally, it is not feasible to establish a rigorous standard for web data

M. Bouzeghoub et al. (Eds.): NLDB 2000, LNCS 1959, pp. 215–226, 2001.

modeling and organization since web page development remains unregulated. Thus, it is impossible to develop a formal web query language.

The objective of this research is to propose a method for searching web data. We develop a *Smart Web Query (SWQ)* engine based on context ontologies. This work is significant in at least two ways. First, it provides a new and feasible approach to searching and extracting useful information from the World Wide Web by using context ontologies. Second, it provides a means to represent context ontologies without using taxonomies.

2 Related Research

2.1 Searches on Web Data

Four main strategies have been employed to search unstructured web data.

- **Syntactic search** is the most common search strategy on unstructured or semi-structured data and is used by most existing commercial and prototype search engines (e.g. [1, 9, 24]). Documents are discovered, classified, and referenced in a search database by human subject experts (e.g. [9]), or by automated agents/spiders (e.g. [24]). Database instances are accessed through boolean or hierarchical searches [1].
- **Metadata search** improves on syntactic search by using relevant aspects of a document's schema. There are two types of metadata search – syntactic and semantic. In syntactic metadata search, syntactic elements of a document such as the title, section headings, and links [17], are considered. Semantic metadata search is usually performed in specialized domains. Domain specific semantics are used to enhance the query's precision and recall. For example, in CiteSeer [3], commonly referenced authors identify the subject category of a publication.
- In **Query by example**, (suspected) relevant documents are identified based on their similarity to a sample document. Query-by-example is traditionally used for non-textual searches, such as those for web images [4].
- **Navigational search** simulates the web browsing search process. A robot, or autonomous agent is given a sample page containing links. The robot traverses the links, evaluating each page for relevance to a search specification [16].

A semantic metadata search strategy appears to be the most promising. Syntactic search is limited, since the context of the search is not considered. Query by example is difficult to deploy for a generic search. An agent that performs navigational search typically must have its search specification represented using one of the other search strategies. Syntactic metadata search is limited for the same reasons as a purely syntactic search. The main difficulty with a semantic metadata search is the rapid deployment of metadata representations for multiple contexts. Most metadata search engines restrict themselves to particular contexts, since context representation is traditionally a difficult and time consuming task.

2.2 Ontology Development

An ontology is an explicit specification of a conceptualization [10] that can be used to support communication among different parties with different internal knowledge representation schemes. Most ontologies consist of terms, their definitions, and axioms relating them [10], with terms usually organized into a taxonomy [13]. Problems in ontology development include the following.

- **Difficulty of Obtaining Domain Expertise:** Traditional ontologies are normally developed by a human domain expert [8]. Internet users however, query the web for a wide range of topics. It is difficult and expensive to obtain a domain expert for the plethora of topics for which users will search. Also, many aspects of ontologies do not require domain expertise. For example, some kinds of relationships among terms are common knowledge to all persons involved in the domain. Even casual investors know that "bonds" and "stocks" are "investment instruments." Thus, a flexible and extensible ontology structure needs to be established so that individuals with varying degrees of expertise can incrementally embed their knowledge within the ontology.
- **Extensibility:** Ontologies based on taxonomies are very difficult to extend. Frequently, the addition of new terms necessitates restructuring of the hierarchy [12]. For web querying, it is necessary for ontologies to be extensible, as languages are vibrant and evolving.
- **Validation Difficulty:** The validation of ontologies is usually performed by measuring the inter-rater reliability of the validating domain experts, or by having a single authoritative domain expert perform the validation. However, it is often difficult to get expert agreement on one ontology [18].
- **Heterogeneous Definitions:** When an ontology is structured as a taxonomy, the definition (interpretation) of a term is based on its position within the taxonomy and its relationship to other terms [13]. However, many terms and their relationships are multi-dimensional [6]. For example, a "stock" and a "bond" are both financial instruments. A person who owns a "stock" has ownership of a company, but a "bond" owner has first rights to the company's assets. Thus, the relationship between terms depends fundamentally on the perspective of the user and not on rigid hierarchies.
- **Ontology Integration:** It is difficult to integrate two ontologies based on taxonomies that represent the same real-world concept. While ontology interchange formats exist (e.g. Ontolingua [8]), the integration of ontologies remains an expensive, time consuming, and manual activity [12].
- **Adaptability:** Ontologies based on taxonomies cater, not only to specific subjects (e.g. 'Financial Trade'), but also to specific tasks [5]. For example, a 'Financial Trade' ontology designed to identify synonyms (e.g. "stock" and "share") would have difficulty identifying the structure of financial publications (e.g. "Assets" always precede "Liabilities" on a balance sheet). Adaptable ontologies are required for web searches.

2.3 Ontologies Adopted for Web Search

Little research has been carried out on the use of domain semantics, represented by ontologies, for web searches. Most research on ontologies for web searches (e.g. [12]) focuses on establishing tools to build ontologies or on post-hoc development of ontologies [22]. Such ontologies are often manually constructed. Domain specific ontologies have been proposed for web searching, (e.g. [15]). However, these ontologies are primarily used to search structured databases or facilitate particular kinds of search, such as e-commerce negotiations, or phone book searches [11]. Research on using ontologies to facilitate generic web search seems to be lacking.

It is not cost effective to develop a generic ontology for the World Wide Web. We advocate the development of context ontologies to enhance web searches. Context ontologies organize not only terms and their relationships (i.e. contents for traditional ontologies), but also domain specific knowledge, best practices and heuristics (i.e., the epistemology).

3 Smart Web Query Approach

An efficient web search can only be achieved if the context and semantics behind the search are explicitly explored and used to guide it. Thus, we propose a Smart Web Query (SWQ) approach for the semantic retrieval of web data, and develop the SWQ engine. The SWQ engine provides a uniform way to perform any context sensitive query by semantics.

The SWQ engine employs context ontologies for identifying semantics to specify and refine web queries. Thus, a flexible, extensible and rapidly deployable structure is required to construct context ontologies for it. We propose a set theoretic representation structure of ontological terms, where every term in the context ontology can be accessed and manipulated in an identical manner. The SWQ engine establishes each web query by comparing context ontologies against user specified search terms. Then, it matches the search terms against a specific ontology, and uses the ontology to guide the search. This section presents the system architecture of the Smart Web Query approach and the design of the SWQ engine. The development of context ontologies is presented in Section 4.

Figure 1 shows the system architecture of SWQ, which consists of the following components:

1. the SWQ engine and its components such as the query parser and context ontology determination engine;
2. the context ontologies for the application domains;
3. the add-on filters for improving search precision based on properties in the context ontology; and
4. heuristics, access patterns and best practices for searching. These are represented as a set of properties of the ontology and are used to enhance the scoping of context, and to identify the media (e.g. sound clip, HTML page, PDF document) that most likely contain relevant information.

The user interface of the SWQ engine is similar to that of traditional search engines. A user must input a set of key terms separated by boolean operators. The user also provides search parameters, such as the maximum number of web sites to consider, and the add-on filters used for the search. The SWQ engine performs seven steps for semantic web search as shown in Figure 2.

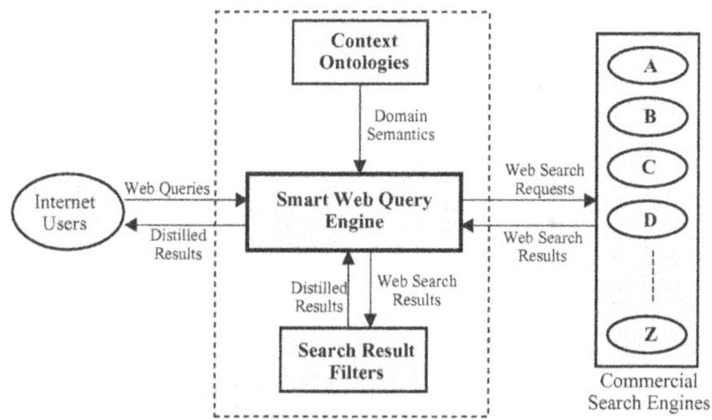

Fig. 1. The System Architecture of Smart Web Query

Step 1: Web Query Parse. The user enters a set of key terms, a set of boolean operators (e.g. and, or, not) and some search parameters. For example, a user might specify "'bond' & 'high grade'" and that only 50 web sites are to be considered. SWQ then builds a parse tree of the users' query.

Step 2: Ontology Determination. SWQ then determines appropriate context ontologies by comparing the user's key terms to those in the available context categories. Ontologies with matching key terms are identified in the order of terms matched, sorted from the ontology by most matching key terms to least matching key terms. The user then selects the relevant ontology for web search. For example, SWQ identifies that the terms "bond" and "high grade" exist in both the 'Financial Trade', and 'Adhesives' ontologies. SWQ then asks the user to identify the relevant ontology.

Step 3: Synonym Determination. Context-dependent synonyms of users' key terms are determined by querying the relevant ontology. The set of key terms, and their synonyms are then passed to boolean search engines such as Altavista and Yahoo. For example, SWQ finds that "investment grade" is a synonym for "high grade", and queries the various boolean search engines with "bond" and ("high grade" or "investment grade"). At the option of the user, the "kind of" relationship (e.g. T-bill is a "kind of" bond) can also be used to increase query precision.

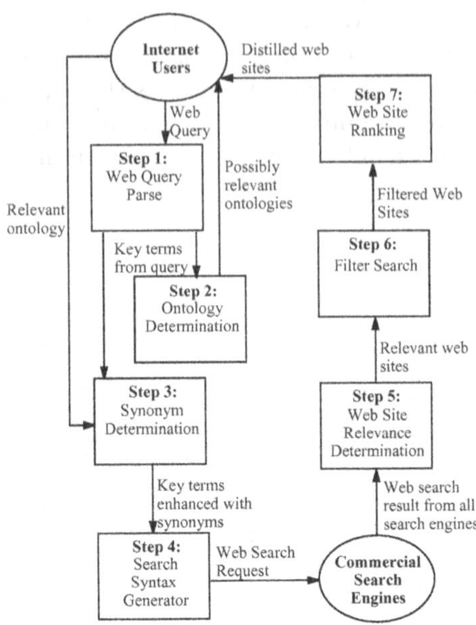

Fig. 2. Semantic Web Search performed by Smart Web Query (SWQ) Engine

Step 4: Special Search Invocation. Some terms in the context ontologies are also associated with particular kinds of data formats. If a *data format term* or its synonym is used in the search query, then SWQ accesses specialized search engines that can query for the desired data format. For example, "technical" in 'Financial Trade' refers to an analysis using charts and graphs that are represented graphically on web pages. When this term is invoked, SWQ sends a query to Altavista's image query search engine to find chart-like images that match the search specification.

Step 5: Determination of Web Site Relevance. Most of the commercial search engines return not only the URL, but also a snippet of text found in the web page. These text snippets are parsed for matching terms in the relevant ontology, which were not used in the search query. The number of matching terms is compared to the total number of words in the snippet. This ratio is used to rank the web sites for relevance. Web sites with a sufficiently low score (e.g. < 0.05) are rejected as out of context. The user can adjust the threshold value (i.e. 0.05). The URLs and text snippets returned from the query are parsed. Terms in those snippets are matched to the relevant ontology. Snippets with terms such as "Moody's", "S&P", "trend", "T-Bill", and "municipal" receive higher scores than those with terms such as "superglue", "adhesive", and "surface".

Step 6: Filter Search. The reduced list of relevant web sites is then passed to a set of filters. These filters adopt other search strategies to improve the precision of the web search. The current set of filters which consider readability, document structure (layout), and word sense, are presented in Section 5.

Step 7: Site Ranking. If the number of relevant web sites is greater than the number of web sites that should be presented (e.g. 50), SWQ offers the user a choice. Either the user can view only the web sites with the highest rankings, or the user can refine the search using matching key terms that were consistently found in the text snippets parsed in step 5.

For example, SWQ determines that 500 web sites are relevant. The user earlier specified that only 50 web sites were to be presented. Furthermore, the user discovers that the highest ranking web sites are inappropriate to the search. The user can refine the search. To facilitate the search refinement, the SWQ engine identifies the list of ontological terms that appeared in the relevant web sites from step 5 (e.g. "Moody's", "S&P", "trend", etc.), sorted according to frequency of occurrence. The user reviews this list, and selects additional terms to reduce the relevant web sites. For example, the term "trend" is chosen. This reduces the number of web sites to be considered to 20. SWQ then presents these 20 web sites for the user's perusal, sorted from highest number of relevant terms to least number of relevant terms.

4 SWQ Ontology Development

Traditional approaches to ontology development (e.g., [8]) represent ontologies as hierarchies of terms. Since taxonomy-based ontologies are inferior for web search engines, we construct an SWQ ontology as an unordered set of terms associated with their relationships and properties pertaining to a particular domain. This makes SWQ ontologies easy to develop. For example, the current 'Financial Trade' ontology consists of 682 terms related to financial trading, such as "stock", "bond", and "mutual fund". Our 'Financial Trade' ontology was developed by analyzing reference documents and a set of web sites (i.e. [2, 7, 19, 20, 23]) concerned with financial trading.

4.1 Conceptual Modeling of SWQ Ontologies

Figure 3(a) presents the conceptual modeling of SWQ ontologies as an Entity-Relationship diagram.

Ontology Hierarchy. Ontologies are related by their common terms. For example, the 'Financial Trade' and 'Accounting' ontologies are strongly related, since terms such as "Annual Report", "Profit", and "Loss" are common to both. Ontologies can be sub-ontologies of other ontologies. An ontology is a sub-ontology if and only if all of its terms are contained in another ontology. The domains of the properties of sub-ontologies are always restrictions of the domains of their super-ontological properties.

Ontological and Term Properties. Ontologies and terms may have *properties* (called ontological and term properties, respectively). Every ontology has identical properties, albeit with different values. For example, every ontology has a `readability` property. Documents concerning 'Financial Trade' are harder to read than documents concerning 'Leadership Self-Help'. Similarly, every ontological term has a `Definition`, and a `Word Sense` (e.g. noun, verb, etc.).

Term Relationship Properties. Terms can interact with other terms to form term relationships, that likewise have properties. There are two kinds of term relationship properties: generic and specific. Generic properties are available to all term relationships. For example, some term relationships are unidirectional (e.g. "bond" is a kind of "instrument"), while others are bidirectional (e.g. "stock" is a synonym of "share"). `Direction` models this term relationship property.

Directed relationships enable the SWQ ontology to establish partial orderings between terms. For example, "bonds" and "stocks" are equivalent level subsidiaries of "instrument" due to the 'kind of' term relationship. However, the ordering of terms is dependent entirely on the term relationship, and not on an absolute hierarchy. Thus, for the 'asset acquisition' relationship, "bond" has a higher ranking than "stock". Term relationships in SWQ ontologies can be transitive. For example, "T-bill" is a kind of "bond", and "bond" is a kind of "instrument". Thus, "T-bill" is also a kind of "instrument".

Some properties are only specific to some term relationships. For example, in the 'Financial Trade' ontology, "stock" and "share" are synonyms. The 'synonym' term relationship has the `Semantic Distance` property (i.e. the degree of synonymity of two terms with values ranging from 0 to 7). It is not necessary to specify all term relationship properties. For example, leaving `Semantic Distance` unspecified does not prohibit SWQ from operating. Furthermore, SWQ ontologies can be extended, enhanced and refined incrementally with additional terms, relationships, and properties.

4.2 Relational Schema of SWQ Ontologies

Since the relational data model is based on set theory, a relational database management system (DBMS) is the optimal choice for organizing and storing SWQ ontologies. For the prototype SWQ engine, we adopt Microsoft Access as the back-end database. Figure 3(b) presents the relational schema for storing SWQ ontologies, which is transformed from Figure 3(a).

The *Ontology* relation captures the name of the ontology, and the ontology's properties (e.g. `Readability` score). The ontologies are treated as subclasses or super-classes if they are presented as such in the *Ontology Hierarchy* relation. The terms (e.g. 'bond', 'high grade') and term properties such as `Word Sense` (i.e. whether the word is a noun or verb) used in the ontology are stored in the *Terms* relation. Term relationships and their generic properties are stored in the *Relationships* relation. The *Relationship Terms* relation stores the intersection data of these two relations. For hierarchical relationships, the *Relationship Hierarchy* relation identifies the parent relationship terms. Finally, the *Relationship*

Properties relation stores the properties of the specific term relationships. These properties are segregated from the *Relationships* relation, since different kinds of relationships have different kinds of specific properties.

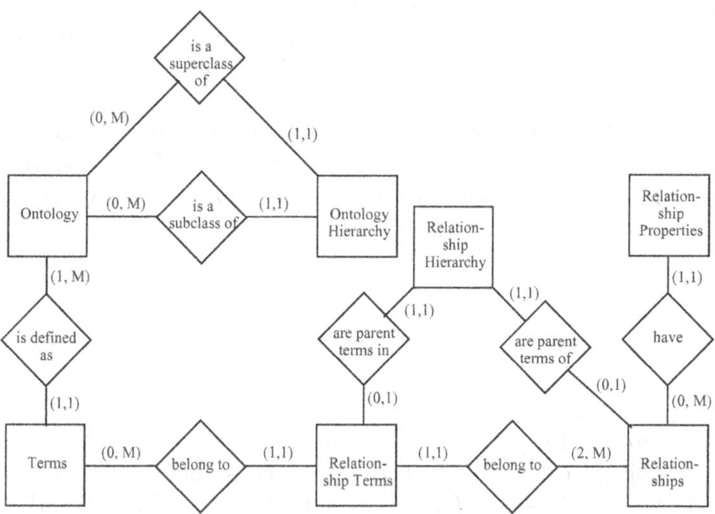

(a) The Entity-Relationship Diagram

Ontology: *Ontology*(Ontology Name, {Ontological Properties})
Ontology Hierarchy(Ontology Name, Super Ontology Name)
Term: *Terms*(Ontology Name, Term, {Term Properties})
Term Relationships: *Relationships*(Ontology Name, Relationship Code, Relationship Type, {Generic Term Relationship Properties})
Relationship Properties(Relationship Code, Relationship Property Name, Relationship Property Value)
Relationship Terms(Relationship Code, Term)
Relationship Hierarchy(Relationship Code, Term)
Schema Definition: *Relationship Definition*(Relationship Type, Has Direction)
Eligible Relationship Properties(Relationship Type, Relationship Property Name)
Relationship Property Definition(Relationship Property Name, Relationship Property Domain)

(b) The Relational Schema

Fig. 3. The Entity-Relationship Diagram and Relational Schema For SWQ Context Ontologies

4.3 Benefits of the SWQ Ontological Structure

The principal benefit of SWQ's ontological structure is that it is easy to deploy an ontology about a subject domain. At minimum, an ontology can be deployed by entering a set of ontological terms. For many domains, the ontological terms can be discovered by identifying a domain dictionary. Human domain experts are only required to define the properties and relationships, which enhance, but are not required, by an SWQ search. In many cases, the ontology can be defined semi-automatically. For example, an ontology developer may identify an electronic collection of works that encapsulate an ontology (e.g. an online dictionary). Furthermore, the base SWQ ontology (i.e. without properties and relationships) can be evaluated on the relevance and authority of the reference sources. Many subject domains have reference sources, whose authority are beyond repute.

5 Filters

We have identified three kinds of add-on filters useful to semantic web search.

Readability Filter. This filter identifies relevant web sites using the Flesch-Kinkaid readability score [21] which is computed as per Equation 1, where w is the number of syllables per 100 words, and s is the number of words in a sentence. Equation 1 produces a score from 0 to 100. The scores have well defined semantics. For example, the scores from 60-69 represent the 8th to 9th grade reading level.

$$R = 206.835 - 0.846w - 1.015s \tag{1}$$

The web sites returned by the search engines are evaluated for their reading levels. These reading levels are compared to the `Readability` ontological property, which contains a range of acceptable readability scores. Web sites whose reading levels fall outside the appropriate ranges are rejected as inappropriate. For example, financial trading reports are typically targeted towards high school graduates (or higher). Thus, taking into account unusually simple or complex financial trading reports, the reading level expected would range from 30-69 (i.e. 8th grade to college level reading). Web sites that match the financial trading ontology key words must have scores within that range.

Document Structure (Layout) Filter. Web sites in particular domains tend to have similar structures. For example, most financial trading web sites have facilities to create trading accounts, advice columns, and price quotes for trading instruments. The layout filter identifies web sites based on their layouts.

Layouts are specified as a set of ontological terms, and web page structures. For example, a financial trading home page will have one of the terms {"connect", "sign on", "open" "source"} (for opening of accounts) , one of the terms {"schedule", "quote", "chart"} (for stock market graphs), and one of the terms {"tips", "news", "facts"} (links to financial advice pages). These terms are often partially ordered. For example, the option for opening a trading account normally precedes the option for financial advice.

Word Sense Filter. The word sense filter parses the text snippets returned from commercial search engines, and identifies the word sense of the ontological terms (i.e. whether the ontological term is used as a noun, verb, adjective, etc.). This word sense is then compared to the `Word_Sense` term property. The Link Grammar Parser [14] is used to identify the word sense of an ontological term from the text snippet. If the text snippet of a relevant web site contains too many ontological terms with the wrong word sense, the web page is rejected as out of context.

6 Conclusion

The Smart Web Query (SWQ) approach enables web search using a context sensitive query. SWQ is founded on the principle of ontologies. However, unlike traditional ontologies that adopt a taxonomy, SWQ's ontologies adopt a set theoretic structure. This structure gives them greater flexibility, extensibility, adaptability, and validity than traditional ontologies. In addition to the ontologies, the SWQ engine employs properties of web sites to improve the precision and recall of the search. These properties include readability, document structure, synonyms, word sense and associated media (e.g. sound, PDF).

We are in the process of implementing and testing the SWQ engine. The prototype SWQ engine is implemented in Java. The ontologies are stored in Microsoft Access. . Once SWQ is completed, we will validate SWQ engine by measuring its recall and precision against commercial search, and meta-search engines.

References

[1] S. Aggarwal, F. Hung, and W. Meng. Wire-a www-based inf. retrieval and extraction sys. In *Ninth Intnl. Wkshp. on Database and Expert Sys. Applications*, pages 887–892, 1998.

[2] The arizona stock exchange. online, 2000. `http://www.azx.com`.

[3] K. D. Bollacker, S. Lawrence, and C. L. Giles. Citeseer: An autonomous web agent for automatic retrieval and identification of interesting publications. In *Second Intnl. Conf. on Autonomous Agents*, pages 116–123, 1998.

[4] M. L. Cascia, S. Sethi, and S. Sclaroff. Combining textual and visual cues for content-based image retrieval on the world wide web. In *IEEE Wkshp. on Content-Based Access of Image and Video Libraries*, pages 24–28, 1998.

[5] B. Chandrasekaran, J. R. Josephson, and V. R. Benjamins. What are ontologies, and why do we need them? *IEEE Intelligent Sys.*, 14(1):20–26, January/February 1999.

[6] K. Dahlgren. A linguistic ontology. *Intnl. Journal of Human-Computer Studies*, 43(5/6):809–818, 1995.

[7] E-trade. online, 2000. `http://www.etrade.com`.

[8] R. Fikes and A. Farquhar. Distributed repositories of highly expressive reusable ontologies. *IEEE Intelligent Sys.*, 14(2):73–79, March/April 1999.

[9] D. Filo and J. Yang. Yahoo inc. online, 1994. `http://www.yahoo.com`.

[10] T. R. Gruber. Translation approach to portable ontology specifications. *Know. Acquisition*, 5(2):199–220, June 1993.

[11] N. Guarino, C. Masolo, and G. Vetere. Ontoseek: Content-based access to the web. *IEEE Intelligent Sys.*, 14(3):70–80, May/June 1999.

[12] J. Heflin, J. Hendler, and S. Luke. Coping with changing ontologies in a distributed environment. In *AAAI Wkshp. on Ontology Mgmt.*, pages 74–79, 1999.

[13] Y. Labrou and T. Finin. Yahoo! as an ontology- using yahoo! categories to describe documents. In *Eighth Intnl. Conf. on Inf. and Know. Mgmt.*, pages 180–187, 1999.

[14] J. Lafferty, D. Sleator, and D. Temperley. Grammatical trigrams: A probabilistic model of link grammar. In *AAAI Conf. on Probabilistic Approaches to Natural Language*, 1992.

[15] F. Lehmann. Machine-negotiated ontology-based EDI. In *Electronic Commerce: Current Issues and Applications. LNCS 1028*, pages 27–45, 1996.

[16] A. K. Luah, W. K. Ng, E.-P. Lim, W. Lee, and Y. Y. Cao. Locating web inf. using web checkpoints. In *Tenth Intnl. Wkshp. on Database and Expert Sys. Applications*, pages 716–720, 1999.

[17] P. Martin, W. Powley, and A. Weston. Using metadata to query passive data sources. In *31st Annual Hawaii Intnl. Conf. on Sys. Sciences*, pages 286–294, 1999.

[18] T. Menzies. Cost benefits of ontologies. *SIGART Intelligence Magazine*, 10(3):26–32, Fall 1999.

[19] E. B. Ocran. *Dictionary of Finance and Funds Mgmt., Investment and Stock Exchange Terms.* African Investor Publishing Co., 1989.

[20] J. Slatter. *Straight Talk About Stock Investing.* McGraw-Hill, 1995.

[21] C. Tekfi. Readability formulas: An overview. *Journal of Documentation*, 43(3):261–273, 1987.

[22] P. Wariyapola, S. L. Abrams, et al. Ontology and metadata creation for the poseidon distributed coastal zone mgmt. sys. In *IEEE Forum on Research and Technology Advances in Digital Libraries*, pages 180–189, 1999.

[23] N. Wice. Glossary: Fifteen terms to help you talk. *TIME Digital*, pages 12–20, 17 May 1999.

[24] B. Yuwono and D. L. Lee. WISE: A world wide web resource database sys. *IEEE Trans. on Know. and Data Engineering*, 8(4):548–554, August 1996.

GETESS: Constructing a Linguistic Search Index for an Internet Search Engine

Ilvio Bruder[1], Antje Düsterhöft[1], Markus Becker[2], Jochen Bedersdorfer[2], and Günter Neumann[2]

[1] University of Rostock, Computer Science Department
A.-Einstein-Str. 21
18051 Rostock, Germany
{ilr,duest}@informatik.uni-rostock.de
[2] DFKI GmbH
Stuhlsatzenhausweg 3
66123 Saarbrücken, Germany
{beders,mbecker,neumann}@dfki.de

Abstract. In this paper, we illustrate how Internet documents can be automatically analyzed in order to capture the content of a document in a more detailed manner than usual. The result of the document analysis is called an *abstract*, and will it be used as a linguistic search index for the Internet search engine, GETESS.
We show how the linguistic analysis system SMES can be used with a Harvest-based search engine for constructing a linguistic search index. Further, we denote how the linguistic index can be exploited for answering user search inquiries.

1 Introduction

Growing amounts of information in cyberspace make it increasingly difficult for network users to locate specific information for certain themes. Even experts sometimes experience the "joy" of becoming "Lost in Hyberspace".

In contrast, a wide variety of tools and services exist that are useful for information searches in the Internet, but whose efficiency is somewhat limited. The majority of tools used for information searches in the Internet concentrate primarily on so-called syntactical attributes, such as TITLE or DESCRIPTION, without considering the actual meaning of the information (cf. [11]).

The bulk of available information in the Internet is provided in natural-language format and supplemented with graphics. Furthermore, user queries are typically formulated using natural–language words and phrases. This, despite the fact, that during the past few years the computer linguistic field has developed a wide variety of tools and mechanisms for partially automatic, natural-language processing taht could be employed as intelligent search support.

Internationally, the English language has established itself in the Internet. Most information in the Internet in Germany is also presented in English and

M. Bouzeghoub et al. (Eds.): NLDB 2000, LNCS 1959, pp. 227–238, 2001.

German. In German-speaking areas, the German language is playing an increasingly subordinate role in the Internet. Presently, a typical Internet user is either an information expert, student or computer freak with some knowledge of the English language. However, as access to the Internet increases, the circle of users is also expected to become more multifaceted. At some point, knowledge of the English language can no longer be assumed .

The project GETESS (http://www.getess.de) [1] [10] focuses on the development of an Internet search engine which analyzes information in German within a defined domain.
The project began with the idea of combining Internet techniques with database and knowledge representation methods, as well as results from the computer linguists. The GETESS architecture subsequently integrates these aspects in order to give more detailed information to the user.

Therefore, the starting point is the idea to combine Internet techniques with database and knowledge representation methods as well as results from the computer linguists. The GETESS architecture integrates the different aspects in order to give more detailed information to the user.
Users can formulate their queries using natural–language phrases, and they will be supported by an ontology. A query's result set consists of so–called *'abstracts'* that are summaries of the contents of web documents.

After motivating the main ideas behind GETESS in *section 2* we illustrate the functionality of the GETESS system, the GETESS Gatherer and the architecture of the information extraction system, SMES in *in section 4*. In *section 5* we discuss integrating SMES into the GETESS-Gatherer and its actual implementation.
In *section 6* we provide a conclusion and consider future work.

2 Motivation

Internet search engines are actually able to answer inquiries (cf. [11]) like

- simple keywords, e.g., "hotel" or "Rostock" or "coast", or
- simple keywords connected via boolean operators, e.g., "hotel and Rostock", or
- strings, e.g., "hotel between Rostock and Wismar".

The possibilities outlined above for describing queries do not satisfactorily meet the users' needs. Users want an easy-to-formulate (natural) query language that allows to describe questions such as

- "ich suche eine Unterkunft an der Küste zwischen Rostock und Wismar" ("I'm looking for an accomodation on the coast between Rostock and Wismar")

[1] GETESS is funded by the German Bundesministerium für Bildung, Wissenschaft, Forschung und Technologie (BMBF) under grant number 01IN802. The partners of the project are AIFB, the University of Karlsruhe, DFKI Saarbrücken, Gecko mbH Rostock, and the University of Rostock.

Additionally, a user may also want the following information:

- an accomodation that can be a hotel or an appartment or a youth hotel or ...
- an accomodation *between* Rostock and Wismar (Rostock and Wismar are cities)
- an accomodation on the coast, in combination with the geographical information that Rostock and Wismar are cities on the Baltic Sea, one can assume that the user wants to be on the coast of the Baltic Sea

The essential information behind the user inquiry has to be extracted, because the user does not explicitly provide it. Consequently, it's important for a search engine to support a user in analyzing the user's inquiry.

– "ich möchte ein Doppelzimmer unter 150 DM"
("I want to have a double room that costs no more than 150 DM")
A search engine capable of answering this query must analyze the Web documents in such a way, so that prices can be read as integer values. In practice, most prices on the Web are integrated into text as strings. An indepth analysis of the text is necessary to classify the correct strings as prices. The same problem we have for addresses of institutions (e.g., hotels), special multi-valued sets (e.g., the set of credit cards), times (e.g., opening times), etc. However, the problem can be solved when a Web information in a particular domain (e.g., tourism) is analyzed and classified within the context of that domain. Important information can then be extracted and stored in the correct way (e.g., for comparisons).
– "ich suche ein Doppelzimmer mit Swimmingpool"
("I'm looking for a double room with a swimmingpool ")
The user's inquiry requests a double room in a hotel (or other establishment) where a swimming pool is located. A problem in answering this inquiry because information about the rooms are often stored on different Web pages. Therefore, a keyword search would never find this complex information because the relevant keywords are not on the same Web page.
This illustrates why information from a particular institution must be connected, i.e., its Web pages must be logically joined in order to answer such questions.

In the GETESS project, we use a domain-related approach in which all specific appearances of items are seen as representations of that particular item. So that specific words that are important in our domain are mapped onto concepts. For instance 'Master card' is a specific appearance of 'credit card'. The search engine subsequently uses these concepts in order to provide search results. The search engine also maps the natural-language user inquiries onto concepts and tries to match the concepts in the analyzed Web documents.

3 Collecting Data from the Web - The GETESS Gatherer

The GETESS project focuses on developing an intelligent Internet search site. It will offer the user an easy–to–operate system and will provide for the description of search requirements in a natural-language. Intelligent systems situated

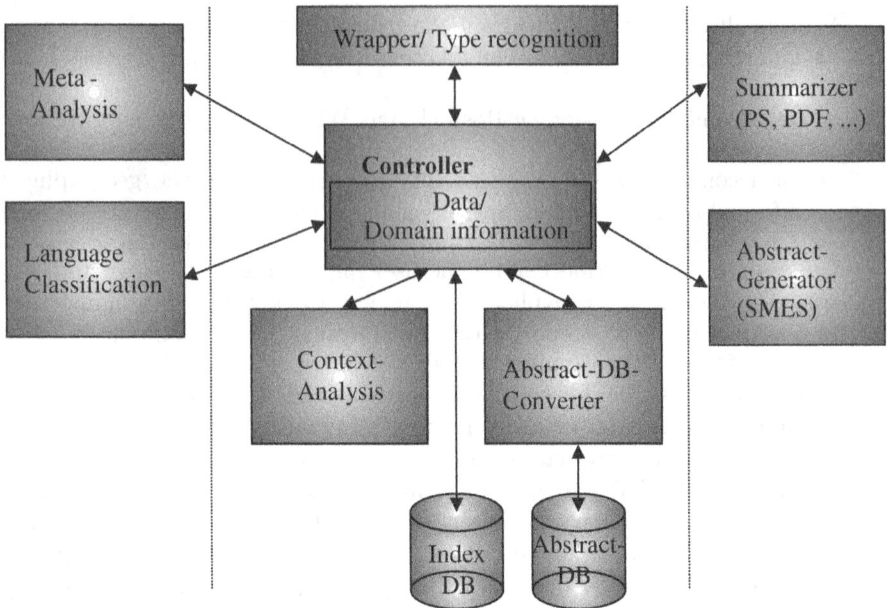

Fig. 1. GETESS Gatherer

between search sites and information will be responsible for condensing extensive and complex data into language-independent, content-weighted summaries (*abstracts*). The sum total of *abstracts* will provide a base and will subsequently be used as results for queries. Results will then be translated into the user's mother tongue.
A fundamental requirement for developing of an Internet search site is an extremely large amount of data. Accordingly, the amount of information allocated to the *abstracts* will also be substantial. Therefore, databases will be used for efficient storage and quick access to *abstracts*.

The GETESS-Gatherer (cf. Figure 2) is one of the main components of the GETESS architecture. The Gatherer works as an Internet agent that periodically collects data from the Internet. After a data type recognition the Gatherer-controller starts the summarizers and and the SMES-*abstract*-generator in order to analyze the documents (**information extraction**). The different summarizers parse e.g. HTML, XML, PS, RTF,... documents and extracting keywords using information retrieval techniques (**keyword extraction**). The *abstract*-generator creates *abstracts* and uses the meta-analysis, where especially HTML-Meta-Tags and the HTML structure are analyzed, as well as the language classification and the information extraction where knowledge about the structure of an complex Internet site will be extracted.
The controller's task is to coordinate the work of the agent with the other Gatherer tools.

Harvest - The Basis of the GETESS-Gatherer. Harvest is actually one of the most imortant search engines, and it serves as the foundation for the GETESS Gatherer[2]. The GETESS Internet agent, the keyword extraction mechanism, and the summarizers are largely based on the Harvest system.
Parallel to the keyword extraction the GETESS gatherer initiates the information extraction (SMES). In any case, we have results either in the form of abstracts based on a linguistic analysis or results based on a keyword analysis. Because of this, we want to integrate the information extraction system, SMES, into the Internet agent. Otherwise additional information collected by specific GETESS tools has to be made available to the harvest components, e.g., meta-information.

Meta-analysis. During the meta-analysis, typical structures of documents as well as significant structures of an Internet domain, will be automatically analyzed. Therefore, an internet agent is working prior to the information extraction in order to find collections of similar documents and special URL-strings.
Document collections are created when documents have comparable HTML structures. An approximation algorithm [3] is used to decide whether a similarity exists between documents.
The meta-analysis agent collects this heuristic information and makes it available for the keyword and information extraction.

Language Classification. The language classification is used to define the document's language [4]. The linguistic analyses SMES combined with an Internet agent will get to know this document language when an *abstract* of a document will be constructed.
Otherwise, documents with the same content but of different languages should be put together via the constructed *abstracts* in the database. So, equal *abstracts* representing documents with the same content but of different language. Lastly, the GETESS search engine takes only one of these *abstracts* as a query result - exactly the *abstract* of this document which is of the language the user want to have.

Abstract Database Converter. Lastly, the GETESS Gatherer has to store the constructed abstracts into a database. Because the abstracts are in XML format, a special conversion into database structures is needed. A discussion about possible database systems and mechanisms for storing the abstracts can be found in [8].

The GETESS Gatherer runs periodically and collects data in the Internet. The result is a linguistic index in *abstract* form that is stored into a database. Furthermore, a keyword index is constructed for the linguistic analysis. Both indexes are used in the natural language dialogue system in order to answer user inquiries.
In the next sections, we focus on the specific problem of integrating the information extraction system, SMES, into the Harvest Gatherer agent.

---

[2] "Currently, there are hundreds of Harvest applications on the Web (for example, the CIA, the NASA, the US National Academy of Science, and the US Government Printing Office), as this software is on the public domain." [1]

4 Information Extraction with SMES

Linguistically based pre-processing of text documents is performed by SMES, an information extraction core system for real-world German text processing (cf. [6], [7]). The system's design provides a set of basic powerful, robust, and efficient natural-language components and generic linguistic knowledge sources that can easily be customized for processing different tasks in a flexible manner. The essential abstract data types used in SMES are

- dynamic tries for lexical processing:
  tries are used as the sole storage device for all sorts of lexical information (e.g., stems, prefix, inflectional endings). Besides the usual functionality (insertion, retrieval, deletion), a number of more complex functions are available, most notably a regular trie matcher and a robust recursive trie traversal that supports recognition of (longest matching) substrings. The latter is the basic algorithm for on-line decomposition of German compounds.
- weighted finite state transducers (WFST):
  WFST are used for representing cascades of grammar modules, such as proper name grammars (e.g., organizations, complex time/date expressions, person names), generic phrasal grammars (nominal and prepositional phrases, and verb groups), and clause level grammars. Using WFST supports efficient and robust representation of each grammar modul.

4.1 The SMES Architecture

The architecture of the SMES system (shown in figure 2) consists of two major components, the Linguistic Knowledge Pool (LKP) and STP, the core shallow text processor of SMES. STP consists of three major components: the tokenizer, the lexical processor, and the chunk parser.

Text tokenizer. Each file is first processed by the *text scanner*. Applying regular expressions, the text scanner identifies some text structures (e.g., paragraphs, indentations) and word, number, date and time tokens (e.g, "1.3.96", "12:00 h"), and expands abbreviations. The output of the text scanner is a stream of tokens, where each word is simply represented as a string of alphabetic characters (including delimiters, e.g. "Daimler-Benz"). Number, date and time expressions are normalized and represented as attribute values structures. For example, the character stream "1.3.96" is represented as (:date ((:day 1)(:mon 3)(:year 96)) and "13:15 h" as (:time ((:hour 13)(:min 15))).

Lexical processor. Each token, that is identified as a potential word form is lexically processed by the LEXICAL PROCESSOR. Lexical processing includes morphological analysis, recognition of compounds, retrieval of lexical information (where retrieval allows fuzzy matching), and tagging, which performs word-based disambiguation. Morphological analysis follows text scanning and performs inflection, and processes compounds. The capability of efficiently processing compounds is crucial because compounding is a very productive process of the German language. The output after morphology is the word form together with all

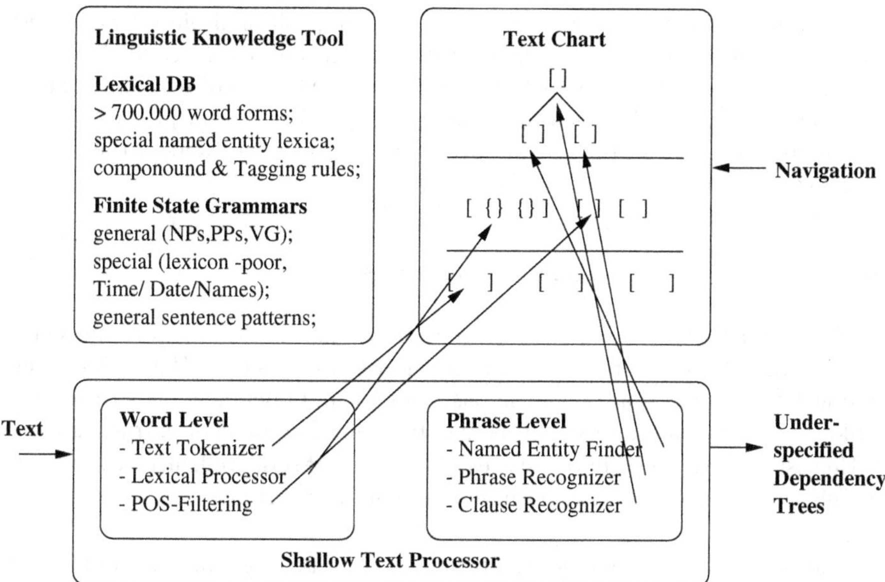

Fig. 2. The blue print of the SMES system architecture

its readings. A reading is a triple of the form tuple{stem,inflection,pos}, where *stem* is a string or a list of strings (in the case of compounds), *inflection* is the inflectional information, and *pos* is the part of speech.

Currently, the morpholgical analyzer is used for the German and Italian language. The German version has a very broad coverage (a lexicon of more then 120,000 stem entries) and an excellent speed (5000 words/sec) without compound handling and 2800 words/sec with compound processing, where all lexically possible decompositions are computed for each compound.

Chunk parser. The chunk parser is subdivided into three components.In the first step phrasal fragments are recognized, like general nominal expressions and verb groups or specialized expressions for time, date, and named entity. The structure of potential phrasal fragments is defined using weighted finite state transducers WFST. In the second step, the dependency-based structure of the sentence fragments is analysed using a set of specific sentence patterns. These patterns are also expresssed by means of finite state transducers (FST), so that step one and three are uniformly realized by the same underlying mechanism. In the final fourth step, the grammatical functions are determined for each dependency-based structure using a large subcategorization lexicon.

SMES has a very broad linguistic knowledge source, i.e., a huge lexical data base (more than 120.000 stem entries, more than 12,000 subcategorization frames, as well as basic lexica for proper names). It has a broad-coverage, special sub-grammar for recognizing unknown proper names on the fly and general grammar for recognizing nominal phrases, prepositional phrases, and verb groups. Complete processing of 400-word text takes about 1second. Most important as it relates to this paper, SMES has a high degree of modularity: each component can be used in isolation. Thus, it is possible to run just a subset of the components, e.g., using only the specialized subgrammars and/or the phrasal grammars for peforming term extraction.

4.2 Creating Domain-Related Abstracts

A document's content is represented in an *abstract*. An *abstract* is composed of tuples whose elements are the results of the term extraction. Heuristics determine which terms are paired on the basis of text and document structures. The employed keys for pairing two terms may be either linguistic or extra-linguistic.

Heuristics are applied in two stages. First, a set of positive heuristics suggests possible tuples. The following positive heuristics are currently implemented:

- The *title heuristic* combines the terms between the starting and ending title tags with those from the rest of the document.
- The *sentence heuristic* conjoins all terms of a sentence with each other.
- The *NP-PP-heuristic* couples all directly consecutive sequences of nominal and prepositional phrases. It thus models minimal PP-attachment.

A merger allows every suggested pairing to appear only once in the set of tuples, however, it tracks every positive heuristic that suggested a tuple. Therefore, if tuple was suggested by more than one heuristic, it can be regarded as more relevant.

In a subsequent step, negative heuristics act as filters on the output of the positive heuristics. There are two negative heuristics.

- The *instance heuristic* rejects all tuples that bear the same instance name. This would be the case for pairings of identical place names.
- The *coordination heuristic* rules out tuples that stem from one coordinated noun phrase. In the example sentence, "Das Hotel hat einen Swimmingpool und eine Dachterasse.", the sentence heuristic would come up with three tuples, and we would reject <Swimmingpool, Dachterasse>.

5 Integrating SMES into Harvest

The aim of the GETESS Gatherer is to construct a linguistic search index in combination with a keyword index [2]. Because Harvest is used for constructing the keyword index, we have to analyze the possibilities of integrating the SMES information extraction.

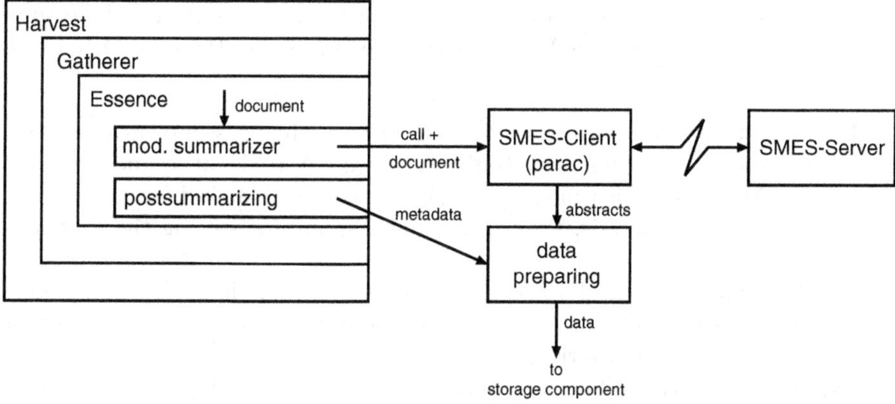

Fig. 3. Integration of SMES into Harvest

Demands. We defined the following demands for using the SMES system:

- modularity/ flexibility: Because of potential changes in the SMES system during project development, a high degree of modularity and flexibility are required. Internal changes in the SMES system should not have direct consequences for the GETESS Gatherer. Similarly, changes in the GETESS Gatherer should not have direct consequences for the SMES system.
- parallelism: The gathering process (especially the work of the Internet agent) and the SMES analysis should work parallel. Because the process of gathering keywords is very time consuming, the SMES analysis should take place parallel to the other GETESS Gatherer processes.
- database-use: The results of the SMES analysis should be stored into a database. The type of database can differ. So it is possible to have a full-text database system (like the database system Fullcrum), an object-relational database system (like DB2), or only a file system. The resulting abstracts of the SMES analysis should be stored in one of these systems and should not be connected to different database systems.

Connecting the GETESS Gatherer and SMES. Figure 3 depicts the approach for connecting the GETESS Gatherer with the SMES system. We have two general parts: the SMES client and the integration as Harvest summarizer.

- The SMES client. The GETESS gatherer interacts with the SMES system via a client-server architecture.
- The GETESS Gatherer and SMES are connected using the Essence system, which is an important part of the Harvest Gatherer (cf. [5]). The aim of the Essence system is to summarize information. Starting from a known information type (e.g., HTML, PS, ...), special summarizers analyze the formatted text in order to find keywords. We decided to integrate the SMES analysis as a special summarizer. Therfore, an HTML text is first analyzed through the

HTML summarizer and then analyzed with the SMES system. The results of the SMES analysis (in XML format) are stored and then converted into a database entry.

Implementational aspects. The GETESS gatherer is implemented with the SMES system and runs periodically. The system needs 40 seconds for analyzing a HTML page. This time-frame includes the time required for the Internet agent, the keyword analysis, the SMES analysis, and for storing the abstracts into the database.
The system completely analyzes the Internet site www.all-in-all.com completely (about 4000 pages in German and English) and is actually tested with other Internet sites within the tourism domain.

Let us consider the following reduced example, the source of http://www.all-in-all.com/1165.htm.

Hotel Mecklenburger Hof
D-19288 Ludwigslust
Lindenstrasse 40 - 44

Das Hotel Mecklenburger Hof liegt verkehrsgünstig in der Innenstadt nahe dem Ludwigsluster Schloss mit seinem Schlosspark und der Schlosskirche.

Hausbeschreibung:
Komfort auf hohem Niveau in 37 Zimmern mit 72 Betten. Das Haus wurde mit viel Liebe zum Detail restauriert und bietet seinen Gästen stilvolle gemütliche Gastlichkeit, verbunden mit einem sehr aufmerksamen Service, einer ausgezeichneten Küche und exzellenten Frühstücksbufett.
Ein gut sortierter Weinkeller gehört genauso dazu, wie der zweimal im Jahr stattfindende Operettenball und weitere interessante Veranstaltungen.
Kostenfreie Parkplätze stehen Ihnen in der Tiefgarage zur Verfügung.

Preise:
Einzelzimmer: von DM 88,00 bis DM 120,00
Doppelzimmer: von DM 130,00 bis DM 185,00

Kreditkarten: EC, Visa, Diners

The following abstract is the result of analyzing the source:

```
<Getess>
  <HOTEL>
     <HOTEL_1> hotel Mecklenburger Hof </HOTEL_1>
  </HOTEL>
  <ORT>
     <ORT_1> Ludwigslust  </ORT_1>
     <ORT_2> Ludwigslust (linde-PL-N-strasse) 40-44 </ORT_2>
  </ORT>
  <GEBIET>
     <GEBIET_1> Mecklenburg </GEBIET_1>
  </GEBIET>
  <ZIMMERAUSSTATTUNG>
     <ZIMMERAUSSTATTUNG_1> telefon </ZIMMERAUSSTATTUNG_1>
     <ZIMMERAUSSTATTUNG_2> bett </ZIMMERAUSSTATTUNG_2>
  </ZIMMERAUSSTATTUNG>
  <ZIMMER>
     <ZIMMER_1> zimmer </ZIMMER_1>
     <ZIMMER_2> einzelzimmer </ZIMMER_2>
     <ZIMMER_3> doppelzimmer </ZIMMER_3>
  </ZIMMER>
  <PREIS>
     <PREIS_1> ez-min 88 </PREIS_1>
     <PREIS_2> ez-max 120 </PREIS_2>
     <PREIS_3> dz-min 130 </PREIS_3>
     <PREIS_4> dz-min 185 </PREIS_4>
  </PREIS>
  <PREIS_WAEHRUNG>
      <PREIS_WAEHRUNG_1> dm </PREIS_WAEHRUNG_1>
  </PREIS_WAEHRUNG>
  <UNTERKUNFT_ZAHLUNGSMOEGLICHKEIT>
     <UNTERKUNFT_ZAHLUNGSMOEGLICHKEIT_1> kredit-karte
     </UNTERKUNFT_ZAHLUNGSMOEGLICHKEIT_1>
  </UNTERKUNFT_ZAHLUNGSMOEGLICHKEIT>
  <BETRIEB_ZAHLUNGSMOEGLICHKEIT>
     <BETRIEB_ZAHLUNGSMOEGLICHKEIT_1> ec  </BETRIEB_ZAHLUNGSMOEGLICHKEIT_1>
     <BETRIEB_ZAHLUNGSMOEGLICHKEIT_2> visa </BETRIEB_ZAHLUNGSMOEGLICHKEIT_2>
     <BETRIEB_ZAHLUNGSMOEGLICHKEIT_3> diners </BETRIEB_ZAHLUNGSMOEGLICHKEIT_3>
  </BETRIEB_ZAHLUNGSMOEGLICHKEIT>
  <HAUSBESCHREIBUNG>
     <HAUSBESCHREIBUNG_1> haus-beschreibung </HAUSBESCHREIBUNG_1>
  </HAUSBESCHREIBUNG>
  <GASTRONOMIE>
     <GASTRONOMIE_1_> kueche (auszeichn) </GASTRONOMIE_1>
     <GASTRONOMIE_2> fruehstuecksbufett (exzellen)
     </GASTRONOMIE_2>
     <GASTRONOMIE_3> weinkeller (sortier) </GASTRONOMIE_3>
  </GASTRONOMIE>
</Getess>
```

6 Conclusion

In this paper, we have shown how an Internet search engine can use linguistic and domain-related knowledge. We have illustrated the GETESS search engine and, in particular the GETESS gatherer. The GETESS gatherer collects data from the Internet for the search engine. In contrast to other search engines, GETESS uses not only keywords to answer inquiries, but also focuses on a linguistic and domain-related approach in which so-called *abstracts* are constructed. These *abstracts* are conceptual descriptions of specific Web documents and are the basis for answering user inquiries.
Future work will consider on algorithms that can be exploited for clustering logically related Web pages that should be analyzed together.

References

1. R. Baeza-Yates, B. Rebeiro-Neto: Modern Information Retrieval. ACM Presse, Addison Wesley, New York, 1999
2. I. Bruder: Integration von Harvest und SMES in GETESS. Studienarbeit, Universität Rostock, Fachbereich Informatik, 1999 (in German)
3. I. Bruder: Integration von Kontextwissen in den GETESS-Gatherer. Diplomarbeit, Universität Rostock, Fachbereich Informatik, 2000 (in German)
4. A. Düsterhöft, S. Gröticke: A Heuristic Approach for Recognizing a Document's Language Used for the Internet Search Engine GETESS. In: Proc. of the 2nd International Workshop on Natural Language and Information Systems, September 2000, Greenwich, UK
5. Harvest-System: http://harvest.transarc.com
6. G. Neumann, R. Backofen, J. Baur, M. Becker, C. Braun: An Information Extraction Core System for Real World German Text Processing. In: Proc. of the ANLP'97, March 1997, Washington, USA, 208-215,
7. G. Neumann, J. Piskorski, C. Braun: A Divide-and-Conquer Strategy for Shallow Parsing of German Free Texts. In: Proc. of the 6th International Conference of Applied Natural Language, April 2000, Seattle, USA
8. M. Klettke, H. Meyer: Managing XML documents in object-relational databases. University of Rostock, Rostocker Informatik-Berichte, No. 24, 1999
9. S. Staab, C. Braun, I. Bruder, A. Düsterhöft, A. Heuer, M. Klettke, G. Neumann, B. Prager, J. Pretzel, H.-P. Schnurr, R. Studer, H. Uszkoreit, B. Wrenger, "A System for Facilitating and Enhancing Web Search", In: *IWANN'99 - Proceedings of International Working Conference on Artificial and Natural Neural Networks*, Alicante, ES, 1999, LNCS, Berlin, Heidelberg, Springer
10. S. Staab, C. Braun, I. Bruder, A. Düsterhöft, A. Heuer, M. Klettke, G. Neumann, B. Prager, J. Pretzel, H.-P. Schnurr, R. Studer, H. Uszkoreit, B. Wrenger, "GETESS - Searching the Web Exploiting German Texts", In: *CIA'99 - Proc. of the 3rd Int. Workshop on Cooperating Information Agents.* Upsala, Schweden, 1999, LNCS, Berlin, Heidelberg, Springer
11. Search Engine Watch: Tips About Internet Search Engines. http://searchenginewatch.com/

Using Semantics for Efficient Information Retrieval

Amalia Todiraşcu[1,2*], François de Beuvron[2], Dan Gâlea[3], Bernard Keith[2], and François Rousselot[2]

[1] University "Al.I.Cuza" of Iasi, Computer Science Department, 16, Berthelot Str., Iasi 6600, Romania, Phone: +4032201529, Fax:+4032201490, amalia@infoiasi.ro

[2] Laboratoire d'Informatique et d'Intelligence Artificielle, ENSAIS, 24, Bd. de la Victoire, 67084 Strasbourg Cedex, France, Phone: +33388144753, Fax: +33388241490 {amalia,beuvron,keith,rousse}@liia.u-strasbg.fr

[3] Computer Science Institute, Romanian Academy - Iasi, 22, Carol Av., Iasi 6600, Romania
dgalea@iit.iit.tuiasi.ro

Abstract The paper presents a system for querying a base of HTML documents in natural language for a limited domain. Different small French corpora (heart surgery, newspaper articles, papers on natural language processing) are used for testing the prototype. The domain knowledge, represented in description logics (DL), is used for filtering the results of the search and is extended dynamically as result of DL inference mechanisms. The system uses shallow natural language parsing techniques and DL reasoning mechanisms are used to handle incomplete or incorrect user queries.

Keywords: semantic information retrieval, NLP querying, description logics

1 Introduction

Searching engines for the Web accept user queries composed by a set of keywords or written in a command language or in natural language. User queries are matched to the index file containing the most frequent words found in the texts. The performances of these systems are evaluated by two parameters: *recall* (the number of retrieved documents/the number of documents) and *precision* (the number of relevant documents/the number of retrieved documents). Keyword-based searching engines provide bad recall (these systems ignore synonyms or generalizations handling) and low precision (the answers contain too much noise). Natural language queries need a deeper understanding of the sense, and adequate tools for this goal, like shallow parsers [1] or conceptual parsers (CIRCUS[9]), using verb categorisation patterns).

* I am Ph.D.student at LIIA, due to a grant from the French government. A part of this work was done during my stay at LIIA, ENSAIS, Strasbourg

M. Bouzeghoub et al. (Eds.): NLDB 2000, LNCS 1959, pp. 239–250, 2001.

Several IR (Information Retrieval) systems use semantic resources as filters for improving search results: keywords with multiple-word terms [9], their semantic variations [5] or lists of synonyms [8]. The development of large thesaurus provides resources for conceptual indexing (EuroWordNet [14], CoreLex [3]). Indexes can be more complex semantic representations:concepts, syntactic structures. Queries are expanded using document summaries which are stored instead of term files [12]. Phrasal terms express more specific concepts and eliminate the ambiguity introduced by the single words used for indexing. An application of this methodology is document summarization, implemented in the project Document Surrogater [16]. The algorithm produces a set of significant terms from a focus file prepared by a human expert. Another system using terminological information is FASTER [5]. The module identifies multi-words terms and to use them as indexes for the document base. A terminological base is used by the system and it is enriched by the new term candidates (applying some morphological transformations on existing terms).

The design of the systems using large semantic resources, like thesaurus, involves big costs for building the resources and provides low flexibility when integrating new knowledge. The disadvantage of these systems is the use of expensive resources. Some systems use deep syntactic or semantic parsing, involving domain-specific patterns ([9]) or complex grammars for identifying syntactic constituents. The systems adopting a bottom-up approach, building the resources from the text, are more flexible and provide better portability.

We adopted an approach using semantic information for filtering the results of the search. We adopted too a bottom-up approach for building the domain knowledge base. The information from the text is used for building semi-automatically a hierarchy of domain concepts. The domain hierarchy is represented in description logics (DL), providing efficiency and fault tolerance when handling incomplete or erroneous data. Logic inference mechanisms provided by DL are used to extend dynamically the domain model (new concepts inferred from the new documents are added to the existing hierarchy), and to complete and correct missing information extracted from the user query. The system was designed to include minimal linguistic and domain knowledge. The system is portable for other domains, due to the dynamic maintainance of the domain knowledge base.

2 System Architecture

The system integrates a natural language interface for querying a base of Web documents about a limited, specific domain. The system integrates several natural language processing modules as well as some logical inferences modules. Some modules were implemented in Java and in Perl. A few small experimental French corpora on heart surgery (70000 words), newspaper articles (300000 words) and NLP articles (250000 words) are used for testing the prototype. Most of the examples presented are from the heart surgery corpus. The system uses the same representation formalism for domain knowledge and sense (in DL), which provides powerful inference mechanisms, capable of dealing with incomplete, erroneous data. It integrates shallow natural language processing techniques for text documents (Figure 1).

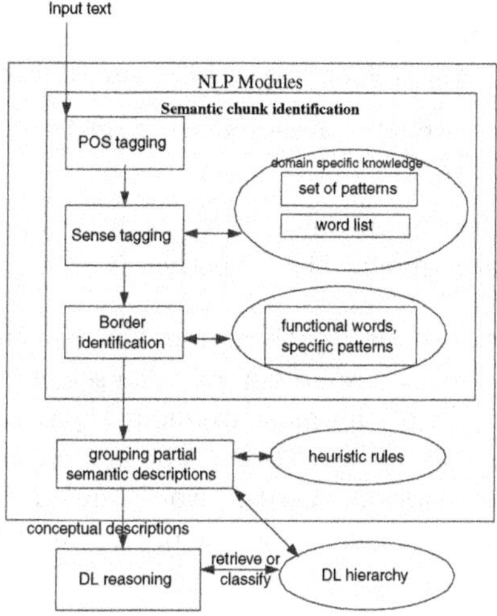

Fig.1. System architecture

The NLP modules use domain knowledge for extracting the sense from the input text and for filtering the results of the search. The main goal is to identify the word sequences corresponding to the most significant domain concepts (*semantic chunks*). A semantic chunk contains a noun and it is delimited by two border words. Border words are functional words, auxiliaries, some composed prepositions. The main assumption we made is that we do not need to identify exactly the syntactic constituents, but to identify approximately the sequence of words containing the relevant information. For this purpose, we use the delimiters and the lexical information.

Example. The phrase

"la présence ou l'absence d'athérosclérose significative des artères coronariennes, de même que le degré de sévérité..."

contains some relevant pieces of information: *"présence", "l'absence", "d'athérosclérose significative", "des artères coronariennes", "le degré", "sévérité".*

NLP modules implement shallow parsing methods:

I. **Semantic chunks identification**. The identification of semantic chunks is done by identifying the lexical information. This module uses several tools: a POS tagger, a sense tagger, a border identifier.

a) *The POS tagging* (use WinBrill, trained for French with a set of data provided by INALF - Institut National pour la Langue Française [6]) identifies the content words (nouns, adjectives, verbs) and functional words (prepositions, conjunctions etc.). Brill's tagger uses a set of contextual and lexical rules learned from annotated texts, for guessing the lexical category for the unknown words.

Example.

```
1)/CD la/FW présence/NN ou/VB l'absence/NN d'athérosclérose/NN
significative/JJ des/FW artères/NNS coronariennes/NN, ...
```

```
1) the occurrence or the absence of significant atherosclerose
of coronary arteries,...
```

where the labels have the meaning: NN - simple noun; FW - functional word; CD - cardinal number; JJ - adjective; NNS - plural noun.

b) *The sense tagger* contains a pattern matcher, consulting a set of syntagms and their sense assigned by a human expert. The set of conceptual descriptions was established from a list of the most frequent repeated segments and words extracted from a set of representative texts. The pattern matcher assigns to each syntagm its semantic description. A list of words and their semantic representations is also used to label the content words of the input text.

Example.

```
il garde [un angor d'effort]/ANGOR_EFFORT en rapport avec [une
dysfonction]/TROUBLE du [pont IVA]/ANATOMIE alors que...
```

```
he has manifested an effort angor due to a disfunction of the
IVA bridge, while...
```

We made some studies for different texts: a set of medical texts, of journal texts and of NLP articles in French.The instances of the concepts are identified as noun phrases in most of the cases.The nouns, the adjectives represent concepts themselves, while prepositions are just used for separating the chunks:

	Medical	Journal	NLP papers
Concepts	453	587	667
Instances	1941	2379	3543

Synonyms included in the word list share the same conceptual descriptions. Synonym handling is possible using a thesaurus (like Wordnet [14]). This extension is not included yet in the system, it is under development.

c) *A module for border identification.* It identifies the words and the syntactic constructions, that delimit the semantic chunks. This module uses the output of POS tagger (for identifying the functional words), as well as a set of cue phrases (syntactic phrases containing auxiliaries, composed prepositions etc.). The set of cue phrases is built as a result of studies done on test corpora. The semantic chunks of this experimental corpus were manually annotated with conceptual descriptions by the human expert. The borders of noun and prepositional phrases (determiners, prepositions) are candidates for chunk border. The borders of the semantic chunks are represented by the following lexical categories and syntactic constituents:

Lexical categories	Percent
Phrase delimiters	37.73
Prepositions	42.52
Conjunctions	6.57
Auxiliaries	4.2
Verbs	4.16
Adverbs	1.88
Other phrases	2.90

II. **Combining partial semantic representations**. This step uses DL inference mechanisms, as well as syntactic heuristic rules for combining the conceptual descriptions associated to each semantic chunk. We extracted a set of 23 different heuristic rules.

Examples of syntactic rules:

1) if a preposition is a delimiter between two semantic chunks and the preposition is relating a noun to its modifier, then we can combine the conceptual descriptions of the two chunks into a more complex semantic description.

   `(1) if` (⟨*Chunk*1⟩ ⟨*Border*⟩ ⟨*Chunk*2⟩)
   `and (Noun in` ⟨*Chunk*1⟩)
   `and (Modifier in` ⟨*Chunk*2⟩)
   `then new concept(and sem(`⟨*Chunk*1⟩`)(SOME Role sem(`⟨*Chunk*2⟩`)))`

   The syntax is specific to DL formalism and it will be explained below. It expresses that a semantic relation exists where a syntactic relation between two elements exists.

2) if a conjunction relates two semantic chunks, then we combine the two descriptions.

   `(2) if` (⟨*Chunk*1⟩ ⟨*conjunction*⟩ ⟨*Chunk*2⟩)
   `then new concept(and sem(`⟨*Chunk*1⟩`) sem(`⟨*Chunk*2⟩`))`

User queries or documents to be included in the base are processed by the NLP modules described above. First, the pattern matcher identifies word sequences matching the patterns, and the sense tagger labels the identified phrases with the conceptual description. A lexical information is assigned to each word by the POS tagger.

Next, the semantic chunks are identified in the input text. Heuristic rules are used for combining partial semantic descriptions. The conceptual descriptions are processed by DL module, and then instances of the text are retrieved, or new concepts will be added to the existing hierarchy.

While a new document is included in the text base, it is first processed by a tokenizer, identifying the list of most frequent words. For each word from the list, we extract the left and the right context (3-7 words). From this list, we extract the most frequent content words (nouns, adjectives, verbs). The contexts of these content words are processed by the NLP modules for identifying new concepts. The DL module validates the new conceptual definitions and they are added to the domain hierarchy. New definitions are first tested if they are not already classified in the hierarchy. Only the most frequent content words are selected (about 5-10 concepts, depending on the size of the document).

3 Description Logics

Description logics (DL) are frame formalisms dedicated to knowledge representation ([2]). DL structures the domain knowledge on two levels: a **terminological level** (T-Box), containing the axioms describing the classes of objects of the domain (*concepts*), with their properties (*roles*) and an **assertional level**, (A-Box), containing objects of the abstract classes (*instances*). DL uses logical operators for creating complex conceptual descriptions as follows in figure 2:

DL Operator	Logic operator	DL Interpretation
D = SOME R C	$\exists R.C$	there is at least one instance of C related by the relation R
D = ALL R C	$\forall R.C$	restricts the co-domain of the relation R
D = AND C1 C2	$C1 \wedge C2$	conjunction of conceptual descriptions
D = OR C1 C2	$C1 \vee C2$	disjunction of conceptual descriptions
NOT C	$\neg$ C	the complement of the concept C

Fig.2. Some DL operators

Examples. The definition

```
(define-concept Mother (AND Woman (SOME hasChild Child)
(ALL hasAge Age)))
```

is interpreted as: a **Mother** is a **Woman** that have at least one child (relation **hasChild**) being an instance of the concept **Child**. For each instance of the concept **Mother**, all the instances related by **hasAge** must be an individual of the concept **Age**.

DLs provide powerful inference mechanisms at terminological level: testing the satisfiability of a concept definition, detecting the subsumption relation between two concepts (detecting which concept is more general than the other one), *classification* (ordering the new concepts in the hierarchy induced by the subsumption relation). The A-Box provides *consistency* test (i.e. contradiction-free), *instantiation* test (i.e. concept subsuming the instance) for the individual descriptions, or *retrieval inference* (retrieving for a given concept all its individuals). Several DLs have been described and provide different expresivities (the possibility of defining concepts, roles, the handling of transitive and inverse roles etc.). Some of the tableaux calculus algorithms have been implemented in several DLs reasoners: CLASSIC [15], Fact [4](used for describing GRAIL, a complete medical terminology).

DLs are appropriate for applications dealing with semi-structured data or incomplete data, like IR systems. Some IR systems, using DL as knowledge representation formalisms, have been developed (integrating CLASSIC [15], for querying a digital library, or a terminological logic specially designed for retrieving multimedia information [7]).

Missing values are allowed in DL, the instances do not define values for all concept attributes (incomplete instances):

Example.

```
(define-primitive-concept Person)

(define-concept Patient (AND Person (SOME hasDisease Disease)
(SOME hasAge Age)))

(instance p1 Patient)
```

The last command [1] is not giving any particular value for the age or the disease of the **Patient**, even if **p1** is an instance of the concept **Person**.

Semi-structured data are difficult to handle because they have no precise schemas. In DL, the concepts do not define the exclusive list of roles for their individuals.

```
(define-concept Patient (AND domainTOP (SOME hasAge Age)(SOME
hasDisease Disease)))
(instance y0 (AND Patient (SOME hasAge 60)))
```

In the example, the instance **y0** of the concept **Patient** gives a value only to the role **hasAge** and has the value "60", then there must be a concept **Age** in the hierarchy having as its instance the value "60".

CICLOP[2] DL reasoner [10], provides the same expressivities as most of the other DL reasoners (role hierarchy, inverse roles, multiple hierarchies, transitive roles and features) and is used for representing the domain knowledge. It accepts reasoning simultaneously in several hierarchies (multiple T-Boxes) and implements an A-Box [13].

4 DL for Indexing

DL provides powerful inference mechanisms for handling incomplete and semi-structured data, as well as validity tests for new inferred facts. On the other

[1] The syntax of the commands for defining concepts and instances is borrowed from the CICLOP syntax

[2] Customizable Inference and Concept Language for Object Processing, developed at LIIA(Laboratoire d'Informatique et d'Intelligence Artificielle), ENSAIS, Strasbourg, France

hand, IR systems handle incomplete or erroneous input data as well as fuzzy knowledge of the domain. For these reasons, we choose DL as domain knowledge representation formalism for our IR system.

4.1 Building the DL Hierarchy

The DL hierarchy is used for filtering the results of keyword based searching. We do not propose to replace keyword indexes with concepts. Building a conceptual index is a difficult task. Conceptual level is an intermediate level between the user query and the document base.

Documents are identified by a basic keyword-based search. The NLP modules then parse these documents. New concepts are identified in the text and the hierarchy is updated.

The DL hierarchy of the domain has as its core a manually built initial hierarchy. The initial concepts are identified by a human expert in the list of repeated segments extracted from a set of initial texts. The expert defines also the relations between the concepts. For the medical corpus, the initial hierarchy contains about 137 concepts selected from the list of the most frequent repeated segments. The complete description of this small hierarchy took one day.

When a new document is added to the index base, it will be parsed paragraph by paragraph by a NLP module. For each paragraph, a concept description is built, it is added to the existing hierarchy and it is classified.

Sense tagging assigns words and syntagms with their DL descriptions. The set of patterns and words (extracted from the list of repeated segments) was annotated manually by a human expert with the DL descriptions. Partial semantic descriptions are combined by applying heuristic rules encoding syntactic knowledge. For example, it is possible to combine conceptual descriptions for a noun and its modifier.

Example. The user query in text format

"Les patients avec un infarctus mais sans angioplastie"
[The patients with a heart attack but without angioplasty.]

The system extracts the primitive concepts: **Patient**, **Infarct** and **(not Angioplasty)** and it combines them obtaining more complex descriptions. We combine **Patient** and **Infarct** (while "avec un infarctus" modifies the noun phrase "les patients") and also **Patient** and **(not Angioplasty)**, using DL reasoning module (there is a role relating the two concepts in the hierarchy). We applied the heuristic rules (1) (combining a noun and its modifier) and (2) (the rule triggered by a conjunction) - rules described in section 2.

Due to DL capabilities of dealing with incomplete and semistructured data, the new concepts identified in the text are combined and dynamically added to the existing hierarchy. Optionally, the human expert will be asked to validate the new concepts or to complete their definitions.

4.2 Indexing with CICLOP

Documents which are candidates to be included in the indexed base are first tagged with lexical categories. Then each document is analyzed by the **Tokenizer** module, extracting the list of the most frequent content words, and their contexts. These words are primitive concepts and they are added in the DL hierarchy. More complex conceptual descriptions are supposed to be created around these primitive concepts. The algorithm identifies the conceptual descriptions in the context of each word. We tested the prototype only for small documents (around 1500-2000 words). Only the new concepts, corresponding to the most frequent words are taken into account (5-10 new concepts per document).

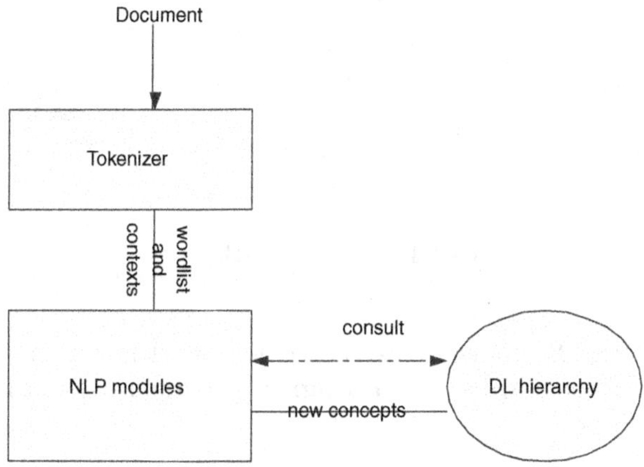

Fig.3. Document preparing for indexing

Example. For the phrase "cardiopathie ischémique" we extract the contexts:

> "...des symptômes de **cardiopathie ischémique**, presentées par le patient, agé de 69 ans,..."
> "...the ischemic cardiopathy symptoms manifested by the 69-old year patient..."

The semantic chunk identifier extracts the following chunks: "des symptômes", "de cardiopathie ischémique", "le patient", "de 69 ans". The concepts **Symptom**, **Patient**, **Iscardiopathy** and **Age** are identified and combined due to heuristic rules. We obtain the following description:

```
(AND Symptom (SOME hasSignfor (AND Iscardiopathy (SOME hasAgent
(AND Patient (SOME hasAge (AND Age (SOME hasVal "69"))))))))
```

A module building document summaries (including the most frequent conceptual descriptions) is still under development (in Java). We intend to use summaries as indexes for the document base.

Multiple T-Boxes

Due to the property of reasoning simultaneously on several T-Boxes, CICLOP is used for representing the domain knowledge and the structure of documents. Each level of knowledge is represented in two separate T-Boxes. The separation of different levels of knowledge increases search efficiency. The references of the concepts are identified in the document with a better precision than a keyword-based system. A keyword-based system identifies only the documents containing the requested keyword. Our approach identifies the places of the instances of the concepts in the text (the paragraph in the document).

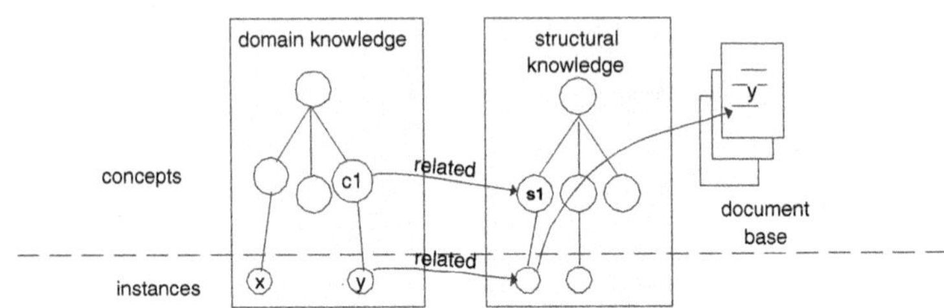

Fig.4. Multiple T-Boxes

The **structure** T-Box contains the structural elements of the document. **Text** is a set of **Paragraphs**. The **Paragraph** contains a set of **References** of the domain concept.

```
(define-concept Paragraph (AND top (SOME hasPart Reference)
(SOME hasNumber (> 0))))
(define-concept Reference (AND top (SOME hasStart (> 0))
(SOME hasEnd (> 0))(SOME hasNumber (> 0))))
```

Domain concepts are related to **structure** T-Box. Instances of these concepts are associated to domain concepts. When the domain concepts are identified in the user query, then their instances are retrieved. Instances of domain concepts are related to instances of structural concepts which are used to locate the information in the documents.

4.3 User Queries

User queries are interpreted by the NLP modules in order to extract a semantic representation. The concepts identified in the user query are related to the instances of the concepts from the T-Box **structure** which contain information about the location of the concepts in the documents.

Example. The user asks

"Donner le patient ayant eu un infarctus mais pas une angioplastie".
"Give me the patients having a heart attack but not an angioplasty".

The sense tagging module will identify the concepts **Patient**, **Heart_attack**, **Angioplasty**. The semantic chunks identified in this query are: "le patient", "un infarctus", "pas une angioplastie". The border identifiers are : "ayant eu" et "mais".

From **Patient**, and **Heart_attack** we can create a more complex conceptual representation while in the domain model there is a role path (**Patient** and **Disease** are related by **hasDisease** and **Heart_attack** is a **Disease**) and because "ayant eu un infarctus" is a modifier of "the patients". We apply again the heuristic rule about noun and its modifier and the rule about conjunctions. **Patient** has a **Treatment**, so we have a relation between **Patient** and **(not Angioplasty)** which is sub-concept of **Treatment**.

We obtain a complex description:

```
(AND Patient (SOME hasDisease Heart_Attack)(ALL hasTreatment
(not Angioplasty)))
```

This concept retrieves the instances **x** and **y** related to instances of the concept **Paragraph** and **Reference** (fig.4).

4.4 Evaluation

The system was evaluated for the small test corpora. To have a good evaluation of the efficiency we need to test the system on real corpora, with a real domain, and this will be the next developpment step. At this stage of the work, we can only evaluate the system without the use of summaries. The medical corpus consists of 52 short documents about patients or coronography descriptions. We used a set of 30 questions for evaluating this corpus.

The evaluation consists in two steps:

- we interpret user queries as a set of keywords and we obtain a set of documents;

- we apply NLP modules for creating a DL representation for the query and use the domain hierarchy for filtering the results of the search.

The keyword-based index file was built by a small module written in Java. For the small hierarchy built on the medical corpus, the precision of the results was better when the ontology is used (74 % of the answers were better as the keyword-based search, 16 % of the answers were as precise as the keyword searching). The use of synonyms which were not known by the system, or the inconsistencies in the domain model were reasons for failures. The great amount of situations were the precision was not improved is due to a poor ontological analysis of the domain.

5 Conclusion and Further Work

The paper presents a semantic-based approach for retrieving information from a base of documents. The system integrates shallow natural language processing for extracting the most relevant semantic chunks. DL reasoning, as well as shallow syntactic knowledge is used for computing semantic representations of texts and queries. Summary extraction techniques will be used in order to optimize the system performances. The approach presented here can be used only on a small subset of documents covering a limited domain. The advantage of using this approach is that the domain ontology is updated during the querying process. However, constraints must be imposed in order to limit the size of the domain hierarchy. The system is still under development and it must be tested on real corpora and in a dynamic environment like Web.

References

1. **S.Abney** - *Parsing By Chunks.* In: **R. Berwick, S. Abney and C. Tenny (eds.)**, *Principle-Based Parsing.* Kluwer Academic Publishers, Dordrecht, 1991.
2. **F.Baader, B.Hollunder** - *A Terminological Knowledge Representation Systems with Complete Inference Algorithms*, Workshop on Processing Declarative Knowledge, PDK'91.
3. **P.Buitelaar** - *CORELEX: Systematic Polysemy and Underspecification*, Ph.D. thesis, Brandeis University, Department of Computer Science, 1998
4. **I.Horrocks** - *Optimising Tableaux Decision Procedures for Description Logics*, Ph.Thesis, University of Manchester, 1997
5. **C.Jacquemin** - *Improving Automatic Indexing through Concept Combination and Term Enrichment*in *Proceedings of the 17th International Conference on Computational Linguistics (COLING'98)*, pages 595-599, Montral.
6. **J.Lecomte** - *Le Catégoriseur BRILL14-JL5/WINBRILL-0.3*, InaLF, InaLF/CNRS report, December 1998
7. **C.Meghini, F.Sebastiani, U.Straccia** - *A System for the Fast Prototyping of Multidimensional Image Retrieval*, in *Proceedings of ICMCS'99*, Firenze, vol II, pp. 603 - 609.
8. **T.Read, E.Barcena** - *JaBot:a multilingual Java-based inteligent agent for Web sites*, in COLING'98, Montreal, Canada, 10-14 August 1998
9. **E. Riloff, J.Lorenzen** - *Extraction-based Text Categorization Generating Domain-Specific Role Relationships Automatically*, in ed. **T.Strzalkowski**, *Natural Language Information Retrieval*, Kluwer Academic Publishers, 1999
10. **D.Rudloff, F. de Beuvron, M.Schlick** - *Extending Tableaux Calculus with Limited Regular Expression for Role Path : an Application to Natural Language Processing*, DL'98, Trento, Italy, 1998
11. **T.Strzalkowski** - *Natural Language Information Retrieval*, Kluwer Academic Publishers, 1999.
12. **T.Strzalkowski, J.Wang, B.Wise** - *Summarization-based Query Expansion in Information Retrieval*, in COLING'98, Montreal, Canada, 10-14 August 1998
13. **A.Todiraşcu, F. de Beuvron, F.Rousselot** - *Using Description Logics for Document Indexing*, IAR 14th Annual Meeting, Strasbourg, 18-19 November 1999.
14. **P.Vossen** - *EuroWordNet - A Multilingual Database with Lexical Semantic Networks*, Kluwer Academic Publishers, 1998
15. **C. Welty** - *An HTML Interface for Classic*, in *Proceedings of the 1996 International Workshop on Description Logics*, AAAI Press, November, 1996.
16. **J.Zhou** - *Phrasal Terms in Real-Word IR Applications*, in **T.Strzalkowski** - *Natural Language Information Retrieval*, Kluwer Academic Publishers, 1999

Guidelines for NL-Based Requirements Specifications in NIBA[1]

G, nther Fliedl*, Christian Kop+ , Willi Mayerthaler*, Heinrich C. Mayr+, Christian Winkler*

+Department of Business Informatics, *Department of Computational Linguistics
University Klagenfurt, Austria

Abstract: In this paper we discuss the linguistic base of standardized sentences as well as their structure and their employment in requirements analysis. Standardized sentences are quite helpful in the automatic analysis of requirements concerning static and dynamic aspects. Since standardized sentences require being filtered out of prose texts, which is a time consuming task we prefer to use standardized sentences in the case of requirements completion. Such completions inevitably emerge in the iterative process of requirements analysis. To enhance the process of requirements analysis we use a special approach called conceptual predesign the results of which are mapped by heuristic rules to conceptual design schemes, e.g. formulated in UML.

1 Introduction

Automatic sentence analysis is generally handled by means of a somewhat restricted language, filtering out several constructional and semantical features of input sentences. As already has been done in [7], [2], [20], the KISS method [14], the DATA-ID method [6] and the CREWS-SABRE approach, we propose a pre-structuring of texts. This structuring is based on the NTMS-model (naturalness theoretical morphosyntax) [16], [8].

The KISS method defines potential input sentences recurring on the grammatical base categories *subject, predicate, direct object, preposition, attributive adjunct* and *indirect object*, only allowing the active voice/mode. ëCandidate listsí (lists of *subjects, actions* and *objects*) are then generated out of linguistic categories.

In contrast to that, the DATA-ID approach is based on the pre-structuring, simplification and classification of texts which are requirements specifications for a database application to be developed. During the process of simplification sentences are checked for homonyms, synonyms, redundancies, implicit information and repetitions. After that, sentences are classified according to specific features that are usually word categories, and sorted into ëdata sentencesí, ëoperation sentencesí and ëevent sentencesí. Parts of a phrase (e.g. words or syntactic projections thereof) are

[1] The NIBA project is partly founded by the Klaus Tschira Stiftung Heidelberg and by the *Jubiläumsfonds* of the Austrian National Bank.

M. Bouzeghoub et al. (Eds.): NLDB 2000, LNCS 1959, pp. 251-264, 2001.

finally transferred into glossary-like schemata which contain more details than pure lists. The last step then consists in transferring the glossaries into a conceptual schema.

[4] also deals with requirements analysis issues and proposes to provide the designer with style guides and content guides he has to comply with. The style guides regulate, similar to DATA-ID and to KISS, the mode as to how requirements have to be disambiguated (e.g. avoiding synonyms/homonyms, substitute pronouns with the corresponding nouns etc.). Content guidelines support the designer in formulating structured sentences. The latter facilitate their automatic treatment and integration into the Requirement Chunk Model [18].

Our approach is driven as well by the goal of enhancing requirements analysis using natural language processing. More or less following the DATA-ID approach, we try to filter and to capture as much as possible information out of natural language requirements specifications and to transform them into glossary-like schemata entries. This information serves both for establishing conceptual schemes and for the later steps of the conceptual design. For this purpose we use a model called KCPM (Klagenfurt Conceptual Predesign Model) [13]. KCPM was introduced in order to minimize the conceptual distance between requirements in natural language and the conceptual design in a first approach. The designer is supposed to realize the universe of discourse (UoD) by means of simple notions and standardized notations and to collect important notions regarding the given UoD, independent of numerous models concerning conceptual design (object model, dynamic models). To allow the end-user (requirements holder) a thoroughgoing validation, we also use glossary notation, thus representing relevant information of the respective UoD in tabular form. Missing entries in columns indicate that the information concerning this point is not yet available. Glossaries can be considered as notepads by use of which the designer prepares the subsequent step of conceptual design (hence the notion *conceptual predesign*). The entries of these notepads (representing notions about the relevant aspects of the given UoD) are then mapped semi-automatically onto conceptual design.

In this paper we describe how to get glossary entries out of structured sentences. First, we give a very short overview of the target predesign model (KCPM) in section 2 and suggest how to proceed in the analysis of natural language requirements (section 3). Section 4 and 5 focus on the linguistic base for standardizing requirement sentences.

2 KCPM

The central KCPM concepts for structure-modeling are *thing-type* and *connection-type*. A thing-type models relevant notions or technical terms occurring in the userís domain. Normally, they are expressed by noun phrases. Typical *things* (instances of thing-types) are natural or juristic persons, material or immaterial objects, abstract notions. Thing-types are generalizations of the notions *class* and *value-type* (e.g. UML class schema) or *entity set* and *value set* (ER-model). Connection-types are

employed to describe relations between thing-types. They can be perceived of as generalizations of the notions *association* and *attribute* (relationship set and attribute) occurring in conceptual design.
To describe functional aspects of an UoD KCPM offers the concept *operation-type*. Operation-types have thing-types as parameters. Operations as instances of an operation-type are carried out by someone or something, the *actor*. An actor can manipulate things, read them or send them to a *recipient*. In the realm of business process modeling, typical actors are organizational units (e.g. departments, offices) performing operations in order to accomplish tasks. In doing so, they exchange documents. In the following example *Manager* and *Clerk* are the actors of the operation-types *übergeben (hand over)* and *unterschreiben (sign)* respectively, which both have the parameter thing-type *Rechnung (bill)*. Furthermore, *Manager* and *Poststelle (forwarding department)* must provide an operation-type such as *übernehmen (take over)*, allowing them to receive something:

- *Der Sachbearbeiter übergibt die Rechnung an den Manager. (The clerk hands the bill over to the manager.)*
- *Der Manager unterschreibt die Rechnung und übergibt sie an die Poststelle. (The manager signs the bill and hands it over to the forwarding department.)*

KCPM characterizes operation-types with properties like

- Duration of executing the operation
- Frequency of execution

Their value(range)s can, but need not be concretized. Linguistic analysis, however, should place a feature indicating whether a given operation is commonly associated with a duration. This feature can then be used for inducing further questions during requirements completion as well as in the transition onto the conceptual level. If the end-user nominalizes an operation-type (e.g. *übergeben* ✎ *Übergabe*), the operation-type itself can be considered as a thing-type. In this case, the thing-type is assigned to the respective operation-type and is called *operation representative*.

UoD dynamics emerge from *actors* performing operations under certain circumstances (*pre-conditions*) and thus creating new circumstances (*post-conditions*). An operation-type or the combination of operation-types to be carried out by one or more actors (concurrently) together with the respective pre-conditions and post-conditions build up what we call a *cooperation-type*[2]. In other words, a cooperation-type is a triple *<vb,(ak,op),nb>*, *vb* and *nb* being sets of conditions, (*ak,op*) a set of actor, operation-type pairs. Consequently, a *business process type* (BPT) consists of a network of cooperation types (CT), and a *business process* (instance of a BPT) consists of a sequence of cooperations (instances of CTís of the

---

2 This term has been taken over from object orientated business process modeling [KK 95]. A cooperation in that sense is an elementary step of a business process to which one or more actors contribute by (concurrently) executing operations (services).

resp. BPT) which again consist of a set of operation executions. Hereby, the beginning and the end of performing a cooperation (or, in modeling details, the beginning and the end of an operation execution) are considered as *events*.

In the realm of modeling static UoD properties conceptually we observe a certain homogeneity due to the fact that from a structural point of view we are confronted with one single ontological perspective (extensions of the ER-approach). In contrast to that modeling dynamics comprises several perspectives [5]:

- Use-Cases
- Scenario-technique
- Event driven processes (Petri-net theorie [19], Activity Charts)
- Behavior of objects (State Charts) [10]
- Communication of/between objects (Collaboration Diagrams).

Each of these models aims at describing one ontological point of view in detail. In that sense, the schemata of these models complete each other. Because of their different focuses they are employed in different parts of requirements analysis and conceptual design. One possibility, a commonly practiced method nowadays, suggests to start modeling dynamics by identification of Use Cases [15] which are described by means of the Scenario-technique [4]. With the help of Scenario-technique one tries to get State Charts after filtering out classes (and with them objects) from Use-Case scenarios [17]. Whereas we still take over the step of identifying Use Cases by the identification of cooperations, we donít do that by using traditional Scenario-technique. In contrast to that we suggest an approach which is first of all event-driven. That means, we ask the user to talk about when and under which conditions and consequences certain activities/actions take place in the context of a given business (process type). Such ë*when' (or conditions)* may be an event or some properties of certain objects (e.g. ë*the order is complete'*) or a time marker like ë*Monday morning'*, so that we talk very generally about pre-conditions under which something has to be done. We thus stick to a block-based approach. A Use Case (or a business process as well) consists of blocks/bundles (the cooperations) of events and operations that can be combined like a puzzle according to Use Case regulations. Thereby, pre-conditions and post-conditions may be considered as interfaces between cooperations. Similarly to the Scenario technique, only in a second step we construct an object-behavior model in the form of State Charts. KCPM does not prefer any special graphic notation but supports the following idea:

- Providing the designer with a kind of notepad during analysis
- Providing the user with notations he is familiar with

Thus, KCPM illustrates notions by means of glossaries (*thing-type glossary, connection-type glossary, operation-type glossary, cooperation-type glossary and some others*). The features of these concepts are reflected in its related glossary columns. Figure 1 shows typical examples of the cooperation-type glossary with relevant parts of the operation-type glossary.

cooperation-type glossary											
pre-condition				operation-type			post-condition				
id	name	thing-types	type	id	name	thing-types & (involvement)	id	name	thing-types	type
b1	Auftrag trifft ein	Auftrag	event	o1	pr, ft f, r jeden Artikel ob im Lager verf, gbar	Auftrags-abteilung (actor) Artikel (parameter) Auftrag (parameter)	b10	jeder Artikel des Auftrags gepr, ft	Auftrag	end_of activity
b2	alle Artikel des Auftrags verf, gbar	Auftrag	property	o2	Artikel den Auftrag zu-weisen	Auftrags-abteilung (actor) Artikel (parameter) Auftrag (parameter)	b11	Artikel ist dem Auftrag zugewiesen	Auftrag	property
				o3	pr, fen ob Zahlung f, r Auftrag autorisiert	Buchhaltung (actor) Auftrag (parameter)		gepr, ft ob Zahlung f, r Auftrag autorisiert ist	Auftrag	end_of activity
b3	Artikel Lagermenge unter Nachbe-stellmenge	Artikel	property	o4	Artikel nachbestellen	Bestell-abteilung (actor) Artikel (parameter)	b12	Artikel in Bestellung	Artikel	property
							b13	Auftrag offen	Auftrag	property
b4	Alle Artikel des Auftrags im Lager	Auftrag	property	o5	Auftrag wird zur Auslieferung freigegeben	Auftrags-abteilung (actor) Auftrag (parameter)	b14	Auftrag ist zur Aus-lieferung freigegeben	Auftrag	property
b5	Zahlung des Auftrags autorisiert	Auftrag	property							
	....									

Figure 1: Cooperation-type Glossary

3 Criteria of Standardization

Prose texts are full of ambiguities and gaps[3]. The resulting complexity cannot be handled satisfactory in all cases by means of linguistic analysis. This is why literature commonly proposes standardizing texts in several steps. Such steps consist of disambiguation (finding and filtering out homonyms, synonyms and redundancies, explaining implicitly present information and gaps) and other simplifications of several types we are not going to discuss here. We propose the following stages:

- Disambiguation
- Substituting pronouns
- Eliminating gaps
- Adding complementary information according to the guidelines of standardization listed below.

Completions of the original text are particularly apt for being entered into the parser in a standardized form. This implies that the designer is required to mentally process

[3] We propose that texts of this type have to undergo first a lexically orientated context analysis. In [9] we describe such content analysis by means of a concordance program. Starting point are free prose texts to be mapped in an initial step into glossary entries.

the mentioned steps in advance. Since completions however are mostly smaller text units than the original text, we consider this a minor task the advantage of which is that the parsing output can be entered automatically into the glossaries, thus providing detailed results. A typical completion possibly omitted in the original text is e.g.

Ist die Zahlung nicht autorisiert, so wird der Auftrag zurückgewiesen. (If payment is not authorized, the order is rejected).

In this case, the designer could translate the text into a standardized form such as

Wenn *die Zahlung nicht autorisiert ist,* **dann** *weist die Auftragsabteilung den Auftrag zurück. (If payment is not authorized then the responsible department rejects the order*).

and then transmit to the parser.

Such proceeding requires first of all general rules like the following ones for making additional changes, as partially mentioned above:

1. Each sentence is terminated by an unequivocal (".", "?", "!" und ";"), see [4].
2. Use sequential order for describing processes.
3. Avoid structural ambiguities (*kissing secretaries can be dangerous*), ellipses and coordinate structures (*and/or*).
4. Use consistent notions in all descriptions. Avoid use of synonyms and homonyms, and anaphoric references such as he, she, them and it.
5. Use present tense and indicative mode. If a verb allows passivization a passive construction is allowed provided that the agent phrase (mostly a prepositional phrase) is made explicit.
6. Modal verbs can be used. They are however interpreted rather under a syntactical point of view than semantically.
7. Extended infinitive clauses are to be avoided (*the computer scientist believes to be able to do this*).
8. Conditional clauses should be complete (no gaps).
9. Avoid verb complexes such as *the mechanic intends to be able to repair the car tomorrow.*
10. Avoid complex nominal phrases but restrict to nominal phrases containing one prepositional phrase at the most.

Complying with these rules yet is not enough. Automatic analysis of natural language sentences implies the representation of a sentence in a reduced form so that the respective rules for transformation can be generated on the base of these sentence patterns. Thus, linguistic treatment as described in the following section is necessary.

4 Standardizing Requirement Sentences by Means of NTMS

As proposed by Content Guidelines (CG) [4], standardizations are used in a modified form for systematic treatment of natural language texts in NIBA as well. The base or our standardization are Predicate-Argument-Structures (PAS) as defined in [8]. Lexicon elements, commonly known as PAS, encode valence and the argument position of the indicated theta-roles. Fine differentiations are done by means of features. PAS are crucial for the wellformedness of a sentence, since the interpretation of sentences in many cases can only be managed with the help of morphosyntactically specified theta-roles. This is why frequently features are anchored, which give informations about case encoding. We distinguish between structural cases such as nominative and accusative on the one hand and non-structural cases which can be defined as direct representations of theta-roles. The distinction between non-structural and structural P-cases is difficult: a structural P-case e.g. is given if in the context of verbs expressing movement directionality is encoded by means of a preposition. E.g. consider the phrases *Er läuft in den Saal* (he runs into the hall) vs. *Er lief im Saal* (*He ran in the hall).* We analyze the second case as locative adjunct-dative. Thematic roles can be considered as semantic parts of verbs. They thus are obligatory parts in the verb lexicon, even if they need not to be represented in the syntactic pattern. The conditions regarding their syntactic representation depend largely on the respective context. We use the following theta-roles for verb classification:

AG, EXP, TH(PATIENT/OBJEKTIVE), CAUS, GO, SO, LOC, BEN, INSTR

- **AGENT (AG)** is the carrier of an action, e.g. a natural or juristic person carrying out or at least intending an action.
- **EXPERIENCER (EXP)** is a person experiencing something or realizing a certain psychologically specifiable experience and having an attitude towards this experience.
- **THEMA (TH)** is an animated or non-animated entity involved in an action or event without being able to influence or control it. In the entity involved is non-animated, TH is often subcategorized as OBJECTIVE, if it is animated and the fact of being animated is relevant in the respective situation, TH is subcategorized as PATIENT.
- **CAUSATOR (CAUS)** is the initiator of an action not carried out by himself.
- **GOAL (GO)** is a concrete or abstract place where an event is terminated or that is reached when the action is considered successful.
- **SOURCE (SO)** is the starting point of a process, an action or an event.
- **LOCATION (LOC)** is the place put in direct or indirect relation with the entity or object involved in the event encoded by the verb.
- **BENEFICIARY (BEN)** is the person taking profit of an action.
- **INSTRUMENT (INSTR)** is an object with the help of which an action is carried out or at least started.

According to [1], we call the arguments of a verb constituting its meaning 'inherent verb-arguments'; e.g. consider the phrases *den Textbaustein* (*the text block*) and *in einen Text* (*into a text*) within the sentence

Er fügt den Textbaustein in einen Text ein (He inserts the text block into a text).
[TH] [GO]

Such arguments characterized by obligatory theta-roles must be distinguished from non-inherent verb arguments. Compare e.g. the BEN-role of *für seinen Betrieb* (*for his firm*) in sentences like *er arbeitet ausschließlich für seinen Betrieb* (*he works exclusively for*

his firm) as opposed to the LOC-role of *in Klagenfurt* in *er wohnte in Klagenfurt* (*he lived in Klagenfurt*).
Non-inherent arguments are mostly domain-specific. They constitute the domain relevant meaning of typical verbs and have to be included in the lexicon if they restrict the verb meaning in a way that consulting a general lexicon does not prognosticate. Consider e.g. sentences like:

Er notiert an der Börse. (He quotes at the stock exchange.)
Er schreibt das Programm für einen Großbetrieb. (He writes the program for a large enterprise.)
etc.

Semantic roles corresponding to adjuncts are not included in the PAS. Normally, adjunct roles are assigned by prepositions. In the context of the verb *laufen* (to run) the prepositions *in* (in), *auf* (on), *unter* (under) can govern the accusative and thus generate the feature [+dir].

The verb specific distribution of theta-roles is shown in the following list of lexicon entries (LE). As for transparency reasons we only note PAS:

Geben (to give):	AG[GO,TH]
Schicken (to send):	AG[GO,TH]
Bleiben (to stay):	TH[LOC]
Wohnen (to live):	TH[LOC]
Interessieren (to interest):	TH[GO]
Sehen (to see):	EXP[TH]
Weggehen (to see):	AG[SO]

Ambiguity is expressed by assigning two PAS, comp. the LE of *interessieren*:
interessieren : TH[GO]
interessieren : AG_i[i, GO]

The PAS of a verb contain all domain-independent meaning constituting arguments specified as theta-roles. They are provided with brackets distinguishing internal arguments from external arguments, as e.g. in the PAS of *sehen (to see)*:
seh: EXP[TH]. The structure indicates that TH is the internal argument and hence the direct object of *sehen.* EXP is located outside the bracket and is therefore the external argument of the verb in function if the subject. A locative verb like *wohnen (to habitate)* carries the PAS: TH[LOC]. The entity with the role TH is assigned to a certain place by the verb. TH is syntactically spoken the subject, LOC has the function of a prepositional object. We employ two types of PAS for verb classification:

- Class defining PAS: Rough grids allowing alternatively specified PAS and characterizing 20 verb classes consisting of 12 main classes and 8 subclasses.
- Verb specific PAS: Unequivocal instances of class-PAS with the task to disambiguate verb meanings.

With the help of this descriptive inventory based on the considerations mentioned above German verbs can be classified as shown below. The restriction of linguistic variety is based on ënaturalí patterns establishing verb classes [8]:

Class	Abbreviation	PAS
1	AUX	<Ø>/V_{-fin}
2	eV	[TH]
3	iV	AG/TH[]
4	LocV	TH[LOC]
5	PossV	GO[TH]
6	PsychV	TH[GO/TH]
7	tVag/2	AG[TH]
7,1	tVag/2d,g	AG[GO/BEN]
7,2	tVag/2pp[4]	AG[SO/GO]
7,3	tVag/2sk	AG[THabstr]
7,4	tV/ppsk	AG[GO/SOabstr]
8	tV/3	AG/GO(TH,GO/SO)
8,1	tV/3ti	AG[TH...,GOabstr]
8,2	tV/3tda	AG[THacc,GOabstr]
8,3	tV/3tdd	AG[THdat,GOabstr]
8,4	tV/3sk,ak	AG[GO,Thabstr]
9	SentV	EXP[TH]
10	Vcop	TH[N2/A2]
11	tV/2	-AG/-EXP[TH]
12.1-12.5	ReflV	AGi/THi[i,(GO/LOC/TH)]

Abbreviations:[5]

AUX(1) stands for ∀-modal auxiliaries. They do not govern θ-roles and form together with the main verb a verb-complex, the verb status of which they govern. Instead of a PAS we note the empty θ-grid and the infinitive governed by the auxiliary. Since it is

---

4 For reasons of transparency we note Ñppì instead of p^2.

5 (1) AUX = auxiliary; (2) eV = ergative verb; (3) iV = intransitive verb; (4) locV = locative verb; (5) possV = possessive verb; (6) psychV = psychological verb; (7) tVag2 = bivalent agentverb; (7,1) tVag/2d,g = bivalent agentverb with dative-object or genitive-object; (7,2) tVag/2pp = bivalent agentverb with prepositional objekt; (7,3) tVag/2sk = bivalent agentverb with sentential object; (7,4) tVag/2pp = bivalent agentverb with sentential prepositional objekt; (8) tV/3 = trivalent verb; (8,1) tV/3ti = trivalent verb with infinitival complement sentence and thematical identity of the antecedent and the logical subjects of the infinitival group; (8,2) tV/3tdd = trivalent verb with infinitival complement sentence and thematical difference of the antecedent and the logical subject of the infinitival group; (8,3) (tV3tdd) = agentive, trivalent verb with concrete theme in the dative and abstract ÑGOALì; (8,4) (tV/3sk,ak) = trivalent verb with infinitival complement and subject control or arbitrary control; (9) sentV = verba sentiendi; (10) Vcop = copula verb; (11) tV/2 = transitive verb, whose subjekt does not carry the AG-Role nor the EXP-role; (12) reflV = reflexive verb.

the auxiliary that carries inflectional endings/finite features in the context of a main verb, the status of the main verb can only be non-finite.

The parser assigns phrase structures to 'text sentences'. These phrase structures contain the verb specific PAS as defined above and can thus be considered as structural representations of text elements that can be semantically interpreted

Verb classes (2) ñ(12) determine the syntactic and semantic structure of sentences. Their elements commonly are called *head verbs*. Their bracketing structures represent in addition to syntactic relations those features which are relevant for an interpretation in the field of conceptual modeling. In [22], all head verb class bracketing structures occurring in our model are listed. These structures may be visualized by trees like the following which represents class (2).

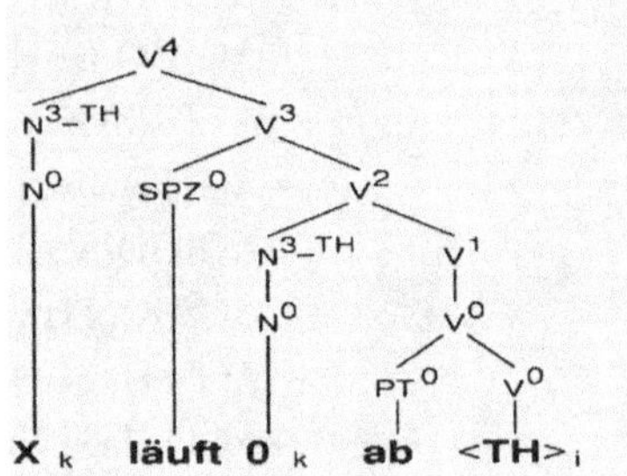

For the purpose of requirement engineering it is now necessary to filter out those verb classes from the ones listed above that can be head verbs of potential requirement sentences (standardized sentence patterns).

5 Standardized Requirement Sentences

In the following we list only such classes implying sentence patterns relevant for modeling. In other words, sentence constructions that hint at the KCPM concepts connection-type, operation-type, cooperation-type (condition/operation-type structure) employed in conceptual predesign.

5.1 Parameters of Modeling Static UoD Aspects

In the default case, connection-types are established by the following verb classes:

4	locV	TH[LOC]
5	possV	GO[TH]
6	psychV	TH[GO/TH]
7	tVag/2	AG[TH]

7,1	tVag/2d,g	AG[GO/BEN]
7,2	tVag/2pp[6]	AG[SO/GO]
7,3	tVag/2sk	AG[Thabstr]
7,4	tV/ppsk	AG[GO/SOabstr]
8	tV/3	AG/GO(TH,GO/SO)
8,1	tV/3ti	AG[TH...,Goabstr]
8,2	tV/3tda	AG[Thacc,Goabstr]
8,3	tV/3tdd	AG[THdat,Goabstr]
8,4	tV/3sk,ak	AG[GO,THabstr]
9	SentV	EXP[TH]
10	Vcop	TH[N2]
11	tV/2	-AG/-EXP[TH]
12.1-12.5	ReflV	AGi/Thi[i,(GO/LOC/TH)]

5.2 Parameters of Modeling Dynamics

As for modeling dynamics, sentences semantically classified by verb classes and PAS are categorized with respect to *activity/action, completion of activity, property/state of thing-type, event, restriction* in order to obtain the parameters *operation-type, condition* and *cooperation-type* (in the sense of a condition/operation-type structure). An operation-type can be derived from the following verb-classes.

Activity/Action Something that is to be done by someone - e.g. agentive verbs.

3	iV	AG/TH[]
7	tVag/2	AG[TH]
7,1	tVag/2d,g	AG[GO/BEN]
7,2	tVag/2pp	AG[SO/GO]
8	tV/3	AG/GO(TH,GO/SO)
12.1-12.5	ReflV	AGi/THi[i,(GO/LOC/TH)]

The noun phrase carrying the semantic role AG become an 'actor' in the operation glossary. Nominal phrases which carry different semantic roles get the status of a parameter in the operation. The parameter *condition* is derived according to the following sub-categories:

Completion of activity An Activity/Action which has been done. e.g. Past participle of transitive and intransitive verbs

[6] For reasons of transparency we note Ñppì instead of p^2.

Property/state — *Properties of thing-types.* E.g. Adjectives to thing-types or adverbials describing properties of activities

4	locV	TH[LOC]
5	possV	GO[TH]
10	Vcop	TH[N2/A2]

Event — *e.g.* Ergative verbs (something happens to a thing-type but the thing-type does not act)

2	eV	[TH]

5.3 The Natural Language Correlate of Cooperation-Types

Having established categories leading to conditions and others leading to operations, we can find out with which of them a cooperation-type can be extracted from natural language. In doing so, we propose to use a if/when constructions as a preliminary standardization. Hereby we distinguish valid sentence patterns for entering a combination of pre-condition/operation and patterns leading to the combination operation/post-condition. Valid patterns for the first alternative are:

(1) Wenn (if) *<Completion of activity>* dann (then) *<Activity/Action>*
Wenn X den Y geprüft hat, dann schickt X Y an Z. (If X has examined Y, then X sends Y to Z.)

(2) Wenn *<Property/state/behaviour potential>* dann *<Activity/Action>*
Wenn der Artikel in ausreichender Menge im Lager verfügbar ist, dann weist die Auftragsabteilung diesen Artikel dem Auftrag zu. (If the article is on stock, the responsible department assigns the article to the order.)

(3) Wenn *<Event>* dann *<Activity/Action>*
Wenn der Auftrag eintrifft, dann prüft die Auftragsabteilung für jeden Artikel ob dieser im Lager verfügbar ist. (If the order comes in, the responsible department checks whether every article is available.)

(4) *<Restriction>* *<Activity/Action>*
Immer Montags wird ein Kassasturz gemacht. (Cash-check is done on Mondays.)

Valid patterns for entering the combination operation/post-condition are:

(1) Wenn *<Completion of Activity >* dann *<Completion of Activity>*
Wenn die Auftragsabteilung den Auftrag geprüft hat, dann ist die erste Phase der Begutachtung abgeschlossen.(When the responsible department has checked the order, then the first step of validation is terminated.)

(2) Wenn *<Completion of Activity>* dann *<Property/state/behaviour potential>* *Wenn die Auftragsabteilung den Artikel nachbesteltl hat, dann ist der Artikel 'in Bestellung'. (When the responsible department has ordered the article, then the article has the state 'being ordered').*

6 Conclusion

In this paper we presented our linguistically motivated model of conceptual predesign. More precisely, we defined the syntactic and semantic filters for sentences to be parsed and illustrated in our system. These filters are necessary because they serve the designer as guidelines for generating predesign entries.

We showed that natural language based glossaries can be used as a tool for notes, filtering processes and checks in requirements analysis. Thus, glossaries are more user oriented than conceptual design schemes. Our future work will focus on mapping information onto conceptual schemes since we intend to obtain state diagrams for objects out of glossaries. Hereby, glossaries can be helpful in finding those objects having a complex live cycle. Moreover, hints at states and transitions as well as events, conditions, actions and activities can be filtered out of specific entry patterns which are described in more detail by the categories *event, property, restriction, end_of_activity* etc.

References

[1] Abraham, W.:"Deutsche Syntax im Sprachenvergleich", Gunter Narr Verlag, T, bingen, 1995.

[2] Batini, C.; Ceri, S.; Navathe, S.B.: ÑConceptual Database Designì, The Benjamin/Cummings Publishing Comp., Inc., 1992.

[3] Becks, Andreas.; K^ller, J^rg.: Automatically Structuring Requirements Scenarios, CREWS Report 99-15.

[4] Ben Achour, C.; Rolland, C.; Maiden, N.A.M.; Souveyet, C.: Guiding Use Case Authoring: Results of an Empirical Study. In: 4th IEEE International Symposium on Requirements Engineering (RE'99), University of Limerick, Ireland, June 7-11 1999.

[5] Booch, G.; Rumbaugh, J.; Jacobson, I.: The Unified Modeling Language - User Guide, Addison Wesley Publ. Comp. 1998.

[6] Ceri, S. (ed.): Methodology and Tools for Database Design. North Holland, 1983.

[7] Chen, P.: ÑEnglish Sentence Structure and Entity Relationship Diagramsì. In Int. Journal of Information Sciences, Vol. 29, 1983. Pp 127-149.

[8] Fliedl, G.: Nat, rlichkeitstheoretische Morphosyntax ñ Aspekte der Theorie und Implementierung. Gunter Narr Verlag T, bingen, 1999.

[9] Fliedl, G.; Kop, Ch.; Mayr, H.C.; Mayerthaler, W.; Winkler, Ch.: "Linguistic Aspects of Dynamics in Requirements Specifications", Appears in DEXA Workshop NLIS.

[10] Harel, D.; Gery, E.: Executable Object Modeling with Statecharts. In: IEEE Computer, 30 (7), 1997.

[11] Jones, C.: Applied Software Measurement : Assuring Productivity and Quality. Mc Graw Hill, 1996.

[12] Kaschek, R.; Kohl, C.; Mayr, H. C.: Cooperations - An Abstraction Concept Suitable for Business Process Reengineering. In: Gy^rk^s, J.; Kripser, M; Mayr, H.C. (eds).: Conference Proc. ReTIS'95, Re-Technologies for Information Systems, R. Oldenburg Verlag, Wien, M, nchen, 1995.

[13] Kop, Ch.; Mayr, H.C.: Conceptual Predesign ñ Bridging the Gap between Requirements and Conceptual Design. In: Proceedings of the 3rd International Conference on Requirements Engineering. Colorado Springs Colorado, April 6-10, 1998.

[14] Kristen, G.: Object Orientation ñ The Kiss Method - From Information Architecture to Information System. Addison Wesley, 1994.

[15] Jacobson, I.; Christerson, M.; Jonsson, P.; ÷vergaard, G.: A Use Case Driven Approach. Addison Wesley Publ. Comp, MA, 1992.

[16] Mayerthaler, W.; Fliedl, G.; Winkler, Ch.: Lexikon der Nat, rlichkeitstheoretischen Syntax und Morphosyntax, Stauffenburg Verlag, Brigitte Narr, T, bingen, 1998.

[17] Rumbaugh, J.; Blaha, M.; Premerlani, W.; Eddy, F.; Lorensen, W.: Object oriented modeling modeling and design. Englewood Cliffs, NJ, Prentice Hall, 1991.

[18] Rolland, C.; Ben Achour, C.: Guiding the Construction of Textual Use Case Specifications. In: Chen, P.; van de Riet, R.P. (eds.): Data & Knowledge Engineering Journal, Vol 25, No 1-2, pp 125 - 160, North Holland, Elsevier Science Publ. March 1998.

[19] Scheschonk, G. (ed.): Petri-Netze im Einsatz f, r Entwurf und Entwicklung von Informations-systemen. Informatik Fachbericht, Springer Verlag, September 1993.

[20] Tjoa, A. M.; Berger, L.: Transformation of Requirement Specification Expressed in Natural Language into an EER Model. In: Elmasri, R.A.; Kouramajian, B.; Thalheim, B. (eds.): 12th International Conference on Entity Relationship Approach. Arlington, Texas. New York, Springer 1993. pp. 127-149.

[21] Weidenhaupt, K.; Pohl, K.; Jarke, M.; Haumer, P.: Scenario Usage in System Development: A Report on Current Practice. IEEE Software March 1998.

[22] Fliedl, G.: "Head Verb Classes - a comprehensive list"; Technical Report; University of Klagenfurt 2000.

Developing Document Analysis and Data Extraction Tools for Entity Modelling

Heather Fulford

Business School
Loughborough University
Loughborough
Leicestershire
LE11 3TU
UK
h.fulford@lboro.ac.uk

Abstract. The entity-relationship approach to conceptual modelling for database design conventionally begins with the analysis of natural language system specifications to identify entities, attributes, and relationships in preparation for the creation of entity models represented in entity-relationship diagrams. This task of document scanning can be both time-consuming and complex, often requiring linguistic knowledge, subject domain knowledge, judgement and intuition. To help alleviate the burden of this aspect of database design, we present some of our research into the development of tools for analysing natural language specifications and extracting candidate entities, attributes, and relationships. Drawing on research in corpus linguistics and terminology science, our research relies on an examination of patterns of word co-occurrence and the use of ëlinguistic cuesí. We indicate how we intend integrating our tools into a CASE environment to support database designers during each stage of their work, from the analysis of system specifications through to code generation.

1. Introduction

When building entity models and representing those models graphically in entity-relationship diagrams, analysts, adopting a top-down approach, typically begin by analysing natural language specifications to identify and extract the relevant entities, the relationships holding between those entities, and the attributes associated with each entity. It is this preliminary task of document analysis for data extraction purposes which forms the focus of this paper.

The task of scanning natural language specifications in search of relevant constructs can essentially be thought of as one of linguistic analysis [15]. Generally undertaken manually, it can be considerably time-consuming, often entailing several ëtrawlsí through a given document to ensure that all the requisite data items are captured. These data items then have to be appropriately categorised as entities, attributes or relationships [5]. In the course of his/her career, the analyst will most probably be

M. Bouzeghoub et al. (Eds.): NLDB 2000, LNCS 1959, pp. 265-275, 2001.

required to perform this task in a range of subject domains, without necessarily possessing expert knowledge of any of the domains he/she encounters.

The interdisciplinary empirical research presented in this paper is devoted to efforts to design and create tools to support database designers in this arguably somewhat laborious task of document analysis, data item identification, and data item categorisation. Following a careful study of technical and specialist documents written in English and spanning a range of subject domains, we have devised an approach to document analysis. We have denoted our approach a ëtext-probing approachí. Using this approach as a starting point, we have developed a prototype program for extracting entities from natural language specifications. More recently, we have extended the approach and incorporated a further prototype program for identifying, in natural language specifications, some of the relationships holding between entities. We are currently conducting some exploratory research into the further enhancement of our text-probing approach to include a program for detecting the attributes associated with entities.

Our approach to document analysis draws on research carried out over the past few decades in computational and corpus linguistics (see for example [20], [2]) and terminology extraction (see for example [4], [18]). Essentially, this approach is based, as we will demonstrate in this paper, on a study of patterns of word co-occurrence and the use of ëlinguistic cuesí in natural language specifications. (Fuller reports of the design and development of the text-probing approach to document analysis and data extraction can be found in [8] and [9].

This paper is structured as follows:
In section 2, we bring together aspects of the relevant literature with our own observations of the language of system specifications and consider some of the issues facing analysts when examining natural language specifications for the purpose of data extraction and categorisation. We note some of the complexities associated with the task, and highlight those aspects of the task that may render its automation difficult. Next, in section 3, we present an overview of our text-probing approach document analysis and data extraction for database design purposes. Finally, in section 4, we present some concluding remarks about our work to date. We give some indications of how we anticipate that our work might be further developed in the future, placing specific emphasis on how we envisage incorporating our prototype analysis and extraction tools into a CASE (Computer-Aided Software Engineering) environment being created to support the database designer through each stage of his/her work, from the analysis of system specifications through to code generation.

2. Examining Natural Language Specifications: Some Issues for Analysts

The initial phase of entity modelling has been described as a subjective task of analysis and categorisation [5]. When discussing entity modelling techniques, authors of textbooks on systems analysis and design typically advocate that analysts adopt what could be denoted a top-down ëlinguistic approachí to the task of analysing natural language specifications and identifying entities, relationships and attributes [3], [13], [5]. Such authors generally recommend that, when searching for entities, the analyst should focus on an examination of the nouns and noun phrases in the natural language specification; when searching for relationships, he/she should focus on the verbs; and when endeavouring to associate attributes with entities, he/she should look again at the nouns, and also in some instances, at the adjectival constructions.

In this section, we consider some of the issues the analyst faces when engaging in this process of linguistic analysis, and highlight those aspects of the process that may render its automation difficult. The issues discussed include some of those raised in the literature as well as some drawn from our own observations and empirical studies of English natural language specifications.

Identifying entities represented by nouns or noun phrases in natural language specifications is arguably not as straightforward as it might initially appear. Perhaps the most obvious issue to note is that, in any given set of natural language specifications, not all nouns will represent relevant entities: the analyst has to examine each noun and noun phrase in turn and decide whether ëdata is likely to be storedí about each one[13]. This suggests that the application of linguistic knowledge alone is unlikely to suffice in the entity identification task. The task is particularly difficult for analysts who do not possess subject domain knowledge [12]. Indeed, interaction with the client organisation (and hence access to a source of the relevant domain knowledge) is often the only means of completing the entity identification task successfully [16]. Similar issues are likely to occur in the search for constructs representing relationships between entities, as well as in the search for attributes.

Another issue analysts have to contend with in the entity identification task is that of synonymy, i.e. different words being used to refer to the same entity [16], [5]. It is possible that an entity discussed in a selection of documents will be represented by various nouns depending, for example, on the author of the document, its text style, and so on. For example, we might find the expressions *sale representative* and *sales person* used interchangeably to refer to the same entity. Further liaison with the client organisation may be necessary to unify such synonymous representations.

Attribute identification arguably presents the analyst with a considerable challenge. Indeed, some have contended that it is extremely difficult to distinguish between attributes and entities [19]. On the linguistic level, for example, one problem is that attributes, like entities, may be represented by nouns or noun phrases. Deciding whether a given noun is an entity or an attribute requires careful study, and probably again the application of domain knowledge on the part of the analyst.

It is widely acknowledged in the literature that automation of the task of document analysis and data extraction is a difficult one (see for example [1], and [16]). Arguably, one of the principal reasons for this difficulty is the range of knowledge types an analyst may require to perform the task successfully. This might include, as we have noted earlier, linguistic knowledge, subject domain knowledge, and perhaps also general world knowledge. Moreover, given the subjective nature of the task, it is likely that the analyst will also have to rely to some extent on ëjudgement and experienceí [5].

The literature contains a number of efforts to automate the task of data item extraction for database design purposes, although as [12] point out, more attention seems to have been devoted to using natural language processing techniques for ëinterfacing databasesí than has been centred on creating databases from natural language representations. The existing efforts to automate the data item extraction task encompass a variety of approaches to tackling the task, and perhaps this in itself serves to reflect something of the complexity of the task. Perhaps the most notable examples of automation attempts include those which rely on parsing-based techniques (see for example [12]); those using an expert system approach entailing a question and answer format; those which rely on transformation techniques (see for example [22]); and those which depend on building ëintermediateí conceptual models and data glossaries (see for instance [7]).

Obviously, each approach has its individual merits and limitations. In our own research on document analysis and data extraction, we do not claim to have designed and implemented a fully automated approach, but rather we have sought to place emphasis on supporting and the guiding the analyst by providing tools that present as output ëcandidateí data items. The analyst can then examine this output, perhaps in collaboration with a member (or members) of the client organisation, to reach an agreed set of relevant entities, attributes and relationships for his/her particular project. We have endeavoured to create an approach which will tackle ërealí texts in real-world domains, rather than artificially-constructed texts from small-scale application areas (an acknowledged limitation of, for example, [12]). From a computational point of view, we have avoided the use of the arguably somewhat cumbersome and time-consuming grammatical tagging and parsing-based techniques. We provide an outline of our approach in the next section.

3. The Text-Probing Approach to Document Analysis and Data Extraction

In developing our text-probing approach to document analysis and data extraction for entity modelling, we have sought above all to take into account the environment in which analysts might typically operate in the course of their careers. As noted earlier, it is likely that an analyst will work in a number of domains, and yet he/she is unlikely to be a domain expert in any of them. In any given project, an analyst will probably encounter, and have to examine, a range of documents written in a wide variety of styles and for various audiences. Mindful of these issues, our approach endeavours to be both domain-independent as well as document-type-independent. Moreover, the programs in which our approach is implemented have been designed with the option to process individual documents as well as batches of documents.

Our text-probing approach to document analysis and data extraction has its origins in the context of our studies in terminology and corpus linguistics. In this earlier exploratory work in natural language processing, our objective was to provide tools to assist terminologists in the task of compiling terminology collections, such as glossaries, of technical terms (see for example [8] and [9]). The role of the terminologist is arguably quite similar to that of the database designer: a terminologist, like a database designer is required to scan technical documents in a range of subject domains, without necessarily being an expert in any of them. Furthermore, like the database designer, the terminologist will be searching these documents for linguistic constructs: terms, for example, will typically be represented by nouns or noun phrases.

We further developed and applied our text-probing approach to the context of knowledge engineering for expert system development. In this application of our work, we sought to develop tools for assisting knowledge engineers in the task of analysing documents (often largely transcripts of interviews with domain experts) for the purpose of extracting facts (typically represented by nouns or noun phrases) and rules. This stage of our work is reported more fully in [10].

Our studies of systems analysis and design have led us to refine our approach still further in order to develop tools to support database designers in the entity modelling task. Specifically, we have introduced the notion of extracting entity sub-types, identifying relationships holding between entities, and begun considering techniques for extracting attributes associated with entities.

We outline here our text-probing approach to document analysis and data extraction for entity modelling purposes, beginning with our work on the design of a prototype tool to help analysts identify entities in natural language specifications.

3.1 Entity Extraction

Our empirical studies of technical documents for terminology extraction purposes, together with our theoretical studies of the literature of text analysis and term extraction (see for example [23] and [21]), led us to the observation that a technical term (typically represented by a noun or noun phrase) is likely to co-occur in text with function words (e.g. determiners, conjunctions, and prepositions) and/or punctuation. In other words, a technical term is likely to be *preceded* in text by a ëboundary markerí comprising a function word or punctuation mark, and *followed* by a ëboundary markerí comprising a function word or punctuation mark. This can be summarised in the following pattern:

Function word/punctuation + TERM + Function word/punctuation **(1)**

This basic premise of the co-occurrence patterns of technical terms formed the basis of our approach to entity identification in natural language specifications. Thus, since entities are typically represented by nouns or noun phrases, the summarised co-occurrence pattern, in the context of entity extraction, becomes:

Function word/punctuation + ENTITY + Function word/punctuation **(2)**

In Table 1 below, we illustrate this pattern with some sample entities and their immediate textual environment (i.e. co-occurrence patterns) taken from the natural language specification extract presented in Figure 1 below.

Table 1. Sample co-occurrence patterns for entity identification

Boundary marker	**ENTITY**	**Boundary marker**
the	*warehouse*	is
a	*pick list*	.
.	*Customer order forms*	have
ì	*master pick list*	ì

Figure 1 below shows an extract from a natural language specification. Using the approach to entity identification outlined above, a number of candidate entities would be identified using this approach (highlighted in bold in Figure 1).

The ***warehouse*** is ***sent*** the ***shipping documents*** for a ***batch*** of ***customer orders***, which cannot be ***filled*** from the ***office inventory***. ***Shipping documents*** consist of a ***copy*** of all the ***customer orders*** in the ***batch*** and a ***pick list***. ***Customer order forms*** have a ***mailing label*** which is ***attached*** to them and which was ***printed*** in the ***sending office***. The ***warehouseman combines*** all of the ***pick lists*** he ***receives*** in a ***day*** into a ë***master pick list'***.

Fig. 1. Sample natural language specification highlighting candidate entities

We observed that these co-occurrence patterns held true for nouns and noun phrases in a variety of subject domains as well as across a range of text types.

Using this observation of co-occurrence patterns of nouns and noun phrases as a basis, we wrote a computer program that scanned natural language specifications and identified as candidate entities those words and phrases residing between boundary markers comprising function words and/or punctuation. The program was essentially designed to ëprobeí texts and identify the candidate entities residing between the boundary markers, hence the designation of our approach as a ëtext-probing approachí. The program was written in Quintus Prolog. Subsequently, we have explored further implementation possibilities.

The basic functionality of the program we have written for entity extraction was relatively straightforward (hence the possibility to port it to a variety of platforms). A particular benefit of the program which we perceive (as noted earlier) was that it did not need to rely on the somewhat computationally cumbersome techniques of tagging and parsing. The program identifies the boundary markers by using a preset file of function words and punctuation marks. It was possible to create such a file because both function words and punctuation marks essentially comprise a closed set, and hence a comprehensive list of them could be compiled using widely-available grammar and linguistics resources.

In common with other programs for noun identification, the output from our text-probing approach to entity extraction typically contains a certain amount of ënoiseí. In order to keep this noise to a minimum, we filter the output using a stoplist (again, this is in common with other approaches to noun identification). This stoplist was created following a study of the theoretical and empirical literature of specialist and technical writing (see for example [17]), and consists of commonly occurring words and phrases that are conventionally used in technical or specialist writing. The list includes reporting verbs (e.g. *to note, to state*, *to say*), and various phrases (sometimes referred to collectively in the linguistics literature as ëlinking wordsí) that are used to ërefer back to points which have already been stated or forward to points which will be made laterí [17]. It further contains a collection of other general linking expressions, such as *consequently*, *furthermore*, *moreover*, and *for example*, as well as some frequently-occurring verbs.

Our entity extraction program, when evaluated across natural language specifications from a variety of subject domains, typically accurately identified between 80 and 90 per cent of the entities. Moreover, the remaining entities not identified were, in most cases, ëpartially identifiedí. By this we mean that the program tended to overgenerate and highlighted as candidate entities strings of words which were longer than the entity itself. An example of this phenomenon (taken from Figure 1 above) is the programís proposal of *warehouseman combines* as a candidate entity. In the sample specification, the string *warehouseman combines* resides between boundary markers comprising function words, and hence the string is proposed as a candidate entity.

Whilst we are naturally investigating means of reducing this noise in the output to a minimum, we believe it is preferable for the program to overgenerate rather than undergenerate. Arguably, it is easier for the analyst to scan the output of candidate entities and filter out the overgenerated items using his/her knowledge, judgement and intuition than it is for the analyst to be presented with undergenerated output. If the program undergenerated, the analyst would be forced to return to the original specification and scan it manually to retrieve the entities not captured by the program.

We believe that the results of our entity extraction program compare very favourably with other programs we have seen for identifying nouns or noun phrases. We further believe that the domain and document-type independence of our approach render it of particular use to database designers. The non-reliance on grammatical tagging and parsing, moreover, means that our approach could be easily portable to a number of platforms and programming languages. In the context of our terminology extraction work, we developed a comprehensive evaluation framework for measuring the success of our text-probing approach. This framework is described in [9], and we anticipate using it in due course to evaluate our text-probing approach to entity extraction.

3.2 Relationship Identification

We turn our attention now to work we have begun on developing a program for identifying the relationships holding between entities. There are two aspects to this work.

First, we have been working on extending our co-occurrence patterns to incorporate patterns of boundary markers for identifying verbs which may (as noted earlier) represent relationships. The boundary markers we have explored include a subset of function words comprising auxiliary verbs (e.g. *have*, *be*), modal verbs (*must*, *should*, *would*), and prepositions (*in*, *on*, *through*), as well as punctuation marks. The program we have written to identify verbs representing relationships essentially operates in the same way as the program for entity extraction (outlined in the previous section). We are currently in the process of testing and evaluating this aspect of our work.

Second, we have been exploring the use of ëlinguistic cuesí to identify relationships such as type-subtype and part-whole holding between entities. This work builds on some earlier research undertaken in the context of knowledge engineering and expert system development, and it draws on discussions of lexical-semantic relationships in the literature of linguistics. In this literature, individual lexical-semantic relationships, such as the type-subtype (hyponymy) and the part-whole (meronymy) relationships are described in terms of ëdiagnostic framesí [6] or ëformulaeí [14]. For example, the type-subtype relationship would be represented by the frame *X is a kind of Y*. In texts, such as natural language system specifications, this frame may not be explicitly used, but rather any one of a wide variety of linguistic expressions might be used to represent the frame. Phrases such as *type of* and *sort of*, *is a* might, for example, be used.

Our contribution to research into the identification of entity types and subtypes has, to date, been to collect and archive linguistic expressions used to express the frame *X is a kind of Y*. We have denoted these expressions ëlinguistic cuesí. This collecting and archiving work was undertaken by studying large quantities of specialist and technical texts, as well as consulting dictionaries of synonyms and thesauri. Table 2 below shows a sample of linguistic cues that we have collected and archived for identifying entity sub-types.

Table 2. Sample linguistic cues for identifying entity sub-types

Kind of	Is a
Sort of	Species of
Type of	Brand of

We have written a prototype computer program that searches natural language system specifications in search of these linguistic cues, the aim being to guide the analyst to the ërichí portions of the specifications that may contain relevant type-subtype constructs. The output of this program currently comprises highlighted sentences containing the relevant linguistic cues. We are now in the process of extending the archive of linguistic cues to incorporate other kinds of relationship, such as causal, material, and so on, in order to provide further support for analysts in their database design work.

3.3 Attribute Extraction

As indicated earlier, one of the major challenges facing the analyst is the task of distinguishing between entities and attributes. Since both data types are typically represented by nouns, the task can be an exceedingly difficult one for the analyst. The application of linguistic knowledge, domain knowledge, experience and intuition is often required to perform it successfully.

In order to assist the analyst in this stage of his/her work, we have studied system specifications and examined the linguistic means used to represent attributes. Following the pattern of our work on relationship identification, we have begun to collect a number of linguistic cues which seem often to be used to ëpointí to the presence of attributes in specification documents. These linguistic cues include words and phrases such as *each*, *every*, *of the*, and *of a*. Furthermore, identifiers (key attributes) might be captured by searching for cues such as *unique*, *only*, and so on. We are now developing a program for searching for these linguistic cues in system specifications, and also further developing the linguistic analysis aspects of this phase of our work.

4. Conclusions and Future Directions

We believe that our text-probing approach to document analysis and data extraction, relying as it does on the identification of co-occurrence patterns and linguistic cues, could provide a useful framework for developing a more comprehensive toolset for supporting database designers in their work. We intend now to begin on a phase of extensive testing and evaluation of the approach, and to compare our results with those of human designers as well as with those of other existing programs for entity extraction.

Moreover, we are exploring the possibility of integrating our analysis and extraction work to date with another aspect of our work into the development of a CASE-based environment for constructing entity-relationship diagrams and generating code.

Aspects of our CASE-based work to date are reported in [11]. There we report on the use of a metaCASE tool (Lincoln Softwareís ToolBuilder) to create a CASE environment incorporating facilities for producing inter alia entity relationship diagrams, data flow diagrams, and data dictionaries. It is our intention to combine our document analysis and data extraction tools with this CASE environment so that the database designer can proceed, with automated support, from the document analysis stage through ER model construction, to code generation. We anticipate that this integration work will form the basis of a future research project.

References

1. Abbott, R. J. Program design by informal English descriptions. In Communications of the ACM, 26(11) (1983) 882-894

2. Aijmer, K. and Altenberg, B. (Eds.) English corpus linguistics: studies in honour of Jan Svartvik. Longman, London and New York (1991)

3. Bowers, D. From data to database. 2nd edition, Chapman and Hall, London (1993)

4. Cluver, A. D. de V. A manual of terminography. Human Sciences Research Council, Pretoria (1989)

5. Connolly, T. and Begg, C. Database systems: a practical approach to design, implementation and management. 2nd edition. Addison Wesley Longman, Harlow (1999)

6. Cruse, D. A. Lexical semantics. Cambridge University Press, Cambridge (1986)

7. Fliedl, G., Kop, C., Mayerthaler, W. and Mayr, H. C. Das Projekt NIBA zur automatischen Generierung von Vorentwurfsschemata f,r die Datenbankentwicklung. In Papiere zur Linguistik, Nr. 55 (Heft 2, 1996) 154-174

8. Fulford, H. Knowledge processing 6: collocation patterns and term discovery. Computing Sciences Report. CS-92-21. University of Surrey, Guildford (1992)

9. Fulford, H. Term acquisition: a text-probing approach. Doctoral thesis. University of Surrey, Guildford (1997)

10. Fulford, H. Griffin, S. and Ahmad, K. Resources for knowledge transfer and training: the exploitation of domain documentation and database technology. In Proceedings of the 6th international conference on urban storm drainage, Volume 2. Eds. J. Marsalek and H. C. Torno. Victoria, Canada: Seapoint Publishing. (1993) 1332-1338

11. Fulford, H., Work, L. B., and Bowers, D. S. Tools for information systems teaching: making a case for metaCASE. In Proceedings of the 7th Annual

Conference on the teaching of computing. Eds. S. Alexander and U. OíReilly. CTI Computing, University of Ulster. (1999) 64-68

12. Gomez, F., Segami, C., and Delaune, C. A system for the semiautomatic generation of E-R models from natural language specifications. In Data and knowledge engineering 29 (1999) 57-81

13. Lejk, M. and Deeks, D. An introduction to systems analysis techniques. Prentice Hall Europe, Hemel Hempstead (1998)

14. Lyons, J. Semantics. Cambridge University Press, Cambridge (1977)

15. Rock-Evans, R. A simple introduction to data and activity analysis. Computer Weekly, Sutton (1989)

16. Saeki, M., Horai, H., and Enomoto, H. Software development process from natural language specification. In Communications of the ACM (1989) 64-73

17. Sager, J. C., Dungworth, D., and McDonald, P. F. English special languages, principles and practice in science and technology. Oscar Brandstetter Verlag KG (1980)

18. Sager, J. C. A practical course in terminology processing. John Benjamins Publishing Co., Amsterdam/Philadelphia (1990)

19. Silberschatz, A., Korth, H. and Sudershan, S. Database system concepts. 3rd edition. McGraw-Hill, Singapore (1997)

20. Sinclair, J. M. Corpus, concordance, collocation. Oxford University Press, Oxford (1991)

21. Sinclair, J. M. The automatic analysis of corpora. In Svartvik, J. (Ed.) Directions in corpus linguistics: proceedings of Nobel Symposium 82. Stockholm 1991. Series: Trends in linguistics studies and monographs 65. Mouton de Gruyter, Berlin and New York (1992) 379-397

22. Tjoa, A. M. and Berger, L. Transformation of requirement specifications expressed in natural language into an EER model. In Proceedings of the 12th Entity-Relationship Approach-ERí93 Conference. Lecture notes in Computer Science, Vol. 823 (1994) 206-217

23. Yang, H. F. (1986) A new technique for identifying scientific/technical terms and describing science texts. In Literary and Linguistic Computing 1. No. 2. (1986) 93-103

On the Automatization of Database Conceptual Modelling through Linguistic Engineering

Paloma Martìnez[1] and Ana Garcìa-Serrano[2]

[1] University Carlos III of Madrid, Department of Computer Science, Avda. Universidad 30, 28911 LeganÈs, Madrid, Spain
pmf@inf.uc3m.es

[2] Technical University of Madrid, Department of Artificial Intelligence, ISYS Group, Campus de Montegancedo S/N, 28660, Madrid, Spain
agarcia@dia.fi.upm.es

Abstract. The aim of this paper is to show an approach to database (DB) conceptual modelling that takes advantage of lexical knowledge (morphologic, syntactic and semantic) in order to (semi) automatically interpret a textual description of an Universe of Discourse (UoD) and to propose a feasible data conceptual schema according to the natural language (NL) description. Main contributions of the present work are: definition of several linguistic perspectives based on syntactic and semantic clues that help to acquire Extended Entity Relationship (EER) conceptual schemata from textual specifications, specification of a grammar for the EER conceptual model, as well as a set of correspondence rules among linguistic concepts and the EER model constructors.

1 Objectives and Motivation

This work is part of a research framework[1] devoted to DB conceptual modelling that integrates various knowledge sources and technologies for helping novice DB analysts and students in different specific DB development tasks using methodological guides (for example, definition of EER conceptual schemata, transformation of conceptual schemata into relational schemata, automatic generation of SQL-92 code and other functionalities). One of the aims of this project is to cover some lacking features in current CASE tools for the overall coverage of DB life cycle, especially in requirements analysis phase, as well as the absence of methodological assistants, that may show what the steps to be followed in DB development are.

In practice, requirements elicitation and collection is mainly done using NL. Thus, it is reasonable to search for methods for systematic treatment of specifications. A conceptual schema, independently of data formalism used, plays two main roles in the

[1] This work takes part of the CICYT project PANDORA (CASE Platform for Database development and learning via Internet) TIC99-0215 and CAM project MESIA 07T/0017/1998.

M. Bouzeghoub et al. (Eds.): NLDB 2000, LNCS 1959, pp. 276-287, 2001.

conceptual analysis phase: a semantic role, in which user requirements are gathered together and the entities and relationships in a UoD are documented and a representational role that provides a framework that allows a mapping to the logical design of database schemata. Related to the data modelling formalisms, the EER model, [3], has proven to be a precise and comprehensive tool for representing data requirements in information systems development, mainly due to an adequate degree of abstraction of the constructs that it includes.

Since the eighties, many efforts have tackled methodological approaches for deriving conceptual schemata from NL specifications, [4], [1], [13], and some of them include NLP technology, [14], [6]. Recent state-of-the-art includes very interesting approaches that take advantage of NL knowledge for conceptual modelling such as COLOR-X (COnceptual Linguistically-based Object-oriented Representation language for Information and Communication Systems), [2], is a requirements engineering method whose linguistic foundation is reflected in two aspects. First of them concerns with the definition of a formal modelling language, Conceptual Prototyping Language, that is quite close to NL. The second is related to the requirements specification process, which transforms a textual document into conceptual models through a word-semantics driven process using a lexical DB. NL-OOPS (NL-Object Oriented Production System), [12], follows a different approach. It is based on a general purpose natural language processing (NLP) system called LOLITA on top of which a NLP-based CASE prototype has been constructed. The object-oriented analysis is an algorithm that extracts objects and their associations to be used in building object oriented schemata. The work described in [7] proposes a NL based ER schema generator, whose semantic analysis produces a logical form for each sentence that is used to extract ER constructors, including ternary relationships.

Our objective is twofold. First, to take into account different kinds of linguistic knowledge, not only semantic knowledge as in COLOR-X, in order to propose conceptual schemata for a descriptive text. Second, to use NLP techniques such as those used in NL-OOPS, not only in a fixed sequential path but using different combinations of NLP tasks.

2 The Role of Knowledge-Based Models for Linguistic Engineering

The system architecture for language applications development (in our case DB Conceptual Modelling from NL) is a structured model defined using KSM, [5]. KSM is a methodology for knowledge-based systems design and implementation, supported by a software platform. It helps developers to build and execute a knowledge model for a particular application through visual facilities with windows and graphics.

The key concept of this architecture is an entity called Knowledge Unit (KU), which behaves as a knowledge based agent. A KU is characterised by what it knows (knowledge area view described by a set of knowledge sub-areas) and what it is capable of (specified by a collection of tasks represented by arrows), that is, a body of knowledge that encapsulates both procedural and declarative knowledge.

Fig. 1 shows the core view of the knowledge organisation that gives rise to the implemented architecture. Each box represents a KU with its knowledge and functionality (upper level KUs make use of immediate lower level KUs). Morpho-syntax and Linguistic Perspectives KUs contain the linguistic knowledge required to analyse texts. Domain KU includes all the knowledge needed to translate results of linguistic analysis to DB Conceptual Modelling schemata.

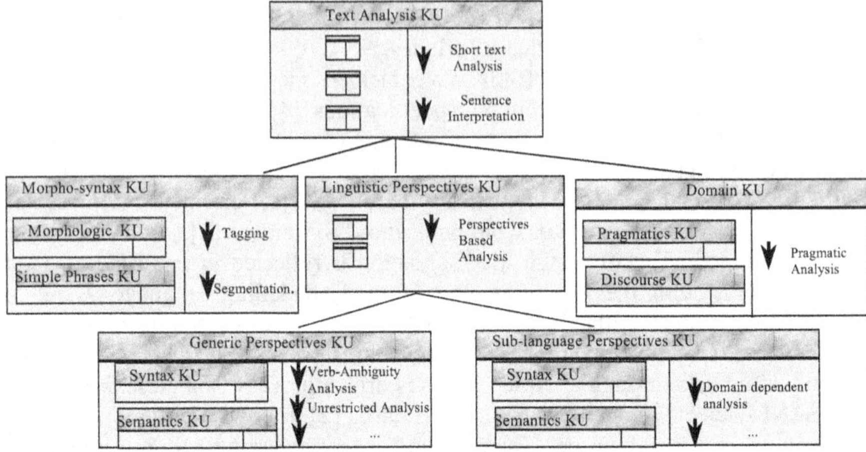

Fig. 1. Top level view of knowledge-based model

Criteria applied to obtain this knowledge organisation are:

- Linguistic knowledge sources (Morphology, Syntax and Semantics) and domain knowledge are subdivided into specialised sub-areas in order to face their inherent complexity.
- Linguistic perspectives represent the different strategies of analysis that can be performed on a sentence according to domain dependent linguistic features.
- Allow the combination of complete and partial NL analysis as well as shallow and deep analysis that are used by a flexible inference strategy so as to achieve a greater level of robustness.

Details about the analysis, design and operationalization of this architecture are found in [8] and [9].

3 Domain-Oriented Linguistic Strategies

The Linguistic Perspectives are different strategies to face text analysis trying to profit from the most promising information for the current domain (DB conceptual modelling). Linguistic Perspetives based analysis is performed after a pre-processing of the text that assigns parts-of-speech (noun, verb, preposition, determiner and others) to the words of each sentence and performs partial sentence segmentation by grouping tags in noun, prepositional and verbal phrases. Every Linguistic Perspective use Syntactic knowledge (about patterns, phrase and sentence structures) and Semantic knowledge (about lexical, phrase and sentence meanings) but in different sequences (Fig. 1). They were designed from an analysis of a corpus of 100 texts (around 15-20 sentences per text) describing DB formulations concerning different subjects. From this corpus, it has been possible to identify various aspects, mainly semantic and syntactic, which can guide the interpretation (as is shown in Fig. 2). Six different Linguistic Perspectives are defined: Sub-language perspectives (P1, P2, P3, P4) if they depend on the DB domain and Generic perspectives (P5, P6) if otherwise. All of them are briefly described below.

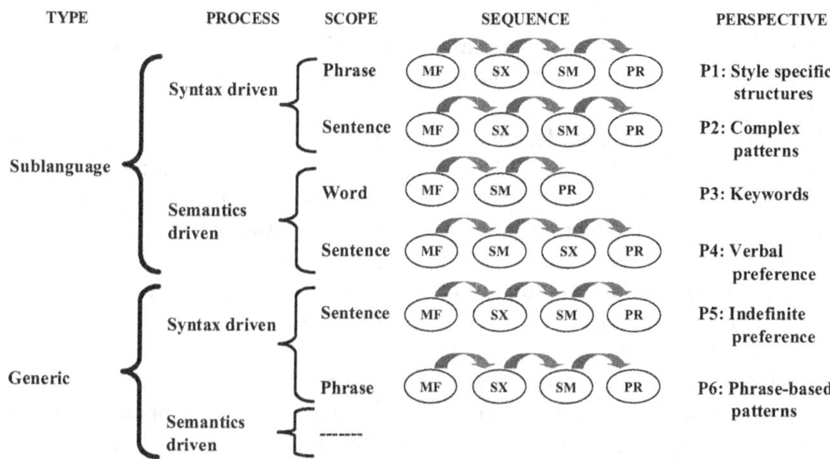

Fig. 2. Classification of Linguistic Perspectives

Style-specific patterns (P1): It is composed of a set of syntactic structures that are prototypical of the texts of the domain, that is, DB designers use them to denote a special meaning. For instance, in DB desciptions it is very usual to find the syntactical structure: np: np,np, ... np[2] mbedded in a sentence. This construction could describe subtypes of an entity type in an EER schema as in ì... *estudiante: licenciado, no graduado, etc*î (ì... *student: graduate, undergraduate, etc*î) but also attributes of an entity type or values of an attribute, depending on the context.

Complex patterns (P2): Some significant sentence structures that provide certain useful cues have been detected in the corpus. For instance, the sentence pattern:

vg np *de dos/tres/... tipos*: np, np,...cc np[3]

in which vg includes the verb ìexistirî (there are) as in ì*Existen participantes de tres tipos: jugador, árbitro y entrenador* î (ì*There are three types of participants: player, referee and coach*î). These types of constructions are commonly used to enumerate the entity subtypes of an entity type, the attributes of an entity type and others.

Keywords (P3): A set of words that belongs to the domain terminology, that is, words with a single meaning in DB modelling domain. For instance, keywords are: ì*código*î (code), ì*identificador*î (identifier), ì*nombre*î (name), etc.

---

[2] np is a noun phrase

[3] vg is a verbal group (main and auxiliary verbs), cc is the conjunction *and/or*. English literal translation of this pattern is vg np *of two/three/... types*: np, np, ...cc np

Verbs with semantic preference (P4): The most important perspective concerns verbs with a lexical preference in the domain. These verbs usually appear in descriptive texts (generally indicating structural relations among concepts) such as ì*incluir*î (to include), ì*ser*î (to be), ì*tener*î (to have), ì*pertenecer*î (to belong) and others. For instance, Spanish verb ì*disponer*î (to dispose) can denote to give instructions, to prepare and to posses. The latter is the preferential meaning in DB domain. This meaning requires two semantic arguments (roles): Beneficiary and Object. These verbs could lead to relationship, generalisation and aggregation types in a conceptual schemata. It is important to underline that the semantic verbal classification that has been defined is general enough to be migrated from one domain to another.

Verbs without semantic preference (P5): Due to the fact that descriptive texts of the corpus are thematically variable (different UoD), verbs without semantic preferences are commonly used. For these verbs, all their meanings have to be kept in the lexicon in order to find the best semantic frame that fits the sentence. For instance, verbs as ì*vender*î (to sell), ì*publicar*î (to publish), etc. do not to have lexical preferences. All these verbs lead to relationship types among entity types denoted by the verbal arguments or relationship types containing attributes among entity types, all of them denoted by the verbal arguments.

Phrase-based patterns (P6): Relationships among components of a noun or prepositional phrase are of great interest. For instance, the noun phrase ì*hospital público*î (public hospital), which includes a noun and an adjective, can inform about a special type of ì*hospital*î, that is, it would be possible to have a generalization whose supertype entity is ì*hospital*î with a subtype entity called ì*hospital público*î. Other important simple phrases are nominal groups (v.g., ë*todos los proyectos*í- every project -, ë*un único departamento*í- a single department -, ë*algunas secciones*í- some sections -) or nominal groups followed by a prepositional group (v.g., ë*los empleados de la empresa*í- employees of the company -, ë*un cierto número de profesores*í- a number of teachers -).

Relationships existing in a nominal group and among nominal and prepositional groups have also been studied, for instance, head-modifier relationship[4]. Table 1 contains some of semantic associations in different types of nominal groups.

4 Database Conceptual Modelling Knowledge

The knowledge about DB conceptual modelling (Domain KU) establishes a correspondence among the knowledge acquired from text and EER model

[4] From a linguistic viewpoint, Spanish morphology is more complex than English one. Syntactically, in English there are almost no constraints on the prepositions of noun modifiers and thus, relationships between the head and the modifier are evident (for instance, the house in the corner *-la casa de la esquina-*, the book on the shelf *-el libro de la estantería-*, the woman with the cat *-la mujer del gato-*). However, English language has nominal compounds (noun + noun) that cause problems in semantic interpretation just the preposition "de" in Spanish does. There are more examples which have influence in semantic interpretation.

Syntax	Semantics	Semantic features	Examples
ng + ëdeí + ng	DESCRIPTION	(*relation* + de + *common*)	tipo de sala
		(*time_period* + de + *time_period*)	plazo de tiempo
		(*instrument* + de + *instrument*)	software de red
		(*human_action* + de + *knowledge*)	oferta de empleo
		(*identification* + de + *room*)	n˙ mero de sala
	POSSESION	(*person* + de + *instrument*)	propietario del coche
		(*instrument* + de + *organization*)	ordenadores del organismo
		(*person* + de + *organization*)	empleado de la empresa
		(*instrument* + de + *building*)	puerta del edificio
	QUANTITY	(*quantity* + de + *instrument*)	n˙ mero de obras
		(*group* + de + *person*)	conjunto de clientes
	PARTICIPATION	(*person* + de + *event*)	jefe de proyecto
		(*person* + de + *social_event*)	monitor de aerobic
	LOCATION	(*organization* + de + *region*)	clubes del paÌs
	USE	(*organization*+de + *human_action*)	secciÛn de administraciÛn
		(*person* + de + *knowledge*)	profesor de pr· ctica
ng + ëení + ng	LOCATION	(*instrument* + en + *point*)	libros en stock
ng +íconí +ng	DESCRIPTION	(*room* + con + *instrument*)	salas con aparatos

Table 1. Some head-modifier semantic relationships

constructors, [10]. The definition of linguistic perspectives leads to a set of heuristics that establish equivalence between results of linguistic analysis and constructors that capture the semantics of an EER model.

The results of perspectives-based interpretation are translated into structures that contain specific domain roles, i.e. EER model elements (entity and relationship types, attributes, relationship cardinalities, generalization and aggregation types, etc.). The pragmatic analysis is a refined semantic analysis that depends on the application domain. Thus, a set of rules (Axioms of Correspondence) that contain in its left side conditions about linguistic attributes and in its right side specific DB conceptual model elements have been defined. Table 2 shows some of these equivalencies among stative[5] verbs and DB conceptual model constructors[6]. Similar correspondences have been defined for the remaining perspectives (style and complex patterns, noun-modifier relationships, etc.). A DB conceptual grammar has been developed to represent an EER DB conceptual schema although in some examples only the graphical representation is shown.

Discourse KU is in charge of studying the relationships among the results of the linguistic perspectives based analysis in order to eliminate inconsistent interpretations (Inconsistencies KU) as well as of update the knowledge acquired from sentences (Case KU).

[5] Stative verbs represent non-dynamic events and they are decomposed in five semantic domains (basic, benefactive, experiential, temporal and locative) each of one having different semantic roles.

[6] Similar correspondences have been defined for action and process verbs, [8].

Stative Verbs					
Verb Semantic Class		**Semantic Roles**	**Verb Pragmatic Class**	**Correspondences to pragmatic roles**	**Conceptual Model Concept**
Basic	An Obj	Obj	Existential	Obj= Entitye Type	**Obj**
	Prop is Atrib	Obj, Prop	Generalisation	Obj= Supertype Entity Prop= Subtype entity	Obj Prop
Benefactive		Ben, Obj	Descriptive	Ben=Entity Type Obj=Attribute	**Ben** Obj
			Association	Ben=Entity Type Obj=Entity Type	Ben Obj
Locative		Loc, Obj	Aggregation	Loc=Entity Type (whole) Obj=Entity Type (part)	Loc Obj
			Association	Loc= Entity Type Obj=Entity Type	Loc Obj
			Generalisation	Obj= Supertype Entity Loc= Subtype Entity	Obj Loc

Table 2. Some semantic-pragmatic correspondences for stative verbs

5 A Case Study

This section is devoted to explain a case study using a descriptive text of the corpus about the Football World Cup that is shown below. Briefly, there are 19 sentences, 3 of which contain verbs with semantic preference in the domain of DB conceptual modelling (P4), 9 contain verbs without semantic preference (P5), 4 style specific patterns (P2), 7 complex patterns (P2) and, finally, 4 keywords (P3).

1. Durante un campeonato se desarrollan varias eliminatorias.
2. De cada eliminatoria interesa su tipo (octavos de final, cuartos de final, semifinal y final), su fecha de inicio y su fecha de finalizaciÛn.
3. Un determinado n˙mero de selecciones participa en el campeonato.
4. De cada selecciÛn interesa su paÌs y su continente.
5. Se asigna a cada selecciÛn un determinado grupo.
6. Cada selecciÛn ocupa una determinada posiciÛn (1, 2, 3 Û4) en un grupo.
7. Cada grupo es identificado por un cÛdigo (A, B, C, D, E o F).
8. Varias selecciones componen cada eliminatoria.
9. Cada encuentro est· caracterizado por el sitio, fecha, hora y resultado.

10. Las selecciones participan en diversos encuentros.
11. Cada selecciÛn est· compuesta de un determinado n˙mero de participantes.
12. De los participantes interesa el nombre, n˙mero de pasaporte y fecha de nacimiento.
13. Entre los participantes distinguimos: jugadores, entrenador y tÈcnicos.
14. Cada jugador ocupa un determinado puesto (ëDefensaí, ëCentrocampistaí, etc.) en el equipo de la selecciÛn.
15. Cada entrenador tiene varios aÒos de experiencia.
16. Cada tÈcnico desempeÒa una funciÛn (por ejemplo, ëMÈdicoí, ëMasajistaí, etc.).
17. Los equipos de liga proporcionan jugadores a las selecciones.
18. De cada equipo de liga interesa el nombre y el paÌs.
19. Los entrenadores preparan a los equipos de liga durante un intervalo de tiempo.

Just the sentence 14[7] analysis will be described because it activates up to perspectives: P1, P5 y P6. Once the morphosyntactical tagging and segmentation is performed on the sentence, it is checked that one style specific pattern (P1) matches the sentence phrase: ì*puesto ('Defensa', 'Centrocampista', etc.)*î and whose semantic analysis returns:

Value_enumeration: order_relationship→ (person, person)

Its correspondent pragmatic interpretation arises two possibilities (E1 and E2)[8]:

E1 = Entity Type : puesto ;
Entity Type : centrocampista ;
Entity Type : defensa ;
Generalization : es1 ,
Supertype : puesto ,
Subtypes : defensa, centrocampista ;

E2 = Attributes : puesto :
Domain : dom1 (defensa, centrocampista)

that is, E1 is a generalization where *puesto* is the supertype and *defensa* and *centrocampista* are the subtypes. E2 contains *puesto* as an attribute that could have the *defensa* or *centrocampista* values.

Following, P5 is activated because the verb *ocupar* (to occupy, to play) is a verb without semantic preference; it has two possible senses as is shown in its verbal lexical entry:

```
verbal_lexical_entry: ocupar
   gen_sx_features:
      f_pas: yes              (% capability for passive constructions %)
      f_exclpron: no          (% only pronominal use %)
      f_pron: yes             (% capability for pronominal use %)
      f_mod: no               (% capability for modal use %)
      f_aux: no               (% capability for auxiliary use %)
   meaning_list: {
```

7 English literal translation is ì*Each player plays a different role in a National Team ('Deffender', 'Midfield', etc.)*î

8 Henceforth, Ei (i=1..n) are the DB sub-schemata that are obtained in the consecutive interpretation steps. Consequently, more than one schema proposal is obtained.

```
meaning:  {
   frame_id: ocupar1                          (% meaning identifier %)
   f_comment: ì tomar posesiÛn o instalarseî  (% brief description %)
   f_aux_ser: yes                             (% if passive construction with ëserí %)
   f_aux_estar: yes                           (% if passive construction with ëestarí %)
   f_sx_frame: tr                             ( % transitive, intransitive, bitransitive,...... %)
   f_prep_req1: [ ]                           ( % prepositions for prepositional argument 1%)
   f_prep_req2: [ ]                           (% prepositions for prepositional argument 2 %)
   f_event_type: action                       (% state/action/process depending of event type %)
   f_sm_frame: loc3                           (% basic/experiential/temp/benefactive/locative %)
   f_sm_arg:[person, [event, location, group]]         (% argument semantic constraints %)
   f_pref_meaning: no                                  (% if preferent meaning %)        }
meaning:  {
   frame_id: ocupar2                          (% meaning identifier %)
   f_comment: ì relaciÛn de orden en algoî    (% brief description %)
   f_aux_ser: yes                             (% if passive construction with ëserí %)
   f_aux_estar: yes                           (% if passive construction with ëestarí %)
   f_sx_frame: bitr3                          ( % transitive, intransitive, bitransitive,...... %)
   f_prep_req1: [ ]                           ( % prepositions for prepositional argument 1%)
   f_prep_req2: [en]                          (% prepositions for prepositional argument 2 %)
   f_event_type: action                       (% state/action/process depending of event type %)
   f_sm_frame: loc5                           (% basic/experiential/temp/benefactive/locative %)
   f_sm_arg:[person, order_relationship, [event, location, group]] (% arg sem constraints %)
   f_pref_meaning: no                                  (% if preferent meaning %)        }
```

This verb has two syntactic frames, transitive (tr) and bitransitive3 (bitr3); the only verbal syntactic schema that the sentence fits is bitr3 that requires Subject, Direct Object and Suplement. This analysis successes with the following instantiation of syntactic functions: Subject= Cada jugador , DirObj= un determinado puesto, Supl = en el equipo de la selecciÛn.

The segment ìel equipo de la selecciÛnî belongs to this perspective because it is a verbal argument but it also activates the syntactic and semantic rules of perspective P6. Lexical entries of ëequipoí and ëselecciÛní denote that ëequipoí could have the semantic features *instrument* and *organization* and ëselecciÛní could have the semantic features *human_action* and *organization*. So, the possible combinations for semantic analysis are:

instrument + de + *human_action* ✐ USE
instrument + de + *organization* ✐ POSSESION
organization + de + *human_action* ✐ USE
organization + de + *organization* ✐ POSSESION

All previous combinations are valid if the segment is analyzed separately. However, the verb centred analysis of the sentence produces:

Verb: ocupar
  Event Type: action
  Semantic Domain: locative
  Essential Roles:
    Agt= (jugador=person)
    Obj= (puesto= order_relationship)

Loc= (equipo=organization, ((selecciÛn=organization ←possesion→ equipo= organization) OR (equipo=organization ←use→ selecciÛn=human_action)))

Note that the interpretations *instrument* + de + *organization* ✎ POSSESION and *instrument* + de + *human_action* ✎ USE have been eliminated because the instrument feature is not compatible with the verbal selectional constraints in the locative role (location, group, event). Finally, the pragmatic interpretation for perspective P5 is:

E3 = E2 ∪ Entity Type : equipo ;
Relationship Type : ocupar ;
Participants : jugador, equipo ;
Attributes : puesto
Relationship Type : posee ;
Participants : selecciÛn, equipo

E4 = E2 ∪ Entity Type : equipo de la selecciÛn ;
Entity Type : equipo;
Generalization : es2 ,
Supertype : equipo,
Subtypes : equipo de la selecciÛn ;
Relationship Type : ocupar ;
Participants : jugador, equipo de la selecciÛn ;
Attributes : puesto

Previous interpretation E1 of perspective P1 has been eliminated because of the inconsistency rule: Entity Type (puesto) is inconsistent with Attribute (puesto)

The remaining sentences are analyzed in a similar way and the resulting interpretations are added to the previous ones, taking into account the inconsistency rules. One of the possible solutions for the previous text is shown in Fig. 3.

6 Conclusions and Future Work

We have shown an approach to DB conceptual modelling that takes advantage of lexical knowledge (morphologic, syntactic and semantic) in order to (semi) automatically interpret a textual description of an UoD. We claim that linguistic knowledge provides decisive information that helps users to carry out conceptual analysis, because of the semantic role of conceptual schemata.

From an application domain viewpoint, in future research a complete methodology for DB development could be defined, along with the implemented prototype because this DB modelling application is part of a framework for DB development and learning. Moreover, an extension and refinement of the EER model constructs obtained from NL interpretation is under study (for instance, high order relationships, cardinality constraints, [11], etc.).

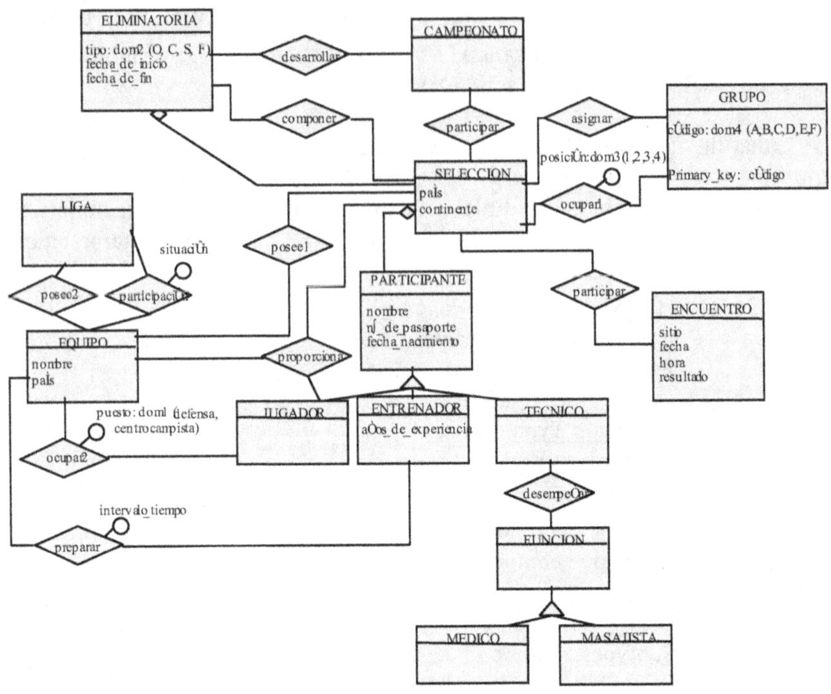

Fig. 3. One possible DB conceptual schema

References

1. Booch, G.: Object-oriented development. IEEE Trans Software Engineering, 12, 2, (1986) 211-221.
2. Burg, J.F.M, van de Riet, R.P.: Analyzing Informal Requirements Specifications: A First Step towards Conceptual Modeling. In Applications of Natural Language to Information Systems. IOS Press (1996).
3. Chen, P.: The entity-relationship model ñ Toward a unified view of data. ACM Transactions on Database Systems, Vol. 1, N.1, (1976) 9-36.
4. Chen, P.: English Sentence Structure and Entity-Relationship Diagrams. Information Sciences, 29, (1983) 127-149.
5. Cuena, J., Molina, M. ìKSM: An environment for Design of Structured Knowledge Modelsî. Knowledge-Based Systems-Advanced Concepts, Techniques and Applications. Publisher: World Scientific Publishing Company (1996).
6. Dunn, L., Orlowska, M. A Natural Language Interpreter for the Construction of Conceptual Schemas. Proceedings of 2nd Nordic Conference on Advanced Information System Engineering (CAISE¥90). Stockholm, Sweden (1990).
7. GÛmez, F., Segami, C., Delaune, C. A system for the semiatomatic generation of E-R models from natural language specifications. Data & Knowledge Engineering, 29, (1999) 56-81.
8. MartÌnez, P. Propuesta de estructuraciÛn del conocimiento ling¸Ìstico para interpretaciÛn de textos: AplicaciÛn al diseÒo de Bases de Datos. PhD. Dissertation. Universidad PolitÈcnica de Madrid, (1998).

9. Martìnez, P., Garcìa-Serrano, A. A Knowledge-based Methodology applied to Linguistic Engineering. In R. Nigel Horspool Ed., Systems Implementation 2000: Languages, Methods and Tools. London: Chapman & Hall, (1998) 166-179.
10. Martìnez, P., De Miguel, A., Marcos, E. A Knowledge-based Approach to Database Conceptual Modelling through Natural Language. International Workshop on Issues and Applications of Database Technology, (IADTí98). Berlin, Germany, July, (1998).
11. Martìnez, P., De Miguel, A. Cuadra, D., Nieto, C., Castro, E. Data Conceptual Modelling through Natural Language: Identification and Validation of Relationship Cardinalities. 2000 Information Resources Management Association International Conference (IRMA 2000), Anchorage, Alaska, May, (2000).
12. Mich, L., NL-OOPS: from natural language to object oriented requirements using the NLP system LOLITA. Natural Language Engineering, 2, 2, (1996).
13. Rumbaugh, J., Blaha, M., Premerlani, W., Eddy, F., Lorensen, W. Object-Oriented Modeling and Design. Englewood Cliffs, NJ, Prentice Hall, (1991).
14. Saeki, M., Horai, H., Enomoto, H. Software development process fromm Natural language specification. ICSI'89, International Conf. on Software Engineering, ACM, (1989) 64-73.

The REVERE Project: Experiments with the Application of Probabilistic NLP to Systems Engineering

Paul Rayson[1], Luke Emmet[2], Roger Garside[1] and Pete Sawyer[1]

[1]Lancaster University, Lancaster, UK. LA1 4YR
{paul, rgg, sawyer}@comp.lancs.ac.uk
[2]Adelard, Coborn House, 3 Coborn Road, London UK. E3 2DA
loe@adelard.co.uk

Abstract. Despite natural language's well-documented shortcomings as a medium for precise technical description, its use in software-intensive systems engineering remains inescapable. This poses many problems for engineers who must derive problem understanding and synthesise precise solution descriptions from free text. This is true both for the largely unstructured textual descriptions from which system requirements are derived, and for more formal documents, such as standards, which impose requirements on system development processes. This paper describes experiments that we have carried out in the REVERE[1] project to investigate the use of probabilistic natural language processing techniques to provide systems engineering support.

1. Introduction

Despite natural language's well-documented shortcomings as a medium for precise technical description, its use in software-intensive systems engineering [1] (henceforth referred to simply as systems engineering) remains inescapable. The products of the systems engineering process (requirements specifications, acceptance test plans, etc.) almost always have to employ natural language in order to describe the desired system properties for a heterogeneous readership. Recognising this, several researchers [2, 3, 4, 5, 6, 7] have used natural language processing (NLP) tools for the analysis, paraphrasing and quality evaluation of documents produced by the systems engineering process. There has been little attention paid to the main focus of this paper, however: tools to assist the analysis of natural language inputs to systems engineering.

In developing the requirements for a system, systems engineers face the need to understand large volumes of information. This information is almost always expressed in natural language. This is true of information elicited from human stakeholders (users, customers, domain experts, marketing experts, etc.), and information derived from technical and business documents. Systems engineers collect this information to build up their understanding of the system requirements

---

[1] REVerse Engineering of REquirements. EPSRC Systems Engineering for Business Process Change (SEBPC) programme project number GR/MO4846.
Further details can be found at: http://www.comp.lancs.ac.uk/computing/research/cseg/projects/revere/

M. Bouzeghoub et al. (Eds.): NLDB 2000, LNCS 1959, pp. 288-300, 2001.

and the constraints on the system and on the development process. Hence, for example, requirements information elicited from stakeholders may need to be analysed in the context of information about the system's operational environment and standards that regulate the system's application domain. A systems engineer for a railway signalling system, for example, might be faced with having to understanding documents describing complex signalling control processes, statements of requirements from many different stakeholders, specifications of equipment to which the system will have an interface, engineering standards and railway legislation.

Whatever the source of the information, its analysis is a difficult task that requires skill, domain knowledge and experience and is almost completely unsupported by tools. This is a particular problem where the volume of the information is large and the sources of information diverse.

In this paper we describe our work in the REVERE project, where we are investigating the feasibility of using probabilistic NLP techniques to improve this situation. The work is illustrated with two examples: analysis of a large corpus of transcripts and field notes of an ethnographic study of an air-traffic control (ATC) application (reported elsewhere [8]), and analysis of a new safety-critical systems standard. These both serve to illustrate the principles involved. In combination, the two examples illustrate the promise of the approach and highlight some issues that require further attention for the approach to be widely exploitable.

2. Natural Language in Systems Engineering

Systems engineering is concerned mainly with identification and analysis of the system requirements, identification of a configuration of components (the system architecture) that will satisfy the requirements, and verification that once completed and integrated, the configuration of components does meet the requirements. To do this, the system requirements must be acquired and analysed. These requirements are always constrained by many factors that include budgetary limits, the operational environment, technical feasibility, the need for standards compliance [9] and many others. Hence, many factors must be understood and balanced by a systems engineer. Natural language invariably plays a large part in the systems engineering process and this fact has attracted sporadic interest in the employment of NLP techniques in systems engineering. Work has focused on both the products of the process and inputs to the process.

2.1 Natural Language Products of the Systems Engineering Process

Products of the process include specifications of the requirements and test plans. The use of natural language is needed to enable these documents to be read by a heterogeneous readership that includes both engineers and customers. However, it is hard to describe complex concepts simply, clearly and concisely in natural language. In recognition of this, several research projects [2, 4, 6, 7] have investigated the synthesis of conceptual models (object models, data-flows, etc) from natural language descriptions. These have employed rule-based NLP and so require documents written using natural language subsets as their input.

2.2 Natural Language Inputs to the Systems Engineering Process

The inputs to the process include human-sourced information and formal documents. Human-sourced information is information elicited directly from system stakeholders. It may comprise, for example, unstructured textual description and transcripts of user interviews. It is one of the raw materials from which the system requirements are derived. Formal documents include standards, process descriptions, user manuals and specifications of other systems. They are often needed to complement human-sourced information as sources of additional requirements and constraints. They are also a crucial source of domain knowledge needed to interpret the requirements and constraints. The crucial point is that a great deal of intellectual work is needed to identify a coherent and cohesive set of system requirements. These are never pre-formed but have to be synthesised from a variety of sources that contain information which may be poorly structured, contradictory, at varying levels of detail and of uncertain relevance.

The systems engineer must use whatever information resources are available to derive the requirements [10]. This typically entails an iterative process of inferring key abstractions (stakeholders, roles, tasks, domain objects, etc.) and verifying these against the structure and behaviour of existing systems. Hence, while work concerned with products of the systems engineering process relies upon a pre-existing formulation of the system requirements, work on inputs to the process must cope with much messier natural language text.

Dan Berry and colleagues have studied this problem over a number of years [11, 12, 13]. Their work is based on the use of pattern matching techniques to extract abstractions. The frequency with which the abstractions occur within the text is taken as an indication of the abstractions' relevance. The authors of the work recognise this assumption has been challenged by work on automatic abstraction in other domains, but argue that it appears to be valid in the context of requirements analysis.

Both Berry's work, and similarly motivated work by [14], explicitly recognise that NLP cannot automate the system engineer's job. The system engineer still has to read the myriad documents. Instead, the tools seek to mitigate the problems of information overload. They do this by compensating for human weakness (such as attention lapses due to tiredness) by helping to flag abstractions that would repay detailed manual analysis. This is a refreshingly realistic view of the potential for NLP that is informed by a real understanding of the problems of system engineering, and one that forms the starting point for our own work.

3. The REVERE Project

Like Berry's work, the REVERE project is concerned with supporting systems engineers faced by the need to extract information from large volumes of unstructured text. We do not believe that it is possible to fully automate this. We do, however, believe it is feasible to help provide a 'quick way in' to unfamiliar documents, in order to help focus system engineers' attention on candidates for important abstractions. An important requirement for REVERE is that the approach must scale. This immediately rules out purely rule-based NLP because of the diversity of the documents that may have to be analysed. We do not believe that the pattern-matching alone can offer sufficient coverage or be sufficiently efficient for the kind of interactive support that we aim to provide.

Our approach is therefore to exploit *probabilistic* NLP techniques. Instead of attempting to model the grammar of a natural language as a set of rules, the class of probabilistic tools that we are interested in classifies words on the statistical likelihood of them being a member of a particular syntactic or semantic category in a particular context. The probabilities are derived from large corpora of free text which have already been analysed and 'tagged' with each word's syntactic or semantic category. Extremely large corpora have been compiled (the British National Corpus consists of approximately 100 million words [15]). For some levels of analysis, notably part-of-speech tagging, probabilistic NLP tools have been able to achieve levels of accuracy and robustness that rule-based techniques cannot approach.

Probabilistic tools do not attempt to automate understanding of the text. Rather, they extract interesting properties of the text that a human user can combine and use to infer meaning. Evidence from other domains suggests that such tools can effectively support analysis of large documents. For example, in [16] probabilistic NLP tools were used to quickly confirm the results of a painstaking manual discourse analysis of doctor-patient interaction. In this application, they were also able to reveal information that had not been discovered manually.

Probabilistic NLP techniques meet the requirement for scalability. The execution time of the tagging process varies approximately linearly with the document size. Once the text has been tagged, retrieval and display tools are needed to allow the user to interact with the document. These use the tags to provide views on the document that reveal interesting properties and suppress the bulk of text. They do this in a way that is largely independent of the size of the document. Hence the user is protected from information overload by being able to be selective about the information they want to extract.

4. The REVERE Tools

We have adapted and experimented with a set of existing NLP tools developed at Lancaster for the processing of English language text. The most important of these is CLAWS [17]. CLAWS uses a statistical hidden Markov model technique and a rule-based component to identify the parts-of-speech (POS) of words to an accuracy of 97-98%. One obvious application of this in a system engineering context is the identification of modal verbs such as 'shall', 'must', 'will', 'should', etc. Expressions of need, desire, etc., consistent with user or system requirements can therefore be located in a document very easily and without the need to construct complex regular expressions or search templates. Even this basic level of analysis goes beyond what is provided by the current generation of requirements and document management tools that are becoming widely used by systems engineers.

A semantic analyser [18] uses the POS-tagged text to assign semantic tags that represent the general sense field of words from a lexicon of single words and an idiom list of multi-word combinations (e.g. ëas a ruleí). These resources contain approximately 52000 words or idioms and classify them according to a hierarchy of semantic classes. For example, the tag *A1.5.1* represents words or idioms meaning *Using*, which is a subclass of *general and abstract terms*. Words that would be assigned this tag (in the appropriate POS context) include *user*, *end-user* and *operator*. Similarly, the tag X2.4 is a subclass of *Psychological actions, states and processes* and would be assigned to terms meaning *Investigate*, such as *search*, *browse* and *look for*. The tagset has been crafted from analysis of a large corpus of English text. One of the things we are investigating is the extent to which it would be applicable to the technical domain(s) of systems engineering.

These tools are integrated into a retrieval and display tool called WMATRIX (a development of XMATRIX [19]). This embodies a process model that leads the user through a sequence of steps needed to apply the POS and semantic tagging and other types of analysis that, once complete, allow the user to interact with abstractions of the text. Many of these abstractions are provided by frequency profiling. At the most basic, this produces a simple concordance of individual words and displays them in the context of their surrounding text. Frequency profiling becomes more useful when a semantically tagged document can be compared against a *normative corpus*: a large representative body of pre-tagged text. Comparison with the normative corpus allows information to be extracted from a document by searching for statistically significant deviations from the frequency norm suggested by the corpus. This exploits the tendency for words or expressions to have different semantic profiles in different domain contexts. A general usage normative corpus is likely to reveal many of the dominant domain entities and roles as words or expressions that occur with a frequency that deviates grossly from the norm. These are the kinds of abstractions that an engineer must identify when analysing the requirements for a system, since they help build up a picture of what the system must do and of the people and objects in the system's environment.

With complex systems, there are often so many diverse requirements that some separation of concerns needs to be imposed on the problem space in order to understand the requirements and roles of different stakeholders. This is sometimes supported by the use of viewpoints on a system. A viewpoint can be thought of as a *partial specification* [20]; a subset of the system requirements that represent those requirements unique to a particular stakeholder's perspective of what the system must do. The engineer can use WMATRIX to search a document for roles, since roles often correspond to stakeholders. By finding the set of candidate roles and viewing where they occur in the body of the text, it is possible for the engineer to verify whether the roles are important and build up an understanding of how they interact with the system's environment.

To provide a snapshot of the results so far, and illustrate some of the key issues, we now briefly describe two examples. These are an analysis of the requirements for an air traffic control system and an evaluation of a new standard for the development of safety-critical systems.

5. Example 1: Air Traffic Control

The target documents are field reports of a series of ethnographic studies at an air traffic control (ATC) centre. This formed part of a study of ATC as an example of a system that supports collaborative user tasks [8]. The documents consist of both the verbatim transcripts of the ethnographerís observations and interviews with controllers, and of reports compiled by the ethnographer for later analysis by a multi-disciplinary team of social scientists and systems engineers. The field reports form an interesting study because they exhibit many characteristics typical of information. The volume of the information is fairly high (103 pages) and the documents are not structured in a way (say around business processes or system architecture) designed to help the extraction of requirements. Two stages in the analysis are shown: a search for candidate roles; and an analysis against a normative corpus.

5.1 Role Analysis

Roles are likely to emerge from several kinds of analysis using WMATRIX. Corpus analysis will often reveal a role as a noun with a semantic category that has a frequency distribution that varies significantly from that of the normative corpus. In formal documents certain parts of speech are often associated with roles (and other entities of the domain). In a standards document, for example, modal verbs often reveal roles by their context, such as: "The **Developer shall** define the safety test to be conductedÖ î

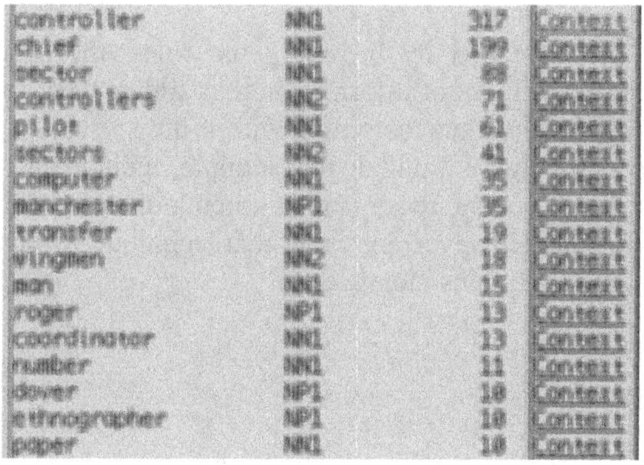

controller	NN1	317	Context
chief	NN1	199	Context
sector	NN1	88	Context
controllers	NN2	71	Context
pilot	NN1	61	Context
sectors	NN2	41	Context
computer	NN1	35	Context
manchester	NP1	35	Context
transfer	NN1	19	Context
wingmen	NN2	18	Context
man	NN1	15	Context
roger	NP1	13	Context
coordinator	NN1	13	Context
number	NN1	11	Context
dover	NP1	10	Context
ethnographer	NP1	10	Context
paper	NN1	10	Context

Fig. 1. Candidate roles in air traffic control

In this early stage of our analysis of the ATC field reports, an initial role analysis was performed by a simple combination of POS analysis and regular expressions. These are often revealed as human agent nouns with common endings for job-titles (such as 'er' or 'or', 'et' or 'ot', 'man' or 'men', etc) and adjectives that are commonly used without their accompanying noun ('head', 'chief', 'sub', etc.). Using this, the candidate roles that occur most frequently in the ATC document (and hence imply significance) are shown in figure 1.

Figure 1 shows a mixture of words that are clearly not roles (e.g. sector, computer, manchester, roger), but also some that are: controller, chief, wingmen, coordinator and ethnographer. Ethnographers are roles in the analysis rather than the application domain, but the other three are all roles or stakeholders, with their own requirements or viewpoint on ATC. Theories about whether the candidate roles are significant or not can be tested by viewing their context. Figures 2 and 3 show examples of the contexts in which occurrences of 'controller' and 'chief' occur.

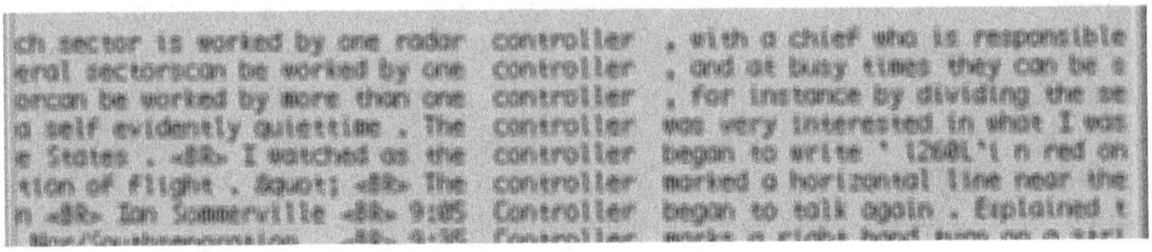

ch sector is worked by one radar controller , with a chief who is responsible
eral sectorscan be worked by one controller , and at busy times they can be s
orcan be worked by more than one controller , for instance by dividing the se
a self evidently quiettime . The controller was very interested in what I was
e States . <&> I watched as the controller began to write ' 1260L'1 n red on
tion of flight . " <&> The controller marked a horizontal line near the
n <&> Ian Sommerville <&> 9:05 Controller began to talk again . Explained t

Fig. 2. References to the role name *controller*

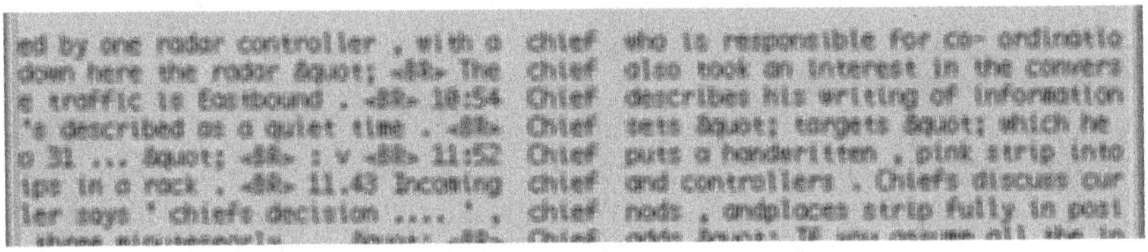

ed by one radar controller , with a chief who is responsible for co- ordinatio
down here the radar " <&> The chief also took an interest in the convers
e traffic is Eastbound . <&> 10:54 Chief describes his writing of information
's described as a quiet time . <&> Chief sets " targets " which he
o 31 ... " <&> : v <&> 11:52 Chief puts a handwritten , pink strip into
ips in a rack . <&> 11.43 Incoming chief and controllers . Chiefs discuss cur
ler says ' chiefs decision .... ' . chief nods , andplaces strip fully in posi

Fig. 3. References to the role name *chief*

The examples illustrate that by browsing the roles, the systems engineer can impose a viewpoint on the mass of information that allows them to build up a picture of the corresponding stakeholders' activities within the system's application domain. The first lines in each of figure 2 and 3, for example, include an explanation of both roles' responsibilities. Of course, there is also much 'noise' and sometimes synonyms are used for a single role. However, by using this technique, we have isolated sets of requirements for each of the roles identified.

5.2 Corpus Analysis

The motivation for corpus analysis is that entities that are significant to the application domain will be revealed by the relative frequency of their appearance in the text when compared against a normative corpus. The normative corpus that we used was a 2.3 million-word subset of the BNC derived from the transcripts of spoken English. Using this corpus, the most over-represented semantic categories in the ATC field reports are shown in table 1. The log-likelihood figure is a statistical measure of deviation from the word's frequency deviation from the normative corpus. The higher the figure, the greater the deviation.

Table 1. Over-represented categories in ATC field reports

Log-likelihood	Semantic tag	Word sense (examples from the text)
3366	S7.1	power, organising (ëcontrollerí, ëchiefí)
2578	M5	flying (ëplaneí, ëflightí, ëairportí)
988	O2	general objects (ëstripí, ëholderí, ërackí)
643	O3	electrical equipment (ëradarí, ëblipí)
535	Y1	science and technology (ëPHí)
449	W3	geographical terms (ëPole Hillí, ëDish Seaí)
432	Q1.2	paper documents and writing (ëwritingí, ëwrittení, ënotesí)
372	N3.7	measurement (ëlengthí, ëheightí, ëdistanceí, ëlevelsí, ë1000ftí)
318	L1	life and living things (ëliveí)
310	A10	indicating actions (ëpointingí, ëindicatingí, ëdisplayí)
306	X4.2	mental objects (ësystemsí, ëapproachí, ëmodeí, ëtacticalí, ëprocedureí)
290	A4.1	kinds, groups (ësectorí, ësectorsí)

With the exception of Y1 (an anomaly caused by an intervieweeís initials being mistaken for the PH unit of acidity), all of these semantic categories include important objects, roles, functions, etc. in the ATC domain. The frequency with which some of these occur, such as M5 (flying), are unsurprising. Others are more revealing about the domain of ATC. Figure 4 shows some of the occurrences of the semantic category O2 (general objects) being browsed by a user of WMATRIX. The important information revealed here is the importance of 'strips' (formally, 'flight strips'). These are small pieces of cardboard with printed flight details that are the most fundamental artefact used by the air traffic controller to manage their air space. Examination of other words in this category also reveal that flight strips are held in 'racks' to organise them according to (for example) aircraft time-of-arrival.

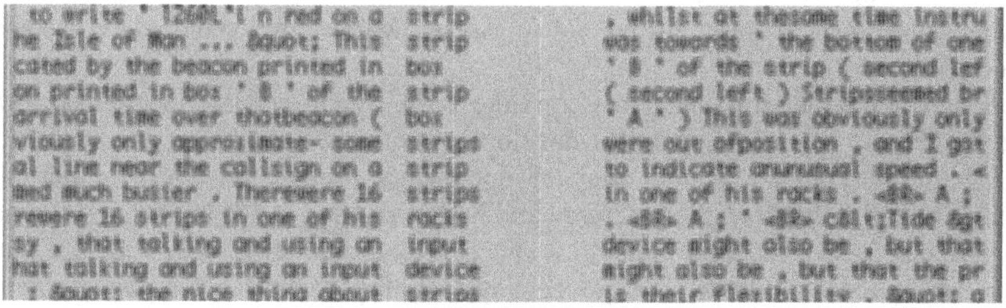

Fig. 4. Browsing the semantic category O2

Similarly, browsing the context for Q1.2 (paper documents and writing) would reveal that controllers annotate flight strips to record deviations from flight plans, and L1 (life, living things) would reveal that some strips are 'live', that is, they refer to aircraft currently traversing the controller's sector. Notice also that the semantic categories' deviation from the normative corpus can also be expected to reveal roles.

In this example, the frequency of S7.1 (power, organising) confirms the importance of the roles of 'controllers' and 'chiefs', identified by the role analysis described above.

Using the REVERE tools does not automate the task of identifying abstractions, much less does it produce fully formed requirements that can be pasted into a specification document. Instead, it helps the engineer quickly isolate potentially significant domain abstractions that require closer analysis. It cannot guarantee completeness. For example, some important abstractions may be overlooked because their frequency of occurrence in the document being analysed is close to that of the normative corpus. In addition, word semantics may be domain-specific leading to them being tagged wrongly (in the domain context), making it easy to overlook their significance. This issue is explored in the next example.

6. Example 2: A Standards Document

This example explores the REVERE tools' utility for assessing the impact of standards in systems engineering. The example is based upon the publication of a new national standard for the procurement of safety-critical military systems (approximately 21000 words). In all domains, systems engineers are constrained by regulations, standards and best operating practice, all of which may be documented in a number of sources. Safety-critical systems engineering processes tend to be particularly tightly regulated and document-centric. Systems engineers working in safety critical domains therefore need to acquire a good awareness of the standards landscape and how individual standards apply to different projects. This obviously requires a lot of reading and interpretation of standards documents. This might be to:

- keep abreast of emerging standards in their domain in order to monitor international best practice;
- anticipate the effect of new standards on future international, national and sector (such as defence) standards;
- build competence for possible future work in the market for which the standard was written;
- identify a set of key attributes to assess against the standard to establish compliance.

Systems engineering standards are like *meta* requirements documents - they specify generic requirements on the development processes and their products within a domain. In contrast to the class of documents used in the ATC experiment, standards tend to be strongly structured and highly stylised in the lexical and syntactic conventions used, and in the semantics attached to certain terms. In particular, modal verbs are frequently used to signify where system properties or development practices are mandatory or advisory.

Our analysis of the standard had two goals: to determine the weight given to different development practices mandated or advised by the standard; and to identify the roles of people who would use or be regulated by the standard. These were performed using POS and role analysis.

6.1 POS Analysis

WMATRIX allows the engineer to isolate words that are assigned any given POS tag. In standards documents, words given the modal verb tag ('VM') are of particular interest. Figure 5 illustrates the frequency profile of all the standard's modal verbs.

shall	VM	199	Context
must	VM	127	Context
may	VM	76	Context
can	VM	68	Context
will	VM	48	Context
should	VM	39	Context
could	VM	13	Context
might	VM	1	Context
would	VM	1	Context

Fig. 5. Modal verbs' occurrence in the standard

The most common modal verb in the standard is 'shall'. In standards (and other types of specification documents) a convention is often adopted in which 'shall' is used as a keyword in clauses that denote mandatory requirements. The convention often extends to using other modal verbs to denote weaker obligations. Any of the modal verbs may also appear in normal English usage in informal, descriptive sections of the document.

ties . </P> <p> 16.2.2 Such a plan	should	include 1 . A list of CSRs (result
tor . <p> 17.5.3.4.4 The Evaluator	should	also be consulted on the choice of
ing 17.6.1.3.1 Software simulation	should	be used to test the functional beha
sing a set of test vectors , which	should	be generated using a test pattern g
Assurance Report , and the design	should	provide adequate margins on critica
s been initiated , the operator(s)	should	be alerted , both visually and aura
(AUST) 5679 66 17.7.6 Operators	should	be qualified and trained to a level
afety issues for such technologies	should	be invoked by the Developer , in co
the form and any additional papers	should	be forwarded to : Assistant Program

Fig. 6. Occurrences of 'should' in the standard

Once identified, the modal verbs were browsed in their context within the standard to build up a picture of the conventions used in the standard. This was essentially to see if their usage complied with our expectations. We started by browsing the occurrences of 'shall', to distill a view of the mandatory requirements of the standard. As expected, most of the occurrences of 'shall' in the standard occur in formal clauses representing mandatory requirements. However, documents cannot always be relied upon to use modal verbs consistently. This is illustrated in figure 6, which shows a subset of the 39 occurrences of 'should'. Normally, where 'should' appears in a formal clause of a standard, it is used to denote an advisory requirement. However, to avoid any ambiguity, it is common for a standards document to contain a definition of the convention used to differentiate between mandatory and advisory requirements. Our suspicion was aroused when browsing the lists of modal verb contexts failed to reveal such any such definition. We then discovered the following occurrence of 'should' in the standard: "*17.7.6 Operators **should** be qualified and trained ...*". This turns out to represent a mandatory requirement and hence represents a violation of the lexical convention that we had assumed for the standard.

Our exploration of the document's use of modal verbs revealed mistaken assumptions about the conventions used by the document. We eventually isolated the clause in the standard that defined the conventions used: mandatory requirements were indicated by bold text and advisory requirements were written in plain text. Our tools were unable to detect this easily because the tools currently do not include any formatting analysis.

Identifying the paragraph that defined the convention was complicated because we had to find words with semantic tags that corresponded to *mandatory* and *advisory*. This requires experimentation with several tags:

- S6 'Obligation and necessity'
- S8 'Helping/hindering'
- X7 'Wanting'

The terminology in the standard for a mandatory requirements was simply the word 'requirement'. This was tagged X7. The terminology used for an advisory requirement was the word 'guidance'. This was the tag S8. Clearly, in a standards document context, these two terms, as well as others such as 'mandatory' and 'advisory' should all be given the same tag. This revealed a problem in the use of a tagset derived from the analysis of general English for the analysis of technical or formal documents.

6.2 Role Analysis

In this stage of the analysis we were interested in discovering the roles identified for people who would apply or be constrained by the standard. This is important because different roles will have different viewpoints on the standard. For example, developers are typically interested in how to comply with a standard, while assessors are interested in how to evaluate a developer's work against a standard. In its introduction section, the standard identifies a set of roles as follows: "This standard applies to the Customer, Developer, Auditor and Evaluator of the system". By applying the REVERE tools' role analysis we identified several other candidates for roles in the text. The most commonly occurring are illustrated in figure 7.

developer	NN1	[illegible]	Context
evaluator	NN1	45	Context
customer	NN1	39	Context
auditor	NN1	35	Context
operator	NN1	28	Context
users	NN2	19	Context
operators	NN2	12	Context
certifier	NN1	9	Context
factors	NN2	8	Context
user	NN1	6	Context

Fig. 7. Candidate roles identified in the standard

Of course, many of these will be synonyms or special cases of the primary roles explicitly identified by the document. For example, the (prime) contractor is treated as the developer. However, others that are not explicitly identified do appear to be significant. For example, Figure 8 illustrates occurrences of references to users (or end users) in the document. While these may not be directly affected by the standard, there is an implication that they will be involved in a development project that complies to the standard.

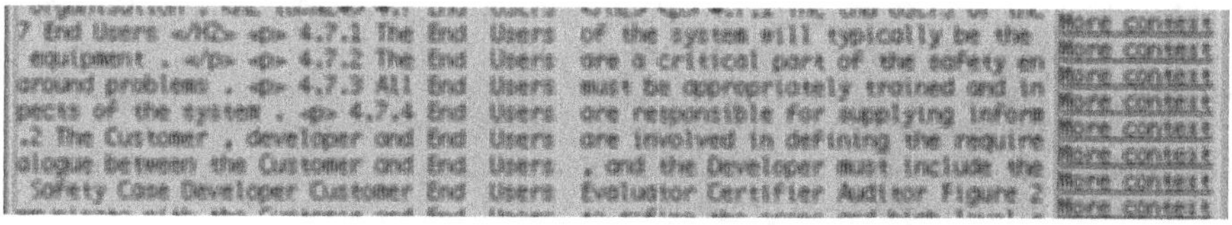

Fig. 8. Occurrences of the role 'users' in the standard

7. Conclusions

Our work on the REVERE project is motivated by the potential to provide the means for rapid analyses of complex and voluminous free text that often forms an input to systems engineering projects. The need for rigour in systems engineering means that a deep understanding of key information has to be acquired by the systems engineer. However, faced with a large volume of information of uncertain relevance and quality, tools that supported rapid but fairly shallow analysis would be of potential value to systems engineers. Although shallow, the analysis supported by such tools would help the systems engineer to identify where they needed to focus their attention. This would mitigate attentional losses caused by information overload.

The paper has described two experiments using a set of tools that we have developed. These include POS and semantic taggers and are integrated by an end-user tool called WMATRIX. The experiments (a third is reported elsewhere [21]) reveal both promise for the approach and limitations of our existing tools.

The principal defects appear to be caused by the need to tailor our semantic tagger to a technical domain. Despite this, the results of our work to date lead us to believe that, just as probabilistic NLP has emerged in commercial products in other domains (notably word processing and speech recognition), it also has the potential to form a key component of next-generation systems engineering tools.

It is crucial to the understanding of our work that we do not aim for completeness; systems engineering will always rely upon human skill and expertise. However, by rejecting as impossible the use of NLP for fully automating any aspect of systems engineering, we are able to focus on our goal of supporting systems engineers' manual analysis of documents. Initial results in a variety of systems engineering domains suggests that the REVERE tools are effective in helping engineers identify crucial domain abstractions and test theories about what abstractions exist, their importance and how they are inter-related in the domain.

References

1. Stevens, R., Brook, P., Jackson, K., Arnold, S.: Systems engineering: coping with complexity, Prentice-Hall, 1998.

2. Rolland, C., Proix, C.: A Natural Language Approach for Requirements Engineering, Lecture Notes in Computer Science, Vol. 593, 1992.
3. Burg, J., van de Riet, R.: COLOR-X: Object Modeling profits from Linguistics, Proc. Second International Conference on Building and Sharing of Very Large-Scale Knowledge Bases (KB&KS'95), Enschede, The Netherlands, 1995.
4. Cyre, W., Thakar, A.: Generating Validation Feedback for Automatic Interpretation of Informal Requirements, in Formal Methods in System Design, Kluwer, 1997.
5. Rosenburg, L., Hammer, T., Huffman, L.: Requirements, Testing & Metrics, Proc. 15th Annual Pacific Nothwest Software Quality Conference, Utah, USA, 1998.
6. Ambriola, V., Gervasi, V.: Experiences with Domain-Based Parsing of Natural Language Requirements, Proc. 4th International Conference NLDB '99, Klagenfurt, Austria, 1999.
7. Steuten, A., van de Reit, R., Dietz, J.: Linguistically Based Conceptual Modeling of Business Communication, Proc. 4th International Conference NLDB '99, Klagenfurt, Austria, 1999.
8. Bentley R., Rodden T., Sawyer P., Sommerville I, Hughes J., Randall D., Shapiro D.: Ethnographically-informed systems design for air traffic control, Proc. CSCW '92, Toronto, November 1992.
9. Emmerich, W., Finkelstein, A., Montangero, C., Antonelli, S., Armitage, S., Stevens, R.: Managing Standards Compliance, IEEE Trans. Software Engineering, 25 (6), 1999.
10. Butler, K., Esposito, C., Hebron, R.: Connecting the Design of Software to the Design of Work, Communications of the ACM. 42 (1), 1999.
11. Berry, D., Yavne, N., Yavne, M.: Application of Program Design Language Tools to Abbottís method of Program Design by Informal Natural Language Descriptions, Journal of Software and Systems, 7, 1987.
12. Aguilera, C., Berry, D.: The Use of a Repeated Phrase Finder in Requirements Extraction, Journal of Systems and Software, 13 (9), 1990.
13. Goldin, L., Berry, D.: AbstFinder, A Prototype Natural Language Text Abstraction Finder for Use in Requirements Elicitation, Automated Software Engineering, 4, 1997.
14. Fliedl, G., Kop, C., Mayr, H., Mayerthaler, W., Winkler, C.: Linguistically Based Requirements Engineering - the NIBA Project, Proc. 4th International Conference NLDB '99, Klagenfurt, Austria, 1999.
15. Aston, G. and Burnard, L.: The BNC Handbook: Exploring the British National Corpus with SARA, Edinburgh University Press, 1998.
16. Thomas, J., Wilson, A.: Methodologies for Studying a Corpus of Doctor-Patient Interaction, in Thomas, J. and Short, M. (eds.) Using Corpora for Language Research, Longman, 1996.
17. Garside, R., Smith, N.: A Hybrid Grammatical Tagger: CLAWS4, in Garside, R., Leech, G., and McEnery, A. (eds.) Corpus Annotation: Linguistic Information from Computer Text, Longman, 1997.
18. Rayson, P., and Wilson, A.: The ACAMRIT semantic tagging system: progress report, Proc. Language Engineering for Document Analysis and Recognition (LEDAR), Brighton, England. 1996.
19. Rayson, P., Leech, G., and Hodges, M.: Social differentiation in the use of English vocabulary: some analyses of the conversational component of the British National Corpus, International Journal of Corpus Linguistics. 2 (1), 1997.
20. Jackson, D. and Jackson, M.: Problem decomposition for reuse, BCS/IEE Software Eng. J., 11 (1), 1996.
21. Rayson, P., Garside, R., Sawyer, P.: Recovering Legacy Requirements, Proc. Fifth International Workshop on Requirements Engineering: Foundations of Software Quality (REFSQí99), Heidelberg, Germany, 1999.

Presenting Mathematical Concepts as an Example for Inference-Rich Domains

Helmut Horacek

Universit%odes Saarlandes
FB 14 Informatik
Postfach 1150, D-66041 Saarbr¸cken, Germany
horacek@cs.uni-sb.de

Abstract. Presenting machine-stored information in human-adequate terms is a challenge in all kinds of domains and applications. Especially in inference-rich domains, this task proves to be difficult, because presentations directly reflecting the organization of the information stored in some knowledge or data base differ significantly from comparable presentations produced by human authors. Motivated by the associated discrepancies, we have developed presentation techniques for machine-stored information in inference-rich domains, and we have elaborated these techniques for mathematical concepts. The presentations obtained are fundamentally reorganized, compared to the uniform representation of domain objects, and they can be produced in varying forms, geared by evidence about the domain knowledge, inferential capabilities, and information intentions of the audience. These techniques prove relevant to assist the inspection of standardized information repositories, and they contribute significantly to the adaptation of interactive teaching material in formal, inference-rich domains.

1 Introduction

Presenting machine-stored information in human-adequate terms is a challenge in all kinds of domains and applications. Especially in inference-rich domains, this task proves to be difficult, because presentations directly reflecting the organization of the information stored in some knowledge or data base differ significantly from comparable presentations produced by human authors, as in text books and interactive presentations. One of the most salient inadequacies of direct presentations constitutes the considerable degree of redundancy, since these presentations widely ignore the inferential capabilities of humans.

Motivated by the discrepancies between machine-generated presentations and those typically produced by humans, we have developed presentation techniques for machine-stored information in inference-rich domains, and we have elaborated these techniques for mathematical concepts. The presentations obtained are fundamentally reorganized, compared to the uniform representation of domain objects, and they can be produced in varying forms, geared by evidence about the domain knowledge, inferential capabilities, and information intentions of the audience. The representations of the domain concepts illustrated are part of the distributed mathematical data base MBASE [22], and the presentations are integrated in the interactive proof development environment ΩMEGA [1]. These techniques prove

M. Bouzeghoub et al. (Eds.): NLDB 2000, LNCS 1959, pp. 301-312, 2001.

relevant to assist the inspection of standardized information repositories, such as MBASE, and they contribute significantly to the adaptation of interactive teaching material in inference-rich domains such as mathematics, and possibly other formal domains, such as physics and theoretical models of economy.

This paper is organized as follows. After reviewing previous work on presentations in inference-rich domains, we introduce the categories of information stored in MBASE, and we characterize some typical presentation goals. Then we describe presentation knowledge which drives the way how pieces from several information categories are composed, followed by presentation techniques which organize these compositions, illustrated by a typical example. We conclude with a short outlook for future work.

2 Previous Work

Not surprisingly, automatically generating presentations in inference-rich domains has primarily been addressed in the domain of mathematical proofs. However, most approaches in this area do not take into account the inferential aspects of these presentations in an in-depth manner. Most systems that can present mathematical proofs in natural language only apply minor modifications to the underlying proof structures, prior to expressing individual proof steps by natural language templates. Systems following this schema include ILF [4], which separates the display of the logical content of proof nodes from their tree-like presentation, THEOREMA [2], which displays the proof in a hierarchical manner, with details temporarily hidden and exposed on demand, and the verbalization component on top of Nuprl [11], which presents proofs on the condensed level of tactics. For the special form of equation proofs, presentation tools of today's theorem provers (e.g., WALDMEISTER [9,10]) linearize the underlying proof structure by promoting multiple referred subproofs into lemmas. This presentation is enhanced by using compact notation formats [6], indicating lemma substitutions by graphical markers, and introducing auxiliary variables for large, locally unchanged subterms [4].

In order to obtain better presentations, some systems describe certain kinds of complex inference steps very densely, and they leave some categories of proof steps implicit in their output. An example is CtCoq [3], which generates compactified proofs by composing text patterns associated with proof object types, thereby abstracting from intermediate inference steps recoverable from inductive definitions. The linguistically most elaborate system is PROVERB [19], the system developed in our own research group, which omits instantiations of axioms, and applies linguistically motivated techniques for text planning, generating referring expressions, and aggregation of propositions with common elements.

In other domains, only a few methods developed within the field of natural language generation try to anticipate a user¥s likely inferences and to exploit them by conveying information indirectly. Zukerman and McConachy [29] select a subset of content specifications for presentation, thereby exploiting inferable relations expressed in a taxonomic hierarchy. Green and Carberry [7] aim at the generation of indirect answers to accomplish complementary discourse goals by modeling potential obstacles that prevent intended achievements. Horacek [12] attempts to capture inference relations between generic and referential pieces of knowledge through rules expressing aspects of conversational implicature [8]. In [13], we have proposed a much simpler version, elaborated for everyday discourse, threreby enhancing the coverage to chains of inferences, and supporting argumentation structure reorganization. In [14], finally, we have adapted these techniques to the presentation of mathematical proofs.

3 Categories of Domain Information

In this section, we informally describe the mathematical concepts to be presented, that is, the content of MBASE and its organization (see [22] for details). MBASE is a server that comprises a relational data base management system embedded in a logical programming environment. Most importantly, this environment offers efficient transformations between complex objects and a binary representation that can be stored as byte-string forms in the data base which, in turn, can be effectively read and restored as objects again. Through this mechanism, the inherent problem of efficiently handling both the representation of complex knowledge base entries and the processes for reasoning about them is distributed among the components of this hybrid architecture. Moreover, a number of mathematical services can access MBASE through a system of mediators that take care of ontological differences between the mathematical service at hand and the view of MBASE (currently supported for three such services). In the following, we abstract from all these technical aspects, such as the distributed organization of the data base, and we concentrate on the conceptual content which is subject to presentation or assists in the presentation of other concepts.

The statement of a mathematical theorem can depend on the availability of an eventually large set of definitions of mathematical concepts which, in turn, may themselves depend on other concepts. Moreover, previously proven theorems or lemmata may be reused within the context of a proof. Going beyond pure representation purposes, a formal reasoning system needs access to other forms of knowledge, including information about control knowledge for automated reasoners (theorem provers) and about (human-related) presentation knowledge.

In order to store and manipulate these kinds of information, MBASE distinguishes several categories of information objects, on which the structure of the underlying data base model is grounded:

- *Primary (mathematical) objects*, such as symbols, definitions, lemmata, theorems, and proofs.
- *Human-oriented (technical) knowledge*, such as names for theorems, and specifications for notation and symbol handling.
- *Machine-oriented information*, to interact with automated reasoning services.
- *Structuring objects*, for supplying constructs to express relations between mathematical objects.
- *Relations to external knowledge sources.*

Based on these categories, the data base model distinguishes the following primary data base objects:

- *Symbols* for mathematical concepts, such as '+' for addition, and 'group' for the property of being a group.
- *Definitions* for associating meanings to symbols in terms of already defined ones.
- *Assertions*, which are logical sentences, including axioms, theorems, conjectures and lemmata, distinguished according to pragmatic or proof-theoretic status.
- *Proofs*, as representations of evidence for the truth of assertions.
- *Proof objects*, encapsulating the actual proof objects in various formats, including formal, informal, and even natural language formats.
- *Examples*, due to their importance in mathematical practice.

In addition, the data base model contains some relations between objects of these kinds, including

- *Definition-entailment*, to relate defined symbols to others and, ultimately, to symbols marked as primitive.
- *Depends-on/Local-in*, which specify dependency and locality information for primary knowledge items. At the present stage of development, this relation is implemented for definitions and proofs, which make explicit the use of symbols/ lemmata in a definition or assertion, as well as for theories, which specifies the organization of mathematical subdomains and the associated inheritance of their properties.

For the task of presentation, most of these objects and relations are relevant, although we do not exploit the full potential at the current stage of development. At present, we make use of human-oriented objects to address technical presentation issues, and we combine definitions, assertions, and proofs along the relations among these objects, selected according to the requirements of a given presentation goal.

4 Presentation Goals

There are numerous purposes which render the selection of information and its presentation to a human audience beneficial. At present, we have elaborated strategies for three presentation goals, as well as techniques for tailoring the content selected to the general needs of humans and to the requirements of a specific audience. These presentation goals are:

- *Inspection of some portion of the data base*, to examine the coverage of the system with respect to certain subdomains or specific aspects, such as variations of proofs. Unlike the other goals, which address users with varying degrees of expertise, this task is of interest to system authors and administrators.
- *Acquire a certain part of the domain knowledge*, to learn about some domain concepts and related information, such as a definition or an assertion, together with relevant information yet unknown to the audience.
- *Getting acquainted with an instance of operational knowledge*, to learn about the use of domain concepts for some task, such as the elaboration of a proof, in a form and degree of exposition suitable to the experience of the audience.

The content selection in pursuing these goals is primarily driven by the domain information stored, and influenced by assumptions about the audience. The inspection of some portion of the data base, which features a specific domain concept, concerns all information dependent on or related to that concept, that satisfies some additional specifications, that is, maximal distance to the concept addressed, and categories of information. Unlike with the other presentation goals, the information selected is presented in a rather telegraphic fashion, and its original structure is widely maintained to make this structure evident. The next presentation goal, acquiring a certain part of the domain knowledge, also features a specific domain concept, but the additional specifications are interpreted in a more selective fashion, geared by assumptions about the background knowledge of the audience. Finally, getting acquainted with an instance of operational knowledge concerns a proof available in one or another form, the most interesting one being a representation of an automatically found proof, which undergoes considerable modifications prior to its presentation.

Pursuing these presentations in adequate terms has to reflect particularities of the domain. In mathematics, presentation of its primary information parts, definitions and theorems, and, in particular, its operational parts, the proofs, have some properties distinguishing adequate presentations from the form in which the information is originally available. These properties are:

Structural organization ñ Theorem provers organize solution paths to proofs as derivation trees, which are typically nested to a large degree. Similar structures are obtained when definitions are expanded. In presentations addressing humans, these tree-like structures must be adequately linearized into chains of argumentation.

Granularity ñ Mathematical definitions are organized in a recursive manner, and the terms used can in principle be expanded to more basic ones, which is what provers do when using nested definitions and checking their applicability in a concrete instance. The proofs themselves are typically made on the level of a general calculus appropriate for the underlying inferencing. For presentations, the associated information must be lifted to some more abstract level adequate for human reasoning.

Explicitness ñ Definitions and reasoning are both extremely explicit, with all details elaborated to the ultimate degree. For presentations, much more compact forms are required, in dependency of the background knowledge and inferential capabilities of the intended audience, otherwise the presentations are largely felt as redundant.

In some sense, these properties are characteristic for inference-rich domains in general, and to argumentative discourse in moderately complex cases.

5 Presentation Knowledge

In order to present the information selected adequately in view of the assumed mental capabilities of the audience, assumptions about capabilities of the audience are stored in a user model. These capabilities comprise the following categories of knowledge and communicative competence:

- *knowledge per se*, including taxonomic and referential knowledge,
- the *attentional state* of the addressee,
- *taxonomic* and *logical* inferences, and
- *communicatively motivated* inferences.

Assumptions about the addressee's taxonomic and referential knowledge are represented by simple stereotypes, which include sections for domain terminology, definitions, axioms, and lemmata (see [5] for details). The domain knowledge comprises concepts that are particular to more or less specialized mathematical (sub)theories such as group theory, as well as concepts that are valid over a significantly large set of varying theories, such as the laws of associativity, commutativity, etc. For example, apprentices are credited with knowing the concepts of integers and ordering relations, mathematical students are additionally assumed to be familiar with the laws of associativity and monotony, and specialists in the area of group theory are also assumed to know the definition of a group and of its components, such as unit element.

The attentional state is modeled by attributing the user with *awareness* concerning the facts needed to mentally reconstruct implicit information, which is more than being acquainted with these facts. For generic knowledge, that is, domain regularities, the user is considered to be aware of those parts of his/her knowledge that belong to 'basic' world knowledge or to special knowledge about the issue presented. For referential knowledge, the user is credited with being aware of all facts mentioned or implied so far within the current discourse segment. For the domain of mathematical proofs, the underlying categorization of knowledge is oriented on relevant mathematical theories: basic axioms and axioms within the particular subarea addressed are considered to be part of the user's awareness, and discourse segments follow the rhetorical structures underlying the domain concept or proof descriptions.

The remaining inference categories, taxonomic and logical inferences, are understood here as elementary clues, either relying on purely taxonomic knowledge, or following a standard logical inference pattern such as modus ponens. Typical reasoning steps are generalizations of terms and relations, and abstractions from individuals, embedded in modus ponens derivations. To assess these skills in our domain, we have categorized the reasoning steps in the derivation of machine-generated proofs, and we have examined the complexity of the inferences involved, in a number of text book examples and in machine-found proofs.

Communicatively motivated inferences, finally, concern the capability to augment logically incomplete pieces of information in a given context. They are expressed by presentation rules, which refer to the other categories of presentation knowledge. Their functionality is explained in the next section.

6 Presentation Techniques

Presenting information from inference-rich domains in adequate terms requires taking the three characteristic properties described in Section 4 into account. This is done by making decisions about appropriate granularities and degrees of explicitness in which content specifications should be presented, and by reorganizing these specifications to meet textual presentation requirements.

For presentations addressing humans, we believe that the best choice for the basic abstraction level for inference-rich content is the *assertion level* according to Huang [18], that is, the application of axioms and lemmata. On the assertion level, the content selected is conveyed completely and in full detail. For expressing the components of this abstracted argumentative structure adequately in natural language, there is a tension between producing too explicit or too implicit utterances, which is underpinned by several empirical investigations. The study in [27] demonstrates that humans easily uncover missing pieces of information left implicit in discourse, provided this information conforms to their expectations in the given context. Conversely, studies on human comprehension of deductive syllogisms [20] have unveiled considerable performance differences among individual syllogisms. These experimental results fit to the empirically validated hypotheses about the impacts human resource limits in attentional capacity and in inferential capacity have on dialog strategies [28]. In particular, an increasing number of logically redundant assertions aim at making certain inferences explicit, in dependency of how hard and important an inference is (modus tollens being an example for a hard inference). Implementing the insights gained through these studies in view of expressing argumentative structures, we apply expansion operations to adjust the level of granularity, and we apply conversationally motivated presentation rules in order to eliminate subjective redundancies, thereby obtaining a suitable degree of explicitness.

The purpose underlying the expansion of assertion levels steps is to decompose presentations of complex theorem applications or involved applications of standard theorems into easier comprehensible pieces. At first, assertion level steps are expanded to the natural deduction (ND) level (see [18]). Thereafter, a partial recomposition of ND-steps into inference steps encapsulating the harder comprehensible deductive syllogisms, modus tollens and disjunction elimination steps, is performed, in case the sequence of ND rules in the entire assertion level step contains more than one of these. To do this, the sequence of ND rules is broken after each but the last occurence of a modus tollens or disjunction elimination, and the resulting subsequences of ND-steps are composed into a sequence of reasoning steps at some sort of *partial assertion* level. Consider, as an example, the application of the transitivity axiom (($a \rho b$) and ($b \rho c$) implies ($a \rho c$)) in reverse direction. While the utterance ì($b \rho c$) and not ($a \rho c$) implies not ($a \rho b$) î, which directly corresponds to the assertion level representation, is hard to understand even for formally trained people, separating the modus tollens inference step ì¨ ($a \rho c$) implies ¨ ($a \rho b$) or ¨ ($b \rho c$) î from the disjunction elimination ìThus, $b \rho c$ yields ¨ ($a \rho b$)î illustrates this inference in a much clearer way.

In order to handle the problem of subjective redundancies, we make use of communicatively motivated *presentation* rules that express aspects of human reasoning capabilities with regard to contextually motivated inferability of pieces of information on the basis of explicitly mentioned facts and relevant background knowledge [14]. These rules provide an interface to stored assumptions about the intended audience. They describe the following sorts of situations:

- Omission of a *proposition* appearing as a justification (by the *Cut-prop*-rule). For example, if the addressee is aware of $0 < 1$, and is able to conclude $0 < a$ given $1 < a$ and $(((0 < 1) \wedge (1 < a)) \rightarrow 0 < a)$, this rule is applicable.
- Omission of a *rule* (axiom instance) appearing as a justification (by the *Cut-rule*-rule). For example, if the addressee is assumed to be able to conclude $0 < a$ from $1 < a$ through transitivity, this rule is applicable.
- Omission of an *intermediate* inference step (by the *Compactification*-rule). For example, if $0 \neq a$ is considered inferable through $0 < a$, which, in turn, is inferable through $1 < a$, and if $0 < a$ and $1 < a$ are considered coherent, this rule is applicable to justify $1 < a$ from $0 \neq a$ directly.

In order to apply these rules successfully, the complexity of an inference step involved must be within certain limitations. This is measured in terms of the numbers of premises used, the number of intermediate steps needed to refer the inference step's conclusion back to known premises (that is, basic axioms or communicated facts), and the complexities of the substitutions required. Moreover, the composition of inference steps (captured by the *Compactification*-rule) attempts to follow insights from psychological experiments. Hence, leaving out intermediate steps in a chain of argumentation should be understood as a 'direct' cause, while 'indirect' causes negatively affect the reasoning effort [27] ñ this criterion needs to be modeled for the domain at hand. In an approach to expert system explanations, we have modeled this aspect by requiring purposes of domain rules involved to be identical [12]. For proofs, we try to capture it by a structural similarity between intermediate and final conclusions.

When an appropriate degree of explicitness for presenting the argumentative structure is obtained, its proper organization needs to be addressed next, which is motivated by general rhetorical considerations rather than by mental capabilities attributed to a particular audience. This issue requires breaking the original, typically deeply nested tree-like structure into several inference chains, each of which can reasonably be expected to be presentable in a linear form. Fulfilling this requirement is supported by a variant of the presentation rules, called *Restructuring*-rule, which gives a justification more general scope in the argumentative structure. Applying this operation is motivated by multiple uses of the same argument, or by the preference of presenting a chain of inferences without an intermitting side step.

The presentation rules are applied to the argumentative structure from its leaf nodes to the root node, without returning to direct or indirect ancestor nodes. In a first cycle, the *Cut-Prop* and the *Cut-Rule* rules are applied to each node followed by the *Compactification* rule; in a second cycle, the *Restructuring* rule is applied. Through this organization, dependencies among individual rule applications are captured appropriately, and also efficiently since each rule application contributes to the final result.

7 An Example

Finally, we illustrate the presentation capabilities of our methods by a small example. Consider the following theorem (adapted from [21])

(1) *Let K be an ordered field. If* $a \in K$, *then* $1 < a$ *implies* $0 < a^{-1} < 1$

The solution found by the theorem prover OTTER [23] and transformed into a structure at the assertion level [18] is graphically illustrated in Figure 1. In this Figure, axioms appear in boxes, multiple used propositions in double boxes, and propositions derived in ovals. Derivational dependencies are expressed by straight lines, in downward direction. Moreover, axioms are identified by their name (Lemma 1.10 being the reference in [21]) and associated with their instantiations in the proof.

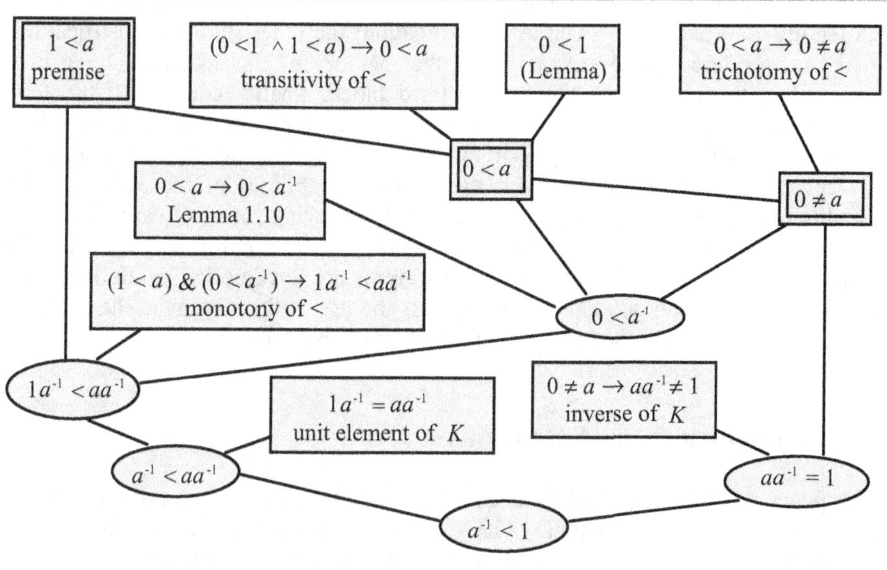

Figure 1: Graphical illustration of the internal representation of the proof of theorem (1)

This structure is further processed by checking the contextually motivated inferability of its parts. At first, the fact $0 < 1$ is considered inferable by virtue of the *Cut-prop* rule. Then the uses of the axioms transitivity and trichotomy, which only require trivial substitutions here, are considered inferable through the *Cut-rule* rule, provided the audience is acquainted with these axioms. Similarly, also the uses of the axioms monotony, unit element, and inverse are considered inferable by an informed audience. Moreover, applying the *Compactification* rule suggests the direct inferability of the facts $0 < a$ and $0 \neq a$ from $1 < a$ only, since these formulas are all considered similar to one another. Finally, applications of the *Restructuring* rule partition the reduced argumentative structure into three blocks: the first one consists of the assumption $1 < a$, which is presented first because it serves as a justification in

(1) ìLet $1 < a$. Since lemma 1.10 holds, $0 < a^{-1}$. Then $0 < a^{-1} = 1a^{-1} < aa^{-1} = 1$. î

(2) ìLet $1 < a$. Since lemma 1.10 holds, $0 < a^{-1}$. Then

a^{-1}	$= 1a^{-1} < aa^{-1}$	because of the unit element of K
	$< aa^{-1}$	since $1 < a$ and $0 < a^{-1}$ hold, and '<' is monotone
	$= 1$	because of the inverse element of K for $a \neq 0$.
	Thus $a^{-1} < 1$. î	

Figure 2: Presentation variants for the proof of theorem (1)

both blocks following it. The second block consists of the intermediate result $0 < a^{-1}$, with lemma 1.10 explicitly given as a justification; the other (indirect) justification, $1 < a$, is considered to be still active in the memory of the audience, since it is mentioned in the preceeding block. The third block, finally, consists of the four inequations appearing in the bottom part of Figure 1, which can be composed into a chain, if the justifications for the reasoning steps involved are considered inferable.

Depending on assumptions about the mental capabilities of the audience, the reasoning underlying this proof can be presented in varying forms of explicitness. In Figure 2, two of these variants are given. The short version on top addresses a well-informed audience, since all references to theorems are left implicit, while the more elaborate version below it additionally explains the use of the axioms in the chain of inequations, in particular the precise scope of their application.

8 Conclusion and Extensions

In this paper, we have proposed techniques for presenting machine-stored information in inference-rich domains, which we have elaborated for mathematical concepts. As particularities of this enterprise, the presentations obtained are fundamentally reorganized, compared to the uniform representation of domain objects, and they can be produced in varying forms, geared by evidence about the domain knowledge, inferential capabilities, and information intentions of the audience. The representations of the domain concepts illustrated are part of the distributed mathematical data base MBASE, whose basic functionality is implemented and will further be extended in the near future. A simplified version of the natural language presentations is also implemented and integrated in the interactive proof development environment ΩMEGA. We are currently working on extending this component to the full functionality described in this paper.

There are at least two aspects in which our methods can be extended beneficially:

- Providing presentations on higher levels of abstraction, as exemplified in [24], which, among others, enables one to include motivations for proof steps, a feature generally missing in presentations obtained from operational specifications (see also [25]).
- Providing partial presentations for extended specifications, which require particular treatment in their organization (see [26]). In addition, the organization of larger proofs needs to be accomodated by more advanced measures, along the lines pursued in [17], which addresses the specific form of equation proofs.

Here, we briefly elaborate on the second aspect. In order to express the underlying reasoning within limited text length, abbreviated forms for its inference steps can be generated, by successively relaxing details about its use, or even combining several inference steps, according to the following options, as addressed in a preliminary fashion in [15]:

1. Omitting the way *how* a piece of knowledge (a domain regularity) is applied
2. Omitting that piece of inferential knowledge, the domain regularity itself
3. Omitting premises of the inference (eventually, only some of them)
4. Omitting intermediate inference steps

Omitting parts of the content may be motivated by increasing the optimism concerning assumptions about the mental capabilities of the audience (a reduction in *convenience*) or by simply reducing the originally intended degree of detail (a reduction in *quality*), following the theoretical model in [16]. The production of longer, but information reduced utterances can naturally serve the purpose of a summary meeting certain length parameters and content preferences. Moreover, these texts are well-suited as first-shot explanations in comparable discourse situations. Subsequently, further details may be exposed, guided by vague hints (ìbe more concreteî) or by specific demands (ìWhy does fact x holdî, ìHow is fact x derived?î).

Our techniques prove relevant to assist the inspection of standardized information repositories, such as MBASE, and they contribute significantly to the adaptation of interactive teaching material in inference-rich domains such as mathematics, and possibly other formal domains, such as physics and theoretical models of economy.

References

1. Benzm¸ller, C., Cheikhrouhou, L., Fehrer, D., Fiedler, A., Huang, X., Kerber, M., Kohlhase, M., Konrad, K., Melis, E., Meier, A., Schaarschmidt, W., Siekmann, J., Sorge, V.: ΩMEGA: Towards a Mathematical Assistant. In Proc. of the 14th International Conference on Automated Deduction (CADE-97), Townsville, Australia (1997) 252-255
2. Buchberger, B., Jebelean, T., Kriftner, F., Marin, M., Tomuta, E., Vasaru, D.: An Overview of the Theorema Project. In ISSAC'97, Hawaii (1997)
3. Coscoy, Y., Kahn, G., ThÈry, L. Extracting Text from Proof. In Typed Lambda Calculus and its Application (1995)
4. Dahn, I.: Using ILF as a User Interface for Many Theorem Provers. In Proc. of User Interfaces for Theorem Provers, Eindhoven 1998
5. Fehrer, D., Horacek, H.: Exploiting the Addressee's Inferential Capabilities in Presenting Mathematical Proofs. In Proc. of the 15th International Joint Conference on Artificial Intelligence (IJCAI-97), Nagoya, Japan (1997) 959-964
6. Fehrer, D., Horacek, H.: Presenting Inequations in Mathematical Proofs. Information Sciences **116** (1999) 3-23
7. Green, N., Carberry, S.: A Hybrid Reasoning Model for Indirect Answers. In Proceedings of ACL-94, Las Cruces, New Mexico (1994)
8. Grice, H.: Logic and Conversation. In Syntax and Semantics: Vol. 3, Speech Acts, Academic Press (1975) 43-58
9. Hillenbrand, T., Buch, A., Vogt, R., Lˆchner, B.: Waldmeister: High-Performance Equational Deduction. Journal of Automated Reasoning **18**(2) (1997) 265-270
10. Hillenbrand, T., Jaeger, A., Lˆchner, B.: System Description: Waldmeister ñ Improvements in Performance and Ease of Use. In Proc. of the 16th International Conference on Automated Deduction (CADE-99), Trento, Italy (1999) 232-236
11. Holland-Minkey, A., Barzilay, R., Constable, R.: Verbalization of High-Level Formal Proofs. In Proc. of AAAI-99 (1999)

12. Horacek, H.: A Model for Adapting Explanations to the User's Likely Inferences. User Modeling and User Adapted Interaction **7** (1997) 1-55
13. Horacek, H.: Generating Inference-Rich Discourse Through Revisions of RST-Trees. In Proc. of AAAI-98 (1998) 814-820
14. Horacek, H.: Presenting Proofs in a Human-Oriented Way. In Proc. of the 16th International Conference on Automated Deduction (CADE-99), Trento, Italy (1999) 142-156
15. Horacek, H.: Generating Deductive Argumentation in Variable Length. In Proc. of the 7th European Workshop on Natural Langauge Generation, Toulouse, France (1999)
16. Horacek, H.: Tailoring Inference-Rich Descriptions Through Making Compromises Between Conflicting Principles. International Journal on Human Computer Studies, to appear.
17. Horacek, H.: Presenting Equation Proofs in a Human-Oriented Style. In Proc. of EMCSR-2000, Vol. 2, Vienna, Austria (2000) 745-750
18. Huang, X.: Reconstructing Proofs at the Assertional Level. In Proceedings of the 12th International Conference on Automated Deduction, Springer-Verlag (1994) 738-752
19. Huang, X., Fiedler, A.: Proof Presentation as an Application of NLG. In Proc. of the 15th International Joint Conference on Artificial Intelligence (IJCAI-97), Nagoya, Japan (1997) 965-971
20. Johnson-Laird, P., Byrne, R.: Deduction. Ablex Publishing (1990)
21. L‚neburg, H.: Vorlesungen ‚ber Analysis. BI Wissenschaftsverlag (1981)
22. Kohlhase, M., Franke, A.: MBASE: Representing Knowledge and Context for the Integration of Mathematical Software Systems. Journal Symbolic Computation **11** (2000) 1-37
23. McCune, W.: Otter 3.0 Reference Manual and Guide. Technical Report ANL-94/6, Argonne National Laboratory (1994)
24. Melis, E., Leron, U.: A Proof Presentation Suitable for Teaching Proofs. In Proc. of 9th International Conference on Artificial Intelligence in Education AI-ED'99, Le Mans, France (1999)
25. Mellish, C., Evans., R.: Natural Language Generation from Plans. Computational Linguistics **15**(4) (1989) 233-249
26. Mooney, D., Carberry, S., McCoy, K.: The Generation of High-Level Structure for Extended Explanations. In Proc. of COLING-90, Vol. 2, Helsinki, Finland (1990) 276-281
27. Th‚ring, M., Wender, K.: Über kausale Inferenzen beim Lesen. Sprache und Kognition **2** (1985) 76-86
28. Walker, M.: The Effects of Resource Limits and Task Complexity on Collaborative Planning in Dialogue. Artificial Intelligence **85** (1996) 181-243
29. Zukerman, I., McConachy, R.: Generating Concise Discourse that Addresses a User's Inferences. In Proceedings of the 13th International Joint Conference on Artificial Intelligence, Menlo Park, Calif.: International Joint Conferences on Artificial Intelligence, Inc. (1993) 1202-1207

Modeling Interaction and Media Objects

Klaus-Dieter Schewe[1] and Bernhard Thalheim[2]

[1] Massey University, Department of Information Systems, Private Bag 11 222, Palmerston North, New Zealand,
K.D.Schewe@massey.ac.nz

[2] Brandenburg University of Technology at Cottbus, Computer Science Institute, PostBox 101344, D-03013 Cottbus,
thalheim@informatik.tu-cottbus.de

Abstract. Interaction of users with computational devices has to meet the users intention on one side and needs to be specified in a formal manner which can be uniquely interpreted by computers. Thus, we need a model of interaction which meets the intensional understanding of users and which has an extensional description that is directly implementable. In this paper we develop a model for interaction on the basis of the notion of interaction objects. We show further how this notion can be specialized to internet-based interaction. In the later case we use media objects for interaction.

1 Introduction

Interaction and information both are buzzwords of everyday's life. In our understanding, *information*, as processed by humans, is data perceived or noticed, selected and organized by its receiver, because of his/her subjective human interests, originating from his/her instincts, feelings, experience, intuition, common sense, values, beliefs, personal knowledge, or wisdom, simultaneously processed by his/her cognitive and mental processes, and seamlessly integrated in his/her recallable knowledge.

Information systems with SQL interfaces are replaced by systems which are usable by 'everybody' without learning efforts and in an intuitive manner, which are intuitive understandable, and which 'philosophy' or 'mission' can be captured within seconds by novel users[1]. Thus, information systems need to have a natural interaction with the user.

Interaction might be considered as "mutual or reciprocal action or influence" (Websters Dictionary). It is based on objects which can be composed to more complex objects. The composition depends on the context of the object. This approach is similar to approaches developed and used in natural language research and linguistics which we shall use and extend.

Interaction has been neglected for a long time in the area of information systems. This ignorance is based on the belief that information systems interaction

[1] We call in our internet and media projects this requirement 'großmuttersicher' (usable by a grandmother).

M. Bouzeghoub et al. (Eds.): NLDB 2000, LNCS 1959, pp. 313–324, 2001.

can be based on the Seeheim model which adds the presentation component on top of application systems. In internet applications this misconception leads to serious performance problems. Thus, we use tight integration of data, functionality and interaction.

Interaction description can be based on notions developed in linguistics and in movie business. The *story* of interaction with the information system is the intrigue or plot of a narrative work or an account of events. Stories can be played in different *scenarios*. The term scenario in the context of information systems stands for the integrated behavioral contents of the interaction with the information system, i.e. what kind of events the information system will consume and what actions will be triggered as a results.

Scenarios are separated into dialogues. A *dialogue* is - in its widest sense - the recorded conversation of two or more persons, especially as an element of drama or fiction. In a literary form, it is a carefully organized exposition, by means of intended conversation, of contrasting attitudes. Dialogues lent itself easily and frequently to presentation of controversial ideas. Thus, a dialogue can be defined as a written composition in which two or more actors are represented as conserving a similar exchange between a person and something else, e.g. an information system.

Basic media objects can be used similar to words. They are characterized by syntactic expressions, have a semantical meaning and are used within a certain pragmatical framework. The utilization is ruled by the *grammar*. We adopt media objects to their environment by declension, conjugation, add prefixes and suffixes and use them for defining other media objects. Media objects have their principal form. The construction of media objects is based on rules similar to rules used for grammars of natural languages. Therefore the framework is similar to the linguistic framework.

Thus, the *paper* is organized as follows: In the second section we introduce an approach to systematic and well-founded specification of interaction objects. We will use a formal description based on [12]. In the third section we discuss the application of the approach to internet information systems and specialize the interaction object to media objects. This approach has been successfully used for the development of internet information sites such as `www.cottbus.de`.

Due to space limitations we do not discuss the grammatical framework for construction of complex media objects and complex interaction objects. Thus, we concentrate this paper on the description of interaction objects and media objects. They serve as a vehicle for communication and interaction between actors and the system.

2 Interaction Objects

We distinguish between *data types* as means for the conceptual description of values, *database types* for describing database objects, and finally *interaction types* for the description of information service content. On all three layers we obtain schemata, i.e. a type system (with set semantics), a database schemata with databases as instances and an interaction schema.

2.1 The Underlying Database

Following our three-layer view, we may assume an underlying type system. Using abstract syntax, such a type system may be defined as

$$t \quad = \quad b \mid (a_1 : t_1, \ldots, a_n : t_n) \mid \{t\} \mid [t] \quad .$$

Here b represents an arbitrary collection of *base types*, e.g. *BOOL* for boolean values **T** and **F**, *OK* for a single value *ok*, *PIC* for images, *MPIC* for video data, *CARD* and *INT* for numbers, *DATE* for dates, *URL* for URL-addresses, *MAIL* for e-mail-addresses, etc. Finally, $(\cdot)$, $\{\cdot\}$ and $[\cdot]$ are constructors for records, finite sets and finite lists.

Of course, the chosen type system may be different from this one. It may contain other constructors or be more restrictive. Each data type then defines a fixed set of values. We omit the standard inductive definition. On the database layer, it is also not extremely relevant, which data model is chosen. We use the Higher-Order Entity-Relationship model [14], but we shall only talk of *database types*. The following definition captures the gist of the model.

A *database type of level k* has a name E and consists of

- a set $comp(E) = \{r_1 : E_1, \ldots, r_n : E_n\}$ of components with pairwise different role names r_i and database types E_i on levels lower than k with at least one database type of level exactly $k-1$,
- a set $attr(E) = \{a_1, \ldots, a_m\}$ of attributes, each associated with a data type $dom(a_i)$ as its domain,
- and a key $id(E) \subseteq comp(E) \cup attr(E)$.

We shall write $E = (comp(E), attr(E), id(E))$. A database type of level 0 may be called "entity type". A database type of level $k > 0$ is a "relationship type".

A *database schema* $\mathcal{S}$ is a finite set of database types, such that for each $E \in \mathcal{S}$ and each component $r : E'$ of E we get $E' \in \mathcal{S}$.

A *database* $\mathcal{D}$ over $\mathcal{S}$ assigns to each $E \in \mathcal{S}$ a finite set $\mathcal{D}(E)$ of record values $(r_1 : e_1, \ldots, r_n : e_n, a_1 : v_1, \ldots, a_m : v_m)$ with $e_i \in \mathcal{D}(E_i)$ for all components $r_i : E_i$ and values v_i of type $dom(a_i)$ for each attribute a_i such that no two records in $\mathcal{D}(E)$ coincide on the key $id(E)$.
As an extension we may extend database types by operations [11,14], but for the moment we only consider structural aspects.
The following database schema is adapted from the ODIN system [6]:

DEPARTMENT = (∅, {*name, homepage, contact*}, {*name*})
LECTURER = ({*in*:DEPARTMENT}, {*name, position, homepage, email*},
{*name, in*:DEPARTMENT})
PAPER = (∅, {*no, kind, name, level, description, regularity, points*}, {*no*})
PREREQUISITE = ({*of*:PAPER, *for*:PAPER}, ∅, {*of*:PAPER, *for*:PAPER})
LECTURE = ({*goal*:PAPER}, {*semester, schedule, literature, comment*},
{*goal*:PAPER, *semester*})

$$\begin{aligned}
&\text{Course} = (\emptyset, \{\mathit{name}, \mathit{degree}\}, \{\mathit{name}\})\\
&\text{Teacher} = (\{\mathit{who}{:}\text{Lecturer}, \mathit{for}{:}\text{Lecture}\}, \emptyset,\\
&\qquad\qquad \{\mathit{who}{:}\text{Lecturer}, \mathit{for}{:}\text{Lecture}\})\\
&\text{Contribution} = (\{\mathit{for}{:}\text{Course}, \mathit{of}{:}\text{Paper}\}, \{\mathit{optional}\},\\
&\qquad\qquad \{\mathit{for}{:}\text{Course}, \mathit{of}{:}\text{Paper}\})\\
&\text{Involved} = (\{\mathit{who}{:}\text{Department}, \mathit{in}{:}\text{Course}\}, \emptyset,\\
&\qquad\qquad \{\mathit{who}{:}\text{Department}, \mathit{in}{:}\text{Course}\})
\end{aligned}$$

As a domain for an attribute we have for example

$$dom(\text{schedule}) \quad = \quad \{(\text{kind} : STR, \text{time} : TIME, \text{day} : STR, \text{room} : STR)\}$$

in the database type LECTURE *and the corresponding string type STR.*

2.2 Extended Views and Interaction Objects

In order to approach the content description of web pages we adopt the idea of extended views exploited for dialogue systems [11,5].

A *view* V on a database schema $\mathcal{S}$ consists of a view schema $\mathcal{S}_V$ and a defining query q_V, which transforms databases over $\mathcal{S}$ into databases over $\mathcal{S}_V$.The defining query may be expressed in any suitable query language, e.g. query algebra, logic or an SQL-variant.

A *raw interaction type* has a name M and consists of

- a content data type $cont(M)$ with the extension that the place of a base type may be occupied by a pair $\ell : M'$ with a label ℓ and the name M' of a interaction type,
- a finite set $sup(M)$ of raw interaction type names M_i, each of which will be called a supertype of M,
- and a defining query q_M with create-facility such that $(\{t_M\}, q_M)$ defines a view.

Let us extend example presented above. Suppose we want to define a raw interaction type PAPER_W_PREREQ containing information about papers (for a certain course) together with its prerequisites. The content data type will be

$$cont(Paper\_w\_Prereq) \quad = \quad (\dots, \text{pre} : \{p : Paper\_w\_Prereq\})$$

with the dots representing the attributes in the database type PAPER together with their domains.

Finally, we can define the *interaction type* by adding to the raw interaction type operations such a d-operations. Typical d-operations are operations defined for OLAP databases [7].

2.3 Storyboards and Scenarios

Same as with information systems [11] the usage of an information service is determined by the activities of the users. Taking the idea of story modeling outlined above the major goal is to describe possible sequences of user activities. These activities should be associated with media objects.

Since interaction objects are only defined via sites and hence via interaction types, it is a natural abstraction to let also stories occur as instantiations. This leads to scenarios, in which alternatives and even iteration will be enabled.

A *scenario* is a finite, directed graph $\mathcal{G} = (V, E)$, where the nodes are called scenes. With each scene sc we associate a view V_{sc} describing the information consumed by sc and an (optional) user type U_{sc}. Each edge from sc_1 to sc_2 is associated with a data type expressing the information communicated from scene sc_1 to scene sc_2.

The picture in Figure 1 describes a scenario without user types. Let the underlying database schema be the one from our main example . The view associated with the scene select_department simply corresponds to the subschema formed by the database type DEPARTMENT. *The view associated with the scene get_lectures corresponds to the subschema defined by the database types* LECTURER, DEPARTMENT, TEACHER, LECTURE *and* PAPER.

The information communicated from select_department to select_semester can be described by values of type (name : ..., homepage : ..., contact : ...).

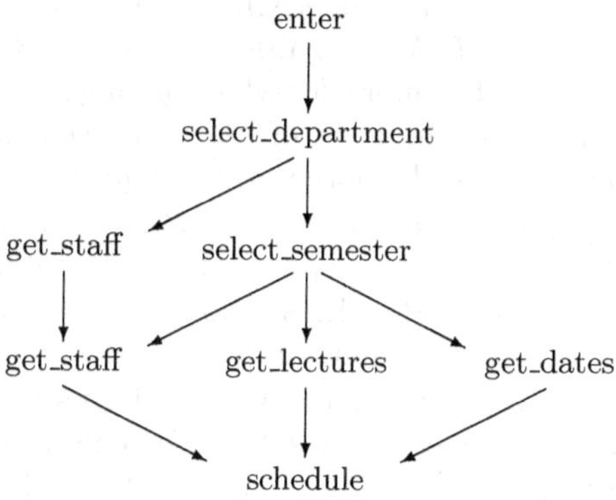

Fig. 1. Sample Scenario

3 Refinement of Interaction Objects to Media Objects

Internet sites can be based on media objects. The content of an internet page is an instance of a complex media object.

3.1 Raw Media Types

For internet site, the introduced interaction object specification is yet not sufficient, since in all these cases the query result will be a set of values. One key concept that is missing in the views is the one of *link*.

In order to introduce links, we observe that links behave similar to references in object oriented databases [11,10]. Therefore, we must allow some kind of "objectification" of values in the query language. This means to transform a set $\{v_1, \ldots, v_m\}$ of values into a set $\{(u_1, v_1), \ldots, (u_m, v_m)\}$ of pairs with new created URLs u_i of type *URL* – more precisely, we first get only surrogates for such URLs. In the same way we may objectify lists, i.e. transform a list $[v_1, \ldots, v_m]$ of values into a list $[(u_1, v_1), \ldots, (u_m, v_m)]$ of pairs. We shall talk of *query languages with create-facility*.

As a second extension we may want to provide also escort information [5], which can be realized by a supertyping mechanism similar to super-dialogue classes [11]. This leads to the definition of *raw media type*.

The *raw media type* is a raw interaction type where we use the above presented extensions. Furthermore, the type t_M is the type arising from $cont(M)$ by substitution of *URL* for all pairs $\ell : M'$. Furthermore operations can be added as shown below.

Same as for database schemata, we may now build finite sets $\mathcal{C}$ of raw media types. If these are closed with respect to supertypes and names occurring in content expressions, we shall talk of a *content schema*.

Given a database $\mathcal{D}$ over the underlying database schema $\mathcal{S}$ the defining queries determine finite sets $\mathcal{D}(M)$ of pairs (u, v) with URLs u and values v of type t_M for each $M \in \mathcal{C}$. Furthermore, for M' occurring in the content expression of M, the URLs occurring in the place of M' must occur in $\mathcal{D}(M')$. The same applies for supertypes. We use the notion *raw site* for the extension of $\mathcal{D}$ to $\mathcal{C}$.

Finally, we collect all raw interaction types $M_1, \ldots, M_k$ with $(u, v_i) \in \mathcal{D}(M_i)$ for a given URL u. The pair $(u, (M_1 : v_1, \ldots, M_k : v_k))$ will be called a *raw interaction object* in the pre-site $\mathcal{D}$. Raw interaction objects provide a formalization and extension of raw information units [5].

For the defining query we first have to create URLs for all papers and prerequisites, then "glue" together the results. We omit the rather complicated expression. The work in [11,14] contains examples for such queries.
The introduction of supertypes in raw interaction types allows repeated parts (structures and operations) to be modeled. In particular, it is possible associate general functionality or escort information with supertypes.

Raw media objects are not yet sufficient for information service modeling. In order to allow the information content to be tailored to specific user needs and presentation restrictions, we must extend raw media types. We shall now discuss the features that make the resulting media types differ from the raw media types.

For many of the values we have to provide not only the type, but also the *measure unit*, e.g. Joule or kcal, PS or kW, cm, mm or m, etc. There exist fixed means for the calculation between the different units. Formally, each base type b should come along with a set $unit(b)$ of possible measure units. Each occurrence of b in the database or the raw media types has to accompanied by one element from $unit(b)$. This lead to an implicit extension of the defining queries q_M. We shall talk of a *unit-extended* raw media type.

Since the raw media types are used to model the content of the information service, order is important. Therefore, we claim that the set constructor should no longer appear in content expressions. Then we need an *ordering-operator* $ord_{\leq}$ which depends on a total order $\leq$ defined on a type t and is applicable to values v of type $\{t\}$. The result $ord_{\leq}(v)$ has the type $[t]$. We shall tacitly assume that ordering operators are used in the defining queries q_M. In this case we talk of an *order-extended* raw media type.

Adhesion as illustrated in [5] on the basis of flat structures introduces a controlled form of information loss. Formally, we define a partial order $\leq$ on content data types, which extends subtyping:

- For any expression exp we have $exp \leq OK$.
- For link expressions we have $(\ell : M') \leq (\ell : M'')$ iff M'' is a direct or indirect (via transitive closure) supertype of M'.
- For record expressions we have $(a_1 : exp_1, \dots, a_m : exp_m) \leq (a_{\sigma(1)} : exp'_{\sigma(1)}, \dots, a_{\sigma(1)} : exp'_{\sigma(n)}$ with injective $\sigma : \{1, \dots, n\} \to \{1, \dots, m\}$ and $exp_{\sigma(i)} \leq exp'_{\sigma(i)}$.
- For list and set structures we have $\{exp\} \leq \{exp'\}$ (or $[exp] \leq [exp']$, respectively) iff $exp \leq exp'$ holds.

Let $cont(M)$ be the content data type of a raw media type M and let $sup(cont(M))$ be the set of all content expressions exp with $cont(M) \leq exp$. A partial order $\preceq_M$ on $sup(cont(M))$ extending the order $\leq$ on content expressions is called an *adhesion order*.
Clearly, $cont(M)$ is minimal with respect to $\preceq_M$. Small elements in $sup(cont(M))$ with respect to $\preceq_M$ define information to be kept together, if possible.

Take the raw media type PAPER_W_PREREQ *sketched in our example. On this we may define an adhesion order* $\preceq = \preceq_{Paper\_w\_Prereq}$ *such that the following holds:*

$$(\text{name} : \dots, \text{level} : \dots) \preceq (\text{pre} : \{p : Paper\_w\_Prereq\}) \preceq (\text{description} : \dots) \preceq (\text{regularity} : \dots, \text{points} : \dots) \preceq (\text{no} : \dots, \text{kind} : \dots) \quad .$$

We omit further details.
Another possibility to tailor the information content of raw media types is to consider dimension hierarchies as in OLAP [7]. Flattening of dimensions results in information growth, its converse in information loss. According to the definitions of the database type and the raw media object type the hierarchy is already implicitly defined by the component or link structures, respectively.

If E' is a component of E corresponding to the role r, then we may replace E by $flat_r(E)$ defined as follows:

$$\begin{aligned} comp(flat_r(E)) &= comp(E) - \{r : E'\} \cup comp(E') \quad , \\ attr(flat_r(E)) &= attr(E) \cup attr(E') \quad \text{and} \\ id(flat_r(E)) &= \begin{cases} id(E) - \{r : E'\} \cup id(E') & \text{for } (r : E') \in id(E) \\ id(E) & \text{else} \end{cases} \quad . \end{aligned}$$

Analogously, we may flatten occurrences of links $\ell : M'$ in content data types cont(M'). We simply substitute cont(M') for $\ell : M'$. The resulting raw media type will be denoted as $flat_\ell(M)$.

Conversely, any subset $P \subseteq comp(E) \cup attr(E)$ allows to replace E by $raise_P(E)$ and a new database type E_{new} defined as follows:

$$\begin{aligned} comp(raise_P(E)) &= comp(E) - P \cup \{r_{\text{new}} : E_{\text{new}}\} \quad , \\ attr(raise_P(E)) &= attr(E) - P \quad , \\ id(raise_P(E)) &= \begin{cases} id(E) - P \cup \{r_{\text{new}} : E_{\text{new}}\} & \text{for } P \cap id(E) \neq \emptyset \\ id(E) & \text{else} \end{cases} \\ comp(E_{\text{new}}) &= P \cap comp(E) \quad , \\ attr(E_{\text{new}}) &= P \cap attr(E) \quad \text{and} \\ id(E_{\text{new}}) &= \begin{cases} id(E) & \text{for } id(E) \subseteq P \\ P & \text{else} \end{cases} \quad . \end{aligned}$$

Analogously, we may define $raise_{exp}(M)$ for a content expression occurring within $cont(M)$. This will introduce a new link expression replacing exp.

For a raw media type M let $\bar{H}(M)$ be the set of all raw media types arising from M by applying a sequence of flat- and raise-operations to raw media types or underlying database types. A *set of hierarchical versions* of M is a finite subset $H(M)$ of $\bar{H}(M)$ with $M \in H(M)$.
Note that the defining queries are changed according to *flat* and *raise*. Furthermore, each adhesion order $\preceq_M$ on M induces an adhesion order $\preceq_{M'}$ on each element $M' \in H(M)$.

A *media type* is a unit-extended, order-extended raw media type M together with an adhesion order $\preceq_M$ and a set of hierarchical versions $H(M)$.
Then a *media schema* is defined in the same way as a content schema replacing raw media types by media types. A database $\mathcal{D}$ over the underlying database schema $\mathcal{S}$ extends to a unique raw site. Furthermore, we may extend $\mathcal{D}$ to all hierarchical versions $M' \in H(M)$ and all $M'' \succ_{M'} M'$ defined by the adhesion orders. This wide extension of $\mathcal{D}$ will be called a *site*.

Finally, we collect all media types $M_1, \dots, M_k$ together with their hierarchical versions and types defined by the adhesion order such that $(u, v_i) \in \mathcal{D}(M_i)$ holds for a given URL u. The pair $(u, (M_1 : v_1, \dots, M_k : v_k))$ will be called a *media object* in the site $\mathcal{D}$. Media objects provide a formalization and extension of information units [5].

3.2 Usage Modeling

The introduction of media objects as instantiations of media types provides a formal mechanism for web site modeling. However, it does not yet answer the questions concerning the purpose of the web site, its anticipated usage and the users to be supported. These questions shall be addressed now.

For a general view of system usage it is advantageous to think in terms of "stories" [3,14], a term adapted from movie production. Basically, a *story* is a sequence of user activities usually called "scenes". In our case we think of each scene to be supported by some visited page. Thus, roughly spoken a *scene* consists of a page and a selected activity on that page.

Sample stories are given by a user entering the site, getting an overview over a certain topic, e.g. a list of lectures in a specific department and a specific semester, selecting a certain portion of the information and finally invoke an action such as booking, registration or simply printing, before leaving the site. Another possible story could have the general overview being replaced by a search access or the user may have a concrete goal and proceed directly to the pages supporting this goal.

Users are characterized by the user profile [1] which is used for adaptation of systems to the actual user. Users experience differs in experience with the system, with computers in general, and the task domain, in their abilities, skills and knowledge. They are abstractly specified as actors. The *actor* specification we are using includes the following:

Roles the actor plays in the interaction with the system. Roles of actors are based on *actors context*, *actors rights* and *responsibilities*, *actors intention* and *actors behavior stereotype*.
Profile of the actor, i.e. *ability profile*, *skill profile*, *knowledge* and *education level*, *interaction profile*, *information profile* and *Experience*.
Tasks the actor has to solve during interaction.

Actors perform tasks which imply the information need of the actor. The description of the actor is used for the selection of the grammatical rules used for the composition of complex interaction and media objects. We design generic, adaptable interaction object and specialize the interaction objects according to the profile of the actor [8,9].

The goal of actor profiles is to support significantly different user behaviour. In order to describe such user profiles, we start with a finite set Δ of *user dimensions*, e.g. Δ = experience, skill, training, goal-orientation, presentation_preferences. The set of dimensions describes the guidelines for user classification.

For each dimension $\delta \in \Delta$ we assume to be given a scale $sc(\delta)$. Formally, a *scale* is a totally ordered set. For example, the scale for goal-orientation may be

$$sc(\text{goal} - \text{orientation}) = \{\text{surfer}, \text{navigator}, \text{searcher}\}$$

with surfer $\leq$ navigator $\leq$ searcher. As another example consider

$$sc(\text{presentation\_preferences}) = \{\text{detailed}, \text{normal}, \text{condensed}, \text{terse}\}$$

with detailed $\leq$ normal $\leq$ condensed $\leq$ terse.

Let $\Delta = \{\delta_1, \ldots, \delta_n\}$ be a set of user dimensions. Then the *set of user profiles* (or the *user-grid*) over Δ is $gr(\Delta) = sc(\delta_1) \times \ldots \times sc(\delta_n)$. A *user type* over Δ is a convex region $U \subseteq gr(\Delta)$.

We already used user types, i.e. sets of user profiles, in the definition of scenarios. This indicates which stories will be supported for which user profiles and consequently show, which media objects will be used for this purpose. This gives rise to certain completeness criteria, e.g. to cover all supported profiles by the media schema and vice versa.

Our remaining goal concerns the presentation of media objects. Most web pages have been developed with HTML, but unfortunately HTML mixes content and layout. We want to follow the ideas of the UFIS project – partly based on

XML – and separate content from layout. Media objects provide the central means for content modeling.

For presentation modeling we adapt the metaphor of a container [5]. The underlying picture is the following: Selected information will be wrapped out loaded into a (generic) container, shipped to the user and then unloaded with the help of a browser. So the goal is to provide such containers.

Ideally, containers should be usable for different contents, but nevertheless the design of container is heavily influenced by the usage of media objects in the scenarios, the user profile and the technical constraint arising from size and presentation facilities of the supported presentation devices.

For instance, we may assume a scale for the size of the devices ranging from tiny (as for WAP handies) over small (for videotext screens) to normal, large and huge (for different kinds of screens). It might be the case that not all sizes are to be supported. Formally, such a scale is a totally ordered set analogous to the scales for user dimensions.

Other technical constraints may be the unability to present images or video / audio information or channel bandwidth (e.g., for mobile devices).

Basically, the possible content of a container can be described by a content data type same as for media types. Any actual content must fit into this type, i.e. it must give rise to a supertype. Furthermore, the content data type must be accompanied by some presentation layout matching the technical constraints. This layout may include constants such as recurring pictures, background, etc. It may be realized by a parameterized HTML document.

A *container* has a name C and consists of a content $cont(C)$ and a presentation layout $lay(C)$.

Loadability of a media object $(u, (M_1 : v_1, \dots, M_k : v_k))$ into a container C holds, if the content data type $cont(M_i)$ is a supertype of $cont(C)$ for at least one i. Since M_i arises from a media type including versions originating from adhesion or hierarchy, this implies that v_i matches the content description of the container C.

The *wrapping* of the media object $(u, (M_1 : v_1, \dots, M_k : v_k))$ into the container C then means the identification of the suitable M_i in order to load a maximum amount of information. Formally, this means to choose $cont(M_i)$ minimal, so that loadability can be guaranteed.

Finally, the *loading* of the container consists in the generation of the page replacing the parameters by the loaded information.

3.3 Media Object Composition and Functional Support

Media objects can be rather complex. For this reason, users need to supported by functionality of the interaction management system. This functionality can be based on generic functions derived from the general specification whenever a media object is specified similar to generic operations such as *insert*, *delete* and *update* in the case of relational databases.

The functionality required for media objects can be classified as follows:

Main functions which need to be supplied for each of the sites are

- ***navigation functions*** enabling the actor in vertical (into the depth of the media objects provided so far), horizontal (local navigation through a neighborhood function) and global (sitemap, landmark, navigation facilities, global search, external) navigation,
- ***search functions*** which allow a more sophisticated search in the sites. Search functions are based on the defining query of the raw interaction object. They can be differentiated into *search functions for selection* of objects, *functions for quick or survey search* among the set of media objects, and *media object generating search functions*]which enable the actor to set-up his/her own search media object.

Import/export functions for the actors purpose such as

- ***export support functions*** for printing, storing, extraction etc. of the (partial) content of media objects,
- ***import support functions*** enabling actors in sophisticated data and information input during interaction with the site.

Support functions supporting the user during utilization of the site such as

- ***indexing functions*** representing similar to dockets the meta-description of the media objects and enabling the actor to use the meta-description for task solution and
- ***marking functions*** which support the user during during utilization of sets of objects.

Representation function for various display types of results obtained during browsing through media objects.

Using the above presented codesign approach we can easily integrate functionality specification into media object specification.

4 Conclusion

Interaction has been neglected for a long time in information systems design. It has become more important with the advent of internet applications. Internet applications which have to be more efficient cannot be based on the classical Seeheim or the Arche architectures separating the interaction engine from the application engine. At the same time, we need a formal model for interaction objects and more specifically for media objects. These objects are based on the local communication structure such as extended views and use a part of the functionality of the used machinery. In order the develop objects which can be needlessly integrated into the information systems environment we based the media and interaction objects on the theory of types.

The proposed approach has successfully been used during the development of sophisticated internet services. The media objects presented in this paper are the basis for information sites such as town and regional information sites. At the same time, automatic adaptation of interfaces can be performed in dependence on the communication profile, the actors profiles and the technical environment currently in use.

Interaction objects and media objects can be composed to more complex objects. The composition is based on a set of grammatical rules. In order to apply those rules we classify the objects according to their utilization. This classification is similar to the classification of words into adjectives, adverbs, pronoun, verbs, etc. The grammatical rules for constructing complex interaction object are beyond the scope of this paper and will be presented in a forthcoming paper.

Acknowledgement

We would like to thank the members of the Cottbus *net* and RADD project teams for their stimulating discussions and their effort to implement our ideas.

References

1. M. Altus, User modeling for conceptual database design based on an extended entity relationship model: A preliminary study. Proc. 3rd ADBIS'96, Moscow, 1996, 46-51.
2. O. De Troyer. Designing well-structured websites: Lessons learned from database schema methodology. Proc. ER'98, Springer LNCS 1507, 1998, 51-64.
3. T. Feyer and B. Thalheim. E/R based scenario modeling for rapid prototyping of web information services. Advances in Conceptual Modeling, Springer LNCS 1727, 1999, 253-263.
4. P. Fraternali and P. Paolini, A conceptual model and a tool environment for developing more scalable, dynamic and customizable web applications. Proc. EDBT '98, Springer LNCS 1377, 1998, 422-435.
5. T. Feyer, K.-D. Schewe, and B. Thalheim. Conceptual design and development of information services. Proc. ER'98, Springer LNCS 1507, 1998, 7-20.
6. O. Kao, G.R. Joubert, T. Ripke, J. Engehausen. ODIN – Online data management via internet. *EMMSEC* poster presentation, Stockholm (Sweden) 1999.
7. J. Lewerenz, K.-D. Schewe, and B. Thalheim, Modelling data warehouses and OLAP applications by means of dialogue objects. Proc. ER'99, Springer LNCS 1728, 1999, 354-368.
8. T. Schmidt, Konzepte, Betrachtungen und Lösungen für die Basistechnologie eines Informationssystems – Clientseite. M.Sc. Thesis. BTU Cottbus 1998.
9. R. Schwietzke, Konzepte, Betrachtungen und Lösungen für die Basistechnologie eines Informationssystems – Serverseite. M.Sc. Thesis. BTU Cottbus 1998.
10. D. Schwabe, and G. Rossi, Developing hypermedia applications using OOHDM. Proc. Workshop on Hypermedia Development. Pittsburgh (Pennsylvania), 1998.
11. K.-D. Schewe and B. Schewe, View-Centered Conceptual Modelling – an Object Oriented Approach. Proc. ER'96, Springer LNCS 1157, 1996, 357-371.
12. K.-D. Schewe and B. Thalheim, Fundamental concepts of object oriented databases. Acta Cybernetica, 11(4), 1993, 49 - 81.
13. L. Seger, Making a script great. Samuel French, Hollywood, 1994.
14. B. Thalheim, Entity-relationship modeling - Foundations of database technology. Springer, Berlin, 2000.

Validating Conceptual Models – Utilising Analysis Patterns as an Instrument for Explanation Generation

Maria Bergholtz, Paul Johannesson

Department of Computer and Systems Sciences
Stockholm University and the Royal Institute of Technology
Electrum 230, S-164 40 Kista, Sweden
{maria, pajo}@dsv.su.se

Abstract. In this paper we outline an architecture and design principles to support the validation of conceptual models by generation of explanations in natural language. The architecture utilises the concept of analysis patterns as a context for explaining implicit dependencies between different parts of the model. In addition Toulminís argumentation model is used to structure the interaction between user and system. We argue that this architecture assists in building explanation generation systems that are highly interactive and provide an adequate amount of information for different user categories.

1 Introduction

The main challenge in systems development is that of building the *right* system ñ one that meets the user needs at a reasonable cost. The key to achieving this goal lies in the early stages of systems development, i. e. in the analysis and representation of the requirements of the system to be built. It is essential that the constructed model of the system correctly represents the piece of reality under consideration and the userís requirements. The process of ensuring that a model possesses these qualities is called validation.

Validation is often an informal process where the different stakeholders participate, including people with limited knowledge of modelling and systems design. However, people who are unfamiliar with modelling languages may have severe difficulties in understanding and thus validating a model. Furthermore, the sheer size and complexity of a model may make it difficult even for experienced designers to validate a model.

Several techniques to ease the validation process have been proposed. One approach is to introduce *graphical symbols*, [11], or *user defined concepts,* [18]. Another approach is to *paraphrase* parts of the conceptual model into natural language [2], [3], [19]. Model *simulation* can be used for observing and experimenting with the dynamic properties of a model, [21]. *Explanation generation* techniques have been used to integrate the techniques mentioned above. Explanation generation extends paraphrasing by including question-answer facilities that interactively supports a user exploring a model. Model simulation can be complemented by explanation generation that guides a user through the execution and

M. Bouzeghoub et al. (Eds.): NLDB 2000, LNCS 1959, pp. 325-339, 2001.

explains the systemís behaviour. Explanation generation has previously been used mainly for expert systems, e. g. the Explainable Expert System (EES), [17], which provides natural language explanations of rule-based systems based on Rhetorical Structure Theory (RST), [14].

Recently, there has also been an interest in using explanation generation for the purpose of validating conceptual models. A problem in this respect is that of finding a domain independent context in which to structure the explanations. Earlier work [8], [5] use RST to create coherent language output. However, this approach require customisation for each domain since typical RST-relations have no correspondence to conventional conceptual model constructs. An alternative is found in [4] where Toulminís argumentation model [20] is mapped onto a conceptual model in order to structure the user dialog. However, the mapping of the constituents of the argumentation model and conceptual model is still rather coarse, which results in relatively unstructured explanations.

In this paper we introduce an additional level into the explanation architecture proposed by [4] by utilising the concept of *analysis patterns* as a context for structuring natural language explanations of conceptual models.

The purpose of this paper is to propose an architecture for explanation generation of object oriented conceptual models. The work reported upon in this paper builds on the work of [4] and extends it by utilising the concept of analysis patterns as a context for structuring natural language explanations of conceptual models. The paper is organised as follows. The next section introduces the modelling language. Section 3 discusses analysis patterns and data abstractions as a context for explaining conceptual models. In section 4 an architecture for explanation generation is outlined. Section 5 and 6 elaborate on this architecture by discussing explanations of static and behavioural parts of the conceptual model. Section 7 summarises the paper and gives directions for future work.

2 Conceptual Models and Modelling Formalism

A conceptual model [1] consists of a conceptual schema and a corresponding information base, i. e. the instances corresponding to the types in the conceptual schema. The conceptual schema, in turn, can be viewed as a language (i. e. enumerations of entity types, attributes, relations) to describe the phenomena in the system to be modelled, a set of derivation rules and integrity constraints and a set of event-rules describing the behaviour of the object system.

For the purpose of explaining conceptual models, the Unified Modelling Language (UML) is chosen as modeling notation. An example UML class diagram and part of the corresponding object (instance) diagram is shown in Figure 1 and Figure 2, respectively.

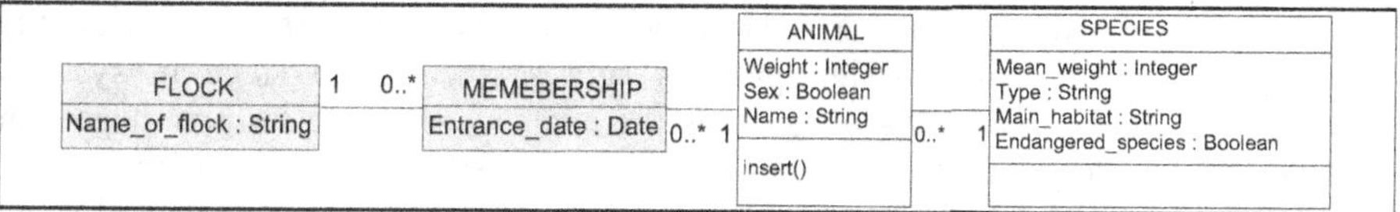

Fig.1. A UML Class Diagram

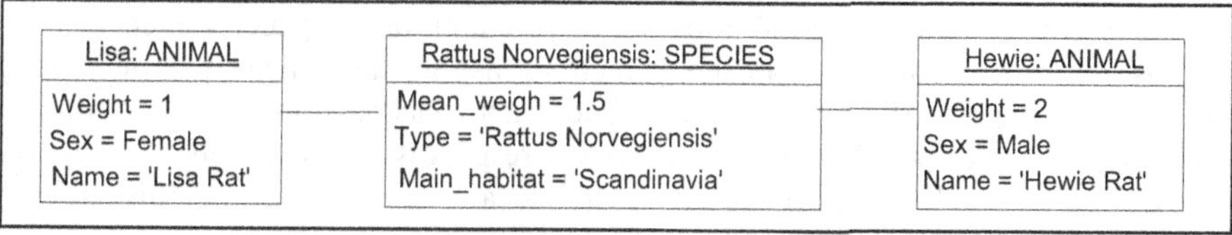

Fig.2. Part of a UML Object Diagram corresponding to the diagram of Figure 1.

3 Patterns and Data Abstractions for Explanation Generation

When designing an explanation architecture for conceptual models it is essential to investigate *what* concepts to explain. Another question is how large parts of the schema should be included in an explanation. Much of the semantics in the conceptual schema is given by the graphical notation itself and an appropriate choice of names for classes and associations. Simply paraphrasing, for instance, an association between two classes may not contribute much to the userís understanding of the schema. Even for a person with only rudimentary knowledge of a modelling language, inspecting a graphical schema-fragment may be more informative than reading a text in natural language describing the same phenomena. What is not explicitly graphically captured is harder to make inferences about. The overall semantics of the conceptual model is a result of dependencies between different parts of the conceptual model. Explanations of too large fragments of the model may, on the other hand, prove counter productive. [8] states that it is not very effective to paraphrase large parts of the conceptual model, since the user may find the paraphrased text too general or unfocused. [4] argues that short texts or visualisations that answer focused questions about the structure or behaviour about a model in the context of a special use case, are much more effective. Especially effective are answers that combine information from different parts of the conceptual model, for instance by combining static and dynamic aspects [2], [4].

3.1 Analysis Patterns

Our approach is that the concept of *analysis patterns* may be part of a solution to the problem of finding a context that provides an adequate abstraction level for effectively explaining the semantics of different model constructs and naturally limiting the scope of the explanations to include a relevant part of the conceptual schema.

The notion of patterns come in a large number of varieties. One of these is the *design pattern*, [7]. While design patterns address the design stage in systems development, an *analysis pattern* concerns the analysis and specification stage. An analysis pattern describes, at an arbitrary level of abstraction, a set of real-world objects, their interrelationships, and the rules that govern their behaviour and state. Examples of analysis patterns are the patterns in [6], the data model patterns of [9] and domain abstractions discussed in [12]. These patterns may be viewed as conceptual patterns (i. e. small parts of a conceptual model), to be used, and reused, as an already constructed solution to a modelling problem. In this paper we are viewing analysis patterns from the opposite direction, as an instrument for generating explanations of relationships between constructs in a conceptual model in a validation situation. The use of patterns, in general, in this respect is not very well investigated. One example is [13] where design patterns are used for validating system requirements.

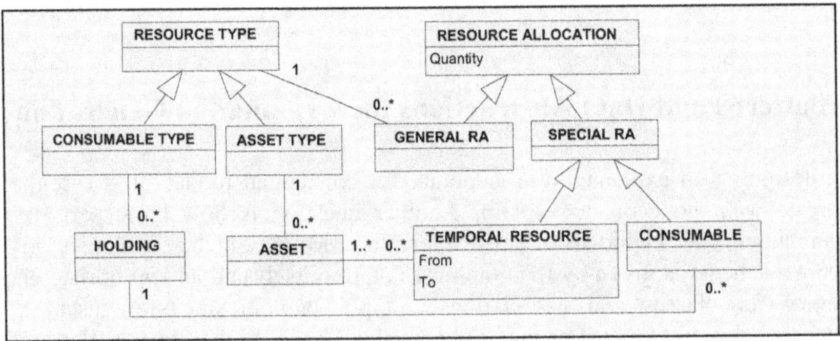

Fig.3. Resource allocation analysis pattern [6] (modified)

In Figure 3 an example analysis pattern, *resource allocation* [6], is given. The resource allocation pattern models different types of allocation of resources. Some resources are consumed in an activity, e. g. in surgery blood plasma is consumed. Other resources, assets, can be reused, e. g. a nurse. The consumable type classifies the consumable resources while individual assets are categorised by the asset type. A temporal resource is a specific resource allocation of an asset, whereas a consumable is a resource allocation of a consumable type from a certain holding (finite store). General resource allocation is used to represent what resource types are required for a certain activity. This feature is shown in the class diagram of Figure 4 where the resource allocation pattern is used to model the allocation of resources for patient activities in a health-care system. Figure 5 shows part of a corresponding object diagram.

3.2 Additional Data Abstractions for Explanation Generation

We will include three additional data abstractions, the semantics of which we believe also offers an adequate context to create explanations in natural language of different parts of conceptual models.

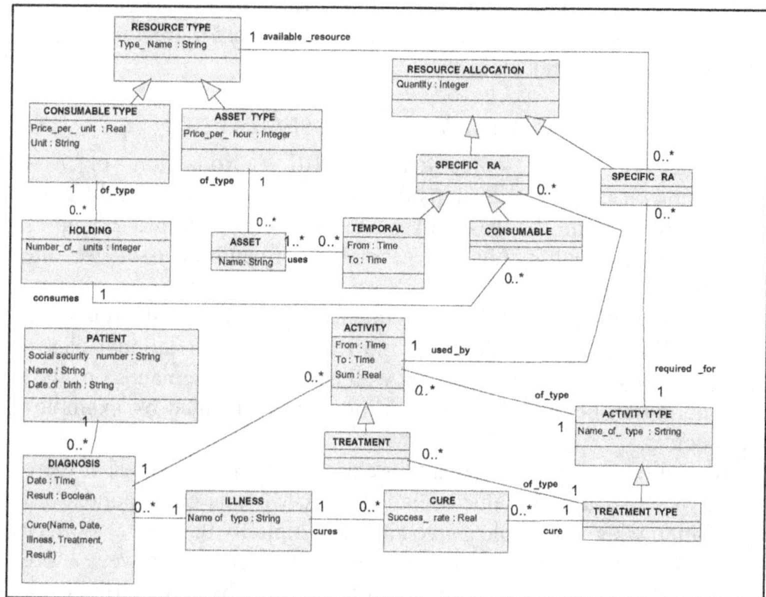

Fig. 4. A class diagram utilising the resource allocation analysis pattern

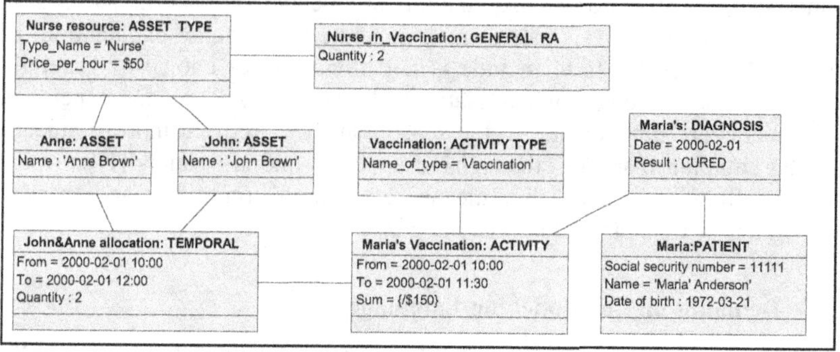

Fig. 5. An object diagram corresponding to the class diagram of Figure 4

GENERALISATION HIERARCHY

A hierarchy of classes related by means of generalisation relations connecting specific classes (subclasses) to general classes (super classes). The subclass inherits attributes, methods and associations from the super class and may also have additional attributes associations and methods (or method implementations) of its own.

POWER TYPE

[15] defines a power type as an object type whose instances are subtypes of another object type. The Asset type class of Figure 4 is a power type for the Asset class.

Instances of the Asset type class are the different categories of recources, for instance a nurse type or surgeon type. Instances of the Asset class are the surgeon ëMolly Browní and nurse ëLisa Andersoní.

RELATIONAL CLASSES (ASSOCIATION CLASSES)

An important concept is objectification [10] (introduction of a relational class/association class) of relationships that occur time and again in different analysis patterns and even form the basis of some of these patterns, examples are the accountability pattern with its numerous variations [6] and the asset structure element models of [9].
We will give an example of a description in natural language of the relational class. In a user dialog, this text will serve as a motivation why a relational class has been introduced into the conceptual schema as well as giving the semantics of the relational class. The definition below should be additionally augmented by example instances from the schema.

> A relational class (or association class) must be introduced if there exists either a multivalued relation (in UML this corresponds to a relation where both roles have either multiplicity 0..* or 1..*) *where the relation has properties of its own* or a relation between more than two classes. The properties of the relation become attributes of the relational class.

One reason to include additional, generally smaller, modelling concepts in addition to the analysis patterns into the explanation architecture is that in some situations explaining an entire analysis pattern may generate too large an explanation. Exactly what modelling constructs to include is not obvious. Our choice of generalisation, power-type and relational (or association) classes is based on our experience that these concepts are fundamental in the sense that they are used more frequently in a modelling situation than are other related concepts and are generally represented in most modelling languages by means of classes (entities) and associations (relationships) without any additional language symbols.

3.3 Demands on the Modelling Language

One problem in utilising analysis patterns in an explanation architecture is that this puts explicit demands on the modelling language to be used. The notation must include language fragments for the purpose of classifying objects and associations as constituting an analysis pattern. One approach is that the language contains explicit (preferably graphical) symbols for different pattern types. It is difficult to envisage how this approach would be carried out in practice, though. The complexity of the language would increase to a level where the advantages of the graphical notation may be diminished by an introduction of too many new symbols. Another approach is to incorporate the use of analysis patterns into CASE tools in the sense that the tool aids the user in constructing conceptual schemas by offering a variety of different domain independent analysis patterns to be used as building blocks in the schema. In either approach the semantics of the different analysis patterns will be present in the CASE tool. An explanation component can thus base the generation of explanations in natural language on the constraints and dependencies pertaining to a generic pattern. One possibility is to make use of ëcanned textí, a hard coded explanation in natural language, describing the semantics of different constructs of the conceptual model. Such a library of explanations in natural language corresponding to different generic constructs of the modelling language may either be maintained by an explanation component for conceptual models or pertain to the specification of the modelling language.

However, state of the art for CASE-tools of today does not generally include the concept of analysis patterns. We are aware of very few tools that aid the user in utilising analysis patterns in requirements engineering even if some attempts to enlarge and refine the diagramming techniques in this direction have been made. One example can be found in the utilisation of stereotypes in the class diagrams of UML where a stereotype can be used to denote the concept of power-types.

4 Argumentation Model

In organising the generation of explanations some problems inherent in text generation must be addressed, for instance what is the focus of the explanation, on what level of detail should an explanation be given, for whom is the explanation given, what sources of information should be used in the explanation, etc. These issues are mainly solved by a *deep generator* (i. e. a planner and organiser of a coherent text, for a detailed explanation please refer to [16]). In addition, a surface generator is needed to realise the output from the deep generator, i. e. a grammar to create syntactically correct sentences and a lexicon to generate the words. The surface grammar and lexicon are not addressed in this paper.

Even if it is natural to explain a certain schema fragment in the context of the analysis pattern to which it belongs, some kind of argumentation model is needed to structure the dialog between user and system. An argumentation model that is domain independent and where the constituents are easily mapped onto the specification of a conceptual model is Toulminís argumentation model [20]. We argue that this argumentation model and its mapping onto the different levels of the conceptual model can be used as a framework for the design of a deep generator.

4.1 Basic Constituents of Toulmin's Argumentation Model

The starting point of an argument is a *claim* which is a sentence asserting some proposition. The claim is related to *grounds* supporting the claim. If the presumed listener to the argument is not convinced that the claim holds on basis of the grounds the argument may continue with a *warrant,* i.e. a relation between a ground and a claim showing that the grounds are indeed relevant for the claim. A warrant has usually the form of a general rule that is applicable to the case at hand. If grounds and warrant should not provide enough evidence for the listener, a supportive argument can be given in the form of a *backing.* Normally backing takes the form of rules at a higher level than the warrant.

4.2 Mapping of Toulmin's Model to a Conceptual Model

The constituents of Toulminís argumentation model can be mapped to a specification of a conceptual model in a way that makes it possible to structure the explanations by gathering information from different levels and components of the conceptual model. If a user questions the grounds for a specific claim, the warrant may include additional information from the conceptual model and forms the basis for a more detailed explanation. User-queries involving phenomena in the conceptual model may be given at the instance-, schema-, or meta-schema levels. On the schema-level we distinguish between a query pertaining to an isolated schema-fragment and queries made in the larger context of an analysis pattern. If the query is given at the schema-level (for instance ìWhat is an *animal*?î) it is appropriate to structure the system answers so that the grounds are given at the schema-level, the warrant at a more detailed schema-level involving a larger part of the schema corresponding the analysis pattern to which the schema fragment belongs and the backing, finally, is given at the meta-schema level. An argument and its mapping to the different levels of the conceptual model can be described as shown in Figure 6.

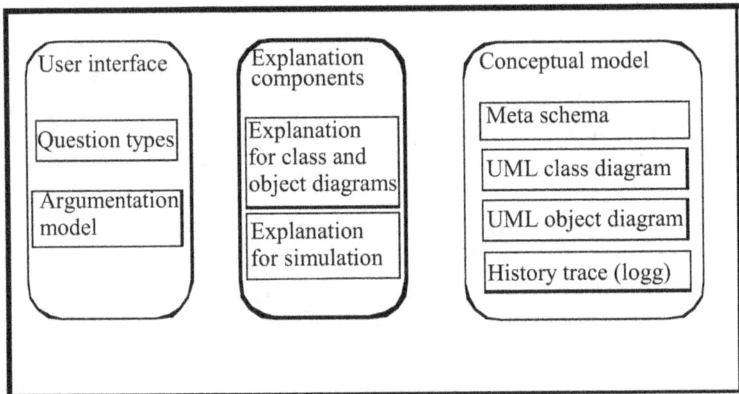

Fig. 6. Mapping of a conceptual model on Toulminís model

The basic idea of Figure 6 is that when a claim is given on a certain conceptual level the system answers by giving an explanation on the same level or the level immediately following the claim-level (corresponding to the grounds). If the user requests more information, the next level of the conceptual model will be utilised in the warrant. The mapping between conceptual levels and constituents of Toulminís argumentation model is complete only in the case when the query is given at the schema level and we believe that explanations designed according to Toulminís model are probably most useful for claims on the instance or schema-level. Queries at meta-level (i. e. queries regarding the modelling language) may be warranted or backed by exemplifications at the instance level as is indicated in Figure 6.

4.3 Query Categories

The issue of how user input should be given has not yet been addressed. For the purpose of this paper, our approach is to let the user interact directly with a graphic view of the conceptual model by means of point and click interaction, in which case no parsing of user input is necessary. Follow up questions from the user could also be managed via a graphical user interface where the system displays the possible alternatives. This includes giving more detailed information as well as letting the user query part of an explanation, for instance by highlighting key-words used in the explanation.

In this respect it is necessary to decide what kind of questions and explanations the system should be able to answer. [4] has addressed the issue and identify at least four different question types that a user may be able to ask when exploring a conceptual model. The first kind of question is the *structural* question that asks about the structure of a construct, its properties and relationships to other constructs as well as the constraints pertaining to the construct. The second type of question is the *causal* question that asks about the cause of a construct, i.e. the events that have made it to come into existence. The third type is the reason question that asks about the *reason* for a construct, i. e. why the construct has been introduced and what purpose it serves. Finally, there is the *procedural* question that asks how something is carried out. The boundaries between the question types are not absolute. A user query may fall into several, if not all, of the identified question categories.

4.4 An Explanation Generation Architecture

The architecture of an explanation generation system is outlined in Figure 7. The first module is the user interface, which defines the argumentation model to be used for structuring the dialog between user and system. In addition to the argumentation model, a set of question types is listed in order to provide alternatives for the user. These question types correspond to the question types identified above. The second module contains the explanation components, which provide two different validation techniques: explanations of class and object diagrams and explanations of the results of simulation. The last module contains the different components of the conceptual model to be explained.

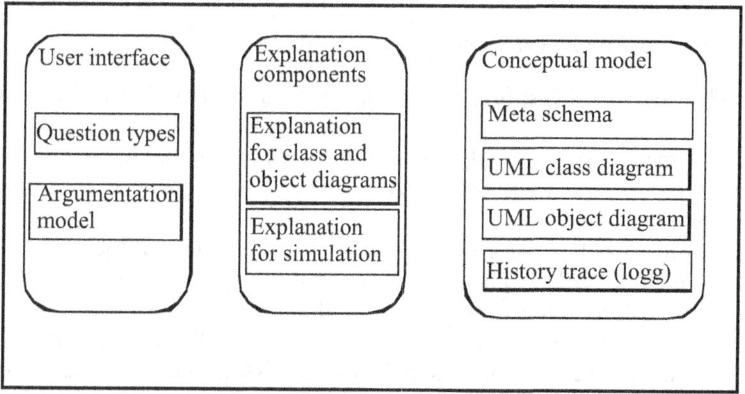

Fig. 7. Architecture of an explanation generation system

The following three design principles are utilised by the explanation system for structuring explanations in natural language of conceptual models:

- For each construct in a conceptual model, determine which type of questions can be asked about it: structural, causal, procedural and reason.
- For each model construct and identified question type, determine what parts of the conceptual model are useful to include in an explanation: *Level of conceptual model, Analysis pattern(s) or data abstraction to which a queried concept belongs, Relevant dynamic rules*
- For each model construct, question type and corresponding information from the conceptual schema, apply the argumentation model to structure the information into appropriate units.

The following sections illustrate how the design principles described above can be applied to generate explanations of conceptual models in natural language. Example UML diagrams are depicted in Figure 1, Figure 2, Figure 4 and Figure 5.

5 Explanation for Class- and Object Diagrams

5.1 Structural and Reason Questions – Combining the Class Diagram and Object Diagram

Queries about the static schema on different levels, instance, schema, detailed schema fragment (for instance an analysis pattern) and meta schema, may be classified into at least three of the types of questions described in the previous chapter. The most obvious question is probably the structural one asking about the structure of a certain phenomenon or why a certain fact holds. The reason question, why a construct has been introduced and what purpose it serves, is very closely related to the structural question and we believe that for the sake of explaining the static class- and object diagrams, the two question types may be merged into one structural-reason question type.

Utilising the semantics pertaining to a UML association class

USER: What is a **membership**? *(Schema-level structural query concerning the class diagram of Figure 1)*
SYSTEM: A membership is used to denote that a certain animal has entered a certain flock on one particular date. *(grounds at the schema-level)*
USER: I donít understand.
SYSTEM: A relational class (or association class) must be used if there exists either a multivalued relation *with properties of its own* or a relation between more than two classes. An animal may enter several flocks and a flock may have many members. To model that an animal became a member of a particular flock on a certain time an association class membership is required to relate exactly one instance of animal to exactly one instance of flock with the property ëentrance_dateí set to the time of the animals admission in the flock. *(warrant at detailed schema-level)*
USER: I donít understand.

SYSTEM: The association class defines only one legal combination of each pair of classes related through the association class. This implies that there can only exist one membership for every pair of animal-flock. *(backing at the meta-schema level where one constraint belonging to the UML association class serves to motivate why the particular schema-fragment is used).*

Utilising resource allocation pattern [6] and generalisation

USER: I doní t understand the purpose of the **temporal class**. (*Schema-level structural query concerning the class diagram of Figure 4*)
SYSTEM: A temporal (allocation) is used to denote that certain resources are allocated for a certain period of time. *(Grounds at schema-level).*
USER: I doní t understand
SYSTEM: A temporal is a special kind of a resource allocation. Certain resources are consumed during usage, for instance a package of plaster, whereas other resources (people, machines etc.) can be reallocated many times. Resource allocations for the different types of resources have different properties which is displayed in the schema as a generalisation hierarchy where the class temporal have additional attributes that do not belong to any other subtype of resource allocation, namely the attributes ëFromí and ëToí. These attributes serve the purpose of allocating certain assets (that is non-consumable resources) for a certain period of time. The resource allocation analysis pattern includes additional subtypes to the class resource allocation. Important is the general resource allocation class, which is used as a dictionary to show what resources are *required*, as opposed to actually utilised or booked, for a certain kind of activity. *(Warrant at detailed schema (analysis pattern) level)*
USER: What is a **generalisation hierarchy**? (Meta-level structural follow-up query in the context of resource allocation)
SYSTEM: A generalisation hierarchy is used to denote that certain phenomena constitute subsets of other phenomena. It consists of several classes related by means of generalisation relations (graphically depicted by a solid arrow with a hollow end). These relations go from the more specific class, the subclass, to the more general class, the superclass. The subclasses implicitly have the same properties, relations and operations as the superclass as well as additional properties, relations and operations (or implementations of operations) of its own. The properties and relations common to all members of a generalisation hierarchy are accordingly placed in the topmost superclass in the hierarchy while more specific properties are propagated down to an appropriate level where the property in question apply to *all* potential subclasses of the superclass of that level. In this case resource allocation constitute the top node of a generalisation hierarchy. There are two subclasses to a resource allocation: general resource allocation and specific resource allocation where special resource allocation, in turn, is the superclass of the temporal and consumable classes. *(Grounds on meta-level exemplified on schema level).*

5.2 Causal Question – Combining Static and Dynamic Model

User queries may be causal, in which case the explanation system must deliver an event or a sequence of events that lead to the introduction of a certain modelling construct or instance of such a construct. There is no clear answer to how many events should contribute to the answer to a causal question. The grounds may include a single event, which may be augmented by an explanation of the pre- and post conditions of the event (corresponding to the warrant). Furthermore, the dialog structure for causal questions are not independent of the dialog structure of the structural and reason questions described above. It may be beneficial to include explanations of structural nature together with the displayed event(s). This is particularly useful when the events execute and maintain dependencies and derivations between instances that belong to a certain data abstraction or analysis pattern. An example of this is given below:

Utilising the semantics of the concept power types

USER: Why has ëRattus Norvegicusí mean weight 1.5 lb? *(Instance-level causal query concerning object diagram of Figure 2)*
SYSTEM: Because there has been exactly two rats inserted, ëHewieí and ëLisaí, belonging to the species ëRattus Norvegicusí and their weights are 1lb and 2lp respectively. The mean-weight of ëRattus Norvegicusí is accordingly updated to 1.5 lb. *(Grounds given at instance level).*
USER: I doní t understand.
SYSTEM: ëRattus Norvegicusí is an instance of the class species, whereas ëHewieí and ëLisaí are instances of the class animal. ëMean-weightí is a derived attribute calculated from the actual individual weights of all animal instances belonging to a certain instance of species. Whenever a new instance of animal is inserted (that is, the method ë*insert'* of class animal is executed) this causes the mean-weight of the corresponding instance of species to be updated. *(Warrant at schema-level).*
USER: What is the difference between an animal and a species? *(Follow-up query on the schema-level)*
SYSTEM: Species can be seen as a *power type* of animal. By this we mean that the class species can be seen as a template for the individual animals belonging to the species. Species have properties of its own, for instance mean-weight, which are not applicable to individual animals but belong to a certain group of animals, represented by the species class. An individual animal has a weight but the attribute mean-weight only applies to the species. Other properties of species are main-habitat, reflecting the natural habitat of the animals related to a certain species as opposed to the actual whereabouts of an individual animal. Every animal is related to exactly one instance of species, while a species may be related to many animals. *(Backing at pattern-level describing the roles of the queried concepts in the data abstraction they belong to)*

6 Explanation for Simulation

6.1 Procedural Question – Combining Dynamic and Static Models

Simulation means to execute dynamic rules in a conceptual model and explore the consequences of these executions. The procedural question can be seen as a reversed causal question. Instead of inspecting the existing instances and asking for the events that made them come into existence the user explores the consequences of executing a certain event. The system exemplifies and justifies the result of the execution by referring to the relevant parts of the conceptual model. This can be done either by displaying the results of the execution of the rule; an insertion, deletion or update of an object(s) or object property (corresponding to giving the grounds in Toulminís argumentation model) or by verifying what preconditions must be met for the event (or method) to execute as well as what post conditions hold after the execution (corresponding to a warrant). If the procedural question involves an event with several alternative execution paths, the system must provide a motivation to why a certain branch is chosen over another.

Utilising the semantics of a relational class

USER: What happens if Mariaís diagnosis is cured? *(I.E. the method cured(Name, Date, Illness, Treatment, Result) of Figure 4 and Figure 5 is executed*)
SYSTEM: First, the property of diagnosis ëResultí is updated reflecting the result of Mariaís treatment for a certain illness. Secondly, the property ëSuccess-rateí of the instance of class cure corresponding to Mariaís diagnosis and treatment type will be updated according to Mariaís result. *(Grounds at instance level)*
USER: I donít understand.
SYSTEM: The treatment type class and illness classes are related by means of the cure class. A relational class (or association class) must be used if there exists either a multivalued relation *with properties of its own* or a relation between more than two classes. An illness may be cured by several treatment types and a treatment type may cure many illnesses. To model that a certain illness is cured by a particular treatment with a certain success-rate, relation class cure is required to relate exactly one instance of illness to exactly one instance of treatment type with the property ëSuccess-rateí set to reflect the mean success rate of the instances undergoing actual treatments with diagnosis of the particular illness. *(Warrant at detailed schema-level utilising the semantics of a relational class)*

In this case the focus of the last warrant is on explaining the semantics of the concept of relational classes as opposed to explaining the concept of power types. Both schema constructs (a relational class and the analysis pattern including power types) are candidates to be highlighted in the system explanation since the relational class in this case relates concepts that, in turn, are part of the power type pattern. The reason for the systemís choice of explaining the relational class is that the user query in this context is interpreted as a procedural one where the effects of executing a certain event are to be explained. The object immediately effected by the execution of method ìcured()î are the instance of class CURE corresponding to Mariaís ILLNESS. Hence the context of the explanation is the semantics pertaining to the generic relational class of which class CURE is an example. If the user requires yet another explanation it is natural to expand the answer by giving the semantics of the power type pattern in which Mariaís TREATMENT is related to its power type TREATMENT TYPE.

7 Conclusions and Future Work

In this paper we have proposed an architecture and design principles for an explanation component for validating conceptual models by generation of explanations in natural language. The focus of explanation generation must be on explaining information that is only derivable from or implicitly specified in the model. We have advocated the use of analysis patterns and data abstractions as a natural context for explaining such implicit dependencies between different constituents of the conceptual model, as well as for focusing the generation of explanations on relevant parts of the model. This approach is integrated with Toulminís argumentation model in order to organise the dialog structure and the detail level of the explanations to meet different user requests.

However, the rules for when and where a certain pattern or data abstraction should be applied have only been vaguely addressed. As can bee seen in the user dialogs of the previous sections, the fact that a queried model fragment may belong to several analysis patterns constitutes a problem in structuring the answers. Clearly, rules for what pattern is best suited in an explanation need to be established. One approach is that the question types of section 4.3 indicate what objects in the schema are related to the focus of the question. This may, in turn, be an indication of what analysis pattern to choose over another. Another approach is to let the system show different suggestions for the user to choose from if there exists more than one applicable analysis pattern by which to explain a user query.

What has not been shown in the paper is an implementation of the proposed framework. In order to follow this line of research a formalisation of rules for how to apply different analysis patterns and data abstractions in the generation of explanations must be made. Furthermore the explanation generation architecture must be extended with a component for surface generation.

References

1. Boman, M., Bubenko, J.A., Johannesson, P., Wangler, B.: *Conceptual Modelling*, Prentice Hall Series in Computer Science, 1997
2. Dalianis, H.: ìA Method for Validation a Conceptual Model By Natural Language Discourse Generationî, *CAISE-92* International Conference on Advanced Information Systems Engineering, Loucopoulos P. (Ed.), Springer LNCS 593, pp. 425-444, 1992
3. Dalianis, H.: *Concise Natural Language Generation from Formal Specifications,* Ph.d. thesis, Department of Computer and Systems Sciences, Royal Institute of Technology, Stockholm 1996
4. Dalianis, H., Johannesson, P.: ìExplaining Conceptual Models ñ An Architecture and Design Principlesî, 16th International Conference on Conceptual Modeling-ERí97, 1997
5. Dalianis, H., Johannesson, P.: ìExplaining Conceptual Models ñ Using Toulminís argumentation model and RSTî, in the Proceedings of The Third International workshop on the Language Action Perspective on Communication Modelling (LAP98) Stockholm, Sweden, pp. 131-140, 1998
6. Fowler, M.: Analysis Patterns: Reusable Object Models, Addison-Wesley, 1997
7. Gamma, E., Helm,R., Johnson, R., Vlissides, J.: *Design Patterns,* Addison-Wesley, 1995

8. Gulla, J.A.: ìA General Explanation Component for Conceptual Modelling in CASE Environmentsî, *ACM Transactions on Information Systems,* vol. 14, no. 2, pp. 297-329, 1996
9. Hay, D.C.: Data Model Patterns: Conventions of Thought, Dorset House Publishing, 1996
10. ter Hofstede, Arthur H.M., Proper, Henderik A., van der Weide, Theo P.: ìExploiting fact verbalisation in conceptual information modellingî, *Information Systems,* vol. 22, no. 6/7, pp. 349 ñ 385, 1997
11. Kung, D.: ìThe Behaviour Network Model for Conceptual Information Modellingî, *Information Systems,* vol. 18, no. 1, pp. 1 ñ 21, 1993
12. Maiden, N.A., Sutcliffe, A.G.: ìExploiting Reusable Specifications through Analogyî, *Communications of the ACM,* vol. 35, no. 4, pp. 55 ñ 64, 1992
13. Maiden, N.A., Cisse, M., Perez, H., Manuel, D.: ìCREWS Validation Frames: Patterns for Validating Systems Requirementsî, Proceedings of The Fourth International workshop on Requirements Engineering: Foundations of Software Quality ñ REFSQí98, Pisa/Italy, June 1998
14. Mann, W., Thompson, S.: ìRhetorical Structure Theory: Description and Construction of Text Structuresî, in *Natural Language Generation: New Results in Artificial Intelligence, Psychology and Linguistics,* Ed. M.Nijhoff, pp. 85 ñ 95, Dordrecht, 1987
15. Martin, J., Odell, J.: *Object-Oriented Methods. A Foundation,* Prentice Hall 1994
16. McKeown, K., Swartout, W.: Language generation and explanation, in Advanced Natural Language Generation, Ed. M. Zock and G. Sabah, Pinter Publishers Ltd, 1988
17. Moore, J., Swartout, W.: ìA Reactive Approach to Explanation: Taking the Userís Feedback into Accoutnî, in *Natural Language Generation in Artificial Intelligence and Computational Linguistics,* pp. 1 ñ 48, Dordrecht 1991
18. Mylopoulos, J., Borgida, A., Jarke, M., Koubarakis, M.: ìTelos: Representing Knowledge about Information Systemsî, *ACM Transactions on Information Systems,* vol. 8, no. 4, pp. 325 ñ 362, 1990
19. Rolland, C., Proix, C.: ìNatural Language Approach to Conceptual Modellingî, in *Conceptual modeling, Databases and CASE: An Integrated View of Information Systems Development,* Ed. P. Loucopoulos and R. Zicari, pp. John Wiley, New York, 1992
20. Toulmin, S.: *The Uses of Arguments,* Cambridge University Press, 1959
21. Zave, P.: ìThe Operational versus the Conventional approach to Software Developmentî, *Communications of ACM,* vol. 27, no. 2, pp. 104 ñ 117, 1984

Conceptual Patterns – A Consolidation of Coad's and Wohed's Approaches

Petia Wohed

Department of Information and Systems Sciences
Stockholm University/Royal Institute of Technology
Electrum 230, 164 40 Kista, Sweden
petia@dsv.su.se

Abstract: The information system analysis process is considered as a difficult phase during the information systems development. The difficulty lies in gathering relevant information from the domain experts. Different techniques for supporting this process have been developed. One of them is provided by Coad, who defines a number of patterns aimed for use during the analysis of an information system. Another one is the work provided by Wohed on automating the information gathering process, which so far is implemented for one domain only. In this paper these two approaches are consolidated in order to continue the work provided by Wohed and extend it into a domain independent effort.

1 Introduction

One of the main activities during the development of an information system is the information analysis, which gives input for the design of the database behind a system. To support information analysis, the conceptual modelling technique has widely been used. The goal of conceptual modelling is to derive a model covering the relevant aspects of the underlying universe of discourse (UoD). The difficulty for the designers of an information system lies in capturing and extracting the relevant information from people working within and knowledgeable about the UoD that is analysed.

To support this process different techniques, supporting the communication between domain experts and information systems developers, have been developed. One of them is the representation of a conceptual schema produced by system developers in a natural language [4],[2] in order to make the schema readable and understandable to domain experts, who will then be able to validate it.

Another approach is the verbalization technique as described by Hofstede in [1]. This technique builds on the assumption that a verbalization of the samples from the UoD gives the structure and rules of the UoD. The point of the departure is a description of the communication in the UoD to be modeled, which builds the set of sample sentences, and the output is a conceptual schema.

Similarly, a description of a system is required for the technique developed by Purao and Storey [8],[9], which provides intelligent support for retrieval and synthesis of patterns for object-oriented design. The required input for this technique is a natural language sentence describing the aim of the system. Then, after applying

M. Bouzeghoub et al. (Eds.): NLDB 2000, LNCS 1959, pp. 340-351, 2001.

techniques for natural language processing, automated reasoning, learning heuristics, pattern retrieval from a patterns library, and pattern synthesis a conceptual model for the UoD is received.

The differences between the two approaches producing conceptual schemas described above are: firstly, the access to a pattern library in Purao and Storeyís approach; and secondly the kind of the description, which is used as input: a set of sample sentences in the first case, and a sentence describing the aim of the system in the second one. However, both these approaches start with a description. If such description is not available the approaches can not be applied. An alternative, for such situations, should be the approach proposed by Wohed [10], which does not require any particularly prepared input. Instead, information for the modeled domain is gathered by posing a number of predefined questions to a domain expert. In order to automate the modeling process, similar to Purao and Storeyís approach, Wohedís approach builds on the access to a pattern library from which the suggested solutions are selected.

The work provided by Wohed has so far been concentrated on one domain only. The work provided here is a continuation of it. It attempts to generalize the predefined questions in order to make them domain independent. Such a generalization is suggested after consolidation of the approach with the work provided by Coad [3], who extracts and defines a number of generic conceptual patterns.

The paper is organized as followed. Section 2 gives a brief description of the notation used in the paper. In Sections 3 and 4 the approaches proposed by Wohed and Coad are described. Section 5 presents the consolidation of the approaches. In section 6 a suggestion for the generalization of the questions is presented and some loss of information is outlined. Finally, Section 7 summarizes the paper and gives directions for further work.

2 Conceptual Schemas

In this section we briefly introduce the modeling language which is used. A formal definition of it, may be found in [7].

The basic construct in conceptual modeling approaches is the object. Objects that are similar to each other are grouped together into object types, such as Person and Country. Objects have different properties, which are modeled by attributes, and they can be related to each other, which is represented by relationships. In our graphical notation (see Figure 1) object types are represented by rectangles, attributes by lists inside the object types, and relationships by labeled lines. A direction of each line is given in its label. The object type initiating a relationship is called the domain of that relationship and the object type in its end is called the range. Generalization constraints are shown by arrows where the head of an arrow points to the super-type. For each relationship, the mapping constraints, represented by a quadruple <1m,1m,tp,tp>, specify whether it is single-valued, injective, total or surjective. A relationship is single-valued, denoted by 1 in the first position of the quadruple, when each instance of its domain is connected to at most one instance of its range. A relationship that is not single-valued is multi-valued, denoted by m. A relationship is total, denoted by t on the third position, when each instance of its domain is connected to at least one instance in its range. A relationship that is not total is partial, denoted by p. A relationship is injective (surjective) when its inverse is single valued (total). The second and fourth positions in the quadruple are reserved for the injective and surjective properties, correspondingly.

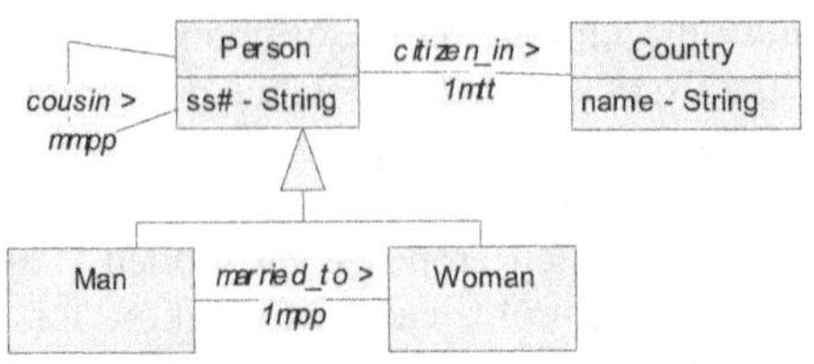

Figure 1 An example of a conceptual schema

The description of the domain represented by the model in Figure 1 is as follows: a Person is a citizen_in a Country and (s)he may have several cousins. The distinction between Man and Woman is kept. A person may only marry_to someone with the opposite sex, and polygamy is only allowed for women.

3 The Modeling Wizard Tool

The conceptual modeling wizard is based, as can be seen from its name, on the concept of a wizard tool, i.e., a tool gathering information from the user by asking her (him) a number of questions and suggesting a solution tailored to the set of the received answers. Applied to the area of conceptual modeling, this wizard poses questions about a domain and suggests a conceptual schema for this domain (a detailed description of the tool can be found in [10]. So far the wizard supports the booking domain only.

Six questions were collected and implemented in the tool (see Figure 2). The questions were identified after a number of different solutions, collected from Hay [6] and Fowler [5], and completed by other relevant solutions for the booking domain, were analyzed. They were aimed to cover the differences between different booking situations so that a satisfactory solution could be identified. A brief description of the questions is given below.

The first question is about the cardinality of a booking, i.e., where a booking may consist of several booking lines (e.g. when booking a trip, both tickets and hotel rooms may be reserved), or not (usually when booking a rental car). The second question is about whether a booking concerns a (number of) concrete objects (like when booking a time to dentist) or not (e.g. when booking a book in a library, not a particular exemplar of a book, but rather a title is booked). The third question investigates whether the bookings made within a system have the same character (as is the case for cinema tickets bookings) or whether they may differ. (In the trip booking example above, tickets bookings require departure and destination places and time for departure, whereas hotel room bookings require arrival and departure times and number of beds.) The fourth question is aimed to clarify whether or not it is necessary to keep information about the request for a booking. (For instance when scheduling room bookings for university courses, booking requests are collected from the head teachers for each course and used as input in the scheduling work.). The fifth

1. Does a booking consist of
   - o one object, or
   - o may it consist of several objects?

2. Does a booking concern a (number of)
   - o concrete object(s), or
   - o does it rather specify the character of the object(s)?

3. Do all the bookings
   - o have the same character

   or may they be divided into several categories?
   - o 2 o 3 o 4
   - o larger than 4

4. Is it necessary to keep information about the request for a booking, before making the booking?
   - o no

   If yes , does the booking request concern
   - o a concrete object(s)
   - o a specification of an object(s)

5. Does a motivation need to be given for a booking?

   5í. Does a motivation need to be given for a booking request? (depending on the answer from question 4)
   - o yes
   - o no

6. May a booking be done on the behalf of someone else?

   6í. May a booking request be done on the behalf of someone else? (depending on the answer from question 4)
   - o no,

   If yes, is it important to keep information about the party who made it?
   - o no
   - o yes.

Figure 2 The questions implemented in the tool

and sixth questions depend of the answer to the fourth question. If booking requests are necessary to keep information about, the fifth and the sixth questions are posed for the booking requests, otherwise the questions are posed for the bookings. The fifth question asks if a motivation (a purpose) for a booking/booking request is necessary. (For the university scheduling work each head teacher gives the course he/she will make the bookings for.) The sixth question asks whether a booking/booking request may be done on behalf of someone else (e.g., a secretary may book the business trips for her/his boss).

For the sake of user-friendliness the questions are placed in sequence by showing a new question only when the previous one has been answered. A conceptual schema solution is gradually built and refined, and graphically presented after each new answer. Figure 3 shows a solution suggested by the tool according to the answers in the right hand side of the figure.

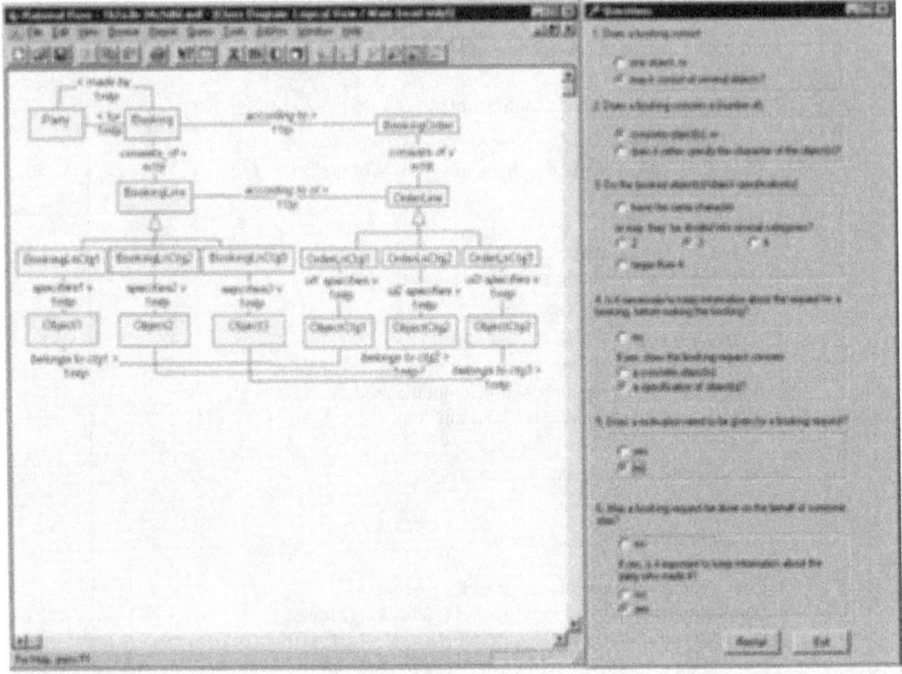

Figure 3 A snap shot from the tool

Initially, the object types Booking and Parties and the relationship for are introduced. This is done because of the totality of this relationship. The answer from the first question, results in the introduction of the object types Booking and BookingLine and the relationship between them. The answer from the second question causes the introduction of an object type called Object, which can not be seen in the final solution, due to changes performed when answering the rest of the questions. The answer from the third question results in specializing BookingLine into BookingLnCtg1, BookingLnCtg2 and BookingLnCtg3. The object type Object, introduced after the previous answer, is divided into Object1, Object2, and Object3. The first part of the fourth question results in the introduction of the object type BookingOrder. The second part results in the introduction of the object types for different object categories (ObjectCtg1, ObjectCtg2 and ObjectCtg3). Beside, the structure of a Booking is mirrored in the structure of the BookingOrder. If the answer from the fifth question is positive a further object type called Motivation should be introduced, but since it is negative, no changes are done. Finally, according to the answer from the last question the relationship made_by between Booking and Party is introduced.

4 Coad's Transaction Patterns

One of the earliest contributions on patterns in information systems analysis was provided by Coad, who in 1995 published ìObject Models: Strategies, Patterns, and Applicationsî [3]. The book presents 148 strategy steps for building systems and 31 object-model patterns for building object models and demonstrates their applicability by using them when building five different systems.

The characteristic of Coadís 31 patterns is that they are very small and generic, usually consisting of no more than two object types and a relationship between them. They do not address a particular problem, but are rather general and may be considered as building bloks of a schema.

Coad divides 30 of his patterns in the following four categories: transaction patterns; aggregate patterns; plan patterns; and interaction patterns. All these patterns follow a template, defined through the first pattern called the fundamental pattern (see Figure 4)

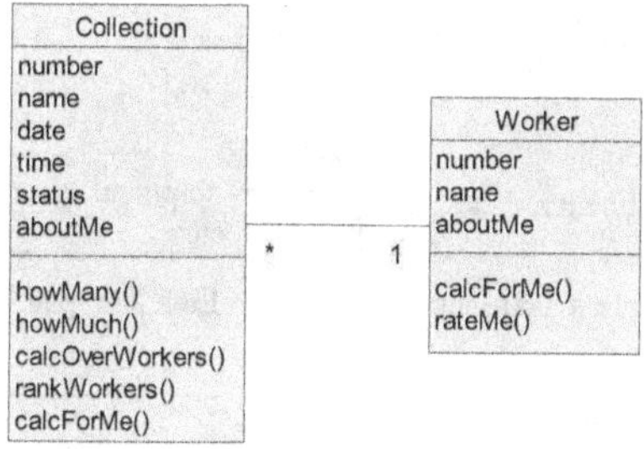

Figure 4 The fundamental pattern - Coadís first pattern (pattern #1) -

Only the patterns classified as transaction patterns are relevant for this work. An extract of Coadís own description of them, including the object typesí names, the relationships between them and some of the examples, is presented in Figure 5. Coadís notation is close to UML. The main difference is the placing of mapping constraints on the opposite side of a relation.

5 Relationships between the Wizard's Questions and Coad's Patterns

In the previous two sections the patterns defined by Coad and a modeling wizard tool built partly on patterns presented by Hay and Fowler and partly on additional patterns relevant for the booking domain, have been presented. In this section, the attention is turned into incorporating these two approaches by analyzing the questions implemented in the tool trough Coadís patterns.

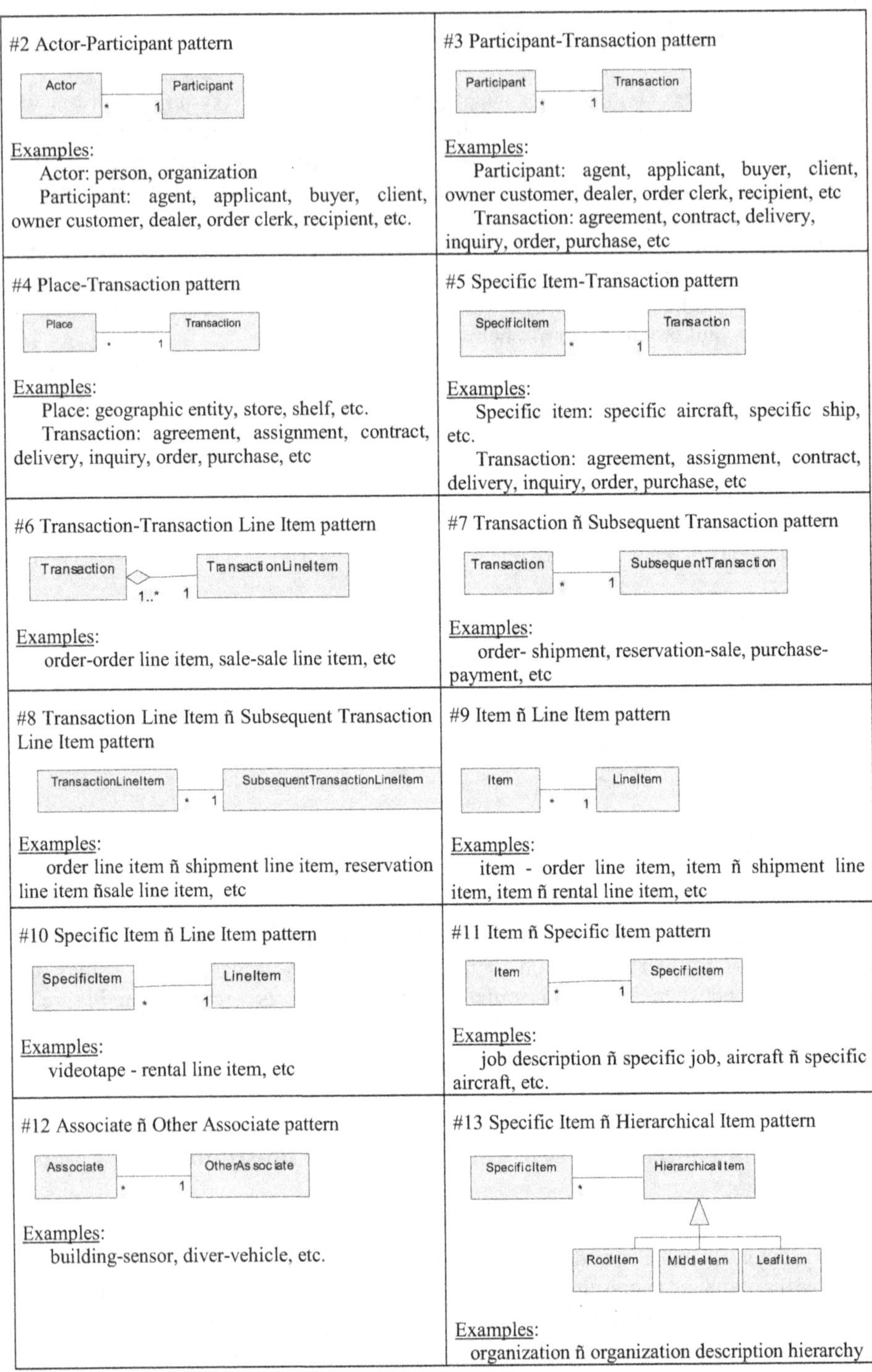

Figure 5 The transaction patterns defined by Coad

Starting with the first question ìDoes a booking consist of one object or may it consist of several objectsî, it may be noticed that an answer, claiming that a booking consists of several object, results in the introduction of the Transaction-Transaction Line Item pattern (pattern # 6 from Figure 5) into the solution (instantiated by Booking - BookingLine in the example from Figure 3). An answer claiming the opposite should not give any change. In this way the first question investigates whether pattern #6 shall, or shall not, be included in the solution.

Going further to the second question, investigating whether a booking concerns a concrete object, or rather the description of an object, can be related to Item-Specific Item pattern (#11). Not the whole pattern is applied at this moment, but the question still focus on the distinction made by this pattern. Furthermore, depending on the answers from the first and the second questions together, one of the following patterns are used for extending the solution after answering the second question: Item-Line Item pattern (#9); Specific ItemñLine Item pattern (#10) (the one used in Figure 3, where it is instantiated by Object and BookingLine), Specific ItemñTransaction pattern (#5); and finally a pattern not defined by Coad, but using his terminology we should refer to it as ItemñTransaction pattern.

The third question, asking whether the bookings in the analyzed domain have the same, or different, characters, is related to the Specific ItemñHierarchical Item pattern (#13). It results in specializing the booking object type into sub types when there are different (but no more than four) kinds of bookings.

Continuing analyzing the fourth question, asking whether information about the requests for a booking shall be kept or not, a relation to the Coadís Transactionñ Subsequent Transaction pattern (#7) can clearly be outlined. Certainly, the name Transaction - Preceding Transaction pattern should be more suitable, in this particular case, but since the semantic should be the same, no new patterns extending the Coadís set are necessary. In our particular example Transaction-Subsequent Transaction is instantiated by BookingOrder and Booking, correspondingly. Moreover, the second part of the question is a repetition of the second question for the BookingOrder and the analysis provided under the second question may be repeated here. The suggested solution after answering the fourth question depends also on the first and the third question. If the TransactionñTransaction Line Item pattern (#6) has been applied, then the Transaction Line ItemñSubsequent Transaction Line Item pattern (#8) is applied now (which resulted in Figure 3 in the OrderLine-BookingLine construction). Similarly the Specific Item-Hierarchical Item pattern (#13) is used depending on whether it has been used in the solution resulting from the third question.

The fifth question asking whether the motivation for a booking (booking request) is necessary or not is related to AssociateñOther Associate pattern (#12). Finally the last question investigating the different participants in a booking is related to Participantñ Transaction pattern (#3).

Summarizing, we would like to note that all patterns from Coadís library, except Actor-Participant pattern (#2), and Place-Transaction pattern (#4) were covered by the questions (see Figure 6). One reason for not having a question related to pattern #4 could be that the place where a booking is done was not identified as potential important information. However there may exist situations where even the physical place for a booking is necessary to keep information about, which should make it necessary to extend the questions in order to cover this aspect as well. Neither is the pattern #2 covered by the questions in their present state. This can be explained by the fact that, within the booking domain, an actor usually has one role only. In the cases where an actor may have several roles, the connection between the different roles is not considered. In domains where it is usual for the actors to be shared between different roles, and in the cases where the connections between the different roles are important, a question covering this aspect should be necessary to include.

Question number	Pattern #
Q1	#6
Q2	#11
Q1 & Q2	#9, #10, #5, and an additional pattern
Q3	#13
Q4 (the second part repeats Q2)	#7 (and the same patterns as for Q2 and Q1 & Q2)
Q1 & Q3 & Q4	#8, #13
Q5	#12
Q6	# 3

Figure 6 The patterns related to each question

Even if the analysis provided above was partly made to reason about the completeness of the questions, i.e., whether all patterns were covered by the questions, it is still not enough for making any conclusion whether the set of questions is complete or not. This is due to the varying number of times a pattern can be applied for building different solutions. To be able to reason about the completeness of the questions according to the iteration of some patterns in a particular solution, some empirical studies have to be provided.

6 Generalization of the Questions

After mapping the wizardís questions into the Coadís patterns successfully, the next step, in the work of making the wizard domain independent, is generalizing the questions. This is done by the support of the terminology defined by Coad, during the construction of the patterns. In Figure 7 the result of this generalization is presented. The following substitutions have been performed: booking → transaction (booking is substituted with transaction); object → item; concrete object → specific item; request and booking request → preceding transaction; motivation → other associate; and finally, party → participant.

1. Does a transaction consist of

   ○ one item, or

   ○ may it consist of several items?

2. Does a transaction concern a (number of)

   ○ specific item(s), or

   ○ does it rather specify the character of the item(s)?

3. Do all the transactions

   ○ have the same character

   or may they be divided into several categories?

   ○ 2 ○ 3 ○ 4

   ○ larger than 4

4. Is it necessary to keep information about the preceding transaction of a transaction, before making the transaction?

   ○ no

   If yes, does the preceding transaction concern

   ○ (a) specific item(s)

   ○ (a) specification of an item(s)

5. Does other associate need to be given for a transaction?
5í. Does other associate need to be given for a preceding transaction?
(depending on the answer from question 4)

   ○ yes

   ○ no

6. May a transaction be done on the behalf of someone else?
6í. May a preceding transaction be done on the behalf of someone else?
(depending on the answer from question 4)

   ○ no,

   If yes, is it important to keep information about the participant who made it?

   ○ no

   ○ yes.

Figure 7 The questions after the substitution

Even if this set of general questions has not yet been empirically tested, it can be observed that some of the semantics we had for the booking domain is lost. For instance, when asking whether the booking requests were necessary to keep information about, or not, it was supposed that the structure for booking requests is similar to the structure of the bookings, i.e., if the bookings consisted of several booking lines, then the requests should also consist of several order lines. It was also supposed that there should be a connection from each booking line to each order line. However, when asking generally if it is necessary to keep information about some preceding transactions, we cannot just presuppose such semantic. Instead, it is necessary to gather information whether such semantics exists by particularly asking about it. Besides, it should also be necessary to ask if it is necessary to keep information about any subsequent, and not only preceding, transactions. These observations indicate that the questions need to be extended in order to make them work for any domain where a transaction is involved. So far the questions work only on domains with the presupposed properties described for the booking domain, e.g., Order-Shipment, Purchase-Payment etc.

7 Conclusions and Further Research

This paper summarizes and consolidates two approaches supporting the information analyses process. The first approach, suggested by Coad, consists of a set of generic patterns to be used during the conceptual modeling process and a set of guidelines for how and when to use these patterns. The second approach, suggested by Wohed, propagates the automation of the modeling process by suggesting a modeling wizard, aimed to gather information about a domain by posing questions to the domain experts and suggesting a solution according to the received answers. The wizard is so far implemented for one domain only, the booking domain. The questions implemented in the wizard were matched to the patterns defined by Coad. This matching was done both to reason about the completeness of the questions and to support their generalization into domain independent questions. During the generalization process some of the semantics relating the questions with each other were lost. Introducing complementary questions for retrieving this semantics is a way to solve this loss of information.

The wizard can in this way be extended to even support other domains where a transaction is involved. Each time the wizard is used it should be tailored to the particular domain it is going to be used for. Such tailoring can be performed by instantiation of the general questions into domain specific ones, going in the opposite direction of the one performed in this paper. It is then necessary to define a set of relevant substitutions for each domain.

After implementing and testing the extensions discussed here, the next step is to further extend the wizard to support other domains then just transaction domains, e.g., to support the modeling process of different product structures. The aggregate patterns defined by Coad could then be used as a point of departure.

Acknowledgments

I would like to thank my advisor Docent Paul Johannesson, my colleague Maria Bergholtz, and the anonymous reviewers for many valuable comments on earlier drafts of this paper.

References

1. A.H.M. ter Hofstede, H.A.Proper, T.P. van der Weide, ìExploiting Fact Verbalisation in Conceptual Information Modellingî, *Information Systems*, vol. 22, no. 6/7, pp. 349-385, 1997
2. M. Bergholtz and P. Johannesson, ìValidating conceptual models ñ utilising analysis patterns as an instrument for explanation generationî, to be presented at the *5th*

International Conference on Applications of Natural Language to Information Systems, NLDBí00, Versailles, 2000

3. P. Coad, D. North, M. Mayfield, *Object Models: Strategies, Patterns, and Applications*, Prentice Hall, 1995.
4. H. Dalianis. ìA Method for Validating a Conceptual Model by Natural Language Discourse Generationî in Loucopoulos, P., (Ed.), *CAISE-92 International Conference on Advanced Information Systems Engineering*, Lecture Notes in Computer Science, No. 593, pp. 425-444, Springer Verlag, 1992
5. M. Fowler, *Analysis Patterns: Reusable Object Models*, Addison-Wesley, 1997.
6. D.C. Hay, *Data Model Patterns: Conventions of Thought*, Dorset House Publishing, 1996.
7. P. Johannesson, *Schema Integration, Schema Translation, and Interoperability in Federated Information Systems*, Dissertation at Department of Computer and Systems Sciences, Stockholm University and Royal Institute of Technology, Sweden, 1993.
8. S. Purao and V.C. Storey, ìIntelligent Support for Retrieval and Synthesis of Patterns for Object-Oriented Designî, in, D.W Embley and R.C. Goldstein., (Eds.), *CAISE-97 International Conference on Advanced Information Systems Engineering, Lecture Notes in Computer Science*, No. 1331, pp.30-42 , Springer Verlag, 1997.
9. S. Purao, ìAPSARA: A Tool to Automate Systems design via Intelligent Pattern Retrieval and Synthesisî, *The Data Base for Advances in Information Systems*, vol. 29, no. 4, 1998.
10. P. Wohed, ìConceptual Patterns for Reuse of Information Systems Designî to be presented at *CAiSE'00, International Conference on Advanced Information Systems Engineering*, Stockholm, 2000.

Patterns Retrieval System: A First Attempt

Catherine Berrut[1] and AgnËs Front-Conte [2]

[1] Laboratoire CLIPS-IMAG, BP 53, 38041 Grenoble Cedex 9, France,
currently visiting: MMIR Group, School of computer applications,
Dublin city university, Glasnevin, Dublin 9, Ireland
[2] Laboratoire LSR-IMAG, BP 72, 38402 Saint Martin díHËres Cedex, France
{Catherine.Berrut, Agnes.Conte}@imag.fr

Abstract. New approaches to the development of information systems, based on components reuse, are now preferred to traditional ones. In particular, patterns are among the most frequently ìre-usedî components in such approaches. Tools must be provided to applications developers to help them to use these patterns during the analysis, design and implementation of applications. In particular, help must be given for the users to retrieve patterns corresponding to their problems. We present in this paper an experiment whose aims are to identify the ability and the quality of the classical techniques provided by the information retrieval field in a pattern retrieval system. In this first attempt, we apply these techniques to a specific library of patterns: Gammaís design patterns corpus, and we evaluate the results of this experiment in order to identify the specific need of the user and the direction in which our patterns retrieval system should evolve.

1 Introduction

The current environments for application development provide tools such as patterns in order to make the specification work and the development as easy and correct as possible. These tools are rich and numerous, but they are still delegated to trained engineers able to easily manage their use. At the moment, these patterns provide a secure way to specify and develop applications providing reuse of know-how on methods and techniques for the analysis, design and implementation of applications. The applications are still reserved for developers who know them well, and who easily retrieve them through for example a browsing system [4]. The biggest existing problem for the actual use of the patterns database is to provide tools that enable the retrieval of thousands existing patterns according to a specific need: it is one thing to know that a pattern exists, quite another to know where it is and retrieve it or to find better alternatives to a specific pattern.

In this work, we made an analysis of the classical techniques provided by the information retrieval field and applied these to the retrieval of patterns. Our objectives are to identify the ability and the quality of these techniques for our pattern retrieval system. In this first attempt, we test our patterns retrieval system on Gammaís design patterns corpus [10]. Giving the qualitative performances of this first system, this will

M. Bouzeghoub et al. (Eds.): NLDB 2000, LNCS 1959, pp. 352-363, 2001.

identify the specific need of the patterns users, and indicate to us which direction our patterns retrieval system should take in order to provide a better qualitative performance identified by real users needs.

This paper is divided into several sections. Section 2 explains the context of the experiment: it first details the notion of design patterns and then, introduces the global principles of information retrieval. Section 3 presents the 6 indexing methods used in the experiment to extract the indexing terms from the patterns. Section 4 briefly shows the information retrieval model (a subset of the boolean model) used in the experiment to retrieve a pattern corresponding to a query. Section 5 presents the experiment made on 6 queries and the obtained results. Finally, section 6 draws some conclusions and perspectives of this work.

2 Context of the Work

2.1 Design Patterns

A pattern is know-how aimed at resolving a recurring problem in a particular domain. Expression of this know-how identifies the addressed problem, proposes a correct solution to resolve the problem and offers the way incorporating the solution into the required application.

In computer science, object-oriented patterns can be compared to patterns in architectural domain [1] or in hydraulic domain [2]. They facilitate the process of engineering of object-oriented systems by proposing predefined artefacts for similar problems and their different implementation techniques. A pattern is defined as a solution to a problem in a context [11].

Patterns are generally classified in relation to the engineering step they address. Analysis patterns [6, 13, 9] are dedicated to a problem appearing during the requirements analysis phase. They may concern a specific application domain or may be of general interest. They help the designer to build object models that represent the system requirements in the best way as possible. Design patterns [10, 5] identify, name and abstract common themes of the object-oriented design domain. They capture experience and knowledge linked to design by identifying objects, their collaborations and their responsibilities. Finally, implementation patterns [7] also called idioms are generally specific to a language; they describe how to implement characteristics away from this language (for example, how to simulate multiple inheritance in Java). The experiment presented in this paper is only focused on design patterns [10].

Representation formalism
The representation formalism used to describe the 23 patterns of [10] is composed of 13 sections. We present here the main headings of this formalism.

Pattern Name

Intention	The problem addressed by the pattern.
Motivation	An application example (a scenario) described in a textual and eventually graphical way.
Description	The proposed semi-formal solution, expressed with UML-like diagrams describing in particular the participants to the pattern and their responsibilities.
Implementation	Advices and techniques which can be used to implement the pattern.

Table 1. The patterns representation formalism

2.2 Information Retrieval Systems

An information retrieval system is designed to retrieve interesting documents extracted from a corpus, according to a user specific need, generally expressed through a semantic expression describing the expected content of the documents [14, 12]. These systems are designed for dealing with corpus of millions of documents, therefore the objectives of the user requirements is not to retrieve a document with external attributes such as title or author, but describing an expected document semantic content. The results from information retrieval is not strict, but generally composed of a list of documents dealing with the query. This list of documents can be a simple or a ranked list where documents are sorted according to the systems view of the link strength between the query and the retrieved documents.
The general architecture is made of two processes:

- An indexing process which aims to extract the semantic content of the documents according to a specific indexing language;
- A querying process which calculates the matching between a user query and the corpus using a matching function.

The qualitative performance of information retrieval systems is evaluated using specific measures which compare the system answer and a user answer to the same query on the same corpus. The nearer the system is to the user answer, the better it is. There exist several measures indicating the quality of this proximity. In this paper, we use the following:

- The recall measure. This measure indicates the ability of the system to retrieve all the relevant documents (as indicated by the user). It is calculated as:

$$(\text{Rel} \cap \text{Ret}) / \text{Rel} \qquad \textbf{(1)}$$

  where Rel indicates the relevant documents according to the userís point of view, Ret the documents retrieved by the system.
  A good recall is close to 1.
- The precision measure. This measure indicates the ability of the system to retrieve only relevant documents (as indicated by the user). It is calculated as:

$$(\text{Rel} \cap \text{Ret}) / \text{Ret} \tag{2}$$

A good precision is close to 1.

- The fallout measure. This measure indicates the ability of the system to retrieve non relevant documents. It is calculated as:

$$(\text{Ret} \cap \text{nonRel}) / \text{nonRel} \tag{3}$$

where nonRel indicates the non relevant documents.
A good fallout is close to 0.

3 Patterns Indexing

The quality of an information retrieval system strongly depends on the selected indexing language and indexing process. These are decided according to the underlying application and users of the system [3]. There exist well-known links with the qualitative performances of a system and the level of the indexing language which is implemented [15]. When a new system must be designed for a new application, you have to identify the real user needs and to deduce the underlying indexing language needed. This is a long and experimental task.

The first questions to answer in an indexing process are the following:

- Which section of the documents must be used for indexing ? This determines the exhaustivity of the indexing process, i.e. its ability to store all detailed data appearing in the documents. The exhaustivity is not always a good quality for the system and may lead to bad precision measures in some circumstances;
- Which indexing language is required ? The definition of the indexing language fixes the specificity of the indexing process, i.e. its ability to store the data as it appears in documents. An indexing language that is too specific may lead to bad recall measures in some circumstances.

In order to work, an indexing process is generally divided in three steps:

- Extraction of terms (in the selected sections of the documents);
- Selection of the indexing terms from the extracted terms (respecting the indexing language model);
- Weighting, which indicates the importance of each indexing terms in each document. This step does not exist in all systems.

In order to start our patterns indexing, we decided to build a benchmark of 6 different indexing methods. We measured their behavior on a same matching function (a subset of the boolean model as described in the following section). These indexing methods are classical indexing techniques adapted to the patterns corpus:

- 3 different extractions of the terms on selected sections of patterns:
  - ♦ document oriented process,
  - ♦ expert oriented process,
  - ♦ query oriented process.

- 2 selection processes:
  - ♦ no selection at all (extracted terms are the indexing terms),
  - ♦ selection of medium frequent terms.

The combination of these different possibilities leads to 6 indexing processes.

3.1 The 3 Extraction Processes

« Document oriented » extraction process

This process extracts the terms directly from abstract of the documents. It is called ì document orientedî because it indexes the document from its available content.

In patterns, the abstract is stated in the Intention section. We only extracted the nouns and the verbs from the intention section of the patterns.

« Expert oriented » extraction process

This indexing process consists of asking an expert of the domain to choose the most significant sentences in the document, i.e. those which carry meaning as possible according to the experts point of view. In those sentences, we extracted adjectives, nouns and verbs.

« Query oriented » extraction process

This indexing process first consists of asking a users expert (a librarian for example) the following question: ì which queries would the user formulate to ask for this documentî ? As an answer, the librarian identifies the different queries the users would ask. All the terms of these queries are extracted and verbs and adjectives are nominalized .

3.2 The 2 Selection Processes

In our experiment, each extraction process was followed ì withoutî and then ì withî selection by filtering:

- Without filtering: each term of each document is taken into account as it is extracted. So, if from a document D_i, a set of terms $\{t_{i1}$, Ö , $t_{id}\}$ is extracted, the document is indexed by this set $\{t_{i1}$, Ö , $t_{id}\}$. The indexing language is formed as the union of all extracted terms.
- With filtering:
  - ♦ The terms present in too many documents are eliminated: these terms are not interesting for querying a corpus as they are equivalent as asking for the entire corpus. In our experiment, the only term eliminated is ì objectî .
  - ♦ The terms ad_i present in only one document are separated from the other terms t_j. They are indeed considered as direct access keys (identifiers) to the documents: querying with such terms is equivalent to querying for the document with its file name. The set of ad_i is called AD.
  - ♦ The other terms (t_j) are agregated in the T set.

- For all document D_i, its indexing is $D_i = \{ad_{i1}, Ö , ad_{in}\} U \{t_{i1}, Ö , t_{im}\}$ where ad_i are the terms only linked to D_i and t_i are extracted from D_i and other documents.
- In this case, the indexing language is defined by: AD U T

3.3 Indexing Results

Table 3 gives the total results obtained through the 6 different indexing processes.

Extraction Selection	Document oriented	Expert oriented	Query oriented
Without filtering	121 terms	69 terms	47 terms
With filtering	87 terms in AD 34 terms in T	57 terms in AD 12 terms in T	33 terms in AD 14 terms in T

Table 2. Results through the 6 indexing processes

These results show that the design patterns are very specific documents. This means that they do not share a lot semantics and that isolating a design pattern appears easier than finding similar documents. The overall vocabulary which really allows information retrieval is quite small (34, 12, 14 T terms) comparing to the (87, 57, 33 AD terms).

These statistics are classical in expert corpus, i.e. in corpus designed by experts for experts. These corpus are well known and use what is called a ìspecificity languageî. That means they are based on a natural language but use a specific vocabulary or syntactic constructions. A typical attitude in such corpus is the use of specific terms that identify a document and this is clearly evident here.

Having established different indexing processes with quite different semantic results, the work now consists in identifying which of these indexing processes provides the best results for an information retrieval system. In the next section we describe the matching function we used before comparing the different qualitative results we obtained.

4 The Used Information Retrieval Model: A Subset of the Boolean Model

The matching functions used are the following:

- **without filtering**

Given a query R composed of a set of terms: $R = \{tr_1, Ö , tr_r\}$,
and a document D_i indexed by a set of terms: $D_i=\{t_{i1}, Ö , t_{in}\}$.

D_i is an answer to R if R is included in D_i, i.e. if each term of R belongs to D_i. The answer to a query R is formed by the documents which contain all the terms of R (the boolean model restricted to ì ANDî).

- **with filtering**

Given a query R composed of a set of terms in which some belongs to the AD set:

$R = \{ad_1, Ö , ad_n\} U \{tr_1, Ö , tr_r\}$

and a document D_i indexed by:

$D_i = \{ad_{i1}, Ö , ad_{in}\} U \{t_{i1}, Ö , t_{im}\}$.

D_i is an answer to R if

- **$\{tr_1, ..., tr_r\}$ C $\{t_{i1}, ..., t_{im}\}$ (all t of R are in D_i)**
- **or if one of the ad_i of D_i exists in $\{ad_1, ..., ad_n\}$.**

To summarize, D_i is an answer to R if R directly asks for D_i (through one of its AD terms) or if D_i contains all of R indexing terms.

The answer to a query R is composed of:

- the documents for which an AD term was in R

  +
- the documents which contain all the terms of R.

5 The Experiment

5.1 The Test-Queries

In order to establish qualitative results, we built a set of test-queries. We asked users to give queries they would like to have on a patterns retrieval system and the relevant documents they would expect as answers from the system. The set of our test-queries is given below, with the accompanying relevant document, and their generality measure which indicates the ability of a query to have a lot of documents as answers. The generality measure is calculated as the proportion of relevant documents by the size of the corpus and is used when a new system is built. The indication of the average generality score of the test-queries gives an idea of typical users attitude. A high generality measure indicates broad search, mostly made for learning from a corpus, whereas a low generality measure indicates expert users whose work mostly consists in retrieving specific documents in the corpus. Identifying a typical attitude from the users helps the tuning of the system either on the expected indexing level or on the provided matching function and the kind of relevance feedback.

Query	Content	Relevant documents	Generality score
R1	Recursive object composition	Composite	0,04
R2	Object state	Memento, Observer, State	0,13
R3	Change of object state	Observer, State	0,09
R4	Creation of object class	Abstract factory, Builder, Factory method, Prototype	0,17
R5	Instanciation of object class	Factory method, Singleton	0,09
R6	Unique instanciation of object class	Singleton	0,04

The analysis of these generality measures confirms the results got from the indexing statistics: the corpus is an expert corpus made for experts. The documents are specific documents and are easier to identify than to cluster. The queries are precise, and expect very few documents as answers. The use of the corpus (considering this first experiment) is not a learning use but an identification use of documents that the user knows.

5.2 Answers to the Queries and Qualitative Evaluations

Answers to the « Document oriented » indexing

	Retrieved documents without filtering	Retrieved documents with filtering	Recall	Precision	Fall-out
R1	Composite	Composite	1	1	0
			1	1	0
R2	Memento, Observer, State	Memento, Observer, State	1	1	0
			1	1	0
R3	Observer, State	Observer, State	1	1	0
			1	1	0
R4	Abstract Factory, Factory Method	Abstract Factory, Factory Method	0,5	1	0
			0,5	1	0
R5	Factory Method	Factory Method, Singleton	**0,5**	1	0
			1	1	0
R6	Factory Method	Factory Method, Singleton	**0**	**0**	0,05
			1	**0,5**	0,05
Average :			**0,67**	**0,83**	**0,01**
			0,92	**0,92**	**0,01**

Answers to the « expert oriented » indexing

	without filtering	with filtering	Recall	Preci-sion	Fall-out
R1	Composite	Composite	1	1	0
			1	1	0
R2	Memento, Observer	Memento, Observer, State	0,67	1	0
			1	1	0
R3	Observer	Observer, State	0,5	1	0
			1	1	0
R4	∅	Abstract Factory, Adapter	0	0	0
			0,25	0,5	0,05
R5	∅	Factory Method, Prototype, Singleton, Adapter	0	0	0
			0,5	0,5	0,1
R6	∅	Singleton, Adapter	0	0	0
			1	0,5	0,05
		Average :	**0,36**	**0,5**	**0**
			0,79	**0,75**	**0,03**

The ìexpert indexingî methods are incompatible with the three last queries on which no valid indexing seems to exist. Due to the first bad extraction, the ìfilteringî process does not bring enough quality to the ìexpert indexingî method and still has very bad results.

Answers to the « query oriented » indexing

	Without filtering	with filtering	Recall	Preci-sion	Fall-out
R1	Composite	Composite	1	1	0
			1	1	0
R2	Memento, Observer, State	Memento, Observer, State	1	1	0
			1	1	0
R3	Observer, State	Observer, State	1	1	0
			1	1	0
R4	Abstract Factory, Factory Method	Abstract Factory, Adapter	0,5	1	0
			0,5	1	0
R5	Factory Method	Factory Method, Prototype, Singleton, Adapter	0,5	1	0
			1	1	0
R6	∅	Singleton, Adapter	0	0	0
			1	0,5	0,05
		Average :	**0,67**	**0,83**	**0**
			0,92	**0,92**	**0,01**

The ìquery indexing without filteringî process has the same results as document indexing, except that it does not bring fallout for the last query. The use of filtering improves the results returned by the ìquery orientedî process.

5.3 Recall / Precision / Fallout Boards per Query

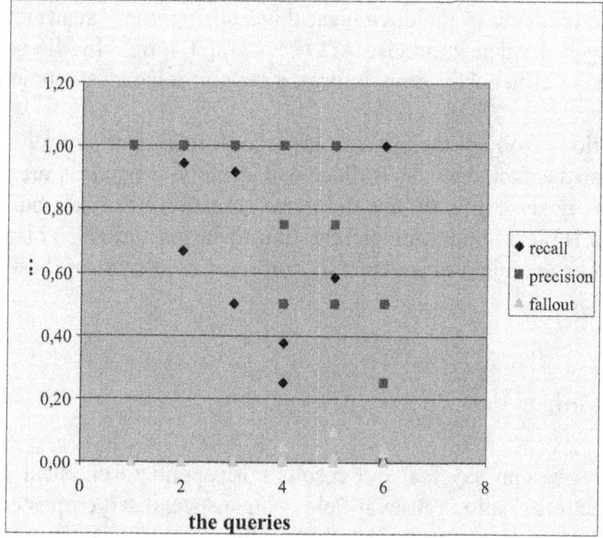

Fig. 1. Best, average and worst scores

Precision is good for all the queries except R6, recall is more variable and never gets to 1 for the R4 query. Fallout does not get high, and appears when recall also increases.

5.4 Analysis of the Results

Indexing with filtering gives better results than indexing without filtering, in particular on the two last queries. Nevertheless we can note that filtering does not enhance the results of the expert-oriented indexing process, whose results were bad to start with. This is not surprising because the job the expert does is not an indexing work but much more a comprehension work (or even a quick memorising work). Remembering a pattern and indexing it are two very different things. Asking an expert user to index documents rarely leads to good results. Indexing really needs dedicated processes or experts, but these experts are not expert users, rather user experts !

Filtering enhances the fallout measure. This is due to the separation of AD and T terms, which are in the query but are now treated differently. Some T terms play a fallout role as they stay in the query processing. Without filtering, these T terms occurred with the AD terms and therefore failed to give fallout results.

The document oriented extraction process gives approximately the same results as the query oriented one. This result is interesting in terms of cost: for equivalent results, the cost of the indexing will be lower if no expertise is needed. This also confirms the results of indexing - we deal with a deep semantic corpus being queried with very specific needs.

Why does R6 (ìUnique instanciation of object classî) lead to precision problems ? Using a ìwithout filteringî indexing process implies that the query is much too precise comparing the indexing of the document: this leads to empty answers. Using filtering, the query is well divided in precise AD terms and T terms. In all cases, this leads to bad precision by either AD terms indicated by non-relevant documents or too many broad T terms.

R4 (ìCreation of object classî) also leads to problems: it never gets a good recall. This is due to the fact that the Builder and Prototype patterns are never retrieved. These patterns never explicitly use the terms ìcreation of classî, but rather the more specific terms ìobjects buildingî or ìcreation of instanciationî. This classically leads to silence and bad recall, and is generally corrected by the use of thesaurus at querying stage or feedback.

6 Conclusion

In conclusion, we can say that our results correspond to classical results generally obtained in the information retrieval field using a specialised corpus context. On a less specialised corpus, the query-oriented extraction process is generally less reliable. Nevertheless, we have to stay vigilant and be careful not to make too many quick decisions because this experiment only ran on a few patterns and queries. A larger attempt has now to be done in order to be sure the results we found still hold true. Finally, one of the aims of this experiment was to know if the Intention section of the generally used formalisms was suited to retrieve a pattern corresponding to a given problem. Once more, we think with this experiment that the Intention section seems to correctly carry the problem and allows us to retrieve the good patterns corresponding to a given problem.

The perspectives of this work are numerous. First we would like to use the specificity of the corpus formed by the patterns in order to get better precision and recall. This corpus has indeed a well-defined structure thanks to its representation formalism composed of several headings, as well as a precise semantics for each heading which have their own meaning. Some techniques already exist to take this structure and this semantics into account in order to improve the information retrieval [8]. Secondly, we would like to develop an environment for the development of applications using patterns, which would include patterns retrieval system in particular. The existing prototypes only offer browsing abilities, allowing the user to navigate from one pattern to another until he finds the pattern that seems to correspond to his problem. As we already said, this supposes he knows the existence of all patterns, which is nowadays impossible due to the increasing number of patterns.

References

1. Alexander C., *The Timeless Way of Building*, Oxford University Press, New York, NY, 1979.

2. Asplund K. and Swift G., *Downstream Water Volume*, http://www.designmatrix.com/pl/ecopl/dswv.html, 1973.
3. Berrut C., *Indexation des données multimédia, utilisation dans le cadre d'un système de recherche d'informations*, Habilitation ‡ Diriger des Recherches, UniversitÈ Joseph Fourier, 1997.
4. Borne I. and Revault N., *Comparaison d'outils de mise en œuvre de design patterns*, NumÈro spÈcial de la revue LíOBJET : Patrons OrientÈs Objet, HermËs, 1999.
5. Buschmann F., Meunier R., Rohnert H., Sommerlad P. and Stal M., *Pattern-Oriented Software Architecture – A System of Patterns*, Wiley and Sons Ltd., 1996.
6. Coad P., North D. and Mayfield M., *Object Models – Strategies, Patterns and Applications,* Yourdon Press Computing Series, 1996.
7. Coplien J.O., *Patterns – The Patterns White Paper*. ISBN 1-884842-50-X, 1996.
8. Franck Fourel, *Modélisation, indexation et recherche de documents structurés*, Ph.D. thesis, UniversitÈ Joseph Fourier, 1998.
9. Fowler M., *Analysis Patterns – Reusable Object Models*, Addison-Wesley, 1997.
10. Gamma E, Helm R., Johnson R. and Vlissides J., *Design Patterns, Elements of Reusable Object-Oriented Software*, Addison-Wesley, 1994.
11. Lea D., *Patterns Discussion FAQ*, http://g.oswego.edu/pd-FAQ.html, 1997.
12. Van Rijsbergen C.J., *Information retrieval*, 1979.
13. Rolland C., *Adapter les Méthodes à l'Objet : Challenges et Embûches*, JournÈes MÈthodes díAnalyse et de Conception OrientÈes Objet des SystËmes díInformation, AFCET, Paris, 1993.
14. Salton G. Mac Gill M.J., *Introduction to modern information retrieval*, MacGraw Hill Book Company, 1983.
15. Soergel D, *Indexing and retrieval performance: the logical evidence*, JASIS 45(8), pp 589-599, 1994.

Ontology Learning from Text

Alexander Maedche and Steffen Staab

Institute AIFB, Karlsruhe University, D-76128 Karlsruhe, Germany
{maedche,staab}@aifb.uni-karlsruhe.de
http://www.aifb.uni-karlsruhe.de/WBS

1 Motivation

Ontologies have shown their usefulness in application areas such as information integration, natural language processing, metadata for the world wide, to name but a few. However, there remains the problem of engineering large and adequate ontologies within short time frames in order to keep costs low. We here present a general architecture for discovering conceptual structures and engineering ontologies from text and a new approach for discovering non-taxonomic conceptual relations from text.

2 The Framework

We present our framework for semi-automatic engineering and learning of ontologies. As described in [2] the framework compromises a *(i)* Text & Processing Management component, *(ii)* an Text Processing Server, *(iii)* a Lexical Database and Domain Lexicon, *(iv)* a Learning Module, and *(v)* the Ontology Engineering Environment OntoEdit. The architecture has been fully implemented in the Text-To-Onto system. The system follows an balanced cooperation approach, i.e. each modeling task can be done by the user or by a learning algorithm. This interaction of system and user contributes to the complex task of ontology learning and semi-automatic engineering.

Within our general architecture, we embed a new approach described in further detail in [1] for discovering non-taxonomic conceptual relations from text. Building on the taxonomic part of the ontology, our approach analyzes domain-specific texts. It uses shallow text processing methods to identify linguistically related pairs of words. An algorithm for discovering generalized association rules analyzes statistical information about the linguistic output. Thereby, it uses the background knowledge from the taxonomy in order to propose relations at the appropriate level of abstraction. We have evaluated our approach against an ontology about the tourism domain that we had hand-modeled before.

References

[1] A. Maedche and S. Staab. Discovering conceptual relations from text. In *W. Horn (ed.): ECAI 2000. Proceedings of the 14th European Conference on Artificial Intelligence*. IOS Press, Amsterdam, 2000.

[2] A. Maedche and S. Staab. Semi-automatic engineering of ontologies from text. In *Proceedings of the 12th International Conference on Software and Knowledge Engineering. Chicago, USA, July, 5-7, 2000*. KSI, 2000.

M. Bouzeghoub et al. (Eds.): NLDB 2000, LNCS 1959, pp. 364–364, 2001.

ISIS: Interaction through Speech with Information Systems

Afzal Ballim, Jean-Cédric Chappelier, Martin Rajman, and Vincenzo Pallotta

Department of Computer Science
Swiss Federal Institute of Technology (EPFL), Lausanne, Switzerland
{ballim,chaps,rajman,pallotta}@di.epfl.ch

We present the result of an experimental system aimed at performing a robust semantic analysis of analyzed speech input in the area of information system access. The goal of this experiment was to investigate the effectiveness of such a system in a pipelined architecture, where no control is possible over the morpho-syntactic analysis which precedes the semantic analysis and query formation. The general applicative framework of the ISIS project[1] was to design an information system NLP interface for automated telephone-based phone-book inquiry. The proposed architecture for the functional prototype contained 3 modules:

- a speech recognition system, taking speech signals as input and providing N-best sequences in form of a lattice.
- a stochastic syntactic analyzer (i.e. parser) extracting the k-best analysis;
- a semantic module in charge of filling the frames required to query the database

The use of domain knowledge has turned out to be crucial since our particular goal is to process a queries without any request of clarification from the system. Due to the inaccuracy and ambiguity generated by previous phases of analysis we need to select the best hypotheses and often recover information lost during that selection. Although robustness can be considered as being applied at either a syntactic or semantic level, we believe it is generally at the semantic level that it is most effective. This robust analysis needs a model of the domain in which the system operates, and a way of linking this model to the lexicon used by the other components. It specifies semantic constraints that apply in the world and which allow us, for instance, to rule out incoherent requests. Taking the assumption that the information system being queried is relatively close in form to a relational database, the goal of the interpretative process is to furnish a query to the information system that can be viewed in the form of a frame with certain fields completed, the function of the querying engine being to fill in the empty fields.

[1] ISIS project started on April 1998 and finished on April 1999. It was funded and overseen by SwissCom; the partners were EPFL (LIA and LITH), ISSCO and IDIAP. A technical report is available on-line at:
`http://lithwww.epfl.ch/~pallotta/rapportfinal.ps.gz`

M. Bouzeghoub et al. (Eds.): NLDB 2000, LNCS 1959, pp. 365–365, 2001.

Effects of Hypertext Navigational Structure on Knowledge Acquisition

Mohamed Khalifa, Rinky Lam

Department of Information Systems, City University of Hong Kong,
Tat Chee Avenue, Kowloon, Hong Kong
{iskhal, isrinky}@is.cityu.edu.hk

Abstract. As web-based learning is becoming more and more popular, the effect of the hypertext navigational structure on knowledge acquisition is gaining interest with both researchers and practitioners. We still, however, lack clear guidelines on how to design such a structure. In this research, we investigate the potential of concept mapping techniques in designing the hypertext navigational structure of web-based learning systems. We also empirically test through a field study the effects of such design methods on the knowledge acquired by the users.

Several researchers argue that the hypertext navigational structure should provide an explicit representation of an expertís schemata. Concept mapping can be used to both elicit and graphically represent the expertís schemata for specific knowledge domains. The resulting concept maps can then form the basis for designing the hypertext navigational structure of web-based learning systems related to these knowledge domains. In this study, we develop a methodology for translating ìexpert concept mapsî into hypertext navigational structures. We also demonstrate empirically the effect of this methodology on knowledge acquisition with both objective measures (assessment of structural knowledge acquired by the learners) and subjective measures (survey of the learnersí perceptions). The objective and the subjective measures provide ample evidence of the superiority of the proposed design method in terms of effects on knowledge acquisition.

M. Bouzeghoub et al. (Eds.): NLDB 2000, LNCS 1959, pp. 366-366, 2001.

MEDIEVAL : A Navigation Tool Through Medieval Documents

Afzal Ballim and Hatem Ghorbel

Swiss Federal Institute of Technology, Lausanne, Switzerland
IN Ecublens, 1015 Lausanne, Switzerland
{ballim,ghorbel}@di.epfl.ch

The integration of databases and natural language is becoming an important research field. Most of the database systems are taking advantage of the large progress of research in natural language to improve user interaction. The other way around is also a plausible approach : the use of databases in the services of NLP. This usage must not be restricted to the static storage of natural language utilities (dictionaries, thesaurus ..), but can be extended to support dynamically the results of linguistic analysis and to improve the information extraction task. In this framework, the aim of MEDIEVAL or "Modèle d'EDition Informatisée d'Ecrits médiévaux, Visualisée par ALignement" is to build a model for medieval text alignment and develop a tool for the navigation through these manuscripts.

In this project we are interested in French medieval manuscripts. As a first step, we worked with extracts from versions of the manuscript l'*Ovide moralisé.* A first approach adopted in this project was based on an annotation task. Because of the particular features of this kind of manuscripts, and in order to achieve consistency in the transcription procedures of the medieval texts, guidelines were established. A second approach was based a structure-driven alignment system[1]. Hypertext data is generated from the alignment results in order to provide comparative view displayed in different windows supporting bidirectional links to locate and describe correspondence between document parts. Since morphology in medieval texts holds linguistic features important to researches, a morphosyntactic analyzer was incorporated in the process of alignment. An XML database of all occurrences of words as well as a full semantic description of the background of the process of infliction or variance so far submitted is generated. During the process of navigation, an XML-parsing will be applied to the hyper-base to extract the needed information.

As previously described, this project uses linguistic applications already developed to build databases holding output data in a structured way. In the course of our work, we have come to realize that using database technologies and structured document concepts in natural language applications is a promising axis. Ongoing work based on discourse analysis will follow the same approach.

References

1. Ballim, A., Coray, G., Linden, A. and Vanoirbeek, C.: The Use of Automatic Alignment on Structured Multilingual Documents. In: Seventh International Conference on Electronic Publishing EP'98, Saint Malo, April 1998.

M. Bouzeghoub et al. (Eds.): NLDB 2000, LNCS 1959, pp. 367–367, 2001.

MESIA: A Web Site Assistant for Document Filtering

Pablo Sanchez Torralba and Ana Garcìa-Serrano

Technical University of Madrid, Department of Artificial Intelligence
Campus de Montegancedo S/N, 28660, Madrid, Spain
{agarcia, psanchez}@dia.fi.upm.es

Abstract. In MESIA project, we tackled the problem of reach an acceptable degree of accuracy in finding links that contains relevant documents to the user consult. The current prototype interacts with the web-pages of the Madrid Local Government (www.comadrid.es) through AltaVista. The filtering process consists in the consult modification, the structural and linguistic analysis of the links texts and the use of the user model and past experience when available to obtain the final answer. The system evaluation has started not only measured by time and space, but also by the retrieved answers set precision.

1. Tool Architecture

The MESIA project (CAM 07T/0017/1998) the user is assisted during the web-search by the transformation of the user query in natural language to a formal one, to be processed by the CAM web searcher, extending the query terms with morphologic variations and with semantically related or synonymous terms. The wrapper module designed for the HTML page analysis is a parser that uses a web-grammar describing the structure of the web pages and the expected relevant short texts that allows a simple analysis to discard some links and a partial linguistic analysis using a semantic patterns set according to the terminology and domain key words to confirm some other links. As a result, it is generated a structure of structural and semantic features which describes superficially the selected pages to be send to both, a presentation module (produces the final answer) and to a store for future queries. In addition, MESIA can also directly get a formal query looking for the answer in the Classified Document Data Base without accessing the web.

2. Prototype

The prototype has been design following a knowledge-based methodology during the different phases of the development cycle, using Java for the interface and data base access (Microsoft Access) and the logic programming environment CIAO-Prolog (www.clip.dia.fi.upm.es/Software/Ciao/) which facilitated the integration of the project available resources: Spanish lexicon ARIES (www.mat.upm.es/~aries/), the EuroWordNet Spanish synset and a preference based analysis module Martinez and Garcìa-Serrano (NLDBí2000).

M. Bouzeghoub et al. (Eds.): NLDB 2000, LNCS 1959, pp. 368-368, 2001.

LExIS
A Query Language to Scan Information Flow

Jérôme Carrère, Frédéric Cuppens, and Claire Saurel

ONERA CERT, 2 avenue Edouard Belin BP4025, F-31055 TOULOUSE, FRANCE
{carrere,cuppens,saurel}@cert.fr

The goal of our research is to define a language that enables a user to express his information needs as well as a language for querying full text semistructured documents. We consider in the context of our research a document as a textual information flow.
In this poster we present LExIS, a language that provides a convenient way for users to easily express queries that identifies a flow containing specified information. Based on the user queries expressed in LExIS, we generate a logical representation of the user information need. This logical representation of the user information needs is matched against the logical representation of the flow as it is processed.
The LExIS syntax is inspired from the grammars++ approach by Salminen and Tompa(Information Systems, 24, 1999). This language is based on syntactic constraints. Constraints only related to the structure of the text are not sufficient to specify information to be retrieved. We exhibit other kinds of constaint and integrate them in a logical query language.
The following expression provides an exemple of LExIS query (Δ stands for conjunction and ∇ stands for disjunction):

$$((\, train \ \Delta \ (crash \nabla victim)\{title\}) \\ \Delta \ (''M.DUPOND'' \ \Delta \ passenger \ \Delta \ victim)\{paragraph\})\{article\} \ . \quad (1)$$

The goal of this query is to retrieve specific paragraphs of articles dealing with train crash or train victims that may contain information about one particular victim called "M. DUPOND".
LExIS is used to specify information to be retrieved over any structured or semi-structured information flow. It can be used to search information over data sheets, reports, ... or even TCP, IP, ... packets as long as an analyser is defined for each kind of data types. By defining an analyser for a data type we also provides a set of specific constraints that can be used by the user to express his information need in LExIS.
We provide a formal semantics for this language and give some directions for future research.

key words: information retrieval, query language, information specification.

M. Bouzeghoub et al. (Eds.): NLDB 2000, LNCS 1959, pp. 369–369, 2001.

A Financial Data Mining Trading System

VÈronique Plihon, Fei Wu, Georges Gardarin

Laboratoire PRISM / UniversitÈ de Versailles Saint-Quentin
45 Avenue des Etats-Unis 78035 Versailles Cedex, France
Email: <Firstname>.<Lastname>@prism.uvsq.fr

Abstract. Data Mining techniques are used to extract hidden knowledge (ex: rules, patterns, regularities) from data in databases. The knowledge discovered can be applied for supporting decision-making, as for instance in the financial domain. The tool demonstrated illustrates first how data mining can support the dynamic clustering and the forecasting of stock trends, and then how XML can support the portfolio management through the definition of trading strategies.

1 Introduction

Recently, many financial trading systems appear on the web. Most of them presents market stock data, computes indicators, and allows to create portfolios. Our tool uses data mining and XML techniques for better supporting the analyse and the forecasting of stock trends [2].

2 Tool Architecture

The data are stored in an Oracle 8i database. An HTML wrapper build using WF4 [1] and an XML parser allow to download the updated stock values every day from several Markets and to store them into the database. Strategies and their trading conditions are defined by the user and stored as XML documents. Client works either through a web browser or through a Java program. Embedded within a web server, servlets are used to fetch query results from database via JDBC and display them to users.

3 Demonstration

The demonstration presents first how stock data can be selected by market and/or by period, manipulated to compute financial indicators (ex. RSI, etc.) and visualised graphically. About ten various charts are available in our system.
The Portfolio management module, is then demonstrated. It allows to visualise the content of the portfolios, the selling and buying orders executed in the past. The definition of strategies is also exemplified here.
Finally, in the Data mining module, the various similarity methods and the clustering algorithms available are presented.

4 References

1. Arnaud Sahuguet and Fabien Azavant. *W4F*, 1998. http://db.cis.upenn.edu/W4F
2. Fei Wu, Veronique Plihon, Georges Gardarin. *Similarity-Based Queries for Time Series Databases*. Prism Research Report, Feb, 2000.

M. Bouzeghoub et al. (Eds.): NLDB 2000, LNCS 1959, pp. 370-370, 2001.

Author Index

Lecture Notes in Computer Science

For information about Vols. 1–1952
please contact your bookseller or Springer-Verlag

Vol. 1953: G. Borgefors, I. Nyström, G. Sanniti di Baja (Eds.), Discrete Geometry for Computer Imagery. Proceedings, 2000. XI, 544 pages. 2000.

Vol. 1954: W.A. Hunt, Jr., S.D. Johnson (Eds.), Formal Methods in Computer-Aided Design. Proceedings, 2000. XI, 539 pages. 2000.

Vol. 1955: M. Parigot, A. Voronkov (Eds.), Logic for Programming and Automated Reasoning. Proceedings, 2000. XIII, 487 pages. 2000. (Subseries LNAI).

Vol. 1956: T. Coquand, P. Dybjer, B. Nordström, J. Smith (Eds.), Types for Proofs and Programs. Proceedings, 1999. VII, 195 pages. 2000.

Vol. 1957: P. Ciancarini, M. Wooldridge (Eds.), Agent-Oriented Software Engineering. Proceedings, 2000. X, 323 pages. 2001.

Vol. 1959: M. Bouzeghoub, Z. Kedad, E. Métais (Eds.), Natural Language Processing and Information Systems. Proceedings, 2000. X, 372 pages. 2001.

Vol. 1960: A. Ambler, S.B. Calo, G. Kar (Eds.), Services Management in Intelligent Networks. Proceedings, 2000. X, 259 pages. 2000.

Vol. 1961: J. He, M. Sato (Eds.), Advances in Computing Science – ASIAN 2000. Proceedings, 2000. X, 299 pages. 2000.

Vol. 1963: V. Hlaváč, K.G. Jeffery, J. Wiedermann (Eds.), SOFSEM 2000: Theory and Practice of Informatics. Proceedings, 2000. XI, 460 pages. 2000.

Vol. 1964: J. Malenfant, S. Moisan, A. Moreira (Eds.), Object-Oriented Technology. Proceedings, 2000. XI, 309 pages. 2000.

Vol. 1965: Ç. K. Koç, C. Paar (Eds.), Cryptographic Hardware and Embedded Systems – CHES 2000. Proceedings, 2000. XI, 355 pages. 2000.

Vol. 1966: S. Bhalla (Ed.), Databases in Networked Information Systems. Proceedings, 2000. VIII, 247 pages. 2000.

Vol. 1967: S. Arikawa, S. Morishita (Eds.), Discovery Science. Proceedings, 2000. XII, 332 pages. 2000. (Subseries LNAI).

Vol. 1968: H. Arimura, S. Jain, A. Sharma (Eds.), Algorithmic Learning Theory. Proceedings, 2000. XI, 335 pages. 2000. (Subseries LNAI).

Vol. 1969: D.T. Lee, S.-H. Teng (Eds.), Algorithms and Computation. Proceedings, 2000. XIV, 578 pages. 2000.

Vol. 1970: M. Valero, V.K. Prasanna, S. Vajapeyam (Eds.), High Performance Computing – HiPC 2000. Proceedings, 2000. XVIII, 568 pages. 2000.

Vol. 1971: R. Buyya, M. Baker (Eds.), Grid Computing – GRID 2000. Proceedings, 2000. XIV, 229 pages. 2000.

Vol. 1972: A. Omicini, R. Tolksdorf, F. Zambonelli (Eds.), Engineering Societies in the Agents World. Proceedings, 2000. IX, 143 pages. 2000. (Subseries LNAI).

Vol. 1973: J. Van den Bussche, V. Vianu (Eds.), Database Theory – ICDT 2001. Proceedings, 2001. X, 451 pages. 2001.

Vol. 1974: S. Kapoor, S. Prasad (Eds.), FST TCS 2000: Foundations of Software Technology and Theoretical Computer Science. Proceedings, 2000. XIII, 532 pages. 2000.

Vol. 1975: J. Pieprzyk, E. Okamoto, J. Seberry (Eds.), Information Security. Proceedings, 2000. X, 323 pages. 2000.

Vol. 1976: T. Okamoto (Ed.), Advances in Cryptology – ASIACRYPT 2000. Proceedings, 2000. XII, 630 pages. 2000.

Vol. 1977: B. Roy, E. Okamoto (Eds.), Progress in Cryptology – INDOCRYPT 2000. Proceedings, 2000. X, 295 pages. 2000.

Vol. 1978: B. Schneier (Ed.), Fast Software Encryption. Proceedings, 2000. VIII, 315 pages. 2001.

Vol. 1979: S. Moss, P. Davidsson (Eds.), Multi-Agent-Based Simulation. Proceedings, 2000. VIII, 267 pages. 2001. (Subseries LNAI).

Vol. 1808: S. Pande, D.P. Agrawal (Eds.), Compiler Optimizations for Scalable Parallel Systems. XXVII, 779 pages. 2001.

Vol. 1980: M. Agosti, F. Crestani, G. Pasi (Eds.), Lectures on Information Retrieval. Proceedings, 2000. XI, 311 pages. 2001.

Vol. 1981: J.M.L.M. Palma, J. Dongarra, V. Hernández (Eds.), Vector and Parallel Processing – VECPAR 2000. Proceedings, 2000. XVI, 580 pages. 2001.

Vol. 1983: K.S. Leung, L.-W. Chan, H. Meng (Eds.), Intelligent Data Engineering and Automated Learning – IDEAL 2000. Proceedings, 2000. XVI, 573 pages. 2000.

Vol. 1984: J. Marks (Ed.), Graph Drawing. Proceedings, 2001. XII, 419 pages. 2001.

Vol. 1985: J. Davidson, S.L. Min (Eds.), Languages, Compilers, and Tools for Embedded Systems. Proceedings, 2000. VIII, 221 pages. 2001.

Vol. 1987: K.-L. Tan, M.J. Franklin, J. C.-S. Lui (Eds.), Mobile Data Management. Proceedings, 2001. XIII, 289 pages. 2001.

Vol. 1988: L. Vulkov, J. Waśniewski, P. Yalamov (Eds.), Numerical Analysis and Its Applications. Proceedings, 2000. XIII, 782 pages. 2001.

Vol. 1989: M. Ajmone Marsan, A. Bianco (Eds.), Quality of Service in Multiservice IP Networks. Proceedings, 2001. XII, 440 pages. 2001.

Vol. 1990: I.V. Ramakrishnan (Ed.), Practical Aspects of Declarative Languages. Proceedings, 2001. VIII, 353 pages. 2001.

Vol. 1991: F. Dignum, C. Sierra (Eds.), Agent Mediated Electronic Commerce. VIII, 241 pages. 2001. (Subseries LNAI).

Vol. 1992: K. Kim (Ed.), Public Key Cryptography. Proceedings, 2001. XI, 423 pages. 2001.

Vol. 1993: E. Zitzler, K. Deb, L. Thiele, C.A.Coello Coello, D. Corne (Eds.), Evolutionary Multi-Criterion Optimization. Proceedings, 2001. XIII, 712 pages. 2001.

Vol. 1995: M. Sloman, J. Lobo, E.C. Lupu (Eds.), Policies for Distributed Systems and Networks. Proceedings, 2001. X, 263 pages. 2001.

Vol. 1997: D. Suciu, G. Vossen (Eds.), The World Wide Web and Databases. Proceedings, 2000. XII, 275 pages. 2001.

Vol. 1998: R. Klette, S. Peleg, G. Sommer (Eds.), Robot Vision. Proceedings, 2001. IX, 285 pages. 2001.

Vol. 1999: W. Emmerich, S. Tai (Eds.), Engineering Distributed Objects. Proceedings, 2000. VIII, 271 pages. 2001.

Vol. 2000: R. Wilhelm (Ed.), Informatics: 10 Years Back, 10 Years Ahead. IX, 369 pages. 2001.

Vol. 2001: G.A. Agha, F. De Cindio, G. Rozenberg (Eds.), Concurrent Object-Oriented Programming and Petri Nets. VIII, 539 pages. 2001.

Vol. 2002: H. Comon, C. Marché, R. Treinen (Eds.), Constraints in Computational Logics. Proceedings, 1999. XII, 309 pages. 2001.

Vol. 2003: F. Dignum, U. Cortés (Eds.), Agent Mediated Electronic Commerce III. XII, 193 pages. 2001. (Subseries LNAI).

Vol. 2004: A. Gelbukh (Ed.), Computational Linguistics and Intelligent Text Processing. Proceedings, 2001. XII, 528 pages. 2001.

Vol. 2006: R. Dunke, A. Abran (Eds.), New Approaches in Software Measurement. Proceedings, 2000. VIII, 245 pages. 2001.

Vol. 2007: J.F. Roddick, K. Hornsby (Eds.), Temporal, Spatial, and Spatio-Temporal Data Mining. Proceedings, 2000. VII, 165 pages. 2001. (Subseries LNAI).

Vol. 2009: H. Federrath (Ed.), Designing Privacy Enhancing Technologies. Proceedings, 2000. X, 231 pages. 2001.

Vol. 2010: A. Ferreira, H. Reichel (Eds.), STACS 2001. Proceedings, 2001. XV, 576 pages. 2001.

Vol. 2011: M. Mohnen, P. Koopman (Eds.), Implementation of Functional Languages. Proceedings, 2000. VIII, 267 pages. 2001.

Vol. 2012: D.R. Stinson, S. Tavares (Eds.), Selected Areas in Cryptography. Proceedings, 2000. IX, 339 pages. 2001.

Vol. 2013: S. Singh, N. Murshed, W. Kropatsch (Eds.), Advances in Pattern Recognition – ICAPR 2001. Proceedings, 2001. XIV, 476 pages. 2001.

Vol. 2015: D. Won (Ed.), Information Security and Cryptology – ICISC 2000. Proceedings, 2000. X, 261 pages. 2001.

Vol. 2018: M. Pollefeys, L. Van Gool, A. Zisserman, A. Fitzgibbon (Eds.), 3D Structure from Images – SMILE 2000. Proceedings, 2000. X, 243 pages. 2001.

Vol. 2020: D. Naccache (Ed.), Topics in Cryptology – CT-RSA 2001. Proceedings, 2001. XII, 473 pages. 2001

Vol. 2021: J. N. Oliveira, P. Zave (Eds.), FME 2001: Formal Methods for Increasing Software Productivity. Proceedings, 2001. XIII, 629 pages. 2001.

Vol. 2022: A. Romanovsky, C. Dony, J. Lindskov Knudsen, A. Tripathi (Eds.), Advances in Exception Handling Techniques. XII, 289 pages. 2001

Vol. 2024: H. Kuchen, K. Ueda (Eds.), Functional and Logic Programming. Proceedings, 2001. X, 391 pages. 2001.

Vol. 2025: M. Kaufmann, D. Wagner (Eds.), Drawing Graphs. XIV, 312 pages. 2001.

Vol. 2026: F. Müller (Ed.), High-Level Parallel Programming Models and Supportive Environments. Proceedings, 2001. IX, 137 pages. 2001.

Vol. 2027: R. Wilhelm (Ed.), Compiler Construction. Proceedings, 2001. XI, 371 pages. 2001.

Vol. 2028: D. Sands (Ed.), Programming Languages and Systems. Proceedings, 2001. XIII, 433 pages. 2001.

Vol. 2029: H. Hussmann (Ed.), Fundamental Approaches to Software Engineering. Proceedings, 2001. XIII, 349 pages. 2001.

Vol. 2030: F. Honsell, M. Miculan (Eds.), Foundations of Software Science and Computation Structures. Proceedings, 2001. XII, 413 pages. 2001.

Vol. 2031: T. Margaria, W. Yi (Eds.), Tools and Algorithms for the Construction and Analysis of Systems. Proceedings, 2001. XIV, 588 pages. 2001.

Vol. 2033: J. Liu, Y. Ye (Eds.), E-Commerce Agents. VI, 347 pages. 2001. (Subseries LNAI).

Vol. 2034: M.D. Di Benedetto, A. Sangiovanni-Vincentelli (Eds.), Hybrid Systems: Computation and Control. Proceedings, 2001. XIV, 516 pages. 2001.

Vol. 2035: D. Cheung, G.J. Williams, Q. Li (Eds.), Advances in Knowledge Discovery and Data Mining – PAKDD 2001. Proceedings, 2001. XVIII, 596 pages. 2001. (Subseries LNAI).

Vol. 2037: E.J.W. Boers et al. (Eds.), Applications of Evolutionary Computing. Proceedings, 2001. XIII, 516 pages. 2001.

Vol. 2038: J. Miller, M. Tomassini, P.L. Lanzi, C. Ryan, A.G.B. Tettamanzi, W.B. Langdon (Eds.), Genetic Programming. Proceedings, 2001. XI, 384 pages. 2001.

Vol. 2039: M. Schumacher, Objective Coordination in Multi-Agent System Engineering. XIV, 149 pages. 2001. (Subseries LNAI).

Vol. 2040: W. Kou, Y. Yesha, C.J. Tan (Eds.), Electronic Commerce Technologies. Proceedings, 2001. X, 187 pages. 2001.

Vol. 2045: B. Pfitzmann (Ed.), Advances in Cryptology – EUROCRYPT 2001. Proceedings, 2001. XII, 545 pages. 2001.

Vol. 2053: O. Danvy, A. Filinski (Eds.), Programs as Data Objects. Proceedings, 2001. VIII, 279 pages. 2001.